BUSINESS

Second Edition

Fred Luthans
University of Nebraska

Richard M. Hodgetts
Florida International University

The Dryden Press / Harcourt Brace Jovanovich College Publishers
Fort Worth Philadelphia San Diego New York Orlando Austin San Antonio
Toronto Montreal London Sydney Tokyo

To the memory of our fathers,
Carl H. Luthans and Harold T. Hodgetts,
who taught us the fundamentals and spirit of business.

Acquisitions Editor: Robert Gemin
Developmental Editor: Kathryn Erley
Project Editor: Karen Shaw
Art and Design Director: Jeanne Calabrese
Production Manager: Robert Lange
Permissions Editor: Doris Milligan
Director of Editing, Design, and Production: Jane Perkins

Copy Editor: Jean Berry
Indexer: Leoni McVey
Compositor: York Graphic Services
Text Type: 10/12 Janson

Library of Congress CIP Data

Luthans, Fred.
   Business/Fred Luthans, Richard M. Hodgetts. — 2nd ed.
      p.   cm.
   Includes bibliographical references and index.
   ISBN 0-03-054624-9
   1. Industrial management — United States.   2. Business
enterprises — United States.   I. Hodgetts, Richard M.   II. Title.
HD70.U5L88   1992
658 — dc20

Printed in the United States of America
 23456-32-987654321
Copyright © 1992, 1989 by The Dryden Press
Copyright © 1993 version

Requests for permission to make copies of any part of the work
should be mailed to: Permissions Department, Harcourt Brace
Jovanovich, Publishers, 8th Floor, Orlando, FL 32887.

Address orders:
The Dryden Press
Orlando, Florida 32887

Address editorial correspondence:
The Dryden Press
301 Commerce Street, Suite 3700
Fort Worth, TX 76102

The Dryden Press
Harcourt Brace Jovanovich

Cover Illustration: © Nicholas Wilton.

Preface

The first edition of *Business* was unique in its focus on change. The theme was "It's not business as usual." Looking ahead to the 1990s as an era of unparalleled change, there was seen to be fundamental shifts in the philosophies, strategies and operating functions and principles of business. Now that the 1990s have arrived and the new millennium is fast approaching, these predictions have become a reality and the rate of change is accelerating. Thus, the dominant theme of this new edition continues to be environmental change.

The 1990s have already taught an important lesson: the environment not only serves as a context for business but also increasingly determines success or failure. Attention to the changing environment makes this second edition of *Business* both distinctive and up-to-date. Introductory Part One includes expanded treatment of the economic environment. This was formerly presented in an appendix but is now the subject of Chapter 2. All of Part Two is devoted to the modern environment of business, with chapters on international business, social responsibility and ethics, and innovation and entrepreneurship. These three environmental themes are then sustained throughout the text in Close-Up examples.

As a second distinctive feature, this edition uses video technology to bring the text alive. Each chapter begins with a high-interest, relevant vignette of an entrepreneurial business accompanied by a short video tape profiling the company. At the end of each chapter a video case uses the opening vignette and accompanying video to provide the opportunity for further analysis, drawing from the chapter material. This text stands alone in its use of a high-interest, relevant video to tie in the real world at the beginning of each chapter and as the case discussion vehicle at the end. Video Close-Ups in the international, ethics, and innovation chapters reinforce the environmental themes. With the accompanying videotapes (e.g., "McDonald's in Moscow"), these can be used in the discussion of the environmental dimension when covering these chapters. Another option is to use them later on in the course as a supplemental reminder of environmental issues.

This new edition fine-tunes, updates, and adds emerging topics to the basic functions of business. New or greatly expanded topical coverage includes innovation and creativity in Chapter 7, service management and total quality management in Chapter 9, management information systems in Chapter 10, and the crisis in the financial industry in Chapter 19. With a few historically important exceptions, examples in the text are drawn from the 1990s. A new appendix on careers supplements the updated career opportunities sections found at the end of each part. A complete *Career Guide* is found in the student *Study Guide*.

Pedagogy

To help make the study of business as effective and enjoyable as possible, we have incorporated a number of pedagogical features into the text itself. They are designed to engage students with the material and to help them master a wide array of concepts and vocabulary.

Learning Objectives   Each chapter begins with a series of objectives that cover the key points of the chapter. The objectives are then reviewed at the end of the chapter as Learning Objectives Revisited.

Vignettes   Each chapter opens with a real-world vignette profiling an entrepreneurial business. The vignettes were selected on the basis of timeliness, high interest, and relevancy to the chapter topic. Most important, the vignettes have an accompanying short video that can be shown to make the example come alive. End-of-chapter video cases expand on the opening vignettes, allowing the student to draw from the chapter material to analyze and answer questions.

Checkpoints   Designed for active learning, the Checkpoints consist of two review questions at the end of each major section of the chapter. They enable students to continually check their progress as they study the chapter material. The Checkpoints can also be used to review important concepts and topics.

Key Terms   A four-way glossary helps to identify and define key terms. Each key term is defined in the text where it first appears and in the margin alongside the text. There is a complete glossary at the end of the book. Additionally, the terms are listed at the ends of chapters as Key Terms Reviewed.

Close-Ups   Examples from real companies and recent business events should be interwoven throughout the text, we believe, rather than inserted arbitrarily in the chapters. Consequently, hundreds of up-to-date examples appear in the main body of the text. Each chapter also contains two longer examples called Close-Ups. Although set apart, they are referenced in the text so that the student will relate them to the text material. They focus on international, ethical, and innovation issues and are used to reinforce the environmental themes of the text. The three environmental chapters comprising Part Two provide Video Close-Ups on the environmental themes. Although these are placed in the respective environmental chapters, they could be used in any part of the course.

Cases   At the end of each chapter are two cases. The first is a video case tied into the company or industry profiled in the opening vignette and video. For the second case, You Be the Adviser, the student assumes the role of a business consultant and deals with a particular issue or solves a problem by applying ideas presented in the chapter.

Review Questions and Applied Exercises   The Review Questions go beyond basic recall to ask students to apply the chapter text to real-world situations. The Applied Exercises are all new to this edition. They are experiential exercises that actively involve the student in problem solving or self-analysis. These exercises draw from the concepts presented in the chapter.

Career Opportunities   Each of the seven parts of the text ends with a Career Opportunities section. These sections identify specific jobs in the areas discussed in that part of the book. Job descriptions, the employment outlook, and earnings are presented. A new appendix on careers included in this edition gives practical advice on finding a job.

Supplements

Each supplement has been developed with the same care as the text to ensure that it fully supports and enhances the material in the text. As an example of this effort, all of the written support material for classroom lectures, discussions, and exercises is organized by chapter in a single volume (the *Instructor's Manual*) rather than in several volumes. Similarly, the student *Study Guide* incorporates all supplementary materials for the student, including a career guide. The questions in the *Test Bank* have been thoroughly checked by the authors for accuracy and consistency with the text.

Instructor's Manual
In the *Instructor's Manual* we have provided a variety of materials, from which the instructor may choose whatever is most appropriate for the class and for each topic. Each chapter of the manual includes the following features:

- Chapter outline
- Chapter overview and summary
- All key terms in the chapter, with definitions
- Teaching notes and review outline
- Supplemental lecture
- Profile of a business leader
- Controversial issue for class discussion
- International perspective (where relevant)
- Supplemental cases with discussion questions and suggested answers
- Discussion topics and in-class exercises
- Out-of-class projects
- Term paper topics
- Guest lecturer suggestions
- Answers to end-of-chapter review questions
- Instructions and answers to end-of-chapter applied exercise
- Analyses and answers to questions with end-of-chapter cases

Computerized Instructor's Manual
The computerized *Instructor's Manual* allows you to load supplemental materials onto your own word processing program and customize lecture outlines.

Test Bank
An accurate test bank is critical for most professors teaching the introduction to business course. Each question in this *Test Bank* has been reviewed and checked for accuracy and consistency with the text. Approximately 3,000 true/false, multiple-choice, and short-answer questions are organized by

chapter learning objective. The key for each question includes the answer, the text page reference, the cognitive type (factual or applied), and the learning goal number. Each multiple-choice question is graded for level of difficulty. Each chapter also includes two minicases with accompanying multiple-choice questions. The *Test Bank* was written by Douglas Hibbert, of Fayetteville Technical Institute, and Mona Levine, of Montgomery College–Rockville.

Computerized Test Bank

In addition to the printed version, the *Test Bank* is available in a computerized format for use with IBM-PC and Apple II microcomputers. The computerized test banks contain the same questions appearing in the printed *Test Bank* and allow the instructor to preview and edit the questions, add questions, and print multiple versions of tests and answer keys.

Study Guide

The *Study Guide* consists of the study guide proper and a career guide.

The study guide proper is designed to help students master the vocabulary and concepts of the text and apply them to real-world situations. After completing the questions and exercises, students will be prepared for class discussions and examinations. The study guide includes the following for each chapter: learning objectives, chapter summary, key-terms matching exercise, true/false questions, completion questions, multiple-choice questions, mini-cases, short-answer questions, and answers to all questions. Each part ends with a crossword puzzle of the key concepts in the part. The study guide proper was written by Robert Cox, of Salt Lake Community College.

The *Study Guide* also includes a career guide that introduces the basic issues of the career search and career management and provides students with exercises that will help them think about the process. It includes sections on occupation choice, the job search, on-the-job issues, and sources of information. The career guide was written by Jeffrey Greenhaus, of Drexel University.

Videos

To maximize student interest and learning, relevant, high-interest video segments from FNN (Financial News Network) support the opening vignette and ending video case for each chapter.

Video Instructor's Manual

The *Video Instructor's Manual* provides complete teaching notes and suggestions on each video. Each chapter of the manual includes a detailed video outline, a list of the chapter concepts covered in the video, teaching objectives, warm-up and recap discussion questions, and in-class and out-of-class experiential activities. This manual was written by Anthony Lucas, of the Community College of Allegheny County, and Gayle Marco, of Robert Morris College.

Transparencies

The transparency package includes approximately 150 full-color acetates of figures not found in the text and over 150 transparency masters of all figures in the text. Acetates and masters of figures are accompanied by detailed teaching notes that describe the figures and draw out the key points that students should note.

Stock Market Game

Developed by Leon Sterdjevich, of Montgomery College, the *Stock Market Game* gives students hands-on experience in investing money wisely and provides them with a better understanding of the stock market. The 8- to 10-week game allows students to select and track four stocks on a week-by-week basis and create a profitable portfolio. The workbook includes an overview of stocks and the stock market, information on gathering and analyzing industry and company information, a list of references, and forms for logging in weekly data.

Business Papers

The set of *Business Papers* contains an assortment of actual business forms and documents — including stock and bond certificates, a small business loan application, a balance sheet, and many others — and teaching notes for each. It was prepared by Leon Sterdjevich.

Chopsticks Computer Simulation

This management simulation, written by Eugene J. Calvasina, James Leon Barton, Jr., and Ava Honan of Auburn University-Montgomery, Richard Calvasina of University of West Florida, and Gerald Calvasina of University of North Carolina at Charlotte, places students in the manager's role and requires them to make decisions about key areas of the business. This is an interactive simulation designed to offer students the opportunity to learn how decisions affect an organization.

Acknowledgments

This book has been developed with the invaluable help of dozens of professors who teach introduction to business. At each stage of development, market surveys, focus groups, past users, and reviewers played a critical role in shaping the book.

We would like to thank the following professors who reviewed the first edition:

Larry Bain, Weatherford College; John Balek, Morton College; John Beem, College of DuPage; Glennis Boyd, Cisco Junior College; Daniel Brady, Highland Community College, Gary Carlson, DeVry Institute of Technology; Helen Davis, Jefferson Community College; Lee Dlabay, Lake Forest College; Carol Ferguson, Rock Valley College; George Hager, College of DuPage; Douglas A. Hibbert, Fayetteville Technical Institute; Garland Holt, Tarrant County Community College; Graham Irwin, Miami University; David Kelmar, Santa Monica College; David Lemak, U.S. Air Force; John Lloyd, Monroe Community College; Paul Londrigan, C. S. Mott Community College; Don Manning, University of Northern Colorado; Jim McAnelly, Waubonsee Community College; Carnella Moore, Glendale

Community College; Pat Plocek, Richland College; Richard Randolph, Johnson County Community College; James Reineman, College of Lake County; Robert Smoot, Northern Virginia Community College; Philip Weatherford, Embry-Riddle Aeronautical University; Charles Woodfill, Franklin University; Larry Zigler, Highland Community College.

We would especially like to express our gratitude to the following professors who reviewed the second edition of *Business:*

Joseph H. Atallah
DeVry Institute of Technology

Brenda Britt
Fayetteville Technical Institute

Judith G. Bulin
Monroe Community College

Gary Clark
Sinclair Community College

Ted Dieck
Thomas Nelson Community College

Janice M. Feldbauer
Austin Community College

Don Gren
Salt Lake Community College

Doug Heeter
Ferris State University

Bob Johnson
Jefferson College

Mona Levine
Montgomery College

John Lloyd
Monroe Community College

Anthony J. Lucas
Community College of Allegheny County

Gayle J. Marco
Robert Morris College

Rieann Spence-Gale
Northern Virginia Community College

Lynn H. Suksdorf
Salt Lake Community College

Juanita Vertrees
Sinclair Community College

We also thank the following professors who have had significant input into the second edition:

Durant C. Black, Salt Lake Community College; John W. Brown, Monroe Community College; Robert J. Cox, Salt Lake Community College; Patricia Eyer, Northern Virginia Community College; Barbara A. Gorman, Montgomery College; Douglas A. Hibbert, Fayetteville Technical Community College; David L. Hofmeister, Mankato State University; Joseph Hrebanek, Community College of Allegheny County; Carolyn Kelly, Mitchell Community College; Jerome M. Kinskey, Sinclair Community College; Philip R. Leftwich, Mitchell Community College; Marcia M. Levingston, DeVry Institute of Technology; Corinne L. Nicholson, St. Andrews Presbyterian College; Katherine A. Olson, Northern Virginia Community College; Richard Rowe, Montgomery College; Celeste M. Sichenze, Northern Virginia Community College; Michele Smith, Mankato State University; Robert M. Stivender, Wake Technical Community College; C. E. Tychsen, Northern Virginia Community College; Leonard C. Vecchiola, Community College of Allegheny County; John Yeamans, Sinclair Community College.

We believe that an important, but often overlooked, part of the review process is to have the specialized functional areas reviewed. We called on our colleagues at the University of Nebraska in the Department of Finance (Richard A. DeFusco, Manferd D. Peterson, and Thomas S. Zorn), the Department of Economics (Campbell R. McConnell), the Department of Marketing (Ronald D. Hampton), and the Department of Accounting (Thomas E. Balke) to review chapters in their areas of expertise. We thank these individuals for the considerable time and effort they gave to us. Interestingly, without exception, they also thanked us for the opportunity to make sure that what was being said in their areas of an introductory business text was indeed current and correct.

We would like to acknowledge the dedication, support, and expertise provided to us by the Dryden Press team. In particular, we would like to thank Robert Gemin, senior acquisitions editor, who has provided inspiration, useful ideas, and enthusiasm on all phases of the project, and our very talented and hard—working developmental editor, Kathi Erley. We received help from the rest of the team at various stages and would like to thank them. Although many deserve credit, we would like to mention the following: our dedicated project editor Karen Shaw, our skilled copyeditor Jean Berry, Martha Beyerlein, Jeanne Calabrese, Bob Lange, Doris Milligan, Patti Arneson and her marketing staff, and, of course, the field sales force who, in the final analysis, represent our book.

Closer to home, we would like to thank the secretarial/word processing support provided by Debbie Burns, and especially Cathy Jensen. Last, but by no means least, we want to thank our families for giving us the time and creating a supportive climate that allowed us to do the best that we could do.

Fred Luthans
Richard M. Hodgetts
September 1991

Preface Annotations

Each chapter begins with a list of Learning Objectives previewing main concepts that the reader should retain.

SUBWAY IS FLYING HIGH

In recent years many entrepreneurs have found it more profitable to buy a franchise than to start and build a business from scratch, and those who opened a Subway Sandwiches and Salads joined the fastest growing franchise operation in the country. Founded by Fred DeLuca in 1965, it already has over 5,500 units. The firm is extremely profitable. Unlike many other franchisors, Subway does not open stores under its own ownership; all are franchises.

Small Business and Franchising

Chapter Learning Objectives

- Define small business and its impact.
- Identify the types of small businesses.
- Analyze some of the major advantages and disadvantages of owning a small business.
- Discuss how to start a small business and effectively operate it.
- Describe how the franchise form of business works.
- Relate the major advantages and disadvantages of franchises.

Among the things that attract people to Subway is that no experience is needed. Everything new owners have to know can be learned. All they need is an intense desire to succeed, in the opinion of Fred DeLuca. Another benefit of this particular franchise is that not much money is needed to start. In 1991, the franchise fee was a relatively low $10,000 (fees for well-known fast-food franchises range from triple digits to over a million dollars), and startup costs were estimated at a modest $30,000 to $80,000 depending on the location.

Another benefit of owning a Subway franchise is that they are highly rated by the experts. For example, *Entrepreneur* magazine has listed Subway as the best franchise in the country for four consecutive years. This rating resulted from a formula that includes factors such as number of years in franchising, number of units in operation, startup costs, and growth rate. After making a thorough analysis of over a thousand different franchise companies, the magazine staff gave Subway a total of over 4,000 points. McDonald's was second with 3,200 points. However, the two companies are not in direct competition. Subway is in submarine sandwiches while McDonald's is mainly in hamburgers. As one franchisee noted, "We can locate across the street from a McDonald's and live off the overflow of its traffic."

Photo Source: Courtesy of Subway.

A short case at the beginning of each chapter illustrates business problems and solutions and introduces key chapter concepts. A video accompanies each case.

CLOSE-UP / *Innovation*

Plasma technology attaches an electric current to each dot on the screen, thus causing a gas to glow and produce an image. Photonics Technology, an American firm, has built 60-inch flat-panel screens for the U.S. Air Force, but there are other American and Japanese firms that also have plasma technology expertise. A third form of HDTV research relies on electroluminescence. A fourth employs tiny movable mirrors on a

High-Definition TV En
While television technology
the years ahead promise a n
evision (HDTV). These TV se
screens that offer near-perfe
Who will bring this technolo
take? At present, American,
pursuing a variety of compe

One is the use of active
are already being used in
Because of their familiarity
nese firms such as Sharp,
over $1 billion to create HDT
ever, in order to hedge their
other approaches such as p

Capital The money an
the factor of production
and use monetary resour
to buy the necessary lar

Although tradition:
money, we have extende
of a business. In today's
Technology is the appli
ment, and machinery. I
modern business. For r
tech — suggests what m

When firms invest
development or advance
useful or attractive. For
television industry to ad
ufacturers to introduce r
one foot deep and mode
Sometimes technology i
TV remote control that
three: power, channel,

The accompanying
the Picture) describes a

Entrepreneurship We
the widely recognized pr

VIDEO CLOSE-UP / *Ethics*

tion that the paint provides to the body and other key parts of the aircraft lessens over time. However, before the plane can be repainted, the old paint must be removed. This is a costly process and, when solvents are used, results in pollution. Now a new process, invented by Cold Jet Inc., makes paint removal simpler and reduces the pollution problem by using dry ice to shatter the old paint. This thermal shock procedure does not

A Matter of Thermal
The word pollution usually
lution caused by factories
power plants. Some more
are also part of the price d
the dirt and soot that hav
plane are removed, it w
plane reduces the operati
fleet of planes make it a p
just for appearance, but
Keeping the plane cl
also be repainted. Air poll
begin peeling off the pain
increase wind resistance

CHECK ✓ P

merism A move
vide buye
d barg
or obt:
cts an

CLOSE-UP / *International*

A Global Venture
About ten years ago Ford began planning a replacement for its one-year-old Escort, the best-selling car in its line. The initial plan called for the company to build a car that could be marketed in the Far East and Europe as well as in the United States. However, this plan soon ran into problems and Ford determined that the best strategy was to enter into a joint venture with Mazda to produce a product that could be sold in Japan and the United States. The Japanese would have responsibility for engineering the inside of the car, while Ford would handle the styling of the outside. In addition, Mazda would take the lead development role and have final say over engineering decisions. The project proved to be a major lesson to Ford in how to handle international joint ventures.

One of the major problems was that Mazda locks in its designs much faster than Ford. Like other American car makers,

Ford would often introduce style changes late in the plan and hurry to incorporate them into the car. This approach had to be changed, and a final design was approved much earlier than Ford was accustomed to doing. Other seemingly minor but important problems included getting agreement on the size of the license-plate recesses, the type of rust-resistant alloy to use for the flooring, and the length of the wheelbase.

Once all of this was worked out, Ford found that the car had too many Japanese parts and this would keep it from being classified as a domestic model. Solution: A Ford engine was put in the car. Then the value of the yen rose dramatically and the project began going far over budget. Solution: Some Japanese suppliers were dropped and more U.S. suppliers were used so that 50 percent of the parts were provided by American suppliers.

Finally, in early 1990, the first cars rolled off the assembly line. In Ford's view, the venture was a success, thanks in large measure to the assistance it received from Mazda. While it is still too early to know with certainty, initial estimates are that the company saved over $1 billion by developing and producing the car on a joint venture basis.

Source: James B. Treece and Amy Borrus, ''How Ford and Mazda Shared the Driver's Seat,'' *Business Week*, March 26, 1990, 94–95.

ownership. The ideal form of ownership may turn out to be a variation of a partnership, such as a joint venture.

Joint Ventures and Syndicates
Particularly important in today's entrepreneurial climate is a special form of ownership called a **joint venture.** In this form of ownership, described in Chapter 1 as a venture, two or more investors or firms share the control and property rights of an enterprise. When viewed as a partnership, it is usually temporary and has the purpose of carrying out a single business project. When the project is completed, the participants dissolve the joint venture. During the life of this form of business ownership, each partner is a general partner.

Joint ventures have become popular in real estate developments. A group of investors pool their funds to build or purchase houses or apartments. Once they are sold, the partnership arrangement comes to an end.

Although joint ventures viewed as partnerships usually involve individual investors, joint ventures can also involve separate corporations serving in a more long-term relationship. For example, high-tech firms use them to combine their talents to develop, manufacture, and market such products as drugs, chemicals, and computer hardware. Automakers from the United States and Japan (for example, GM and Toyota, Ford and Mazda) have used joint ventures to attempt to gain market share by combining their manufacturing and marketing efforts. The accompanying International Close-Up (A Global Venture) provides details of the Ford-Mazda joint venture. Although

Joint venture A type of joint ownership that, when viewed as a partnership, is usually temporary and is created for the purpose of carrying out a single business project.

"Close-Up" boxes throughout the text integrate coverage of international issues, ethics and social responsibility, and innovation.

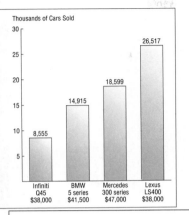

Thousands of Cars Sold

Infiniti Q45 $38,000	BMW 5 series $41,500	Mercedes 300 series $47,000	Lexus LS400 $38,000
8,555	14,915	18,599	26,517

When Toyota introduced the Lexus in the United States, over a third of the buyers traded in an American luxury car. The accompanying graph shows the number of different foreign luxury cars sold in the United States between January and August 1990. An increase in imports such as this, unless other products of equal or greater value are exported, lowers the gross national product.

Source: Courtesy of Lexus.

Fiscal policy The use of government spending and tax collection to attain full employment and a noninflationary high level of GNP.

Monetary policy Government regulation of the money supply to attain full employment and a noninflationary high level of GNP.

At the same time, lems. Some of the imp panying International

Causes of Business cies, and good and ba or more of them are in economy or every pa same time. If a dowr manufactured goods, east and large urban a Conversely, if the pri rural communities wi city dwellers will no ripple effect. Eventua crunch. The far-reach business cycles.

In a purely comp lated through supply the government attem tary policies. **Fiscal p** tion to attain full em **Monetary policy** is g employment and a n policies, which chang on business cycles.

Farmers Jim and Keith Boysen harvest corn on their 800-acre family farm in eastern Iowa. Today's seed corn produces plants with higher yield and greater drought and pest resistance than seed of 50 years ago because of special breeding by DEKALB Genetics and other companies. The United States has a comparative advantage in crops such as corn thanks to climate and terrain, the availability of tractors and equipment (capital equipment), and skilled farmers and agriculture specialists (human resources).

Source: Courtesy of DEKALB Genetics Corporation.

So while the United States still has a ready supply of college-graduate professionals, entrepreneurs, and intrapreneurs (see Chapter 7), there may be a need for more skilled workers in order to remain competitive in the future.

The newly industrialized countries (NICs), which include South Korea, Singapore, Hong Kong, and Taiwan (sometimes called the "Four Asian Tigers"), have made their mark in world trade largely through their human resources. Employee wages in the NICs have traditionally been lower than their counterparts in Japan, Europe, and the United States. Not only are their human resources less costly, but they are becoming increasingly educated and skilled. Once dismissed as marginal producers of low-quality clothes and toys, the NICs have become producers of complex, high-quality goods because of their skilled workers. They now produce everything from VCRs and computers to cars and planes. In recent years, however, like their more advanced competitors such as Japan and the United States, they have had some economic setbacks. Their workers are demanding a share of the economic miracle and want higher wages. Only time will tell if the Asian tigers will continue the phenomenal economic growth they experienced in the 1980s.[14]

In the underdeveloped countries of Africa, the Middle East, and South America, businesses have been unable to take full advantage of high-tech markets. For example, even if they buy sophisticated computers, they are unable to use them to the fullest if they lack a well-trained, skilled workforce that knows how to get the most out of these machines. Human resources help explain some of the productivity differences between businesses in the developed countries, the NICs, and the underdeveloped Third World nations.

FIGURE 1.2
Per Capita Income in Selected Countries

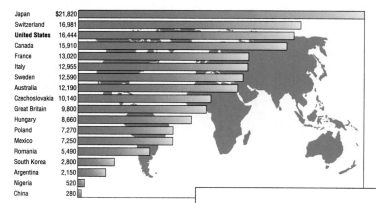

Japan	$21,820
Switzerland	16,981
United States	16,444
Canada	15,910
France	13,020
Italy	12,955
Sweden	12,590
Australia	12,190
Czechoslovakia	10,140
Great Britain	9,800
Hungary	8,660
Poland	7,270
Mexico	7,250
Romania	5,490
South Korea	2,800
Argentina	2,150
Nigeria	520
China	280

Source: *Information Please Almanac*, 1990; and Craig R. Whitney, "East Europe Joins
Preview of the Pain," *New York Times*, January 7, 1990, 3E.

Clear and precise figures help illustrate major points and reinforce concepts for students.

CHECK ✓ POINT

families are members
recent trend toward t
husband work, has he
greater purchasing po

1. What are the fact
2. How do the right
    over these factors

Alternative Eco

Until the end of the
under which America
only one type of econ
ion's Mikhail Gorbach
nomic and political re
all of the formerly C
market economies in

FIGURE 4.2
Sales and Growth of Franchising

Sales (in Billions of Dollars)

1970	120
1979	287
1982	376
1983	423
1984	492
1985	530
1986	576
1987	625
1988ᵃ	640

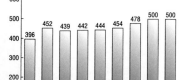

Number of Establishments (in Thousands)

1970	396
1979	452
1982	439
1983	442
1984	444
1985	454
1986	478
1987	500
1988	500

ᵃ estimated

Source: "Why Franchising Is Taking Off," *Fortune*, February 12, 1990, 124.

Suddenly Slender and Designer Body weight-loss centers are all franchises.
    Companies that service other businesses also frequently use franchises.
These organizations include collection agencies, employment services, printing and copying services such as Postal Instant Press, and tax preparation
companies such as H&R Block. The accompanying Innovation Close-Up (A
Postal Franchise of Your Own) provides another example.

The Franchise Agreement
While the products of franchises vary widely, the basic business arrangements have much in common. These arrangements are contained in a franchise agreement, which is a contract between the supplier and dealer that
spells out what each party will do. Typically the dealer (franchisee) agrees to:

*   Pay a franchise fee for the right to run the operation
*   Pay a percentage of the gross revenues to the supplier (franchisor)
*   Follow the operating procedures that have been set forth by the fran-
    chisor

The buyer of a franchise might be required to pay as much as $575,000 for a
McDonald's or as little as $10,000 for a new H & R Block tax-help shop[10] or
$10,000 for an Auto Critic unit, which provides mobile used car inspection
services, or $8,500 for an Albert Andrews Ltd. unit, which offers custom
men's clothing services.[11] If the franchise must operate out of a special unit
such as a restaurant, the buyer must lay out the facilities in a manner speci-

Burger Buddies
Two mini-cheeseburgers with ketchup
and pickles
NEW!

Eighty-five percent of Burger King restaurants are franchised. Franchisors add new products to their menus only after carefully developing and test marketing them, as with these Burger Buddies. This is a benefit to the franchisees, because pretesting increases the chance that new products will succeed. The cost of such benefits is covered by franchise fees.

Source: Courtesy of Burger King Corporation.

and workshops on topics such as business forecasting, sources of financing, types of business organizations, and choosing a site location.

1. What are two kinds of services the Small Business Administration (SBA) offers?
2. Suppose that you owned a small business and were struggling to make ends meet. What help could you expect from the Small Business Administration?

CHECK ✓ POINT

"Checkpoints" follow each major section to encourage active reading and help students review important chapter topics.

...ld-be entrepreneurs have been attracted to a spe-... the **franchise.** Under a franchise arrangement, a ...s for dealers to handle a product or service under ...ions. The supplier is known as the **franchisor;** ...**franchisees.**

...e most popular ways of getting into a small ...peals to many people wanting to get into busi-... starting a business from the ground up and ...g firm. Franchising is an excellent way to ...rship with the lessons of a proven system. ...f the fastest growing and most important ...4.2 graphs the tremendous growth in the ...the past several years. At present, franchising accounts for one-third of retail sales and, sometime in the 1990s, the International Franchise Association (IFA) forecasts that franchising's share of retail sales will reach 50 percent.[9]

Franchises meet many different customer demands. Some of the best-known franchises are in the fast-food industry, including McDonald's, Burger King, Wendy's, and Kentucky Fried Chicken. Franchises are popular in other service industries as well. For example, Ramada Inn Motels, Maids International, Dollar Rent a Car, One Hour Martinizing Drycleaner, and

Franchise A system of distribution in which a producer or supplier arranges for a dealer to handle a product or service under mutually agreed-upon conditions.

Franchisor The supplier in a franchise system.

Franchisee The dealer in a franchise system.

Key terms are bold faced and defined in a marginal glossary. These terms are repeated at the end of each chapter and included in a comprehensive, end-of-text glossary.

and the Far East. At the same time, large American banks such as Chase Manhattan and Citibank continue to maintain their financial relationships with nations around the world from Poland to Peru.

A major ethical challenge facing many multinational firms is how to conduct business in other countries. Does management follow its own home's rules and ethical standards, or those of the country in which it is doing business? Sometimes these standards are conflicting ones but, as the next chapter on social responsibility and ethics will point out, short-run ethical compromises may lead to long-run disasters. Businesses are learning that they must use the highest ethical standards not only as the right way to do business (even in another culture), but as the profitable way to do business in the long run.

In any event, we live in a global economy, and the future of business is surely an international one.

CHECK ✓ POINT

1. What are three ways businesses can expand to overseas markets?
2. Why are small companies going international more likely to use licensing than foreign subsidiaries?

Closing Comments

The global economy is a growing challenge for business. Many firms sell goods and services with appeal in the markets of several countries. This means that international trade offers both the additional opportunity of new markets and the additional challenge of new competition. Modern businesses need to think "international" rather than just in national terms. This includes having an expanded perspective of social responsibility to the people in every nation, not just to those on the home front. To the extent that businesses can meet these important challenges, they stand a good chance not only of surviving, but also of being leaders in their respective industries.

"Closing Comments" sections provide a summary of each chapter.

VIDEO CASE / *A Foreign Invasion*

During the past 10 years, Japan has become one of the world's largest exporters of goods. The American "Big Three" found out just how big as their market share for cars declined in the face of competition from Honda, Toyota, Mazda, Nissan, and other Japanese manufacturers. However, automaking is not the only essential manufacturing industry in which the Japanese have made inroads into the American market. Three other key industries are machine tools, computers, and semiconductors.

In the late 1970s, American machine tool manufacturers had large backlogs of orders and dominated the market. During the 1980s, however, imports began flooding the market and by 1986 almost 50 percent of all machine tools were being imported. Since then American manufacturers have been able to regain a small percentage of the market, but the Japanese are now the major competitors. At the beginning of this decade, Japanese machine tool manufacturers had built $10 billion worth of equipment, three times the

U.S. output. And in the United States much of the machine tool output is produced by foreign-owned firms including Mazak, the most productive machine tool operation in the country, which is owned by Japan's Yamazaki Mazak.

In computers, the U.S. global share has slipped from 76 percent in 1984 to less than two-thirds today. The strongest area for American firms is workstations, where they command an overwhelming presence thanks to superior design and their lead in micropro-

A video case at the end of each chapter relates back to the chapter's opening vignette, further discussing the company or industry profiled at the beginning of the chapter.

rs — and the United
his area. However,
in chipmaking tech-
t all the world mar-

apanese have done an
ading the American
shing a strong pres-
acturing arena. The
are: Can the United
e and take back lost
w much danger does
p pose to the Ameri-

Source: Edmund Faltermayer, "Is 'Made in U.S.A.' Fading Away?" *Fortune*, September 24, 1990, 62–73.

Case Questions

1. In which manufacturing industries is Japan currently dominating the U.S.? What conclusions can you draw from these findings?
2. What are the advantages of Japanese investments in the United States? What are the drawbacks?
3. Is the United States in economic danger if the present trend of foreign investment continues?

Learning Objectives Revisited

1. **Discuss the global economy and international business.** International trade is the sale of exports (goods shipped to other countries) and purchase of imports (goods brought in from other countries). The balance of trade is total exports minus total imports. In recent years, the United States has had a negative balance of trade, or a trade deficit. Therefore, although the United States is a major exporter of goods, an important part of international business affecting the United States is overseas businesses selling in domestic markets.

2. **Present the major reasons for international business.** Businesses sell in international markets when they have an absolute or comparative advantage. Sources of advantages include abundant natural resources, favorable climate and terrain, sufficient capital equipment, skilled personnel, accessible geographic location, and a stable political climate.

3. **Identify some government-imposed barriers to international trade.** Some of the principal barriers to international trade include quotas (import restrictions in terms of quantity or value) and tariffs (duties levied on imported goods). The government also restricts trade for security reasons and may impose regulations that make business operations more complex and costly. To keep money in the country, the government may limit conversion of funds.

4. **Relate some cultural differences that make international trade challenging.** Cultural differences create barri-

ers when business people disregard them. Language and communication style are basic differences, but customs and manners may
The concept of time differs a
punctuality being mo
than in ot
duri

5. **Expla**
Som
the
coop
eral
com
(EC
have
inter
Ban
Inte
opm

6. **Disc**
tiona
used
tional are
port use merchants o
own sales office or branch. La
want more control use joint ventures, bra
nizations, and subsidiaries.

The "Learning Objectives Revisited" section reviews main chapter concepts and reinforces the Learning Objectives introduced at the beginning of each chapter.

Key Terms Reviewed

Review each of the following terms. For any that you do not know or are unsure of, look up the definitions and see how they were used in the chapter.

multinational corporation (MNC)
transnational corporation (TNC)
balance of trade
exports
imports
trade deficit
balance of payments
absolute advantage
comparative advantage
quota
tariff

culture
free-trade zone (FTZ)
General Agreement on Tariffs and Trade (GATT)
Export-Import Bank (Exim Bank)
International Monetary Fund (IMF)
International Bank for Reconstruction and Development (World Bank)

International Finance Corporation (IFC)
International Development Association (IDA)
license
joint venture
branch organization
subsidiary

Review Questions

1. If the United States has a negative balance of trade this year, will it also have a negative balance of payments?
2. What is the trade deficit? Why are some people concerned about the U.S. trade deficit?
3. What would give a country's businesses an absolute advantage? A comparative advantage? What is a comparative advantage possessed by an American firm such as Touchstone Pictures (Walt Disney Company's movie-making firm)?
4. South Korean companies are beginning to produce durable goods such as automobiles and computers and ship many of them halfway around the world to sell in the United States. Why would these companies expand to such a distant market? What advantages do they have to offer U.S. customers? What advantages does the U.S. market offer the companies?
5. Imagine a country with few natural resources and land that is not particularly fertile. What advantages could such a country develop as a trading partner?
6. Why do governments restrict imports? Who benefits from such actions?

7. Managers of J&J Sweets are thinking of building a candy factory in Czechoslovakia. However, the Czech government would require J&J to take on a local partner. Would this be disadvantageous to the company? What should the company's managers weigh in making this decision?
8. How do cultural differences make international business more difficult? How can U.S. managers cope with these differences?
9. How can businesses take advantage of free-trade zones?
10. Tina McCormick wants to expand her line of shoe stores into South America, but her bank has turned down her request for financing. Where else can Tina look for funding?
11. How do American businesses benefit from organizations that provide financing to underdeveloped nations?
12. Telephone Tech, a small research-based American firm, usually enters international markets by licensing or exporting rather than by creating a subsidiary. What might be two reasons for this action?

Applied Exercise

How much do you *really* know about international business practices and developments? Take the following quiz. Most students answer only 50 percent of these statements correctly.

T F 1. In Latin countries, decisions typically are made by the manager and communicated to the subordinates without very much feedback or participative management.

Key terms are listed at the end of each chapter to aid in reviewing important concepts. End-of-chapter Review Questions go beyond basic recall, asking students to apply chapter material to real-world situations.

"Applied Exercises" follow each chapter to encourage critical thinking and provide an active review of key concepts.

A "You Be the Advisor" case at the end of each chapter puts students in the role of business consultant as they help a business firm solve a problem using chapter concepts.

YOU BE THE ADVISER / *Going International with Real Estate*

Falworth Real Estate is a large landholder in Arizona and Florida. The firm owns a total of 1.2 million acres in these two states. Falworth both sells and develops land. The biggest revenues come from building speculative or customized homes, duplexes, and condos. However, the company also sells lots to those who want to build their own houses or hold the property as an investment.

Over the past 5 years the company has sold over 200,000 acres to smaller real estate developers and 400,000 acres to individual investors. The latter is the most profitable market niche and the one that the firm has targeted for the 1990s. The primary way in which Falworth sells this land is through agents working throughout the United States. For example, there is one agent who has the state of Illinois. He is authorized to sell Falworth land to Illinois residents and is given a percentage of the sales price. There are sales agents throughout all 50 states (some covering more than one state) and they have been selling a combined total of 1,250 acres a week.

Over the past year, James Falworth, the founder and president, has been thinking about opening up new sales territories in Europe and Asia. Foreign agents would be given exclusive sales territories and receive a commission on their sales. They could sell to anyone in their territory who is a native of that country. For example, an agent in France could sell an acre of land in Florida to a French couple but could not sell the land to an American family that was vacationing in France. Falworth would offer the same basic arrangement as that given to agents in the United States: each would be given a monthly draw of $1,000 that would be offset by sales com-

missions. There would also be an allowance for advertising, travel, and out-of-pocket expenses.

Mr. Falworth intends to make a final decision on this matter within the next two months. He and his staff have done considerable research and the major stumbling block appears to be the identification of overseas sales agents and the allocation of sales territories. But, as he reported in a preliminary report to the board of directors, "If we can sell 50,000 acres a year to Europeans and Asians, we can triple our annual profits. What we need to do now is to plan our strategy so that we have the same success overseas that we are having here in the states."

Your Advice

1. What should Falworth do? Prioritize your answers.
   ___ a. Have the company advertise overseas and handle sales through the home office.
   ___ b. Let local state agents advertise overseas and handle all international sales themselves.
   ___ c. Invest the necessary time and effort and appoint overseas sales agents in both Europe and Asia.
2. What cultural challenges will Falworth face if it decides to go into the European market? The Far East market?
3. What major pitfalls does the company face beside cultural problems if it decides to go international? Explain.
4. What would you specifically recommend the company do in preparing to go international?

Fred Luthans and Richard Hodgetts bring a well-rounded combination of teaching, research, and business experience to this text. Each has been teaching business courses for over 25 years, and each has written several successful textbooks. They have teamed up on a number of books, including *Social Issues in Business*, now in its sixth edition, and *Real Managers*, which has been acclaimed as the most comprehensive study of how successful and effective managers spend their time. Their most recent text is *International Management*, published in 1991 by McGraw-Hill.

Fred Luthans is the George Holmes Distinguished Professor of Business at the University of Nebraska–Lincoln, with a Ph.D. and an MBA from the University of Iowa. In 1986 he won the University of Nebraska Distinguished Teaching Award. He has been a visiting scholar at a number of colleges and universities and has lectured in most countries in Europe and Asia and in Mexico and Australia. In addition to extensive training and consulting work with many local and regional businesses, he has worked with a number of national organizations, including the Rural Electric Cooperative Association, Brunswick, Hormel, Wal-Mart, Blue Cross/Blue Shield, 3-M, U.S. West, Burger King, U.S. Savings and Loan League, and the FDIC. He has been president of the Academy of Management and is one of the few professors who are fellows of both the Academy of Management and the Decision Sciences Institute. Professor Luthans serves as a consulting editor for the McGraw-Hill Management Series and is editor of *Organizational Dynamics*. He is the author of *Organizational Behavior*, sixth edition; coauthor with Robert Kreitner of *Organizational Behavior Modification*, which won the American Society of Personnel Administration Association Award for outstanding contribution to human resource management; and author of several other texts.

Richard M. Hodgetts is a professor of business at Florida International University, with a Ph.D. from the University of Oklahoma and an MBA from Indiana University. He has twice been named an outstanding teacher of the year at both the University of Nebraska and Florida International University, most recently in 1988. He has lectured in many countries in South America, the Caribbean, Europe, and the Middle East. He has worked with Burger King, Exxon International, CIGNA Dental, and Wal-Mart, among many others. Professor Hodgetts is a fellow of the Academy of Management, serves on the review boards of several journals, and is the book review editor for *Organizational Dynamics*. He is the author of *Modern Human Relations at Work*, and *Management: Theory, Process, and Practice;* coauthor with Donald Kuratko of *Entrepreneurship;* and author of several other texts. He also writes a weekly column on small business and entrepreneurship for the *News and Sun Sentinel* (Ft. Lauderdale).

Brief Contents

Contents

PART FOUR
Managing People   373

Chapter 11 Motivation and Leadership   274

Chapter 12 Human Resource Management   300

Innovation Close-Up / Information at
Your Fingertips **391**

Ethics Close-Up / A Bleak Financial
Future **396**

International Close-Up / Cracking
the Japanese Market **430**

Innovation Close-Up / Pulling
Them In **431**

Ethics Close-Up / Bringing Order Out of Chaos   **572**

International Close-Up / Operating Around the Clock   **579**

PART SEVEN
Special Topics 595

Ethics Close-Up / Are New Car Consumers in Danger? **602**

Ethics Close-Up / Get Well, Stay Well **614**

Ethics Close-Up / Bringing an
Antitrust Suit Against
Universities **627**

International Close-Up / Getting
Tough on Foreigners **629**

PART

One

Foundations of American Business

MORE THAN JUST THE MONEY

Fred Livingston has a wide number
of business interests including at last
count a half dozen real estate firms,
three restaurants, an art gallery, an
ad agency, and a radio station. Not
bad for a native of Chicago who
started out in marketing and
advertising. Early in his business
career, Fred became unhappy
working in the Midwest and moved
to Hawaii for the better climate.
Since arriving in Honolulu, where he
became interested in real estate, Fred
has managed to build a small business

The Nature and Challenge of Business

Chapter Learning Objectives

- Explain the basic rights of the free enterprise system.

- Describe the factors of production.

- Discuss ways of measuring economic well-being.

- Define alternative economic systems.

- Identify the major challenges currently facing American business.

- Relate the benefits of studying business.

empire in the 50th state. From the beginning, Fred recognized that his people play an important role in running his businesses and that they need to be rewarded. Fred sticks to his strengths of marketing and advertising and turns over to his valued subordinates the job of managing the individual operations. Those who run his businesses on a day-to-day basis are all given much freedom to make decisions and are included in a revenue-sharing plan. The more money the business makes, the more money they make.

What drives Fred to be so successful in business? Certainly to make a profit and money for himself and his wife is an important consideration. For example, when Fred bought the radio station, he knew that the previous owner was losing money. However, Fred conceived a plan to limit losses and to turn around the operation. When it comes to new ventures, he openly admits that he is looking for a return of $1 million or more in 3 or 4 years. Even so, profit and monetary gain are not the only reason Fred Livingston

is in business. He also gains satisfaction from success itself. He already has all the money he needs, but getting involved in the exciting world of business, accomplishing personal and business goals, and making business ventures successful are driving forces that prevent Fred from just sitting back, relaxing at his beautiful beach-front home, and watching the surfers ride the big ones.

Photo source: Photo by Dana Edmunds.

Introduction

Now that you have skimmed the preface and the table of contents, you are ready to begin your study of business. This chapter will show you the big picture. After defining business in general, it describes the American business system of free enterprise and the market economy. Then it describes some of the world's other economic systems, the major challenges currently facing American business, and the benefits you can derive from studying business.

What Is Business?

Business An organized, profit-seeking approach to providing people with the goods and services they want.

Profit The difference between revenues and expenses.

The study of business begins with a simple definition of a complex process: **Business** is an organized, profit-seeking approach to providing people with the goods and services they want. The "profit-seeking" part of the definition distinguishes business from nonbusiness activity. **Profit** is the difference between money received from the sale of products or services (revenues) and the costs of doing business (expenses). Business activity plays a vital role in the United States because of its significance in the overall economy and in our daily lives. For example, business provided the textbooks you purchased at the college bookstore, the tapes you bought at the record shop, the car you drove to school, and the pizza you ate last Saturday night.

Even governments depend on business for goods and services. Business built the publicly owned commuter trains that carry people from the suburbs to the inner cities and the buses that crisscross the streets and avenues of our cities. Business also built the large courthouse that dominates the town square of many small towns. In fact, government agencies spend a large portion of tax revenues in the business arena, purchasing a variety of goods and services. For example, the federal government spends billions of dollars every year purchasing computers from IBM, airplanes from Boeing, and electronic goods from General Electric, to name but a few of the thousands of firms with which it does business.

CHECK ✓ POINT

1. What is business?
2. How has business contributed to life in the United States?

Free Enterprise and the Market Economy

Free enterprise system
An economic system under which businesses are free to decide what to supply and are rewarded based on how well they meet customer needs.

Market economy
An environment in which prices and wages are determined by the competitive environment, rather than by central planners, as in socialist countries.

More than a half century ago, President Calvin Coolidge declared, "The business of America is business." This is still true today. In the United States the process of providing people the goods and services they want takes place within a **free enterprise system** and a **market economy.** Free enterprise allows businesses to decide what is supplied and to be rewarded on the basis of how well customer needs are met. In a market economy, prices and wages are determined by the competitive marketplace, rather than by central planners as in socialist countries. Although the terms free enterprise and market economy are often used interchangeably, the perspective is a little different. This chapter takes more of a free enterprise approach and the next chapter gives specific attention to the mechanisms of the market economy.

The millions of dollars that American businesses spend each year on advertising should create a positive image for the company and its products. So when the Professional Golfer's Association held its 1990 championship tournament at all-white Shoal Creek Country Club, Anheuser-Busch, a leading sports advertiser, canceled the Budweiser advertising it had scheduled for the telecast of the tournament. So did other advertisers. They exercised the freedom of choice to do what was in the best interest of their companies.

Source: Courtesy of Anheuser-Busch Companies.

Rights in a Free Enterprise System

The free enterprise system is based on three fundamental rights. These are the right to private property, freedom of choice, and the right to rewards.

Private Property   The **right to private property** is the right to own, buy, sell, or give away property. For example, if you see a For Sale sign in front of a rundown but formerly beautiful old home, you have a right to make an offer to buy it. If you do buy it, you might decide to make just enough repairs to go into business renting inexpensive housing to students. Or you might take out a big loan, make major improvements, and ultimately sell the renovated house for a substantial sum. You could even buy the house and then give it away, although this is not a typical business decision.

Right to private property   The right to own, use, buy, sell, or give away property.

   The right to private property applies in many circumstances. The owner of a printing press can decide whether it would be more profitable to print books or business cards or to sell the operation to someone else. The owner of a small building might want to operate a boutique or to lease the space. Because of the right of private property, the owners of a fast-food restaurant can enforce a dress code on customers, such as "no shirt, no shoes, no service." They own the business. All these options are available to owners under the free enterprise system.

Freedom of Choice   The second basic right, **freedom of choice,** means that businesses can hire people, invest money, purchase machinery and equipment, and choose the markets where they wish to operate. Quite simply, a business is free to function in any way it sees fit as long as no laws are broken. This freedom extends to employees and customers. A person working at the college bookstore is free to quit and go to work at a local supermarket. Or the person can try for a better salary and benefit package at a local Sears outlet and go to work there. As long as the product is legal and they have the money, customers can buy whatever they would like. People are free to make whatever career or purchase choices they feel are best.

Freedom of choice   The freedom of businesses to hire people, invest money, purchase machinery and equipment, and choose the markets where they wish to operate.

Right to Rewards   The third basic right in the free enterprise system is the **right to rewards.** This is the owner's right to all of the profits, after taxes, that accrue from business activity. The owners of a business may take the

Right to rewards   The owner's right to all of the profits, after taxes, that accrue from business activity.

profits and use them in any way — put them back into the business or distribute them.

For example, a student group could go into the campus-calendar business. They could round up appropriate campus models, photograph them, and produce the calendars at a local printer. The costs involved, such as the photographer's and models' fees and the printing charge, are the expenses. The revenues would come from selling the calendars. If the revenues exceed the expenses, the students have made a profit. After paying the appropriate taxes, they can use the profits to buy photography or printing equipment for future calendars, distribute the profits to the members of the group, or donate the profits to their favorite charity. The owners of a business can even sell the business, pay tax on the gains, and retire on what is left.

The right to profits drives the free enterprise system to continually grow and become more effective. Unfortunately, the profit motive has sometimes been abused; owners have been known to attempt to exploit employees or customers. Nevertheless, most business people realize that they can earn the greatest long-term profits when customers and employees are satisfied.

Factors of Production

Besides the three basic rights, free enterprise and a market economy depend on four factors of production: land, labor, capital, and entrepreneurship. These are the resources on which businesses draw to produce the goods and services they sell. Although other economic systems use some of these factors, notably land and labor, and some free enterprise businesses rely more heavily on one factor than on another, all free enterprise businesses use some combination of the four.

The first three — land, labor, and capital — have been recognized through the years. We have added the fourth — entrepreneurship — because it has now become clear that this is also a vital factor of modern business. Entrepreneurship receives special treatment in Chapter 7; this discussion introduces it along with the other, more traditional factors of production.

Land The geographic territory, including water and natural resources, used in producing goods and services.

Land The term **land** refers to the geographic territory, including water and natural resources, used in producing goods and services. Land is literally the foundation of business and includes the site where the enterprise is located. It also includes natural resources for building, heating and cooling, and supplying the raw materials for making the products or providing the services.

Labor The people who produce the goods and services that the business provides.

Labor Another factor of production has traditionally been called **labor:** the people who produce the goods and services that the business provides. Although the term labor has the connotation of operating employees in factories, today this would be expanded to include white-collar workers and even top-level executives, professionals such as accountants or engineers, middle managers, first-line supervisors, and support personnel. All the human resources of the business fall into the category of labor. People, not buildings or capital, run the business. The Diversity Close-up (Assets Must Be Able to Read) describes one way in which business is improving the quality of the labor force.

The labor component represents a significant proportion of the costs involved in operating most businesses. In labor-intensive manufacturing concerns, labor costs may be as much as two-thirds of the budget for operations. At your college, about 90 percent of costs are for administrators, faculty members, and supporting employees.

CLOSE-UP / *Diversity*

Assets Must Be Able to Read

Business firms have long argued that their people are their most important asset. Today, many firms are finding that in order for this asset to maintain its value, they must fight a growing problem: illiteracy in the work force. About 23 million Americans cannot read, and many of them hold full-time jobs. There are a number of reasons for this problem. One is that many employees dropped out of high school and have never had any formal education since then. Some people have simply never learned how to read. Others have forgotten much of their education, so they are unable to meet growing demands brought on by increasingly more sophisticated technology.

What can be done about this? One major step being taken by many businesses is that of teaching their people to read at a level commensurate with job requirements. These programs are taking a wide variety of forms, but there is one common theme: The workers are being taught to read materials that are job-related. In this way, the individuals can take what they are learning and apply it directly back on the job. Here are some specific examples:

At the Stone Savannah River Pulp & Paper Corporation, the company has spent $200,000 on an on-site classroom with a full-time teacher and a dozen personal computers. After three years, the firm has been able to get almost all of the 153 employees who have participated in the program to reach the necessary reading level required to operate high-tech, computerized equipment.

At the Adolph Coors Company the firm spends $80,000 a year to teach employees to read and work toward general equivalency diplomas. The program is run by company personnel and retirees.

At Motorola's plant in Mesa, Arizona, reading courses are offered to workers who test below the eighth-grade level, and the company is experimenting with self-paced and home-computer programs.

Currently, American businesses are spending more than $3 billion a year to teach workers to read. The price is high — but not as high as that of employing human assets who cannot read, and hence, perform, effectively.

Source: Troy Segal, Karen Thurston, and Lynn Haessly, "When Johnny's Whole Family Can't Read," *Business Week*, July 20, 1992, pp. 68–70.

Capital   The money and technology used for operating the enterprise form the factor of production called **capital.** You will learn how businesses obtain and use monetary resources in Part Six. Simply put, businesses need money to buy the necessary land and labor to operate.

Although traditionally capital has been associated primarily with money, we have extended this factor to the concept of the physical resources of a business. In today's businesses the factor of capital includes technology. **Technology** is the application of knowledge to production, physical equipment, and machinery. It has become increasingly visible and important to modern business. For many people, the term high technology — or high tech — suggests what modern business is or should be all about.

When firms invest in technology, usually in the form of research and development or advanced equipment, their goods and services are often more useful or attractive. For example, in recent years technology has enabled the television industry to add stereo. Other developments are enabling TV manufacturers to introduce models that have a very large screen but are less than one foot deep and models that can display multiple channels on one screen. Sometimes technology involves simplifying things, as in the case of a new TV remote control that reduces all the complicated buttons down to just three: power, channel, and volume.[1]

Entrepreneurship   We have added a fourth factor, **entrepreneurship,** to the widely recognized production factors of land, labor, and capital. It is the

Capital   The money and technology used for operating the enterprise.

Technology   The application of knowledge to production, physical equipment, and machinery.

Entrepreneurship   The process of organizing, operating, and assuming the risks associated with a business venture.

Entrepreneur The creator and/or organizer of a venture.

Venture A new business or a new or different approach or product/service in an existing business.

Intrapreneuring Creating and controlling of new, usually risky projects by managers and staff experts within an existing business.

Standard of living The measure of how well off people of a country are economically.

Houston's Fiesta Mart is pioneering the growing of fresh vegetables and herbs a few feet from the grocery store's produce counters. This venture combines entrepreneural spirit with the technology of special Sylvania lighting from GTE and the other factors of production, land, labor, and capital.

Source: © 1989 Jeff Smith.

process of organizing, operating, and assuming the risks associated with a business venture. Entrepreneurship is not new — the founders of American business, including famous businesspeople such as John D. Rockefeller and Cornelius Vanderbilt, were certainly entrepreneurs. It used to be recognized as a factor of production, but only recently has this process resurfaced as the factor that pulls the others together. As one economic analyst has pointed out: "Without this innovative, risk-taking propensity the other factors are basically sterile."[2]

Two important roles are involved in the entrepreneurial process: entrepreneurs and intrapreneurs. The **entrepreneur** is the creator and/or organizer of a venture. A **venture** is a new business or a new or different approach or product/service in an existing business. Typically, the term entrepreneur is used for the individual who founds or develops the enterprise. Three well-known examples are Richard Sears, who started what today is Sears, Roebuck; Edwin Land, who founded the Polaroid Corporation; and Steven Jobs, who cofounded Apple Computer and has now started NeXT, Inc.

In recent years, management experts have expanded their understanding of the factor of entrepreneurship to include innovative risk-takers within existing businesses. This is known as **intrapreneuring.**[3] The intrapreneuring process consists of managers and staff experts creating and controlling new, usually risky projects within an existing business.

Intrapreneurs do not create new businesses; they move existing ones ahead. For example, on the 25th anniversary of Raychem, a high-tech firm, founder and chairman Paul Cook estimated that the company had developed about 200,000 products. This phenomenal activity was not the work of the entrepreneurial founder, but of in-house intrapreneurs — managers, engineers, and operating employees throughout the firm. At smaller firms, such as Convergent Technologies in Southern California, two- and three-person in-house teams have developed successful intrapreneurial projects. Large, well-known companies such as 3M and Hewlett-Packard also depend on the intrapreneurial approach. IBM recently reorganized to promote such a spirit among its executives.

Measuring Success in a Free Enterprise System

The economic well-being of Americans suggests that the free enterprise system is succeeding in the United States. The measure of how well-off economically the people of a country are is called their **standard of living.** The overall economic activity of a country, measured by the gross national product (GNP), covered in Chapter 2, reflects the standard of living. However, a more specific way to measure standard of living is to divide the value of a country's total production by its population. If a nation's businesses produce a great deal compared to the size of its population, then many goods and services will be available to the average citizen, and the standard of living will be high. Conversely, if businesses produce little relative to the size of the population, there will not be as much to go around, and the standard of living will be low.

The American standard of living is high. For example, most American students own a Walkman transistor radio; many also have TVs, stereos or CDs, and cars. An increasing number have their own personal computer (PC). This wealth is not typical of young people in most other parts of the world. Keep in mind that this standard is the average for all citizens. Some

FIGURE 1.1
Modern Communication Technology in Selected Countries

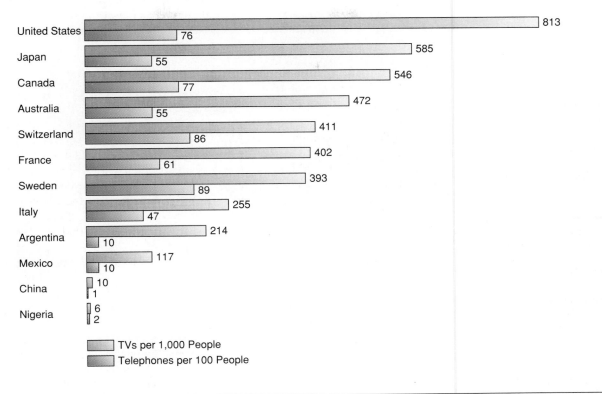

Source: *Statistical Abstracts of the United States, 1989, 826.*

glaring exceptions need attention; pockets of poverty exist in urban and rural areas across the United States. Nevertheless, most Americans enjoy a very high standard of living, which is due in no small part to business.

More consumer goods (televisions, CDs, telephones, VCRs, PCs, autos, and clothes) are available to consumers in the United States than anywhere else in the world. Figure 1.1 compares the quantities of TVs and telephones owned by the people in selected countries. The difference between the standard of living in the United States and in other countries is even greater if we include popular consumer goods such as houses, automobiles, stereos, VCRs, and PCs. In the early 1990s, for example, basic necessities were still rare in the Soviet Union,[4] let alone VCRs and PCs. Clearly, American consumers enjoy a higher standard of living than those in the Soviet Union and most other countries.

Statisticians also measure a country's standard of living by determining how much money the average person earns. Such a measurement is called per capita income, or income per person. Figure 1.2 shows examples of per capita income in various countries. Notice that in the United States average income per person is over $16,000, greater than for most countries.

Of course, this is not distributed equally. Some people make a large amount of money, and others make much less. Overall, however, most U.S.

FIGURE 1.2
Per Capita Income in Selected Countries

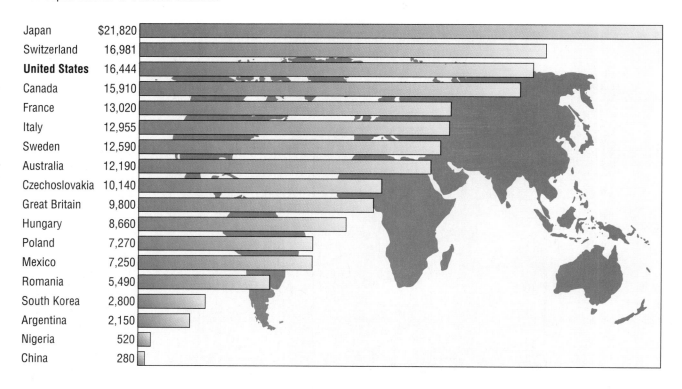

Japan	$21,820
Switzerland	16,981
United States	16,444
Canada	15,910
France	13,020
Italy	12,955
Sweden	12,590
Australia	12,190
Czechoslovakia	10,140
Great Britain	9,800
Hungary	8,660
Poland	7,270
Mexico	7,250
Romania	5,490
South Korea	2,800
Argentina	2,150
Nigeria	520
China	280

Source: *Information Please Almanac*, 1990; and Craig R. Whitney, "East Europe Joins the Market and Gets a Preview of the Pain," *New York Times*, January 7, 1990, 3E.

families are members of the middle class (earning $25,000 or more). The recent trend toward two-income families, in which both the wife and the husband work, has helped to increase income per person and to provide even greater purchasing power per family.

CHECK ✓ POINT

1. What are the factors of production?
2. How do the rights of the free enterprise system affect businesses' control over these factors?

Alternative Economic Systems

Until the end of the past decade free enterprise and the market economy, under which American businesses have operated since the beginning, was only one type of economic system in the world. Then, with the Soviet Union's Mikhail Gorbachev's policies of *glasnost* (openness) and *perestroika* (economic and political restructuring), the Berlin Wall came tumbling down and all of the formerly Communist countries in Eastern Europe moved toward market economies in varying degrees. Going into the 1990s, the People's

FIGURE 1.3
The Basic Economic Systems

U.S. Japan	U.K. Sweden Norway	China Cuba

Free Enterprise People are free to determine the goods and services they need.	**Socialism** Government owns and controls primary industries, but others are in private hands.	**Communism** Property is owned by government, and all decisions regarding goods and services are made by government.

Republic of China and Cuba were the only notable countries that held to a relatively strict Communist economy. Even the Soviet Union, the long-time center of the Communist world, began moving slowly toward a market system. Yet, despite these dramatic developments, it is important to understand the alternative economic systems of communism and socialism. Although no pure form of any of the economic systems exists in any country, one of the three types usually predominates, as indicated in Figure 1.3.

Communism

At the opposite extreme from free enterprise is **communism,** in which the government (or technically, the people) owns all property and makes all decisions regarding production of goods and services. Under this system, a central planning committee decides what will be produced and made available to the people. If the government decides to manufacture radios and few individuals want them, the government pressures the people to buy the radios.

This Laneco supercombination store offering groceries and nonfood items represents what American shoppers expect: a wide selection in a pleasant atmosphere. Without the rewards of the free enterprise system there is little incentive to produce goods. Consumers then face empty store shelves and constant shortages, as has been the case in the Soviet Union.

Source: Courtesy of Wetterau Incorporated; © Gamma Liaison.

Communism An economic system in which the government owns all property and makes all decisions regarding production of goods and services.

Conversely, if the government decides to concentrate on manufacturing defense equipment and to deemphasize consumer goods such as TV sets, most people are forced to go without TV sets even if they want them. The same is true with regard to food and clothing. People are allowed to purchase whatever is available, but if there is no match between the supply of a good and the demand for it, everyone must live with the imbalance. This imbalance became so extreme by the end of the 1980s that it was a major cause for the demise of the Communist regimes in Eastern Europe.

Under pure communism, profits theoretically are nonexistent, and equality should exist between workers and managers. However, Communist countries found that profit was a good way to measure performance and that managers strive to do a good job if the government rewards them with a promotion to a better position or with other special benefits. For example, going into the 1990s, the Soviet government was rewarding managers with a car, a better apartment, or access to stores that sell consumer goods unavailable to the average worker. Although communism is no longer a major economic system in the world today, it is still important historically and may surface again in the future, although probably not in its pure form.

Socialism

Socialism An economic system under which the government controls primary industries, but most other businesses remain in private hands.

Another major economic system is **socialism.** Under this system, the government controls primary industries, but most other businesses remain in private hands. If the government does take over these private companies — an act called "nationalizing" — it pays the owners for the business. Usually, however, the price is below fair market value.

Nationalized industries are usually heavy industries such as steel and large-scale manufacturing, banking, and transportation industries such as the airlines and the railroads. To run these operations, the government often employs a large staff. In fact, the governments of Socialist countries such as England and the Scandinavian countries often employ a large percentage of the population. Many jobs are given out on the basis of political friendship. If new government officials take charge, many top managers are replaced by individuals more closely aligned with the new party leaders.

As in communism, a major goal of socialism is to enhance the public welfare, and the government often provides many services, including transportation, utilities, housing, education, and medical care, at low or no cost. Consequently, many Socialist countries have extremely high tax rates. Anyone making much more than the average worker pays taxes on the additional income at rates that may run as high as 90 percent. This is in contrast to the United States, where under current tax laws hardly anyone pays more than about one-quarter of his or her income in federal taxes and the additional state and local taxes may bring it up to about one-third of one's income.

Mixed Economies

Mixed economy An economy combining the characteristics of free enterprise, Communist, and/or Socialist economies.

Over the years, the various economic systems have been merging. This trend came to a head at the end of the 1980s in Eastern Europe. Pure forms no longer really exist. Most nations have a mix of government ownership and private enterprise. A **mixed economy** is one that combines characteristics of free enterprise, communism, and/or socialism.

Although the United States is known for its free enterprise or market economy, the government still owns considerable assets. For example, it is

Ford Motor Company, like many other U.S. businesses, owns and operates manufacturing plants in Mexico. Despite the socialistic traditions of the Mexican economy, Mexico's government has been encouraging foreign investment and selling off some state-owned industries as they move more toward a market economy and trade with the outside world.

Source: Courtesy of Ford Motor Company.

the largest landholder in the country. National parks, wilderness lands, government buildings, and military installations are only some of the property the federal government directly owns and controls. State and local governments also have large holdings. On the other hand, the U.S. government owns few businesses that directly provide goods and services. The government fills practically all its needs by purchasing from private business firms. In addition, municipal governments are beginning to turn more public services over to private industry. With shrinking tax dollars, many cities are turning to private business to provide their services more efficiently and at a lower cost. The remaining government-supplied services are also becoming more efficient. The potential for competition from private industry spurs government workers to try harder.

In contrast, Communist governments are directly responsible for providing goods and services. Yet in recent years both the Soviet Union and China have softened this position somewhat. Especially the Soviet Union, under Mikhail Gorbachev, has tried to stimulate a deteriorating economy by encouraging plant managers to run more efficient operations and by giving them pay incentives and greater autonomy within their operations. A law allows thousands of Soviet citizens to work for themselves in small family businesses. The Soviet government has also licensed over 135,000 private organizations to run restaurants, operate taxis, repair cars and TV sets, and manufacture everything from dresses to bathroom tiles.[5] China, on the other hand, had made some dramatic reforms toward a market economy in both rural and then later urban centers under the leadership of Deng Xiaoping. Then, when things began to move too fast, Deng ordered a bloody crackdown on the prodemocracy protestors in Tiananmen Square in June of 1989. Going into the 1990s, the situation remains very uncertain in China and doing business there is very difficult.[6]

Despite last-ditch efforts of the entrenched leadership in China and Castro in Cuba, "pure" communism is a thing of the past. In the meantime, former Communist Eastern European countries such as Poland and Hungary are moving toward free enterprise or market economies and letting prices for consumer goods float free, a dramatic change over the previously government-imposed pricing system.[7]

Socialist countries use a combination of state-owned and privately owned enterprise. In Sweden, for example, the government owns 50 percent of the mining industry but only 2 percent of the chemical industry. This pattern is not uncommon. Many countries that have flirted with government control of industries have found themselves unable to manage some of them and thus have returned them to private hands and this trend continues worldwide. Great Britain has sold British Gas for $7.9 billion to private investors. Italy has raised over $3.6 billion by selling ownership in such well-known enterprises as Alfa Romeo and Alitalia. Sweden has sold 30 percent of its nationalized steel company to a private Swedish insurance firm, and Spain has sold its automaker, SEAT, to Volkswagen for $600 million.[8]

CHECK ✓ POINT

1. What are the other two basic economic systems besides free enterprise found in the world today?
2. In what ways are the economies of the United States and the Soviet Union mixed economies?

Challenges Facing American Business

U.S. business has provided Americans a high standard of living, but to continue doing so, it must rise to new challenges. Currently, businesses in the United States need to improve productivity, keep up with technology and innovation, combat unemployment on the one hand and labor shortages on the other, fulfill their ethical and social responsibilities, meet foreign competition, and generate and utilize information more effectively.

Productivity

Productivity The amount of output divided by the input.

The term **productivity** is one of the buzzwords of the 1990s. Although it means different things to different people, perhaps the most common measure of productivity is the amount of goods produced (output) divided by the labor or expense required to produce those goods (input). This formula indicates that productivity increases when output is greater or when costs (inputs) are less.

If Company A produces 500 units a day (output) with 10 hours of labor (input), its productivity is: 500 units ÷ 10 hours = 50 units per hour. If Company B produces 600 units with 10 hours of labor, its productivity is 60 units per hour. Clearly, Company B is more productive; every hour, it produces more than Company A. Assuming that the wages and cost of materials are the same for both firms, this means that the more productive firm should be able to sell its product at a lower price than its competitor. Why? Because the cost per unit is less.

This idea applies to many different projects. For example, a student who types term papers with the use of a computer will turn out more completed pages per hour than a student typing with an electric typewriter. This is because the student using a computer can correct errors and make changes more quickly. The student can use the time saved to type additional pages.

Clark Material Handling Company's Lexington, Kentucky, plant manufactures forklift trucks. Through greater involvement of line employees in production processes and scheduling, line employees were able to eliminate an entire paint shift and increase output dramatically.

Source: Courtesy of Clark Equipment Company.

The Productivity Challenge   In the past, other countries of the world, especially Asian countries such as Japan, have paid their workers much less than U.S. businesses have paid their workers, and thus have had a decided edge in competitive battles for world markets. The wage differential between American and Japanese workers has now almost disappeared, but other problems such as the costly Persian Gulf War, stiff competition from a united European Community (EC), and newly developing countries, such as Taiwan and South Korea, provide new challenges.

Over the past couple of decades, productivity in the United States has grown more slowly than it has in many other countries. For example, the manufacturing output per hour in the United States has grown, but not as much as in Japan, Germany, or even the United Kingdom. The past few years have shown considerable improvement in U.S. manufacturing productivity, but the service sector still remains pretty bleak. Over the past ten years, manufacturing productivity has jumped a vibrant 44 percent, but U.S. nonmanufacturing productivity has risen by just 1.4 percent.[9]

This is especially disheartening in light of the growing dominance of service sector employment in America. Employment in service industries is projected to grow 21 percent in the 1990s. By the new millennium (the year 2000), four out of five employees will be in service jobs.[10] With all of this employment growth in services, where productivity problems are the greatest, the challenge is clear.

Although the productivity of both manufacturing and service is most visible and disturbing in relation to foreign competitors, it must be remembered that businesses must also stress productivity to compete domestically. Those firms with the highest productivity rates will grow and prosper.

Meeting the Productivity Challenge   How can American businesses meet this productivity challenge? In manufacturing, one way is by using the most up-to-date facilities and equipment. For example, Timken, the giant steel maker, has recently spent $500 million to build an advanced steel mill, and General Motors has invested eight years and $3.5 billion in research and development and production facilities to launch its new car, Saturn.[11]

Another, probably even more important, way to improve productivity, especially in the service sector, is to give more attention to new approaches to managing employees. American managers should not necessarily mimic Japanese management techniques, because U.S. workers are different, but they should learn the lesson of giving top priority to human resource management. For example, successful American firms such as Wal-Mart Stores, Inc., and W. L. Gore Company call their employees "associates" to emphasize their importance and to give formal recognition to human resources as a top priority. Lakeway Industries encourages its people to use "aggressive hospitality" with the customers. So while using up-to-date facilities and equipment is certainly one answer to productivity problems, it is not necessarily the *only* answer. People and the way they are managed are also vital to improving productivity. Chapter 11 will discuss motivating and leading today's employees in greater detail.

Technological Change and Innovation

Even though the human side of productivity is vital, managers cannot slight the technological side and the need for information and new ways of doing things. Innovation Close-Up (Touch-Screen Computers) provides an example of an impending technological development. Technology and innovation remain important in helping firms stay up-to-date and effective. Companies use technology and innovation in at least two ways:

1. They can invest in the most efficient, state-of-the-art machinery and equipment. For example, auto producers with the most advanced technology use computerized robots to perform much of the work. The result is higher quality and a lower rejection rate.
2. Companies can discover innovative uses for high-technology equipment. For example, they can use existing equipment to create new goods or services or provide more timely information.

Over the past decade or so, a number of high-tech regions have developed in the United States. In these locations, companies that expend considerable sums for research and development and hire well-trained employees are creating new technologies and products. These regions are located throughout the country, including the famous Silicon Valley (from Palo Alto to San Jose, California), with firms such as Apple Computer and Silicon Systems; the Research Triangle (Durham, Chapel Hill, and Raleigh, North Carolina), with firms such as Northern Telecom and SCH Corporation; and Route 128/95 (Boston, Massachusetts, and its surrounding area), with firms such as BBN Laboratories and Gen Rad. Recently, other high-tech areas have sprung up in such places as Denver, Colorado, and Austin, Texas.

How can business meet the challenge to keep up with technological change and innovation? It can ensure that it has state-of-the-art equipment and processes so that it can produce its goods and services as attractively and cheaply as possible and can train its people to use the latest technology. There is even some discussion at national levels regarding a government-sponsored high-tech industrial policy. Such a policy would encourage American firms to develop greater technological capability and thus better fend off foreign competition in the electronics and computer fields.[12]

CLOSE-UP / *Innovation*

Touch-Screen Computers

Touch-screen computers are a good example of technological change and innovation that will be of use to more and more businesses. A touch-screen computer is an audio-video computer that can provide a wealth of information. Now that most people seem comfortable with automatic teller machines, many businesses believe that American consumers are ready to retrieve information and order products via touch-screen computers.

One of the most interesting versions of these touch-screen machines is the computer kiosk, an innovation frequently found in malls around the country. Some supermarket deli counters in New England have installed kiosks so that shoppers can order their favorite sandwiches and cold cuts without having to wait in line. At Expo '92 in Seville, Spain, visitors were able to use these machines to preview pavilions, find their way around the exhibits, and make reservations at restaurants. At auto shows, it is common to find these units providing information on various models and accessories such as the cost of a new car with specific extras added.

There are a wide variety of functions that kiosks can perform. They can radically alter the costs of service businesses by replacing $6- to $8-per-hour workers. Not only are kiosks less expensive, but the machines can be programmed to provide product and pricing data that would be extremely difficult for people to memorize, especially if there is a wide variety of products and the prices change frequently. Those who analyze the growth of computer kiosks have noted that:

While kiosks are a fairly small business now — about $250 million annually — giant IBM is aggressively pursuing it. "We think it can become a multi-hundred-million-dollar business for us," says Linda D'Angelo, manager of consumer multimedia for IBM. Her group builds complete kiosks, including computer, cabinet, speakers, and credit-card reader. And programmers at IBM's Thomas J. Watson Research Center have studied the best "human interface" for the masses.

The touch-screen computer industry seems to hold a great deal of promise for providing a wealth of different types of services. Of course, some people are going to miss the human touch. However, for those who are pressed for time or simply demand convenience, touch-screen computers may well become a necessity. In the future, more and more people may be saying, "Excuse me for a minute, but I have to run down to the corner kiosk."

Source: Evan I. Schwartz, *et al.*, "The Kiosks Are Coming, The Kiosks Are Coming," *Business Week,* June 22, 1992, p. 122.

Unemployment and Labor Shortages

Another challenge facing American business is to help solve economic ills. One such problem is **unemployment,** the involuntary idleness of people who are actively seeking work. Unfortunately, many people in the United States are still without jobs. Some are seeking **blue-collar jobs,** which are jobs in manufacturing or ones that call for employees to work with their hands. Others are seeking **white-collar jobs,** which involve clerical, office, or managerial work. A recently emerging third category of jobs includes the so-called **steel-collar jobs,** which are jobs performed by robots and computers. These have replaced many of the jobs traditionally done by humans.

This development has resulted in **structural unemployment,** the loss of work because of basic changes in the structure of the economy. The closing of large, inefficient steel mills, for example, has resulted in structural unemployment because many of these workers lack the skills to find jobs in other industries. Efforts by newspapers such as the *Chicago Tribune* and the *New York Daily News* to replace old printing presses with modern ones, if successful, are another example. Many of the presspeople who will lose their jobs will not be able to find new ones because they are ill-equipped to do other work.

How can business reduce unemployment? One way is to retrain unemployed workers and managers so that they can find jobs in new or emerging

Unemployment The involuntary idleness of people who are actively seeking work.

Blue-collar jobs Jobs in manufacturing or ones that call for employees to work with their hands.

White-collar jobs Jobs that involve clerical, office, or managerial work.

Steel-collar jobs Jobs performed by robots and computers.

Structural unemployment The loss of work because of basic changes in the structure of the economy.

The three basic job categories are blue-collar, white-collar, and steel-collar. The employees of Haliburton Company, shown working on a well, are blue-collar; their jobs largely consist of working with their hands. The customer service representative for CompuServe has a white-collar job — he works in an office assisting customers using a computerized information service. The robot shown welding auto electronic components is part of the steel-collar workforce used by Delco Electronics.

Sources: © John Olson for Haliburton Company; Courtesy of General Motors Corporation; Courtesy of CompuServe Incorporated.

industries. For example, Xerox has undertaken an expensive retraining program that, in nine months of intensive, full-time study, prepares outdated employees for new, high-tech careers. Similarly, Rockwell International helped set up a retraining program designed to assist laid-off auto workers in making the transition to high-demand aerospace and defense jobs.

Another approach to reducing unemployment is to remain alert to changing market conditions and to maintain a strong demand for the company's goods and, especially, services. Keeping on top of the changing job market allows business firms to retain employees and even hire more people. To date, these efforts seem to be working. Since 1970, the U.S. economy has produced more than 33 million net new jobs, for an increase of over 40 percent. Moreover, between 1982 and 1990, the United States created more new jobs than Europe and Japan *combined*.[13]

Interestingly, however, even though unemployment remains a challenge, so does a possible upcoming labor shortage. Beginning in the late 1960s, the birthrate started to decline and there may soon be a shortage of entry-level workers. This possibility prompted a General Electric executive to note: "For U.S. corporations, tomorrow's competitive battles will be won or lost on the strength of their ability to build and retain a skilled work force."[14] Table 1.1 shows the jobs of the future.

Ethics and Social Responsibility

Social responsibility The obligation of business to the society in which it operates.

Closely related to the unemployment problem is the challenge of meeting ethical and social obligations. **Social responsibility** is the obligation of business to the society in which it operates. This responsibility takes a number of different forms. One is providing equal opportunity in employment to everyone, including women and minorities. A second is protecting the environment by conserving energy and not polluting or causing any damage to it. A third is providing customers with safe, high-quality goods and services. **Ethics** is the use of proper conduct and behavior. This is achieved by providing the standards of honesty and integrity that govern the conduct of business.

Ethics The use of proper conduct and behavior.

How can business better meet its ethical and social obligations? It can start with several basic approaches:

- Adopting a code of ethics and then rewarding specific incidents that reflect the code in actual practice. For example, ITT adopted a 16-page "Code of Corporate Conduct," ranging from antitrust issues to fire prevention, and publicly recognizes incidents that reflect the code.

- Striving to hire the best possible people regardless of race, color, sex, religion, or ethnic origin. Eastman Kodak and Coca-Cola are two companies that have excellent reputations for initiating programs to ensure equal opportunity in employment.

- Working to provide a safe environment within and outside the organization. The Union Carbide disaster in Bhopal, India, where 2,500 people lost their lives from leaking toxic gases, and the Exxon oil spill in Alaska point to problems that can arise when businesses neglect to pay close attention to their environmental responsibilities.

- Providing consumers with information about the way products work and responding to any complaints or inquiries. For example, General Electric has a toll-free number customers can use to inquire about any of its products.

These are only a few of the ways business has responded to its ethical and social obligations. Chapter 6 will give specific attention to all aspects of ethics and social responsibility.

Competitiveness in World Markets

Another challenge facing American business is to become more competitive in the global marketplace. In recent years, Americans have bought more from foreign countries than we have sold to them. Major ways that U.S. companies can compete more effectively are by increasing productivity, keeping abreast of advancing technology, retraining and hiring the unemployed, being socially responsible, and working more harmoniously with government. These goals are not easy, but they are attainable.

For example, companies such as Motorola and whole industries such as steel, which had some very bleak years throughout the 1980s, are showing some definite signs of a comeback and are competing favorably with the Europeans and Japanese. Some of this comeback can be attributed to the weakening dollar compared to the Japanese yen and European currencies, making imports more expensive and U.S. goods cheaper overseas. But there has also been a major overhaul in these American firms and industries to raise efficiency, slash costs, make better quality products, and sell them more aggressively. Even the battered auto industry is showing signs of improvement in areas such as quality, if not sales. For example, between 1980 and 1989 the Big Three (General Motors, Ford, and Chrysler) reduced the average number of defects per car by over 75 percent![15] The quality gap, if not the sales growth, between American and Japanese cars is beginning to close.

To date, however, even with these changes, U.S. firms are still not competitive in many product areas with Japan and the European Community (EC) or with the newly industrialized countries (NICs) such as Korea, Taiwan, Hong Kong, and Singapore. This inability to compete stems from a number of problems such as wage rates and trade relations. The U.S. government is trying to help by limiting some of the trade privileges, but a definite challenge remains for American business to be more competitive in

TABLE 1.1
Occupations Expected to Have the Largest Number of New Jobs, 1986–2000

Salesclerks	1.2 mil.
Waiters, waitresses	752,100
Registered nurses	612,000
Janitors, cleaners, maids	604,000
General managers and top executives	582,000
Cashiers	575,000
Truckdrivers	525,000
General office clerks	462,000
Food-counter workers	449,000
Nursing aides, orderlies, attendants	443,000

Source: U.S. Department of Labor.

world markets. Chapter 5 discusses in detail all aspects of international business and how American business can meet this challenge.

The Need For Information

Today's world of business increasingly relies on information. Managers have to know what is going on if they are to carry out their jobs effectively. They need enough information and the right kind to make good decisions. For example, in making a long-range plan for the enterprise the manager or planning group must know the resources the company has available and must be able to predict changes that are likely to occur in the environment.

In recent years many managers have found that they are buried with data from computer printouts and reports. However, they do not have the information they need because they lack either the time or the ability to sift through these data to find what they need to know. Another problem is that the managers are unable to obtain accurate, up-to-date information. So they make decisions based on incorrect or incomplete data. Regrettably, much of what managers "know" about what is going on around them is not accurate and they need to gather additional information in order to correct their erroneous view. For example, which of the following statements are true and which are false?

1. The United States is the most productive nation in the world.
2. The United States currently produces 25 percent of the world's industrial output even though it has only 5 percent of the world's population.
3. American firms are making very little money selling their goods in Japan.
4. The country holding the largest amount of investments in the United States is Japan.
5. The country with the largest international holdings is Japan.

The first two statements are true. The United States, not Japan or Germany, is still the most productive nation in the world. At last count, Japan's productivity is about three-fourths of that of the United States (over 90 percent in manufacturing, but less than two-thirds in the service sector, which is the sector that dominates both economies).[16] The United States also produces one-quarter of the world's industrial output with only 5 percent of the population.[17] The last three statements are false. American firms such as IBM, Exxon, and Mobil sell more than $20 billion of goods annually in Japan.[18] The country with the largest investments in the United States is Great Britain, followed by the Netherlands. Although the Japanese are now investing more each year in the United States than is any other country, the value of the British and the Dutch holdings has increased dramatically over the past two decades, and assets they bought for $1 billion in 1970 are now worth many times that amount. Finally, the United States has the largest international holdings in the world.

Most students, and practicing managers for that matter, would not answer these questions correctly. Why? Because they lack up-to-date, accurate information. In this book we are going to focus attention on the need for accurate, timely information and how managers are getting it, because this will be a key criterion for business success in the years ahead.

CHECK ✓ POINT

1. What are two of the major challenges facing American business today?
2. How can businesses meet those challenges?

Why Study Business?

Why study business? What can you gain from such an effort? Studying business pays off in personal and career growth.

Career Choice

Most people spend too little time thinking about what they want to do for a living. They take a job, stay with it for a while, and then move on to something else. In the beginning, this career pattern is neither uncommon nor dangerous. However, over time, these people find that their careers are undirected; they are simply drifting. By the time they finally decide what they want to do, many are well along in age, and the jobs they want are already filled by younger people. As a result, their progress up the ladder is slower than it could have been.

Studying business can help you avoid this pitfall. As you read this book, think about careers in the areas of business discussed in the various chapters. If some area particularly interests you, investigate it further, starting with the Careers Appendix at the end of the book. Perhaps you would like a job in production or sales or accounting. Maybe you would like to go on to law school. All of these are promising career fields — and it is never too early to start thinking about where you want to be in 5 or 10 years. Many successful people have taken such an approach, and many students are already doing it.

Self-Employment   One career option open to you is working for yourself. Small business is one of the major areas of opportunity now and in the foreseeable future. To be successfully self-employed, you need to know many different areas: personnel, operations, marketing, accounting, finance, and management. The study of business can help provide this needed base of knowledge. To that end Chapter 3 covers sole proprietorships and partnerships, Chapter 4 covers small business and franchising, and Chapter 7 is concerned with entrepreneurship.

Service to Others   With membership in our society goes the obligation to contribute to its betterment. Business can help you fulfill this obligation by teaching you how to identify and solve problems, from working on alternative energy sources to hiring those challenged with a disability to providing quality goods and services. By studying business you will not only gain insights into how you can help others in a humanitarian sense but, through involvement in the greatly expanding service sector, you also may be able to improve society by providing services such as education, health care, financial and tax planning, and travel arrangements.

Relevance

Many fields of study are important to personal enrichment, but they are not always directly relevant to everyday living. Business is. This book applies ideas that you can use in everyday living. A better understanding of the world of business will help you better cope with life in the real world. For example, your knowledge of business may help you make better informed decisions as a consumer.

American Home Products Corporation employs more than 2,300 scientists and technicians to develop new drugs and therapies for preventing, eliminating, or reducing health problems such as diabetes, asthma, arthritis, hypertension, hepatitis, and AIDS. The opportunity to serve others can be one of the greatest satisfactions of a career in business.

Source: © 1990 Kelly/Mooney Photography.

Personal Profit and Growth

Business also offers a chance for personal financial gain and psychological growth. On the financial side, successful businesspeople are able to make a good living. On the psychological side, they know they have contributed to society by providing meaningful job opportunities and a better way of life for others.

As you read this book and study for your exams, keep these reasons in mind. Business is an exciting and enriching field to study and practice. As you study business, remain alert to its applications. Keep asking yourself how you can use this information. Also keep in mind a career in business. Millions of Americans have profited from the study of business. You can, too!

CHECK ✓ POINT

1. What are three reasons for studying business?
2. Why have you chosen to study business?

Closing Comments

This chapter lays the foundation for your study of business. Its purpose is to prepare you for getting involved or, in probably the most famous business manager of our time Lee Iacocca's words, "getting out of your chair and doing something" in the exciting world of business. The chapter provided an understanding of free enterprise and the market economy, the alternative economic systems of communism and socialism, and the current challenges facing American business. This knowledge provides a point of departure and perspective for the rest of the chapters.

VIDEO CASE / *Looking for New Opportunities*

Fred Livingston, the successful Hawaiian businessperson described in the opening vignette, proves that with insight, ingenuity, and luck it is possible to become rich in the world of business. Yet, in spite of what most of us would consider an ideal lifestyle of sun and surf, every morning he is the first one in the office. The excitement of the business world brings more enjoyment than anything else. The same can be said for David Geffen, who is the richest of the rich in the glamour capital of Hollywood.

David Geffen, only 47 years old, is already worth about $1 billion. To his friends and business associates, this billionaire status comes as no surprise. Before he was 30, Geffen was already a millionaire thanks to his success in the music business. In 1970 he started a

record company and managed to sign well-known performers such as Linda Ronstadt, Joni Mitchell, and the Eagles. He eventually sold his record firm to Warner Brothers for $7 million. In 1980 he returned to Warner with a contract that allowed him to put together singing talent. Warner Brothers agreed to pay for all the distribution and manufacturing costs and would assume any losses, but Warner and Geffen would split all profits. Within a year, this arrangement paid off handsomely for Geffen.

He tried to sell his share of the business back to Warner Brothers, but they did not want to pay his price. Instead, they made him an offer by which he promised to work for them for 6 more years and they, in return, gave him the rights to the business at the end

of this time. Geffen agreed, and it proved to be a tremendously profitable decision. During this time, he signed more new talent including the then unknown band Guns 'N Roses, which sold over 14 million copies of its first two records. At the same time that Geffen was gaining control of his company, the music industry was consolidating. By the end of the 1980s, Geffen Records was the only major independently owned company in the industry. Then Geffen got a call from the president of MCA, who offered him 10 million shares of MCA stock for his record company. Geffen agreed. Next, MCA sold out to Matsushita for $66 a share, which translated to $660 million for David Geffen. In addition, of course, he has many other investments that have also earned him millions. For example, he owns other securities, a TV station, a real estate firm, a movie company, and Broadway theater investments.

What is David Geffen doing now? Like Fred Livingston in Hawaii, Geffen is looking for new investments that will allow him to continue using his considerable creative and business talents. Also like Fred Livingston, Geffen says that making money is certainly a motivating factor for him, but having fun in the process is what really counts.

Source: Lisa Bugernick and Peter Newcomb, "The Richest Man in Hollywood," *Forbes*, December 24, 1990, 94–98.

Case Questions
1. Is Fred Livingston an entrepreneur? Is David Geffen an entrepreneur?
2. Which of the four factors of production most account for the success of these two businesspeople? Defend your answer.
3. Which of the three rights in a free enterprise system is most important to Fred Livingston and David Geffen?

Learning Objectives Revisited

1. **Explain the basic rights of the free enterprise system.** The basic rights provided by the free enterprise system are the right of private property, which is the right to own, use, sell, or give away property; freedom of choice, which is the right to make business decisions, such as hiring people, investing money, purchasing machinery and equipment, and selecting markets in which to operate; and the right to rewards, which is the owner's right to all of a business's after-tax profits.

2. **Describe the factors of production.** The factors of production are land, which consists of the geographic territory and natural resources used in producing goods and services; labor, which is the people who produce the goods and services; capital, which includes the money used for operating the enterprise and the technology used in producing the goods and services; and entrepreneurship, which is the process of organizing, operating, and assuming the risks associated with a business venture. The first three have been traditionally recognized, but entrepreneurship has only recently re-emerged as an important factor of production.

3. **Discuss ways of measuring economic well-being.** The measure of economic well-being is the standard of living. Often, this is measured as the value of a country's total production divided by its population. Although there are exceptions, Americans currently enjoy a higher standard of living than the people of most other countries.

4. **Define alternative economic systems.** America has a free enterprise or market economy in which people are basically free to determine the goods and services they want, while the competitive marketplace determines prices and wages. There are other forms of economic systems. Under communism, the government (the people) owns all of the factors of production and decides the goods and services that will be produced. Under socialism, the government controls primary industries, but most other businesses remain in private hands. Today we are living in dramatically changing times. The formerly Communist stronghold of Eastern Europe has collapsed and the countries are moving toward a more market-oriented economy. Most accurately, these countries, as well as others around the world, have mixed economies, that is, economies that combine characteristics of free enterprise and a competitive marketplace, communism, and/or socialism. For example, even the economy of the United States combines free enterprise and a market economy with a little socialism. The People's Republic of China and the Soviet Union combine communism with a limited market economy.

5. **Identify the major challenges currently facing American business.** Some of the major challenges currently confronting business include increasing productivity, keeping abreast of technological change and innovation, helping reduce unemployment and cope with a possible labor shortage, fulfilling social responsibilities and being ethical, being internationally competitive, and getting timely, accurate information.

6. **Relate the benefits of studying business.** Some of the benefits of studying business include gaining greater insight into career choices, determining whether self-employment is personally appealing, learning how to contribute to the betterment of society, gaining knowledge of a field that offers relevance to everyday living, and achieving financial gain and psychological growth.

Key Terms Reviewed

Review each of the following terms. For any that you do not know or are unsure of, look up the definitions and see how they were used in the chapter.

business	capital	mixed economy
profit	technology	productivity
free enterprise system	enterpreneurship	unemployment
market economy	entrepreneur	blue-collar jobs
right to private property	venture	white-collar jobs
freedom of choice	intrapreneuring	steel-collar jobs
right to rewards	standard of living	structural unemployment
land	communism	social responsibility
labor	socialism	ethics

Review Questions

1. What are the fundamental rights of the free enterprise system? Explain the meaning of each right. Why are these rights critical to the survival of the system?
2. George Waterstreet is the accountant for a light manufacturing firm. At the end of last year, George calculated that the company received $2.5 million in revenues for the products it sold. The same year, the company spent $2 million on wages, raw materials, equipment, supplies, and rent for the factory. What is the company's profit? Does the company have a right to this entire sum?
3. What are the four factors of production? Explain how each would be used in starting a restaurant, an assembly plant, and a bookstore.
4. What are the primary differences between the economic system of communism and the economic system of the United States? If the Soviet Union begins giving salary increases and bonuses to managers and workers who do an outstanding job, is it changing the economic system? Why or why not?
5. What is productivity? In general, how can businesses improve productivity?
6. Identify two ways in which companies use technology to stay up-to-date and effective. How can this affect productivity?
7. Nancy Norris is a management consultant. One of her clients has asked her to develop guidelines for how the company can meet its social responsibility. What areas should Nancy's guidelines cover?
8. Another one of Nancy's clients is a shoe manufacturer concerned about foreign competition. Nancy's assignment is to suggest ways to meet the competition. What possible activities might Nancy investigate?
9. How can the study of business help in career planning?

Applied Exercise

Along the top of the accompanying matrix are five industries that are critical to the economy of a country. Running down the left side of the matrix are 12 countries that rely heavily on these industries. Go to as many sources as needed (for example, books on these countries in the library) and gather information on the status of these industries in each of the 12 countries. Then, referring to the legend below the matrix, fill in the matrix by indicating the type of control that is exercised over each of the industries. For example, if the airline industry in the United States is privately owned, place a *P* at the top of the first column; if electric power in Italy is mostly government-owned, although there is some private ownership, place a *G/P* in the appropriate box of the matrix. Fill in all 60 of the boxes.

Private and Government Control of Enterprises in Selected Countries

	Airlines	Electric Power	Postal Service	Railroads	Telecommunications
United States					
Australia					
Brazil					
England					
Canada					
China					
France					
Italy					
Japan					
Sweden					
Germany					

P Privately owned.

P/G Mostly privately owned, with some government ownership.

G/P Mostly government-owned, with some private ownership.

G Government-owned.

YOU BE THE ADVISER / *Helping Tony*

Tony Fascell owns a restaurant that specializes in Italian food and is located in the heart of the business district. Tony does a brisk lunch business, and on weekends his establishment is jam-packed from 6:00 p.m. until 2:00 a.m. In the six months he has been in operation, Tony's business has gone from serving an average of 110 customers a day to over 400. In the process, he has expanded the number of tables from 22 to 45.

Tony started out with $25,000 of his own money and another $75,000 he borrowed from relatives and friends. A local bank gave him an additional line of credit of $100,000. He used these monies to buy equipment, tables, dinnerware, and other necessities to carry the business for the first six months. By this time, Tony felt, the operation should be paying its own way. As it has turned out, business has done even better than he expected. As of last week, Tony had doubled the number of people originally working in the restaurant, and sales are 3½ times his expectations.

Unfortunately, Tony has found that most of the new waiters are unable to provide good enough service and process as many orders as he would like. The same is true for the two new cooks he recently hired. However, Tony is convinced that with more on-the-job experience, they will become as proficient as the regulars.

Yesterday, one of Tony's customers, a manager with a British firm, asked him if he had ever thought of expanding operations. "Your restaurant is distinctive and would do well in Europe," he said. "Have you ever thought about opening another one in, say, London's financial district? I have some partners who would be more than willing to put up the money. Think about it and get back with me, won't you?" Tony promised to do so.

Your Advice

1. What do you recommend that Tony do? Read each of the following choices and rank them in order of preference by putting (1) next to your first choice, (2) next to your second choice, and (3) next to your last choice.
   ___ a. Tony should keep his current operation but not expand internationally.
   ___ b. Tony should keep his current operation and also expand internationally.
   ___ c. Tony should close up his current operation and focus all of his efforts on international expansion.
2. What factors of production would Tony be using if he set up a restaurant in London? Which one of these factors would be most important? Why?
3. What types of problems is Tony beginning to have in his current business, and what types of problems will he face if he opens a London restaurant? How can he solve them? Offer some specific advice.
4. What rights of the free enterprise system does Tony have now? Would he also have these in London? If he had a profit in London, would he be as well off as he is in the United States? Why or why not?

THE MARKET ECONOMY IN ACTION

Throughout the Cold War years the United States and the Soviet Union did very little business. Under Mikhail Gorbachev's policies of glasnost (openness) and perestroika (restructuring), this changed. At the start of the decade the Soviet Union began moving toward a market economy that encouraged foreign investment and private ownership. Yet the transition proved to be very difficult. Besides the major political issues, the practical problem was that Soviet currency (the ruble) was not easily convertible in the world market. Foreign investors had trouble converting profits earned in the

Economic Foundations of Business

2

Chapter Learning Objectives

- Identify key economics terms: supply, demand, macroeconomics, microeconomics, and gross national product.

- Describe the four components of gross national product.

- Discuss the four phases of the business cycle.

- Explain the causes of business cycles.

- Identify and describe the four basic market structures.

Soviet Union into their own dollars or other currency. Some companies such as PepsiCo innovatively solved this problem when it sold soft drinks bottled in the Soviet Union by taking payment in vodka, which it in turn sold in the world market. Most companies, however, do not want to become involved in trading their products for other products.

A second problem faced by the Soviet government was the difficulty in getting trade credit from the West so that it could purchase much-needed food for its people. The Soviet agricultural system is extremely inefficient and as the improvements promised by

Gorbachev's perestroika failed to materialize, the Soviets had to turn to the West for economic help. The United States and the European Community (EC) assisted by providing massive amounts of food and giving trade credit. In addition, Western banks loaned double-digit billions. This helped the Soviet Union's short-run economic problems.

Only time will tell how the explosive political situation will end up, but one thing is certain: In order to survive in the long run, the Soviet Union is going to have to make some fundamental changes in its economic system. Many of its organizations

will have to become privately owned businesses, and the industrial sector will have to be completely overhauled because the machinery and equipment is out of date and inefficient. The government will also have to attract foreign investment and become more active in the international economic and political community. As all of this happens, the Soviet Union of the 21st century will be markedly different from that of the Cold War years or even today.

Photo source: Vladmir Vyatkin/Time Magazine.

Introduction

Chapter 1 described the types of economies under which businesses operate around the world — particularly free enterprise and the competitive marketplace in the United States — and also the major challenges to business. This chapter focuses on the market economy and its mechanisms. Businesses must recognize and operate successfully in their economic environment if they are to grow, or even survive. You will learn about both the overall economy (macro) and that of the individual firm or industry (micro) as you study Chapter 2.

The General Economic Environment

Economics The study of how societies use limited resources to fulfill their needs and wants for goods and services.

How societies use limited resources to fulfill their needs and wants for goods and services is explored in the study of **economics.** A simple example would be the need for textbooks in college classes. To produce college textbooks, publishing firms enter into contracts with knowledgeable authors (usually university professors). Under the terms of such a contract, the publishing firm agrees to pay the authors, who in turn research a subject, write about it, and submit a completed manuscript. The publishing firm and the authors are fulfilling society's needs and wants for textbooks.

The process uses resources — labor, capital, and raw materials. Economists call these resources "scarce" because they are limited. This limited supply means that none of us can have as much of everything as we would like.

Economic environment
An environment in which buyers and sellers are brought together through an elaborate series of markets.

The exchange of goods and services takes place in the **economic environment,** which consists of buyers and sellers who are brought together through a series of markets. In the textbook example, the buyers are the students. The sellers consist of all the publishing firms that offer textbooks for a particular course (introduction to business, history of western civilization, principles of accounting, and so forth). The market in this case is your bookstore, where sellers and buyers meet.

Why Business Managers Need to Know Economics

The economic environment is very important for business. To a large degree, it dictates the types of decisions businesspeople will make. Consequently, most successful business managers have a basic understanding of how the economic environment works and the changes taking place within it. They can read economic news and know how these developments are likely to affect their industry in general and their company in particular. For example, book publishers know that as the birthrate slows, so will the number of future students. They also know that in good economic times, many young people bypass college, but in tough economic times, many cannot find jobs and so they go on to college. When enrollment increases, so does the demand for textbooks. An understanding of economic activity in the United States begins with a basic knowledge of supply and demand.

The Role of Supply and Demand

Supply The various amounts of a product that will be provided at varying prices.

The primary driving forces of the market economy are supply and demand. **Supply** indicates the amounts of a product that will be provided at varying

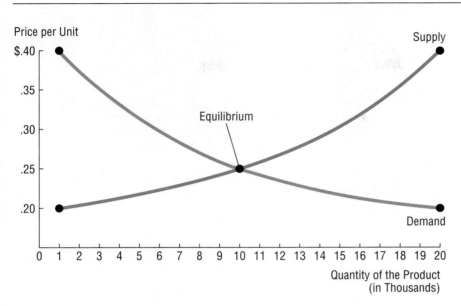

FIGURE 2.1
Supply and Demand for a Product

prices. **Demand** indicates the amounts of a product that will be purchased at varying prices. Sellers will provide a great deal of a product at a high price, while buyers will purchase a great deal of a product at a low price. Business-people are interested in supply and demand because, as the next example illustrates, these forces determine the price at which they can sell their products.

Figure 2.1 provides a simple example of supply and demand. It shows various prices for a simple manufactured product; it also indicates how many units of the product the manufacturer would supply at each price and how many units a store would sell at each price. The supply and demand is also graphed. The graph makes it clear that the buyers (stores) will buy more at a low price, while the sellers (manufacturers) will sell more at a high price. At 40 cents per unit, manufacturers will ship 20,000 units of the product to stores, but the stores will be willing to buy only 1,000 units at this price. However, at 20 cents a unit, the stores will be willing to buy 20,000 units, but the manufacturer will ship only 1,000 units. At 25 cents per unit, the suppliers will ship 10,000 units, and the stores will pay for the same amount. So this is the price at which the parties will strike a deal — the price at which demand equals supply. This price is called the **equilibrium price.**

The relationship between supply and demand is vital to a basic under-standing of economics. It is the way prices are determined in a competitive market economy. In market structures other than a competitive one, prices are set differently; this will be discussed later in the chapter.

The Levels of Economic Analysis: Macro and Micro

The forces of supply and demand provide a general overview of the competi-tive economic environment for American business. But to gather enough information to make effective decisions, today's business managers try to fill

Demand   The various amounts of a product that will be purchased at varying prices.

Equilibrium price   The price at which demand equals supply.

VCRs are now found in about 70 percent of American homes. In 1978 a basic machine cost about $900 and videotapes, on sale, cost $20. The equivalent machine now sells for about $200 and tapes for about $5. Increased demand led to an increase in supply and a resulting decrease in price.

Source: Courtesy of Panasonic Distribution Center.

Macroeconomics The branch of economics that is concerned with the overall economy.

Microeconomics The branch of economics that is concerned with the individual firm or household.

CHECK ✓ POINT

Gross national product (GNP) The total market value of all goods and services produced in the economy in one year.

in the details. They do so by learning more about economics, by studying its two major branches: macroeconomics and microeconomics.

Each of these branches examines the economy on a different level. **Macroeconomics** is the branch of economics that is concerned with the overall economy. For example, when the local newspaper reports that unemployment is down and the number of new housing starts is up, this tells business managers something about the economy in the aggregate, rather than about a particular firm or industry group. The other branch of economics, **microeconomics,** considers the individual firm, industry, or household. Microeconomics provides information about how prices are set in an industry, what influences consumer behavior, and how managers decide how much their business should produce. The rest of the chapter introduces you to these two levels of analysis.

1. Why do business managers need to know economics?
2. How do supply and demand determine the price of a good or service?

Macroeconomics

Business firms are interested in macroeconomics because they want to know the state of the economy at large. Managers need some idea of where the economy is headed if they are to effectively plan for the future. There are many ways of focusing on and measuring macroeconomic activity. The two major measurements are gross national product (GNP) and leading indicators.

Gross National Product

Most attention in macroeconomics focuses on **gross national product (GNP),** the total market value of all goods and services produced in the economy in one year. GNP is a good gauge of the health of the overall economy. When GNP is growing, managers assume that demand is strong. A flat or falling GNP may signal trouble and suggest that a business may have difficulty expanding.

In evaluating GNP, managers have to keep in mind the influence of price. To understand this, imagine a very simple economy in which the only goods produced are fish (to eat) and tents (to live in). Suppose that 2 years ago

Real GNP (in Billions of 1982 Dollars)

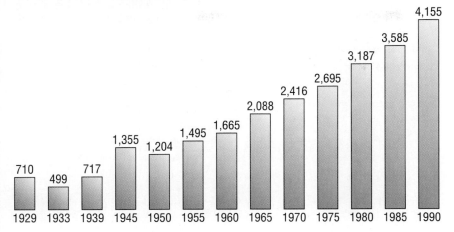

FIGURE 2.2
U.S. Gross National Product
for Selected Years

Source: *Survey of Current Business*, United
States Department of Commerce, January
1991, 6.

businesses caught five million fish and made one million tents, and they produced the same number this year. The GNP for both years is the same, right? Not necessarily. Remember that GNP is the *market value* of these goods and services. If the price of tents has risen from $70 to $75, the GNP will increase, implying that the economy has grown, when really the only change is in prices. We say that the growth is in "nominal" GNP—growth in name only. But if you're a manager and want to know whether the economy is really growing, not just prices, how can you tell?

Statisticians can perform calculations that correct for price changes. In statistical language, this is called holding price constant, and the resulting GNP figures are called "real" GNP, or GNP stated in "constant dollars." As shown in Figure 2.2, the real GNP reflects the actual quantity of goods and services produced. If real GNP goes up, more goods and services were produced this year than last year. Business usually views this as a good sign because it means more people were working and earning incomes, and more goods and services were produced and sold.

GNP is the sum of four different types of spending: personal consumption expenditures (C), private investment (I), government purchases (G), and net exports (X_n) of goods and services, or $GNP = C + I + G + X_n$. Each of these components is defined and discussed in the sections that follow. If the total of all four expenditures this year is greater than it was last year, GNP will rise. If the reverse is true, GNP will fall.

Personal Consumption Expenditures   Personal consumption expenditures consist of all purchases made by individuals and families. As Table 2.1 shows, about two-thirds of every dollar spent in the U.S. economy goes for personal consumption.

Personal consumption comprises several subcategories. One is **durable goods,** which are goods that do not quickly wear out. Examples include

Durable goods   Goods that do not wear out quickly.

TABLE 2.1
Breakdown of U.S. GNP

Type of Spending	Amount (in billions of 1988 dollars)	Percentage of Total
Goods and services purchased by individuals	$3,227.5	66%
Private investment	766.5	16
Government purchases of goods and services	964.9	20
Net exports of goods and services	−94.6	−2
Total	$4,864.3	100.0%

United States Department of Commerce, Bureau of Economic Analysis, "Survey of Current Business," January 7, 1991, 8.

washers, dryers, autos, television sets, stereos, and newly developed electronic goods.[1] For years, American manufacturers dominated the market for durable goods. Since then the market has been dominated by Japanese and, more recently, Korean manufacturers.

Another category of personal consumption is **nondurable goods.** These are goods that are used up or wear out quickly. Examples include toothpaste, soap, food, and gasoline.

Other personal consumption expenditures include services, such as medical care, education, domestic help, and legal and accounting assistance. Purchases of services by Americans have been dramatically increasing in recent years and have become a dominant component of American consumer spending.

Nondurable goods Goods that are used up or wear out quickly.

Private investment Total expenditures for capital goods during a year.

Capital goods Machinery, equipment, tools, and facilities.

Private Investment   The **private investment** area of GNP is total expenditures for capital goods during a year. **Capital goods** include machinery, equipment, tools, and facilities. In other words, as Chapter 1 pointed out, these capital goods represent the technological dimension of business. Another major part of private investment is changes in business inventories, which take such forms as raw materials, work in process, and finished goods. Notice that this definition excludes what we often think of as investing: buying stock, for example, or putting money into a certificate of deposit.

Government Purchases of Goods and Services   The government spends billions of dollars every year. The pie chart in Figure 2.3 shows that at the federal level a large percentage of the money is spent on running the military and for health and human services. At the state and local level, governments spend billions on education, police and fire protection, and road and building maintenance. At the present, government purchases account for approximately one-fifth of GNP.

Imports Goods or services brought into one's own country.

Exports Goods or services sold to other countries.

Net exports The amount by which foreign spending on American goods and services exceeds American spending on foreign goods and services.

Net Exports of Goods and Services   The fourth component of GNP is net exports of goods and services. The United States utilizes both **imports** (goods or services brought into the country) and **exports** (goods or services sold to other countries). Rather than treating them separately, in calculating GNP the difference between the two is taken. Thus, **net exports** refers to

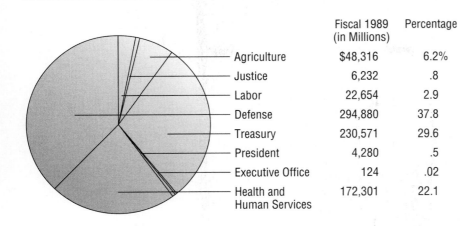

	Fiscal 1989 (in Millions)	Percentage
Agriculture	$48,316	6.2%
Justice	6,232	.8
Labor	22,654	2.9
Defense	294,880	37.8
Treasury	230,571	29.6
President	4,280	.5
Executive Office	124	.02
Health and Human Services	172,301	22.1

FIGURE 2.3
U.S. Government Spending (Selected Departments)

the amount by which foreign spending on American goods and services exceeds American spending on foreign goods and services. For example, if foreigners buy $100 billion worth of U.S. exports and Americans buy $50 billion worth of foreign imports in a year, then net exports will be a positive $50 billion.

Unfortunately, in recent years the United States has been importing more than it has been exporting, so this figure is negative, as Table 2.1 shows. In recent years imports have exceeded exports by billions of dollars. The biggest part of this deficit was accounted for by trade with Japan.[2]

Leading Business Indicators

Business is particularly interested in changes in GNP because these reflect changes in the economy at large, at the macro level. However, rather than wait for changes to occur, businesspeople like to anticipate or forecast what is going to happen and prepare for it. For example, if the economy is likely to grow, business managers want to be ready to expand appropriately. If a downturn is likely, they want to cut back operations and prepare to weather the economic storm.

For this reason, managers pay close attention to the **composite of leading indicators,** which is a set of measurements that provides clues about which way the economy is moving. Table 2.2 shows the 12 indicators that the U.S. Department of Commerce tracks. The Commerce Department combines these indicators into one composite index.

A brief review of some of these variables shows why they are good indicators of what is going to happen in the economy. For example, if the average work week of production workers (#1) is up, layoffs are down (#2), new orders for plant and equipment are up (#6), and inventories are up (#8), business is beginning to pick up and the economy is likely to spurt ahead. If just the opposite is happening, the economy is beginning to slow down. In either case, the length of the lead may be weeks or months. Many business managers keep close track of these leading indicators for clues about how to adjust their strategies appropriately.[3]

Composite of leading indicators
A set of measurements that provides clues about which way the economy is moving.

In recent years, more than a million bars of Dial soap have been sold every day, making Dial the nation's leading deodorant bar. Soap is classified by economists as a nondurable good, that is, a product that wears out quickly. Durable goods, on the other hand, last longer. The total goods and services that individuals and families buy for their personal use represent about two-thirds of the gross national product.

Source: Courtesy of Greyhound Dial Corporation.

TABLE 2.2
Leading Business Indicators

1. The average work week of production workers in manufacturing
2. The layoff rate in manufacturing
3. The value of manufacturers' new orders for consumer goods and materials in constant dollars
4. New business foundations
5. Standard & Poor's index of 500 common-stock prices
6. Contracts and orders for plant and equipment in constant dollars
7. The number of new private housing starts
8. Net changes in inventories on hand and new orders
9. The percentage of companies reporting slower deliveries
10. Changes in prices of key raw materials such as foods, feeds, and fibers
11. Changes in liquid (easily sellable) wealth held by private investors
12. The money supply in constant dollars

Business Cycles

The GNP and the leading indicators provide information about whether the economic environment is growing, shrinking, or stagnant. This behavior of the economy is part of another area of macroeconomics, **business cycles.** These cycles are fluctuations in business activity that progress through four major phases.

Business cycles Fluctuations in business activity.

The Phases of the Business Cycle   The **peak** phase of the business cycle is the period when national output reaches its highest level. This peak or period of prosperity is followed by **recession,** an economic period during which the economy begins to slow and move downward. Recessions are typically characterized by sales declines, employee layoffs, and a general business retrenchment. If economic conditions do not stabilize, the result can be a **depression,** an economic period characterized by prolonged recession and massive unemployment, low wages, and large numbers of people living in poverty. When the cycle bottoms out it reaches a "trough." As the economy begins to turn around, it enters a **recovery,** an economic period during which demand for goods and services is on the rise. During this period, production increases, employees are called back to work, and wages start to rise.

Peak The phase of the business cycle when national output reaches its highest level.

Recession An economic period during which the economy begins to slow and move downward.

Depression An economic period characterized by prolonged recession, massive unemployment, low wages, and large numbers of people living in poverty.

Recovery An economic period during which demand for goods and services is on the rise.

Trends in the Business Cycle   The past 60 years provide a good picture of business cycles in action. This history is shown in Figure 2.4. The Great Depression came to an end with the start of World War II. At the end of the war, some people predicted that the economy would enter a recession. However, except for a dip in 1949, the economy stabilized and experienced positive growth through the 1950s.

The 1960s started slowly, but a tax credit for purchases of new machinery (capital goods) and an $11 billion tax cut for individual taxpayers helped spur the economy on. However, the latter part of the decade saw a rise in **inflation,** which is a general increase in the level of prices. Under inflation, purchasing power is eroded; it costs more and more to buy less and less.

Inflation A general increase in the level of prices.

FIGURE 2.4
The Business Cycle in Action

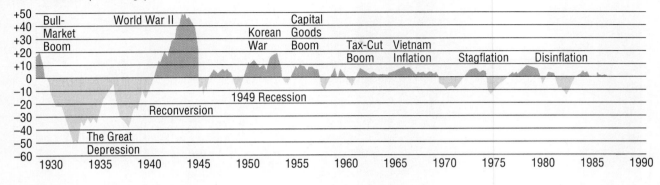

Inflation has had a particularly strong impact on expenditures in such areas as energy, medical care, and transportation.

The 1970s saw the emergence of a new economic phenomenon: stagflation. **Stagflation** is stagnant economic growth coupled with inflation. Before the 1970s, economists believed that inflation occurred only after the economy was at full employment. Now, they realize that it could occur in an economy in which economic growth was still quite low and there was a good deal of unemployment. The Arab oil embargo worsened the situation and, by the end of the 1970s, the United States was bogged down in the worst economic decline since the Great Depression.

The 1980s began on a sour note. For the first couple of years, unemployment remained high, while inflation and interest rates for loans (which had reached 20 percent and more) slowly came down. By the middle of the decade, the group of Arab oil exporters known as OPEC had all but collapsed, leading to a decrease in oil prices, and inflation was under control. On the other hand, economic growth remained fairly slow, and the government was running massive deficits. Overall, however, the economic climate for business, except for the escalating trade deficit, was better than it had been the decade before.

In the early 1990s a recession surfaced. Unlike the previous recessions in the early 1980s, this latest recession seemed to be the logical outgrowth of some long-term problem trends of the previous decade. Specifically, inflated commercial and residential property values started to decline, the banking system came under severe earnings and regulatory pressure, and the national debt remained very high.[4] This recession hit industries such as real estate, retail trade, and financial services particularly hard. For example, Citicorp, the country's largest bank, announced plans to trim 8,000 jobs.[5] Also, similar to the 1970s and 1980s, the Middle East may play a significant role in the American economy of the 1990s. The war with Iraq could have a positive or negative impact. Whereas defense spending can pump up an economy, escalating oil prices and political uncertainties can lead to deferred orders and purchases by businesses of all types and have a dampening effect.[6]

Stagflation Stagnant economic growth coupled with inflation.

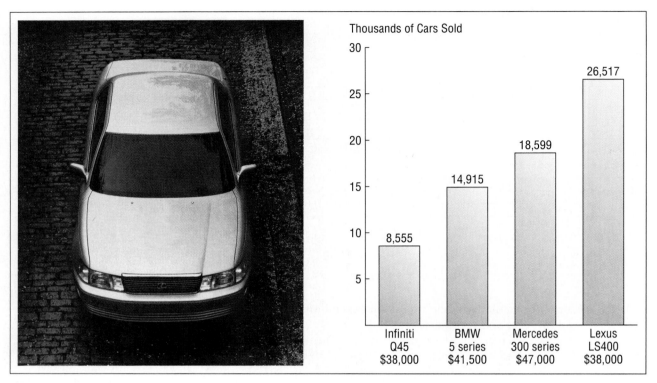

Thousands of Cars Sold

Infiniti Q45 $38,000	BMW 5 series $41,500	Mercedes 300 series $47,000	Lexus LS400 $38,000
8,555	14,915	18,599	26,517

When Toyota introduced the Lexus in the United States, over a third of the buyers traded in an American luxury car. The accompanying graph shows the number of different foreign luxury cars sold in the United States between January and August 1990. An increase in imports such as this, unless other products of equal or greater value are exported, lowers the gross national product.

Source: Courtesy of Lexus.

Fiscal policy The use of government spending and tax collection to attain full employment and a noninflationary high level of GNP.

Monetary policy Government regulation of the money supply to attain full employment and a noninflationary high level of GNP.

Another recent development that is having an economic effect is the Los Angeles riots that have helped call attention to the economic plight of the cities. Some of the implications of these riots are discussed in the accompanying Diversity Close-Up (Is There a Lesson in the L.A. Riots?).

Causes of Business Cycles What causes business cycles? Wars, tax policies, and good and bad economic times are obvious contributors. Often two or more of them are influential at the same time. Also, not every sector of the economy or every part of the country faces the same business cycle at the same time. If a downturn starts with, say, a slowdown in the demand for manufactured goods, then industrial areas of the country such as the Northeast and large urban areas will feel the effect quickly, but rural areas will not. Conversely, if the price of farm products begins to decline, farmers and small rural communities will feel the negative effects almost immediately, while city dwellers will not. If these problems persist, however, there will be a ripple effect. Eventually the entire country will begin to feel the economic crunch. The far-reaching changes can stem from any of the factors that cause business cycles.

In a purely competitive market situation, business cycles would be regulated through supply and demand alone. However, in the American system, the government attempts to influence the economy through fiscal and monetary policies. **Fiscal policy** is the use of government spending and tax collection to attain full employment and a noninflationary high level of GNP. **Monetary policy** is government regulation of the money supply to attain full employment and a noninflationary high level of GNP. These government policies, which change spending or the money supply, can have a big impact on business cycles.

CLOSE-UP / *Diversity*

Is There a Lesson in the L.A. Riots?

The Los Angeles riots of 1992 brought home to everyone in the U.S. the socioeconomic reality and challenge of providing equal opportunity and well-paying jobs for all citizens. Governmental agencies estimate that poverty costs the United States approximately $230 billion annually. Half of this comes in the form of public assistance in terms of food and housing. Another $50 billion is accounted for by the cost of police and correctional institutions. The remaining billions can be attributed to the increase to gross national product that would be realized if the poor were fully employed.

Approximately 42 percent of America's 36 million impoverished people live in the cities. Somewhat surprisingly, 40 percent of household heads of these urban dwellers have high school diplomas, so education alone is not a causal factor of poverty.

More economic opportunities are needed, and the Los Angeles riots have helped to galvanize business attention to the problem. The Bank of America has pledged $25 million in loans to help L.A. businesses rebuild. J.C. Penney is rebuilding two of its outlets in the riot-torn part of the city, as is Circuit City. In addition, the city has appointed Peter V. Ueberroth to head a group that will work to persuade companies to establish businesses in the area. At the same time, the federal government is working to free up $600 million in aid.

Will these efforts be enough to turn things around in L.A.? Not even the most optimistic observers believe it will be. They hope, however, that business will work closely with the local community to create jobs, and that Los Angeles' urban poverty will slowly begin to decline. If it does, Los Angeles will serve as a model for other major cities around the country. As one observer put it, "The urban poor, black and white alike, need a sustained public and private investment so that they, too, can become part of the American dream. And if we fail to act, we will all be the poorer. Morally and ethically."

Source: Christopher Farrell, *et al.,* "The Economic Crisis of Urban America," *Business Week,* May 18, 1992, pp. 38–43; and Ronald Grover, Gloria Lau, and Jane Birnbaum, "Can Anything Rise from the Ashes," *Business Week,* May 18, 1992, pp. 42–43.

Changes in Total Spending The major immediate cause of business cycles is changes in total spending. For example, if the federal government decided to spend no more than it collected in taxes (a balanced budget), deficit spending would end. As a result, the government would spend dramatically less. The government might, for example, cut expenses for military weapons and supplies, research and development, and computers. The resulting decline in the demand for these products may hurt the sales of many industries: defense contractors and aerospace, high-tech, and computer firms to name but a few.

By the same token, by balancing the budget, the cost of the debt would be reduced and there might be a positive long-range impact on trade with other countries. Traditionally, most economists have called for deficit spending to spur employment and economic growth, but, especially after the stock market crash in 1987 and the recent recession, a growing number of economists and politicians began calling for a reduction in the national debt, which means less government spending and/or increased taxes.

Changes in the Money Supply Another influence on business cycles is changes in the money supply. These changes result from federal government activities described in Chapter 19. An increase in the amount of money in circulation makes it easier to obtain; a decrease makes it more difficult to obtain. When money is easy to obtain, interest rates for loans are low. Businesses and people borrow more and spend more, and the economy expands. When money becomes more difficult to obtain, interest rates for loans will rise. Businesses and people cut back on their borrowing; they have less to spend, and the economy slows down.

By monitoring and manipulating the amount of money in circulation, the government can help move the economy forward or slow it down. During a recession, the government wants to turn things around, so it will tend to

Raytheon Company is prime contractor for the Patriot air-defense system shown here deployed with U.S. forces in Europe. The Patriot's successful showing in the war with Iraq may save it from funding cuts that will reduce overall Defense Department spending by 25 percent until the mid-1990s. Changes in the federal government's total spending, however, may cause diversified companies like Raytheon to increase commercial and nondefense businesses.

Source: Courtesy of Raytheon Company.

increase the supply of money. This is called an "easy-money policy." When the economy is moving ahead too quickly, resulting in inflation, the government will slow it down by reducing the amount of money in circulation. This approach is a "tight-money policy."

Changes in Business Investments   A third cause of business cycles is changes in business investments. Businesses invest in many things, including factory buildings, machinery, equipment, warehouses, and inventory. As companies spend money in these areas, their expenditures help increase GNP and move the economy forward. But if the demand for goods and services declines, managers will begin reducing inventory and will avoid expanding facilities or replacing or upgrading equipment. Instead, they will wait for the economy to turn around.

Although managers may make investments based on expectations, changes in business investment often directly follow trends in the economy. As managers notice that the economy is starting to turn down, they will begin trimming purchases. As they see the economy starting to turn up, they will begin increasing inventory and expanding facilities and equipment and upgrading their technology.

Expectations   Besides changes in spending patterns and the money supply, business cycles are also greatly responsive to expectations such as pessimism and optimism. If people believe that prices are going to rise rapidly next year,

CLOSE-UP / *Innovation*

Stay the Course

Economic cycles are a major concern to many Third World countries that are finding themselves beset by high debt and low economic growth. How can they fire up their economies? Some are looking to Harvard economist Jeffrey Sachs to help answer this complex and difficult question.

Sachs is well known in a number of Third World countries for his innovative approaches to economic planning. He worked closely with the government of Bolivia to help stem that country's unbelievable annual inflation rate of 24,000 percent. His prescription for the problem was to immediately institute deep cuts in both wages and state spending. His approach worked. Within 2 years the annual inflation rate had fallen to 15 percent. Now Sachs is working with Eastern European countries such as Poland and Hungary. As these countries moved toward market economies, it became painfully clear that the size of their debts would require some radical action. In Poland Sachs convinced the government to balance the budget and eliminate most consumer subsidies. As a result, the cost of household heating fuel jumped 600 percent and gasoline prices doubled. This has resulted in much hardship, but because they "bit the bullet" early and made some radical changes, the Poles appear to be ahead of their neighbors in moving toward a market economy. As Sachs puts it, if these governments hold the course and stick to their guns, inflation can be whipped and economic growth can be stimulated. It's all a matter of staying the course.

Source: Robert E. Norton, "The American Out to Save Poland," *Fortune*, January 29, 1990, pp. 129–134.

they are likely to buy this year. If people believe the economy will continue its prosperity for another couple of years, they will be more likely to take a loan and buy a home or car or go on a dream vacation.

The behavior that results from these expectations can influence the economy. A strong economy can be thrown into a recession if consumers suddenly stop spending because they believe the economy is going downhill. Actually, it would be their own lack of spending that caused the economic decline, but it is often difficult to get people to recognize this fact. The good news is that expectations are unlikely to start a change in the business cycle, and they can facilitate or speed up an economic turnaround. The bad news is that expectations can worsen an economic downturn. Some of these implications for the economies of underdeveloped countries are discussed in the accompanying Innovation Close-Up (Stay the Course).

CHECK ✓ POINT

1. What are two ways business people evaluate the macroeconomic environment?
2. If you were planning to expand your taxicab business, in which measurements would you be most interested?

Microeconomics

Besides the general economic environment, business managers want to know about their particular industry and their particular company. What price should they charge? How much should they produce? How will consumers respond to a price increase? For these answers, managers turn to microeconomics, the branch of economics that helps explain how businesses make decisions.

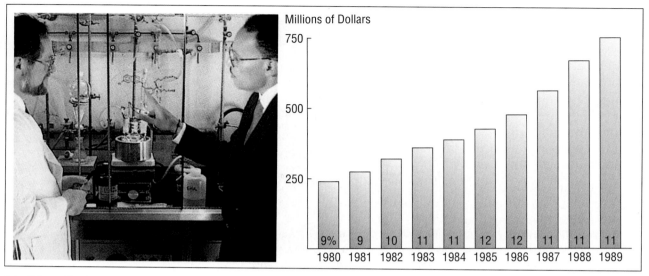

Millions of Dollars

	1980	1981	1982	1983	1984	1985	1986	1987	1988	1989
	9%	9	10	11	11	12	12	11	11	11

Scientists at Merck & Co., Inc., discuss ongoing research on a new drug for asthma. Investment in research and development is one of the strategies businesses employ to assure long-term profits. Over the past 10 years, Merck has consistently raised its R&D expenditures, as illustrated in the graph in millions of dollars and percent of sales.

Source: Courtesy of Merck & Co., Inc.

The Economic Basis of Business Decisions

When economists analyze business decisions, they assume that managers are rational — that when managers make decisions, they weigh the costs and benefits and choose the option with the greatest net benefits. To use a simple example, if you can spend 50 cents for one apple or the same amount for two apples of comparable quality, you will choose two apples. (If you aren't hungry enough to eat two apples, you can save the second one or exchange it for something else.) Likewise, if you were the owner of a business and could choose between earning $1 million and $2 million this year, chances are you'd opt for $2 million, other things being equal. This would be the rational thing to do.

In a free enterprise economy, the benefit that businesses seek to maximize is profit. Remember from Chapter 1 that profit is the company's total revenue minus its expenses. Therefore, to obtain the maximum profit, which is the rational approach, managers must keep production costs as low as possible and revenues as high as possible.

Long-Term versus Short-Term Profits   If the objective of business is to maximize profits, there may be a conflict with being socially responsible. The resolution of this conflict may be found in the difference between long-term and short-term profits. Companies that want to remain profitable over the long term need good relationships with customers and the community. For example, a hair-styling business may decide that it can save a lot of money by hiring untrained stylists fresh out of high school and using substandard or even dangerous supplies, but after a few customers had their hair styled there, word would get around and the shop would be out of business.

When effective businesspeople seek to maximize profits, they consider the lifetime of the company. They try to make products and provide services that people will value enough to buy again, and they try to develop a good reputation in the community. This approach makes some decisions complicated — a more expensive manufacturing process, higher wages, or fewer sales may seem to hurt the company in the short run but may be beneficial in the long run. In addition, a focus on long-term profitability may seem expensive at the outset, but it increases earnings and growth over the company's existence.

Measuring Profits Chapter 18 discusses in detail the accounting statements used for measuring a company's profits, but for purposes of the present discussion it can simply be said that, to measure profits, managers have to calculate the company's total revenue and total expenses. To find total revenue, they multiply the price of their product by the quantity sold. To calculate total costs, they multiply the cost of producing one unit of their product by the number of units produced and add the costs that are there no matter how many units are produced (for example, lights, heat, and rent). In general, the amount the company will want to produce is the quantity at which the difference between revenues and costs is greatest.

One way a company could increase profits would be to sell the same quantity at a higher price. But remember that, in a competitive economic environment, demand falls with an increase in price. If the quantity sold decreases sharply, the company can actually earn less profit by charging a higher price. Therefore, businesspeople try to determine how sensitive consumers are to the price of their product. For example, because some consumers are relatively insensitive to the prices of luxuries such as designer clothing, sellers of designer clothes can charge high prices. In general, sensitivity to price is influenced by the type of competition the supplier faces.

Competition and Market Structure

To learn about the kind of competitive environment they face, owners and managers try to understand the type of market structure in which their business is operating. The market structure influences how buyers and competitors make decisions. In particular, knowing this helps owners and managers determine price and develop other competitive strategies.

The market structures in which businesses in a free enterprise economic system operate fall into four major categories: pure monopoly, oligopoly, monopolistic competition, and pure competition.

Pure Monopoly A **pure monopoly** is a market in which there is only one seller or producer and there are no substitutes for the product or service. The most common examples are public utilities, which are established and regulated by the government. These utilities, such as the local power company, have the exclusive right to sell their output to area residents and businesses.

Pure monopolies are discouraged legally and philosophically in a free enterprise or market economy and thus rarely occur in the private sector. Nevertheless, some companies such as Polaroid come close. When Polaroid first produced the "instant picture" camera, it had a monopoly because, as their major competitor Kodak learned the hard way, no one else was able to duplicate this product. The company was able to maintain its monopoly because it applied for, and was granted, a **patent,** a federal government grant of exclusive control over and use of a discovery or a new product or process for 17 years. Although seldom associated with monopolies, patents can temporarily create a monopoly-like situation for a company.[7]

Another possible way for a firm to resemble a monopoly is to own the raw materials for a particular product. For example, the DeBeers Company

Pure monopoly A market in which there is only one seller or producer and there are no substitutes for the product or service.

Patent A federal government grant of exclusive control over and use of a discovery or a new product or process for 17 years.

Simple Pleasures® frozen dairy dessert tastes like ice cream but lacks fat. Simplesse® all natural food substitute, an ingredient made with egg whites and skim milk protein through a patented process, gives Simple Pleasures its rich taste. There are several different patents issued on Simplesse technology that give the patent owners the right to exclude others from using the technology and thus from producing Simplesse. This provides The Simplesse Company, the opportunity to recoup investment in the product and make a profit before competing with imitators.

Source: Simplesse® is a registered trademark of The Simplesse Company for its brand of all natural fat substitute. © 1990. Used with permission.

of South Africa owns most of the world's diamond mines and, through agreements, controls other sources it does not own. The International Nickel Company of Canada controls most of the world's known nickel reserves. In essence, these companies have monopolies. They are practically the only seller, and their products have no close substitutes.

Still another possible way for a private firm to create a monopoly-like situation is to obtain the exclusive rights to sell a particular good or service. The local garbage collection service, for example, may provide all of the refuse collection for a given area. Because of the investment needed to provide this service, it is cheaper for one company to do this than many small ones. This is why a city or town may create a monopoly position for the refuse firm by granting it an exclusive contract.

The way a monopoly sets prices depends on whether it is regulated. A regulated monopoly such as a utility can charge only what the regulating agency will allow. The firm requests periodic price increases to allow it to keep up with inflation and plant maintenance and expansion, but the regulators determine the final price. In an unregulated monopoly, the business sets the price that provides the greatest profit. This does *not* mean charging the highest price, because at the highest price there will be very few customers. Although there are no substitutes, the customer may choose to go without. Nor does it mean charging an extremely low price, because at this level the profit may be very small.

Oligopoly A market in which a small percentage of the firms dominate the industry.

Oligopoly An **oligopoly** is a market structure in which a small percentage or number of firms dominate the industry. For example, of, say, 40 companies in an industry, three or four of them may account for 70 or 80 percent of the sales. In the automobile business, General Motors, Ford, Chrysler, and a handful of foreign competitors dominate the industry. In the Pacific market, two airlines, Northwest and United, account for over 70 percent of the market among U.S. carriers.[8] In the long-distance telephone industry American Telephone & Telegraph (AT&T), Sprint, and MCI dominate the market.

In an oligopoly, the strategy of each firm affects the others. If one lowers its price, the others must follow or will lose customers. If one raises its price and the others do not follow, the first must lower its price or lose customers. An illustrative case is the airline industry. Before deregulation in 1978, many major airlines competed for passengers. The same was true several years after deregulation. Eventually, however, only a small number of the companies survived the fierce price competition. By 1990, at the top 15 airports, half the airline passenger business was either controlled by one carrier, or two carriers shared at least 70 percent. Among small commuter airlines the same thing happened. From 1978 to 1989 the number of commuter airlines declined by 28 percent while the number of passenger miles served by the airlines increased by 236 percent.[9] Because few survive in the end, firms in an oligopoly typically try to avoid competing on the basis of price and turn to nonprice competition instead.

Nonprice Competition   Competition in an oligopoly usually consists of **nonprice competition** — trying to win over customers with advertising and personal selling rather than price. This form of promotion (covered in Chapter 17) traditionally has been used to differentiate a standardized product or service. For example, everyone wants good telephone service, and it is irrelevant who provides it. In the early 1990s AT&T was using an effective advertising program to convince customers that its prices were as low as the competitors and lure those who had switched to other companies to return and be hooked back up to AT&T for free. This fight for market share is also being waged by the Baby Bells (the regional firms spun off from AT&T) in the international arena.[10] To the extent that AT&T is successful in this advertising effort, it will be able to differentiate itself from the competition, even though all firms in the oligopolistic market structure are selling a standardized service. Besides advertising, quality[11] and service[12] have become increasingly important ways that firms in oligopolistic markets differentiate themselves. Chapter 9 will discuss quality and service in detail.

Nonprice competition   The effort to win over customers with advertising and personal selling rather than price.

Barriers to Entry   Another important characteristic of an oligopoly is that entry into the industry is difficult. It costs a lot of money to enter an oligopolistic industry because the firms already there have made huge capital outlays for large plants or other facilities, up-to-date expensive equipment, research and development laboratories staffed by specialists creating new products, and patents to protect their current products and processes. Taken as whole, these assets constitute what are called "barriers to entry." Any firm that cannot overcome these barriers is effectively blocked from entering the oligopolistic market.

Monopolistic Competition   In contrast to the few firms dominating an oligopoly, in **monopolistic competition** there are many firms, each offering only a small share of the total output demanded. Firms readily enter such a market because there are relatively few barriers to entry. Under monopolistic

Monopolistic competition   A market structure in which there are many firms, each producing only a small share of the total output demanded.

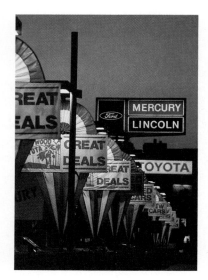

When many firms compete for a share of the market, each business looks for ways to attract and keep customers, who might be lured away by one of the many competitors. Automobile dealers face this situation, called monopolistic competition. Automakers, on the other hand, have only a few, large competitors; their market situation is called oligopolistic.

Source: © Don Smetzer/Tony Stone Worldwide.

Pure competition A market structure in which there are many independent sellers, each offering products at the current market price.

CHECK ✓ POINT

competition, each firm attempts to differentiate its products and services from those of the competition. Similar to oligopolistic firms, nonprice competition is important because the large number of competitors makes it difficult to raise prices. Customers have access to too many other sources of the product at a better price. Video stores are a good example. Mass merchandisers like Wal-Mart and K mart have begun buying huge quantities of tapes and selling them at cutthroat prices. They have begun driving out the smaller video stores that cannot compete with these low prices.[13]

As in an oligopoly, to be successful in a monopolistically competitive environment, businesses must develop a reputation among their clientele and work to improve quality and service. In fact, many consumers today are more concerned with quality and service than they are with price.[14] Service stations are a good example. While one gallon of gasoline is much like another, the services that accompany the gas may vary. At some service stations, when the customer drives in, employees check under the car's hood, wash the windows, and ensure that the tire pressure is correct. Many customers will pay the extra money for the gas because they think that the accompanying services are worth it.

Pure Competition   Under a **pure competition** market structure, there are many independent sellers, each offering products at the current market price. Just as there are no absolutely pure monopolies in modern America, there are also no really pure competitive markets. Although the U.S. government to a degree does influence price and the amount produced, agricultural products come the closest. These products are standardized; consumers cannot distinguish one farmer's or company's offerings from those of another. Also, no supplier is large enough to influence the price. Each is selling only a small percentage of the total output being demanded. For example, a farmer selling corn or wheat will sell at the going price per bushel. Buyers cannot distinguish between Farmer Anderson's corn or wheat and Farmer Brown's corn or wheat, so the farmer simply brings the crops to market and sells them at the going price. The same is true in dealing with vegetables or cattle.

In pure competition, supply and demand are critical to the price of goods and services. Additional factors such as advertising and personal selling, used to influence the transaction in other market structures, are unimportant to those operating in pure competition.

To summarize, Table 2.3 compares and contrasts the four market structures. Managers find that understanding the type of structure in which they are operating is an important part of making effective business decisions involving, say, pricing and advertising, and of making a profit.

1. What are the four basic market structures found in the micro analysis of the American economy?
2. How do business people decide how much to produce?

Closing Comments

The economy directly affects business performance. Few firms do extremely well during a major depression; most are profitable during periods of prosperity. In most cases, however, businesses operate in an economic cycle that

TABLE 2.3
Characteristics of the Four Basic Market Structures

Market Structure

Characteristics	Pure Monopoly	Oligopoly	Monopolistic Competition	Pure Competition
Number of firms in the market	One	A small number	Many	Many
Control over price	A great deal	Depends on what the others do	Some	None
Type of product	Unique	Unique or differentiated	Differentiated	Standardized
Ease of entry into the industry	Not possible	Very difficult	Relatively easy	Very easy
Use of nonprice competition	Some; mostly public relations, advertising	Quite a lot; advertising, quality, and service	Quite a lot; advertising, quality, and service	None
Examples	Local utilities, garbage service	Steel, autos, household appliances, banks	Retail stores, household items, clothing, restaurants, beauty salons	Agriculture

is moderately good to moderately bad, and they must determine how to adjust to short-term economic fluctuations and market conditions. In particular, businesses must evaluate their market structures and decide which strategies will be most effective in helping them compete with other firms in that market or industry. In doing so, major consideration is given to both price and nonprice competition. Companies that are able to do this effectively are often the most profitable in their industry.

VIDEO CASE / *Economic Change*

The Soviet Union is in the throes of dramatic change. At the beginning of the 1990s, representatives from the New York Stock Exchange went to Moscow to discuss how a stock exchange works and to explain why the Soviets could benefit from having one. At least up until the crackdown by the Soviet military on Baltic states and other political unrest, investors from all over the world have been coming to Moscow to talk trade deals.

Foreign investment would be good news for the Soviet Union, which at the beginning of the 1990s was facing very difficult economic times. For years the Soviet economy had been controlled by a central planning com-

mittee that drew up a master economic plan. If a particular product was designated for production, it was made regardless of consumer demand. Similarly, if a product was not assigned for production by the central planners, it was not manufactured even though there was a tremendous demand for it. Under Mikhail Gorbachev's perestroika (restructuring) the government began changing its approach. The Soviet government realized that unless it moved to a market economy and revitalized major sectors such as agriculture and industry, the Soviets were going to suffer economic and political ruin. At the beginning of the decade, the Soviet economy was so weak that some inter-

national banking analysts dropped the Soviet credit standing down to the level of bankrupt Bulgaria.

In the short run, the Soviets need help from the West in the form of credit guarantees so that they can purchase goods such as corn, grain, and other foodstuffs. The Soviet economy also needs investment that can help modernize factories and produce consumer goods as well as investments that will help with long-term projects such as exploring for oil and gas and developing the commercial passenger airline industry. These, of course, are only a few of the things on the Soviets' shopping list and may all change if they fail to get their political house in order. However, the need is clear for a transition to a market economy as fast as possible. Unless foreign investors feel that they have the control needed to run the business efficiently, they are not going to make the needed investments.

Investors from many countries are looking for opportunities, and the Soviet Union must make itself an attractive place for them. Most analysts would also agree that the Soviet government must figure out how to take money out of the defense budget and transfer it into the private sector for the production of goods and services for the

average consumer. This will help gain public support for other needed economic reforms and help speed the realization of perestroika. Can the Soviets accomplish this economic miracle? The jury is still out, but on one point everyone agrees: The Soviet economy is going to have to change dramatically during the years ahead.

Source: Paul Hofheinz, "The Soviet Winter of Discontent," *Fortune*, January 28, 1991, 78–85; Igor Reichlin, "Brother, Would You Lend Moscow a Dime?" *Business Week*, December 10, 1990, 44–45; R.C. Longworth, "European Community to Send Soviets $1 Billion in Food Aid," *Chicago Tribune*, De-

cember 15, 1990, Sec. 1, 3; and "What Gorbachev Wants from Business," *Fortune*, December 31, 1990, 62–64.

Case Questions

1. What are some of the major economic problems being faced by the Soviet Union?
2. How will the GNP breakdown in the Soviet Union change during the years ahead? What is likely to increase? What is likely to decrease?
3. How is the market structure within the Soviet Union likely to change during this decade? What effect is this likely to have on the economy?

Learning Objectives Revisited

1. **Identify key economics terms: supply, demand, macroeconomics, microeconomics, and gross national product.** Economics is the study of how societies use limited resources to fulfill their needs and wants for goods and services. Supply is the various amounts of a product that will be provided at varying prices. Demand is the various amounts of a product that will be purchased at varying prices. Macroeconomics is the branch of economics that is concerned with the overall economy. Microeconomics is the branch of economics that is concerned with the individual firm or household. Gross national product, or GNP, is the total market value of all goods and services produced in the economy in one year.

2. **Describe the four components of gross national product.** The four components of gross national product are (a) the total spent on goods, both durable and nondurable, and services purchased by individuals; (b) private investment in capital goods; (c) government purchases of goods and services; and (d) net exports of goods and services.

3. **Discuss the four phases of the business cycle.** One phase of the business cycle is the peak that occurs during a period of prosperity when national output reaches its highest level. This is often followed by recession, an economic period during which the economy begins to slow and move downward. If economic conditions do not stabilize, the next phase can be depression, characterized by prolonged recession and massive unemployment, low wages, and large numbers of people living in poverty. Finally, there is recovery, an economic period

during which the demands for goods and services begin to rise, production increases, people are called back to work, and wages start to rise.

4. **Explain the causes of business cycles.** There are three basic causes of business cycles. One is changes in total spending, which result in a decline in demand. A second cause is changes in the money supply, which occur when the federal government begins expanding or contracting the amount of money in circulation. A third is the expectations of people regarding whether the economy is going to get better or worse.

5. **Identify and describe the four basic market structures.** A pure monopoly is a market structure with only one firm in the market; the firm is unique and has a great deal of control over price; and other firms cannot enter the industry. An oligopoly is a market with a small number of interdependent firms with unique or differentiated products; control over price is dependent on what the other firms do; the industry is difficult to enter; and companies make wide use of nonprice competition. A monopolistically competitive market has many firms with differentiated products, and they have some control over price. Entry into the monopolistically competitive market is relatively easy and heavy emphasis is given to nonprice competition. A purely competitive structure has many firms offering standardized products; no firm has any control over price; entry into the industry is very easy; and there is no use of nonprice competition.

Key Terms Reviewed

Review each of the following terms. For any that you don't know or are unsure of, look up the definitions and see how they were used in the chapter.

economics
economic environment
supply
demand
equilibrium price
macroeconomics
microeconomics
gross national product (GNP)
durable goods
nondurable goods
private investment

capital goods
imports
exports
net exports
composite of leading indicators
business cycles
peak
recession
depression
recovery

inflation
stagflation
fiscal policy
monetary policy
pure monopoly
patent
oligopoly
nonprice competition
monopolistic competition
pure competition

Review Questions

1. In what way do supply and demand influence the equilibrium price? Use an example and graph your data.
2. If the company supplying the products in your answer to Question 1 were to limit its supply to some point to the left of your equilibrium price, what conclusion could you draw regarding the selling price of these goods? If the company supplying the products were to provide a number of units that were to the right of equilibrium price, what conclusion could you draw regarding the selling price of the goods?
3. Which of the four components of gross national product is most important?
4. What are the four phases of the business cycle? Describe each. In what phase of the cycle is the United States operating currently?
5. What is the difference between inflation and stagflation?
6. If the government begins spending less money on the military, how might this affect gross national product? Would GNP decline? Why or why not?
7. What is the difference between monetary and fiscal policy? Compare and contrast the two.
8. Ned Overton is a small banker who follows economic news closely. Ned has drawn a number of conclusions regarding what is likely to happen in the economy over the next 6 months. Review each of these conclusions and determine if it is good or bad news for Ned.
   a. Total spending will increase by 7 percent.
   b. The government is going to start reducing the amount of money in circulation.
   c. Business people are beginning to increase the size of their inventories.
   d. The number of people in the local area will increase by 10 percent over the next 18 months.
   e. Most people Ned talks to believe that the economy will grow strongly for the next 24 months.
9. Roberta Ogilvy is in an oligopolistic industry. As head of the planning department, she recommends strategies to the executive committee. What should Roberta recommend in each of the following situations?
   a. One of her firm's major competitors has announced that it will increase price by 10 percent effective the beginning of next month.
   b. One of her firm's major competitors has announced that it will decrease price by 10 percent effective the beginning of next month.
   c. One of her company's major competitors has announced an increase of 15 percent for research and development for improving product quality.
   d. One of the major competitors has just increased the amount of its advertising by 20 percent.
   e. One of the major competitors has raised its warranty coverage and now offers a longer, more comprehensive service contract on all new products.
   f. A large company in a totally unrelated industry has announced plans to enter her firm's industry.

10. Pat Jefferson owns a pizzeria. The many competitors in the local area include some nationally known outlets such as Pizza Hut and Domino's. What should Pat do in each of the following situations?
    a. Over half of the competitors just announced that they are going to increase the price of their pizzas by 15 percent effective next week.
    b. Four other competitors have announced that they will cut their prices by 10 percent effective next week.
    c. Three competitors have announced plans to provide home delivery service and the price of the pizzas will remain the same as they are charging in their pizzerias.
    d. The biggest three sales months of the year are coming up and the local newspaper has just called and asked if Pat would like to place any advertisements.
    e. Two new pizza parlors are being built on the other side of town.

Applied Exercise

One of the Big Three automakers determined the supply and demand curves in the accompanying graph for a new sports coupé that the company is introducing next year. Using the information in the graph, answer the following questions:

1. How much will the firm charge for each coupé if it produces only 1,000 units?
2. How much will the firm charge per unit if 12,000 units are manufactured?
3. How many units would you recommend that the firm produce? Why?

Supply and Demand for a New Sports Coupé

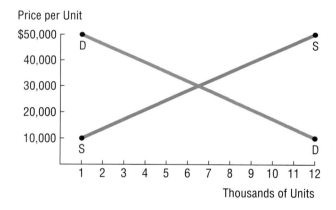

The average cost of a taxi ride to Metro airport is $10 plus a tip, and approximately 1,500 people a day take taxis to and from the airport. Hilda Kramer recently started her own transportation service to and from the airport. Hilda purchased three stretch limousines that are capable of carrying six passengers, and she charges a flat rate of $10 per person each way. An individual who wants to go to the airport in the early morning will call the evening before to make a reservation. Hilda will then have the customer picked up at a preassigned time. If the customer wants transportation home after the return flight, this too will be scheduled. On a typical day each limo will carry a total of 60 customers to and from Metro.

In addition to the convenience, passengers like the extra room in the limo, the coffee and newspapers that are available to them, and the cellular phone that can be used for local calls (50 cents per minute). The service is becoming so popular that Hilda believes she will be able to add two new limos next year.

The taxi firms are feeling the effect of Hilda's service and have countered with a strategy of their own. Beginning next week all four taxi firms will offer a round-trip airport ticket for $18. The ticket can be purchased at the airport or from any cab driver and is good for any locale within 18 miles from the airport.

Your Advice

1. What strategy should Hilda employ in response to the cab firms? Rank order your answers.
   - ____ a. Cut her price to $16 for a round trip and thus undermine their low-price strategy.
   - ____ b. Cut her price to $18 and eliminate the price differential.
   - ____ c. Leave her price at $20 and compete on the basis of better service.
2. How would the supply and demand functions enter into Hilda's pricing decision?
3. Is Hilda affected by outside factors in the success of her business? Name some of the most important.

FROM CHEF TO OWNER

The most common form of business
ownership is the sole proprietorship.
At LA Nicola, a Los Angeles
restaurant, Larry Nicola is the sole
proprietor. His restaurant is located
away from popular Diners' Row in
west Los Angeles. Yet it is able to
attract a waiting-line customer base
for two major reasons: great food and
customer service. Larry runs the
financial side of the business, but he
also makes the final menu choices
and, in his role as chef, runs the
operational side by seeing that the
food is cooked to perfection. At the
same time, Larry has to be people
oriented to work with his staff and to
go out into the restaurant and "work
the crowd." He ensures that
everything is running smoothly,

Forms of Business Ownership

3

Chapter Learning Objectives

- Describe the nature of sole proprietorships.

- Describe the nature of partnerships.

- Explain how a corporation is structured.

- Analyze the advantages and disadvantages of corporations.

- Discuss acquisitions, mergers, and divestitures.

greets old customers, and welcomes new ones. He keeps on top of new trends and knows how to manage change so that his menu reflects the current and emerging tastes of customers. For example, before health foods became a fad, Larry's restaurant was already cutting down on creamy sauces and fatty foods and offering more healthy menu items.

What does Larry like best about being a sole proprietor? He says it is the challenge and the freedom to do things his own way. He is not alone. In recent years, more and more sole proprietorships are being formed by those who used to work for large companies and have now broken away and started their own businesses. In the restaurant industry, chefs often learn the

business through experience and then, like Larry Nicola, open their own restaurants. Because the chef is the most important person in the restaurant, he or she is at a distinct advantage when it comes to starting a new one. A restaurant cannot succeed without a good chef — but there is also a need for management, marketing, and financial skills.

Over the past few years thousands of managers who worked for others have left their jobs and set up successful companies of their own. These sole proprietorships extend from the trucking business to consulting firms. They have several things in common with LA Nicola. Their owners have identified a particular market that they want to serve. They have the talent and are

willing to work hard to reach this market and provide customers with the goods and services they desire. And they have the business structure with the necessary management, marketing, and finance functions in place so that they are able to fend off competition, make a profit, and create a protected niche for themselves. As Larry Nicola would be the first to admit, when a sole proprietorship can accomplish these objectives and throw a little luck in for good measure, then business success will surely follow.

Photo source: © 1991 Suzanne Titus.

The most frequently started small businesses include eating and drinking establishments, automotive repair shops, and residential construction businesses, according to *Inc.* magazine. However, the businesses most likely to survive include veterinary services, funeral services, hotels and motels, and barbershops. Shown here is a bed-and-breakfast hotel, The Victorian Rose, in Cape May, New Jersey. Because a B&B can start out very small, this type of business lends itself to a sole proprietorship.

Source: Craig Hammell/The Stock Market.

Introduction

The first two chapters provided the basic foundation for an understanding of business. This chapter begins to build the structure of business on that foundation. It explains each form of business ownership — sole proprietorship, partnership, and corporation — and identifies some of the advantages and disadvantages of each.

The Sole Proprietorship

An entrepreneur often strikes out alone, for example, starting a construction firm to build homes or setting aside space in the garage to make a product. Sometimes the business grows to a point where the owner wants to share ownership, but often the entrepreneur enjoys and profits from going it alone. A business owned by one individual is called a **sole proprietorship.**

Sole proprietorship A business owned by one individual.

This is the most common form of business ownership in the United States, and because of the entrepreneurial spirit sweeping America, the number of sole proprietorships is still growing. At present they are increasing at the rate of about 400,000 annually.[1] Figure 3.1 shows the proportion of proprietorships relative to partnerships and corporations in terms of number, sales, and profits.

Advantages of the Sole Proprietorship

The sole proprietorship is a popular form of ownership for good reason: It offers many benefits. The major ones are the ease of starting and dissolving the company, the retention of all profits, and the control over operations and information.

Ease of Formation   Setting up a sole proprietorship is relatively simple. Except when the owner needs a license, such as for a liquor store or a barbershop, he or she need not obtain government permission. Furthermore, other than some paperwork pertaining to registering the name of the company and/or sales tax, the government does not require the owner to fill out special forms. And in many areas, businesses selling services don't even have to contend with sales tax. In sum, getting started merely entails laying out a plan of action and beginning operations. For example, a student who wants to earn extra money doing word processing simply needs to advertise in the student newspaper; as soon as a customer submits a paper, the student is in business.

Retention of All Profits   After paying taxes, the owner keeps all profits. The owner of the word-processing business does not have to share the money with anyone. An owner who can figure out how to increase profits by working harder or being more efficient can enjoy the entire benefit of the extra effort or insight. Additionally, the federal government taxes all business revenues under this form of ownership at the same rate as individuals pay. Depending on how much the business makes, this rate can be lower than that for corporations. Also, whereas corporations are taxed and then the shareholders pay tax again, sole proprietors are only taxed once.

Direct Control   The sole proprietor controls operations directly. The owner does not have to hold meetings, consult with or get approvals from partners or stockholders, or secure compromises from business associates. This allows the owner to respond quickly to changes in the marketplace and to take advantage of developments. For example, the owner of the word-processing business could decide to specialize in statistical typing. No co-owners would protest that this would be dull or overly difficult. In recent years, some sole proprietors have also been able to effectively fend off competition from major firms thanks to their ability to take direct control. For example, the Manhattan Toy Company with less than 25 employees beat back giant Gerber toy division's patent violation and the little Blue Mountain Arts company forced Hallmark Cards to discontinue their copycat card line.[2]

Ease of Dissolution   The sole proprietor can cease operations quickly and easily. Someone who has had enough of the business merely has to pay any outstanding bills, such as rent, utilities, salaries, and loans, and meet any contractual obligations, such as lease arrangements. Aside from these limitations, virtually nothing can stop the proprietor from going out of business.

FIGURE 3.1
Sole Proprietorships, Partnerships, and Corporations in the United States

Number (in Millions)

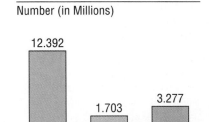

Sales (in Billions of Dollars)

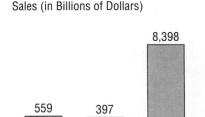

Profits (in Billions of Dollars)

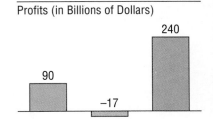

Sole Proprietorships
Partnerships
Corporations

Source: *Statistical Abstracts of the United States*, 1989, 503.

At the end of the school year, the student with the word-processing business could stop working and go home for the summer.

Secrecy Because the owner is seldom burdened with government forms or reports and is not required to divulge operating information to stockholders or partners, operations can remain relatively secret. They are nobody's business but the owner's. The owner can personally formulate strategy and then implement it without telling anyone what he or she is up to. This can be important, considering how closely competitors try to keep tabs on one another.

Disadvantages of the Sole Proprietorship

Even though business owners enjoy the freedom of running a sole proprietorship, this form of ownership does have some distinct disadvantages. Some of the major ones are unlimited liability, difficulty in borrowing money, limited expertise, long hours, limited opportunities for subordinates, and the fact that the life of the business is tied to the owner's involvement.

Unlimited liability Total responsibility for all debts of a company.

Unlimited Liability The owner of a sole proprietorship is subject to **unlimited liability,** which means that the owner has total responsibility for all debts of the company. This liability extends to the owner personally as well as to the business. Under the sole proprietorship, the business and personal property are legally considered to be the same. If the proprietorship cannot pay its debts, the creditors can force the owner to sell his or her car, home, and other personal assets to meet the business's outstanding bills.

Often, a proprietor who goes bankrupt (commonly called going "belly up") loses everything he or she owns. For example, if the student with the word-processing business had borrowed to buy a computer and found that the business's income did not cover the monthly bank payments, the bank could force the student to sell off personal assets such as a car or stereo system to cover the debt of the word-processing business.

Difficulty in Borrowing Money A sole proprietorship has more limited ability to borrow money than do other kinds of businesses. This is because the owner is the only person who stands behind the loan; banks are reluctant to extend large sums of money unless the individual has substantial assets to back up the loan. Thus, the proprietor's ability to borrow money is limited not only by the past and potential profitability of the firm, but also by his or her personal wealth. In the case of the word-processing business, a bank would probably require that a big down payment be made on the computer if it felt that the student would have difficulty generating a great deal of monthly income or if the student owned little of value.

Limited Management Expertise A sole proprietor must excel at many things: planning for the goods and services, supervising operations, promoting and selling the product or service, hiring competent personnel, keeping books and financing operations, and so forth. But it is difficult to excel at any one of these functions, let alone at all of them. The owner's limitations inhibit the ability of most proprietorships to expand and grow. For example, the student's word-processing business would have difficulty competing with larger companies that have experts in selling, financing, and word-processing technology.

Long Hours   Because sole proprietors are totally responsible for day-to-day operations, most of them have to put in considerable amounts of time in order to succeed. If the sole proprietor takes a vacation, no other owners are around to keep an eye on the business. Hired employees seldom share the owner's intense commitment to the business's success.

Nevertheless, the owner can sometimes reduce the time commitment by delegating authority to well-trained, trusted subordinates and by effectively managing his or her time. For example, the student in the word-processing business can work "smarter" (say, by setting up control reports and procedures) rather than "harder" (personally checking all manuscripts for errors).

Lack of Opportunities for Subordinates   Employees in a large corporation typically receive very specialized experience while those in a sole proprietorship may gain valuable wide-ranging experience. However, because they tend to be small, sole proprietorships sometimes offer only limited opportunities to those who work for proprietors. As a result, owners may have a difficult time attracting and keeping talented people. Proprietorships sometimes cannot afford to pay high salaries or offer the benefits, such as a pension plan for retirement, that a larger company can, and they usually do not turn over as much decision making to others. Thus, talented subordinates may move on to other organizations that offer greater opportunities. They may even try to set up a competing business of their own that duplicates what they have learned from their employer. It may be hard for the student owner of the word-processing business to get good help. As soon as a good employee learns the ropes, that person might quit and start his or her own business.

Noncontinuous Business Life   The business's life ends with the end of the proprietor's involvement. If the owner dies, the business usually does, too. If the owner becomes ill and is hospitalized for an extended period of time, the business may have to close its doors. Regrettably, many proprietorships depend exclusively on their owners, and the business cannot be passed on after death. Heirs and subordinates cannot replicate the insight, judgment, and business skills of the disabled or deceased owner. To offset some of the problems that could accompany such a development, many banks or creditors require a proprietor to carry a life insurance policy that will cover financial obligations outstanding after the person's death.

In deciding whether to use a proprietorship, the owner must balance the advantages against the disadvantages in each particular situation. If the disadvantages outweigh the advantages, or if other circumstances such as size come into play, then another form of ownership such as a partnership or corporation would be preferable.

CHECK ✔ POINT

1. What is a sole proprietorship?
2. What are two major advantages and two major disadvantages of this form of ownership?

Bertram M. Lee (left) and Peter C.B. Bynoe were among the group of investors who purchased the National Basketball Association's Denver Nuggets. Lee headed the group, who were the first African-American owners of a major sports team. Typically such groups form a partnership to operate the business.

Source: AP/Wide World.

The Partnership

Rather than go it alone, many entrepreneurs team up with one or more partners. According to the Uniform Partnership Act, in effect in most states, a **partnership** is an association of two or more persons to carry on as co-owners of a business for profit. As Figure 3.1 shows, over a million and a half partnerships are operating in the United States, with total business receipts of more than $397 billion. Most partnerships have two partners, although the law permits more. Each of these partnerships started with an agreement between the partners.

Partnership An association of two or more persons to carry on as co-owners of a business for profit.

The Partnership Agreement
The agreement to form a partnership may be informal, but the partners usually sign a formal written agreement to avoid future misunderstandings. This partnership agreement is a contract that sets forth the specific terms for operating the business. Some of the most common provisions of such a contract include:

- Date of the agreement
- Name of the partnership
- Partnership's business and principal place of operation
- Names of the partners, amount of their investment, and the way profits and losses will be distributed
- Duties of each partner
- Provisions for paying salaries and withdrawing capital from the firm
- What to do if a partner withdraws or dies
- Length of time the agreement will be in force

Types of Partners
The partners need not necessarily share the same involvement in the business and the same liability for the company's debts. Based on differences in shar-

ing involvement and liability, partnerships fall into different categories, the most basic of which are general and limited partnerships.

General Partners   A **general partner** is active in the operation of the business and has unlimited liability. Every partnership must have at least one general partner. General partners have the authority to enter into contracts on behalf of all the partners. A group of students who form a partnership to paint houses during the summer would usually opt to be general partners. Everyone agrees to be responsible for the debts of the business and to make joint decisions.

General partner   A partner who is active in the operation of a business and has unlimited liability.

Limited Partners   A **limited partner** is a partner whose liability is limited to his or her investment in the business. The partnership agreement usually specifies that the limited partners are not active in the business operation. If the parents of one of the students were to put up $500 to help them get started in the painting business, the parents would most likely be specified as limited partners. They would not participate in the business's day-to-day operations and could lose no more than their $500 investment. Big real estate deals and many other popular investment partnerships consist of numerous limited partners and only one or a few general partners.

Limited partner   A partner whose liability is limited to his or her investment in the business.

Special Kinds of Partners   Depending on their role in the partnership, general and limited partners fall into special categories, including:

Silent partner — A partner who is known as an owner in the business but who plays no active role in running the operation

Secret partner — A partner who is not known as a partner to the general public but plays an active role in running the company

Dormant partner — A partner who is not known as a partner to the general public and plays no active role in the company

Nominal partner — A partner who lends his or her name to the partnership but plays no role in the operation

Silent partner   A partner known to be an owner in the business but who plays no active role in running the operation.

Secret partner   A partner who is not known as a partner to the general public but who plays an active role in running the business.

Dormant partner   A partner who is not known as a partner to the general public and plays no active role in the company.

Nominal partner   A partner who lends his or her name to the partnership but plays no role in the operation.

Secret partners are usually general partners; the others are usually limited partners. In the students' painting business, the parents who put up some of the money could be any of these, but typically would be dormant partners. A highly visible, respected member of the community, such as a football coach in a college town, often may be a nominal partner in a business such as a restaurant or sporting goods store.

Sometimes, partners with a limited role come to regret their lack of involvement. For example, Mary Garvey, a silent partner in Grocery Express, was dismayed by the performance of the San Francisco phone-order grocer. The Internal Revenue Service was about to padlock the warehouse for overdue payroll taxes, and Garvey discovered that the store was losing customers because it was constantly out of stock and delivery service wasn't always reliable. Garvey wrested control of the business from her partners, improved services, restocked the shelves, and turned Grocery Express into a prospering enterprise.[3] In so doing, she abandoned her status as a silent partner but turned the business into a success.

Advantages of the Partnership

Like proprietorships, partnerships offer advantages and disadvantages. Some of the more important benefits are ease of formation, expanded financial capacity, the opportunity to draw on complementary skills, the potential for profits, and lower taxes.

Ease of Formation   Forming a partnership is relatively easy. The legal requirements are typically limited to registering the name of the business and securing whatever licenses are needed. If the partners want a formal agreement, they have to pay an attorney's fee, which is relatively small. In the case of the house-painting partnership, start-up costs might involve getting a license and, if a formal arrangement is felt to be needed, arranging for an attorney to draw up the agreement. In total, only about $100 is needed to get started in most locations.

Expanded Financial Capacity   A partnership expands the financial capacity of a business. In contrast to the sole proprietorship, which relies exclusively on the financial resources of one person, the partnership can draw on the funds of two or more owners. This usually makes the business a much better risk, meaning that lenders are more likely to grant a line of credit (a specified amount of funds that the partnership can draw from a bank) or make a loan. Additionally, suppliers and other creditors are usually more willing to extend credit because the general partners are personally responsible for the debts. Two or more partners in the house-painting business would be more likely to have the needed money themselves, to receive a loan for needed equipment, and to get credit from a paint store than would a single student starting this business.

Complementary Business Skills   Because the partnership has two or more owners, the business can draw on complementary business skills. For instance, one partner may be effective at selling, while another is a whiz in financial matters. A third may know a great deal about the technical aspects of the operation. Collectively, the partners can make better decisions than the average sole proprietor. In the painting partnership, one partner might be good at soliciting new jobs. Another might be good at keeping the books and getting the best deals on supplies. Still another might be a good on-site supervisor, assuring quality and keeping everybody motivated and working hard. These complementary skills also have a beneficial side effect. By sharing and dividing up the work, the partners can reduce the number of hours each has to work.

Profit Potential   Although many large partnerships such as real estate ventures are set up so that the limited partners can show losses for tax purposes in the early years, there is nevertheless great potential for profit in the partnership form of ownership. The expertise and resources of the partners often allow the partnership to develop and cater to a market that is beyond the capabilities of a sole proprietor but is too small to attract the competitive attention of a large corporation. In contrast to a sole proprietorship, the painting partnership could cover a larger area and do more work. It might also receive quantity discounts on painting supplies.

Lower Taxes   Partners, like sole proprietors, are taxed as individuals. Depending on the amount of profits the partnership generates, a partner's tax liability could be lower than if the business paid corporate rates and he or she paid taxes on income from the corporation. Thus, the painting partners may pay less tax than if they had incorporated.

Disadvantages of the Partnership

Businesspeople considering a partnership need to be aware of the drawbacks of this form of ownership. Some of the major disadvantages are unlimited liability, the potential for conflicts among the partners, lack of continuity, lack of flexibility, and a complex procedure for dissolution.

Unlimited Liability   General partners face unlimited liability for the partnership's debts. If the partnership's obligations exceed its income and ability to borrow, the general partners must make up the difference from their personal assets.

In a general partnership, where all owners are general partners and therefore have unlimited liability, the agreement usually states that partners will share profits and losses according to the percentage of their contribution. For example, a partner who puts up half of the initial capital and does half the work receives half of the profits and must pay half of the losses. On the other hand, a partner who puts up only one-fifth of the capital and does little of the work will get one-fifth of the profits and must pay one-fifth of the losses.

If any of the partners are unable to pay their share, the other general partners are personally liable. The same is true of lawsuits; each general partner is liable for the actions of all the partners. Even if just one of the partners is involved in something illegal, the other partners are liable for damages. Because of the unlimited liability, relatively wealthy partners could find their liability expanded to include the operating debts of their less well-off partners. If the painting partnership owed $800 at the end of the summer and one of the partners was unable to pay, the other partners would have to come up with the whole amount. Although the paying partner or partners can sue the delinquent partner, they may not get anything.

Interpersonal Conflicts   Sometimes conflicts arise among the partners. While partners often initially agree on which areas of operation each will handle, this agreement often breaks down. A partner begins making decisions that one of the others is supposed to handle, or the partners begin challenging each other's judgment.[4] This squabbling and interpersonal conflict can seriously cut into business efficiency and, in some cases, can set the business back financially. For example, if one of the partners had agreed to paint full-time but now wants to start soliciting business for the partnership or keeping the books instead, the consequences could be arguments, hard feelings, and inefficient operations.

Lack of Continuity   If one of the partners dies, becomes disabled, moves out of town, goes to jail, or simply wants to withdraw from the partnership, the existing partnership terminates. When there are only two partners, this is seldom a major problem. The remaining owner may choose to operate the enterprise as a sole proprietorship and having each partner take insurance on

Employees of Armco Steel Company, LP, monitor a strip of the company's patented aluminum-coated steel as it progresses down the coating line. Armco Steel is a joint-venture limited partnership between Armco Inc. and Kawasaki Steel Corporation formed in 1989 to produce new products like aluminized stainless steel.

Source: © John Madere for Armco Inc.

the other in the amount of his or her ownership would ease the transition. However, when several partners are involved, one partner's withdrawal may spell trouble for the entire operation. For example, if the wealthiest member withdraws out of dissatisfaction at having been obligated to pay more than her share of last year's losses, the business may be unable to continue under any circumstance.

Lack of Flexibility Closely related to the continuity problem is the inflexibility of adding new partners. This may happen when some, but not all, of the existing partners want to bring in another partner. The agreement usually spells out that everyone must concur with such a decision, but as the number of partners increases, unanimous agreement usually becomes extremely difficult to achieve. Thus, flexibility suffers. In the painting partnership, one partner might welcome the enthusiasm of a prospective new partner, while the other partners might doubt the prospect's reliability.

Complex Dissolution Dissolving a partnership is more complex than ending a sole proprietorship. The agreement usually spells out the method of dividing up and dissolving the business. In the case of a two-person partnership, this seldom presents a major problem. However, if there are a number of partners, even a written partnership agreement may fail to prevent disagreements about how much the enterprise is worth and who gets what. The problem is worse when some of the partners feel, rightly or wrongly, that they contributed relatively more to the business. Another problem arises if only some of the partners want to dissolve the current partnership and start a new one. This entails buying out some of the present partners at a mutually agreed-upon price. In the painting partnership, the wealthy partner who bailed out the business during a bad year might object to a final distribution that does not favor her.

Businesspeople considering a partnership must weigh its pros and cons in a given business situation to determine whether this is the best form of

C L O S E - U P / *International*

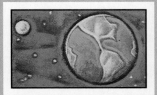

American, Japanese, and German Partners

A few years ago, many computer industry observers were doubting that IBM would be able to survive in the memory chip business. The competition was fierce, and the cost of staying in the game was getting higher every year. It seemed that the Japanese (Toshiba, in particular) would become the major player in the industry. However, this has not happened. The cost and risks of developing new computer chips rose so quickly that even the giant Japanese firms such as Toshiba were unable to keep pace. Despite its large investment and vigorous market effort, Toshiba lost money in the memory chip market. Now these problems may be a thing of the past for IBM, Toshiba and another major competitor, Siemens of Germany.

IBM, Toshiba, and Siemens have found a solution by joining forces in a joint venture to develop state-of-the-art memory chips. These chips will be able to store 256 million bits of data each, which is equivalent to 10,000 pages of typed text. These large-capacity chips are also likely to open the door for computer scientists to achieve breakthroughs in areas such as computer speech recognition, machine vision, and computer reasoning.

If the joint venture partners can achieve their ambitious goal of the 256 million bit chip, they are all likely to prosper greatly. However, the costs are extremely high. In 1992, it cost approximately $500 million to build a manufacturing plant capable of producing the most advanced chips, which at that time could store 16 million bits of information. As the decade progresses, the cost of these high tech plants is going to rise rapidly and is predicted to be in the neighborhood of $1 billion by 1999, a prohibitively large risk for any one organization.

The jury is still out on whether or not the venture partners will be able to reach their objective and do so at price that is low enough to ensure profitability. However, one thing is certain: No company in the computer memory chip market will be able to afford the necessary investment to develop new generation chips. The joint venture of IBM, Toshiba, and Siemens is a sign of things to come in an industry where yesterday's rivals are likely to be tomorrow's partners.

Source: Otis Port, *et al.*, "Talk About Your Dream Team," *Business Week*, July 27, 1992, pp. 59–60; and John Markoff, "IBM in Chip Deal with Toshiba and Siemens," *New York Times*, July 13, 1992, pp. C 1–2.

ownership. The ideal form of ownership may turn out to be a variation of a partnership, such as a joint venture.

Joint Ventures and Syndicates

Particularly important in today's entrepreneurial climate is a special form of ownership called a **joint venture.** In this form of ownership, described in Chapter 1 as a venture, two or more investors or firms share the control and property rights of an enterprise. When viewed as a partnership, it is usually temporary and has the purpose of carrying out a single business project. When the project is completed, the participants dissolve the joint venture. During the life of this form of business ownership, each partner is a general partner.

Joint venture A type of joint ownership that, when viewed as a partnership, is usually temporary and is created for the purpose of carrying out a single business project.

Joint ventures have become popular in real estate developments. A group of investors pool their funds to build or purchase houses or apartments. Once they are sold, the partnership arrangement comes to an end.

Although joint ventures viewed as partnerships usually involve individual investors, joint ventures can also involve separate corporations serving in a more long-term relationship. For example, high-tech firms use them to combine their talents to develop, manufacture, and market such products as drugs, chemicals, and computer hardware. Automakers from the United States and Japan (for example, GM and Toyota, Ford and Mazda) have used joint ventures to attempt to gain market share by combining their manufacturing and marketing efforts. The accompanying International Close-Up (American, Japanese, and German Partners) provides details of a new joint

TABLE 3.1
Types of Corporations

Type	Definition	Example
Public corporation	A business that operates for the purpose of making a profit for the shareholders and has its stock traded in the open market.	General Electric
Private corporation	A profit-making enterprise whose stock is held by a small group of owners and is unavailable for purchase by the general public.	Levi-Strauss
Municipal corporation	A city or township that carries on its governmental functions under a charter granted by the state.	City of Chicago
Government-owned corporation	A federal, state, or local business that is controlled by the government and functions for the welfare of the public.	Tennessee Valley Authority
Quasi-public corporation	A business that is partly owned by the government and partly owned by private investors; can also be a private venture that is subsidized by the government because its operation is important to society.	Comsat (Communication Satellite Corporation)
Nonprofit corporation	An enterprise that is incorporated in order to limit liability and whose purpose is for social service rather than profit.	Stanford University
Single-person corporation	A corporation owned by one individual, usually with the purpose of escaping high personal income taxes.	Authors, consultants, athletes, movie stars
S corporation	A corporation that elects to be taxed as a partnership, while maintaining the benefits of incorporation such as limited liability. Used to be called a "subchapter S" corporation.	Several investors (fewer than 35 under current law) who get together for a real estate project or to buy a small business

Syndicate An association of individuals or corporations formed to conduct financial transactions.

CHECK ✔ POINT

venture. Although the risks are getting increasingly higher, to date there are also planned ventures within the Soviet Union by companies such as Occidental Petroleum, Pfizer, Hewlett-Packard, and Colgate Palmolive.[5]

A **syndicate** resembles both a general partnership and a joint venture. However, rather than come together for the purpose of managing a business, individuals or corporations usually form a syndicate in order to conduct financial transactions. For example, it is common to find syndicates being formed for the purpose of buying sport franchises. Specifically, syndicates were put together to purchase professional basketball teams such as the Miami Heat and baseball teams such as the New York Yankees.

1. Define three types of partners.
2. What are two advantages and two disadvantages of partnerships?

The Corporation

Some business owners seek a form of ownership that is more durable than a sole proprietorship or partnership, which have no legal existence apart from

Company	Sales (in millions)	Profit (in millions)
General Motors	$126,974	$4,224
Ford Motor	96,932	3,835
Exxon	86,556	3,510
IBM	63,438	3,758
General Electric	55,264	3,939
Mobil	50,976	1,809
Phillip Morris	39,069	2,946
Chrysler	36,156	359
Du Pont	35,209	2,480
Texaco	32,416	2,413

TABLE 3.2
The Ten Largest Industrial Corporations in the United States

Source: *Fortune*, April 23, 1990, 346.

Corporation A body established by law and existing distinct from the individuals who invest in and control it.

their owners. They might prefer a business that constitutes a separate artificial entity in the eyes of the law. These owners would want to form a **corporation,** a body established by law and existing distinct from the individuals who invest in and control it. The corporation may take one of a variety of forms, described in Table 3.1.

The corporate form is particularly important in the study of modern business because so many of the country's largest and most powerful firms are incorporated. In fact, while corporations constitute just about 20 percent of all business firms, they account for about 90 percent of all sales and 80 percent of all profits. Corporations also account for more than 70 percent of all wages paid to workers in the United States. Many corporations have payrolls of over 100,000 employees. No wonder that in most people's minds, American business — especially big business — and corporations are one and the same.

Table 3.2 reports the sales and profits of the 10 largest industrial corporations in the United States. These corporations, of course, are much larger than any sole proprietorships or partnerships. However, despite the visibility and power of these large corporations, some of which generate more revenues than the economies of many countries around the world, most corporations are relatively small. In fact, over 80 percent of U.S. corporations generate less than $1 million in annual sales.[6]

Forming a Corporation

To incorporate, the owners must obtain the permission of the state in which they want to incorporate. Most firms incorporate in the state where they intend to do business. However, large corporations, or those that intend to do business nationwide, typically compare the benefits different states offer. Many prefer Delaware because of its lenient tax structure. An incorporated

The panda, a highly endangered species, is the symbol of the World Wildlife Fund. WWF is a nonprofit corporation dedicated to preserving fragile biological resources around the world. The money it raises supports projects like saving the panda from extinction.

Source: Courtesy of World Wildlife Fund.

Compaq Computer Corporation employees inspect new models. Compaq was a three-person start-up company when it incorporated in 1982. By 1990 it had more than 11,000 employees worldwide.

Source: Reprinted with permission of Compaq Computer Corporation.

Domestic corporation
A business operating in the state where it is incorporated.

Foreign corporation A business that has been incorporated in another state.

Alien corporation A business incorporated in one country but operating in another.

business is called a **domestic corporation** in the state where it is incorporated, and a **foreign corporation** in all other states. Not to be confused with a foreign corporation, an **alien corporation** is incorporated in one country but operating in another. Most large corporations are all three — domestic in the state where they incorporate and, because they have facilities in other states and countries, they are also foreign and alien corporations.

The first step in forming a corporation is to submit articles of incorporation to the appropriate state official, usually the secretary of state. These articles are documents that describe such things as:

Name of the corporation

Purposes for which the business is being organized

Number and types of stock that the corporation will have the authority to issue

Rights and privileges of the stockholders

Address of the office of the corporation

How long the company will remain in existence

Names and addresses of the initial board of directors

When the filing is complete and the state gives its approval, the secretary of that state will issue the company a corporate charter. This charter is a contract between the corporation and the state and recognizes the formation of the company in the eyes of the state. Any major changes in the way the company does business will require a change in this charter.

Corporate Structure
According to the corporate charter, the stockholders own the corporation and have the right to elect a board of directors to oversee the company's activities.

The board appoints officers; the officers, in turn, hire the personnel to run the organization. Figure 3.2 illustrates this process.

Stockholders   The corporation's **stockholders** are individuals or institutions, such as employee retirement systems,[7] who have purchased shares of stock in the corporation. The stockholders who own shares in the company and elect the board of directors are called common stockholders. (Preferred stockholders are a special case, and their rights are described in Chapter 20.) Each stockholder receives a stock certificate that indicates the number of shares purchased. Figure 3.3 is an example of such a certificate. Each share entitles the stockholder to one vote.

The number of shareholders of a corporation varies greatly. Small privately owned corporations often issue relatively few shares of stock, perhaps 1,000. The owners of these shares are typically the president of the firm and perhaps immediate family members or those who helped start the company. On the other hand, large public corporations, such as General Motors or IBM, issue millions of shares. The average stockholder generally holds only a few shares, perhaps 100 to 200.

Stockholders typically have the following rights:

To sell their stock whenever they want

To buy newly issued stock before it is made available to the general public

FIGURE 3.2
The Corporate Structure

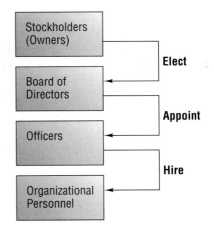

Stockholders   Individuals or institutions who have purchased shares of stock in a corporation.

FIGURE 3.3
Sample Stock Certificate

Source: Reproduced with permission of NCR Corporation.

FIGURE 3.4
Sample Proxy Card

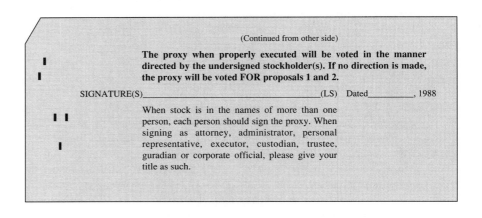

(Continued from other side)

The proxy when properly executed will be voted in the manner directed by the undersigned stockholder(s). If no direction is made, the proxy will be voted FOR proposals 1 and 2.

SIGNATURE(S)_____(LS) Dated_____, 1988

When stock is in the names of more than one person, each person should sign the proxy. When signing as attorney, administrator, personal representative, executor, custodian, trustee, guradian or corporate official, please give your title as such.

Source: Courtesy of Freedom Federal Savings Bank.

To inspect the company's records if good cause can be shown for requesting such action

To vote on proposed amendments to the corporate charter

To vote on the certified accounting firm that will audit the company's books

To vote on the retirement or pension plans the company will offer its employees

To elect the board of directors

Common stockholders are entitled to cast their votes to elect whichever board member(s) they want. If a common stockholder does not attend the annual meeting, which is usually the case, that person may cast votes by **proxy.** This is a written authorization that allows a specified person to cast a stockholder's vote. Often, the corporation will ask its stockholders to give their proxy to management to vote for its own proposed slate of directors. Figure 3.4 shows such a proxy card.

Proxy A written authorization that allows a specified person to cast a stockholder's vote.

Board of Directors   The **board of directors** is the top governing body of the corporation. Its duties include:

Appointing and reviewing the performance of the officers

Helping formulate long-range strategies

Approving top management plans

Setting major policies within which all operations are carried out

Declaring dividends from earnings to be paid to the stockholders

Board of directors The top governing body of a corporation.

Large boards usually consist of a combination of inside and outside directors. **Inside directors** are directors who are employees of the firm. These people are often members of top management, such as the president, the executive vice president, and the controller. **Outside directors** are directors who come from outside the company. They are generally experienced execu-

Inside directors Directors who are employees of the firm.

Outside directors Directors who come from outside the company.

tives with proven leadership ability or specific talents. For example, a corporation that needs help in raising funds might benefit from having a banker or financial analyst on the board. The outside directors are usually from firms in other industries, so that their interests will not conflict with the corporation's.

Boards under Attack In recent years, board members of public corporations have increasingly come under attack from irate stockholders. In fact, it is estimated that the number of shareholder rights suits filed has quadrupled over the past decade.[8] Stockholders have brought negligence lawsuits against boards that have not kept up with the competition by merging with other firms, buying other enterprises, or increasing market share or profits. For example, when the Penn Central Railroad collapsed a number of years ago, the stockholders sued the directors for negligence in their duties. As a result of these developments, some board members now refuse to serve unless the corporation insures them against any claims arising from such lawsuits.

Officers of the Corporation Besides stockholders and directors, the third major group in the corporate structure consists of **corporate officers.** They are legally empowered to represent the corporation and to bind it to contracts. The board of directors designates officers through election or appointment. Typical officers include the chairperson of the board, the president, the executive vice president, the corporate secretary, and the treasurer.

Officers have several responsibilities. They help the board formulate plans, implement strategy, and manage day-to-day operations of the business. They also report to the board and keep it apprised of what is going on in the firm. They usually do this through monthly or quarterly meetings, in which they report on operating activities and results. The officers are answerable to the board, which gives the board overall control of operations and enables it to fulfill its responsibilities to the stockholders.

Corporate officers Individuals legally empowered to represent the corporation and to bind it to contracts.

Advantages of the Corporation

Businesspeople incorporate because this form of ownership offers a number of important advantages. The major ones are limited liability, simple transfer of ownership, continuous existence, ease of raising capital, and professional management.

Limited Liability The owners of a corporation limit their liability to the money they have invested in the purchase of shares of stock. If an investor buys 100 shares of stock in, say, Chrysler Corporation, and this firm declares bankruptcy (which it almost did a number of years ago), the most the stockholder would lose would be the price of the 100 shares. Suppliers and bankers could sue the corporation for their unpaid bills and uncollected debts, but they could not get a legal judgment against the stockholders, officers, or managers of the corporation. This gives considerable protection to and greatly reduces the risks of those who incorporate.

Nevertheless, if a corporation is small and the owner wants to borrow a large sum of money for expansion, the bank is likely to ask the individual to sign the loan both as the corporation president *and* as a private individual. In this case, if the corporation goes bankrupt, the bank would bring action against the president as a private individual and force him or her to sell off personal assets in order to meet the outstanding debts of the business. But except for this case of borrowing as an individual, the bank's only recourse is against the corporation as a legal entity that can both sue and be sued.

Simple Transfer of Ownership   If stockholders want to sell their shares of ownership in the corporation, they can do so relatively easily. For major corporations, where the stock is traded on regulated stock exchanges such as the New York Stock Exchange or the American Stock Exchange, the stockholder merely needs to contact a stockbroker at a bank or brokerage house, such as Merrill Lynch or Dean Witter, and have the stock sold. The broker will sell the stock quickly and issue the seller a check for the amount that the stock was trading for at that moment, minus a commission. If the corporation is a small one that is not listed on a stock exchange, or if it is a privately held corporation, the stockholder may have to seek out a buyer for the stock. Having found such a person, the shareholder is then free to transfer the shares of ownership to the buyer at the agreed-upon price.

Continuity of Existence   Although the articles of incorporation specify the life of corporations, practically speaking, they can exist for an indefinite period of time. The founders of the company can die, the officers can leave, or the stockholders can pass their shares to their heirs or sell them to outsiders; none of this affects the corporation's life. In fact, many of the major corporations in America have existed for decades. For example, Standard Oil of Indiana was founded in 1889, General Electric in 1892, IBM in 1911, and General Motors in 1916.

Ease of Raising Capital   Corporations have a relatively easier time raising capital than do sole proprietorships or partnerships. The reason is that corporations generally have more assets and greater profits than most proprietorships and partnerships. Size alone makes corporations more attractive investment prospects. Large, successful corporations, such as Merck, Rubbermaid, and Procter & Gamble, the top 3 on *Fortune*'s most admired corporations list,[9] can raise millions of dollars in short-term loans by simply going to the large banks and asking for money. Such corporations are able to raise long-term funds through the sale of bonds (long-term loans, which receive detailed attention in Chapter 20) or additional stock. This is attractive to potential investors because they know that there is a ready market for corporate bonds and stocks, so they are not tying up their funds forever. Thus, if Rubbermaid decided to build a highly modernized plastics plant, it could readily raise the necessary funds by selling bonds or by issuing and selling more stock.

Professional Management   Corporations have the advantage of professional management. While sole proprietorships and partnerships are generally managed by the self-employed manager or one of a few general partners, the owners of corporations, especially large ones, are not necessarily the managers. The owners purchase stock and elect the board of directors, which in turn brings in professional managers to run the operation. Although corporate managers generally own shares of stock in the company, they generally do not represent a significant percentage of the ownership.

To finance the creation of facilities and expansion of service — such as the establishment of this hub in Anchorage, Alaska — Federal Express borrows short-term funds from banks and issues bonds to cover long-term debt.

Source: John Madere.

The top managers (the corporate officers) hire specialists to handle areas such as advertising, accounting, engineering, and legal duties. They also employ skilled functional managers to handle the areas of production, marketing, personnel, and finance. These professional managers and specialists bring a degree of skill and knowledge that the average proprietor or general partner simply cannot match. The International Close-Up (AT&T Reaches Out to Touch Someone Overseas) provides an example.

Disadvantages of the Corporation

Along with these benefits of corporate ownership come some disadvantages. The primary ones are taxation, costs of formation, and government restrictions.

The Tax Burden   Although tax laws are constantly changing, the owners of corporations traditionally have a relatively heavy tax burden. Corporations may be subject to higher tax rates than sole proprietorships or partnerships, which are taxed at individual rates. Additionally, any dividends the stockholders receive come from after-tax earnings of the corporation, and these dividends are *again* eligible for taxation on the individual stockholder's income tax return. As pointed out earlier, sole proprietors and partnerships can avoid this double taxation.

Some states provide tax relief to businesses that take the form of **S corporations.** These are small corporations (fewer than 35 stockholders) that are taxed as partnerships but maintain the rights and liabilities of the corporate form of ownership. S corporations were formerly called subchapter S corporations, taking their name from Chapter S of the Internal Revenue Code. The major advantage to S corporations occurs if there is a wide difference between the tax rate for corporations and individuals. As this gap narrows, the S corporation becomes less attractive.[10]

S corporation A corporation that has fewer than 35 stockholders and is taxed as a partnership but maintains the rights and liabilities of a corporation.

CLOSE-UP / *International*

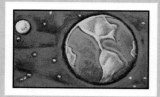

AT&T Reaches Out to Touch Someone Overseas

Professional management is useful not only for domestic operations but in providing companies with the talent needed to manage their overseas businesses. AT&T, the giant communications firm, has been doing business overseas for decades. In the beginning AT&T was quite successful, but during the 1980s it began to realize that competition was much stiffer than before. Since then the company has had to rely heavily on its managerial expertise to compete against very well-managed, well-financed international competitors. For a while the phone giant appeared to be outclassed. For example, in China AT&T sold 10 big switches but then the company lost the business to suppliers because of an unwillingness to show China how to make integrated circuits. Management's reluctance to follow through on this phase of the operation cost the company dearly. In another case AT&T teamed up with Olivetti of Italy in a joint venture. However, the project never produced the anticipated sales because the managements of the two companies could not synchronize their efforts.

The future, however, looks quite bright. AT&T management clinched a major equipment order in Indonesia, thanks to the company's decision to help build a "mini Bell Lab" in that country. The contract should be worth about $500 million to AT&T. In another case the company transferred chip-making technology to its joint venture partner, Compania Telefonica Nacional de Espana, and this phone company helped AT&T land a contract with a local switchmaker. In addition, AT&T is getting millions of dollars from Telefonica's switch business. In a third instance, AT&T and its Thailand partner, Shinawatra Computer, bid on equipment orders that could reach $1 billion or more. AT&T's management is learning how to interact more effectively with overseas partners and clients and the bottom line is beginning to show results. In 1985 the company was making 7 percent of its revenue in overseas markets; in 1991 the firm was expected to gross 19 percent from these sources.

Source: Dinah Lee, Jonathan Levine, and Peter Coy, "AT&T Slowly Gets Its Global Wires Uncrossed," *Business Week*, February 11, 1991, 82–83.

Cost and Trouble of Formation Forming a corporation can be expensive. Corporations encounter a number of different types of organizing fees, such as expenses associated with securing the original charter, fees that must be paid to do business in states where the business is not incorporated, and legal expenses associated with the start-up activities. Besides these monetary costs, the original owners must expend time and trouble to go through all the procedures required for incorporation. The previously discussed student-run businesses of word processing and house painting would not be good candidates to form corporations, because the expense and effort required may outweigh the potential benefits.

Government Restrictions The government regulates public corporations more closely than sole proprietorships or partnerships.[11] For example, they must file reports related to any sale of stocks or bonds, and these sales are monitored by governmental agencies. All corporations must comply with certain laws if they decide to merge or consolidate their holdings with those of another firm. Corporations must also file financial reports with the government and, in the case of regulated industries such as utilities, must submit them periodically. Thus, not only is starting a corporation relatively difficult, but the business must follow many procedures and regulations once it gets going.

When starting a new business or evaluating an existing one, entrepreneurs, managers, and investors must weigh the advantages and disadvantages of each form of ownership in order to determine which is best for them.

TABLE 3.3
Advantages and Disadvantages of Sole Proprietorships, Partnerships, and Corporations

	Advantages	**Disadvantages**
Sole proprietorships	1. Ease of formation 2. Retention of all profits 3. Direct control 4. Ease of dissolution 5. Secrecy	1. Unlimited liability 2. Difficulty of raising capital 3. Limited management expertise 4. Lack of employee opportunities 5. Lack of continuity
Partnerships	1. Ease of formation 2. Expanded financial capacity 3. Complementary business skills 4. Profit potential	1. Unlimited liability 2. Interpersonal conflicts 3. Lack of continuity 4. Difficulty of dissolution
Corporations	1. Limited liability 2. Simple transfer of ownership 3. Continuity of existence 4. Ease of raising capital 5. Professional management	1. Heavy taxation 2. Cost of formation 3. Government restrictions

Table 3.3 summarizes the advantages and disadvantages of the three major forms: sole proprietorships, partnerships, and corporations.

1. What is a corporation?
2. What are two advantages and two disadvantages of the corporate form of ownership?

CHECK ✓ POINT

Corporate Trends: Acquisitions, Mergers, and Divestitures

Business ownership is constantly changing. Fast-growing sole proprietorships and partnerships often incorporate. Businesses of all kinds enter into joint ventures with one another. Among corporations, major changes that have been important in recent years include acquisitions, mergers, and divestitures.

Acquisitions

When one company buys another and takes over its operations and property, this is called an **acquisition.** Over the past decade in the auto industry, for example, Ford has bought Jaguar, General Motors has purchased Lotus, and Chrysler has acquired Lamborghini and American Motors. In other industries Georgia Pacific acquired Northern Nekoosa, United Air Lines purchased Pan American's Pacific routes, Unilever acquired Chesebrough-Pond's, LTV bought Republic Steel, Triangle Industries acquired both

Acquisition The purchase of one company by another, in which the purchasing company takes over the acquired company's operations and property.

J.L. Kraft's wholesale cheese business started in 1903 as a sole proprietorship. His company grew and in 1930 was acquired by National Dairy Products Corporation (later renamed Kraft, Inc.). In 1980, Kraft, Inc. merged with Dart Industries, Inc. which owns Tupperware and Duracell; in 1986 Dart & Kraft, Inc. spun off most of the company's non-food business and changed its name to Kraft, Inc. The new entity was then acquired by Philip Morris companies in 1988. In 1989 Kraft was merged with another Philip Morris subsidiary, General Foods Corporation, to form Kraft General Foods, Inc.

Source: Reproduced with permission of Kraft General Foods, Inc.

American Can and National Can, Wells Fargo purchased Crocker National Can, Conagra bought Beatrice, and Honeywell acquired Sperry Aerospace.[12]

In some cases entrepreneurial so-called "corporate raiders" such as Carl Icahn, who purchased TWA, and T. Boone Pickens, who owns a large stake in Koito Manufacturing of Japan, have been responsible for major acquisitions. However, for the most part these typically involve corporate purchases. The corporate raiders of the 1980s, who with their frenzied buyouts struck fear into the hearts of those firms they targeted, now appear to be waning.[13]

Mergers

Merger The joining together of two companies to form a new company.

A **merger** is the joining together of two companies to form a new company. Some of the nation's largest corporations have been formed through mergers. For example, General Motors merged with Chevrolet and with Cadillac in creating its modern automotive empire.

A number of mergers have taken place in recent years. The airline industry in particular has experienced a number of mergers in the aftermath of deregulation. Other industries that have witnessed many mergers include insurance, publishing, and retailing. For example, INA and Connecticut General merged to form CIGNA Insurance. Another major example is the mainframe software business, where Dun & Bradstreet has merged with Management Science America, Duquesne Systems and Morina have joined hands, and Integral Systems and Data Design Associates have now merged.[14]

Divestitures

Divestiture The selling off of a business holding.

While many companies have been getting bigger by merging, some large corporations have recently been getting smaller by divesting. A **divestiture** involves selling off a business holding. This process has had a dramatic effect on forms of business ownership. Some companies such as Manville have found divesting to be the appropriate strategy in order to survive.[15]

Some divestitures have resulted from court orders for antitrust reasons (preventing monopolies and restraining free trade). For example, as was noted in Chapter 1, one of the biggest divestitures in American business history occurred when the courts forced American Telephone & Telegraph Company (AT&T) to release control of its 22 operating companies. These were formed into seven independent regional firms, the "Baby Bells," that now handle local phone service.

Besides court action, divestitures result from a firm's decision that it cannot profitably operate one of its holdings. The company therefore decides to sell it. In recent years, Gulf & Western spun off 65 diverse subsidiaries worth more than $4 billion, Coca-Cola sold its Taylor Wine division to Seagrams, and ITT sold off more than 100 businesses in an effort to drop its marginally profitable lines and focus more attention on its high-profit products.

1. What is an acquisition? A divestiture?
2. What are two reasons a company might acquire or merge with another company? Why would a company want to get rid of one of its holdings?

CHECK ✓ POINT

Closing Comments

One of the most basic decisions in the field of business involves how the business is to be owned. The choices are for the organization to be a sole proprietorship or some form of partnership or corporation. Because each of these forms has distinct advantages and disadvantages, skilled business owners have to weigh the alternatives and often use more than one form of ownership during the course of their business career.

VIDEO CASE / *Out on Their Own*

Larry Nicola's restaurant is a good example of the type of small businesses that are now being started. An increasing number of people are getting into a business that allows them to run things their own way. If they see a mistake being made, they want to be able to correct it immediately. If a customer asks for something that they are not providing, they want to be able to make a quick decision regarding whether to add this to their product or service offerings or to recommend another firm that can meet the need. Simply put, they want to be in charge of their own destiny.

Many executives have found that big companies say the right things in the ads or policies, but they may not be really responsive to customer needs. In recent years, an increasing number of experienced managers from the corporate giants have left to create small businesses that can address these needs. In the process, they often capture their former company's business and use this as a base for their own firm.

Walt Mitchell started his career with United Parcel Service (UPS) when he was in college, and he eventually made it all the way to national marketing manager. However, he found

that the competition was beginning to erode some of UPS's markets and he felt UPS was too slow in responding to these threats. In particular, Walt found it difficult to get his bosses to adopt an idea he and his people had developed for offering volume discounts on small parcels. As he put it, "We knew from day one that this would be an $80-million-a-year business, and somewhere around 87 percent of it would be new business. But nobody wanted to take hold of something new."

Walt left UPS and started his own company, ZoneSkip. It focuses on low shipping rates for small companies that are sending goods from coast to coast. ZoneSkip puts together truckloads of small parcels from various sources and delivers them directly to strategic UPS distribution centers. By using his own trucks and bypassing intermediate UPS zones, Walt is able to cut 20 percent off the price and move the goods faster. The operation is already grossing $25 million annually and has the potential to do at least twice this amount.

Leslie Christian is another example. Leslie's first job was as a federal funds trader for Crocker National Bank in San Francisco. From there she moved on to a brokerage house where she sold government bonds and then to

Salomon Brothers in New York City, where she sold Treasury futures. Her salary was in the "mid-six figures," but she was not happy. There was insufficient recognition for accomplishment and the job became boring to her. She quit and moved back to the West Coast. There she decided to combine her strongly held feminist views and her continuing interest in the stock and bond markets. She opened her own business, which specializes in financial planning for women. Leslie commented on her decision to do this as follows: "I have finally concluded that I really do have something to offer. All the pieces feel good to me."

Source: Kenneth Labich, "Breaking Away to Go on Your Own," *Fortune*, December 17, 1990, 40–56.

Case Questions

1. Why have the people described in this case opted for a sole proprietorship? Why did they not look for partners with whom to combine their talents?
2. What type of liability do these sole proprietors have if their businesses suffer large losses this year?
3. Why do you think so many people who work for large corporations are now starting their own businesses?

Learning Objectives Revisited

1. **Describe the nature of sole proprietorships.** A sole proprietorship is a business owned by one person. Some of the major advantages of this business form are ease of formation, retention of all profits, direct control, ease of dissolution, and secrecy. Some of the major disadvantages are unlimited liability, difficulty in borrowing money, limited management expertise, long hours, lack of employee opportunities, and lack of continuity.

2. **Describe the nature of partnerships.** A partnership is an association of two or more persons to carry on as co-owners of a business for profit. Some types of partners are the general partner, who is active in the business and has unlimited liability; the limited partner, whose liability is limited to his or her investment in the business; the silent partner, who is known as an owner but who plays no active role in running the operation; the secret partner, who is not known as a partner to the general public but is active in running the business; the dormant partner, who is not known to the general public as a partner and plays no active role in the company; and the nominal partner, who lends his or her name to the partnership but plays no role in the operation. The advantages of the partnership include ease of formation, expanded financial capacity, complementary business skills, and profit potential. The disadvantages include unlimited liability, interpersonal conflicts, lack of continuity, lack of flexibility, and complex dissolution.

3. **Explain how a corporation is structured.** A corporation is a body established by law and exists distinct from those who invest in and control it. Its owners are the common stockholders. Common stockholders elect the board of directors; sell their stock whenever they want; purchase additional shares of newly issued stock before the corporation offers it to the general public; inspect the company's records if they can show good cause; and vote on amendments to the corporate charter, on the accounting firm that will audit the company's books, and on the retirement plans the corporation will offer the employees. The board of directors appoints and reviews the performance of the officers; helps develop and approves long-range strategy, management plans, and major policies; and declares dividends. The officers are legally empowered to represent the corporation and to bind it to contracts. They also help formulate plans, implement strategy, and manage day-to-day operations.

4. **Analyze the advantages and disadvantages of corporations.** The major advantages of the corporate form of ownership include limited liability, ease of transfer of ownership, continuity of existence, ease of raising capital, and professional management. The major disadvantages include heavy taxation, cost and trouble of formation, and government restrictions.

5. **Discuss acquisitions, mergers, and divestitures.** In an acquisition, one company takes over the property and operation of another, whereas in a merger, the companies join together to form a new company. Sometimes acquisitions are friendly (the officers and employees welcome the buyer), but sometimes the officers and employees are leery of what will happen to them and they resist the takeover. A divestiture is the selling off of a business holding. By enlarging or shrinking an enterprise, the corporation attempts to make the enterprise more competitive and profitable.

Key Terms Reviewed

Review each of the following terms. For any that you do not know or are unsure of, look up the definitions and see how they were used in the chapter.

sole proprietorship	joint venture	board of directors
unlimited liability	syndicate	inside directors
partnership	corporation	outside directors
general partner	domestic corporation	corporate officers
limited partner	foreign corporation	S corporation
silent partner	alien corporation	acquisition
secret partner	stockholders	merger
dormant partner	proxy	divestiture
nominal partner		

Review Questions

1. What are the major advantages of a sole proprietorship? What are the major disadvantages of this form of business ownership?
2. Three neighborhood friends want to form a partnership to sell neck and shoulder massages to weary executives. What steps should they take to form the partnership? What should they specify in their partnership agreement?
3. Sandra Longstreet invests $10,000 as a limited partner in a partnership set up to construct and lease an office building. A total of 100 partners participate. Unfortunately, so many other buildings are being constructed in the area that the competition overwhelms Sandra's partnership, and it goes bankrupt, owing $1.5 million. Sandra has $20,000 in the bank. How much of this will she have to spend toward the debts of the partnership?
4. Identify each of the following types of corporations.
   a. Tandy's stock trades on the New York Stock Exchange; anyone who has enough money can buy shares.
   b. ABC Real Estate Group, Inc., consists of 20 investors who have formed a company to develop a parcel of real estate; they have elected to be taxed as a partnership.
   c. The City of Seattle has a state charter to carry on its governmental functions.
   d. ComSonics, of Harrisonburg, Virginia, is a cable TV contractor owned by its founder and employees.
5. What rights do common stockholders have?
6. What is a proxy? Why do you think stockholders often vote by proxy?
7. Why do corporations include outside directors on the board of directors?
8. The neighborhood friends' massage business is prospering (see Question 2), and they are thinking of incorporating. What are some reasons they might want to do this? What are some potential pitfalls?
9. What is the difference between a merger and an acquisition?
10. Why do successful corporations such as General Electric divest themselves of business holdings?

Applied Exercise

In each of these situations, one form of business ownership is preferable to the others. Indicate which one is preferable by placing a checkmark (✔) in the appropriate column.

	Business Form		
Situation	**Sole Proprietorship**	**General Partnership**	**Corporation**
The founder wants to totally control all operations.	_____	_____	_____
The company wants to raise $10 million for expansion.	_____	_____	_____
The owner wants to be able to transfer her or his ownership as simply as possible.	_____	_____	_____
None of the owners wants to be liable for any more than the amount of their own investment.	_____	_____	_____
The company needs to raise $10,000 but cannot get a bank loan.	_____	_____	_____
The owner does not want any problems if it becomes necessary to dissolve the business.	_____	_____	_____
The owner wants to give his or her son and daughter a share in the business without a lot of legal red tape.	_____	_____	_____

Sara Holmes owns a successful porcelain shop in a major metropolitan area. Sara's store is located in a large shopping mall in midtown. Although she pays a substantial monthly rent, Sara's store is so well situated that she has three times the walk-in traffic of her nearest competitor. Additionally, while porcelain carries a high markup, Sara's prices are 20 percent lower than those of the competition. In the 3 years she has been located in the shopping mall, Sara's sales have increased 47 percent annually.

Despite her high sales volume, Sara must carry a large inventory. The reason is that most of the porcelain is imported from Europe and delivery time runs 6 to 7 weeks. As a result, Sara must reinvest much of her profits in inventory.

Last month, Sara learned that a store farther down the mall was going out of business. She would like to move into this new location because it is twice the size of her current shop. However, to do so, she would have to double the size of her inventory, and she does not have the necessary funds. Her banker has offered to give her a line of credit equal to 20 percent of the value of her inventory, but Sara believes there may be an easier way to finance the move.

She has two ideas. One is to take in two new partners who would each put up a sum of money equal to her current investment in inventory. For this investment, each would receive 25 percent ownership in the partnership. Sara knows two people who are willing to do this. The second idea is to form a corporation and sell these two people a total of 50 percent of the stock for the same amount of money as they would have invested in the partnership. Both of these ideas sound good to Sara, but she cannot decide which course of action to take.

Your Advice

1. What do you recommend that Sara do? Rank order your choices.
    ___ a. Take the 20 percent line of credit from the bank and remain a sole proprietorship.
    ___ b. Create a partnership and sell these individuals 50 percent of the business.
    ___ c. Create a corporation and sell them 50 percent of the stock.
2. What are the benefits to Sara of forming a partnership? What are the drawbacks to this arrangement?
3. What are the benefits to Sara of forming a corporation? What are the drawbacks to this arrangement?
4. What would you recommend that Sara do? Why? Be complete in your answer.

SUBWAY IS FLYING HIGH

In recent years many entrepreneurs have found it more profitable to buy a franchise than to start and build a business from scratch, and those who opened a Subway Sandwiches and Salads joined the fastest growing franchise operation in the country. Founded by Fred DeLuca in 1965, it already has over 5,500 units. The firm is extremely profitable. Unlike many other franchisors, Subway does not open stores under its own ownership; all are franchises.

Small Business and Franchising

Chapter Learning Objectives

- Define small business and its impact.

- Identify the types of small businesses.

- Analyze some of the major advantages and disadvantages of owning a small business.

- Discuss how to start a small business and effectively operate it.

- Describe how the franchise form of business works.

- Relate the major advantages and disadvantages of franchises.

Among the things that attract people to Subway is that no experience is needed. Everything new owners have to know can be learned. All they need is an intense desire to succeed, in the opinion of Fred DeLuca. Another benefit of this particular franchise is that not much money is needed to start. In 1991, the franchise fee was a relatively low $10,000 (fees for well-known fast-food franchises range from triple digits to over a million dollars), and startup costs were estimated at a modest $30,000 to $80,000 depending on the location.

Another benefit of owning a Subway franchise is that they are highly rated by the experts. For example, *Entrepreneur* magazine has listed Subway as the best franchise in the country for four consecutive years. This rating resulted from a formula that includes factors such as number of years in franchising, number of units in operation, startup costs, and growth rate. After making a thorough analysis of over a thousand different franchise companies, the magazine staff gave Subway a total of over 4,000 points. McDonald's was second with 3,200 points. However, the two companies are not in direct competition. Subway is in submarine sandwiches while McDonald's is mainly in hamburgers. As one franchisee noted, "We can locate across the street from a McDonald's and live off the overflow of its traffic."

Photo Source: Courtesy of Subway.

Introduction

Those who hear the word "business" and automatically think of giant corporations are overlooking an important component of today's business world: small business and franchising. This chapter describes common types of small businesses and the advantages and disadvantages of owning one. It explains how to start a small business and how to keep it going, with some suggestions for enlisting the help of the Small Business Administration. Because franchises have become a very popular form of small business, this chapter describes how they work and their advantages and disadvantages.

Nature of Small Business

Small business Independently owned and operated business that is not dominant in its field of operation and meets certain standards of size in terms of employees or annual receipts.

According to the Small Business Administration (SBA), a **small business** is one that "is independently owned and operated, [is] not dominant in its field of operation, and meets certain standards of size in terms of employees or annual receipts." The standards vary with the industry in question. Using this definition, over 99 percent of all nonfarm businesses in the United States are small businesses with fewer than 500 employees. Over the last few years, about two-thirds of all new jobs in the United States have been created in firms with fewer than 1,000 employees. Table 4.1 lists some of the most entrepreneurial cities in the United States, places where the tax structure and the community give particularly strong support for the development of small business.[1]

The Backbone of the American Economy

Small businesses are the backbone of the American economy. They not only provide millions of people with jobs, they also help big businesses remain profitable by filling small or specialized orders. Large firms cannot fill such orders profitably because the special equipment and personnel needed are not economical for a company that serves a broad market. Small businesses, in contrast, have lower overhead and can handle all sorts of specialized, piecemeal jobs at a profit. Estimates indicate that for every large manufacturing firm in this country, there are 600 small ones, many of which supply the large firm with services, parts, and materials vital to its production process.

Taking up the Slack

In some markets, small firms have secured themselves a niche by catering to the needs of customers who can't get what they want from larger firms. Banking is a good example. In particular, minority bankers (blacks, Hispanics, and Chinese-Americans) have provided services, financed ventures, and reached out to customers in areas the larger banks have ignored or avoided.

Small business also offers career prospects to people who have traditionally had limited opportunities in major corporations. The SBA reports that approximately 6 percent of all businesses in this country are owned and operated by minorities and take in over $30 billion a year in receipts. In addition, an estimated 4.4 million women own small businesses. This represents about 30 percent of all U.S. businesses. Minorities and women who have been stifled by the lack of opportunities in large organizations often have found successful careers in small businesses.

TABLE 4.1
The Most Entrepreneurial Cities in the United States

Source: *Inc.*, March 1990, 42.

1. Las Vegas, Nevada
2. Washington, D.C.
3. Orlando, Florida
4. Tallahassee, Florida
5. San Jose, California
6. Atlanta, Georgia
7. Charleston, South Carolina
8. Lincoln, Nebraska
9. Raleigh-Durham, North Carolina
10. Anaheim, California

C L O S E - U P / *Ethics*

A Growing Business Treating Injured Workers

An important, but often overlooked, social issue facing business is job safety and the care of injured workers. Every year thousands of workers are injured on the job. In most cases, the injuries are nothing more serious than a strained back or sprained ankle. After a few days of bed rest, the employee can usually return to work. However, many companies are now realizing that physical therapy can be extremely helpful in both preventing and treating these ills. This is where National Rehabilitation Centers Inc. enters the picture. National Rehab's objective is simple: Get people well and back to work as soon as possible.

Traditionally, worker injuries have been treated by doctors and chiropractors. However, National Rehab offers rates that are lower than those of traditional clinics or hospitals. The company does this by carefully monitoring diagnostic and treatment charges, in a manner similar to that used by health maintenance organizations or preferred provider networks. Moreover, because the company works towards getting the worker back to the job as soon as possible, it helps employers save money on lost wage claims.

National Rehab is doing so well in attracting new business that is primary concern now is being able to hire enough physical therapists. However, the firm can afford to pay highly competitive rates for therapists because its net income has been increasing by over 50 percent annually. In fact, things are going so well that National Rehab plans to open as many as 10 more centers within the next three years. The timing is right because dramatically escalating health care costs continually push up workers' compensation costs. The company estimates that the dollar value of claims will quadruple to $88 billion by the year 1999 — an estimate that is supported by the National Council on Compensation Insurance. Even if these estimates are only partially correct, there is going to be more than enough business to take National Rehab well into the 21st century.

Source: Walecia Konrad, "Getting Injured Workers Back on the Job Fast," *Business Week,* May 25, 1992, p. 92.

Common Types of Small Businesses

Small businesses most often operate in one of three broad nonfarming areas: light manufacturing and construction, merchandising (retailers or wholesalers), and small firms in the service sector. The accompanying Ethics Close-Up (A Growing Business Treating Injured Workers) is an example of the latter.

Light Manufacturing and Construction Many types of small firms do light manufacturing — machine shops, bakeries, ice cream plants or dairies, and furniture makers — and construction of buildings (residential and commercial) and other projects. They take raw materials and convert them into finished products. For example, machine shops turn iron and steel into special parts used by big auto or appliance factories, bakeries turn flour into bread, dairies turn milk and cream into ice cream and specialty items, furniture shops turn wood and cloth into furniture, and construction firms turn lumber, bricks, and mortar into buildings.

As a whole, a small number of manufacturers account for a large percentage of total employment; only 3 percent of the firms account for almost three-fourths of all manufacturing employment. Thus, there are many very small manufacturing firms that employ fewer than 10 people.

Merchandising Merchandisers are of two kinds: retailers, which sell products to the final customer, and wholesalers, which buy goods to sell to retailers. Retailers are more common than wholesalers. Typical retailers include auto dealers, department stores, discount stores, clothing stores, drugstores, supermarkets, and service stations. Although some department stores, such as Lord & Taylor's in New York, Dillards in Little Rock, or Dayton's in Minneapolis, are large, most of the retail establishments in the United States

Job discrimination early in his career led Henry F. Henderson, Jr., to start his own small business. In 1954, H.F. Henderson Industries began manufacturing industrial scales. Since then Henderson has guided the company into the design and manufacture of automatic weighing systems, control panels, and electrical systems. Today Henderson Industries is one of the top minority-owned businesses in the United States.

Source: © Ken Kerbs Photography, 1991.

have fewer than four employees. Wholesalers, on the other hand, are slightly larger, averaging between four and ten employees. In recent years, wholesalers have grown more slowly than retailers, but they still manage to generate over $1.6 trillion annually.[2]

Services   The modern economy includes many small service firms. Although large financial and insurance firms covered in Chapters 19 and 22 are service industries, some examples of small service firms are restaurants, dry cleaners, auto repair shops, and accounting services. Most of these small service companies are labor-intensive, which means that a large part of their costs goes for employee-related expenses. Restaurants are a good example. A waiter can serve only a limited number of tables. As the size of a restaurant increases, the restaurant manager eventually has to hire more waiters.

As the economy has grown in recent years, service has proved to be one of the fastest-growing sectors. Experts predict that small businesses, mostly in the service sector, will generate most of the new jobs. For example, in the past decade the 500 largest firms slashed 3.5 million jobs, but small businesses, mostly offering services, generated 20 million new jobs.[3] This portion of the economy also promises a good chance for success for the small business. As Chapter 1 pointed out, the productivity record in the service industry is poor and, unlike in the manufacturing sector, new technologies and human resource management techniques are untapped. There is considerable potential for improvement in the service sector.

One important area for growth among service businesses has been that of convenience services. The growth in the number of single-parent households and especially the growth in the number of two-earner households has created a pool of people for whom time for household chores is scarce and who are willing and able to spend money to make their lives easier. The result has been a boom in services geared toward providing convenience. For example, Video-Van of Salem, New Hampshire, will bring video rentals to your door.

Special Selections of Boise, Idaho, will provide personal shopping services, and Entrees on Trays of Ft. Worth, Texas, will deliver dinner to your home.[4] Other businesses do household chores, manicure the lawn, baby-sit, or shine your shoes in your home. Many of the providers of these services are small businesses.

Advantages of Owning a Small Business

Many businesspeople would rather own a small business than head up a division of a larger company. Both positions offer many responsibilities and rewards, but the owner of a small business has the additional benefit of independence. The small-business owner can run the operation the way he or she thinks is best. Closely tied to this freedom is the challenge of pitting one's skills and abilities against those of competitors and the possible satisfaction of success. When the business succeeds, the owner often is able to make more money than would be possible working for someone else. Along with this reward is the intangible satisfaction of providing a community service by supplying needed goods and services. In fact, small-business owners ranked pride in offering a product or service as their most important source of satisfaction.[5]

Besides the intangible benefits derived from small business ownership, there also are some practical advantages. In particular, small businesses may have advantages over large enterprises such as lower costs through simplified record keeping and less overhead, more personalized attention given to customers and employees, and better opportunities for innovation and adaptation.

Disadvantages of Owning a Small Business

Owning a small business is not for everyone. For some people, independence and challenge sound more threatening than inviting. These fears have some justification. Business owners risk losing their money and perhaps having to declare bankruptcy. Thousands of businesses fail each year. The great majority of these are in restaurants, retail trade, construction, light manufacturing, and wholesale trade — the strongholds of small business.

One source of this risk of failure is that small-business owners are often unable to raise large sums of money for expansion. In most cases, small firms have to rely on internal profits as their main source of funds. Running a small business also places stringent demands on the owner's time and ability to make decisions that will keep the business competitive and ensure that it has the financial resources to continue operating. Small-business owners also are often dismayed when they find that the government requires them to comply with a myriad of regulations and a frustrating amount of red tape. Another drawback is the difficulty faced by small businesses in hiring due to the growing shortage of both skilled and unskilled employees.[6] Recently, a large survey of small business owners found that the most critical concern was availability and cost of employee benefits, especially health care.[7]

CHECK ✔ POINT

1. What are three common types of nonfarm small businesses?
2. Name one advantage and one disadvantage of owning and running your own small business.

Starting a Small Business

A person who wants to start a small business needs to do three things before obtaining the needed funds and finding a location and facility: assess his or her abilities and interests, look for a viable opportunity, and draw up a business plan.

Personal Assessment

To reduce the likelihood of failure, prospective business owners should start by assessing their strengths and weaknesses. Some small-business owners try out a number of different business opportunities before settling on the one they like best. An honest personal appraisal can help eliminate the time-consuming and potentially costly (in terms of both money and pride) experiments.

A candid personal assessment helps a potential owner decide whether he or she is able to run a business. For example, the average small-business owner works 70 to 80 hours per week. A person thinking of going into business has to ask, am I *willing* to work long hours? Even if the answer is yes, a follow-up question is, am I *able* to work long hours? Good physical and mental health and a full-time commitment are mandatory to success.

For example, it would be difficult, though not impossible, for a full-time student to go into most businesses, simply because of the amount of time and physical and mental energy required. The same is true of some individuals with full-time jobs who want to run a business as a sideline. These ventures usually fail because the owner cannot give them the necessary attention. Before embarking on a small-business venture, the potential owner should undertake some form of self-assessment, such as completing the questionnaire in Figure 4.1.

Opportunity Identification

Businesses don't prosper just because their owners are hard workers; they have to meet a need. Therefore, the next step before starting a small business is to identify an opportunity to meet a need.

One way to do this is to spend several years working in a field that interests you. While you are working, keep your eyes open. What products and services are companies already providing? Who is buying them? Are the customers satisfied? Are the existing companies meeting the full demand for these products and services? Do customers want something that existing companies aren't providing? The answers to questions such as these may suggest an opportunity for a new business. You might also find the answers to these questions by doing research in the library and by interviewing people who might be a potential market for the product or service you are interested in providing. You might also choose a field based on your particular knowledge, interests, skills, or personal contacts. In this way, you build on your strengths. Table 4.2, which presents some of the major reasons for small business success and failure, illustrates this point.

The Business Plan

Prospective small-business people today usually draw up a business plan. In fact, most banks consider lending only to a small business that has such a

Check the statement that best describes you.

1. Are you a self-starter?
   ☐ I can get going without any help from other people.
   ☐ Once someone helps me get started, I can maintain the momentum.
   ☐ I take things nice and easy and do not get started until the last minute.

2. Can you assume responsibility?
   ☐ I can take charge and see things through to completion.
   ☐ I can take the reins if it is necessary, but I prefer to let someone else handle the responsibility.
   ☐ I prefer to let others handle responsibility.

3. Can you lead people?
   ☐ I can get most people to follow me once I get something started.
   ☐ If someone can help me understand what needs to be done, I can usually take it from there.
   ☐ I prefer to let other people lead and go along if I like it.

4. How good an organizer are you?
   ☐ I am orderly and work from a predetermined plan or design.
   ☐ I can usually get things organized, but if the situation gets too confusing, I give up.
   ☐ Most situations change so rapidly that I find it is a waste of time to organize anything, and I never do.

5. Can you make decisions?
   ☐ Yes, and they usually turn out well.
   ☐ If I have to, but I like plenty of time to think things through.
   ☐ I prefer to let others make decisions and then react to them.

6. How well can you get along with others?
   ☐ Very well. I like people and they like me.
   ☐ I'm as good as the next person and can usually get through just about any situation.
   ☐ I'm a little nervous around people and sometimes find it hard to work with them.

7. How hard a worker are you?
   ☐ I have tremendous drive and stamina and can keep going for a long time.
   ☐ I can work hard for a while, but then I taper off.
   ☐ I do not care to work hard and seldom do.

8. Can people rely on your word?
   ☐ Absolutely. I always stick by what I say.
   ☐ I usually stand by my word, but sometimes it is necessary to change my mind.
   ☐ I often break my word, but that's because things have changed so much that I just don't feel I should go through with my promise.

9. How good are you about seeing things through to completion?
   ☐ Once I set my mind to it, I can see anything through to the end.
   ☐ I usually stick with a task until it is completed.
   ☐ I try hard, but if the situation gets too complicated, I usually bail out.

10. How good is your health?
   ☐ Excellent.
   ☐ Good.
   ☐ All right, but it has been better.

Although there are no right or wrong answers, the first response can be considered the best, the second the neutral, and the last the worst in terms of going into business for oneself. To score yourself, give 3 points for each first response box checked, 2 points for each middle response box checked, and 1 point for the bottom response box checked. As a guideline, if you scored 25–30 points, you may be a very good candidate for going into business for yourself. If you scored 20–24 points, you may not be suited for self-employment. If you scored below 20 points, self-employment is probably not for you.

TABLE 4.2
Major Success and Failure Factors in
Small Business

Success Factors	Failure Factors
• Existence of a business opportunity • Management ability • Adequate capital • Adequate credit • Use of modern business methods	• Incompetence • Lack of experience • Neglect of the business • Fraud (by owner or other key personnel) • Disaster (such as tornadoes, hurricanes, and other acts of God)

Source: Richard M. Hodgetts and Donald F. Kuratko, *Effective Small Business Management,* 4th ed. (San Diego, CA: Harcourt, Brace, Jovanovich, 1992, in press).

formal plan. Table 4.3 provides a summary of a typical business plan. The finance part of the plan is most relevant to lenders because it explains how the owner will keep the business afloat. The statistics are frightening: Most small businesses close their doors within 5 years of their founding. Although overall poor management is the primary underlying reason for most small-business failures, the last straw is often a lack of money for continuing the operation. The business plan should address the major financial considerations of obtaining funds needed to get started and then having the money to keep the operation going.

CHECK ✓ POINT

1. What three activities are required before starting a small business?
2. What information should go into a business plan?

Operating a Small Business

Operating a small business is in many ways similar to running a large firm, but it takes place on a smaller scale. The smaller size means that managing a small business is unique in some ways. In general, small-business owners must be concerned with three major areas: management, marketing, and finance.

Management

Small-business owners need to pay particular attention to two areas of management: staffing and operations. Staffing a small business is especially critical because the company has only a few employees, each with a great deal of responsibility. If only one employee leaves, day-to-day operations could change drastically, and the remaining employees must share the work until the company finds a replacement. Another dimension of staffing in small businesses is the development of managerial succession. Who will replace the manager or owner when he or she dies, retires, or quits? In many small firms, managers never answer this question; when the head person leaves, chaos results and the small business may even fail.

The operations function, which is covered in Chapter 9, addresses several questions: What types of machinery and equipment does the enterprise need? What is the best layout for the facilities? How much inventory and

TABLE 4.3
Outline of a Business Plan

Section I: Summary of the Overall Plan

Section II: Business Description Segment
    A. General description of the venture
       (product or service)
    B. Industry background
    C. Company history or background
    D. Goals/potential of the venture and
       milestones (if any)
    E. Uniqueness of the product or service

Section III: Marketing Segment
    A. Research and analysis
       1. Target market (customers)
       2. Market size and trends
       3. Competition
       4. Estimated market share
    B. Marketing plan
       1. Market strategy: sales and distribution
       2. Pricing
       3. Advertising and promotions

Section IV: Research, Design, and Development Segment
    A. Development and design plans
    B. Technical research results
    C. Research assistance needs
    D. Cost structure

Section V: Manufacturing Segment
    A. Location analysis
    B. Production needs: facilities and
       equipment
    C. Suppliers/transportation factors
    D. Labor supply
    E. Manufacturing cost data

Section VI: Management Segment
    A. Management team: key personnel
    B. Legal structure: stock agreements,
       employment agreements,
       ownership, etc.
    C. Board of directors, advisers,
       consultants, etc.

Section VII: Critical Risks Segment
    A. Potential problems
    B. Obstacles and risks
    C. Alternative courses of action

Section VIII: Financial Segment
    A. Financial forecast
       1. Profit and loss
       2. Cash flow
       3. Breakeven analysis
       4. Cost controls
    B. Sources and use of funds
    C. Budgeting plans
    D. Stages of financing

Section IX: Milestone Schedule Segment
    A. Timing and objectives
    B. Deadlines/milestones
    C. Relationship of events

Section X: Appendix and/or Bibliography

Source: Donald F. Kuratko and Richard M. Hodgetts, *Entrepreneurship: A Contemporary Approach,* 2d ed. (Hinsdale, Ill.: Dryden Press, 1992, 234–235).

what types of storage facilities will the business require? The answers to these types of questions will influence the small company's ability to produce its goods efficiently and to store them at minimum cost. For example, small firms such as Lifeline Systems of Watertown, Massachusetts, and Fireplace Manufacturers of Santa Ana, California, have recently converted to modern but simple production and inventory systems that have had a dramatic impact on their efficiency and profits.[8] The effective small-business owner is as interested in maintaining high productivity and low cost as is the president of a large corporation. Part Three discusses management in greater detail.

Marketing

A vital area of running a small business is marketing (covered in Part Five). The hard fact is that inadequate sales will force small businesses to cease operations. Well-planned marketing activities can minimize these problems. Particularly important dimensions of marketing in small business are personal selling and advertising. For a retail establishment, location is also a primary concern in the marketing effort. A well-placed business helps attract customers and increase sales. For example, a men's or women's apparel shop or other specialty stores could benefit from locating near a large department

A business opportunity can sprout from personal experience. Tim (left) and Tom Karl and two of their brothers designed motorized wheelchairs to give the twins, who have muscular dystrophy, better mobility. They outfitted the chairs with Centel cellular phones for added independence. The brothers plan to market the wheelchairs with the cellular phone as an option.

Source: Bruce Davidson/Magnum Photos and Centel Corporation.

store, because this location would help generate customer traffic. Restaurants, barbershops, candy stores, and jewelry stores often prosper near movie theaters. Women's clothing and shoe stores are grouped together. Furniture stores often do better if they are located near each other, because most people comparison shop for furniture. Two furniture stores located down the block from each other will generate more total sales than if they are located across town from each other. In most cities, you will find a Burger King and a McDonald's near to one another for the same reason.

Financing

Like managing and marketing, financing is important to the success of a small business. The general topic of financing receives more detailed coverage in Part Six. Managers of small businesses need to pay particular attention to two areas: credit and expansion capital.

Credit   Most businesses are givers and receivers of credit. Few businesses, large or small, pay cash for the things they buy. Most use credit and then pay the bills at the end of the month. However, the company may be short of cash when bills come due, in part because it extends credit to its own customers.

Business managers usually resolve this problem by securing a "line of credit" from a bank. This is a bank's agreement to let the business borrow funds as needed up to a specified limit. An example of this type of credit would be a wholesaler whose biggest sales season is September 15 through November 1. Most of these sales are on credit to retailers who pay for them within 90 days, so between December 15 and February 1 the wholesaler will be getting a large inflow of cash payments. However, before this period, the wholesaler will need money to stay afloat. After all, this wholesaler spent a lot of money to acquire the inventory that it has sold but not received payment for. A line of credit from the bank that the company repays by February 15 will tide the wholesaler over.

Jane G. Haley is president and chief executive officer of Gosiger Inc., a machine-tool distribution company started by her father. Since taking over in 1972, she has faced typical staffing and operations management problems: how to attract capable employees, how to make the transition from manual to computer-controlled equipment, how to serve large customers. Her strategy has been to expand the company. It has grown from $2 million to $55 million in annual sales.

Source: T. Michael Keza/Nation's Business.

The big question is whether the small business will be able to secure such a line of credit from a bank. This depends on the owner's ability to show the financial institution that the business is a good risk. The owner does this by demonstrating to the bank that the company has a good record of paying off debts in a timely fashion and that the sales forecast is accurate. A company that can show this, along with the owner's personal guarantee backed by personal assets, seldom has trouble obtaining credit.

Expansion Capital Besides credit for daily operations, a small business needs funds for expansion. For such funding, most small businesses reinvest profits from the business or rely on the owner's personal funds. However, a company that can generate outside sources of capital can more easily accomplish expansion plans. Small businesses have various sources of expansion capital. One source of funding is a **venture capitalist,** an investor who specializes in small firms that offer potential for rapid growth and high returns. In some cases, state and local governments also provide funding.

1. Why is location so important to small businesses?
2. What are two ways in which small-business owners obtain financing?

Venture capitalist An investor who specializes in small firms that offer potential for rapid growth and high returns.

CHECK ✓ POINT

The Small Business Administration

The principal government agency concerned with the economic welfare of small firms in the United States is the **Small Business Administration (SBA).** Congress created the SBA in 1953 with the Small Business Act. Since then, the SBA has played an important role in American small business. In recent years, however, it has been the target of budget-cutting efforts, and its future is uncertain.

The Small Business Administration provides services in several areas. It helps small businesses receive a share of government contracts, in accordance

Small Business Administration (SBA) The principal government agency concerned with the economic welfare of small U.S. firms.

with federal regulations requiring the government to make some of its purchases from small businesses. The agency also has available limited financing assistance and information on business management.

Financing Assistance

The SBA offers several programs to help businesses obtain financing. It guarantees repayment of loans of up to $750,000 that private lenders make to businesses that have been unable to obtain a loan from at least two banks. The guarantee makes lenders more willing to take the risk of extending a loan to a small business. For businesses that have been unable to obtain a guaranteed loan, the SBA also loans up to $175,000 directly. These loans are not easy to obtain; the borrower must fill out a detailed credit application, and funding has always fallen short of the demand for loans.

The SBA also offers loans to special groups. Groups qualifying for such loans include businesspeople with a disability, those involved in conservation endeavors, and development companies helping small businesses in rural or urban areas. Loans are also available to assist small businesses in moving into international markets.

Small business investment company (SBIC) A company licensed by the SBA for the purpose of providing venture capital to small businesses.

Minority enterprise small business investment company (MESBIC) An SBIC that provides capital and equity financing to small businesses whose owners are economically or socially disadvantaged.

The SBA licenses **small business investment companies (SBICs)** to provide venture capital to small businesses. The SBIC borrows from the government on attractive terms and then invests the money in small businesses. It may be willing to consider less glamorous enterprises than a private venture capitalist would. A type of SBIC called a **minority enterprise small business investment company (MESBIC)** provides financing to small businesses whose owners are economically or socially disadvantaged.

Information and Advice

Besides money, the Small Business Administration provides small enterprises with information and advice. Management assistance officers provide individual assistance and counseling to small-business owners. The SBA sponsors publications, both free and for sale, that discuss management, marketing, finance, and other technical aspects of small-business ownership.

The SBA sponsors and administers special programs that provide free counseling to small businesses. Two of these programs are the Service Corps of Retired Executives (SCORE) and the Active Corps of Executives (ACE). These two groups consist of experienced volunteers who want to help small businesses. Today, 750 SCORE and ACE chapters are in operation, staffed by 13,000 volunteers, in all 50 states, Puerto Rico, Guam, and the Virgin Islands.

Another education program is the Small Business Institute (SBI). In cooperation with colleges and universities, SBI conducts programs in which student teams assigned to small businesses provide free management counseling and work alongside the owner in identifying solutions to operational problems. Today over 500 universities have SBIs. Besides helping the small businesses involved, they provide valuable learning and hands-on experience for business students.

Small Business Development Centers (SBDCs) are still another program funded by the SBA that provides a full range of services to assist small businesses by drawing together local, state, and federal resources. With public and private educational institutions and business associations, the SBDCs sponsor courses in small-business management. They also run conferences

Burger Buddies
Two mini-cheeseburgers with ketchup
and pickles
NEW!

Eighty-five percent of Burger King restaurants are franchised. Franchisors add new products to their menus only after carefully developing and test marketing them, as with these Burger Buddies. This is a benefit to the franchisees, because pretesting increases the chance that new products will succeed. The cost of such benefits is covered by franchise fees.

Source: Courtesy of Burger King Corporation.

and workshops on topics such as business forecasting, sources of financing, types of business organizations, and choosing a site location.

1. What are two kinds of services the Small Business Administration (SBA) offers?
2. Suppose that you owned a small business and were struggling to make ends meet. What help could you expect from the Small Business Administration?

CHECK ✓ POINT

Franchising

In recent years, many would-be entrepreneurs have been attracted to a special form of small business, the **franchise.** Under a franchise arrangement, a producer or supplier arranges for dealers to handle a product or service under mutually agreed-upon conditions. The supplier is known as the **franchisor;** the dealers are known as the **franchisees.**

Franchises are one of the most popular ways of getting into a small business. This arrangement appeals to many people wanting to get into business because it avoids the risk of starting a business from the ground up and the expense of buying an ongoing firm. Franchising is an excellent way to combine the spirit of entrepreneurship with the lessons of a proven system. Consequently, franchises are one of the fastest growing and most important modern forms of business. Figure 4.2 graphs the tremendous growth in the number and sales of franchises over the past several years. At present, franchising accounts for one-third of retail sales and, sometime in the 1990s, the International Franchise Association (IFA) forecasts that franchising's share of retail sales will reach 50 percent.[9]

Franchises meet many different customer demands. Some of the best-known franchises are in the fast-food industry, including McDonald's, Burger King, Wendy's, and Kentucky Fried Chicken. Franchises are popular in other service industries as well. For example, Ramada Inn Motels, Maids International, Dollar Rent a Car, One Hour Martinizing Drycleaner, and

Franchise A system of distribution in which a producer or supplier arranges for a dealer to handle a product or service under mutually agreed-upon conditions.

Franchisor The supplier in a franchise system.

Franchisee The dealer in a franchise system.

FIGURE 4.2
Sales and Growth of Franchising

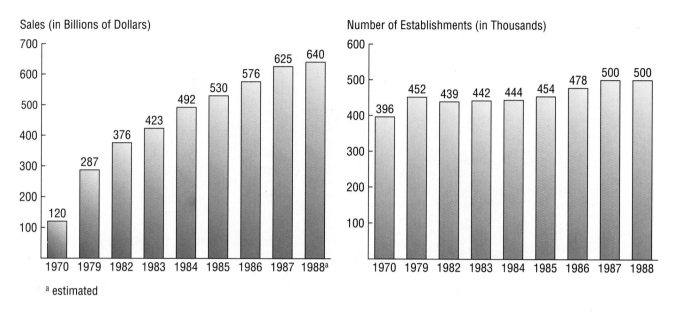

Sales (in Billions of Dollars)

Number of Establishments (in Thousands)

ᵃ estimated

Source: "Why Franchising Is Taking Off," *Fortune,* February 12, 1990, 124.

Suddenly Slender and Designer Body weight-loss centers are all franchises.
Companies that service other businesses also frequently use franchises. These organizations include collection agencies, employment services, printing and copying services such as Postal Instant Press, and tax preparation companies such as H&R Block. The accompanying Innovation Close-Up (New Franchises for Old Markets) provide other examples.

The Franchise Agreement

While the products of franchises vary widely, the basic business arrangements have much in common. These arrangements are contained in a franchise agreement, which is a contract between the supplier and dealer that spells out what each party will do. Typically the dealer (franchisee) agrees to:

- Pay a franchise fee for the right to run the operation
- Pay a percentage of the gross revenues to the supplier (franchisor)
- Follow the operating procedures that have been set forth by the franchisor

The buyer of a franchise might be required to pay as much as $575,000 for a McDonald's or as little as $10,000 for a new H & R Block tax-help shop[10] or $10,000 for an Auto Critic unit, which provides mobile used car inspection services, or $8,500 for an Albert Andrews Ltd. unit, which offers custom men's clothing services.[11] If the franchise must operate out of a special unit such as a restaurant, the buyer must lay out the facilities in a manner speci-

CLOSE-UP / *Innovation*

New Franchises for Old Markets

Every year hundreds of new franchises come into existence. Quite often these only offer goods and services similar to those already on the market. However, there are also a few franchise start-ups that offer an innovative twist that creates or exploit a market that has been ignored or abandoned. One such innovative new franchise operation is the Great Golf Learning Center in Blackwood, New Jersey. While golf is certainly not a new market, the founders of this franchise have developed a golf club with a small laser light that shines from the grip of a 5-iron club. The purpose of the laser light is to project a beam from the top of the club that lets the golfer know whether he or she is swinging the club correctly. While the club has not yet caught on with golfers, its developers have expanded the concept and opened their first Great Golf Learning Center. This 4,000-square-foot course has nine nets, a putting green, a simulated bunker, lounge area, analysis room, and video recording equipment. Customers come to the learning center for instructional programs as well as for an extended six-month training program (cost: $499) that includes unlimited, scheduled 30-minute training sessions and lifetime personal use of the facility. The company currently has five franchises and is looking to open more.

Another new franchise system is Diaper Dan's Delivery of Beltsville, Maryland. While most of today's parent purchase disposable diapers for their baby, this franchise is taking advantage of consumers' increasing environmental awareness by offering cloth diapers. The delivery service is akin to the local milkman's: friendly, reliable, and timely. For $12 per week, drivers deliver diapers as well as demonstrate and sell add-on products such as baby food, infant formula, bottles, rattles, mobiles, pacifiers, and body-care products — all in the convenience of the customer's living room. The franchise system is also working with hospital baby-care classes, representatives from support groups for nursing mothers, and baby product retailers, in order to gain market recognition and customers. By the end of the second year of operations this franchise was grossing almost $800,000 annually. Now the firm is starting to franchise units and there appears to be strong investor interest.

Source: Kevin McLaughlin, "New Arrivals," *Entrepreneur*, April 1992, pp. 128–137.

fied by the franchisor; all franchisees often have the same external and internal decor, table arrangements, menu, and preparation techniques. The result is that a customer in Dallas and one in Detroit will be eating the same food in the same basic environment. The customer will always know what to expect from the business, regardless of location.

The franchisor, in turn, usually promises to do the following things:

- Allow the franchisee the right to use the company's name, logo, and symbols (such as the golden arches in the case of McDonald's)
- Provide advertising and marketing support at both the local and the national levels
- Provide professional, standardized training so the franchisee learns how to run the unit correctly
- Provide the franchisee with merchandise (food and equipment) at wholesale prices
- Assist the franchisee in getting financial assistance, such as a line of credit with a local bank
- Provide ongoing help for the duration of the contract

If you want to enter into a franchise agreement, begin by learning what franchises are available. Excellent sources of information are the *Franchise Annual Handbook and Directory* and the *International Franchise Association Membership Directory*. When you have identified a local franchise that looks promising, investigate it by talking to some of the current franchise owners.

JoAnne Shaw is the founder and head of The Coffee Beanery Ltd., a gourmet coffee business. She opened her first shop in 1976; the company currently has more than two dozen franchises. Shaw is working to expand the business by offering mail-order service and gift packets.

Source: © A. David Kryszak/Black Star.

When you receive a contract, have a lawyer look it over and comment on the advantages and disadvantages of the agreement. Also have an accountant or banker examine the initial investment, the likely annual revenues, the potential return on investment, and the overall financial risks. In entering the world of franchising, as with other small-business ventures, you must look before you leap.

Advantages of Franchising

Franchising offers a number of important advantages. One is that the franchisor provides you with management and operational training, showing you how to organize and operate the unit. Since the franchisor knows the best ways to produce the product or service, keep records, control inventory, and manage cash, you quickly learn what to do and what not to do. This greatly increases your chances of making the venture a success. However, there is also room for innovative approaches. For example, Pizza On The Run, a Miami-based franchisor, sells franchises that include a truck in which the pizza is made. When customers call orders into the franchisor's central dispatcher, the individual sends the nearest truck to that location. As the driver heads for the locale, the baker in the back of the truck prepares and cooks the pizza. Because a typical pie takes only 7 minutes to bake, the pizza arrives nice and hot.

A second advantage is that the good or service has already been tested in the marketplace, has proved to be in demand, and has instant name recognition. You need not worry about whether anyone will buy the hamburgers or auto parts. The franchisor has already identified and demonstrated the market demand and has the name before the public.

In addition, the franchisor often helps with advertising and promotion. For example, the franchisors pay for the TV ads for national franchises such as Holiday Inn, Kentucky Fried Chicken, and Burger King. However, the franchisee pays for these benefits with the original franchise fee and may pay a percentage of sales to the franchisor for such services.

Finally, in many cases, the franchisor helps secure financial assistance. For example, a bank might refuse to lend money to Carl and Jennifer Smith, who want to open "Smith's Muffler Shop." The bank would more likely make a loan if the Smiths had a Midas Muffler franchise. Also, the SBA and about 1,000 private lenders participate in a program that provides loans, and franchisors themselves will often provide necessary start-up capital.

Disadvantages of Franchising

As does any other area of business, franchising has some disadvantages. One of the first drawbacks is that the larger and better known the franchise, the greater the initial fee and the percentage of revenues that must be paid to the franchisor. To avoid this, many people invest in small, unknown franchises with the hope that they will become well established. Unfortunately, many of them do not make it, and the franchisees lose their investment.

A second drawback is that the franchisor usually maintains strong control over the way the operation is run.[12] Local conditions may call for a modification, but if the business is not operated according to the book, the franchisor can terminate the arrangement. This is why those with a strong entrepreneurial orientation or those who managed in large corporations may have trouble as franchisees. As the head of Precision Tune Inc., an automobile tune-up franchise, recently noted, "True entrepreneurs are used to doing things their own way, a franchisor needs someone who can be a team player and follow the system."[13]

Another drawback arises because the franchisee usually agrees to buy all equipment, materials, and supplies from the franchisor. This gives the franchisor a ready, profitable market for its goods. The franchisor may promise to sell all equipment, materials, and supplies at wholesale, implying low prices, but the franchisee might be able to find a local source of these goods at much lower prices. Furthermore, some franchisors might not deliver on their promises. For example, management training may be scheduled for one week a year, but the franchisor may only pay for the initial training. Additionally, in recent years some franchisors have found the quality of their products being challenged. For example, McDonald's food has been called "fatty" by critics.[14]

Finally, some franchisees have found that their agreement allows the franchisor to buy them out at the end of their original contract, say, after 5 or 10 years, at a price stipulated by the contract. If the franchise has done well, the unit may be worth a lot more money, with even greater future potential. However, if the product or service does not sell, franchisees lose their investment, while the franchisor goes right on selling to other franchisees.

Trends and Outlook

Despite its drawbacks, franchising is proving to be extremely attractive to small enterprises that want to expand (by becoming franchisors) and to individual entrepreneurs who are looking for a chance to operate their own businesses (by becoming franchisees). Many franchises are even being run out of the home. For example, Michael Courtney runs his franchised disc-jockey service out of his house[15] and Beverly Dietz of Coral Gables, Florida, operates a very successful catering business from her own kitchen.[16] Franchising enables enterprises to move out of their local area and into regional and national markets. For example, the owners of a popular local sandwich shop may feel their sandwiches are so good and unique that they could become a franchisor. They could sell their name, recipes, and style of service to franchisees in surrounding cities or in other parts of the city. The opportunities are so good that franchisees of some chains are buying units in several locations, and some franchisors are beginning to buy back units or build company-owned units.

The Department of Commerce predicts that restaurants will continue to be the most popular sector of franchising. These restaurants are likely to move toward more diversified menus, including salad bars, fish, and poultry, as personal health concerns influence the consumption of such items. There is also a shift toward ethnic foods, allowing franchises to more effectively win a market share in a local area. Other fast-growing categories in the 1990s will include educational products, cleaning services, business aids, and equipment rental.[17]

International Markets   U.S. franchisors are rapidly moving into overseas markets. Going into the 1990s, the number of foreign outlets is in the five figures with Canada and Japan having the most but with all parts of the world represented. Large franchisors (those with 1,000 or more units each) dominate this international market. About 50 companies account for the majority of international franchise establishments with Kentucky Fried Chicken, Holiday Inn, and McDonald's leading the way.

Because the young people in many foreign countries like to try new products and concepts, overseas franchises often gain quick acceptance. Once again, fast-food outlets are a good example. McDonald's has made the hamburger an international food. Even areas where foreigners have seemed to have traditional ways of doing things may be a franchising market in the future. For example, as building owners examine the costs of keeping cleaning crews on the payroll, they may turn to outside maintenance companies. This is what Dallas-based Jani-King commercial cleaning franchises are counting on as they expect to sell franchises in Mexico, Europe, Australia, and the Far East.[18]

Minority Franchises   Minorities are finding franchising to be an excellent route for getting into business. Many of the start-up hassles and barriers are eliminated and the probabilities of success are greatly enhanced by the franchise arrangements discussed. The Department of Commerce recently reported an increase in minority ownership of franchises. Some of the major increases have occurred in automotive products and services, restaurants, business services, and retailing.

Another development in franchising has been the designing of units to accommodate those challenged by a disability. For example, Heavenly Hot Dogs of Cape Coral, Florida, had modified its units so that they can be operated by franchisees in wheelchairs, and the franchisor is now designing mobile units that can be driven by people with a disability.[19]

CHECK ✓ POINT

1.   How does a franchise work?
2.   Name two advantages and two disadvantages of the franchise form of small business.

Closing Comments

As you learned in this chapter, small-business ownership offers many advantages but is not for everyone. Those who conclude that they are suited for this role should look for an opportunity and prepare a business plan. In operating a small business, the owner should focus especially on management, marketing, and finance. A possible source of assistance is the Small Business Administration, and a business arrangement that might simplify the owner's role is the franchise. Some experts predict that by the year 2000 franchising will generate $1 trillion annually.

VIDEO CASE / *"We're Number One"*

Potential business owners and entrepreneurs can choose from a wide variety of franchises. One of the most popular is proving to be Subway, a submarine sandwich franchise that was started in 1965 by Fred DeLuca and amazingly has over 5,500 units. A recent analysis of over a thousand franchise companies found that not only was Subway ranked as the best franchise operation in the country, but there are only a very few, such as McDonald's, that come even remotely close. In particular, among submarine sandwich franchises, a far distant second was Blimpie, followed by Mr. Submarine, Togho's Eatery, and Sub Station II. Although these four competitors of Subway were ranked well in relation to franchises in general, ranging from 98th to 298th out of the 1,111 rated, Subway was still thought to be head and shoulders above them.

What accounts for the success of the Subway franchise? One answer is the rapid growth. A large number of franchisees are interested in joining the "bandwagon" of the fastest growing franchise operation in the country. A second is that the cost of starting and running this franchise is relatively low. Subway's sandwiches and salads require no cooking and minimum preparation. The stores are only about 1,000 square feet, so rent and overhead costs are low. A third is that there really are no prerequisites for getting into the business other than a desire to succeed. Anyone with the drive to make the business a success and the initial funds to get started has the opportunity.

Of course, Subway is not the only franchise that is doing well. Others that got good marks include the following:

- McDonald's — the hamburger king
- Jani-King — commercial cleaning
- Little Caesar's Pizza — pizza
- Hardee's — miscellaneous fast food
- Chem-Dry — upholstery and drapery cleaning
- Arby's Inc. — miscellaneous fast food
- Electronic Reality Associates Inc. — real estate services
- Kentucky Fried Chicken — chicken
- Jazzercise Inc. — fitness centers

This list shows that there are franchise opportunities in a wide variety of businesses. The vision of fast-food outlets comes to most people when they think of franchise opportunities. However, of the 10 highest ranked franchise companies, four had nothing to do with food. Moreover, among new franchisors, food-related units are in the minority. Some of the most popular new franchises are commercial cleaning, income tax services, signs, optical

products, television magazines, used-auto rentals, and mailing and shipping services. Of the top 12, three are food-related and three are sign companies that produce specialized signs for specific needs. Simply put, a great deal of opportunity exists in the current business climate for franchising, and while fast-food outlets will continue to dominate, they are only one of many that will be important during the years ahead.

Source: *Entrepreneur*, January 1991, 113–115; 164–165.

Case Questions

1. What are the advantages of opening a Subway franchise? Identify and describe two of them.
2. What are the major drawbacks to a franchise like Subway? Identify and describe two of them.
3. Overall, why is Subway so well rated as a franchise? Identify and describe two important factors.

Learning Objectives Revisited

1. **Define small business and its impact.** A small business is independently owned and operated, is not dominant in its field of operation, and meets certain standards of size in terms of employees or annual receipts. Small businesses account for over 99 percent of all nonfarm businesses and the vast majority of all new jobs.

2. **Identify the types of small businesses.** Some of the most common types of small businesses can be found in three main areas: light manufacturing and construction, merchandising, and service enterprises.

3. **Analyze some of the major advantages and disadvantages of owning a small business.** Some of the major advantages of owning a small business include independence, a chance to make a good living, the challenge involved, and the opportunity to provide a community service. The disadvantages of owning a small business include the risk of losing money,

great time demands, difficulty raising large sums of money for expansion, and the need to comply with government regulations and red tape.

4. **Discuss how to start a small business and effectively operate it.** The small business should start with a plan, which usually covers marketing, operations, and finance. The financial portion is especially important to lenders. Effectively operating the small business involves three functions: management, marketing, and finance. Management focuses on staffing and production. Marketing addresses personal selling, advertising, and location. Finance considers credit and expansion capital.

5. **Describe how the franchise form of business works.** A franchise is a system of distribution in which a producer or supplier arranges for a dealer to handle a product or service under mutually agreed-upon conditions. The dealer, known as the franchisee, pays a fee and a percentage of the revenues to the

supplier and operates the unit in a specified manner. The supplier, known as the franchisor, allows the franchisee to use the company's name and reputation; provides professional, standardized training in running the unit; provides merchandise at wholesale prices; and assists the franchisee in getting financial assistance.

6. **Relate the major advantages and disadvantages of franchises.** Some of the major advantages of franchising are that the franchisor provides management and operational training to the franchisee; the good or service has already been tested in the marketplace; the franchisor often helps with the advertising and promotion; and, in many cases, the franchisor helps the franchisee secure financial assistance. Some of the major disadvantages are that the franchisee must pay a high initial fee and percentage of revenues; the franchisor usually maintains strong control over the way the franchisee runs the operation; the franchisee usually has to buy all operating equipment, materials, and supplies from the franchisor; some franchisors do not deliver on their promises; and, in some cases, the franchisor has the right to buy out the unit at the end of the original contract.

Key Terms Reviewed

Review each of the following terms. For any that you do not know or are unsure of, look up the definitions and see how they were used in the chapter.

small business

venture capitalist

Small Business Administration (SBA)

small business investment company (SBIC)

minority enterprise small business investment company (MESBIC)

franchise

franchisor

franchisee

Review Questions

1. In what ways are small businesses important to the economy of the United States today?
2. Anita Summers is considering whether to go into business for herself. Anita is punctual and meticulous and works best when she has clear instructions. She doesn't like surprises and avoids risks. She is willing to work long hours. Based on this information, do you think Anita is a good candidate to be a small-business owner? Support your answer with principles described in the text.
3. Peter Dreyfuss likes dogs and thinks he has the characteristics of a good business owner. Therefore, he has decided to start up a business to provide dog-sitting services. What else should Peter consider before he arrives at such a decision?
4. What aspects of marketing are especially important to the owner of a small business? Why?
5. How do small-business owners obtain financing?
6. What is the Small Business Administration (SBA)? In what ways has this organization helped small businesses? If you were starting a small business, would you count on this organization for financing help? Why or why not?
7. Under a typical franchise arrangement, what are the responsibilities of a franchisee and a franchisor?
8. Lisa Crawford wants the independence of being in business for herself. What advantages and disadvantages of franchising should she consider?
9. If Lisa goes ahead with the franchise, what steps should she take to get started?

Applied Exercise

The list below contains a series of characteristics and behaviors that are commonly found among small-business owners. In each case, indicate whether each would be an advantage or a disadvantage in running the unit efficiently and making a profit.

Characteristic or Behavior	Advantage	Disadvantage
Is a self starter	_____	_____
Enjoys working hard	_____	_____
Believes that if you want something done right, you should do it yourself	_____	_____
Enjoys delegating responsibility	_____	_____
Gives his or her word and stands behind it	_____	_____
Sees things through to completion	_____	_____
Is often sick but tries to make up for it by working on weekends	_____	_____
Has a pleasant personality and can usually get along with anyone	_____	_____
Fires individuals who are unable to keep up with the work pace	_____	_____
Is not afraid to make difficult decisions	_____	_____
Is more interested in making a lot of money than in building a business that will last	_____	_____
Is highly ethical	_____	_____

YOU BE THE ADVISER / *A Lack of Funds*

When Delores Reyes opened her office supply store, she was sure she would be successful. After 10 years as an office manager with a large insurance firm, she knew what types of supplies businesses need. In fact, whenever she had ordered supplies for her employer, Delores had personally gone to the store and talked to the manager. Because the insurance company was the store's biggest account, the owner had gone out of his way to give Delores the best prices and fastest delivery. About 3 months ago, the supply store had been late in delivering a crucial order, and the insurance firm had to delay an important customer mailing by 10 days. Top management decided that it would no longer do business with the store. Delores's boss asked her to find another supplier who would be reliable.

After thinking the matter over, Delores approached her boss with the idea of opening her own store and bidding on the company's business. "You don't have to bid on our business," he told her. "If you want to go into this business, I'll give you a 2-year contract for all of our office supplies." With this amount of business guaranteed, Delores was able to get her operation up and going within 30 days. Unfortunately, a problem has now developed.

The insurance company does about $10,000 a month of business with Delores. Her walk-in business, much of it from other insurance companies she knows from her years in that field, adds another $12,000 monthly. This is much more than

Delores thought it would be, but because of payment delays, she is running out of operating money. The insurance companies pay within 90 days of delivery, which means that Delores has approximately $12,000 in bills outstanding at any time. She also needs expansion capital so she can carry more supplies and negotiate a lease arrangement for the vacant store next to hers. If she can get this store, she will be able to double her current floor space.

Delores cannot continue for more than 2 weeks unless she gets additional capital. She estimates that she will need about $5,000 for day-to-day working cash, $25,000 for additional inventory, and $20,000 to renovate the store next door.

Your Advice

1. How should Delores raise the $50,000 she needs? Rate your choices.
   ___ a. Contact a local venture capitalist and get this person to finance her needs.
   ___ b. Get a line of credit at a local bank.
   ___ c. Contact the Small Business Administration and apply for the necessary funds.
2. How important would a business plan be to Delores's efforts? Support your answer.
3. What areas of business should Delores emphasize? Identify and describe what she should do to make her business a success.

Career Opportunities in Business

The end of Chapter 1 suggests that the study of business pays off in personal and career growth. The chapters themselves provide the necessary background for learning about business, and they should help people be more effective in making career choices. The purpose of these Career Opportunities in Business sections, one at the end of each part of the book, is to focus on the specific careers most closely related to the content of the preceding chapters. Each one briefly describes representative jobs and summarizes the employment outlook and earnings. These short profiles of jobs are intended only to stimulate interest and serve as a starting point in career planning. The Careers Appendix at the end of the book provides more depth and specific guidelines and informal hints on how to find and obtain jobs.

Jobs related to Part One content include economist, small business owner, and franchisee. However, there are many other possibilities, and the employment outlook and earnings change with economic conditions. The earnings figures are highly variable, depending on the area of the country. Also, even though these salary figures represent averages, education and experience will greatly affect the actual pay.

Economist

An economist carries out research that provides information about the economy. Economists are employed in both the private sector, such as banks and insurance companies, and the public sector, such as educational institutions and government agencies at the local, state, and federal levels. Economists have extensive academic training in economic theory, statistics, and research methodology.

Job Description. Economists conduct research on a wide variety of economic topics including employment, inflation, wage rates, international balance of trade, and the effect of government policy on the economy at large. Their findings are of particular interest to groups such as corporate managers, governmental agencies, banks, trade associations, and labor unions.

Employment Outlook and Earnings. There currently are about 40,000 economists, many of whom are employed in academic institutions as teachers and researchers. The demand for this career field is expected to be average during the mid-1990s. Individuals with a bachelor's degree in economics can expect to earn a starting salary of $20,000 to $25,000. However, there is upward mobility. In government and industry, junior-level economists can work their way up the ranks to senior-level positions. The average salary for a federal government economist is around $42,000; in private industry it is approximately $54,000.

Small Business Owner

Small business is the backbone of the economy and these enterprises are found in every sector of the economy. In recent years, small businesses have grown rapidly and today they provide the majority of all new jobs.

Job Description. The specific job of the small-business owner depends on the particular goods and services that the enterprise is providing. Besides conducting day-to-day business, those who run a small business must be able to judge the marketability of their offerings, finance operations, and work well with both customers and employees. Other critical responsibilities include planning, budgeting, record keeping, advertising, and overall problem solving.

Employment and Earnings. Small business opportunities continue to grow and flourish. While most small businesses do not last more than 5 years, and many lose money, some owner-managers close up shop in order to open a new business that they believe offers greater potential. Earnings can vary widely. Most small business owners make less than $40,000 annually, but there are some who earn well over $100,000 and, for the most successful, annual earnings can be much higher.

Franchisee

A franchisee is an individual who pays a franchise fee and, in exchange, receives the right to operate a particular unit in a predetermined location.

Job Description. A franchisee is an independent businessperson who finances and manages his or her own business. In some cases the individual must go through a special training program offered by the franchisor in order to learn how to most effectively run the unit. In other cases the person simply pays the fee, is provided with general instructions, and begins operations. A franchisee must often be able to work with lenders in raising the initial capital to buy the franchise. The franchisee must also be able to carry out many of the responsibilities of a small business owner: work well with both customers and employees, plan effectively, keep accurate records, advertise, and handle day-to-day problems.

Employment Outlook and Earnings. Franchises continue to increase in number and there are many opportunities in a wide variety of areas. Two of the major areas are fast food and personal services. A franchisee who can pay the franchise fee and meet the other requirements set forth by the franchisor can obtain a unit and, in some franchises, can buy additional units over time. Earnings will depend on the franchise sales. Franchisees of new franchises or those that are not well known often earn less than $30,000 annually and they have to work hard to establish the business. Well-established franchises or those that have been in operation for 5 or more years often generate earnings of $50,000 or more annually to the franchisee.

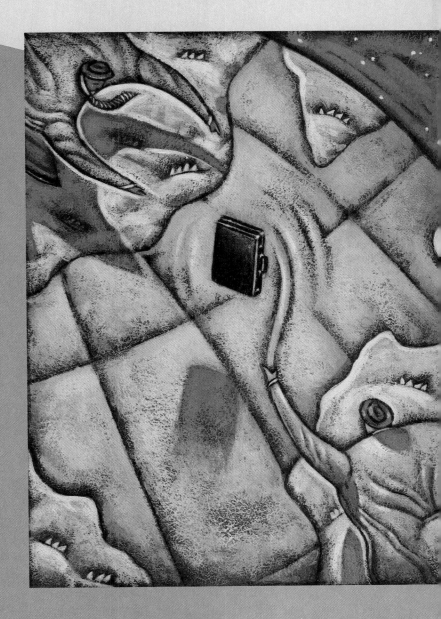

MADE IN JAPAN

What do Pebble Beach, Columbia Pictures, Firestone Tire, Rockefeller Center, and one out of every ten American banks have in common? They are at least partially owned by Japanese investors. In fact, over the past decade, Japanese investment in the United States by firms such as Honda, Mazda, Nissan, Sony, and hundreds of others has skyrocketed. At the beginning of this decade, only the British had more investment in America than did Japan. At the same time, many people are becoming concerned that the United States is too foreign-owned.

A look around the average American home is likely to reveal a

International Business

5

Chapter Learning Objectives

- Discuss the global economy and international business.

- Present the major reasons for international business.

- Identify some government-imposed barriers to international trade.

- Relate some cultural differences that make international trade challenging.

- Explain some efforts to stimulate international business.

- Discuss some common approaches to entering international markets.

---

large number of products that have been made in Japan or in U.S.-based firms that are owned by the Japanese. They include televisions, computers, cameras, radios, VCRs, and watches, not to mention the car sitting out in the garage. Despite the concerns of many people that the Japanese are taking over the manufacturing of consumer goods, others argue that Japanese investment helps the American economy. For example, Japan has bought a large percentage of U.S. government securities every time there has been an offering. If this did not happen, the interest rate on government loans would rise and the American taxpayer would have to foot an even larger bill. Another argument is that Japanese firms in the United States employ more than 250,000 people and their investments in new plants and equipment are helping revitalize Rust Belt industries. And, on the other side of the coin, unknown to many Americans, U.S. firms such as Coca-Cola, DuPont, IBM, McDonald's, and Motorola have significant operations in Japan and sell billions of dollars of merchandise to Japanese consumers every year.

While there are concerns that Japan is trying to dominate the U.S. economy, there is a positive side as well as a negative side to overseas investment in the U.S. economy. We are now in a largely borderless global economy, like it or not. Gone are the days of total economic independence. Now nations focus their efforts on hammering out reciprocal trade agreements that give each party more than it could have obtained by acting alone. Critics may point out that thousands of Mazda, Isuzu, and Mitsubishi vehicles are sold in the United States each year, but Ford, General Motors, and Chrysler also sell many of their autos overseas. In addition, the American "Big Three" hold substantial ownership in Mazda, Isuzu, and Mitsubishi.

Photo Source: © Craig Aurness/Westlight.

In Copenhagen a Danish consumer carries his purchase home. The transnational Colgate-Palmolive Company, maker of Dynamo, sells detergent in 41 countries. Colgate began the manufacture of detergents in Denmark in 1964.

Source: Courtesy of Colgate Palmolive Company.

Multinational corporation (MNC) A company having operations in more than one country, foreign sales, and/or a nationality mix of managers and owners.

Transnational corporation (TNC) A firm that views the world as one giant market; it is "stateless" or "borderless."

Balance of trade The difference between the value of a nation's exports and the value of its imports.

Exports Goods or services sold to other countries.

Imports Goods or services brought into one's own country.

Introduction

Many American businesses have "gone international." They range from huge corporations that do more business overseas than at home, such as Coca-Cola and Xerox, to tiny firms that export a few thousand dollars worth of product a year. This chapter explains what it means to operate in a global economy and why more and more American companies are taking on the challenge. It also discusses the know-how needed by people who work for these companies.

The Nature of International Business

Most businesses today are affected by the global economy. Some businesses directly engage in trade with suppliers and customers in other countries. When a company has operations in more than one country, has foreign sales, and/or has a nationality mix of managers and owners, it is commonly called a **multinational corporation (MNC).** Although only one or two of the criteria have to exist for a company to be considered an MNC, most large corporations today — such as the auto companies, DuPont, United Technologies, IBM, and Eastman Kodak — meet all the characteristics and are truly MNCs. In fact, if a large company is not an MNC in today's global marketplace, it is probably headed for trouble. Even the term multinational corporation may be becoming out-of-date in today's one world, global economy.

More accurate in the global economy would probably be the term **transnational corporation (TNC).** Sometimes called the "stateless" or "borderless" corporation, the TNC goes beyond an MNC by viewing the world as one giant market; national boundaries become irrelevant. The TNC will go anywhere to buy and sell its goods and the location of the headquarters is immaterial.[1]

As Table 5.1 shows, well-known American MNCs such as Gillette, IBM, and Coca-Cola have really become TNCs because they sell more of their products outside the United States than at home. Non-U.S. MNCs such as Switzerland's Nestlé, Sandoz, and Hoffman-La Roche, Sweden's SKF, and the Netherland's Philips all have over 94 percent of their sales outside their home boundaries.[2] Representative of the true global manager today would be five-language-speaking Jan Prising, a Swede who runs an American-owned company out of an office overlooking Lake Varese in Italy.[3]

Because the effects of international trade are so far-reaching, businesspeople try to keep abreast of international business activity. They measure the extent of a country's international trade activity by looking at the balance of trade and the balance of payments.

The Balance of Trade

The **balance of trade** is the difference between the value of a nation's exports and the value of its imports. **Exports** are goods or services sold to other countries. **Imports** are goods or services brought into one's own country. As the definitions imply, one country's exports are another country's imports. Figure 5.1 shows trends in the U.S. balance of trade.

TABLE 5.1

Transnational Corporations (Those with More than Half Their Sales Outside the United States)

Company	Percentage of Sales Outside U.S.	International Influence in Management
Gillette	65%	3 foreigners among top 21 officers
Colgate	64	CEO, other top executives have held several foreign posts; many multilingual
IBM	59	Relies on locals to manage non-U.S. operations; increasing number of foreigners in top ranks
NCR	59	Nationals run foreign operations
CPC International	56	A third of officers are foreign nationals
Coca-Cola	54	Thoroughly multinational management group making big international push
Digital	54	5 of top 37 officers are foreign; most foreign operations run by locals
Dow Chemical	54	20 out of top 25 managers have experience outside United States
Xerox	54	Major joint ventures with Rank, Fuji have shaped top management thinking
Caterpillar	53	4 out of top 5 executives have foreign experience including the new CEO

Source: Adapted from William J. Holstein, ''The Stateless Corporation,'' *Business Week,* May 14, 1990, 103.

FIGURE 5.1

The U.S. Balance of Trade

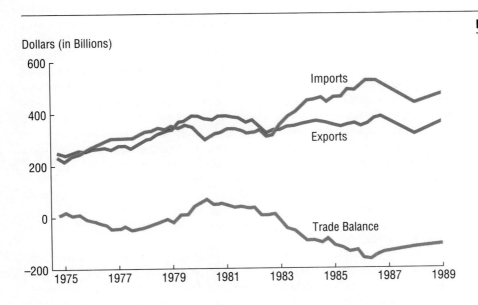

Dollars (in Billions)

FIGURE 5.2
Share of World Exports

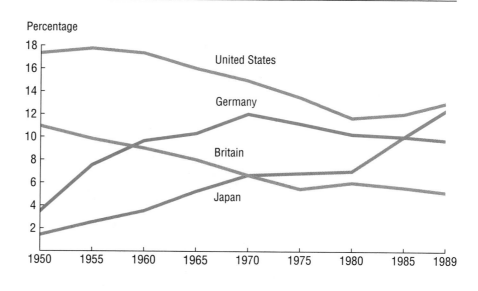

Source: *Fortune,* April 23, 1990, 59.

Trade deficit A negative balance of trade.

As Figure 5.1 shows, imports to the U.S. currently exceed exports. Because American companies and consumers have spent so much on imports in recent years, the United States has a **trade deficit.** This is a negative balance of trade, resulting from exports having a lower value than imports. The U.S. trade deficit caused concern in recent years because it reached record levels. However, the past few years have shown improvement and there are recent signs that the U.S. trade balance may be getting better. For example, as seen in Figure 5.2, the U.S. continues to have the largest share of the world export market. Moreover, although the Germans (especially since the merger of East and West Germany)[4] and the Japanese may overtake America in overall exports during the 1990s, the United States remains strong in some areas. One is manufacturing, where America still accounts for over 30 percent of all industrial production, providing an important base for export activities.[5] In addition, even during the past several years of trade deficits, the U.S. economic growth has been about the same as Japan and more rapid than Germany.[6] Nevertheless, most economists would agree that America needs to cut back the trade deficit for the long-term economic well being of the country.

The Balance of Payments

Balance of payments The total cash flow out of a country minus the total inflow of cash.

A broader way to measure international trade is the **balance of payments,** which is the total cash flow out of a country minus the total inflow of cash. This measure thus incorporates not only purchases and sales, but also investments and government foreign aid. For almost four decades following World War II, the United States was the world's largest investor in other countries. Today, the country is still a big investor, but foreign investment in our debt makes the United States a net debtor (we owe more to other countries than

Washington state-based Boeing Company, the world's leading manufacturer of commercial aircraft, completes five 747-400 airplanes like the one shown here each month for customers like British Airways, Japan Air Lines, and American Airlines. Although Boeing's export sales tally on the positive side of the U.S. trade balance, components for the planes are imported from around the world.

Source: Courtesy of The Boeing Company.

they owe to us). Our huge budget deficit led to high interest rates that in turn attracted foreign investors. America in recent years has been the largest debtor nation. By contrast, Japan is the world's largest creditor.

International Business and the American Economy

As the measures of exports, imports, and cash flows show, international business influences the American economy from two directions: American businesses participate in the economies of other countries, and foreign businesses participate in the U.S. economy. For example, IBM sells billions of dollars of computers and software annually in virtually every major area of the world including Japan, where the computer giant grosses well over $8 billion a year. Other high-tech American firms including Hewlett-Packard, Digital Equipment, and Texas Instruments also do well in Japan. By the same token, Japanese MNCs such as Canon, Sony, and Honda do about two-thirds of their business outside of Japan.[7]

U.S. products often meet with a warm reception overseas. This is particularly true for consumer goods and for products based on high technology. For example, the trademarks of Coke, Levi's, McDonald's, and Mickey Mouse (Disneylands are in Tokyo and near Paris) are known and appreciated worldwide. High-tech firms such as AT&T do business that amounts to 15 percent of sales in countries such as Spain, Indonesia, and South Korea.[8] And U.S. auto firms such as General Motors and Ford, collectively, are bigger than any of the other major passenger car manufacturers in Europe.[9] American firms have also relied heavily on acquisition strategies to purchase firms in other countries. This approach was quite popular during the 1960s and 1970s, but became much less popular during the 1980s. Now, however, there has been a renewed interest in acquisitions. The accompanying International Close-Up (Europe for Sale) provides some examples.

CLOSE-UP / *International*

Europe for Sale

By the end of the 1980s, many observers were concerned that the United States was allowing too many foreign investors to buy American assets while we were not purchasing very much overseas. Recent purchases by U.S. firms, however, indicate that, if anything, the Americans were simply biding their time and trying to acquire the best assets for the dollar. Some of the most recent purchases include the following:

- Ford Motor bought automaker Jaguar for $2.5 billion and opened a new auto components plant in Hungary for $80 million.
- PepsiCo bought Smiths Crisps and Walkers Crisps, two British makers of snacks, for $1.4 billion.
- General Motors acquired 50 percent of Saab Scania's passenger car operations for $600 million.
- Emerson Electric paid $460 million for Leroy-Somer, a French maker of electric drives and motors.
- DuPont bought Howson-Algraphy, a leading British maker of printing plates, for $445 million.
- International Paper paid $300 million for French paper-maker Aussedat Rey.

In addition, there are a wide variety of other investments including Intel's $400 million microprocessor facility in Leixlip, Ireland, and Motorola's decision to set up an export platform in Scotland for the European Community.

These investments are designed to put the American firms in an ideal position to take advantage of the growing European market. AT&T, for example, feels that its stake in the Italian state-owned telephone company will help position it to capture a big share of the $35 billion that Italy has earmarked for upgrading its phone system. Ford and General Motors are following similar strategies. The European passenger car market is 30 percent larger than the U.S. market, and by adding plants in this area of the world, the American car makers are in a good position to meet the demand of the local population.

Another reason for setting up operations in Europe, and one that is often overlooked by observers, is the subsidies that are offered to the firms. Italy put up over $600 million of the $1.2 billion that Texas Instruments will be spending in the southern region of that country. Scotland offered Motorola generous aid with training, temporary facilities, and capital in convincing the firm to settle there rather than in Spain or Ireland, the other two prime locations that were under consideration. Meanwhile, Ireland will hold Intel's taxes to 10 percent through the end of this century in return for its commitment to build a plant outside Dublin that will employ 2,600 people. With potential profits high and the promise of local assistance, many American firms are finding Europe to be an ideal area for acquisition and expansion.

Source: Blanca Riemer, "America's New Rush to Europe," *Business Week*, March 26, 1990, 48–49; John Templeman, Ken Olsen, David Greising, Jonathan Kapstein, and William Glasgall, "Eastward Ho! The Pioneers Plunge In," *Business Week*, April 15, 1991, 51–53.

At the same time, the United States is an important market for foreign companies. The size of the market alone draws foreign businesses to the United States. American consumers snap up Mercedes Benz automobiles, Sony electronic equipment, and Corona beer. Foreign companies also participate in the U.S. marketplace by investing in American companies and even buying them outright. Today, Ball Park hot dogs and French's mustard are owned by a British conglomerate; a Japanese firm owns a large interest in New York's Rockefeller Center. In addition, foreign businesses invest in the United States by purchasing government securities and by providing private firms with needed investment capital. For example, the Arden Computer Corporation of Sunnyvale, California, has raised $50 million from foreign investors; Rasna Corporation, a software firm in San Jose, California, obtained $10 million this way; and Exabyte Corporation, a maker of high-capacity cartridge-type subsystems for data storage got $6 million.[10] Nevertheless, to put this in perspective, foreign investments in the United States still account for only a small percentage of total investments.

International trade therefore opens opportunities for U.S. business owners and U.S. consumers. American business owners can try to make the whole world — the global market — their marketplace and thus acquire more sources of funding. However, the influx of foreign competitors can also make maintaining their domestic market share a challenging job. Consumers can benefit from the greater choices and the sometimes lower prices available when more companies compete for their dollars.

1. What is the balance of trade?
2. Should the United States be concerned about having a negative balance of trade and being the world's largest debtor nation?

CHECK ✓ POINT

Reasons for International Business

Why do some companies expand into international markets, while others stay close to home? How do companies decide which countries to operate in? The managers of a company weigh its resources, opportunities, limitations, and strengths in an effort to determine what the company can do most effectively and profitably.

The Broader View: National Advantages

The types of products a nation's companies trade internationally depend in part on the things businesses in that nation tend to do well. These strengths stem from the nation's resources, such as raw materials, the work ethic and educational levels of the people, and the degree of industrialization. Nations may have an absolute advantage or a comparative advantage. Businesspeople looking for international opportunities might start by determining whether their company has such an advantage relative to businesses in other countries.

Absolute Advantage   Some nations have a monopoly on certain products or can produce them for considerably less than anyone else. This advantage is an **absolute advantage.** For example, South Africa has most of the world's diamonds. Because of its monopoly in this natural resource, South Africa has an absolute advantage in the sale of diamonds. Most resources are distributed more widely, so absolute advantages are rare.

Absolute advantage
A monopoly on certain products or the ability to produce them for considerably less than anyone else.

Comparative Advantage   More often, a nation has a **comparative advantage** — it can sell certain products for relatively less than most other nations can. The reasons for this include cheap labor, abundant natural resources, a favorable climate, and an abundance of technical skill. For example, the United States has many skilled engineers and scientists who can develop products, such as computers and jet engines, that depend on sophisticated technology. Saudi Arabia has a generous supply of oil, so it sells oil to many countries.

Comparative advantage   The ability to sell certain products for relatively less than producers in most other nations can.

The Narrower View: Sources of Advantage

Businesspeople considering international trade might start by weighing whether their product has an absolute or comparative advantage over products supplied by companies in other countries. But at some point, a business's managers must consider the business's own advantages. Some sources of advantage include natural resources and climate, capital equipment and skilled personnel available, geographic location, and political climate.

Natural Resources   Some countries have an abundance of certain natural resources. For example, the United States has about one-third of the entire world's known coal reserves. Mideast countries are rich in oil. Bolivia has tin, and Malaysia has natural rubber. These natural resources can be exported in raw form or converted or refined into a finished component or product. Companies that sell or use these resources are likely to engage in international trade.

Climate and Terrain   A favorable climate or terrain makes it possible to produce certain crops more efficiently than others. In the United States, for example, the Great Plains have a favorable climate and terrain for growing wheat. Farmers in Kansas, Nebraska, South Dakota, and North Dakota produce wheat for the United States and provide millions of tons of wheat for export. Farmers in other countries specialize in products suited to their climate and terrain; for example, farmers in Colombia and Brazil grow coffee beans, those in Cuba raise tobacco. Costa Rican farmers grow bananas, and Brazil is rich in rubber trees.

Capital Equipment   Manufacturers rely on capital resources such as high-tech plants, machinery, and equipment. The more capital equipment a company has, the greater its opportunity to meet domestic demand and have capacity left to produce exports. Businesses with idle capital equipment often turn to international selling as a means of using their productive capacity more fully.

Capital equipment also allows companies to diversify. Although Japanese companies have taken over the market for mass-produced silicon memory chips, America's Silicon Valley chip makers such as Cypreso Semiconductor have competed very well by offering diversity. This company makes 80 different types of chips in a facility that can accommodate several daily tool changes. Meanwhile, IBM, the world's largest chip producer, is now developing X-ray methods of printing chips, a process that should come to fruition in the early 1990s.[11]

Human Resources   Skilled workers are an important supplement to capital equipment. The United States, for example, has the high-tech equipment and there is a growing need for skilled personnel who are able to produce and operate this complex equipment. For example, a maintenance worker at Swift Textiles Inc. used to lug around a 30-pound tool belt so he could manually repair broken looms. Today, he has shed the heavy belt for a hand-sized terminal that can diagnose 100 different problems on new computer-driven equipment. A study for the Department of Labor estimates that, by the year 2000, below-average skills will be good enough for only 27 percent of the jobs, and over 40 percent of the new jobs in the coming years will require average or better skills.[12] The problem is that American workers may not be prepared for this upgrading of skill requirements. For example, 20 percent of Motorola applicants flunked an entry-level exam requiring 7th-to-9th-grade English and 40 percent flunked the 5th-to-7th-grade math exam.[13]

Farmers Jim and Keith Boysen harvest corn on their 800-acre family farm in eastern Iowa. Today's seed corn produces plants with higher yield and greater drought and pest resistance than seed of 50 years ago because of special breeding by DEKALB Genetics and other companies. The United States has a comparative advantage in crops such as corn thanks to climate and terrain, the availability of tractors and equipment (capital equipment), and skilled farmers and agriculture specialists (human resources).

Source: Courtesy of DEKALB Genetics Corporation.

So while the United States still has a ready supply of college-graduate professionals, entrepreneurs, and intrapreneurs (see Chapter 7), there may be a need for more skilled workers in order to remain competitive in the future.

The newly industrialized countries (NICs), which include South Korea, Singapore, Hong Kong, and Taiwan (sometimes called the "Four Asian Tigers"), have made their mark in world trade largely through their human resources. Employee wages in the NICs have traditionally been lower than their counterparts in Japan, Europe, and the United States. Not only are their human resources less costly, but they are becoming increasingly educated and skilled. Once dismissed as marginal producers of low-quality clothes and toys, the NICs have become producers of complex, high-quality goods because of their skilled workers. They now produce everything from VCRs and computers to cars and planes. In recent years, however, like their more advanced competitors such as Japan and the United States, they have had some economic setbacks. Their workers are demanding a share of the economic miracle and want higher wages. Only time will tell if the Asian tigers will continue the phenomenal economic growth they experienced in the 1980s.[14]

In the underdeveloped countries of Africa, the Middle East, and South America, businesses have been unable to take full advantage of high-tech markets. For example, even if they buy sophisticated computers, they are unable to use them to the fullest if they lack a well-trained, skilled workforce that knows how to get the most out of these machines. Human resources help explain some of the productivity differences between businesses in the developed countries, the NICs, and the underdeveloped Third World nations.

Geographic Location   A business's geographic location also influences its use of international trade. If demand exists in a nearby country, businesspeople may sell there because the shorter distance keeps transportation costs down and makes foreign operations easier to control. For example, the West Coast has an advantage over the East Coast in trade with Asia. Also, as the International Close-Up earlier in the chapter indicated, American companies scrambled at the beginning of the 1990s to have a presence in Europe to take advantage of the tremendous market opportunities available in the European Community (EC). U.S. firms wanted to be geographically close to the EC, which opened up the largest single market in the industrialized world with 320 million people.[15]

Political Climate   The political climate of a country can attract or discourage businesses. For example, many foreign countries are attracted to the stable political situation of the United States. Businesses tend to stay away from nations in turmoil. For example, after war broke out in the Persian Gulf at the beginning of 1991, many Western businesses pulled out or have refused to go into that part of the world because of the unsettled political climate and associated risks.[16] The aftershocks of the crackdown on the movement toward democracy in China also affected doing business in Hong Kong, which will be taken over by the Chinese in 1997.[17]

Governments may also set policies specifically to encourage or discourage international trade. For example, the United States is interested in maintaining trade with the Philippines and Costa Rica because it wants to exert economic influence in order to discourage unfriendly governments there. Mexico has recently reversed its policies of the 1980s and is encouraging private investment and is denationalizing its telephone company and its agricultural operations.[18] The same trend is occurring in South American countries.[19] On the other hand, the United States has been involved in prolonged negotiations with the Japanese to encourage them to open their doors wider to imports in return for selling their goods here.[20] In doing so, the United States must be careful not to adopt a highly protectionist policy that could be self-defeating.[21]

Another area of political interest is that of lobbyists who work for foreign firms and attempt to influence legislation that is favorable to their clients. There currently is talk about more closely regulating these individuals.

CHECK ✓ POINT

1. How does absolute advantage differ from comparative advantage?
2. What are three sources of advantage businesspeople consider in determining whether to engage in international trade?

Barriers to International Trade

Government policy can make it expensive or even illegal to engage in international trade. In addition, cultural differences can be a barrier to conducting business in the international arena.

Government Restrictions

Most governments erect some barriers to limit foreign businesses, because it is to the government's benefit when domestic businesses prosper and create more jobs and income for the citizenry. Most economists would also argue that trade restrictions lead to higher prices and limited choices, but these effects are more subtle.

The government also restricts foreign trade for security reasons. To avoid dependence on other countries for critical defense materials, the home government protects defense-related industries by limiting competition and foreign acquisitions. Another reason the government erects trade barriers is to help the country reduce the trade deficit. Advocates of protectionist measures say that they would boost profits and reduce unemployment. To help this situation, the government imposes quotas, tariffs, and other regulations.

Quotas   One of the most common government-imposed trade barriers is a **quota.** This is a restriction on the quantity or value of an item that may be imported. For example, a quota could restrict the amount of Scottish wool imported into the United States in any calendar year to 5,000 tons. Another quota could restrict the amount of French wine imported into the United States to $10 million a year. In recent years Japanese automakers have used voluntary quotas on exporting autos to the United States to avoid having a quota imposed on them by the United States. Most quotas are expressed in terms of physical quantity, because goods are easier to measure and control on this basis.

Tariffs   The government might also discourage imports by taxing them. A **tariff** is a duty or fee levied on imported goods. It discourages imports by making them more expensive in the hope that more consumers will switch to domestic brands. However, if a country's producers are less efficient than those of another, and the country competes by raising its tariff duties, the consumers in that country will pay more for their products than they would otherwise have to.

Regulation of Business   Some governments regulate businesses more heavily than others. Sometimes these regulations discourage businesses from entering a market. In some nations, all international businesses must have local partners, meaning that a foreign company may not set up an operation without at least one national in the top management. Because of the success of some overseas firms, there has been talk in the United States about the need for a high-tech industrial policy to coordinate the effort to fend off foreign competition. Although this is unlikely to happen, it does illustrate the steps that governments can take in attempts to regulate efforts by overseas firms to tap the American market.[22]

Currency Differences

Each nation issues its own currency, and the complications that result are another type of barrier to international trade. International business involves the extra task of converting money from the currency of one nation to that of another. For example, an American company that sends salespeople to London would exchange dollars for pounds for spending there. A company that operates stores in Japan would have to convert yen into dollars. A major challenge for the EC to become a true reality is for the member countries to have a common currency. The same is true for the Eastern European countries; they must have a currency that can be exchanged if they ever hope to

Quota   A restriction on the quantity or value of an item that may be imported.

Tariff   A duty or fee levied on imported goods.

Americans are accustomed to seeing Hondas being unloaded from Japanese freighters in the United States, but these are U.S.-made Hondas arriving in Japan! Honda overcomes some trade barriers by building factories in countries where it wants to sell. By creating jobs in the United States, Honda alleviates the concern that buying from foreign businesses leads to domestic unemployment. In the United States, where Honda sells more cars than in Japan, it has two plants. Some cars produced at these plants end up in Japan.

Source: Courtesy of American Honda Motor Co., Inc.

FIGURE 5.3

The Trade Deficit with the United States' Major Trading Partners

Source: *Fortune,* April 23, 1990, 23.

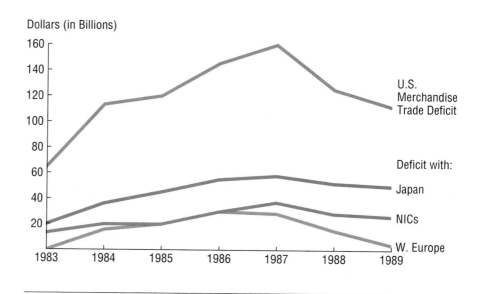

Dollars (in Billions)

U.S. Merchandise Trade Deficit

Deficit with:

Japan

NICs

W. Europe

become a major player in the global economy. The agreement of a monetary union between West and East Germany was a major reason why Germany unified and has become so economically powerful.[23]

The arithmetic of dealing with the exchange rate is fairly simple, but planning for it is difficult in today's constantly changing world. For various reasons, the rate of exchange between the dollar and other currencies frequently changes. For example, if it currently does not take many U.S. dollars to buy a certain foreign currency, then Americans who travel in that country and American businesses who buy from that country can get a great deal more for their dollars than they can if later in the year it takes more dollars to buy the same amount of foreign currency. Obviously, American tourists and managers would have wanted to make purchases as early as possible that year, but predicting shifts in the exchange rate can be as tricky as forecasting the stock market.

In general, a strong dollar (worth more relative to foreign currencies) helps buyers of imports, because it keeps the price of imports down. A weak dollar (worth less relative to foreign currencies) helps exporters by making their products relatively less expensive in other countries. As shown in Figure 5.3, the shrinking U.S. trade deficit with the major trading partners is largely attributed to the weaker dollar.[24] On paper, the earnings of an international business seem to change, too, with a strong dollar making overseas profits seem smaller than they would be with a weak dollar. For example, in recent years some American firms in Japan have found that the rise in the value of the yen has been so great that they have sold their local holdings for astounding dollar profits.[25]

Besides uncertainty over exchange rates, international businesses risk being unable to convert foreign earnings into the currency of their own country. Some countries try to keep funds in the country by refusing to allow companies to convert their currency, thus limiting the ways businesses can

VIDEO CLOSE-UP / *International*

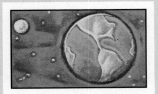

A Big Mak, Please

When the Canadian subsidiary of McDonald's and the Moscow city council decided to open a McDonald's restaurant in the Soviet Union as a joint venture, no one realized how long it would take. Talks between McDonald's and Soviet officials began in 1976, and a contract was finally signed in April 1988. The unit finally opened in 1990 in Moscow's Pushkin Square.

Thousands of Russians now go to Pushkin Square to order a *Big Mak* and *kartofel-fries*. This McDonald's, with a seating capacity of 700, is the largest unit in the entire chain. It can serve up to 15,000 customers a day. The prices are equivalent to those in the United States, which means they are fairly high because the average Russian earns only a fraction of what an American earns. To an American the menu seems quite limited, offering only the Big Mac, Filet-o-Fish, double cheeseburger, milk cocktail (milkshake), soft drinks, french fries, and ice cream sundaes. Nevertheless, business is brisk. Russian customers like the friendly service and high-quality food.

McDonald's hopes to repeat this success and will open many more units throughout the Soviet Union. The Soviets are delighted with the decision to expand. The economy, already suffering food shortages, could benefit from the efficiency and visibility of fast food outlets. In addition, working at McDonald's is considered a prestigious job. When the Moscow unit advertised for employees, it received over 27,000 applications. Of these, 2,100 were interviewed for the 605 openings. Every new hire went through a training program and learned several jobs — punching orders into the computerized cash register, cooking and serving the food on the menu, and keeping the facility clean. To ensure adequate on-time supplies, McDonald's built a $40 million distribution plant outside Moscow. The plant has its own bakery, dairy, and meat-processing departments.

Besides the quality and variety of food, another reason this first McDonald's in the Soviet Union is very popular is that customers can pay with rubles, which are currently not convertible into dollars. Of course, McDonald's has to figure out what to do with all of the rubles. In order to limit this problem, company officials decided that, at the second McDonald's unit in Moscow, customers would have to pay for their food in convertible currency.

---

spend their earnings. Besides the uncertainties surrounding the Soviet Union's political situation in the early 1990s,[26] the biggest practical problem a Western MNC faced with doing business there was how to convert its largely worthless ruble[27] earnings into real money. Experienced MNCs such as PepsiCo reverted to a barter system whereby they swapped their soft-drink syrup for Russian-made vodka.[28] On the other hand, McDonald's agreed to accept rubles in its first outlet in Moscow to gain a foothold in this market, as described in the accompanying International Video Close-Up (A Big Mak, Please).

Cultural Differences

When people from different parts of the world come together, they often have trouble communicating. Even people with the best of intentions may baffle or even insult one another. Such problems arise because of cultural differences. **Culture** consists of the beliefs, attitudes, values, and behaviors that people learn in their society.[29] When doing business abroad, incorrect assumptions about culture can be a major stumbling block. This is true not only for Americans doing business overseas, but also for people from foreign countries doing business in the United States.

Culture The beliefs, attitudes, values, and behaviors that people learn in their society.

Language and Communication Style While English is becoming the language of business, it is not the primary language of most people in the world.

Reaching consumers worldwide requires the use of other languages, and foreign languages are also important in communicating with other business-people. Most people appreciate the effort it takes to learn their language. When businesspeople do not speak or read another country's language, they rely on translators. This can be very costly. At the rate of $20 to $25 a page to translate, some companies are spending millions and not even realizing it. But even when they use skilled translators, businesspeople must be aware of differences in the way people of various cultures communicate.

Speaking styles, including the distances speakers maintain between themselves, are culturally based. For example, many Israeli businesspeople speak English in an aggressive way, leading Americans who are unfamiliar with their speech habits to believe that their Israeli business counterparts are angry about something. However, this is simply the way many Israelis are accustomed to communicate. Arabic businesspeople, in contrast, tend to speak softly and stand very close to their listener, which makes many Americans nervous. They may feel threatened by the closeness, which may seem pushy. Japanese businesspeople, who value politeness above frankness, may seem to agree with all of an American visitor's ideas. However, the American might be dismayed later to discover that when saying yes, the Japanese businessperson merely meant, "I hear you," not "I agree with you."

Another language-related problem is the use of humor. Many Americans love to exaggerate, and some foreigners may take things literally. The American managers of a German subsidiary referred to the bald salesperson in their group as "Curly." They called their 6'10" engineer "Tiny," and the heavyset accountant "Slim." Most of the German managers were baffled by these names and simply wrote them off as the notions of those "crazy Americans."

Customs and Manners   To make their foreign customers and colleagues comfortable and to avoid insult, managers need to be aware of customs and manners. For example, a U.S. custom is for people to wear black as a sign of mourning, but in China mourners wear white. In the United States, most businessmen go to work in a suit and tie, while in Israel almost no one does, and in Latin American countries, businessmen commonly wear a *guayabera* (a long overshirt).

These cultural differences in customs and manners need to be recognized by managers in the international business arena. Unfortunately, Americans have too often ignored cultural differences and have sometimes earned the title of "ugly Americans."

Concept of Time   Most Americans have a high esteem for time and punctuality. In the United States, northern European countries, and England, for example, meetings are expected to start on time. However, in Latin countries, the pace is more leisurely; as a result, many American managers find themselves angrily cooling their heels for 15 to 30 minutes waiting for an appointment or meeting. In warm climates like Mexico, managers often take a long afternoon break but then go back to work after their evening meal, expecting their American counterparts to join them. American managers can save themselves a good deal of discomfort by learning these patterns in advance.

Culture in Perspective   The way businesspeople behave often varies from one country to another. But making business deals often depends on bonds of trust. To build these bonds, managers need to make the extra effort required to understand foreign cultures. Sometimes this involves finding out about a whole different way of looking at the world. Making a product that meets a need is the heart of successful international business, but those efforts will be lost unless the company can overcome cultural barriers.

CHECK ✓ POINT

1. What are some major ways governments erect barriers to international trade?
2. How do business practices vary among cultures?

Promoting International Trade

Despite the many barriers to international trade, which are mainly used to discourage imports, most countries have also made special efforts to promote trade. These efforts consist of creating free-trade zones, constructing trade agreements, and providing financial support.

Free-Trade Zones

A **free-trade zone (FTZ)** is a geographic area into which foreign goods can be imported without payment of duties. Applied to the United States, the importer moves the goods from the FTZ into the United States, where a duty is then imposed. In other cases, the importer ships the products from the FTZ to other countries without ever paying a duty.

> **Free-trade zone (FTZ)**
> A geographic area into which foreign goods can be imported without payment of duties.

The primary benefit of FTZs is that they provide jobs for American workers and markets for U.S. goods. For example, the Brooklyn Navy Yard is now an FTZ at which over 150 firms do business. Many U.S. workers there repackage goods for shipment to foreign markets. Other firms use an FTZ as a temporary business site when they relocate from overseas back to the United States. This gives them a place from which to operate while their local facilities are being constructed. In still other cases, companies use an FTZ to delay customs duties on goods that are not yet ready for market. For example, a company in the New Orleans FTZ is aging its wine for future distribution.

Agreements among Nations

Sometimes groups of nations agree to work together to promote trade among one another's businesses. One of the important existing trade agreements is the General Agreement on Tariffs and Trade. In addition, groups of nations form economic communities.

General Agreement on Tariffs and Trade (GATT)   Over 90 nations have joined together in the **General Agreement on Tariffs and Trade (GATT),** an international agreement and organization designed to eliminate tariff barriers to worldwide trade. Since 1947, member nations of GATT have met periodically to negotiate tariff cuts and to remove other trade barriers. A number of significant steps have been taken over the years. For example, the Kennedy Rounds (1962–1967) brought about an average tariff reduction of

> **General Agreement on Tariffs and Trade (GATT)**
> An international agreement and organization designed to eliminate tariff barriers to worldwide trade.

FIGURE 5.4
Common Market Countries

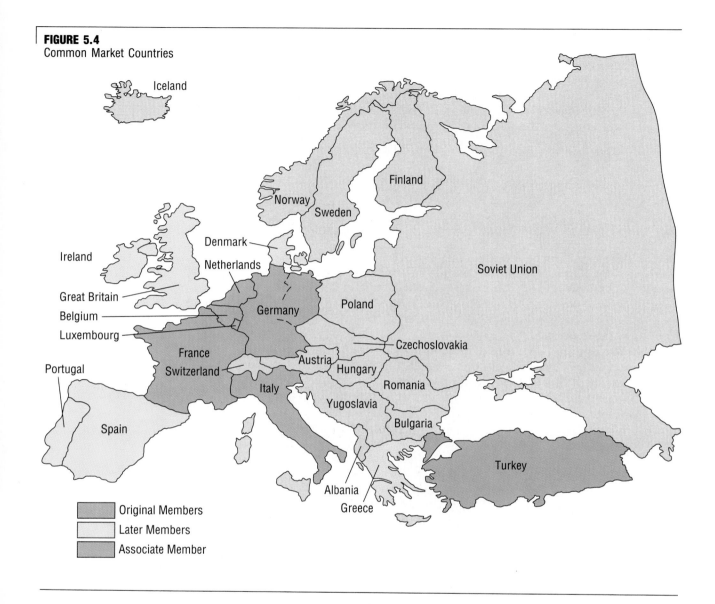

Original Members
Later Members
Associate Member

40 percent on 60,000 separate items. The Tokyo Rounds (1973–1979) reduced tariffs by approximately 33 percent on 6,000 items. Recently, the United States has attempted to use GATT to solve disputes regarding international piracy of patents and copyrights.[30]

Economic Communities   Another way nations have attempted to remove trade barriers is by forming economic communities or unions. The best-known example is the European Community (EC), traditionally known as the Common Market. The 12 member countries shown in Figure 5.4 are Belgium, Denmark, France, Germany, Greece, Ireland, Italy, Luxembourg, the Netherlands, Portugal, Spain, and the United Kingdom. As mentioned earlier, the EC has the goal to become a United Europe that would eliminate trade barriers so that the member countries would be no different than the states in the United States. The goal is to have the free movement of goods, people, service, and capital.

Many of the 300 legislative directives to accomplish a United Europe have been enacted, but some significant barriers remained in 1991.[31] The cultural, language, political, and monetary barriers are the most difficult to overcome. But one thing is sure, the EC has emerged as a powerful player in the global economy and has affected the international trade and business of the United States and other nations.

Financial Support for International Trade

Laws promoting free trade can encourage international business, but some companies need money to reach an international market. The U.S. government and the United Nations have created a number of financial institutions to help foster international trade:

- The **Export-Import Bank (Exim Bank)** is a U.S. government lending agency that makes loans to importers and exporters that are unable to obtain adequate financing from private agencies.
- The **International Monetary Fund (IMF)** is a UN organization that tries to stabilize exchange rates between world currencies.
- The **International Bank for Reconstruction and Development (World Bank)** is an agency supported by about 150 member nations that lends to underdeveloped nations to help them stimulate their economy and grow.
- The **International Finance Corporation (IFC),** an affiliate of the World Bank, invests in private enterprises in underdeveloped nations.
- The **International Development Association (IDA),** an affiliate of the World Bank, makes loans to underdeveloped countries on more liberal terms than does the World Bank.

1. What are two ways international trade is encouraged?
2. How does the federal government provide financing for international trade?

Going International

Many American firms have "gone international." The auto companies and aircraft companies export billions of dollars in goods each year, and United and American Airlines battle for global supremacy.[32] Smaller firms often use a much different approach from that employed by their larger counterparts. Small firms often start off by licensing or exporting their product, while larger firms are more likely to opt for a joint venture or to use a branch, subsidiary, or world company.

Licensing

When a company is small or simply does not want to underwrite the expense of entering a foreign market, it will sometimes seek a licensing agreement with an overseas firm. A **license** is a legal agreement in which one firm gives another the right to manufacture and sell its product in return for paying a royalty. This royalty is often a percentage of the income from the sale of the product.

Export-Import Bank (Exim Bank) A U.S. government lending agency that makes loans to importers and exporters unable to obtain private funding.

International Monetary Fund (IMF) A UN organization that tries to stabilize exchange rates between world currencies.

International Bank for Reconstruction and Development (World Bank) An agency that lends to underdeveloped countries to help them grow.

International Finance Corporation (IFC) An organization that invests in private enterprises in underdeveloped nations.

International Development Association (IDA) An organization that lends to underdeveloped countries.

CHECK ✓ POINT

License A legal agreement in which one firm gives another the right to manufacture and sell its product in return for paying a royalty.

Uniform building codes are one concern of the new European Community. Employees of Armstrong World Industries, Inc., are working to help EC officials establish product specifications, performance standards, and testing methods for flooring and insulation.

Source: Courtesy of Armstrong World Industries, Inc.

Businesses with patents or trademarks that protect them against counterfeiters often use licensing because they have something special to bring to the licensing agreement, and both sides can profit from the deal. The licenser receives royalties and international marketing expertise. The licensee gains a successful product and the know-how required to manufacture it. The licenser often exercises strict quality control over the production of the goods, because its reputation is on the line. However, the specific selling practices are often up to the licensee, who typically knows more about how to sell the product in the foreign market.

Exporting

Businesses that want greater control over manufacturing can manufacture the product at home and then export it to foreign markets. The exporter's degree of involvement in the marketplace depends on its marketing strategy. In formulating such a strategy, exporters need to carefully examine basic demographics, growth potential, and political and economic climate.

Some firms sell their products to an export/import merchant, who assumes all of the selling risks. This merchant is similar to a wholesaler (discussed in Chapter 16), who takes goods off the manufacturer's hands and arranges for resale to retailers. For example, Oracle, a computer software firm in Redwood, California, uses this approach in selling its specialized products in faraway places such as Zimbabwe;[33] Tracom Inc. of Ft. Worth, Texas, uses it in selling used diesel engines and parts to remanufacturers in Europe and Australia.[34] In other cases the company will use an export/import agent. In this case the manufacturer retains title to the goods until the agent sells them to wholesalers or retailers in the foreign country. Rad Elec, a small Maryland-based firm that sells test kits for absorbing radon gas, uses this approach.[35] In still other cases, the exporter may set up its own sales offices or branches and take over distribution and sales of the product in the foreign country. Alcoa uses this approach in Asia to sell sheet aluminum to be used to make beverage cans.[36] This arrangement is more expensive than the other sales approaches, and it is usually limited to large firms.

Joint Ventures

In going international, smaller firms usually use the approach of licensing or exporting. Large firms may try a **joint venture** with a company in the targeted country. As discussed in Chapter 3, this is an arrangement in which two companies pool their resources to create, produce, and market a product. Many firms have used this arrangement because it helps them get a foothold in the international market without having to start from scratch. In the typical joint venture agreement, the American firm provides most of the funding and technical know-how for producing the product. The overseas firm takes responsibility for handling government red tape and fine-tuning the sales pitch to the local market.

Joint venture An arrangement in which two companies pool their resources to create, produce, and market a product.

In some countries it is almost impossible to sell goods without having a local partner, hence the popularity of the joint venture. Samsonite is using this approach to make luggage in Hungary.[37] Tambrands of Lake Success, New York, has a joint venture with the Ukrainian Health Ministry in the Soviet Union to manufacture women's health products.[38] General Electric of the United States has completed a $150 million deal for 50 percent of Tungsram, Hungary's state-owned maker of light bulbs.[39] Such joint ventures have become very commonplace in the global economy.

Branches and Subsidiaries

If a company's managers decide the company should handle the sales of its products abroad, they often establish a branch. A **branch organization** is an operation set up by a parent company in another country for the purpose of accomplishing specific goals such as sales. The branch manager typically assumes the role of an overseas sales manager.

Branch organization
An operation set up by a parent company in a foreign country for the purpose of accomplishing specific goals such as sales.

If the managers decide to go further and set up the company's own production facilities as well as marketing operations overseas, they typically will create a subsidiary. A **subsidiary** is a company organized under the laws of a foreign country for the purpose of carrying out tasks, such as production and sales, assigned by the parent firm. Some subsidiaries are highly dependent on the parent company for instructions and directions. Other subsidiaries operate autonomously because the home office management believes the on-site people are in the best position to make decisions.

Subsidiary A company organized under the laws of a foreign country for the purpose of carrying out tasks, such as production and sales, assigned by the parent firm.

The Future of International Business

Multinational and transnational firms continue to be a growing presence in the global economy. U.S. firms continue to push into every corner of the globe to offer both goods and services. Some of the most recent expansion has involved international franchises, such as McDonald's and Kentucky Fried Chicken, and financial services, such as the offices of large securities firms including Merrill Lynch, Morgan Stanley, and Salomon Brothers in Europe and the Far East. At the same time, large American banks such as Chase Manhattan and Citibank continue to maintain their financial relationships with nations around the world from Poland to Peru.

A major ethical challenge facing many multinational firms is how to conduct business in other countries. Does management follow its own home's rules and ethical standards, or those of the country in which it is doing business? Sometimes these standards are conflicting ones but, as the next chapter on social responsibility and ethics will point out, short-run ethical compromises may lead to long-run disasters. Businesses are learning that they must use the highest ethical standards not only as the right way to do business (even in another culture), but as the profitable way to do business in the long run.

In any event, we live in a global economy, and the future of business is surely an international one.

CHECK ✓ POINT

1. What are three ways businesses can expand to overseas markets?
2. Why are small companies going international more likely to use licensing than foreign subsidiaries?

Closing Comments

The global economy is a growing challenge for business. Many firms sell goods and services with appeal in the markets of several countries. This means that international trade offers both the additional opportunity of new markets and the additional challenge of new competition. Modern businesses need to think "international" rather than just in national terms. This includes having an expanded perspective of social responsibility to the people in every nation, not just to those on the home front. To the extent that businesses can meet these important challenges, they stand a good chance not only of surviving, but also of being leaders in their respective industries.

VIDEO CASE / *A Foreign Invasion*

During the past 10 years, Japan has become one of the world's largest exporters of goods. The American "Big Three" found out just how big as their market share for cars declined in the face of competition from Honda, Toyota, Mazda, Nissan, and other Japanese manufacturers. However, automaking is not the only essential manufacturing industry in which the Japanese have made inroads into the American market. Three other key industries are machine tools, computers, and semiconductors.

In the late 1970s, American machine tool manufacturers had large backlogs of orders and dominated the market. During the 1980s, however, imports began flooding the market and by 1986 almost 50 percent of all machine tools were being imported. Since then American manufacturers have been able to regain a small percentage of the market, but the Japanese are now the major competitors. At the beginning of this decade, Japanese machine tool manufacturers had built $10 billion worth of equipment, three times the

U.S. output. And in the United States much of the machine tool output is produced by foreign-owned firms including Mazak, the most productive machine tool operation in the country, which is owned by Japan's Yamazaki Mazak.

In computers, the U.S. global share has slipped from 76 percent in 1984 to less than two-thirds today. The strongest area for American firms is workstations, where they command an overwhelming presence thanks to superior design and their lead in microprocessor chips and software. In fact, American firms have about two-thirds of the Japanese market for workstations. On the other hand, except for IBM, many American computer makers have their disk drives, monitors, and memory units built in other countries. Overall, however, the U.S. computer industry's manufacturing trade surplus is $2 billion annually.

In semiconductors, the Japanese dominate the industry but Americans are gaining market share. Additionally, the most important part of the industry is the microprocessor — the logic chips that drive computers — and the United States leads in this area. However, Japan is the leader in chipmaking technology, with almost all the world market share.

Overall, the Japanese have done an excellent job of invading the American market and establishing a strong presence in the manufacturing arena. The two big questions are: Can the United States stem the tide and take back lost markets? If not, how much danger does Japanese ownership pose to the American economy?

Source: Edmund Faltermayer, "Is 'Made in U.S.A.' Fading Away?" *Fortune*, September 24, 1990, 62–73.

Case Questions
1. In which manufacturing industries is Japan currently dominating the U.S.? What conclusions can you draw from these findings?
2. What are the advantages of Japanese investments in the United States? What are the drawbacks?
3. Is the United States in economic danger if the present trend of foreign investment continues?

Learning Objectives Revisited

1. **Discuss the global economy and international business.** International trade is the sale of exports (goods shipped to other countries) and purchase of imports (goods brought in from other countries). The balance of trade is total exports minus total imports. In recent years, the United States has had a negative balance of trade, or a trade deficit. Therefore, although the United States is a major exporter of goods, an important part of international business affecting the United States is overseas businesses selling in domestic markets.

2. **Present the major reasons for international business.** Businesses sell in international markets when they have an absolute or comparative advantage. Sources of advantages include abundant natural resources, favorable climate and terrain, sufficient capital equipment, skilled personnel, accessible geographic location, and a stable political climate.

3. **Identify some government-imposed barriers to international trade.** Some of the principal barriers to international trade include quotas (import restrictions in terms of quantity or value) and tariffs (duties levied on imported goods). The government also restricts trade for security reasons and may impose regulations that make business operations more complex and costly. To keep money in the country, the government may limit conversion of funds.

4. **Relate some cultural differences that make international trade challenging.** Cultural differences create barriers when business people disregard them. Language and communication style are basic differences, but customs and manners may also vary. The concept of time differs among cultures, with punctuality being more important in some cultures than in others, and managers do not always work during the same hours.

5. **Explain some efforts to stimulate international business.** Some countries set up free-trade zones (FTZs) in the effort to promote trade. Countries have also cooperated through agreements such as the General Agreement on Tariffs and Trade (GATT) and communities such as the European Community (EC). The United Nations and U.S. government have established financial institutions that foster international trade, including the Export-Import Bank, the International Monetary Fund, and the International Bank for Reconstruction and Development (the World Bank).

6. **Discuss some common approaches to entering international markets.** The two most common approaches used by small businesses that want to go international are licensing and exporting. Firms that export use merchants or agents, or they set up their own sales office or branch. Large businesses that want more control use joint ventures, branch organizations, and subsidiaries.

Key Terms Reviewed

Review each of the following terms. For any that you do not know or are unsure of, look up the definitions and see how they were used in the chapter.

multinational corporation (MNC)
transnational corporation (TNC)
balance of trade
exports
imports
trade deficit
balance of payments
absolute advantage
comparative advantage
quota
tariff

culture
free-trade zone (FTZ)
General Agreement on Tariffs
  and Trade (GATT)
Export-Import Bank (Exim Bank)
International Monetary Fund
  (IMF)
International Bank for
  Reconstruction and Development
  (World Bank)

International Finance Corporation
  (IFC)
International Development
  Association (IDA)
license
joint venture
branch organization
subsidiary

Review Questions

1. If the United States has a negative balance of trade this year, will it also have a negative balance of payments?
2. What is the trade deficit? Why are some people concerned about the U.S. trade deficit?
3. What would give a country's businesses an absolute advantage? A comparative advantage? What is a comparative advantage possessed by an American firm such as Touchstone Pictures (Walt Disney Company's movie-making firm)?
4. South Korean companies are beginning to produce durable goods such as automobiles and computers and ship many of them halfway around the world to sell in the United States. Why would these companies expand to such a distant market? What advantages do they have to offer U.S. customers? What advantages does the U.S. market offer the companies?
5. Imagine a country with few natural resources and land that is not particularly fertile. What advantages could such a country develop as a trading partner?
6. Why do governments restrict imports? Who benefits from such actions?

7. Managers of J&J Sweets are thinking of building a candy factory in Czechoslovakia. However, the Czech government would require J&J to take on a local partner. Would this be disadvantageous to the company? What should the company's managers weigh in making this decision?
8. How do cultural differences make international business more difficult? How can U.S. managers cope with these differences?
9. How can businesses take advantage of free-trade zones?
10. Tina McCormick wants to expand her line of shoe stores into South America, but her bank has turned down her request for financing. Where else can Tina look for funding?
11. How do American businesses benefit from organizations that provide financing to underdeveloped nations?
12. Telephone Tech, a small research-based American firm, usually enters international markets by licensing or exporting rather than by creating a subsidiary. What might be two reasons for this action?

Applied Exercise

How much do you *really* know about international business practices and developments? Take the following quiz. Most students answer only 50 percent of these statements correctly.

T   F   1. In Latin countries, decisions typically are made by the manager and communicated to the subordinates without very much feedback or participative management.

T   F   2. Germans make wider use of participative communication than do managers in other countries.

T   F   3. Money is a bigger motivator among the British and Americans than among workers in any other industrialized country.

T   F   4. In France being on time for meetings is important, whereas in Peru meetings often start late.

T   F   5. The Japanese make very effective use of participative management at the lower levels of the hierarchy.

T   F   6. In Switzerland, managers often go outside their formal authority and make decisions that interfere with the personal lives of their subordinates.

T   F   7. Recent research shows that many Japanese firms are beginning to copy American management practices because they are more effective in running large companies.

T   F   8. The Japanese are finding it more difficult to do business in Europe than in the United States because the Europeans have more controls on foreign firms doing business in their countries.

T   F   9. American firms are currently finding that the quality of their products is so inferior that they are losing markets throughout the world.

T   F 10. Despite all negotiation efforts, Japanese markets remain basically closed to foreign goods.

YOU BE THE ADVISER / *Going International with Real Estate*

Falworth Real Estate is a large landholder in Arizona and Florida. The firm owns a total of 1.2 million acres in these two states. Falworth both sells and develops land. The biggest revenues come from building speculative or customized homes, duplexes, and condos. However, the company also sells lots to those who want to build their own houses or hold the property as an investment.

Over the past 5 years the company has sold over 200,000 acres to smaller real estate developers and 400,000 acres to individual investors. The latter is the most profitable market niche and the one that the firm has targeted for the 1990s. The primary way in which Falworth sells this land is through agents working throughout the United States. For example, there is one agent who has the state of Illinois. He is authorized to sell Falworth land to Illinois residents and is given a percentage of the sales price. There are sales agents throughout all 50 states (some covering more than one state) and they have been selling a combined total of 1,250 acres a week.

Over the past year, James Falworth, the founder and president, has been thinking about opening up new sales territories in Europe and Asia. Foreign agents would be given exclusive sales territories and receive a commission on their sales. They could sell to anyone in their territory who is a native of that country. For example, an agent in France could sell an acre of land in Florida to a French couple but could not sell the land to an American family that was vacationing in France. Falworth would offer the same basic arrangement as that given to agents in the United States: each would be given a monthly draw of $1,000 that would be offset by sales com-

missions. There would also be an allowance for advertising, travel, and out-of-pocket expenses.

Mr. Falworth intends to make a final decision on this matter within the next two months. He and his staff have done considerable research and the major stumbling block appears to be the identification of overseas sales agents and the allocation of sales territories. But, as he reported in a preliminary report to the board of directors, "If we can sell 50,000 acres a year to Europeans and Asians, we can triple our annual profits. What we need to do now is to plan our strategy so that we have the same success overseas that we are having here in the states."

Your Advice

1. What should Falworth do? Prioritize your answers.
   ___ a. Have the company advertise overseas and handle sales through the home office.
   ___ b. Let local state agents advertise overseas and handle all international sales themselves.
   ___ c. Invest the necessary time and effort and appoint overseas sales agents in both Europe and Asia.
2. What cultural challenges will Falworth face if it decides to go into the European market? The Far East market?
3. What major pitfalls does the company face beside cultural problems if it decides to go international? Explain.
4. What would you specifically recommend the company do in preparing to go international?

FEELING GOOD AND PAYING TAXES

Modern business firms are recognized
to have a number of important social
responsibilities. One of them is to
provide an equal opportunity to
everyone for jobs that are challenging
and rewarding. The Women's Self-
Employment Project (WSEP) based
in Chicago offers an interesting twist
on this social goal. WSEP is a nonprofit organization that provides
training, technical assistance, and
business loans to low and moderate
income women interested in starting
their own businesses. Potential
entrepreneurs and small-business
owners may have the motivation, but
they lack the experience and know-
how that will enable them to
successfully run a business.

Social Responsibility and Ethics

6

Chapter Learning Objectives

- Explain the overall nature of social responsibility.

- Describe the social issue of equality in employment.

- Identify the social issue of environmental protection.

- Explain the social issue of consumerism.

- Discuss the nature of business ethics.

Especially those below the poverty level may have good ideas, but they lack the skills, and thus the confidence, to carry them out.

WSEP self-employment training is directed toward overcoming this problem. Women who go through the 12-week program acquire knowledge and confidence about management, marketing, and finance in order to effectively produce and deliver quality goods and services. To date, more than 1,500 women have attended orientations, more than 350 have completed the program, and over 100 new businesses are open. This means that more than 100 women, many of whom used to be receiving financial assistance because they were living below the poverty line, are not only making a living and feeling good about themselves, but they are also paying taxes and providing incomes for others that they employ.

WSEP is continuing its efforts to help women improve their business skills and move ahead. Many large firms are also taking steps to ensure equal opportunities for their female and minority employees. An example is Procter & Gamble. P&G fills its upper level management positions only from within the company. Such a policy helps ensure equal opportunities for all employees. The women and minorities hired by P&G are assured that they will be considered for future promotion and not be passed over by people brought in from the outside. Another example is Xerox. This company has recently set goals for increasing the number of minorities and women in each division and at every level. As a result, in some large divisions the number of executive level positions held by women is expected to triple by 1995. Many of today's businesses have placed social obligations such as equal opportunity in employment among their primary goals. They believe not only that these efforts are good for society as a whole and for their employees but that they enhance their own profits and growth while being good corporate citizens.

Photo Source: Courtesy of Robert K. Gemin.

Introduction

This chapter is placed near the beginning of the book to provide an important social framework and perspective for understanding modern business. It focuses on four major issues that concern everyone directly or indirectly. The first is the legal right of minorities and women to equal employment opportunities. Next, and perhaps the biggest business issue of the 1990s, are the twin environmental concerns: energy and pollution. The third issue is consumerism. Finally, at the core of social responsibility, are the standards that govern business behavior — that is, business ethics.

The Nature of Business's Social Responsibilities

As you learned in Chapter 1, businesses in a market economy depend on certain resources, or factors of production: land, labor, capital, and entrepreneurship. For example, a construction company might require a plot of land, healthy workers, state-of-the-art equipment, raw materials such as plastic pipes (made from a petroleum product) and wood for doors, and a developer to raise the funds and sell the new construction. But what if the workers are unhealthy because the air they breathe is polluted? What if the supply of petroleum and wood runs out? What if the equipment is unsafe and injures the workers? What if the company loses sales — and hence a supply of capital — because it has a reputation for shoddy work? Businesses depend on society and on the environment. Consequently, many observers believe that business should in turn accept some responsibility for these resources.

Business's obligation to the society in which it operates is called social responsibility. Four areas in particular call for social responsibility on the part of business: equal opportunity in employment, environmental protection, consumerism, and business ethics. Each of these areas will be given detailed attention, but first some of the background of social responsibility is presented.

Past and Present Views of Social Responsibility

Paternalistic approach Taking care of employees similar to the way that parents take care of children.

The social role of business is certainly not new. During the 19th and early 20th centuries, some business owners and managers took a **paternalistic approach,** which means that the owners/managers took care of their employees similar to the way that parents take care of children. If a worker was sick, the company would bring in a doctor. Likewise, a long-time employee with a large family would receive a bigger salary than a long-time employee with a small family. These paternalistic owners/managers were genuinely concerned for their employees and basically treated them as if they were family members.

Unfortunately, paternalistic managers were in the minority. Too often employees were paid low wages, product quality and safety were poor, and personal profit was the only objective of the owner/manager. As a result, early in this century, the public began to pressure the government to regulate some business practices. The government responded by requiring businesses to abide by minimum standards of socially responsible behavior. For example, the government eventually passed child labor laws, minimum-wage legislation, and occupational health and safety acts.

Today these and many other laws regulate business. Among them are laws designed to ensure equal opportunity in employment, prevent unnecessary pollution of the environment, protect consumers, and establish ethical levels of behavior in business practices.

Is legislation necessary to ensure fair and responsible business dealings? The general public obviously thinks so. Most business people agree. While noting that they would never do anything illegal or immoral, they suggest that the laws prevent their competitors from doing these things. But while these laws receive broad support, the general concept of social responsibility has stirred some controversy.

The Case for and against Social Responsibility

Aside from obeying the laws of the country, does business have any social obligations? Most consumers believe so, arguing that business has to be responsible for the quality and safety of its products. Most Americans also believe that business must keep the environment clean and pay for any damage it does, and that it should give all people, regardless of race, color, creed, or sex, an equal opportunity in employment. Most business people would agree. They believe in taking a proactive approach; an approach that does not just react to problems or meet minimum standards of the law, but actually prevents problems and goes beyond what the laws require.

Numerous reasons support this view. The most basic is that because business is a vital part of society, it therefore cannot afford to ignore society's problems. By assisting society, business can create a stable environment that is more conducive to its own long-term profit. In addition, business has the managerial, financial, and technical know-how to help solve many of society's problems, so it is obligated to use these abilities to help out. Also, by taking a proactive approach, business can reduce the likelihood that the government will force it to get involved. Governmental guidelines could actually cost business firms more in terms of paperwork and more costly equipment and operating procedures than if the businesses had tackled the social problems on their own.

On the other side of the coin, a few still argue (especially off the record) that social involvement is not business's responsibility. This view contends that devoting company time, money, and talent to social issues will interfere with business's primary responsibility: to make a profit for its owners. Furthermore, since social problems affect the entire nation or the local community, they are the public's responsibility, not private business's. Consequently, elected public officials and government employees should assume the responsibility for society's problems, not business managers. Those who reject social involvement contend that their social obligation begins and ends with running an effective business.

Who is right: those who favor involvement in the social arena or those who oppose it? Most *successful* managers believe that business must not only be socially responsible but also socially active. Enlightened managers view the costs associated with social involvement as wise investments in a better society. The rest of the chapter will take this perspective and examine the various ways that businesses involve themselves in the social arena.

Increased social responsibility in recent times translates into increased market demand for recycling programs. Companies like Browning-Ferris Industries provide curbside collection of recyclable aluminum cans, glass, plastics, and newspapers on a contract basis. Browning-Ferris also sponsors an office paper recycling program and uses the proceeds for charitable purposes.

Source: Courtesy of Browning-Ferris Industries, Inc.

Profits and Social Responsibility

Concern with profits is not inconsistent with fulfilling social responsibility. That is because, in addition to business's responsibilities to consumers and employees, companies are also responsible to their investors. Those who invest money in a company expect to receive an acceptable return in exchange for the risks they take. To give the investors a return, the company must be profitable over the long term. Companies can even use social responsibility to directly contribute to profits. For example, a company could reclaim refuse and wastes and remake them into salable products or they could develop pollution control equipment and sell it to others. It is currently estimated that there is a $100 billion market for pollution control and cleanup and this market is growing at more than 10 percent a year as demand rises for pollution control and for cleaner air and water, less toxic processes, and new technologies and products.[1]

More indirectly, a firm's managers fulfill their responsibility to investors by being honest and avoiding personal gain at the expense of the company. Padding expense accounts or stealing supplies cheats investors of their rightful profits. Besides these relatively small problems, recent scandals in corporate America involving the use of inside stock information to make investments for the personal gain of managers, officers, and directors have led many investors to be wary of unethical conduct on a grander scale.[2] More subtly, recruiting employees from a single ethnic group or of a single sex can also reduce profits by robbing the company of the opportunity to choose the best employee for the job. Also, recent research indicates that when equal-

TABLE 6.1
Some of the Best Firms on the
Environment

Industry	Firm	Reason for High Ranking
Chemicals	H. B. Fuller	Environmental initiatives in construction of its headquarters
Computers	Apple Computer	Recycles; lets environmental groups solicit on site
Electric utilities	Louisville Gas and Electric	Leader in installing smokestack scrubbers
Environmental services	Safety-Kleen (tied)	Leading recycler of solvents and motor oil
	Wellman (tied)	Leading recycler of plastic
Forest products	Jefferson Smurfit	Leading recycler of paper
Natural gas	Consolidated Natural Gas	Promotes new, clean-burning technologies
Oil	Amoco	Strong waste-minimization program
Photo equipment	Polaroid	Strong waste-minimization program
Steel	Nucor	State-of-the-art mills, uses recycled metals
Retailing	Wal-Mart	Promotes environmental products, recycling

Source: David Kirkpatrick, "Environmentalism: The New Crusade," *Fortune*, February 12, 1990, 47. The ratings were compiled by Franklin Research & Development of Boston.

opportunity laws are imposed to erase workplace bias, all workers are spurred to greater efforts.[3] In such cases, managers who fulfill their social responsibility to investors are also fulfilling the broader social responsibility of fair employment practices.

Balancing profits and other responsibilities can be a difficult task. Pollution control, for example, may be costly, and safe products may be more expensive to make than products without safety features. For example, Kodak will spend $100 million to make its facilities more environmentally safe and $46 million to cut back pollution by 70 percent by 1995, Monsanto planned to spend $600 million on environmental programs in the first two years of the decade, and Union Carbide will spend $310 million a year on the environment.[4] Meanwhile, H.J. Heinz (owner of Star-Kist tuna) stopped buying tuna that is caught in nets that also kill dolphins; and Van Camp Seafoods (Chicken of the Sea tuna) and Bumble Bee Seafoods (Bumble Bee tuna) followed suit.[5] Nor are these firms alone in trading profit for social responsibility. Table 6.1 shows the leading socially responsible firms in relation to environmental protection in 10 different industries.

Realistically, managers try to strike a balance in meeting their responsibilities to all parties (sometimes called stakeholders): investors, consumers, and employees. In the long run, however, by taking a proactive approach to meeting its social responsibilities, business benefits both itself and society at large (see Figure 6.1).

FIGURE 6.1

Balancing the Social and Profit Responsibilities of Business

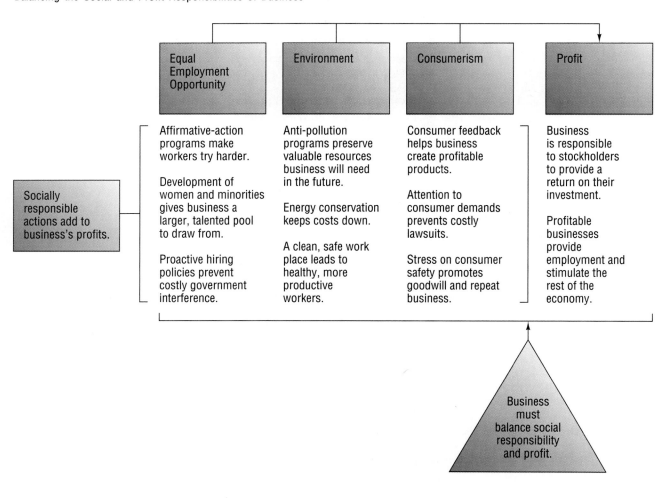

1. What are the social responsibilities of business?
2. What are two reasons why businesses should be socially responsible?

Equality in Employment

Perhaps the most obvious and immediate way a company meets its social responsibilities is by being a fair employer. This social role involves offering equal employment opportunity to women and racial minorities. Efforts at equal opportunity should also extend to others who have suffered employment discrimination, such as those with a disability or older workers. For example, earnings of disabled workers are lower than of those without disabilities and this gap has been getting worse[6]; and of course age discrimina-

TABLE 6.2
Major Legislation Affecting Equality in Employment

Federal Law	Provisions Affecting Business
Fifth and Fourteenth Amendments, U.S. Constitution	Prohibits deprivation of employment rights without due process.
Davis-Bacon Act, 1931	Requires firms engaged in federal construction projects valued at more than $2,000 to pay the prevailing wage rate.
Walsh-Healey Act, 1936	Requires firms with federal supply contracts in excess of $10,000 to pay a minimum wage and overtime for all hours worked in excess of 40 per week.
Fair Labor Standards Act, 1938	Requires virtually all businesses engaged in interstate commerce to pay the minimum wage and overtime for all hours worked in excess of 40 per week.
Equal Pay Act, 1963	Forbids employers to discriminate on the basis of sex by paying higher wages to one sex than to the other for equal work on jobs requiring equal skill, effort, responsibility, and similar working conditions.
Civil Rights Act of 1964	Prohibits discrimination based on race, color, sex, and national origin.
Age Discrimination in Employment Act, 1967	Originally prohibited discrimination in employment of those 40 to 65 years of age; in 1978, was amended to move the top age from 65 to 70 years; and in 1986, the upper limit was removed.
Vocational Rehabilitation Act, 1973, 1978	Prohibits discrimination against persons with mental or physical handicaps. Employers must make a reasonable effort to accommodate them.

tion has long been a problem in the United States. These groups receive specific attention in Chapter 12 when we discuss personnel and human resource management.

Legislation to Ensure Equality

Congress has passed a number of laws designed to ensure equal employment opportunity. Table 6.2 summarizes the major ones. The landmark legislation is the Civil Rights Act of 1964, which specifically prohibits discrimination based on race, color, sex, or national origin. This law established the **Equal Employment Opportunity Commission (EEOC),** which is charged with overseeing enforcement of the act by investigating complaints and taking appropriate action.

Many firms do more than just comply with this act; they have set up **affirmative-action programs.** These programs are designed to seek out minorities, women, those with a disability, and others who are more likely to have problems finding work, and to hire, train, develop, and promote them. These groups have been discriminated against in the past and still face many problems. In particular, women and minorities have stirred concern in government, private industry, and the public at large. If not carefully conceived

Equal Employment Opportunity Commission (EEOC) The commission charged with overseeing enforcement of the Civil Rights Act of 1964 by investigating complaints and taking appropriate action.

Affirmative-action programs Programs designed to seek out minorities, women, those with a disability, and others with problems finding work and to hire, train, develop, and promote them.

FIGURE 6.2
The New Diverse Workforce

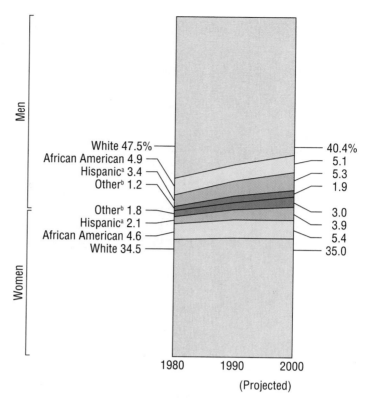

Men

White 47.5% — 40.4%
African American 4.9 — 5.1
Hispanic^a 3.4 — 5.3
Other^b 1.2 — 1.9

Other^b 1.8 — 3.0
Hispanic^a 2.1 — 3.9
African American 4.6 — 5.4
White 34.5 — 35.0

Women

1980   1990   2000

(Projected)

[a]Persons of Hispanic origin may be of any race.
[b]Includes American Indians, Alaskan natives, Asians, and Pacific Islanders.

and planned, affirmative action programs can be interpreted as reverse discrimination (discrimination against the majority), which, of course, must also be avoided to meet the goals of equal opportunity for all.

The Status of Women and Minorities in the Workplace

In spite of laws expressly forbidding discrimination in employment and requiring that all employees receive equal pay for equal work (see Table 6.2), women and minorities still lag far behind white males in these areas. White males tend to earn much higher salaries than do African-American or Hispanic males. White women do better than African-American or Hispanic women, but not nearly as well as white men.

Overall, women still make only about two-thirds of what males earn and this gap has narrowed by less than 10 percent over the past two decades. Although professional and managerial women do better (they earn about three-fourths as much as their male counterparts), very few have broken through the so-called glass ceiling into top level management. Among Fortune 500 firms, fewer than 2 percent of top executives are female. And even when the few do break through, their salaries are relatively low. For example, a recent report by the U.S. Chamber of Commerce found that corporate

AT&T funds an Arizona State University program that encourages young Hispanic women to remain in high school and attend college by including each student's mother in courses and counseling. Here participants Genevieve Perez and her daughter Cathy speak with Ted Trujillo, an AT&T manager active in the program. Businesses ensure a bigger pool of skilled workers from which to draw by sponsoring such programs for women and minorities.

Source: Reproduced with permission of AT&T.

women at the vice presidential level and above earn 42 percent less than their male peers.

Minorities are even worse off than women. Their unemployment rate is much higher than whites and only a small percentage have broken through the glass ceiling into the professional and managerial ranks. For example, although African-Americans currently make up about 10 percent of the workforce, only about 5 percent of corporate executives and 3 percent of the doctors and lawyers are African-Americans. Also, on average, the median family income of African-Americans and Hispanics is about $10,000 lower than whites.

This fairly bleak picture for women and minorities becomes more important when it is realized that the U.S. Bureau of Labor Statistics indicates that, going into the 1990s, 70 percent of all new hires will be women or members of minority groups. As shown in Figure 6.2, this trend will continue so that, by the year 2000, white males will make up only 45 percent of the workforce. Managing this diversity and providing equal opportunities for this so-called "rainbow coalition" will be a key challenge. It has become generally recognized that companies which aggressively hire, train, and promote women and minorities — the growing segments of the U.S. labor market — will succeed.[7] In fact, the coming workforce shortages and diversity of races and gender may accomplish what the activism of the 1960s could not: get corporations deeply involved in social issues.[8]

The Response of Business

To meet the challenges, business has taken some steps to manage the diversity and ensure equal opportunity in employment. These efforts include the following:

- Establishing affirmative-action programs designed to target women and minorities with potential.
- Training these people and then moving them up the ranks as quickly as possible.

Mentor An outstanding, experienced manager who provides an identified person with advice and assistance and helps the person achieve career goals.

Companies have found that assisting employees with their family commitments makes it easier to retain employees and fosters company loyalty. Genentech's 2nd Generation is a child development and day care center for employees' infants, toddlers, and preschoolers. It is located a few blocks from the company's offices and labs.

Source: Courtesy of Genentech, Inc.

CHECK ✓ POINT

- Establishing **mentor** programs, whereby an outstanding, experienced manager takes an identified woman or minority member under his or her wing, provides advice and counsel, and helps the person to achieve career goals. Women, in particular, report that mentors have been extremely helpful to them.

Taking an affirmative-action approach, McDonald's cut in half the turnover rate of its minority managers, and General Motors was able to double its proportion of female managers and increase by 50 percent its number of minority managers. Other companies such as AT&T, Johnson & Johnson, and IBM have become committed to provide child care as a way to retain women employees — and some men, too. Xerox identifies pivotal jobs that lead up the corporate ladder and makes sure women and minorities are considered for them. They have 26 African-American and 17 women vice presidents, out of 270, well above the average for U.S. industry.[9] Digital Equipment meets the newly emerging diverse workforce of the 1990s by holding workshops in "valuing differences" every month with core groups consisting of both genders and all races.[10]

For over 20 years, the courts have ruled in favor of affirmative-action programs for minorities. In a landmark case in 1987, the Supreme Court ruled that employers may give special preference in hiring and promoting women in order to create a more balanced workforce. In this particular case, a man was denied a promotion and the job went to a woman who the man claimed was less qualified. The man charged that he was a victim of reverse discrimination. The court ruled in favor of the woman, even though the justices felt the man might be slightly more qualified (he had scored a little higher on the evaluation). Although this might be interpreted as okaying reverse discrimination, the justices pointed out that their ruling does not mean that unqualified people will be hired or promoted. Instead, they simply stated that sex is now one of several factors that may be taken into account in evaluating qualified applications for a position. Although most companies have been tentative in their use of affirmative-action programs for fear of charges of reverse discrimination, with the Supreme Court ruling they now feel that they have legal backing in their efforts to correct the underemployment of women.

Besides using affirmative action, businesses can assist minorities and women in setting up their own small-business ventures. Established firms can provide managerial and/or technical expertise as well as support in the form of orders and subcontracts. As Linda Johnson Rice, the chief operating officer of Johnson Publications, the largest publisher of magazines for African-Americans, has observed, "There are more opportunities today for the black entrepreneur than in many years. They have learned how to acquire capital, how to put together business plans, and how to start enterprises."[11] Although ventures owned by African-Americans have received the most publicity, women also are starting their own companies in record numbers. The number of firms owned by women is growing at twice the rate of male-owned business.

1. What are two laws designed to ensure equal opportunity in employment?
2. How can businesses help ensure equality in employment?

Environmental Concerns

Equality in employment has the greatest impact on workers and their dependents, but all members of society are directly affected by how business is or is not protecting the environment. A growing number of experts and the general public feel that environmentalism may be the biggest business issue of the 1990s.[12] The threat was made real when the very grim, sick environment of Eastern Europe was revealed to the Western World. The rivers, forests, and health of Eastern Europeans were ruined by years of uncontrolled environmental damage caused by their businesses.[13]

Environmental issues stem from the biological concept of **ecology,** which is the interrelationship of living things and their environment. Any change, however small, can affect life throughout the environment. Businesses affect this environmental strain in a variety of ways, most of which fall into the categories of energy conservation and pollution control. As explained by one environmental expert, "Think of a freeway. You're driving along at 65 mph and everything is going fine. Then one thing goes wrong and the whole system collapses. Our environment is under a similar kind of strain."[14]

Ecology The interrelationship of living things and their environment.

Pollution Contamination of the air, water, land, or environment in which life exists.

Energy Conservation

Business is certainly one of the largest energy consumers. Thus, conservation measures taken by business can generate tremendous savings of society's natural resources. In addition, by conserving energy, business firms can reduce their costs and eventually benefit individual consumers by keeping prices down.

Companies are taking a number of actions to help meet the challenge of energy conservation. One action is the development of long- and short-range conservation plans. General Motors, DuPont, Exxon, and AT&T, among others, have such plans in operation. At AT&T, for example, business grew by 50 percent in a recent 10-year period, while its consumption of energy remained the same. Other firms are studying ways of operating machinery more efficiently or replacing it with more up-to-date, energy-efficient equipment. Some organizations have even installed paddle fans in their offices and shut off the air conditioning. The results of these types of efforts have had dramatic results. Since the 1974 oil crisis, the highly industrialized countries of the world have actually reduced their energy consumption by 20 percent while producing much, much more.[15]

Pollution control systems installed by General Electric clean the smoke released through this 730-foot chimney at the Intermountain Power Project in Utah. The system removes more than 99.75 percent of fly ash and over 90 percent of sulfur dioxide.

Source: Photo by Tom Tracy for General Electric Company.

Pollution Control

Besides energy problems, the public is rightfully concerned with pollution of the environment. **Pollution** is any contamination of the air, water, or land in which life exists. For business, there are a number of pollution problems, such as noise and solid-waste, but the two biggest concerns are with air and water pollution. The accompanying International Close-Up (Soviet Bloc Breakup Reveals Environmental Disaster) shows that this problem is not limited to the United States.

Air Pollution Pollution of the air is a major problem. Approximately 200 million tons of pollutants are released into the air each year. The average person breathes about 35 pounds of air each day, and for those in air-polluted

CLOSE-UP / *International*

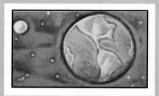

Soviet Bloc Breakup Reveals Environmental Disaster
Protection of the environment has become a major concern for everyone in the United States. However, Eastern European countries are just beginning to realize the tremendous problem they have. With the breakup of the Soviet Union, outsiders are beginning to get their first look at the way the communists ran the countries — into the ground and into the air. It is painfully obvious that these governments have historically cared little about environmental protection. Most people around the world clearly remember the Chernobyl nuclear power plant disaster in which 4 percent of the radioactive reactor core was released into the atmosphere. Unfortunately, this is only one of numerous environmental disasters in the Communist Bloc countries.

In the 1950s, Russian scientists started dumping radioactive waste in local lakes and rivers around the city of Chelyabinsk. Today, a person standing on the banks of nearby Karachai Lake can get a lethal dose of radiation in less than one hour. Meanwhile, at the Techa River, also located in this vicinity, radioactivity, caused by years of hazardous waste dumping, has been found 100 miles away where the river empties into the Arctic Ocean.

Another example is the tragic effect of a 30-year irrigation project on the Aral Sea. In just three decades, this body of water, which is larger than Lake Huron, has shrunk to less than half its original size. The shrinking sea has dramatically changed the local climate as well as released carcinogenic salts from the former seabed into the air. When combined with heavy pesticides, these salts have led to an upsurge in local infectious diseases for both humans and plants. As a result, hospitals in the region now report dramatic increases in infant mortality and throat cancers.

While these examples only scratch the surface, they clearly show that Eastern Europe faces a tremendous environmental problem. Although the economic woes of the former communist countries currently receive all of the attention, the environment of Eastern Europe may be an even bigger problem and challenge.

Source: Paul Hofheinz, "The New Soviet Threat: Pollution," *Fortune*, July 27, 1992, pp. 110–114.

environments, the physical effects can be extremely harmful. Experts estimate that the respiratory ailments and heart disease from breathing polluted air cost the United States approximately $5 billion in medical treatment, lost wages, and reduced productivity. In an effort to address environmental concerns, the federal government has enacted a number of important laws, which are summarized in Table 6.3. In addition, new emission standards are being set for autos,[16] pesticide bans are being extended,[17] and cigarette taxes are being raised.[18]

Besides complying with these laws, businesses are taking proactive steps of their own. An increasing number of firms have designated nonsmoking areas or banned smoking altogether. For example, the *Pittsburgh Press* bans smoking in its newsroom, and McKesson Corporation and Hewlett-Packard adhere to local bans against smoking in public places. The 3M Company is investing in a wide array of pollution controls for its manufacturing facilities. Pacific Gas & Electric has a $10 million joint venture project with environmental groups to study ways of more efficiently producing energy. The Big Three auto manufacturers have designed their engines to dramatically cut auto pollution[19] and companies such as Atlantic Richfield have offered their employees $100 per month to take buses to work.[20] Utilities and industrial firms have installed special equipment to greatly reduce smokestack pollution. This equipment, which includes filters, afterburners, gas-washing devices, and electrostatic precipitators, is beginning to get results. Although the problem is far from solved, some of the traditional causes of air pollution are being eliminated through legislation[21] and, importantly, the social responsibility actions of business.

TABLE 6.3
Major Environmental Laws

Federal Law	Provisions
Clean Air Act, 1963	Designed to assist local and state government in establishing control programs and coordinating research. Later amendments, among other things, established standards for auto exhaust emissions, set up air-quality regions with acceptable regional pollution levels, required states to meet deadlines for complying with Environmental Protection Agency (EPA) standards, and gave citizens the right to bring suit to require the EPA to carry out approved standards against undiscovered offenders.
Federal Water Pollution Control Act, 1965	Set standards for treatment of municipal water waste before discharge. Later amendments set a national water-quality goal of restoring polluted waters to swimmable, fishable waters.
Noise Control Act, 1972	Required the EPA to establish noise standards for products that are major sources of noise. Also set standards for aircraft noise.
Pesticide Control Act, 1972	Required that all pesticides used in interstate commerce be approved and certified as effective for their stated purpose. An amendment to the act established deadlines for registering, classifying, and licensing pesticides.
Clean Water Act, 1974	Set federal standards for water suppliers serving more than 25 people, having more than 15 service connections, or operating more than 60 days a year. Later amendments required that pollutants be monitored using the best available and economically feasible technology.

Water Pollution   There are many sources of water pollution.[22] Industrial toxic wastes are one of the most common. So are oil spills such as those caused by Exxon's Valdez tanker, which devastated the Alaskan environment and resulted in one of the most costly cleanups of all time.[23] The recent war in the Persian Gulf could, among other ecological disasters, lead to the gulf becoming a dead sea.[24] Other sources of water pollution are fertilizers, sewage, leakage of underground waste dumps, and acid rain (caused by sulfur emissions from industrial smokestacks) that falls into rivers and lakes.

Business is taking several actions to control water pollution. The most common actions are to treat waste materials before disposing of them in lakes, streams, or underground dumps, and to recycle the treated water and reuse it in the production process. Many firms are also looking at different ways of handling water discharge, such as alternatives to underground dumps. Other firms, including fertilizer manufacturers, are investigating ways of developing pesticides that, when washed into streams and lakes by the rain, will not pollute the water. For example, Florida Power and Light has a huge grid of cooling canals to prevent its nuclear power plant's warm water discharge from harming the surrounding marine life. The canals have become a breeding ground for endangered crocodiles, and the utility's staff goes out regularly to make sure the nests are protected. Like air pollution, the

Thousands of sea otters and other wildlife were treated by volunteer veterinary technicians at this Alaskan rescue center following the Exxon Valdez oil spill. In response to an urgent request from the rescue center, Abbott Laboratories donated a Vision blood analyzer to test contaminated otters for levels of toxicity in the liver, kidneys, and other internal organs. With Vision, test results were reported immediately and hundreds of animals were saved.

Source: © Mark Joseph.

FIGURE 6.3
The Garbage Situation in the United States

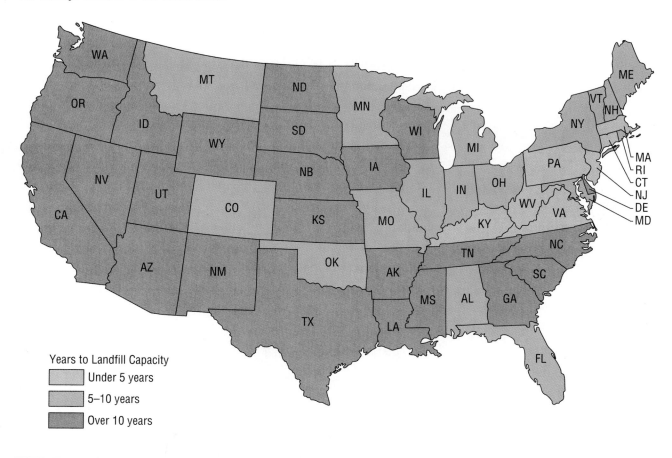

Years to Landfill Capacity

Under 5 years

5–10 years

Over 10 years

Source: *Newsweek*, November 27, 1989, 89.

problems of water pollution are not solved, but businesses are making progress in many areas.

Solid Waste   Another of the major polluters is solid-waste disposal. Research shows that the average American family produces over 4,500 gallons of garbage a year. This is enough to fill a bumper-to-bumper convoy of garbage trucks halfway to the moon,[25] and this amount is forecasted to increase by 20 percent by the year 2000! Meanwhile, landfills are teeming with garbage. Fresh Kills, Staten Island, the largest city dump in the world, is a good example. Over 24,000 tons of New York City garbage are brought in every day and the dump is now leaking 2 million gallons of contamination into the ground each day and, to make matters worse, the fill is beginning to reach its capacity.[26] As shown in Figure 6.3, many other landfills around the country are also beginning to reach capacity, and other methods of handling solid-waste disposal must be implemented.

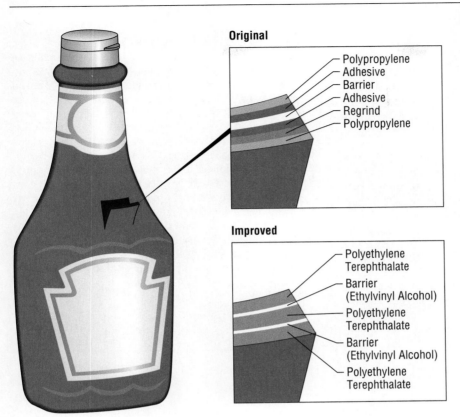

FIGURE 6.4
A Recyclable Ketchup Bottle

Source: *The New York Times*, April 10, 1990, C5. Copyright © 1990 by The New York Times Company. Reprinted by permission.

One of the primary responses is recycling. For years, this approach has been used in Japan,[27] and it is now becoming popular in the United States. McDonald's, which produces hundreds of millions of pounds of paper and plastic annually, now has become a crusading component of recycling.[28] Wal-Mart has asked its suppliers to provide it with more recycled or recyclable products.[29] K mart and a dozen small to medium-sized grocery chains have also announced similar programs.[30] H.J. Heinz has introduced a new plastic ketchup bottle that is more recyclable than its original squeezable bottle, which consisted of six layers that were hard to separate (see Figure 6.4). Many newspaper firms are now using recycled paper.[31]

Another approach is the conversion of garbage into energy through such means as incineration. Two of the leading firms in this area, Ogden Projects and Wheelabrator Technologies, are proving that solid waste disposal can be a profitable business.[32] Another example of an innovative, high-tech process that reduces both solid waste and air pollution problems in paint removal is given in the accompanying Ethics Video Close-Up (A Matter of Thermal Shock). These are only a small number of the efforts that are currently underway to deal with the solid-waste pollution problem, but if they are successful they will help stem the tide in what is going to be one of the major environmental challenges of the years ahead.

VIDEO CLOSE-UP / *Ethics*

A Matter of Thermal Shock

The word pollution usually brings to mind highly visible air pollution caused by factories or possibly water pollution caused by power plants. Some more subtle forms of pollution, however, are also part of the price of doing business. For example, when the dirt and soot that have gathered on the outside of an airplane are removed, it will fly more efficiently. Washing the plane reduces the operating cost per mile. Companies with a fleet of planes make it a practice to wash them periodically, not just for appearance, but because it is cost effective.

Keeping the plane clean helps, but at some point it must also be repainted. Air pollution and the weather will eventually begin peeling off the paint and creating nicks and pockets that increase wind resistance and reduce fuel mileage. The protec-

tion that the paint provides to the body and other key parts of the aircraft lessens over time. However, before the plane can be repainted, the old paint must be removed. This is a costly process and, when solvents are used, results in pollution. Now a new process, invented by Cold Jet Inc., makes paint removal simpler and reduces the pollution problem by using dry ice to shatter the old paint. This thermal shock procedure does not produce toxic vapors or toxic solid waste, as did some of the older processes of paint removal. In addition, from the standpoint of safety, avoiding the use of corrosive materials or toxic solvents means that the metal is not weakened.

Although the thermal shock process is more expensive per se than old methods of paint removal, the speed at which the job can be completed and the savings on waste disposal make it economically sound. It is now being used on trains and automobiles as well as planes. Boeing, Ford, the air force, and the navy are among the major users of the process.

Paying the Bill

How much will it cost to clean up the environment, and who will pay? One way is to fine the polluters. For example, Ashland Oil was recently fined $2.25 million, Ocean Spray was fined $400,000, and Exxon's oil spill disaster in Alaska will have a potential settlement cost of $1.2 billion.[33]

Clean air legislation alone is estimated to cost U.S. industry $21.5 billion annually — more than General Motors, General Electric, Ford, IBM, and Exxon collectively earned in 1989.[34] But the real key is that businesses are recognizing their social responsibilities and proactively spending money on their own that is not required of them by legislation. For example, DuPont is pulling out of a $750 million-a-year business because it may — just may — harm the earth's atmosphere, and 3M is investing in numerous pollution controls for its facilities that go well beyond what the laws require.[35] In the end, however, society will bear much of the cost of environmental protection in the form of higher prices and taxes. However, people report that they are willing to pay these costs even if it means a lower standard of living.[36]

CHECK ✓ POINT

1. What are the two major types of pollution?
2. How are businesses conserving energy?

Consumerism A movement designed to provide buyers with the information and bargaining power necessary for obtaining high-quality, safe products and services.

Consumerism

The third major social issue facing business is **consumerism,** which is a movement to provide buyers with the information and bargaining power necessary for obtaining high-quality, safe products and services. Consumerism takes many forms, including the following:

- **Class-action suits,** in which a group of buyers join together in a lawsuit against the seller
- **Boycotts,** in which consumers organize to convince people to refrain from buying goods or services from targeted businesses
- Individual letters of complaint from dissatisfied customers to the company's management

Consumerism became popular in the 1960s as a result of the work of Ralph Nader and his action groups. Consisting mostly of college students from across the country, Nader's Raiders raised the consciousness of the general public about product information and safety and helped mandate safety features (such as seat belts in American automobiles) in consumer products.

Customers have a number of specific gripes, such as with health spas that sell long-term memberships and then close; manufacturers that offer warranties covering errors in workmanship but fail to point out that the guarantee covers only the cost of the parts and not the labor; and retailers who give dissatisfied customers a merchandise refund but refuse to return their money. The problem is not unique to America. For example, a consumer advocate in Mexico claims that because of mismarked labels customers pay for $370,000 worth of tortillas per year that they never see and that many brands of tequila are mostly water. He also found breaded "steak sandwiches" sold at some Mexican soccer stadiums that were really breaded paper. One pet shop sold talkative parrots that fell silent when bought and taken home. It turned out that the proprietor was a ventriloquist.[37] To handle such consumer abuses case by case can be difficult, so consumerism today generally focuses on two major concerns: information and safety. Consumers want information so they can make informed purchase decisions. Consumers also want product safety to avoid injury. Many laws address these two concerns; Table 6.4 summarizes some of the major legislation.

Incomplete Information in Advertising

A common area of consumer complaint is advertising. Many ads give incomplete information or are ambiguous.[38] For example, some companies advertise personal computers at prices hundreds of dollars below those of the competition; however, the ad fails to tell the consumer that the machines are not new, they are reconditioned. Another common practice involves advertising the computer at a low price and, when the customer comes into the store, telling the individual that in order to take advantage of the lower price, it is necessary to buy other equipment and software.[39]

Still another tactic is **bait and switch,** in which a store advertises a product at a very low price and then tells customers that the product is either out of stock or of low quality and recommends a higher priced alternative. This is a common practice in many discount retail stores. The store will advertise, say, an RCA video camera at a comparatively low price in mid-December. When the consumer comes in to buy the camera, the salesclerk says the store is out of the RCA and will have to order it, which will take 2

Class-action suit A lawsuit in which a group of buyers join together to sue the seller.

Boycott An organized effort to convince people to refrain from buying goods or services from targeted businesses.

Bait and switch Advertising a product at a very low price and then telling customers the product is either out of stock or of low quality and recommending a higher priced alternative.

TABLE 6.4
Major Consumer Laws

Federal Law	Provisions
Wheeler-Lea Act, 1938	Enlarged the Federal Trade Commission's power to prohibit deceptive practices in commerce and false advertising of foods, drugs, and cosmetics.
Fair Packaging and Labeling Act, 1966	Requires that packages and labels identify the article and give the manufacturer's name and location, quantity of contents, and presentation of servings, uses, and/or applications.
Truth-in-Lending Act, 1968	Requires creditors to inform borrowers of the amount of the financing charge and the annual percentage interest rate.
Child Protection and Toy Safety Act, 1969	Forbids the manufacture and interstate distribution of toys and other children's articles that have electrical, mechanical, or other hazards.
Fair Credit Reporting Act, 1970	Requires agencies reporting consumer credit data to follow procedures that ensure the accuracy of their information. If a person is refused credit because of a credit report, the user of the information must inform the consumer of the source of the information.
Consumer Product Safety Act, 1972	Created a Consumer Product Safety Commission to maintain standards for product safety, to require a warning label on potentially dangerous products, and to order recalls of hazardous products.

to 3 weeks. The consumer wanted it for Christmas, so the salesperson offers to sell a GE model, which the salesperson says has better features anyway. The catch is that the GE model costs substantially more. After the consumer has been baited to come in, the salesperson switches to pushing a similar but more profitable product.

Efforts to Solve the Information Problem

One way business solves information-related consumer problems is to educate employees. A business can make personnel aware of the types of information that buyers need and insist that employees convey this to the customer. Managers must also reward this behavior by attention and specific feedback daily and in performance appraisals.

Companies can also communicate with consumers. They can provide brochures and other written materials that spell out the terms and conditions of the transaction. They also can establish a customer complaint department. Retailers can designate one individual in the store to report all complaints directly to higher management.

When managers know the types of problems customers have, they can work to correct them. Willard Marriott, the founder of the giant hotel chain, was known for reading all customer complaints. As you can guess, he didn't was known for reading all customer complaints. As you can guess, he didn't get many to read because employees worked extra hard to see that he didn't receive any complaints from their hotel.

Product Safety

For many products, safety is an important issue. Consumers are commonly injured using bicycles, sports-related equipment, and playground climbing apparatus (such as swings, slides, and seesaws). Other injuries involve mechanical equipment (household appliances, tools, and lawn and snow machinery) and products that fail to work as intended, including autos with defective brakes, electrical toys that shock the user, and plastic soft-drink containers with tops that can come loose under pressure and explode in a person's face. The Consumer Product Safety Commission reported that from toys alone there were 142,000 injuries in one year and the number is going up.[40] Other examples include food and diets that could be very harmful.

In some cases, problems with product safety result from inadequate engineering or testing. For example, when some American cars first came out with front-wheel drive, a number of problems arose with parts such as the water pump, which would break, causing belts to come off and disable power steering and power brakes. Perrier had problems because some employees failed to clean filters that remove impurities and traces of harmful benzene ended up in the water.[41]

In other cases, problems stem from failure to anticipate the way the product will be used. For example, some people have been injured when using their household vacuum cleaner to pick up puddles of water. Others have been seriously hurt while using their lawn mower as a hedge trimmer.

Business has taken many steps to solve these problems. Here are some of the major actions:

- Product recalls, which are common in the auto industry, designed to repair, replace, or simply check the assembly of various parts to ensure that there is no danger to the user
- Warranties or guarantees that cover parts, and often labor, associated with making any necessary changes in the product to ensure its safety
- Greater use of in-house checks of product quality and safety engineering to ensure that units are properly designed and built and errors corrected before shipment from the factory
- Evaluation of feedback from users
- Continued product testing in the research and development laboratory

These are only a few of the steps that business is taking in its effort to meet the challenge of product safety. Although much more needs to be done, most businesses now realize that, with today's safety regulations and litigation-prone customers, they must assume proper responsibility for product safety. Companies that do not are subject to costly lawsuits and the accompanying publicity, which is sure to damage their reputation and future sales. For these reasons, product safety will continue to be a challenge for business.

CHECK ✓ POINT

1. What are the two major concerns of consumerism?
2. What are three ways that businesses can address these concerns?

An EG&G Vactec technician inspects optoelectronic sensors before they are shipped to an electronics manufacturer. These light-sensitive devices are used in automobiles, medical instruments, office equipment, television sets, and smoke detectors. Inspections help assure the proper functioning of final products.

Source: Courtesy of EG&G Inc.

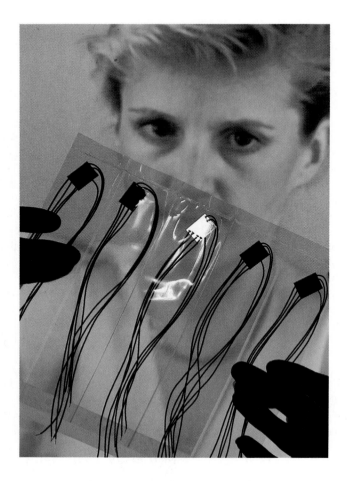

Business Ethics

Recognizing and trying to solve the problems involving equality, the environment, and consumerism represent the major part of the social responsibility of business. At the core of social responsibility, though, are the ethics of business. **Business ethics** are standards that govern business behavior.

Business ethics Standards that govern business behavior.

The honesty and integrity of American business are always under the watchful eye of the public and the media. In recent years, however, this scrutiny does not seem to have prevented what some consider a crisis in ethics. In fact, some critics have begun calling "business ethics" an oxymoron (an expression that combines contradictory words, such as jumbo shrimp). Although most businesspeople are honest, law-abiding citizens, the head of a large accounting firm admits, "We have all been embarrassed by the events that make *The Wall Street Journal* read more like the *Police Gazette*."[42]

Examples of misconduct abound. The Exxon tanker Valdez created one of the world's major oil spills because of improper procedures by the crew. The Bell Atlantic Corporation was suspended from bidding on government work because of material misrepresentations in previously submitted bids.[43] Michael Milken, the junk bond king, pleaded guilty to six criminal charges and agreed to pay $600 million in fines.[44] Conversations secretly taped by government agents depict Chicago futures traders routinely conspiring to make illegal trades and boasting about stealing from the public.[45] Industrial espionage has gone on in the defense industry, where the big contractors allegedly routinely received classified information about the military's long-range spending plans.[46] The federal government is investigating and, in some cases, is charging manufacturers with illegally fixing prices.[47]

Obviously, these are the rare exceptions; the day-to-day ethical business dealings never make the news. Yet unethical practices do seem to be increasing and questions are being raised about the overall ethical climate in business. At the operating level, not only are ethical questions being raised about practices such as drug testing, but also the conduct of some employers who are bugging and taping workers, monitoring them at their computers and phones, and even using special chairs to measure wiggling (wigglers aren't working as hard).[48] Also at the managerial levels, there is some disturbing evidence that the ethical climate may be deteriorating. For example, in a survey of over 1,000 graduates from the classes of 1953 through 1987 of a prestigious business school, it was found that 40 percent said they had been implicitly or explicitly rewarded for taking some action they considered to be ethically wrong — twice as many as were rewarded for refusing to do something wrong.[49] To prevent an antibusiness backlash from the legal system, which is threatening to give federal judges sweeping authority to oversee business operations and level criminal fines that could reach hundreds of millions,[50] business must take proactive steps to ensure ethical behavior.

Communicating Business Ethics

A poll of senior executives found that they believed that a code of ethics was the most effective way to encourage ethical business behavior.[51] Sometimes these codes are written down. For example, United Technologies has a 21-page code of ethics. Figure 6.5 shows the mission statement for General Motors Corporation, including a statement of ethics. Often, however, a code of ethics is communicated orally or even through the overall climate or cultural values of the organization. A stated expectation about ethical behavior often implies a broader standard. For example, when top management tells its salespeople, "We do not allow kickbacks," this statement probably covers more than just giving customers money under the table in return for placing orders. It probably also refers to giving customers anything that might be construed as a bribe or attempt at influence, no matter how small its value. The converse applies to employees who do business with outside vendors. In many companies, a purchasing manager who accepts an expensive gift from a supplier at Christmas is subject to reprimand and possible dismissal.

Creating a Climate for Ethical Behavior

How can business create a climate that promotes ethical behavior among its personnel? Communicating a code of ethics is a start but may be too little. Some companies, especially those that have had ethical problems, such as General Dynamics, have turned to experts like the Washington-based Ethics Resource Center to help them put teeth into their codes. For example, General Dynamics has a committee of board members to review the firm's ethics

GENERAL MOTORS MISSION

The fundamental purpose of General Motors is to provide products and services of such quality that our customers will receive superior value, our employes and business partners will share in our success, and our stockholders will receive a sustained, superior return on their investment.

GENERAL MOTORS GUIDING PRINCIPLES

- We will establish and maintain a Corporation-wide commitment to excellence in all elements of our product and business activities. This commitment will be central to all that we do.
- We will place top priority on understanding and meeting our customers' needs and expectations.
- General Motors is its people. We recognize that GM's success will depend on our involvement and individual commitment and performance. Each employe will have the opportunity, environment, and incentives to promote maximum participation in meeting our collective goals.
- We recognize that our dealers, suppliers, and all our employes are partners in our business and their success is vital to our own success.
- We recognize that a total dedication to quality leadership in our products, processes, and work-places is of paramount importance to our success.
- We are committed to sustained growth which will enable us to play a leading role in the worldwide economy.

- We will continue to focus our efforts on transportation products and services, both personal and commercial, but will aggressively seek new opportunities to utilize our resources in business ventures that match our skills and capabilities.
- We will offer a full range of products in the North American market and participate with appropriate products in other markets on a worldwide basis.
- We will maintain strong manufacturing resources at the highest levels of technology and be cost competitive with each manufacturing unit.
- We will operate with clearly articulated centralized policies with decentralized operational responsibilities to keep decisions as close to the operations as possible.
- We will participate in all societies in which we do business as a responsible and ethical citizen, dedicated to continuing social and economic progress.

policies, a steering group to oversee policy execution, and a corporate ethics director. They also installed a hot line that allows employees to get instant advice on ethical issues involving their jobs. The stock exchanges have also set up a hot line for investors to report trading abuses. If someone thinks a broker has inside information or is manipulating the markets, they can call exchange officials who then set in motion a variety of surveillance measures.[52]

One way of strengthening a code of ethics is to make it clear that the company will punish violators and reward ethical acts. A company that fires a manager for giving kickbacks will find that others who are guilty of this behavior will stop and those who are merely thinking about it will not proceed any further. For example, Harris Corporation warns that failing to report a violation by others could bring discharge.[53] Likewise, when employees receive attention or even an award for ethical behavior, the message quickly gets out that acting ethically is the way to get ahead. For example, the head of Colgate-Palmolive encourages and gives recognition to those who come forward with ethical dilemmas by meeting with them in 80 breakfast meetings a year and at American Express management encourages employees to voice ethical concerns and supports those who speak out.[54]

In order to promote ethical behavior by Martin Marietta employees, the company created an ethics office. George Sammet, Jr., vice president of corporate ethics, and an on-site ethics representative follows up on every report to a Martin Marietta facility of unethical behavior. If they find that the report is true, appropriate action is taken by company officials.

Source: Courtesy of Martin Marietta Corporation.

A second way of encouraging ethical behavior is to reward those who see illegal or unethical practices and call them to the attention of the company or public bodies. These so-called **whistle-blowers** can be particularly helpful in stopping the production or sale of defective products and in helping management maintain high standards of ethical behavior throughout the company.

Unfortunately, in some companies, whistle-blowers find out that their actions lead to harassment and punishment from those who have been a party to the unethical practices. To prevent such retaliation, the law protects federal employees, and an increasing number of states and cities are also passing laws that prevent private employers from threatening, firing, or discriminating against an employee who reports suspected violations of the law to a public body.

Whistle-blowers Employees who alert management or public bodies to illegal or unethical practices.

1. What are two ways that a business can promote ethical behavior among its personnel?
2. What are whistle-blowers, and how can they play a role in promoting business ethics?

CHECK ✓ POINT

Closing Comments

This chapter provides the social foundation for the study of modern business. For many outsiders, this is their only view of business. As many of today's headlines attest, the view is not always flattering. Many of today's problems surrounding equality, the environment, consumerism, and business ethics rightfully make news.

But, as this chapter points out, business is responding and making progress. Sometimes these efforts are on business's own initiative, and sometimes they are a response to laws and public pressure. In most cases, being socially responsible makes good business sense. For example, by banning smoking in the workplace, the company can benefit from reduced health costs and even maintenance expenses (burned rugs or painting). Businesses can also avoid costly problems such as the $5 million paid by the Tennessee Valley Authority to settle a sex discrimination suit or Exxon's $1.2 billion settlement cost for the Alaskan oil spill. An increasing number of businesspeople realize that being socially responsible and ethical pays off. In fact, it not only pays off, it may even determine survival. The reasons for the collapse of the financial services firm Drexel Burnham Lambert and the retailer Allied and Federated stores included the questionable ethical, if not illegal, wheeling and dealing of their top managers.[55] In any case, the way business responds to the remaining social challenges will determine how business is conducted and may even affect the very survival of business in its present form.

VIDEO CASE / *Equal Opportunity for All*

Chicago's WSEP (Women's Self-Employment Project) is a good example of what can be done to help motivated people get off welfare rolls and into the mainstream. Many large corporations are also trying to fulfill their social responsibilities by ensuring that minorities and women are hired and then given an equal opportunity for promotion and higher salaries.

Corning Glass, for example, has established quality improvement teams throughout the company. One team's assignment is to ensure that women are provided equality in all aspects of employment. The company also has set up a nationwide scholarship program that provides summer jobs for college students, with an emphasis on women and minorities, and follows up by trying to recruit them for full-time jobs when they graduate. Another example is provided by Avon. The cosmetics firm provides its managers with awareness training that it feels is the key to recruiting, retaining, and promoting

minorities. As managers begin to gain insights regarding how to manage a diverse workforce, the chances of equality in the workplace increase.

Other companies make a point of comparing the salaries of their male and female employees to ensure that those doing equal work are in fact being paid equal salaries. In the area of promotions, considerable evidence exists that women face a glass ceiling in being promoted into the upper ranks. Some companies are trying to solve this problem by setting goals or quotas for the number of women or minorities for departments and levels, including the top levels, and then evaluating those in charge in terms of reaching these goals. For example, the CEO may be given a bonus by the board of directors for promoting a woman into an opening for a vice-president.

These efforts are likely to result in increased opportunities for women and minorities in the workplace. No one is projecting that in the near future salary

differentials will disappear or promotion opportunities will increase dramatically. However, the efforts of companies such as Corning and Avon are a step in the right direction and, in an increasing number of companies, social responsibility is more than a catchword; it is slowly becoming a reality.

Source: R. Roosevelt Thomas, "From Affirmative Action to Affirming Diversity," *Harvard Business Review*, March–April 1990, 107–117.

Case Questions
1. How well are women in the workplace doing in terms of promotion opportunities?
2. Are women at work paid the same as men who do similar work? Why or why not?
3. In addition to the data provided in this video case, what else can business firms do to help ensure equality for women and minorities in the workplace?

Learning Objectives Revisited

1. **Explain the overall nature of social responsibility.** Social responsibility is the obligation that business has to the society in which it operates. These responsibilities include equal opportunity in employment, environmental protection, consumerism, and business ethics.

2. **Describe the social issue of equality in employment.** Minorities and women still lag behind white men in

terms of employment and earnings. Unemployment is much greater among minorities than whites, and salaries are lower. Women are still paid less and are underrepresented in management ranks. Business's efforts to resolve these problems include affirmative-action programs, training and promotion, the use of mentors, and assisting small-business ventures.

3. **Identify the social issue of environmental protection.** In particular, the areas of energy conservation and pollution control are most critical. Business is taking many steps to conserve energy, including developing long- and short-range plans and replacing old equipment with more up-to-date, energy-efficient machinery. In controlling air pollution, business is using special devices on its machinery and equipment and is designing and building products that create less air pollution. Many companies are limiting or banning smoking in the workplace. In controlling water and solid-waste pollution, business is treating waste materials before disposing of them and recycling materials for reuse in production.

4. **Explain the social issue of consumerism.** Consumerism is a movement designed to provide buyers the information and bargaining power vital to obtaining high-quality, safe products and services. In meeting this responsibility, business is providing more information to consumers about the terms of sale and the specifics of the product and building safer products.

5. **Discuss the nature of business ethics.** Business ethics are standards that govern business behavior. Some of the ways companies can create a climate for ethical behavior include punishing violators, rewarding those who exemplify ethical behavior, and rewarding those who point out problem areas (whistle-blowers).

Key Terms Reviewed

Review each of the following terms. For any that you do not know or are unsure of, look up the definitions and see how they were used in the chapter.

paternalistic approach	ecology	boycott
Equal Employment Opportunity Commission (EEOC)	pollution	bait and switch
affirmative-action programs	consumerism	business ethics
mentor	class-action suit	whistle-blowers

Review Questions

1. During the 19th century, how did business owners and managers view their responsibility to society? Compare this to the dominant view today.

2. What are some arguments against the notion that businesses have a social responsibility? Are these valid arguments? Why or why not?

3. How does the Civil Rights Act of 1964 protect employees against discrimination? What federal laws protect employees from discrimination based on age and handicapped status?

4. Consider the following hypothetical ad, placed in the Help Wanted section of the local newspaper.
   SALESMAN: Looking for a smart, young (age 21–30) man who is eager to get ahead in the financial world. Must have own car. Call 555-5555 and be prepared to send in resume and photo.
   What federal laws might the advertiser be violating? Explain.

5. How can the company that placed the ad in Question 4 live up to its social responsibility to ensure equal employment opportunity?

6. How do business efforts at energy conservation benefit society?

7. Is it fair to require everyone to pay to clean up the environment? Why not have businesses pay directly for their share of pollution, so that the biggest polluters pay the most? Explain your answer.

8. What steps have businesses taken to alleviate the safety problems connected with their products?

9. "I'm not worried about ethics," says the owner of a hardware store. "I let the preachers worry about that. I'm a business manager, and my interest is in profits. Being ethical would just cut into my profits." Respond to this statement. Do you agree with the store owner's views? Why or why not?

10. When defense contractors pad their bills to increase their earnings, who benefits? Who loses? What can these companies do to promote ethical behavior among their employees?

Applied Exercise

Carefully read each of the following social responsibility/ethics scenarios and determine whether the action is legal/illegal and ethical/unethical. In the case of legality, base your answers on your best judgment of how the court would rule if these facts were all presented in evidence.

1. Paul is walking down the street and sees a note lying on the sidewalk. The note reads, "I have checked out the situation and learned that Big Corporation has landed a major contract with AT&T. The announcement is due tomorrow, so buy as many shares as you can today." Paul immediately calls his stockbroker and learns that Big's stock is selling for $1.25 a share. He places an order for 1,000 shares and 2 days later he sells them for $4.25 each.

   ___ Legal   ___ Illegal
   ___ Ethical   ___ Unethical

2. Claire is on the city council and the president of a major bank has approached her regarding a boat dock he would like to build on the lake beside his house. Five years ago the council voted to stop construction of any additional boat docks on this lake, but the president would like a special variance from the council. He asks Claire's advice on the best way to present his case to the council. She offers him some ideas, but she believes he is wasting his time. Two days later Claire receives a check in the mail for $5,000 for "management consulting." When the vote is taken, Claire supports the variance and it passes on a 5–4 vote. The next day she cashes the check and puts the money into a savings account.

   ___ Legal   ___ Illegal
   ___ Ethical   ___ Unethical

3. Tim is at a baseball game and sees a college friend sitting nearby. He moves behind him to say hello, but waits because the man is engaged in a quiet conversation with his father. Tim hears the father say, "The lowest bid we got on supplying us with those computers was $1,690,000. If we don't get a lower bid by noon tomorrow, we'll take this one." Tim immediately goes back to his seat, waits two innings, and then places a call to his uncle Ted, who owns a computer firm. Ted gets complete information on the computer bid the next morning and submits a bid of $1,680,000 at 11:45 am. Ted gets the contract and a month later sends Tim a check for $10,000.

   ___ Legal   ___ Illegal
   ___ Ethical   ___ Unethical

4. Terrence, a member of the board of directors of High Venture Inc., calls his girlfriend and tells her that he believes this is a good time to sell her stock in the company. She does so immediately, at $11 a share, and 2 days later the company declares bankruptcy. The price drops to 25 cents a share within a week.

   ___ Legal   ___ Illegal
   ___ Ethical   ___ Unethical

YOU BE THE ADVISER / *Charlie's Dilemma*

For a long time, Charlie Wadkins had wanted to own his own company. Six months ago, the opportunity presented itself. A local manufacturer and golfing buddy of Charlie's told him that he wanted to sell his firm and retire. The terms of sale were attractive, and after having an accountant and lawyer go over the books to verify that everything was in proper order, Charlie closed the deal.

What the financial accounts did not show Charlie is that his golfing friend has two problems in the social arena that are threatening to become major lawsuits. One is a complaint filed by three women who applied for jobs at the firm. They were turned down, and in their complaint to the Equal Employment Opportunity Commission, they have noted that of the 492 people working in the company only 6 are women. "Quite obviously," reads the complaint, "this firm does not hire women." The personnel department, which provided the court with preliminary employment data, reported that over the past 5 years, 109 women have applied for work at the firm and 10 of them have been hired. During this same period, 604 men applied and 573 of them were hired. The personnel department's data also show that no woman is in a management position, and, on average, each woman earns about two-thirds of the salary of male workers doing the same job.

The other problem is a formal charge by the union that the company has not done enough to reduce smoke in the plant. According to the union, "in the machine area the environment is dangerous to the health and well-being of the workers, and if nothing is done by the 15th of next month, we intend to file a formal complaint with the Environmental Protection Agency." If Charlie is to resolve this particular problem, he has less than 10 days to take the necessary action.

Charlie is determined to resolve both issues. He also wants to examine the company's overall response to its social obligations over the past couple of years. He intends to conduct this evaluation when he is finished with these two pressing issues.

Your Advice

1. What should Charlie do?
   ___ a. Start immediately to take steps to end discrimination of women, and sit down with the union and reach a mutually agreeable decision regarding how to handle the smoke problem.
   ___ b. Deal immediately with the smoke problem and put together a committee to formulate a 5-year plan regarding how the company might deal with employment practices regarding female applicants and employees.
   ___ c. Hire and promote as many women as possible and, as soon as this is done, devote full attention to the smoke problem.
2. Based on the personnel department's data, do the women seem to have a legitimate case? What would you recommend that Charlie do about the situation? Offer some useful recommendations.
3. What should Charlie do about air pollution?
4. How should Charlie go about making an overall evaluation of the firm's social responsiveness over the past 5 years? Be specific in your recommendations.

CREATIVE COSTUMES FOR SALE

Ed Breed creates and then sells costume characters. Before going out on his own, he gained considerable experience working for Lucas Films, where he learned how to blend technology and creativity in film making. Now he uses this innovative approach at his own company, Entertainment Research Group.

Most of Ed's work is with large corporations and businesses that want someone to create a logo or character for them. The resulting costume creations can take a number of different forms such as a large pitcher

Innovation and Entrepreneurship

Chapter Learning Objectives

- Examine the creative process.

- Present some creative techniques.

- Explain the roles of entrepreneurs and intrapreneurs.

- Relate the work ethic to entrepreneurship.

- Identify some innovative techniques and approaches of successful intrapreneurs.

---

of Kool-Aid or a dinosaur costume that is specially made so that the person inside remains comfortable and can move around easily. This is no simple task. Many stores with their own cartoon-like characters find that they cannot keep someone in the costume for more than an hour at a time because it is both uncomfortable and hot. Ed's creations overcome these practical problems through technological innovations such as inflating the costumes.

More important, however, Ed creates characters that his clients can use to attract customers and keep them coming back. For example, many shopping centers look for a theme to build a promotion campaign around. Ed helps by developing a character or logo that creates a tangible, entertaining vision of what the client is trying to portray. When shoppers see Ed's creation, they associate the happy-go-lucky character with the shopping center. The character also makes radio, TV, and print advertising come to life. The bottom line is that these characters draw back shoppers whose small children ask, "Can we go to the place where they have the big dinosaur, Daddy?"

Ed works with clients as far away as England and Japan. The Japanese in particular are interested in using his characters to represent their products and services. As with the other dimensions of business, when it comes to innovation and entrepreneurship, there are no national boundaries.

Introduction

The "spirit" of American business is innovation and entrepreneurship. New businesses start up and existing ones grow as employees generate unique ideas. Alternatively, novel ideas come through group techniques such as brainstorming. This chapter describes innovative thinkers, where they come from, and what companies can do to nurture them. Besides creativity, another important characteristic of entrepreneurs and intrapreneurs is their commitment to the modern work ethic.

Innovation

Innovation is critical to the success of modern business. Its importance was explained by one manager as follows:

> You need creativity in any business. Everybody can do the normal. For a business to be successful, it has to be 1 percent better. To do that, you have to have unique approaches to standard situations. You have to be creative.[1]

Innovation The introduction by business of a new product or service or the application of a new way to produce a product or service.

Simply defined, **innovation** involves the introduction of something new or unique. It may be a creative product or service or a new way of doing things. For the 1990s, innovation may provide the competitive edge, the 1 percent the manager earlier described, or the very success or failure of today's large and small businesses. Some examples of innovative products and approaches in business follow.

Boy Oh Buoy Sporting Lines Inc. has developed a unique life preserver called Sospenders. The preserver, which contains special safety devices such as an oral inflation valve, reflector tape, and a whistle, is so comfortable that people hardly realize they are wearing it. The unit is gaining popularity with oil rig workers, commercial fishermen, dam workers, and others who have to wear preservers while doing their jobs.[2]

The Second Time Around Most people buy their books, records, and magazines new. Half Price Books, Records, Magazines, Inc. sells used or unsold merchandise at half price. The idea is so appealing that the founder of the firm turned a profit within the first 30 days. Within 5 months, a second store was opened and the founder planned to take the business from coast to coast and to overseas locations.[3]

Video Wise Even sophisticated "video-wise" consumers have trouble and become frustrated trying to program their VCRs. Henry Yuen and Daniel Kwoh, who work for Gemstar Development, came up with an innovative product. Their $60 VCR Plus offers a very simple way to tape The Simpsons while studying for an exam. All you have to do is punch in the short numerical code printed in an increasing number of TV listings, and the device will do the rest. There is no need to go through the complicated steps of a typical recording procedure.[4]

These examples of innovation are becoming more and more common as businesses search for new ways of creating goods and services to compete in the global economy. In doing so, they typically rely heavily on the creative talents of entrepreneurs and intrapreneurs. (Entrepreneurs were defined in Chapter 1 as creators of new ventures or products and services.) **Intrapreneurs** are in-house people who help create new products or services and ways to move the organization ahead.

Types of Creativity

Two types of creativity are typically used by entrepreneurs and intrapreneurs in formulating new goods and services: new-new and new-old. "New-new" creativity applies to inventing goods and services that have never been offered before. One example of this is the Polaroid camera, which revolutionized the industry by helping create a market for instant pictures. This camera did not merely improve upon an existing model; it was an original idea.

"New-old" creativity refers to goods and services that are modifications of past offerings. For example, before McDonald's, there were other fast-food chains such as White Castle and Horn and Hardart. However, under the direction of entrepreneur Ray Kroc, McDonald's revolutionized the fast-food business by offering fast, high-quality, inexpensive food at easy-to-reach locations all across the country. Another example is Holiday Inns. When entrepreneur Kemmons Wilson built the first Holiday Inn in Memphis in 1952, motels already existed in America. However, Wilson offered additional services such as free cribs for babies, free TVs in every room, telephones in every room, a swimming pool in every motel, and no charge for children who shared a room with their parents. Holiday Inns soon became the largest motel chain in America. These types of innovative approaches are still being used. Moreover, some companies have developed a climate for "new-old" creativity. For example, firms such as Merck, Rubbermaid, and 3M have been consistently rated as having the best reputations for creativity and innovation.[5]

More business successes result from new-old creativity, which is more closely associated with intrapreneurs, than from new-new creativity, which is more closely associated with entrepreneurs. For example, the original ideas for a microwave oven lay around Raytheon, a U.S. defense equipment company, for more than 20 years before Japanese competitors developed the idea and obtained the largest share of the market.[6]

Researchers and practitioners generally agree that entre- and intrapreneurs do not necessarily learn how to be creative; it is more like a talent. However, understanding the creative process and learning some creative techniques can help develop entre- and intrapreneurship.

The Creative Process

The **creative process** is a way of generating unique or novel ideas, many of which can be used in a business. As illustrated in Figure 7.1, this process has four steps: preparation, incubation, illumination, and verification. A closer look at each step shows what is involved in generating a creative idea to start a new business or to make an existing one grow and become more profitable.

Preparation   The first stage of the creative process is **preparation.** This step involves gathering information on the problem or issue under analysis through such methods as reading, asking questions, and gaining hands-on

Intrapreneur Manager or staff expert who creates and controls new, usually risky projects within an existing business.

The first roller skates, made in Holland in the 1700s, were in-line skates. In 1980 Americans Scott and Brennan Olson, displaying old-new creativity, put in-line polyethylene wheels and toe brakes on boots and began selling them to hockey players and skiers for summer training. Later, Rollerblade Inc. redesigned the skates, added bright colors such as neons, and marketed in-line skates to the general public for recreation and fitness.

Source: Courtesy of Rollerblade, Inc.

Creative process Generating new or unique ideas, involving four steps: preparation, incubation, illumination, and verification.

Preparation Stage of the creative process that involves gathering information on the problem or issue under analysis.

FIGURE 7.1
The Four Steps of the Creative Process

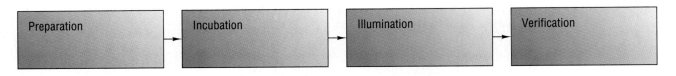

| Preparation | | Incubation | | Illumination | | Verification |

experience. For example, consider Ray Kroc, the McDonald's entrepreneur who many years ago made a deal with the person who invented a machine to make thick frozen milkshakes (the kind sold at McDonald's). Originally, when employees put this frozen milkshake into a regular blender, it burned out the machine. The blender was not built to mix a thick, frozen drink; it was designed to mix regular malts and other light drinks. When Kroc, then a salesperson for a paper cup company, saw the new machine, which could mix six milkshakes at a time, he began to think about how restaurants and other food establishments could use the machine.

Incubation   Stage of the creative process that involves sitting back and letting the subconscious mind work on the problem.

Incubation   The second stage, **incubation,** involves sitting back and letting the subconscious mind work on the problem. Often the brain rearranges information in a logical, straightforward way that makes the solution easier to understand.

The more information collected in the preparation stage, the more likely the incubation period will provide an answer or a general direction to take in resolving the matter. If no ideas surface after a period of time (the length depending on the problem), the creative process returns to the preparation stage. In the case of Ray Kroc's frozen-milkshake problem, he allowed time to mull over the problem and think about solutions. His experience in calling on retail food establishments helped him decide who would be the best targets for this machine.

Illumination   Stage of the creative process during which the answer to the problem or issue becomes apparent.

Illumination   In the third step of the creative process, **illumination,** the answer to the problem or issue becomes apparent. In the case of the milkshake, Kroc realized that frozen milkshakes were going to become a major food offering in fast-food units. So he made a deal with the inventor to let him sell these multimixers nationwide.

Verification   Stage of the creative process that involves testing the solution and, if necessary, modifying it.

Verification   The final step, **verification,** involves testing the solution and, if necessary, modifying it. As Kroc traveled his route selling paper cups to retail food establishments, he would bring one of the multimixers with him. He would demonstrate how the machine worked and then take the order. Today, fast-food franchises use this type of machine to mix their "frosties" and thick milkshakes. Kroc's entrepreneurial creativity led to the development of a new technique and resulting product, helping spur the growth of fast-food franchises in America.

Notice that the example used the term entrepreneur instead of intrapreneur. Ray Kroc is usually considered to be an entrepreneur because he

Dave Packard, at left, and Bill Hewlett work on their first product, an audio oscillator (Walt Disney Studios used one in developing the soundtrack for *Fantasia*.) They founded Hewlett-Packard Company in 1939 in the Packards' garage in Palo Alto, California. Today, HP is one of the 100 largest industrial corporations in America, and creative ideas continue to be an important source of growth.

Source: Courtesy of Hewlett-Packard Company.

popularized the fast-food industry with McDonald's. This came about because the McDonald brothers placed a large order for multimixers. Kroc was pleasantly surprised and decided to look in on their operation and see how it worked. When he did, Kroc became convinced that the McDonald's approach to fast food was brilliant. He talked them into letting him franchise the operation nationally — and the rest is history.

Individual Techniques for Creativity

Although the creative process is quite complex, psychologists are in general agreement that creative individuals have the ability to generate new, useful, responses to questions or problems. The profile of creative people shows that they display a wide range of interests, are independent, and are interested in philosophical or abstract problems. Importantly, however, creative individuals are not necessarily more intelligent (if intelligence is defined by standard tests or grades in school).[7]

In recent years, certain techniques have emerged to help trigger creativity in individuals. One useful approach is to use mental exercises that force the individual to look at problems differently. The following guidelines can be used for thinking more creatively:

Look at the space around the problem rather than just the problem. For example, if an employee is showing up late for work and not producing up to expectations, look at the environment in which the person works. Is this person's desk tucked away in the corner? Does the individual have trouble breaking into the office's social circle? Is the person being assigned boring work? Rather than assume that the employee is at fault, look for conditions in the environment that may be adding to the problem and work to change these.

CLOSE-UP / *International*

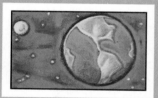

Why Do Flies Fly Straight?

Not all creativity in business today is restricted to small entrepreneurial firms. Many large companies are also encouraging creativity and some, such as NEC of Japan, have gone as far as hiring American scientists to work in their research labs to develop ideas for product development and technological advantage. However, much of what these scientists do may appear to be unrelated to computers or electronic products for which NEC is so well known. For example, William Bialek, one of the top scientists at the NEC Research Institute in Princeton, N.J., is currently trying to understand how flies are able to fly straight, even in the wind. How do signals move from their elaborate eye cells, through tiny nervous systems, to their fast-reacting flight muscles? Notes Bialek, "I'd like to know whether there are some general principles working here." This kind of unrestricted curiosity is exactly what NEC wants from its scientists because it can open the door for new discoveries such as how nervous systems process information.

Researchers at the NEC lab are also researching seemingly more relevant areas such as software that may eventually help computers handle ambiguity. In another project, they are looking into building powerful computers that use light beams and microscopic lasers in lieu of electronic circuitry. They are also trying to unravel the mysteries of superconductivity by studying how gallium arsenide and other materials behave when lasers are fired through them at temperatures approaching absolute zero.

Will these research efforts result in useful, profitable products for NEC? Perhaps not, but the important thing is that without such creative research, the company would not be able to develop 21st century products. Many of these research investigations will end up being blind alleys, but the few that do pan out may prove to be the breakthrough for a market winning product. The scientists who work in these labs are delighted with their environment and the opportunities that are available to them. As one of them put it, "I think what I'm doing here is . . . good for humanity."

Source: Joseph Weber, Neil Gross, and John Carey, "Pure Research, Compliments of Japan," *Business Week*, July 13, 1992, pp. 136–137.

Visualize the opposite of the situation. Instead of focusing on the fact that absenteeism is at an all-time high, assume that it is nonexistent. Write down why there is no absenteeism. What is causing people to come to work every day? Now ask yourself how it is possible to change current conditions so that they look like those that exist in a situation without absenteeism. Start working in that direction.

Reverse the physical characteristics of every object in the problem. For example, suppose a warehouse is filled with material, and there is no way of squeezing any more units onto the floor. How can more units be stored? One way is by making the units smaller or retractable. Another is by using the space between the units and the ceiling above. Can shelves or racks be installed to hold more goods? Can some units be suspended from the ceiling? Is it possible to convert the roof to a storage area by installing inexpensive plastic bins?[8]

These exercises are not difficult, but they do require practice and a desire to break out of some old ways of thinking and to look at problems in new and different ways. Many intrapreneurs are doing just this as they develop new goods, services, and procedures that the business they own or work for will use to gain a competitive edge. Another good example is provided in the accompanying International Close-Up (Why Do Flies Fly Straight?)

Group Techniques for Creativity

At the opposite extreme of highly individualized creative techniques for creativity are group techniques for creativity. The intrapreneur brings together those who are actively involved in the operations to offer new ideas or solu-

FIGURE 7.2
The Brainstorming Process

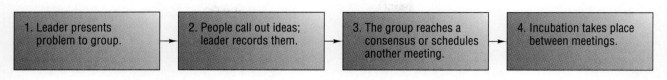

| 1. Leader presents problem to group. | → | 2. People call out ideas; leader records them. | → | 3. The group reaches a consensus or schedules another meeting. | → | 4. Incubation takes place between meetings. |

tions. Companies that have lost out to foreign competition in recent years are trying such group or team approaches to regain ground. For example, East-man Kodak set up what it calls small entrepreneurial business units. It also uses informal group techniques, such as the monthly pizza lunches held by the bio-products division, where employees are encouraged to come up with new ideas in a relaxed atmosphere. In other examples, a team of clerks at Federal Express spotted and solved a billing problem that saved the company $2.1 million a year and at 3M cross-functional teams working on product development tripled the number of new products.[9] Besides such company-specific approaches, there are a number of formal group techniques available. The most popular is brainstorming.

The Brainstorming Technique **Brainstorming** is a creative technique for groups in which the leader presents the problem and encourages participants to generate as many ideas as possible for solving it (see Figure 7.2). Brain-storming has four important rules:

1. Anyone can put forth any idea that seems useful to the problem under discussion.
2. Everyone is encouraged to come up with as many ideas as possible.
3. Participants may improve on someone else's idea or combine it with another idea.
4. Criticism and evaluation of ideas are forbidden.

Brainstorming sessions generally follow a set procedure. The leader, who may be an intrapreneur, begins by presenting the problem to the group. If the participants need some specific technical or descriptive information, they receive it at this time. For example, if the problem involves a small product, such as a hand-held calculator, samples would be available for everyone. Then the brainstorming begins. As people call out their ideas, the leader records them. By the end of the session, which usually lasts about an hour on most small-business problems, the group reaches a consensus about how to handle the problem, or another meeting is scheduled to continue the process.

If the latter happens, the information generated at the first meeting serves as the preparation step in the creative process. During the period between meetings, incubation takes place. By the next meeting, or perhaps during it, illumination may occur. Then the final recommendations can be modified and tested in the verification stage.

Brainstorming A creative technique for groups in which participants generate as many ideas as possible for solving a problem without considering at first the merits of each idea.

Scientists, like this group of researchers at Bristol-Myers Squibb Company, often meet to share ideas that can lead to creative approaches for solving problems and new product development. In such circumstances brainstorming can be a useful technique for producing many ideas.

Source: Courtesy of Bristol-Myers Squibb Company.

Delphi and Nominal Grouping Techniques   Two group techniques that have received increasing attention in recent years are Delphi and Nominal Grouping. They use the brainstorming approach as a point of departure to further attempt to overcome typical group problems, such as one person dominating the discussion or individuals being shy or not completely open in front of the group. Both techniques help trigger creativity and effectively solve problems.

The **Delphi** process (named after the oracle of Delphi in ancient Greece) has four major steps:

1. A panel is formed (usually of experts, but in some cases nonexperts may be deliberately chosen). The members are not in face-to-face contact with one another. Thus, the expenses of bringing a group together are eliminated.
2. Each member is asked to make anonymous predictions or input into the problem/decision the panel is charged with.
3. Each panel member then receives composite feedback from the others' input. In some variations the responses are listed anonymously, but most often a composite figure is used.
4. On the basis of the feedback, another round of anonymous inputs is made. This cycle repeats for a predetermined number of times or until the composite feedback remains the same, which means everyone is sticking with his or her position.[10]

Delphi   A group technique in which a panel of experts (and sometimes nonexperts) makes anonymous contributions, receives composite feedback, and then repeats the process until completion.

The key to the Delphi technique, and its main difference from brainstorming, lies in its anonymity. Keeping the responses anonymous lets the group members be open, flexible, and, hopefully, creative. Companies such as McDonnell Douglas, Weyerhaeuser, and Smith, Kline and French use Delphi panels to come up with new products and to predict technological and economic trends.

A related technique involves **nominal groups** (groups in name only, consisting of individuals whose independent ideas are pooled or combined; they are not allowed to have face-to-face interaction with one another.) A branch of research in social psychology found that nominal groups outperformed regular groups whose members were in face-to-face interaction. However, over time, there is still an additive or **synergistic effect** (the whole is greater than the sum of its parts) from group members interacting with one another. As a result, the **Nominal Grouping Technique** (NGT) evolved. NGT uses the following steps to take advantage of the strengths of both nominal grouping and normal interacting groups:

1. Silent generation of an individual's ideas to take advantage of nominal grouping.
2. Round-robin input from each group member on the ideas that were generated in Step 1. This forced participation gets everyone involved but is not threatening to anyone.
3. Full discussion of the pool of information gathered in Step 2. This is where the fully interacting group members build on one anothers' ideas and come up with new, creative ones.
4. Decision. In this final step, closure is added to the process. The members can make a decision by consensus, vote and let the majority decide, or have the group's leader decide based on what had come out of the first three steps.

An example of applying NGT would be to come up with a new, creative process to increase productivity in the production department. At the weekly staff meeting, the department head would first have all the group members write down ideas on their own. Next, she would go around the table in round-robin fashion and have each member contribute an idea, which would be written down. This would continue until all ideas were in the pool. Then the department head would open up the meeting for full discussion, and members could state their opinions and new ideas. Finally, after the discussion was no longer productive or agreement seemed to be emerging, the decision of what to do would be made by consensus, by majority vote, or by the leader. There is research evidence that such an approach can be very effective.[11]

1. What are the steps in the creative process?
2. How can intrapreneurs use brainstorming to generate creative ideas?

Nominal group A group in name only, consisting of individuals whose independent ideas are pooled or combined; they are not allowed to have face-to-face interaction with one another.

Synergistic effect An effect that leads to the whole being greater than the sum of the parts.

Nominal grouping technique (NGT) A group technique including benefits of both nominal grouping and normal interacting groups; it follows these steps: silent generation of ideas, round robin input, full interactive discussion, and decision making.

CHECK ✓ POINT

The Nature of Entre- and Intrapreneurship

Innovation is very closely linked to the process of entre- and intrapreneurship and entrepreneurs and intrapreneurs have been used thus far in the discussion of innovation. Chapter 1 defined entrepreneurship as the process of

Number of Businesses (in Millions)

Year	1977	1979	1981	1983	1985	1987
Value	1.9	2.3	2.7	3.3	3.7	4.5

In 1975 Liz Claiborne began designing clothes that gave women viable alternatives for the workplace. Today, Liz Claiborne Inc. has become an alternative workplace, where two-thirds of the over 5,000 employees are women. The accompanying graph shows the number of U.S. businesses owned by women.

Source: © E. J. Camp/Outline Press.

organizing, operating, and assuming the risks associated with a business venture. It also pointed out that some businesspeople play an entrepreneurial role in existing businesses. This is the intrapreneurial process.

Successful enterprises require the innovativeness of both entrepreneurs and intrapreneurs. An entrepreneurial type starts the enterprise and comes up with original ideas, products, and services, as well as creative or unique ways of doing things. For example, at Next Inc., Steven Jobs was responsible for developing an innovative easy-to-use method of executing basic on-screen computer commands, or what is called user interface.[12] Intrapreneurial types, on the other hand, keep the enterprise growing and make it more profitable. For example, Alfred P. Sloan did not found General Motors, but through innovative organization design and reward policies, he was able to shape the giant automaker into a growing and prosperous concern.

Some start off as entrepreneurs, by founding a company, and then use intrapreneurship to develop it. Jobs was not able to make this transition from creative founder to developer at Apple Computer. However, some are able to do it. For example, a few years ago Robin Wolaner started *Parenting* magazine with $175,000 she raised from venture capitalists. In an industry where competition is fierce and circulation growth is difficult to attain, her magazine was selling 500,000 copies monthly going into the 1990s and had advertising revenues of $10.7 million. Wolaner then sold out to Time Warner, but she continues as publisher of the magazine. Now she is an intrapreneur looking for new, innovative approaches to market circulation and advertising growth.[13]

Who Are Entrepreneurs and Intrapreneurs?

Entrepreneurs and intrapreneurs are quite similar. As pointed out by one expert, "They are leaders who have an impact on their cultures, particularly those around them who share in their vision of the creation of something new

VIDEO CLOSE-UP / *Innovation*

Jeremy's Place

Entrepreneurs with an innovative idea launch hundreds of businesses every week. Unfortunately, most of these new enterprises do not survive. However, some are careful to make sure that the product or service they envision relates to an actual market need. They then develop and offer specialized goods or services to fill that need, organize and control the operation of the business, and end up making a very profitable living. Starting a successful business does not necessarily involve something brand new, but the chances for success are improved greatly if the business answers a need that has not been adequately addressed in the market. Jeremy Sage has done this with his toy store and party business.

Jeremy gives parties for children aged 4 to 11. He has given new meaning to children's parties by offering a location outside the home and entertainment that is much better than the usual games such as musical chairs or pin the tail on the donkey. In fact, once children have attended a party at Jeremy's Place, they almost never want another party of their own at home. Whether for a birthday or another event, they want to go to Jeremy's, where they receive a bunch of prizes and, most important, fun and laughter for 90 minutes. In many cases an hour and a half party costs $700 to $800.

What makes Jeremy so successful is his ability to combine his many talents. With a background in theater and a genuine love of children, he knows just the type of parties that turn them on. As a result, his parties need to be booked well in advance and any adult who attends one can see why the children enjoy themselves so much.

The particularly interesting thing about Jeremy's successful business is that it is so simple, yet innovative. Like most successful entrepreneurs, Jeremy has special creative talents and job-related experience. During his acting days he acquired the important skill of being able to work in front of an audience. He understands and relates to his customers, the children. Jeremy knows what children want out of a party and how to react effectively to them. This too comes from his acting experience along with a sensitivity toward the feelings of others, especially children, that he developed through the years.

---

of value and wealth with potential for new employment."[14] Liz Claiborne is an entrepreneur who has made such an impact. For 25 years, she was a fashion designer until in 1976 she founded Liz Claiborne Inc. with $50,000 in savings and $200,000 raised from family and friends. She created a line of soft, attractive, colorful clothing styled for the women who were flooding into the working world. The rest is history. Going into the 1990s, Liz Claiborne Inc. was the second-largest American apparel company with one of the highest profit percentages in all business. This venture earned Liz around $100 million.[15]

Not all entrepreneurs and intrapreneurs are as well-known as Steven Jobs or Liz Claiborne. For example, an actor turned entrepreneur who founded a highly successful, enjoyable business specializing in children's parties is described in the accompanying Innovation Video Close-Up (Jeremy's Place). A sampling of other successful entrepreneurial ventures follows. Lyn Peterson and her husband, Karl Friberg, used $9,000 to get their wallpaper store off the ground in 1975. Since then they have expanded the business and manufacture upscale wallpaper and home fabrics. The firm designs and produces its own brand of wall covering and is also licensed to handle the Ralph Lauren line of wallpaper and home fabrics. Today the New Rochelle, New York, business is grossing in excess of $10 million annually.[16]

Intrapreneurs in particular do not necessarily develop new products or services for customers. They may develop new approaches to human resource management, such as in Publix, a Florida-based retailer, where someone was responsible for across-the-board employee ownership long before it was popular. They also develop new perspectives and new ways of doing business, such as at Sunset Scavengers, a San Francisco-based garbage company where the boss, Len Stephanelli, says he "loves garbage," requires that employees own their trucks, and stresses customer service.[17]

Where Do Entre- and Intrapreneurs Come From?

In recent years, many employees have been realizing that the experience they are gaining in everyday operations can help them become entrepreneurial and intrapreneurial. For example, one research effort found that three-quarters of the 161 rapidly expanding firms studied had been started by people who had previously worked for big industrial companies.[18] From their former large employers, these entrepreneurs learned how to organize operations, order inventory, sell products, and finance and manage the business. This experience proved to be invaluable in their entrepreneurial activities.

The same is true of intrapreneurs. People with valuable job experience in an organizational and supervisory climate that is open to change and innovation can make valuable, creative changes in existing processes, products, or services. Their intrapreneurial activities can help their present company grow and profit.

Many entrepreneurs and intrapreneurs also come from the ranks of minorities. In the past, minority entrepreneurs largely were concentrated in mom-and-pop businesses such as groceries, barbershops, and cleaners. Today, there is evidence that they are increasingly moving into fields such as electronics, health care, advertising, real estate development, insurance, and computer software. For example, the percentage of Hispanic-owned computer-related businesses in the United States more than doubled in the 1980s[19] and is continuing to increase in the 1990s. Today's minority entrepreneurs are better educated than their predecessors, and many are gaining valuable experience in large companies before starting their own.

The backgrounds of female entrepreneurs are quite similar to males except that women tend to be a little older when they embark on their new venture (35 to 45 versus 25 to 35). Also, women tend to start businesses in service-related areas (retail, public relations, or educational/training services) whereas men are more likely to enter manufacturing, construction, or high-tech fields. On balance, however, opportunities for entrepreneurial women are greater than ever and, according to the Small Business Administration, they are starting new businesses at three times the rate of their male counterparts.[20]

CHECK ✓ POINT

1. What are entrepreneurs and intrapreneurs?
2. What kind of background do these people have?

Hard Work as a Dimension of Entre- and Intrapreneurship

Entre/intrapreneurs have a strong work ethic. Many people claim that the work ethic in America is dead. "You can't get good help anymore," they say. "No one works hard the way people used to in my day." Yet recent research indicates that not only is the work ethic in America still alive, it is actually thriving. In fact, middle managers may be working too hard with resulting stress and burnout. The norm in many companies has become 12 to 14 hour days, 6 days a week.[21]

The Early Work Ethic

Those who came to America in its early days were said to possess a **work ethic,** which holds that people should work hard and save their money. This work ethic helped the American economy get rolling because it encouraged hard work, savings, and entrepreneurial activities. Savings were reinvested in the economy, allowing businesses to expand and hire more people, and entrepreneurial activities led to new businesses and expansion of existing ones. In turn, new employees had money to spend on goods and services, so business created more customers in the process. At the same time, new employees who believed in the work ethic would save their earnings and strike out on their own in entrepreneurial activities. Simply stated, the work ethic helped the American economy grow because it fostered the ambition to work hard, save, and start new ventures, the very elements needed for economic growth in a market economy.

Work ethic A belief that people should work hard and save their money.

The Modern Work Ethic

Surveys find that the work ethic is still very much alive. Regardless of pay, a majority of respondents indicated they had the old-fashioned work ethic. In fact, one survey comparing job attitudes in the 1970s with those in later years found "important and meaningful work" still more than twice as important as any other job characteristic.[22] As expected, this work ethic was even more common among entrepreneurial types.

Entre/intrapreneurs like to attain goals and to feel that what they are doing is important and meaningful. A couple of examples of these characteristics are found in the intrapreneurs responsible for the Post-It notepads and the anti-ulcer drug Tagamet. Even 3M, a company known for fostering innovation, almost managed to stifle the breakthrough Post-It notepad. The intrapreneur on the project got the product accepted only after persistence, belief in what he was doing, and much hard work. The same was true of Tagamet, the world's first drug to achieve sales of over $1 billion. It was turned down by Britain's largest chemical firm and was accepted by the American firm Smith-Kline only because of the persistence and hard work of the intrapreneur. Like innovation, the capacity for hard work cannot be taught, but it seems to be a necessary requirement for entre/intrapreneurship.

1. What is the work ethic?
2. Why do so many people value hard work today?

CHECK ✓ POINT'

Innovative Approaches to Intrapreneurial Success

Besides creativity and hard work, intrapreneurs can ensure success by getting a new or modified idea to work and be carried out. Study of innovative companies has uncovered some clear guidelines for managing this process. In their "search for excellence," Peters and Waterman found eight common approaches that characterized the firms they admired.[23] Peters has subsequently stated that "excellence" has become an overused term and well-run companies today are even more intrapreneurial — they believe in constant improvement and constant change.[24] The eight approaches can be used as guidelines and a framework for intrapreneurial success.

Bias for Action

Successful intrapreneurs avoid long, complicated delays. If an idea does not work out as intended, intrapreneurs analyze the situation, learn a lesson from the failure, and implement a new course of action. If intrapreneurs have an idea for a new product or service, management should encourage them to explain it orally or to write it down in comprehensible, short reports. Procter & Gamble has a one-page memo rule: If you can't say it in one page, you don't say it.

The active company's focus is on determining what has to be done and then doing it. Peters and Waterman summarize this bias for action with the slogan: "Ready, fire, aim." What this unique slogan says is that you have to be ready; successful intrapreneurs prepare and gather information, they don't fly by the seat of their pants. But, also important, they "fire"; they try things now. Then they "aim"; they verify, they learn, and they perfect.

Closeness to the Customer

Successful intrapreneurs also keep in close touch with their customers. Survey after survey points out that customers want personal attention.[25] Successful companies treat customers as human beings and listen to them. They find out what customers want and what bothers them. The 3M Company estimates that half of its current products are the result of customer complaints. In a manufacturing firm, successful intrapreneurs examine how product modifications can permit the company to tailor-make the good to the customer's specific needs; in an advertising firm, intrapreneurs find out how their clients view their goods and services and what image they would like to convey. Additionally, successful intrapreneurs get out from behind clean desks and closed doors and into the field to talk directly with customers and get firsthand feedback. For example, Al Boyajian, who owns and runs the popular Sears Restaurant in San Francisco, is constantly in touch with his customers. Although his breakfast and lunch restaurant averages 800 to 900 checks a day and the wait is up to 45 minutes to be seated, he still personally interacts with customers, asks for their suggestions, and believes that "my customers should be treated like guests in my own home."[26]

Peters recommends that managers in general, and we would say intrapreneurs in particular, should spend up to three-fourths of their time "managing by walking around" (MBWA). In other words, they should put a priority on going out and talking to customers and people they work with. When successful intrapreneurs are asked how can they afford to spend so much of their time in MBWA, they shoot back: "How can *you* afford to spend so much of your time on paperwork and attending meetings?" Sam Walton, one of the most successful entrepreneurs of all time with his chain of Wal-Mart stores, makes a point of visiting all of the more than one thousand stores and talking to customers and employees firsthand. He appears at a store unannounced and asks how things are going and how things can be improved.

Autonomy

One source of personal development and creative thinking is autonomy. Peters and Waterman found that excellent firms give their personnel the

AT&T Bell Labs creates a climate for intrapreneurship by tapping the scientific knowledge of employees such as Michael Prise. He is part of a research team who built the first digital optical processor. This experimental machine processes information using light instead of electricity and theoretically could lead to computers that operate 1,000 to 10,000 times faster than today's models.

Source: Reproduced with permission of AT&T.

freedom they need to think independently, make decisions, and, in essence, act like intrapreneurs. In companies with a series of products, each division or group is encouraged to act like a small firm within the overall structure. For example, Saturn acts like a separate company within General Motors.[27] Even in large organizations such as GM, this creates the feeling of entrepreneurship and the resulting dynamism, energy, and new ideas that are often generated in small enterprises, where intrapreneurs have wide latitude in making decisions.

Productivity through People

Successful intrapreneurs encourage their workers to contribute to productivity. These managers know that maximum productivity does not result from relying exclusively on technology and machines; subordinates also have important contributions to make. One way to inspire people-generated ideas and effort is with increased autonomy. Some intrapreneurs put their people into autonomous work groups and let them operate any way they want as long as the job gets done. This "free" environment often results in creative, productive ideas that help the firm stay ahead of the competition. For example, in Kodak's apparatus division, workers track their own quality and suggest changes in product design and the manufacturing process. As the general manager notes, "We used to want them to work harder and faster and perspire a great deal. Now we ask for recommendations. And workers are overlapping with engineers and financial people."[28] Part Four will give more detailed attention to this human side of enterprise.

Emphasis on Key Business Values

Another way to encourage an intrapreneurial climate is to emphasize key business values. Every successful intrapreneur has one or two business values that are the keys to success. In some firms, such as Dana Corporation, the focus is on reducing costs and improving productivity. Intrapreneurs in this company direct all their efforts toward these two aims. Other firms, such as 3M Corporation, emphasize new-product development. Others, such as Deluxe Check Printers Inc., value superior service. At this successful firm (they have about 50 percent of the check printing market, making them three to four times larger than their nearest competitor), they do things such as closely monitor the average "ring time" — the number of times the phone rings before it is answered. This simple but generally ignored measure is highly correlated to customer satisfaction with service.[29] These business values become focal points for the effort of the intrapreneurs in these firms. The result is that intrapreneurs move in the same general direction, driven by the same values, and eventually achieve and maintain their lofty goals of growth, profit, and personal achievement.

Sticking to the Knitting

Successful intrapreneurs find out what they do best and specialize in it. In other words, they stick to their knitting. If they are good at new-product development, they enter markets where new products tend to capture large market share and redesigned or revamped products find it hard to compete. If they excel at personal service, they choose markets where price is less important than service. If they are a low-cost producer, they pick markets where people buy based almost exclusively on price. If they merge or acquire another firm, they choose one that is in a business they understand. Successful intrapreneurs emphasize doing what they know best but in a new and creative way.

Simple, Lean Organization Structure

Successful intrapreneurs depend on simple structure. For example, at Hewlett-Packard, product development intrapreneurs face no bureaucratic obstacles. In this no-nonsense system, all employees know to whom they report and who reports to them. In few instances, if any, do intrapreneurs have two or more bosses. If a department or division contains a large number of people, the company breaks it into smaller groups — sometimes even moving people to other geographic locales — so as to reduce the inefficiency that often accompanies large size. Intrapreneurs also minimize the number of support staff.

Many major firms today are trying to make their organizations into a series of small firms all operating under one roof. This gives them the benefits of being small while remaining quite large overall. Organization structures receive more detailed attention in Chapter 8.

Simultaneous Loose-Tight Controls

Successful intrapreneurs apply some controls tightly, leaving others flexible and loose. For example, some intrapreneurs use stringent profit and other financial controls. If a product is unprofitable or fails to achieve anticipated sales, the company drops it. These same intrapreneurs may then apply many other controls loosely. For example, in day-to-day operations, some intrapreneurs may allow their employees a great deal of leeway in the routine aspects of their jobs. Successful intrapreneurs know when to use tight controls and when to loosen the reins.

Innovative Approaches in Perspective

These guidelines for innovation are not guarantees for success;[30] they are important lessons from which intrapreneurs can learn how things are done in the "excellent" firms in America. Perhaps the best way to summarize how to get innovation was stated by the founder and head of highly successful Raychem Corporation. He declared, "There is no secret. To be an innovative company, you have to ask for innovation. You assemble a group of talented people who are eager to do new things and put them in an environment where innovation is expected. It's that simple — and that hard."[31] The ideas themselves are innovative and in some ways contradict traditional notions about effective management. By the same token, intrapreneurs can also draw on the management concepts in Parts Three and Four.

CHECK ✓ POINT

1. What are three ways intrapreneurs can ensure that their ideas will be successfully implemented?
2. What does the slogan "Ready, Fire, Aim" mean?

Closing Comments

Innovation is critical to the success of today's organizations. It is not enough to do something well; the entrepreneur must do it better than the competition, and this requires some degree of ingenuity and creativity. Fortunately for the United States, many people have the entrepreneurial spirit. A good example is Lynette Samuel of Rahway, New Jersey, who owns Lunch Box Napkins, a firm that produces napkins with inspirational messages on them such as "I love you" and "You're a winner!" Today they are carried by gift shops and stationery stores throughout the state and are a popular item among parents who like to include them in their children's school lunch box.[32] Entrepreneurs like Samuel are needed to start new ventures, and intrapreneurs are needed to make existing companies grow and prosper.

This topic has not traditionally been included in the introductory study of business. Although innovation and entrepreneurship played a vital role in the founding of the American business system, it has only recently been recognized as a vital part of modern business. Intrapreneurship has emerged even more recently. It recognizes that the entrepreneurial spirit of discovery, innovation, and change is important in all employees — managers, staff specialists, and operating employees.

VIDEO CASE / *Innovation and Success*

Ed Breed of the Entertainment Research Group has an innovative approach to business. He uses his technological expertise to create inflatable costume characters that are used by companies and shopping centers to represent and promote their goods and services. What makes Ed's business so interesting and successful is the way he combines innovative technology with an entrepreneurial spirit. Although Breed's company is a great example of innovation and entrepreneurship in action, in recent years there are a number of successful firms that have used the same approach, perhaps none better than Nintendo.

Mention Nintendo and most people think of computer games. There is a good reason for this. Nintendo has more than 200 games on themes ranging from baseball to medieval warfare. However, its most successful game is Super Mario Brothers, the all-time best-selling series of games (39 million copies and counting) that involves quests through fantasies by an Italian plumber who can transform himself into a raccoon. Mario is so popular that a recent poll of U.S. school children found that he was better known than Mickey Mouse. This helps explain why Nintendo has been able to capture and retain over 50 percent of the computer game market in the United States. Of course competition has come from a number of different firms. A few years ago, NEC, the giant computer company, offered a console that had far superior images to those of Nintendo. However, NEC was able to capture less than 10 percent of the U.S. market. Nintendo is so well established that competitors have had great difficulty gaining a foothold.

Even more interesting, perhaps, is that many of Nintendo's titles are not created in-house. They are developed by outside entrepreneurs who sell their creative innovations to Nintendo for a "piece of the action." Nintendo, in turn, tests their games, works out the bugs, evaluates the market potential, charges the entrepreneur a fee for manufacturing the game and promoting it, and then pays a royalty on all sales. How well does this work out for the innovative entrepreneurs that develop such games? Nintendo has created a cadre of millionaires whose small firms have developed successful offerings. By following a "spread the wealth" policy, and taking advantage of others' innovative game ideas, Nintendo itself has managed to establish an innovative and entrepreneurial climate. Innovation and entrepreneurship are what a big company such as Nintendo and a small firm such as the one run by Ed Breed have in common.

Source: Susan Moffat, "Can Nintendo Keep Winning," *Fortune*, November 5, 1990, 131–136.

Case Questions

1. How does Ed Breed get ideas for new characters?
2. What do entrepreneurs developing new games for Nintendo do in the verification stage of the creative process?
3. Do entrepreneurs have a strong work ethic? Is this necessary for success?

Learning Objectives Revisited

1. **Examine the creative process.** The creative process involves a series of steps: preparation, collecting information on the problem; incubation, letting the mind work on the problem; illumination, when the solution to the problem becomes apparent; and verification, testing and possibly modifying the solution.

2. **Present some creative techniques.** Some of the ways to trigger creative thinking include: looking at the space around the problem rather than just the problem, visualizing the opposite of the situation, and reversing the physical characteristics of every object in the problem. A popular group technique is called brainstorming, which is a creative thinking process in which the participants generate as many ideas as possible for solving a problem. Other group techniques that extend brainstorming include Delphi, which utilizes anonymous input and composite feedback, and Nominal Grouping Technique, which takes advantage of both nominal grouping and interaction.

3. **Explain the roles of entrepreneurs and intrapreneurs.** An entrepreneur is the organizer or manager of a venture. An intrapreneur is a manager or staff expert who creates and controls new, usually risky projects within an existing business. Successful enterprises need both, because organizations need bold, creative people to start ventures and to maintain and change them.

4. **Relate the work ethic to entrepreneurship.** The work ethic places high value on working hard and saving money. This ethic has helped move the U.S. economy forward, because by saving their money and investing in entrepreneurial activities, people helped generate sources of capital for business expansion and growth; and by working hard, they helped businesses operate efficiently. People today still adhere to the work ethic.

5. **Identify some innovative techniques and approaches of successful intrapreneurs.** Some innovative techniques and approaches drawn from Peters and Waterman's analysis of "excellent" firms include the following: Have a bias for action. Stay close to the customer. Use autonomy. Achieve productivity through people. Emphasize key business values. Stick to the knitting. Have a simple, lean organizational structure. Use simultaneous loose/tight controls.

Key Terms Reviewed

Review each of the following terms. For any that you do not know or are unsure of, look up the definitions and see how they were used in the chapter.

innovation
intrapreneur
creative process
preparation
incubation

illumination
verification
brainstorming
delphi
nominal group

synergistic effect
nominal grouping technique
 (NGT)
work ethic

Review Questions

1. Pete Dunlop's supervisor has asked him for suggestions for modifying the company's billing procedure. Peter has been thinking all afternoon about the request without coming up with a single idea. He is discouraged and almost ready to give up. Does Pete's situation sound hopeless? Use what you know about the creative process to offer some guidelines to help Pete with his problem.

2. You work for an advertising agency that has obtained a new account from a company that sells athletic shoes. The new client wants your agency to come up with a new, creative advertising campaign that will help it capture a large share of the market for athletic shoes. How can you use brainstorming to accomplish this objective? Whom would you include in the brainstorming session(s)?

3. You are leading a brainstorming session to consider possible markets for an electric dish dryer. "Well, working women would really be the key market," says one participant. "I think housewives would be more receptive," says another. A third participant objects: "Hey, what about men? You're wrong to exclude them, because they do dishes, too." As the group leader, what should you say at this point?

4. How are entrepreneurs and intrapreneurs different? How are they the same? Can a person be both an entrepreneur and an intrapreneur?

5. Is the work ethic dead? Explain.

6. How can intrapreneurs stay close to their customers? Give a practical example.

7. In explaining how her business has prospered, owner Kate Kesler says, "I stick to the knitting." What does this expression mean? How do business people stick to the knitting?

Applied Exercise

Read each of the following statements and indicate your answer. If you have at least 80 percent of the same responses as successful entrepreneurs, you have a profile similar to these individuals. If you do not, start working to change these personal beliefs, behaviors, and attitudes that are different from those of successful entrepreneurs.

1. As a child, did you have a paper route, sell candy or magazine subscriptions, or do some other job in order to raise money?

 _____ Yes   _____ No

2. Have you ever been fired from a job?

 _____ Yes   _____ No

3. Are you inquisitive, inventive, and aggressive?

 _____ Yes   _____ No

4. Do you prefer solving simple problems rather than difficult or complex ones?

 _____ Yes   _____ No

5. Do you enjoy having a boss?

    _____ Yes   _____ No

6. Do you have a high need for achievement?

    _____ Yes   _____ No

7. Do you take rejection personally?

    _____ Yes   _____ No

8. Do you believe that most things that happen are a result of fate?

    _____ Yes   _____ No

9. Are you a consistent goal setter and a result-oriented individual?

    _____ Yes   _____ No

10. Are you unwilling to work longer hours for the same salary you now make?

    _____ Yes   _____ No

11. Do you dislike people?

    _____ Yes   _____ No

12. Do you have a low energy level?

    _____ Yes   _____ No

13. Do you follow through with implementation when a decision has been made?

    _____ Yes   _____ No

14. Do you believe in your own power to accomplish goals?

    _____ Yes   _____ No

15. Do you have low moral and ethical standards?

    _____ Yes   _____ No

16. Can you inspire and motivate other individuals?

    _____ Yes   _____ No

17. Do you wake up unhappy 99 percent of the time?

    _____ Yes   _____ No

18. Do you dislike power, control, and authority?

    _____ Yes   _____ No

19. Would you be willing to quit your job today and start at the bottom?

    _____ Yes   _____ No

20. Are you willing to participate in both the profits and losses of a business?

    _____ Yes   _____ No

YOU BE THE ADVISER / *Reducing Turnover*

Management turnover at the Jefferson Company has been unusually high this year. The firm, which has over 15,000 employees in a 12-state area, typically has to replace 5 percent of its workers and 3 percent of its managers every year. However, this year it lost 14 percent of its management staff, including seven senior-level managers.

Jefferson was founded 19 years ago and has witnessed dramatic growth over the past 7 years. During these latter years, the number of employees quadrupled, and management moved from an informal structure to a highly complex, bureaucratic design. To maintain efficiency, top management introduced a series of control measures that ensure everyone is following the rules and abiding by company policy. The president of Jefferson likes to say, "Around here, we are all one big team, and like any successful team, we all have to be moving in the same direction at the same time."

The heavy turnover in the management ranks has not escaped the attention of the board of directors. The chairman of the board has asked the head of the personnel department to put together a brief report indicating why the firm is losing senior-level people. In doing so, the personnel manager contacted the seven executives who had left to find out what they were doing and why they had left. Here is what he discovered:

Five of them left to start their own company.

The other two are partners in new ventures that are just getting off the ground.

Four of them said that they wanted the opportunity for more freedom and decision-making authority.

The other three said they wanted to use what they had learned in the business to run an operation of their own.

All said that they wanted the chance to make more money than they could earn at Jefferson.

Your Advice

1. What should the company do?
   - ___ a. Try to attract back some of those who have left by offering them more money.
   - ___ b. Admit that it is difficult to keep good people, and fill the vacant positions as soon as possible by promoting from within.
   - ___ c. Look into developing an approach that gives employees more autonomy and offers monetary rewards tied to performance.
2. Using the innovative approaches drawn from Peters and Waterman's study of "excellent" firms, specify areas in which Jefferson needs to make changes.
3. What advice would you give to the chairman of the board about how to change each of the areas you have identified in Question 2?
4. How can your advice help the company recruit and maintain people with intrapreneurial tendencies?

Career Opportunities in Business

Many of the most exciting careers in today's business world are in areas related to international operations and entrepreneurship. The shortage of internationally oriented people is creating a major demand for global managers. At the same time many people are choosing to leave large organizations and set up their own operations because of the freedom and the opportunities offered by this career choice. Some of the promising occupations that are emerging as a result of the changing environment of business are examined in this section.

International Manager

An international manager handles the overseas operations of multinational corporations. These managers can be found throughout the world, from highly industrialized nations to Third World countries.

Job Description. The specific responsibilities of international managers vary greatly from firm to firm, but in many ways they resemble those of their counterparts back home. An international manager typically helps to formulate overall strategies and determine marketing plans, ensures that the financial plans are adequate to support operations, and reviews progress periodically. Most international managers have had a great deal of overseas experience and can communicate in the language of the country in which they are assigned.

Employment Outlook and Earnings. At the present time, the few chief executive officers that head up multinational corporations can be thought of as international managers. However, managers who are assigned to various international operations number in the thousands. The demand for these international managers is going to increase greatly during the years ahead. The salary can range from $30,000 up to the hundreds of thousands.

Import-Export Manager

Import-export managers are critical to the success of a firm's international operations. Many companies conduct business overseas, but far more are importers or exporters and they need a manager to oversee this operation.

Job Description. An import-export manager administers shipping, receiving, and billing activities. This manager typically deals with domestic customers and shippers as well as with international freight haulers. The import-export manager is also responsible for ensuring that all shipments comply with international trade regulations, which includes having the proper documentation and filling out all the necessary forms for reporting shipments or receipts of goods.

Employment Outlook and Earnings. The number of import-export managers will continue to grow during the years ahead as the number of companies involved in international shipping and receiving increases. Growth is expected to be faster than average and, depending on the company and the industry, salaries range between $25,000 and $40,000 annually.

Venture Capitalist

As small businesses continue to grow and entrepreneurial ventures seek capital for expansion and funding of critical projects, the venture capitalist will be an important career field.

Job Description. A venture capitalist raises money to help entrepreneurs fund new business start-ups and innovative projects in ongoing operations. The venture capitalist typically invests money provided by others who are looking for high returns on their investment, which is possible when a new venture does well. A venture capitalist works closely with banks and other financing sources, on the one hand, and with entrepreneurs who are seeking funds on the other. Quite often a venture capitalist will specialize in particular types of businesses or industries and thus develop an expertise in that area. This expertise is very useful in evaluating new business proposals and other requests for financial assistance.

Employment and Earnings. The number of venture capitalists is tied closely to the state of the economy and to the emergence of new ventures in growing industries. In recent years some banks have also entered this field, creating and financing their own venture capital department. Earnings of those who work in the venture capital field will vary by the number and size of deals put together, but it is possible to make considerable money, $100,000 or more, in good years.

Entrepreneur

An entrepreneur is one who creates and/or organizes a new venture. These ventures usually end up being a small business and the entrepreneur is directly responsible for all critical decisions. Quite often the profitability and growth will decline if the entrepreneur reduces his or her interest and involvement in the business.

Job Description. Most entrepreneurs start a new venture by seeing a consumer need for a particular good or service and then opening a small business in order to meet that need. Sometimes this entrepreneurial process is a result of gut feel or personal experience; other times it is a result of more formal marketing research. The entrepreneur is most often responsible for financing the new venture, interacting with bankers, and submitting loan requests to both financial institutions and the Small Business Administration. Once the business is established, the entrepreneur becomes a small business owner like those discussed in the Career Opportunities section in Part One. That is, he or she spends a great deal of time on day-to-day operations, interacting with employees and customers, advertising and promoting the firm's goods and services, and evaluating and controlling results.

Employment Outlook and Earnings. Entrepreneurs have been around since the beginning of market economies, but the number of opportunities continues to increase. Women in particular are increasingly establishing their own firms and, if the present trend continues, will control more than 50 percent of all small business in the United States by the year 2000. Earnings vary widely, but entrepreneurs can either go broke and lose everything or become millionaires through their creative ideas and hard work.

TRAINS FOREVER

Except for Coca-Cola, Pepsi, and perhaps Xerox, few companies are as closely associated with their product as Lionel. It is the number-one firm in the model train market and has been for decades. Inventor Joshua Lionel Cowen founded the company about the turn of the century, after developing a fuse for igniting magnesium powder for use by photographers. He then began to produce fuses for exploding mines, which were bought by the United States Navy. The company soon was producing not only fuses but small

Management and Organization Structure

8

Chapter Learning Objectives

- Explain what skills are involved in the management process.

- Present the dimensions of the management function of planning.

- Describe the principles of the management function of organizing.

- Analyze how an informal organization works.

- Discuss the various aspects of the management function of controlling.

- Identify characteristics of organizational culture and ways to change it.

low-voltage motors and electrical novelties. Cowen also developed the first dry cell battery. In 1901 he put an electrical motor in a model railroad car and offered the toy to stores. It quickly became popular, and the company started manufacturing model trains and publishing a Lionel train catalog.

Lionel trains dominated the market for many years. By 1969, however, Lionel Corporation had fallen on such hard times that manufacture of the toy trains was discontinued. The train line was sold to General Mills in 1970. After a number of lackluster years, Richard P. Kughn bought the train line in 1986. He brought in his own management team and started restructuring operations. A host of new products have been introduced and more effective financial controls put into place. Today Lionel is posting record sales. The company carefully plans for the future, yet it does so with an eye on the past, because many adults want to have model trains exactly like those owned by their parents and grandparents. Responding to this nostalgia-based demand, Lionel Classic offers direct reproductions of metal Lionel trains of the 1920s and 1930s. At the same time, high technology is employed to provide new features; for example, computer chips inside the locomotive produce exact sound reproductions from prototype trains. Thanks to effective management and organization, Lionel will continue to be a household word in toy trains — and the company will celebrate its 100th birthday in a few years.

Photo source: Reprinted by permission of Lionel Trains Inc.

Introduction

A successful manager sees what needs to be done and makes an overall plan, organizes the necessary people and materials, provides direction, and heads off problems by setting up a control system. These functions of the management process are the focus of this chapter. Throughout the process, managers must take into account how the company is organized — for example, whether the people who report to them actually have two bosses — and how the company sees itself, that is, its cultural values.

The Overall Management Process

Management is the cornerstone of all business organizations. Like business, the term management has many dimensions and definitions. A simple yet comprehensive definition is that **management** is the process of setting objectives and coordinating employees' efforts to attain them. When managers do this well, the company prospers. Usually this means the company is growing and its profits and share of customers are increasing.

Management The process of setting objectives and coordinating employees' efforts to attain them.

Managerial Skills

Every manager — whether the supervisor on a construction crew, the executive of a large high-tech firm, the accounting manager of a nonprofit organization — needs the same kinds of skills. Each manager must have technical skills, human relations skills, and conceptual skills.[1] What makes management jobs different is the way these skills are emphasized and combined.

Technical Skills   Managers must be able to use the techniques and knowledge of a particular functional area or type of business; these are called technical skills. In the case of the construction supervisor, these skills might include understanding how to use and maintain the heavy equipment, fill out time sheets, and read blueprints. For the head of the high-tech firm, technical skills would include a basic understanding of the company's manufacturing processes, the ability to evaluate budget proposals, and insights into market trends and new product needs. For the accounting manager, these skills would include knowledge of accepted accounting practices and the administrative procedures of the company. In other words, technical skills are associated with the areas of production, accounting, information systems, marketing, and finance.

Human Relations Skills   Managers also have to be able to understand, motivate, and lead people. In fact, one management expert has recently noted that "the major difference between nonmanagers and managers is the shift from reliance on technical skills to focus on human skills."[2] Managers use these human skills when they motivate their subordinates to do their best, when they effectively coordinate efforts of the work group, and when they recognize and reward employee performance. These human relations skills are used by managers at all levels as they motivate and lead subordinates.

Conceptual Skills   Finally, managers must be able to interpret information, provide policy guidelines, and see the relationship of the parts to the

A supervisor at AAR Corporation checks repairs of aircraft accessories. Like other lower level managers, this supervisor needs strong technical skills. Here the skills involved are understanding how the accessories work and knowing how to fix them. Managers at this level but in other departments need skills ranging from being able to prepare a budget to knowing how to make a sales call. Importantly, these supervisors also need conceptual and human relations skills to be effective in their jobs.

Source: Courtesy of AAR Corporation.

whole. For top executives, this may mean defining what business their company is really in.[3] (For example, is Union Pacific in railroading or transportation, are Hollywood studios in film making or entertainment?) Or it may mean seeing an immediate difficulty such as a fall in profits as a symptom of a larger problem such as a failure to keep up with a change in customer tastes and demand.[4] Lower-level managers also must be able to understand how the parts relate to the whole. Often, this involves seeing how one's department fits into the big picture of the entire company. These conceptual skills are operationalized by managers at all levels by the functions of planning, organizing, directing, and controlling.

Levels of Management

The relative importance of these three managerial skills varies at different levels of the organization, because the perspective and day-to-day activities of management jobs change. In general, technical skills are relatively more important at the lowest levels of management. Lower-level supervisors, depending on the job, need to know how to run the equipment, set up the accounts, program the computers, and provide answers to technical questions. However, a large part of the supervisor's (e.g., first level management in charge of operating employees) job is still concerned with human relations and conceptual skills. For middle managers (e.g., department heads, office managers, and product managers), the three skills are about evenly divided. For top-level managers (e.g., vice presidents and the chief executive officer, or CEO), the conceptual skills dominate, the human skills are still important, but the technical skills have a decreased importance. Figure 8.1 shows this relative proportion of the managerial skills by organizational level.

FIGURE 8.1
Management Skills by Level in the Organization

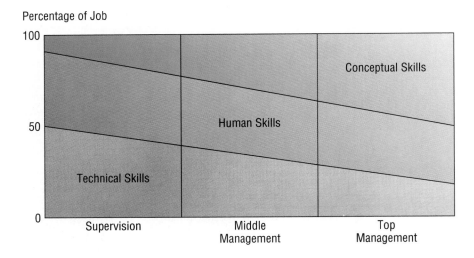

Percentage of Job

FIGURE 8.2
The Functions in the Management Process

Traditionally, American managers at all levels have stressed and been very good at the technical skills. However, recent successful company experience and comprehensive research shows that effective management is more than just a series of routine activities and technical know-how.[5] It is a complex process in which the effective manager uses the conceptual and human skills as well. This chapter focuses primarily on the conceptual managerial skills expressed through the functions of planning, organizing, and controlling. Chapter 11 discusses the human relations skills expressed through the directing function of motivating and leading. Figure 8.2 illustrates these functions in the management process. Other sections of the book, such as

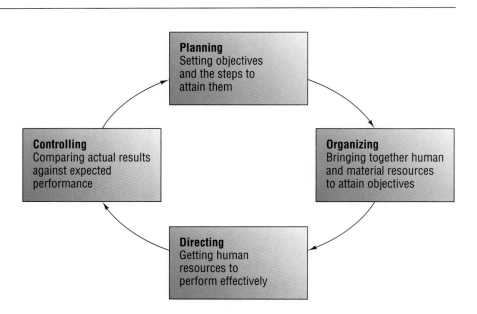

FIGURE 8.3
The Planning Process

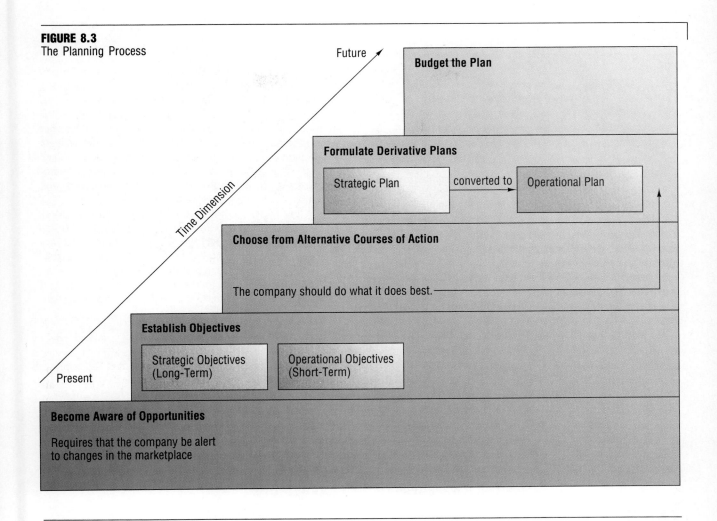

Future

Time Dimension

Present

Budget the Plan

Formulate Derivative Plans

| Strategic Plan | converted to | Operational Plan |

Choose from Alternative Courses of Action

The company should do what it does best.

Establish Objectives

| Strategic Objectives (Long-Term) | Operational Objectives (Short-Term) |

Become Aware of Opportunities

Requires that the company be alert
to changes in the marketplace

Chapter 9 on operations, Chapter 10 on information systems and computers, Part Five on marketing, and Part Six on finance are more related to the technical skills.

1. What skills must managers have?
2. If you were a lower-level supervisor, how would your job differ from that of a top-level manager? Identify two differences.

Planning

The modern management process starts with **planning,** which involves setting objectives and formulating the steps to attain them. The planning process incorporates five specific steps. As shown in Figure 8.3, planning starts when the manager becomes aware of an opportunity and ends with budgeting the overall plan. Today, as changes occur more frequently, many companies develop both long- and short-run plans.[6] For example, McDonnell-Douglas and Boeing are looking into the development of a passenger plane by

CHECK ✓ POINT

Planning Setting objectives and formulating the steps to attain them.

CLOSE-UP / *Innovation*

Xerox Reorganizes for New Business Opportunities

In taking advantage of emerging business opportunities, a company often needs more than just new products or services. Sometimes a new approach to organizing can help generate the necessary stimulation for getting things off the ground. Xerox is a good example. Although this well known company was a pioneer in photocopiers, it eventually lost its market to Canon and Ricoh. Most recently, Xerox let Canon get a big head start in color copiers. However, the company plans to fight by reorganizing into nine product divisions and three geographical sales divisions. The objective of this dramatic reorganization is to make the company smaller, more entrepreneurial, and thus better able to take advantage of market opportunities.

Today, Xerox has three major product/service lines in which it competes: copiers, printers, and software and services. The copiers group is organized to sell in three areas. One is personal document products, the second is office document products, and the third is document production systems. The printer division is also organized into three areas: printing systems for mainframe attached laser printers; office document systems such as office laser printers; and engineering systems which prepare engineering drawings. The software and services group also has three areas: software packages for desktop computers; software to connect faxes to personal computers; and business services provided at customer offices.

Will this new organizational arrangement be more effective and more adaptable to new market opportunities? The results to date appear quite favorable. The group provide software for desktop computers has already brought out two new software packages and is pushing ahead with plans for a dozen more. If this is any indication of things to come, Xerox will indeed be taking advantage of a lot new business opportunities.

Source: Lisa Driscoll, "The New, New Thinking at Xerox," *Business Week*, June 22, 1992, pp. 120–121; and Kathy Rebello, "The Model for Xerox' Reform is Still Being Molded," *Business Week*, June 22, 1992, p. 121.

As more people began to work outside the home creating a need for quick ways to fix meals, they discovered microwave ovens. Alert managers at food processing companies saw that these lifestyle and technological changes resulted in new demands. They soon were planning full lines of microwavable foods, such as Chef Boyardee™ Microwave Meals.

Source: © 1991 Kelly/Mooney Photography.

the year 2000 that can fly up to 2,000 miles an hour over distances of at least 6,000 miles.[7] On a shorter time continuum, Nucor is investing in new technology to beat their competitors in producing flat-rolled steel used for oil pipelines and auto parts,[8] and Philips, the Dutch electronics giant, is working to rapidly position itself for growth in the TV, computer, and semiconductor markets.[9]

Awareness of an Opportunity

The first step in the planning process, becoming aware of an opportunity, requires that the company's managers remain alert to changes in the marketplace. As customers' needs change or the competition offers new goods and services, management must look for ways to exploit these developments. Sometimes companies have a successful product but do not know how to take advantage of the market. Raytheon developed the microwave oven but failed to see that the product would be of value not only in restaurants but also in the typical home kitchen.[10] On the other hand, many firms have exploited their opportunities. For example, the fastest growing producer of custom-made wood windows and doors, Marvin Lumber & Cedar, produces its products on a made-to-order basis. Aware that people like specialty doors and windows that make their homes look distinctive, Marvin offers a wide range of products. All the customer has to do is pick the desired windows and doors out of its catalog and the company does the rest. The idea has been so successful that during the last 10 years Marvin's sales grew 500 percent.[11] Another example is provided by Gillette with its Sensor razor. This high-tech product is helping the company beat back the disposable razor competition and reestablish its market position.[12] The accompanying Innovation Close-Up (Xerox Reorganizes for New Business Opportunites) provides some additional examples.

Outboard Marine Corporation builds a variety of boats and motors. Examples are this bassboat and outboard motor shown here. Its operational objective is to meet the demands of boaters in every segment of the recreational powerboat market. Meeting this operational objective assists the company in fulfilling its strategic objective of providing shareholders with above-average returns on their investments over the long term.

Source: Courtesy of Outboard Marine Corporation.

Establishment of Objectives

In light of the opportunities they see, managers set objectives. These may take two basic forms: strategic and operational.

Strategic Objectives An organization's **strategic objectives** are long-range objectives that help it compare itself with the competition. Increased profits, growth, and market share are typical strategic objectives. Another long-range objective is improving the organization's reputation in the industry and the business community at large. Achievement of strategic objectives requires the efforts of more than one department. For example, profits are greater when the production department keeps costs low and salespeople keep the orders coming in. A good reputation depends on a variety of accomplishments, including financial soundness and a quality product. Gillette's Sensor razor, for example, earns the company 8 cents more per cartridge than its competitors earn, thanks to careful financial investment and product quality. Management also uses strategic objectives in developing a long-range plan, called a **strategic plan.**

Strategic objectives Long-range objectives that help an organization compare itself with the competition.

Strategic plan A long-range plan.

Operational Objectives A company's **operational objectives** are short-range objectives that help management control its internal resources and implement the strategic plan.[13] For example, to increase profits (a strategic objective), managers want high productivity, low costs, and low employee turnover (operational objectives). The operational objectives are the basis for a firm's short-range plan, called its **operational plan,** or sometimes its tactical plan. To ensure that the company is meeting its objectives and carrying out its plan, management will often evaluate progress each month or quarter. For example, when Perrier water was found to contain tiny amounts of potentially harmful benzene, the manufacturer immediately made a global recall of its product and began closely monitoring the quality of future shipments.[14] In the telephone long-distance market, AT&T carefully followed

Operational objectives Short-range objectives that help management control its internal resources and implement the strategic plan.

Operational plan A short-range plan.

MCI[15] and Sprint's market share growth, and lowered its prices to prevent loss of business.[16] At the local level, the Bell companies were working hard to get Congressional clearance to enter the cable TV business and to own at least a portion of the programming.[17]

Choice of Alternative Courses of Action

After setting objectives, managers must choose the courses of action that will achieve the objectives. In doing so, they follow the first rule of strategy: Lead from strength. This means the company should do what it can do best. If the company is a large manufacturer with low cost per unit, it will seek markets where price is important in selling the product. If the firm is small but provides excellent service, it will seek markets where customers are willing to pay more because the company caters to their needs.

Some industries use both of these approaches profitably. For example, in the airline industry, a low-price strategy will attract many vacationers who find it cheaper to fly than to drive or take a bus. The airfare wars that resulted from deregulation have clearly illustrated this. Other passengers fly first class because they want the comfort and convenience. This group includes businesspeople who need to work during the trip. Even though it costs quite a bit more to fly first class, the extra comfort and convenience may be worth the price.

Formulation of Derivative Plans

Derivative plan The plan for a series of actions that convert the strategic plan into an operational plan.

The chosen courses of action become part of the organization's derivative plan. A **derivative plan** outlines a series of actions that convert the strategic plan into an operational plan. The example in Figure 8.4 focuses on the objectives that are part of these plans. Notice how the strategic objectives of profit, sales, and market share are broken down into operational objectives. The derivative plan helps convert the strategies into more and more specifics going from top to intermediate to lower levels of management.

Budgeting of the Plan

The last step in the planning process is budgeting the plan. A budget is a statement of expected results expressed numerically. (For more detail, see Chapter 18.) Examples include the sales budget, the production budget, the purchasing budget, the maintenance budget, the advertising budget, and the personnel budget. The budget indicates the goals in each area and may list the amounts the company plans to spend to achieve the goals. For example, most companies spend money on salespeople and advertising in order to meet sales goals. They don't spend the money arbitrarily; they follow a budget. The budget may also contain nonfinancial information on resources such as people, equipment, or materials that are needed to attain the objectives.

Management by Objectives

Management by objectives (MBO) The system in which managers and subordinates jointly set objectives to use as the basis for operating the business and evaluating performance.

One way to plan formally is to use a technique outlined a number of years ago by management consultant Peter Drucker. This technique, called **management by objectives (MBO),** is a system in which managers and subordinates set objectives jointly and use these objectives as the basis for operating the business and evaluating performance. Although not always labeled as such, MBO helps planning in many organizations today, from the biggest corporations to the local department store.

FIGURE 8.4
Hierarchy of Objectives for Derivative Plans

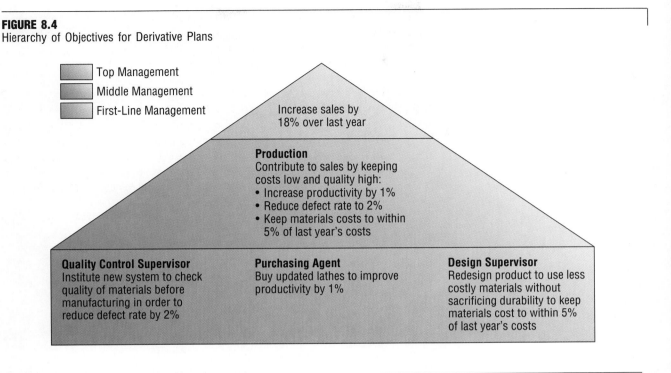

Top Management
Middle Management
First-Line Management

Increase sales by
18% over last year

Production
Contribute to sales by keeping
costs low and quality high:
• Increase productivity by 1%
• Reduce defect rate to 2%
• Keep materials costs to within
  5% of last year's costs

Quality Control Supervisor
Institute new system to check
quality of materials before
manufacturing in order to
reduce defect rate by 2%

Purchasing Agent
Buy updated lathes to improve
productivity by 1%

Design Supervisor
Redesign product to use less
costly materials without
sacrificing durability to keep
materials cost to within 5%
of last year's costs

The generally recognized steps of MBO are to (1) identify the overall goals, (2) have superior-subordinate pairs mutually set specific goals for each area of responsibility, (3) periodically appraise progress, (4) evaluate overall results, and then start the cycle over again.

The MBO process has received its share of criticism over the years. When applied, problems can enter at each step. For example, top management may not communicate the purpose of the system, and subordinates may feel pressured to go through a "paperwork exercise" and "keep score" of how many objectives they did or did not attain. If carefully implemented, these problems can be overcome, and MBO can be an effective way of linking the overall goals of the enterprise to those of the various departments and units.

For proper implementation, the manager must consider the overall company goals when setting departmental goals. Then, the manager links departmental objectives to employee objectives when planning subordinates' responsibilities and discussing their objectives with them. The link to overall goals provides a basis for managers and subordinates to determine objectives jointly and get everyone moving in the same direction.

MBO also stimulates communication between managers and subordinates. It encourages frequent follow-up to discuss performance and to offer assistance. Employees usually appreciate knowing exactly what is expected of them, stated in the form of goals they helped set. The evaluation, which occurs at the end of a predetermined period, usually one year, also lets employees know what to expect.

FIGURE 8.5
The Organizing Process

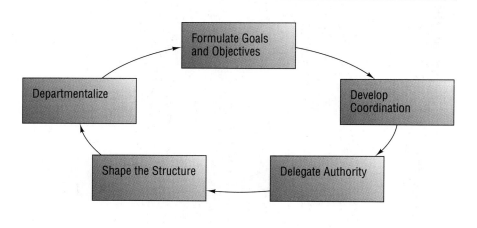

CHECK ✓ POINT

1. What are the major steps in the planning process?
2. What are two reasons managers use management by objectives?

Organizing

Whereas the management process in general can be thought of as the cornerstone of business, organizing could be called the skeletal framework of business. The management function of **organizing** involves efficiently bringing together human and material resources to attain objectives.

Organizing Efficiently bringing together human and material resources to attain objectives.

The Impact of Organizing on Performance

Organizing can greatly affect performance for two reasons. First, work proceeds more smoothly at a well-organized company. If employees must cut through a mass of red tape or forward all decisions up the line for a final OK, they may waste time and effort and grow frustrated in the process. To avoid this, managers must develop an organization that facilitates decision making, communication, and work performance. The importance of an effective organization structure was brought out by the intensive investigation following the explosion of the space shuttle *Challenger*. The investigation concluded that management failure in general and an ambiguous system of authority in particular led to the disaster. Although there were technical problems such as with the O-rings, the organization structure did not allow the essential communication to reach critical decision makers before and during the launch process.

Organizing is also important because it enables managers to meet the challenges of the external environment, so that they can keep up with competitors. This often requires flexibility and change. Some innovative managers have responded by greatly reducing or eliminating levels of bureaucratic structure and accompanying rules and regulations. For example, Marcus Sieff, the former chairman of the British retail chain of Marks & Spence, took a year off to search through, evaluate, and then eliminate 80 percent of the company's paperwork. At the end of the year, Sieff piled up 5 tons of useless paper and hosted a companywide bonfire.[18] This extreme approach to

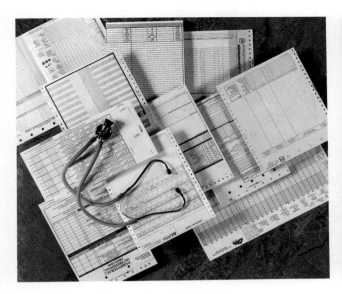

Reynolds and Reynolds, a leading supplier of management information systems and related professional services, markets its products in two major areas: business forms and computer systems. Primary markets include automotive, general business, and healthcare. In 1990, Reynolds studied its automotive forms business to uncover strategies for increasing market share and maintaining profitability. In general business forms, a new management team and a realignment of production and sales responsibility positioned the group to improve profitability in all of its market segments by focusing on vertical markets, like healthcare, that offer superior volume and profit margin opportunity.

Source: Courtesy of Reynolds & Reynolds.

streamlining the organization helped make this company more efficient and let it focus on important areas such as customer service. Other firms, however, have found that as they grow and need more consistency, they need to tighten up operations and create formal rules and procedures for paperwork.

Determining the Organization's Structure

The process of determining the best structure for an organization follows the steps shown in Figure 8.5. These steps involve formulating goals and objectives, developing coordination, delegating authority, shaping the structure, and dividing the overall structure into departments.

Formulation of Goals   The first step in creating the organization structure is similar to the planning process in its emphasis on goals. The goals of the company need not be set forth in an elaborate policy manual, but they should be in writing. For example, Dana Corporation, an Ohio firm that manufactures axles, has no overall policy manuals but instead has a one-page policy sheet.[19]

Goals should be specific. This helps management break them down and assign them to existing organization units or create new ones. Examples of goals that would start the organizing process are:

Attain a 15 percent growth in productive capacity.

Expand sales regions to cover the Pacific coast states.

Develop two new product lines.

Establish branch offices in Paris and Singapore.

Development of Coordination   For separate divisions to attain overall company objectives, their work must be coordinated. **Coordination** is systematic, unified group effort in the pursuit of common objectives. When coordination exists, everyone works in harmony. Coordination depends on two things:

Coordination A systematic, unified group effort in the pursuit of common objectives.

1. Well-defined tasks and objectives. When people know and agree about what they are supposed to be doing and when they should do it, coordination increases.
2. Willingness of managers to cooperate. The desire for teamwork is necessary for coordination.

Coordination is particularly important when more than one unit or department is involved. For example, Hallmark's biggest selling season for Christmas cards is November and early December. Thus, the production department must have enough cards made and distributed before November. Because Hallmark sells to retailers, the retailers need to receive the cards a few weeks in advance, in order to properly price and display them on the sales floor. Hallmark's wholesalers who sell to retailers need even greater lead time. It may be necessary to have the cards in the wholesalers' hands by October 15. Thus, the marketing and production departments at Hallmark must coordinate their efforts so that the Christmas cards arrive in the marketplace at the right time.

Authority The right to command.

Delegation of Authority   After developing coordination, managers next decide how they will delegate authority. **Authority** is the right to command. All managers have authority, but unless they intend to do everything themselves, they must also delegate. **Delegation** is the distribution of work and authority to subordinates.

Delegation The distribution of work and authority to subordinates.

How much should the manager delegate? This depends on the nature of the business or the particular task. Some firms, such as ITT and Polaroid, employ strong **centralization,** which means that the upper levels of management retain most of the important decisions. Other firms, such as Sears, Exxon, Mobil, Dean Witter, and DuPont, use strong **decentralization,** which means delegating many important decisions to the lower levels of management. Some companies switch back and forth from centralization to decentralization, depending on the situation they are facing. For example, to be flexible and respond faster to changing market needs, IBM uses a highly decentralized organization in order to give more decision-making authority to division managers. The manager's job is to determine the right amount of work and authority to delegate to each subordinate.

Centralization An approach to delegation in which upper management levels retain most of the important decisions.

Decentralization An approach to delegation in which many important decisions are made by lower management levels.

In highly decentralized firms, managers delegate important work, freeing themselves for other tasks. One example of extreme delegation occurs at the Ford Motor plant in Edison, New Jersey, which allows its assembly-line workers to use the Japanese-derived "stop button" to halt the entire line in order to correct a quality defect. This gives the lowest level worker a feeling of control over the whole operation. An example in the service industry would be the general manager of a Marriott hotel who tells all employees (from desk clerks and bellhops to department managers) they have the right to make on-the-spot decisions (concerning refunds or any customer request). For example, when a customer complained that he was told that the hotel had free strollers (which they never have had), the desk clerk made a decision to rent a stroller for the customer's use at the hotel's expense. Obviously, such a policy of delegation to front-line employees can have a tremendous positive impact on customer satisfaction.

When delegating, managers must keep in mind two important principles of organizing. Both principles consider responsibility, the obligation to meet the demands of the job. The first is the principle of equal authority and responsibility, which holds that if people are given responsibility, they must have the authority to carry it out. The manager should not delegate one without the other. The second is the principle of absoluteness of responsibility, which holds that while authority can be delegated, the manager still has responsibility. While managers may realistically pass on some responsibility, according to this principle, they cannot try to use delegation as a way to shirk their duties.

The extent to which managers delegate authority and the way they treat responsibility vary among cultures as well as among organizations. For example, no American executives of the Union Carbide Corporation resigned after the poison gas leak in Bhopal, India, several years ago, and no executives of Morton Thiokol resigned over the company's involvement in the loss of the space shuttle *Challenger*. In contrast, when Toshiba was accused of allowing a subsidiary to sell militarily sensitive technology to the Soviet Union, the Japanese company's two top executives resigned. In contrast to the executives at Union Carbide and Morton Thiokol, the executives at Toshiba assumed ultimate responsibility for their company's problems.

Shaping the Structure   Most important to developing an appropriate structure is to allow the enterprise to function in a way that is most effective for its particular situation. To achieve this, businesses often adhere to a number of basic organizing principles:

The principle of flexibility. An organization must be able to adjust to changing conditions. For example, 3M Company uses a "biological organization." To preserve the flexibility of smallness within a large organization, 3M creates a new division for any product that sells well enough. Because 50 percent of the firm's revenue is generated by products developed in the past 10 years, this means that new divisions are being continuously created. This principle of flexibility has also contributed to the highly successful Worthington and Chaparral steel companies (in a depressed industry) who use minimills for flexibility in making specialty products.

The principle of minimum levels. A firm should have as few levels in the hierarchy as possible. For example, Dana Corporation successfully went from 11 levels to 5, even while growing rapidly. Because there were fewer levels, the company avoided many of the problems associated with bureaucracy, such as breakdowns in communication and rapid response to changing conditions.

The principle of span of control. The **span of control** refers to the number of subordinates directly reporting to a supervisor. The principle holds that supervisors should have only as many subordinates as they can manage efficiently. While classic management theorists have recommended that the span be kept small, many successful firms such as Sears deliberately increased the span in order to give subordinates more autonomy. Thus the length of the span may vary widely, depending on the manager and the situation.

Span of control   The number of subordinates directly reporting to a supervisor.

The principles of minimum levels and span of control help determine the "shape" of the structure. For example, if managers can effectively handle only two subordinates, the structure needs a different shape than if all of the managers have ten subordinates. Figure 8.6 illustrates this concept. Notice that a **tall structure** is one with many levels and short spans, and a **flat structure** is one with few levels and wide spans.

Tall structure   Structure with many levels and short spans of control.

Flat structure   Structure with few levels and wide spans of control.

FIGURE 8.6
Organization Shapes

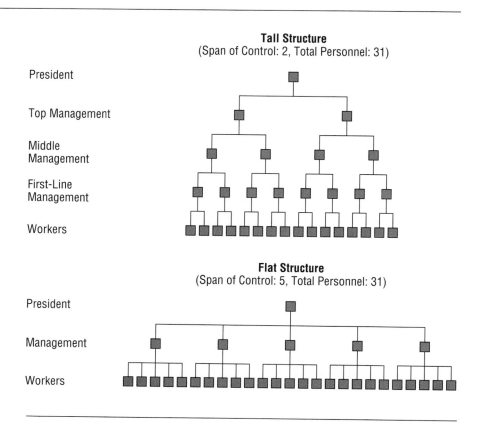

Tall Structure
(Span of Control: 2, Total Personnel: 31)

President

Top Management

Middle
Management

First-Line
Management

Workers

Flat Structure
(Span of Control: 5, Total Personnel: 31)

President

Management

Workers

Departmentalization The
structure of a given level of an
organization on the basis of some
common characteristics.

Functional departmentalization
The structure of a level of an
organization on the basis of major
activities.

Product departmentalization
The structure of a level of an
organization on the basis of
product lines.

Departmentalizing the Structure   Taking into account a given level, managers structure the organization on the basis of some common characteristics. This process is called **departmentalization.** The most popular forms of departmentalization are by function, product, geographic area, and customer.

Managers use **functional departmentalization** when they structure an organizational level on the basis of major activities. For example, in a manufacturing firm, the primary activities or functions are personnel, production, marketing, and finance. The heads of these four functions would be located far up the hierarchy, in most cases reporting directly to the general manager at the plant level or the president at corporate level. In an insurance company such as State Farm, departmentalized functions reporting to the president include actuarial, personnel, public relations, claims, underwriting law, and data processing.

Structuring a level of the organization on the basis of product lines is **product departmentalization.** Many communications firms are organized this way, with major departments or divisions for TV production, movie production, music publishing, TV stations, and radio stations. General Motors has divisions for its automotive lines, such as Chevrolet and Cadillac, and for its nonautomotive lines, such as General Motors Acceptance Corporation, which finances auto loans. Other large multiproduct firms such as Procter & Gamble are also organized by product. Large companies such as IBM have moved to product departmentalization in order to create larger numbers of smaller entrepreneurial units. The five departments consist of

FIGURE 8.7
Departmentalization by Product and Function (Portion of Organizational Chart)

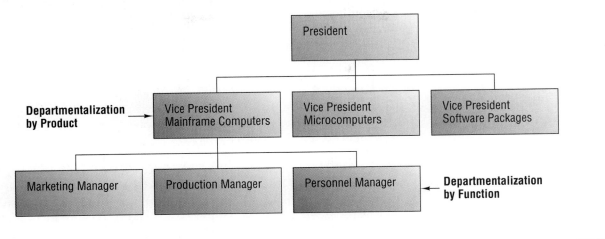

separate, relatively autonomous units for IBM's large, mid-range, and small computers and for its communications and semi-conductor products.

Structuring a level of the organization along territorial lines is **geographic departmentalization.** For example, Dallas-based Southland Corporation has about 7,000 7-Eleven stores grouped into five regions: eastern, central, western, southwestern, and southeastern. Each region is then divided into territories.

The final form, **customer departmentalization,** structures a level of the organization on the basis of customer needs. For example, many banks have departments such as corporate banking, community banking, international banking, real estate lending, and portfolio and investment banking. Each department addresses the needs of a particular group of customers.

Depending on the industry and the nature of the good or service, any one of the departmental arrangements can work well. In fact, most large companies use combinations of them. For example, in a company that uses product departmentalization, the division handling a particular product is typically responsible for producing, marketing, and financing the product line. Within the product division, the organization is based on functional departments. Figure 8.7 illustrates this arrangement.

Types of Organization Structures

When an enterprise adheres to the principles of effective organizing, an overall structure for the organization begins to take shape. While it can take many forms, the structure usually fits one of four basic designs: line, line and staff, functional, or matrix and project. Each type gives management a framework for coordinating overall organizational activity. In practice, most managers prefer to combine types of organizations.

Line Organization Structures   A **line organization structure** is one in which authority flows directly from the top of the organization to the bottom. This structure adheres to the organizing principle known as **unity of**

Geographic departmentalization
The structure of a level of an organization along territorial lines.

Customer departmentalization
The structure of a level of an organization on the basis of customer needs.

Line organization structure
A structure in which authority flows directly from the top of the organization to the bottom.

Unity of command The principle that every person should have only one boss.

command, which holds that every person should have only one boss. Moving from the top of the hierarchy to the bottom, there is a scalar chain of command, meaning that every subordinate is a superior to another subordinate, on down to the lowest member of the enterprise. Every manager has direct control over his or her subordinates. Additionally, department or unit managers have authority over their own operations; they do not share control with other managers.

The line structure offers the advantage of being easy to understand and put into action. Authority and responsibility are clearly spelled out. Everyone has a single boss, so no one is left wondering who gives orders or whom to see with problems or questions. This means that decisions can often be made quickly and efficiently.

Most of the disadvantages of line organizations stem from the heavy responsibilities of the managers. Managers have to be good at handling many different situations, because all problems or decisions come directly to them. Being responsible for every aspect of their unit's operations may also mean that managers are swamped with work. When managers retire or are transferred, it often takes a great deal of time to train replacements and give them the experience necessary to meet the challenges they face each day. In addition, each department or unit is primarily concerned with its own goals and work assignments. Employees pay little attention to what is going on in other areas. When interdepartmental coordination is required, employees often have trouble working with outside groups.

Line-and-staff organization structure A structure in which specialists help those directly responsible for attaining organization objectives.

Line position Those who give orders and make decisions in their area of responsibility.

Staff position Those who give advice and assist the line manager.

Line-and-Staff Organization Structures When companies are relatively small, the line organization can often handle management's needs. As firms get larger, however, they need staff specialists in areas such as personnel management and law. As the enterprise adds these types of specialists, a line-and-staff organization emerges. A **line-and-staff organization structure** is one in which specialists help those directly responsible for attaining organization objectives.

A simple distinction between line and staff positions in an organization is that those holding a **line position** give orders and make decisions in their area of responsibility, while those in a **staff position** give advice and assist the line manager. Although it doesn't always happen in actual practice (except in the military), staff personnel are technically not supposed to give direct orders or make final decisions. Figure 8.8 illustrates what the line-and-staff structure looks like in a manufacturing firm.

Line-and-staff organizations are common in large companies. Several advantages underlie this popularity:

> Skilled professionals are available to provide advice and assistance in areas where the average manager is not particularly knowledgeable.

> Line managers are free to devote their time and energy to producing goods and services. They do not have to be concerned about handling highly specialized matters.

> While the structure is more sophisticated than a line organization, it still follows the principle of unity of command, ensuring a clear line of reporting relationships throughout the structure.

Despite these advantages, the line-and-staff organization may encounter additional tensions and costs. Although technically line managers do not

FIGURE 8.8
Line-and-Staff Organization of a Manufacturing Firm

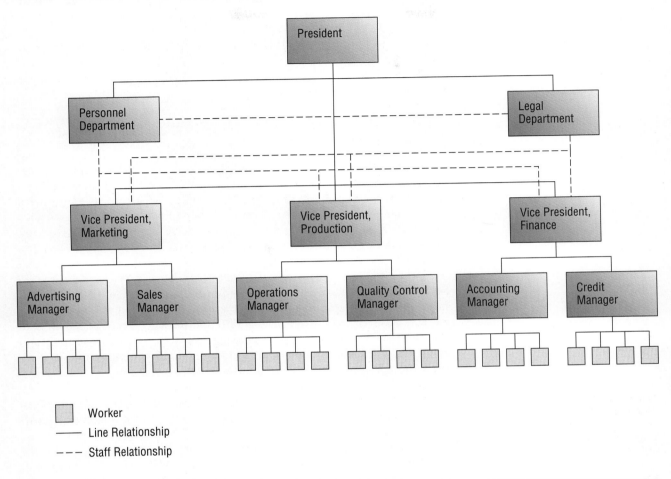

have to accept staff input, they still may resent getting advice from staff people. Staff specialists may come on strong by telling experienced line managers what they are doing wrong and how they should be doing the job. If the staff people give wrong advice, it is the line managers who must bear the ultimate responsibility for the decision, because they are held accountable for results.

Line-staff conflicts can be overcome if staff would sell rather than tell their ideas to line managers. Furthermore, the use of staff specialists can greatly increase the administrative expenses of running the organization. Many large companies in recent years have been cutting back on their staff positions to reduce expenses in the face of economic downturns and improved staff utilization.[20]

Functional Organization Structures In a functional organization structure, specialists are placed in line positions and have the authority to give orders in their areas of expertise. Figure 8.9 illustrates this arrangement.

FIGURE 8.9
Line versus Functional Organizations

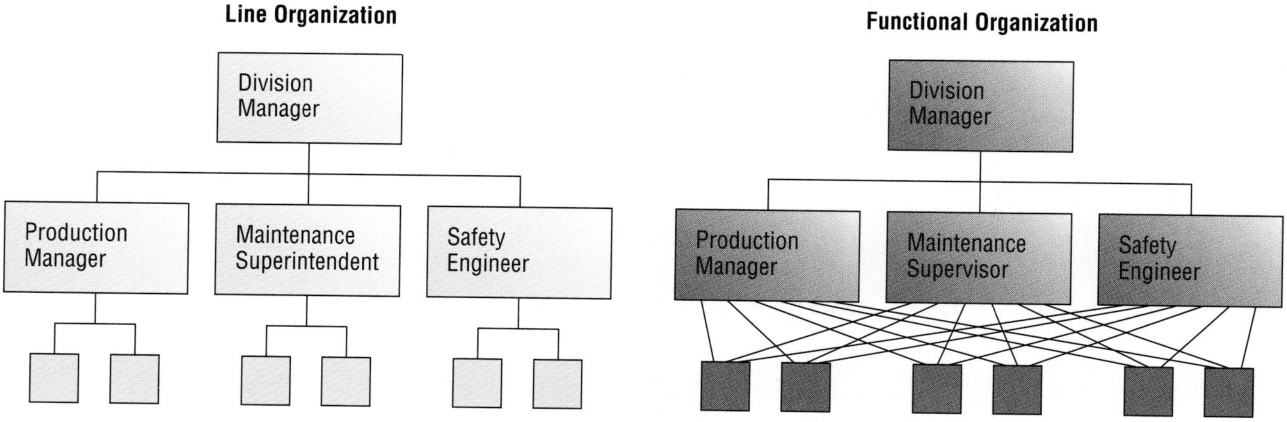

Some managers dislike a functional design because it violates unity of command and so may lead to confusion. For example, in Figure 8.9 each of the workers receives orders from several different managers, each of whom is an expert in his or her area. Conflicting orders may lead to frustration and confusion. Nevertheless, some managers feel that the benefits of this arrangement more than offset its shortcomings.

Project and Matrix Structures   The line, line-and-staff, and functional structures are the traditional types used in most businesses. Recently, however, certain industries have become interested in two newer types: project and matrix structures. A **project organization structure** is formed for the purpose of attaining a particular objective and is then disbanded. For example, a high-tech firm will create a special project team to design a telecommunications satellite. When the team is finished the group members will be reassigned to other work. A **matrix organization structure** combines elements of a line organization with elements of a project organization. These structures were first adopted by, among others, the aerospace industry. Now some large construction firms, such as Bechtel; banks, such as Citibank; and professional service businesses, such as certain accounting and consulting firms, use these matrix forms as well. In a matrix structure people are assigned to a project by their functional department head. As shown in Figure 8.10, the individual now takes orders from and is responsible to both the project manager (the horizontal lines on Figure 8.10) and the functional line department manager (the vertical lines on Figure 8.10). This, of course, violates the principle of unity of command because now the person has two bosses. This can lead to conflict and problems of loyalty and communication breakdown, but some firms feel the trade-off for increased flexibility and responsiveness to change that the matrix structure allows is worth it. For example, projects can be added or eliminated with little disruption to the rest of the organization and, unlike the usual project structures, the matrix struc-

Project organization structure
A structure formed for the purpose of attaining a particular objective and then disbanded.

Matrix organization structure
A structure that combines elements of a line organization with elements of a project organization.

FIGURE 8.10
Matrix Structure of an Aerospace Firm

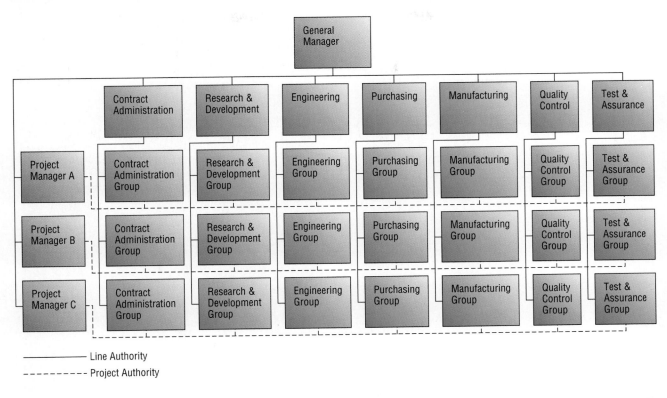

— Line Authority
- - - - - - - - - Project Authority

ture gives the project manager formal authority and a direct line of communication to the specialists on the project team.

Informal Organizations

Through the organizing function described so far, management designs the **formal organization structure,** the explicitly established lines of authority and responsibility. But not all work takes place along formal lines. Often, employees find that using informal channels enables them to avoid red tape, cut across departmental boundaries, and get things done much faster and more efficiently. Research has found that successful managers, those experiencing relatively fast promotions, engage in significantly more of these informal network activities than do their less successful counterparts.[21]

The **informal organization structure** consists of the paths of communication and work created by the personnel themselves, on the basis of friendship and common interests. People who work with each other informally do so because they like each other or because it brings them certain benefits, such as mutual assistance or information. This informal organization exists within the formal organization structure. Rather than boxes on a formal organization chart, the informal organization involves people talking and interacting with each other. The communication part of this network is often called the company's "grapevine." Employees using the grapevine are following

Formal organization structure
The explicitly established lines of authority and responsibility designed by management.

Informal organization structure
The structure created by the personnel on the basis of friendship and common interests.

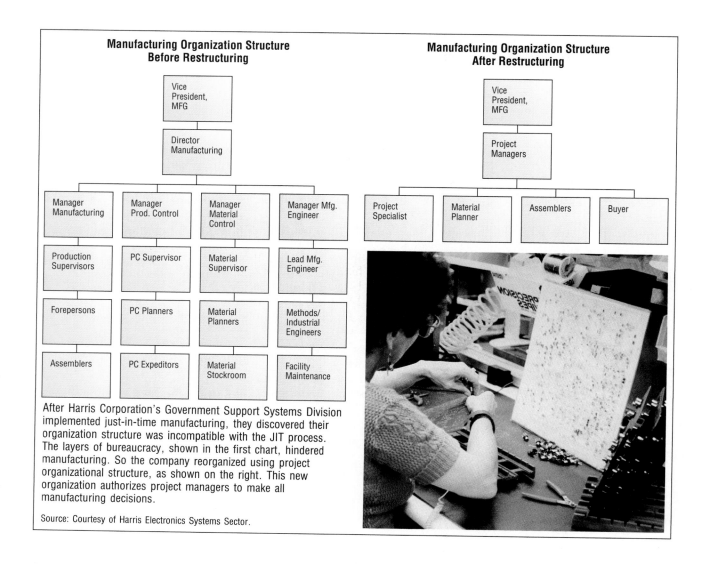

Manufacturing Organization Structure Before Restructuring

- Vice President, MFG
  - Director Manufacturing
    - Manager Manufacturing
      - Production Supervisors
        - Forepersons
          - Assemblers
    - Manager Prod. Control
      - PC Supervisor
        - PC Planners
          - PC Expeditors
    - Manager Material Control
      - Material Supervisor
        - Material Planners
          - Material Stockroom
    - Manager Mfg. Engineer
      - Lead Mfg. Engineer
        - Methods/ Industrial Engineers
          - Facility Maintenance

Manufacturing Organization Structure After Restructuring

- Vice President, MFG
  - Project Managers
    - Project Specialist
    - Material Planner
    - Assemblers
    - Buyer

After Harris Corporation's Government Support Systems Division implemented just-in-time manufacturing, they discovered their organization structure was incompatible with the JIT process. The layers of bureaucracy, shown in the first chart, hindered manufacturing. So the company reorganized using project organizational structure, as shown on the right. This new organization authorizes project managers to make all manufacturing decisions.

Source: Courtesy of Harris Electronics Systems Sector.

CHECK ✓ POINT

lines of communication they established themselves rather than the formal chain of command.

1. What steps do managers follow when they organize?
2. Why do employees create informal organizations?

Directing

The management process is concerned with getting the job done through people. Managers have responsibility for the performance of subordinates. The manager has to see to it that subordinates do their part in helping to achieve the organization's objectives. Managers do this through the function of **directing,** or getting employees to work effectively and efficiently.

Directing today's employees is complex. It involves the two major human relations dimensions, motivating and leading. Because of the com-

Directing Getting human resources to work effectively and efficiently.

plexity of the subject, we investigate motivation and leadership in depth in Chapter 11. For now it can simply be said that, along with planning, organizing, and controlling, directing is usually considered to be one of the major functions of management. However, since it draws mainly on the important human relations skills of the manager, it is given separate, detailed attention in this text.

Controlling

Controlling is the process of comparing actual results against expected performance within a predetermined time. Effective control systems are designed to prevent problems or to catch them early enough so that management can take corrective action.[22] For example, the Marriott Corporation has now dropped its poorly performing restaurant operations and bailed out of some of its hotel partnerships in an effort to deal with the slumping hotel market.[23] Colgate-Palmolive has started boosting earnings by marketing pet food products through veterinarians because profits at this end of the market are much greater than those for similar products sold through supermarkets.[24] The Quill Corporation, the nation's largest mail-order supply store, has sharply reduced its prices in response to competition from Office Depot, BizMart, and other low-price firms.[25]

Controlling, like planning and organizing, begins with setting objectives or standards for performance. Without them, employees will cast about aimlessly, trying to guess what they should be trying to achieve, and any evaluation managers try to make will be arbitrary. Using the initial performance standards, the manager compares the actual performance with the standard. Are salespeople meeting quotas? Are inventories at the target level? Have complaints about customer service dropped to meet goals? If actual performance meets or exceeds the standards, the manager may want to recognize and reward those who are responsible.

If performance falls short of the standards, the manager is responsible for finding ways to correct the problem and to ensure that it does not happen again. This is called feedback control. In addition, effective managers monitor on the "front end"; for example, they carefully watch sales trends, inventories, and machine usage so that they can correct problems before they become serious. This is a proactive approach to control and is sometimes called feedforward control. Seagate Technology, the world's leading manufacturer of hard disk drives for personal computers, was able to use such feedforward control in order to gain a competitive advantage over Japanese rivals.[26] By absorbing the cost of delivery to customers and by guaranteeing delivery within 4 days, Seagate was able to move faster than the competition and prevent customer dissatisfaction for timely needs.

Requirements of Effective Control Systems

To be effective, a control system must be useful, timely, economical, and action oriented. To meet the first requirement, the system must provide the manager with information that is useful and understandable. If managers receive volumes of computer printouts filled with columns of statistics, they aren't likely to know what to do with the information, have time to get through it, or be able to understand it. For example, a manager in a metal-fabricating company received no less than 600 pages of computer printout describing his operation each day. He said it would take him 3 full days to

Controlling Comparing actual results against expected performance within a predetermined time.

A woman shops at T.J. Maxx, the nation's leading off-price retailer. When competitors began an unusually intense promotional campaign, the alert retailer adjusted its advertising and marketing strategy and redirected already budgeted advertising dollars. Effective control systems allowed managers at T.J. Maxx to see the trend early and take action.

Source: Courtesy of The TJX Companies, Inc.

simplify one day's information into understandable, usable form. The manager's solution was to stack the printouts in an empty storage room and subcontract with a trash-removal firm to remove them, untouched, once a month.[27]

The information must also be timely. Daily reports are better than weekly reports, weekly reports are better than monthly ones, and monthly reports are better than quarterly ones. Semiannual and annual reports are necessary for legal purposes and long-range, strategic planning but do little for day-to-day managerial control.

The system must be economical. The benefits it provides should exceed the costs of using it. It makes no sense to install a $50,000 control system that saves the company $50 a year.

The system must lead to corrective action by helping managers identify where the problem areas are and who is responsible for them. Managers can use this information to decide how to correct the problem. This action requirement makes the control system a reality in today's effective organizations.

Useful Control Techniques

In controlling operations, many managers rely heavily on two simple techniques: management by walking around and management by exception.

Management by walking around (MBWA) The management practice of visiting the workplace to find out what is going on.

Management by Walking Around   To practice **management by walking around (MBWA),** managers visit the workplace and find out what is going on with employees and customers. Often they learn more by directly talking to people out on the floor and in the field than they do by studying quality-control reports and other types of formal feedback. For example, top managers of Campbell Soup Company do their own grocery shopping and regularly visit household kitchens to see how meals are prepared. Many retail stores deliberately do not construct an office for the store managers, so they are forced to get out in the store and practice MBWA.

Firsthand information allows managers using MBWA to assess more accurately what is happening and why it is happening. Many times, employees and customers know what is going wrong and how it can be corrected. By actively listening to them, the manager is able to identify problems and formulate corrective actions. For example, the head of 3M notes that: "Our people get close to the market, close to their customers, see what their problems are, and then come back to the laboratories and solve them."[28]

Exception principle The principle that management should concern itself only with significant deviations or exceptions.

Management by Exception   A second control technique is the **exception principle,** which holds that management should concern itself only with significant deviations or exceptions. For example, if the company projects sales of 8,000 units for the month and sells 7,991, the forecast was accurate, and no corrective action is needed. Minor problems do not warrant attention.

On the other hand, major discrepancies do require action. If sales were only 4,300 units, then the manager would want to follow up and find out what had gone wrong. The product may be falling short of customer expectations; the price may be too high; the competition may have increased dramatically; the sales force may not be selling the product properly; the advertising or promotion campaign may have been poorly implemented; or perhaps the standard was set unrealistically high. Whatever the reason, the exception principle calls for an evaluation and correction of the situation.

1. What are the four basic requirements of an effective control system?
2. Describe two ways by which managers can effectively control operations.

Organizational Culture

Managers perform the planning, organizing, directing, and controlling functions within the context of the organization's culture. This culture is all-encompassing. An expert on organizational culture notes:

> The organization itself has an invisible quality — a certain style, a character, a way of doing things — that may be more powerful than the dictates of any one person or any formal system. To understand the soul of the organization requires that we travel below the charts, rule books, machines, and building into the underground world of corporate culture.[29]

More precisely, **organizational culture** consists of the organization's norms, beliefs, attitudes, and values. This culture was initially shaped by the beliefs and values of the entrepreneur who founded the company and is maintained by the managers who follow. In successful companies, these managers shape and encourage the "right" values. The accompanying Innovation Close-Up (American Greetings Meets the Challenge) provides some examples of how this is done.

Organizational culture
An organization's norms, beliefs, attitudes, and values.

Cultural Values

What values are the right ones? Research shows that successful firms share three common cultural characteristics:

1. They stand for something; that is, they have a clear and explicit philosophy of how they should conduct their business.
2. They pay a lot of attention to shaping and encouraging values that conform to the environment in which they operate.
3. These values are known to and shared by the organization's personnel.[30]

Federal Express is often cited as a good example of a company with the right cultural values for success. The dominant values of the culture of this company are customer service and loyalty to the company. Federal Express shapes and encourages these values by *doing* customer service (not just having a slogan) through personalized follow-up and assistance. Management promotes employee loyalty with an up-the-ranks complaint system and by rewarding employee performance. An interesting contrast, and a growing competitor for Federal Express overnight mail, is United Parcel Service. UPS's culture has values of efficiency. The differing cultures of Federal Express and UPS are symbolized by such contrasts as the lively orange and purple colors of Federal Express versus the dull brown trucks and uniforms of UPS, and the easygoing velvet-glove management of Federal Express versus the stopwatch, highly engineered UPS style. Even though they have vastly different cultures, both companies are successful.[31]

Types of Organizational Cultures

One of the easiest ways to describe an organization's culture is in terms of risk and feedback. The decisions managers make can involve high or low risk

C L O S E - U P / *Innovation*

American Greetings Meets the Challenge

Many companies are downsizing their work forces by encouraging early retirement, not hiring new people, and implementing layoffs, and personnel cutbacks. Under these traumatic conditions it can be difficult to keep employees motivated and committed. However, firms like American Greetings are finding that if management shows a genuine concern for the people who remain by redesigning jobs and changing corporate culture, motivation and commitment may not be a problem.

American Greetings is a major greeting card company that recently redesigned almost 400 jobs in its creative division. In the past, the employees in this division focused on one particular aspect of developing greeting cards: design, illustration, lettering, etc. Now employees work in teams that focus on a particular product, and if they want to move to another team they are free to do so. Individuals who for years have specialized in writing Easter or Christmas cards can now transfer to teams that are working on Valentine's Day gift bags or humorous mugs or birthday ribbons. Artists who used to choose dyes can now try their hand at illustration and lettering.

There are a number of reasons for this job redesign. One is that American Greetings does not want to lay off any of the employees. A second is that the firm wants to unleash their employees' creative potential. By allowing them to switch jobs and do those things that appeal to them (in other words, giving people more control over their jobs), the company hopes to tap their creativity. A third reason is that the company is trying to reduce the cost of doing business, and this job redesign approach may cut production costs by as much as 50 percent in some cases. A fourth is to keep employees on board during a time when raises and promotions are going to be less than ever before. The big challenge is going to be convincing employees that they should learn new skills or do new jobs without receiving salary increases.

Although the job redesign approach can be very helpful, the overall culture of American Greetings will have to change if the company hopes to remain competitive. Functional specialization is going to have to give way to interfunctional teamwork, with everyone contributing to the overall good of the company. Sometimes this is easier said than done. Eastman Kodak tried a similar approach and found its profitability declining because workers were unable to quickly change from one job to another.

Only time will tell whether the changes occurring at American Greetings will be successful, but one thing is certain: By getting their employees more involved in all of the aspects of the work, the firm is attacking cultural change at one of its critical cores — the ability to maintain a highly motivated and committed work force in the face of difficult, rapidly changing times.

Source: Joan E. Rigdon, "Using Lateral Moves to Spur Employees," *Wall Street Journal*, May 26, 1992, pp. B 1, B 9.

to the company and the manager's career. Feedback on whether the decisions worked can be fast or slow. Combining these characteristics results in the following four categories of organizational culture.[32]

- The *tough-guy macho culture* is common in organizations such as those in the construction industry, where people have to make high-risk decisions and thrive on fast feedback. Those who do well in this environment are often young and stress speed over endurance. They tend to be individualistic and enjoy winning.

- The *work hard/play hard culture* is characterized by low-risk and fast feedback. Many sales organizations such as insurance agencies or car dealerships fall into this category. Successful people in this organizational culture tend to be team players who are also high achievers.

- The *bet-your-company culture* offers high risk and slow feedback. Firms that have to wait a long time before knowing the outcome of their decisions fall into this category. Examples are oil-well explorers and manufacturers who design and produce expensive, tailor-made equipment. In this culture, successful people tend to be technically competent and able to withstand long-term ambiguity.

- The *process culture* is characterized by low risk and slow feedback. Bureaucratic organizations such as accounting offices or routine manufacturing fall into this category. Successful people in this culture tend to be cautious and to follow the rules meticulously.

How Organizational Culture Develops

Despite their differences, the types of cultures develop and change through similar processes. The process of cultural development is complex. Creation of a culture is based on three important elements: heroes, rites and rituals, and communications networks.

A hero is a role model who embodies the organizational culture — someone employees look up to and admire. The public sees such heroes as representatives of the company. Well-known heroes in today's business world include Fred Smith at Federal Express, Sam Walton at Wal-Mart, and Mary Kay Ash at Mary Kay Cosmetics.

Rites and rituals reinforce desired behavior. Examples are an employee-of-the-month award and an awards dinner at which the company's leading salespeople are honored. Some organizations have even created their own reward rituals. When an employee of the Intel Corporation does a good job, he or she gets a handful of M&Ms as a sign of recognition. The ceremony began years ago, and everyone now keeps a supply of this candy available.

Communications networks are used to keep alive the stories of heroes and to ensure that employees adhere to the corporation's culture. For example, stories about Sam Walton bringing donuts to dockworkers and having a can of tuna fish and crackers for lunch with employees in their lounge are well known throughout the more than 1,200 Wal-Mart stores. The important roles in communications networks are storytellers and organizational priests.

A storyteller is a person who has been around for a long time and who tells stories of the "good old days" to reinforce the organizational culture. While these stories vary from one storyteller to another, the basic themes are usually that hard work will get you ahead and the firm really cares about its people.

An organizational priest helps guard the group's values, keeps everyone together, and offers recommendations for action. These people have usually been around the company for a long time and are familiar with its history. They use this experience to guide other employees. If a new manager has a proposed plan of action, the boss may say, "Check your idea out with Harry." Harry, the organizational priest, will either give the idea his blessing or tell the manager that it will not fly because top management always turns down such ideas. If the priest approves the idea, the manager then proceeds; otherwise the manager drops it.

Changing an Organization's Culture

Sometimes a corporate culture must change. This need for change often arises when the environment changes quickly. For example, Apple Computer was initially able to dominate the personal computer market with a culture stressing innovation. When IBM entered the market, followed by a host of other competitors, Apple tried to compete by selling costlier machines to the business market. The strategy failed. Apple found that in a more competitive environment, it needed a new culture that emphasized marketing. With a changeover in top management, Apple has since shown signs of moving toward a marketing-oriented culture that responds to customer needs.

Culture also must change when a firm starts growing. The culture that worked when a company was small seldom remains the best one. A small company's strong focus on individuality must give way to a concern for the management functions. To remain successful, fast-growing companies, such as Federal Express and Wal-Mart Stores, which had or still have a culture shaped by the founders, have had to change, but not too much or too fast.

Changing an organization's culture usually takes a long time, but managers can guide the process. Experts recommend guidelines such as the following:

- Put a hero in charge of the process.
- Use rituals such as meetings to let people talk about their concerns and to win support for the new values.
- If necessary, bring in outside consultants to help out.
- Ensure that no one is fired as a result of the change. This helps generate further support for the new culture.

CHECK ✓ POINT

1. What are the types of organizational culture?
2. Under what circumstances does an organization's culture need to change?

Closing Comments

This chapter identified the technical, conceptual, and human skills needed for effective modern management. The heart of the chapter described the management functions of planning, organizing, and controlling. Following the steps of the processes outlined in this chapter can simplify management and improve performance. The challenge for managers of today's organizations is to understand and prioritize managerial problems and to apply some of the emerging, proven approaches to planning, organizing, and controlling in a way appropriate to the organization's culture.

VIDEO CASE / Stronger Than Ever

When Joshua Lionel Cowen founded the Lionel Manufacturing Company in 1900, no one realized the impact that this company would have on the toy market. One of the reasons for Cowen's early success was that his model railroad car was operated by an electrical motor, and this was at just the time that homes were being wired for electricity. By 1906 he had developed a transformer to reduce household current to a safe voltage, so model trains no longer needed to use dry cell batteries.

The management history of Lionel is an interesting one in terms of both successes and failures. For example, during the 1920s the company expanded manufacturing facilities and bought out its major competitor. It seemed that nothing could stop the Lionel train. Even the Great Depression hardly slowed up Lionel. During this period the Lionel management team cooperated with Walt Disney to produce a Mickey Mouse handcar that sold a million units at $1 each. Also during this decade the company introduced

the steam whistle and streamlined its products to make them more appealing.

Unfortunately, by the 1950s and 1960s things were turning sour. Management no longer focused exclusively on trains, having become interested in other things. The company was sold to a financier. General Mills eventually bought the company and improved operations but not marketing. In 1986 Lionel was sold to Richard P. Kughn, a Detroit-area real estate entrepreneur. Under his guidance, Lionel has done very well indeed.

In addition to introducing Lionel Classics, which are direct reproductions of trains from the 1920s and 1930s, management is using high technology so that products are more realistic reproductions than ever. The company offers (a) a traditional line, which now includes old-time engines, rolling stock, famous name boxcars, transformers, and trackside accessories; (b) a collector line, which includes operating cars, the Santa Fe passenger series, the GS-2 Daylight Locomotive, and the Chessie Steam Special locomotive and caboose; and (c) the classic line, which includes the Blue Comet train, the #2-400E locomotive and tender, and

racing automobiles. In addition, the company offers a wide assortment of large-scale electric trains and accessories.

The company has reorganized under Kughn so that management includes a chairman of the board, a chief executive officer, a president, and a vice president of sales and marketing. They and other functional managers are responsible for the planning and control of the "new" Lionel Trains, Inc. In particular, these managers are making sure that the firm does not run into the marketing and financial problems it faced back in the 1970s and 1980s. One of the company's overrid-

ing strategic planning goals is to make the name Lionel as popular with today's children as it was with their parents and grandparents. Given that the company is now stronger than ever, this appears to be achievable.

Case Questions

1. What types of managerial skills do the senior Lionel managers need in order to keep the company healthy? Explain.
2. Describe two things Lionel is doing to take advantage of new opportunities in the environment
3. How can management use the control process to more effectively run the firm? Provide an example.

Learning Objectives Revisited

1. **Explain what skills are involved in the management process.** Management is the process of setting objectives and coordinating employees' efforts in attaining them. It consists of planning, organizing, directing, and controlling. While all managers use technical, human relations, and conceptual skills, the nature of the job changes by level in the company hierarchy. Technical skills are relatively more important at the lowest level of management, but the conceptual and human relations skills are also important. At middle management levels, the three managerial skills are about equally weighted. At top management levels, the conceptual and, secondarily, the human relations skills take on relatively more importance, while the technical become relatively less important.

2. **Present the dimensions of the management function of planning.** The planning function of management involves setting objectives and formulating the steps to follow in attaining them. This involves being aware of an opportunity, establishing objectives, choosing alternative courses of action, formulating the derivative plan, and budgeting the plan. Many firms today conduct their formal planning with the management by objectives (MBO) approach.

3. **Describe the principles of the management function of organizing.** Organizing involves efficiently bringing together human and material resources to attain objectives. The steps involved are formulating or-

ganizational goals and objectives; coordinating work; delegating authority; shaping a tall or flat structure; and departmentalizing the structure along functional, product, geographic, or customer lines. The resulting structure may be a line organization, a line-and-staff organization, a functional organization, a project organization, or a matrix organization, which combines elements of line and project organizations.

4. **Analyze how an informal organization works.** Unlike the formal organization, which is designed by management, the informal organization is created by personnel on the basis of friendship and common interests. It consists of people interacting and communicating with one another outside the formal organization structure. Research indicates that successful managers use the informal network.

5. **Discuss the various aspects of the management function of controlling.** Controlling involves establishing initial performance standards, measuring actual performance, determining whether the performance was adequate, and taking corrective action if performance has been inadequate.

6. **Identify characteristics of organizational culture and ways to change it.** Modern management functions within the context of the organization's culture. This culture contains the organization's norms, beliefs, attitudes, and values. The four types of culture are tough-guy macho (high risk and fast feedback),

work hard/play hard (low risk and fast feedback), bet-your-company (high risk and slow feedback), and process (low risk and slow feedback). Managers can change an organization's culture in a number of ways, including putting a hero in charge of the pro-cess; using rituals such as meetings to let people talk about their concerns and to win support for the new values; bringing in outside consultants to help if needed; and ensuring that no one is fired as a result of the change.

Key Terms Reviewed

Review each of the following terms. For any that you do not know or are unsure of, look up the definitions and see how they were used in the chapter.

management
planning
strategic objectives
strategic plan
operational objectives
operational plan
derivative plan
management by objectives (MBO)
organizing
coordination
authority
delegation
centralization

decentralization
span of control
tall structure
flat structure
departmentalization
functional departmentalization
product departmentalization
geographic departmentalization
customer departmentalization
line organization structure
unity of command
line-and-staff organization
    structure

line position
staff position
project organization structure
matrix organization structure
formal organization structure
informal organization structure
directing
controlling
management by walking around
    (MBWA)
exception principle
organizational culture

Review Questions

1. Jose is an upper level executive, Pat is a middle manager, and Frank is a supervisor. What management skills does each need to be effective? Is there any difference in the importance of these skills for the three managers?

2. Priscilla Hanley is president of a cellular telephone manufacturing firm. What are two strategic objectives in which she would be interested? Operational objectives?

3. Why is organizing important in a retail store? A bank? An insurance firm?

4. Christina King works in the payroll department of a corporation with six divisions. Two weeks ago, Christina's boss said, "You've been doing a great job, and I think you're ready to take on something else. From now on, each Friday I want you to follow up with each division to make sure they get their time sheets in by 2 o'clock." When Friday came, Christina found that she had a difficult time persuading two division administrators to turn in the time sheets by the deadline. When she talked to her boss, he said, "It's up to you to take care of that

now." Does Christina have authority? Does she have responsibility? Why or why not? Has Christina's boss followed the principles of delegating? Explain.

5. How do managers decide on a shape for the organization's structure?

6. What is unity of command? Which organization structures adhere to this principle? Which do not?

7. How does a matrix organization work? Would it be a suitable arrangement for a store with 10 employees? Why or why not?

8. How are informal organizations created? How can lower level operating employees benefit from them? How can upper level managers benefit from them?

9. Pete Maahs is the president of Wonderful Home Improvement Company. He has hired a consultant to develop a control system for his business. Pete has always thought that consultants only give answers and don't ask questions, so he was surprised when his consultant asked him what criteria the control system should meet. Pete said he'd think it

over and give the consultant some specifications the next day. What requirements should Pete ask for?

10. What is the exception principle? How can managers use this principle to control operations?

11. Over the past 5 years IBM has encountered much more competition. In what way does this development influence the company's culture?

Applied Exercise

Each of the statements below describes an individual who is very successful in his or her organization. Based on the information provided, determine the organizational culture in which the person is working by using the following key:

T = tough-guy macho culture   B = bet-your-company culture
W = work hard/play hard culture   P = process culture

___ 1. Mary is well known for her work in designing and building sophisticated computer systems.
___ 2. Sam is a very successful car dealer.
___ 3. Tim has made millions in the construction industry and intends to make even more.
___ 4. Paula enjoys her job as a mail sorter.
___ 5. Harry is a very effective door-to-door vacuum cleaner salesman.
___ 6. Regina is highly individualistic and enjoys winning big.
___ 7. Robert takes incoming bills and posts them in the accounting ledger.
___ 8. Helen designs complex telecommunication satellites that cost millions of dollars.

YOU BE THE ADVISER / *An Expansion Proposal*

The Merkoff Corporation was founded over 80 years ago when a group of wildcatters pooled their funds and drilled for oil in Oklahoma. Their first well was one of the biggest in the region, and the Merkoff brothers not only became rich but took their early profits and used them to buy out the rest of the group. Since then, the Merkoffs have been in the business of oil exploration and drilling.

Over the past 3 years, the family members who now run the company have been thinking about expanding its scope of operations. They would like to do more than just discover oil and sell it to the large refiners. They would like to buy some refineries and a large number of service stations and move the oil from the ground right through to the final user. Although it will cost approximately $1 billion to implement this plan, the chief financial officer for the corporation has reported that the necessary financing can be arranged. It is now up to the board of directors to decide whether to go ahead.

Management believes that a number of steps are necessary before it approves the plan. Most important is to anticipate how this change will affect the current organization. "We're going to be getting into new areas, and this will mean having to hire plenty of personnel, while still hanging on to the ones we have now," the chairman of the board reminded the other members. "Also, it will mean a major revision in our strategic plan and the need to control operations in a lot more than the five states where we now operate. Before we do anything, I think we need to discuss the impact of the change." The other board members agreed.

Your Advice

1. What should Merkoff do?
   ___ a. Do not proceed with the plan to expand operations.
   ___ b. Drop the oil exploration side of the business and move into refineries and service stations.
   ___ c. Keep the oil exploration business and expand into refineries and service stations.

2. If you were a member of the board, how would you describe the company's current organization structure? How would you describe the organization's culture? How will this culture change if it expands into the proposed new areas? Explain.

3. What types of objectives would you expect the Merkoff Corporation to be pursuing in its strategic and operational plans? How would these objectives change if it expanded into the proposed new areas? Explain.

4. Would management by objectives be of any value to this firm if it decided to pursue its acquisition plans? What would be the steps they would follow to implement MBO?

5. Could the control mechanisms of MBWA and/or management by exception be used by Merkoff's managers in this business? How?

MANUFACTURING A TEXTBOOK

Most people would guess that the publisher of books such as this one is also the manufacturer. In truth, very few publishers today manufacture their own books. Costs are far too great to justify gearing up and running a printing and binding operation for the relatively small number of books that one publisher would have. Instead, most publishers send the type and artwork prepared from their manuscripts to firms such as R.R. Donnelley, the largest U.S.

Managing Production and Service Operations

9

Chapter Learning Objectives

- Describe the operations system.

- Examine the specifics of operations planning and scheduling.

- Identify the important factors of facility location and layout.

- Discuss the automatic factory.

- Explain the important dimensions of purchasing and inventory control.

- Discuss quality control in manufacturing and service industries.

printing company. Donnelley has both the equipment and the personnel expertise to manufacture books more cheaply than a typical publishing house.

Headquartered in Chicago, Donnelley manufactures countless hardcover and softcover books at plants across the United States and in England, Scotland, Mexico, and Hong Kong. High-tech machines allow it to manufacture high-quality output at very rapid speed. Continuous paper feed, for example,

allows thousands of pages to be printed every hour without having to stop the press to put in new rolls of paper. The printed ribbons of paper are heated to dry the ink, then cut into groups of pages, automatically folded, and gathered in correct order so that they are ready for binding. Hard covers, such as the one on this book, are made separately and joined to the gathered pages. The completed books are put in cartons, and the cartons are stacked on pallets, ready

to be shipped. In capsule form, this is the book manufacturing process.

Most publishing houses would not be able to break even if they printed their own books. However, Donnelley has the facilities, the people, and the volume to promise continued success as the major U.S. book manufacturing firm for some time to come.

Photo Source: © Randy Duchaine/The Stock Market.

213

Introduction

Turning out a product or service involves broad responsibility. It means paying attention to profits, product design, scheduling, facility location and layout, inventory control, quality control, and even whether robots are worth their keep. Operations managers are key players in seeing that customers receive what they want when they want it — and that the company makes money in the process. This chapter uses the overall management process discussed in Chapter 8 as a point of departure to emphasize and focus on managing operations.

Nature of Operations

The Industrial Revolution, which began toward the end of the 18th century in the textile mills of Great Britain, revolutionized the way goods were produced and dramatically altered the way people lived. In particular, the factory system of work employed millions of people and provided mass-produced, standardized, inexpensive goods. Today, the economy of every developed country depends heavily on the production of both goods and services.

Components of the Operations System

Operations The process of transforming inputs such as raw materials and labor into outputs, or finished products or services.

Input Any resource needed to produce a desired good or service.

As illustrated in Figure 9.1, **operations** consist of three distinct components: input, transformation process, and output. An **input** is any resource needed to produce a desired good or service. The figure shows some typical inputs for a restaurant (chefs, equipment, and food) and a manufacturing plant (raw materials, workers, and managers). As will be shown throughout the chapter, managing operations of service organizations is as important as manufacturing organizations. Thus, in a bank, input includes money, managers, tellers, computers, and a building. For colleges, which are another type of service organization, the inputs consist of professors, students, administrators, a library, and classrooms. In general, the inputs consist of raw materials and other resources.

Transformation process Those activities that change inputs into the desired outputs.

The **transformation process** consists of activities that change the inputs into the desired outputs. This is the heart of operations. In Figure 9.1, some of the activities included in the transformation process for a restaurant are waiting on customers and cooking and serving food; for a manufacturing plant, drilling, assembling, and inspecting. In a bank, this process includes waiting on customers, accepting deposits, making loans, investing funds, and keeping records. At a college, this process involves registering students, giving lectures, assigning work to students, administering tests, and carrying out student-professor interactions.

Output The finished good or service that results from the production process.

An **output** is the finished good or service that results from the transformation process. Figure 9.1 shows that the output of a restaurant is a well-fed diner; for a manufacturing plant it is a finished product. For a bank, the output is a satisfied depositor and/or borrower. For a college, it is an educated student.

The output of one business may be the input of another. For example, a steel company might convert iron ore (input) into steel auto bodies (output).

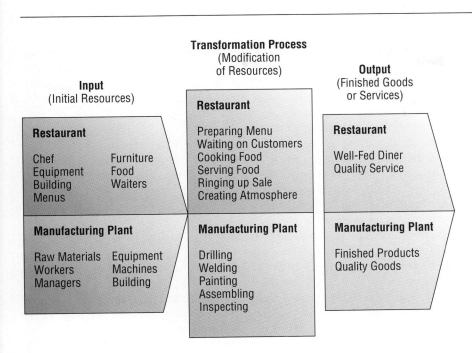

FIGURE 9.1
The Operations System

This output for the steel firm will become an input for the auto manufacturer, which is producing a totally assembled car. Unfortunately, another output of the steel company may be air pollution. As Chapter 6 discussed, socially responsible firms attempt to minimize such undesirable outcomes of their production processes.

Technological Development

Technology and research and development modify the operations system. Engineers are designing new machines that can do the work of many people and do it more cheaply and efficiently. Recently, a number of businesses have adopted computer-integrated manufacturing, in which machines and robots perform many of the activities previously carried out by people. The robot frame can do the work of a human arm, and its microprocessor (a computer) can substitute for a human brain. For example, in automobile manufacturing, robots have been programmed to weld, assemble, paint, lift, dip, inspect, and carry parts.

Most manufacturing facilities are quite small, and advanced technological developments such as robotics will have less impact on their operations.[1] Nevertheless, even these small firms will be able to profit from using some of the latest developments on a piecemeal basis;[2] they need not rip out all of the machines and replace them with state-of-the-art technology.

CHECK ✓ POINT

1. What are the three components of the operations system?
2. Does operations management apply to services, or only to goods produced in a factory?

Operations Planning

Operations planning The process whereby managers determine the most profitable way to produce the goods and services the company will sell.

Through **operations planning,** managers determine the most profitable way to produce the goods and services the company will sell. As you have already learned, long-term profitability depends on keeping productivity and quality high and costs low.

Profitability and Breakeven Analysis

Whether a good or service is new or already part of the firm's offerings, management must determine how much it can produce profitably. One way to determine this is to calculate the breakeven point. The **breakeven point** is the level of production at which total revenues from selling the products equal total expenses incurred in making them. The firm neither makes nor loses money at the breakeven point.

Breakeven point The level of production at which total revenues from selling the products equal total expenses incurred in making them.

Determining the breakeven point for a particular product requires knowledge of fixed costs, variable costs, and selling price. The product manager has cost information and can obtain price information from the marketing department.

In the short run, certain expenses remain the same, regardless of how many units the firm produces. These expenses are *fixed costs*. An example is insurance on the building. Whether the company operates 80 percent of its machines or all of them, and no matter how much raw material it uses, it must still pay its insurance premium. The same is true for property taxes; they do not depend on how many units the firm produces.

The expenses that change in relation to output are *variable costs*. If production goes down, these expenses drop; if production goes up, these expenses rise. An example of a variable cost is raw material. The more units the firm produces, the greater its expense for raw material. The same is true for labor. If the firm adds individual workers or a second shift to produce more, its labor expenses will rise.

The price at which the firm sells the goods is the selling price. The higher the selling price, the fewer goods the company has to sell to reach breakeven.

Calculating the Breakeven Point   The manager enters this information into an equation to compute the breakeven point. As an example, assume that the fixed cost for a particular product line is $100,000, the selling price per unit is $50, and the variable cost is $25. Here's how to arrive at the breakeven point in units:

$$\text{Breakeven point} = \frac{\text{Fixed cost}}{\text{Selling price} - \text{Variable cost}}$$

$$= \frac{\$100,000}{\$50/\text{unit} - \$25/\text{unit}}$$

$$= \frac{\$100,000}{\$25/\text{unit}}$$

$$= 4,000 \text{ units}$$

FIGURE 9.2
Finding a Breakeven Point

Price/Cost and Revenues

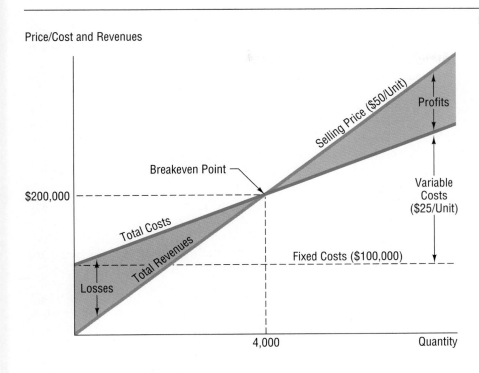

Of course, a business is unlikely to produce a good or service just to
break even; a business needs to make a profit in order to grow, to provide a
decent return to the owners, and, as Chapter 1 pointed out, to survive in a
market economy such as that existing in the United States. In the above
example, forecasted demand will thus have to be greater than 4,000 units for
the company to profit. Perhaps the firm will set 4,400 as the minimum for
this product line. At this point, the company will make a total profit of
$10,000 (4,400 units at the selling price of $50 per unit minus the $100,000
fixed cost and the variable cost of $25 per unit times 4,400 units).

The company must sell 4,000 units to break even on this product line. At this
level of production, it has revenures of 4,000 units × $50/unit, or $200,000.
Its expenses are 4,000 units × $25/unit in variable expenses plus $100,000 in
fixed expenses, or a total of $200,000. Thus revenues and expenses are equal.
Figure 9.2 graphs the relationship of these variables to the breakeven point.

How Companies Use Breakeven Analysis   In the past decade, Chrysler
effectively used breakeven analysis to bring itself back from the edge of bankruptcy. Under the leadership of Lee Iacocca, this company dramatically reduced its costs by closing inefficient factories, reducing wages and salaries,
laying off personnel, and reducing its inventory levels. The result: Chrysler
was able to break even at a lower sales level. The struggling auto firm began
losing market share in the early 1990s[3] and may have to use the same approach in the years ahead in order to survive. Other well-known U.S. firms
such as AT&T, IBM, United Airlines, Citibank, and Sears have reduced
their costs by downsizing (laying off personnel and closing facilities).[4]

There are other ways to reach breakeven besides letting people go through downsizing. For example, at Affiliated Computer Systems, which provides a variety of data processing services, breakeven was reduced by purchasing mainframe computers and automated teller networks from savings and loan institutions that were in trouble.[5] Southwestern Bell was able to garner over 300,000 cellular customers and, while most competitors were losing money in this part of the business, it passed breakeven and operated at a profit.[6] In other words, layoffs and cutbacks aren't the only way to reach breakeven. Most managers try to keep control over costs with efficient designs for products and improved production facilities and techniques.

Product Design

Besides helping the company plan how much it can produce profitably, operations managers participate in the design of products. Based on information about what customers want, operations personnel determine how to make a product that meets the demand. Some companies design new products infrequently; others, such as Hewlett-Packard, design several a week.

Product design The process of deciding the specific dimensions of the good or service to be produced.

The process of deciding the specific dimensions of the good or service to be produced is referred to as **product design.** For example, restaurant managers would design the menu, the decor, special services such as valet parking or a wine steward, and standards for the food and service. Designers of waterbed liners would take into account size, durability, and the functions the liners perform. A well-designed product can save management millions of dollars in product recalls or changes.

Value engineering The evaluation of new products and the application of research and development to design the highest quality, lowest priced output.

The two areas of design that many successful firms emphasize today are value engineering and value analysis. **Value engineering** is the evaluation of new products and the application of research and development to design the highest quality, lowest priced output. Value engineering is extremely important when a new product is on the drawing board.[7] A good example is provided by Cincinnati Milacrin, which developed an injection molding machine that was faster, more flexible, easier to assemble, and 40 percent cheaper than the previous model. The machine sold 2.5 times as many units in its first year of production as its predecessor had done in its best year.[8]

Value analysis The evaluation of current products to determine how they can be improved.

On the other hand, **value analysis** is the evaluation of current products to determine how they can be improved.[9] For example, manufacturers of liquid detergent redesigned their containers with a handle so that they are much easier to carry. Brewers now use snap-top beer cans and twist-off caps on bottles, making the can opener obsolete. IBM has designed a new printer that has fewer parts so it is easier to assemble and to service.[10] LSI Logic makes semifinished computer chips that require only a few last-minute instructions to be customized and ready to go.[11] These companies know that for every dollar spent on value engineering and analysis, they get a considerable return or value added to their products, and eventually their profits.

Another development in product design is computer-aided design (CAD). Using CAD, engineers are now able to produce blueprints by drawing directly on the computer screen and then ordering the computer to provide them with a copy of the design. They can also leave the design on the screen and have the computer rotate the drawing, stretch it out, produce a three-dimensional version of it, or even color or shade it in. A graphic approach called CAID (computer-aided industrial design) can produce free-form designs by artists or architects without technical training. Whereas CAD has revolutionized high-tech product design in manufacturing, CAID has revolutionized packaging and styling. Architectural firms of all sizes now use both CAD and CAID.

1. What is a breakeven point?
2. What are two techniques that help production department personnel design quality products?

C H E C K ✓ P O I N T

Production Scheduling

Once they have planned what to produce, operations managers formulate a master production schedule. A **master production schedule** coordinates all of the raw materials, parts, equipment, manufacturing processes, and assembly operations necessary to produce the goods. This schedule helps everyone involved keep track of what is to be done and when. It also provides a basis for making changes should something go wrong. For example, if there is a power outage in one area, can the materials be sent to another area and processed on those machines? The answer is on the master schedule. It will tell whether the other area can accommodate the extra work.

In developing and maintaining a production schedule, managers often depend on specific production-scheduling techniques. Two of the most widely recognized and used are Gantt charts and PERT networks.

The Use of Gantt Charts

While many types of charts and graphs are suitable for production scheduling, the oldest and still most popular is the Gantt chart. Developed by Henry Gantt, a pioneering expert in scientific management, the **Gantt chart** is a tool for production scheduling and control that keeps track of projected and actual work progress over time.

Figure 9.3 provides an example of a Gantt chart. One of the reasons such charts are so popular is that they allow management to determine the status of work progress merely by looking at the chart. Based on this feedback, the operations manager can decide how to make up lost time on those jobs that have fallen behind and what new jobs to assign to those who have finished their current job orders.

Networking Techniques

When a project becomes more complex, requiring simultaneous scheduling, Gantt charts are no longer adequate. The manager needs to use networking techniques linking the activities of many areas. One of the best known is the **program evaluation and review technique (PERT).** This planning and control tool is useful on projects requiring considerable coordination. For instance, if five or more different jobs must be coordinated in producing a finished product, it may be difficult to determine the overall status of the entire project. PERT enables the manager to do this.

Figure 9.4 shows a sample PERT chart in which five parts (A through E) must eventually be assembled into a finished product. You may have followed a similar scheduling process yourself if you've ever made a Thanksgiving dinner. You identify the tasks you need to do: roast the turkey, bake the

Master production schedule
A plan that coordinates all of the raw materials, parts, equipment, manufacturing processes, and assembly operations necessary to produce goods.

Gantt chart   A tool for production scheduling and control that keeps track of projected and actual work progress over time.

Program evaluation and review technique (PERT)   A planning and control tool useful on complex projects requiring coordination.

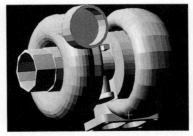

Mercedes-Benz engineers created this surface model of a turbocharger using computer-aided design (CAD). The advantages of CAD over traditional design techniques are flexibility and speed. With a few keystrokes the designer can rotate the part design on any axis, zoom in to see details or back off to see the whole object, change the scale or revise the design, and test its functioning.

FIGURE 9.3
A Gantt Chart

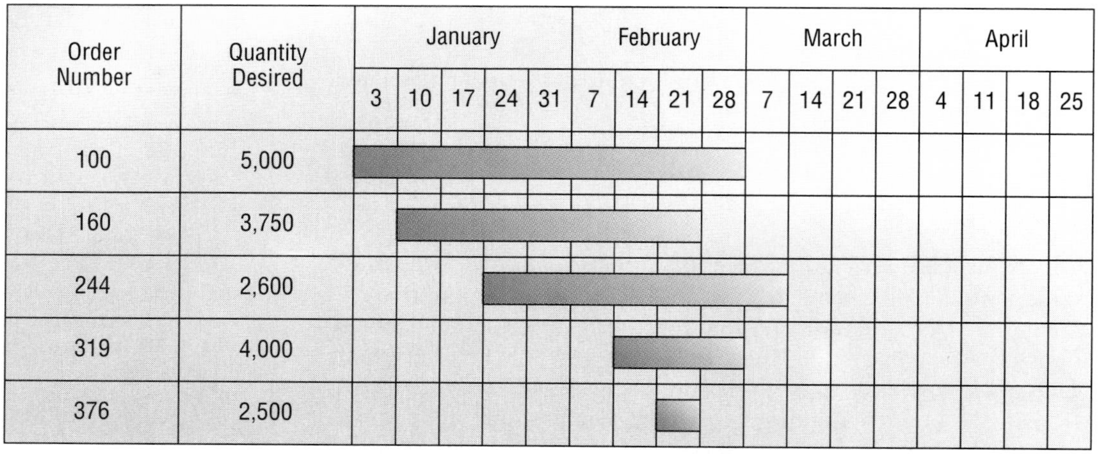

Order Number	Quantity Desired	January					February				March				April			
		3	10	17	24	31	7	14	21	28	7	14	21	28	4	11	18	25
100	5,000																	
160	3,750																	
244	2,600																	
319	4,000																	
376	2,500																	

pies, prepare the side dishes. Then you try to start each one of them at the right time to have everything ready to eat at a specified time. If you want to eat at 4:00 p.m. and the turkey will take 6 hours, you know you have to have it stuffed and in the oven by 9:30 a.m. (allowing it half an hour for cooling and slicing). That means you have to start making the stuffing even earlier, say, at 9:00 a.m. Then perhaps you make a salad at 2:30 p.m., start the potatoes at 3:00 p.m., and cook some peas at 3:30 p.m. Working within a specific time frame, you have juggled many tasks to create a finished product — Thanksgiving dinner. Operations managers follow a similar, though more complex, process to schedule the manufacture of many products.

An important piece of information managers uncover with PERT is the **critical path.** This is the longest possible time the project will take. To determine the critical path, simply add up the time required to follow the longest sequence or path. In Figure 9.4 the critical path is the one that runs through the middle of the project and begins with making part C. (You can check this by adding all of the other paths and comparing the time totals.) In the case of preparing Thanksgiving dinner, the critical path is the 7 hours required to stuff, roast, and slice the turkey. Notice that you planned your other tasks around this one.

As long as this critical path takes no more time than is allowed for the overall project, the project will be completed on time or ahead of schedule. If progress along the critical path falls behind, the manager can take people off the shorter paths and have them help out with the activities along the critical path. Thus PERT helps management keep control over the project and reallocate equipment, materials, and people should it be necessary to prevent the project from coming in late.

Critical path The sequence of activities that identifies the longest possible time a project will take.

CHECK ✓ POINT

1.   What are the two major production scheduling techniques?
2.   If you were in charge of a complex project requiring simultaneous scheduling, what production scheduling technique would you use?

FIGURE 9.4
A Simple PERT Diagram

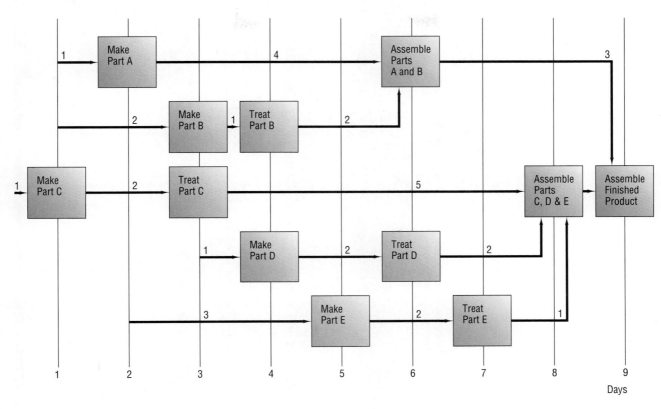

Location of the Facility

The location of the facility is another important variable in the operations function. Location of the manufacturing plant or other business facility can often mean the difference between profit and loss. For example, a company that makes bricks should be located near its customers, because the cost of shipping such a heavy but inexpensive product is great. Aluminum and chemical companies should locate in areas where there is sufficient electric power, because they need a great deal of energy to make their products. Service firms should be located near related services. For example, a public accounting office may locate in, or near, a bank; a doctor's office may want to be next to a hospital; and a real estate office might be near a law office.

There are three location factors that are especially critical: proximity to customers, raw materials, and a labor supply. Proximity to customers is a key consideration for most businesses. For example, Ford assembly plants are placed near population centers so that the finished cars can be shipped only a short distance to the dealers. Most service businesses try to locate near customers because production of a service usually involves interaction with

To encourage businesses to locate in Iowa, the state's Department of Economic Development ran this ad in business magazines. Here winning a race is a metaphor for making a profit in business. By describing the state's workforce and living conditions, and by appealing to business owners' need for quality, the ad suggests that locating in Iowa will make businesses winners.

Source: Courtesy of Iowa Department of Economic Development.

YOUR BUSINESS WINS WITH IOWA QUALITY

In the race for profit, Iowa quality gives business the winning margin.

Iowa winners, including **Amana, Maytag** and **Winnebago,** credit their success to **Iowa's quality work force** — the third most productive in the nation, according to the U.S. Department of Commerce.

Productivity begins in the classroom. And, **in Iowa, public education is synonymous with Iowa quality.** Iowa sets the pace with 93% of the state's schools running ahead of the national average in scholastic achievement.

Iowa quality continues after the race is won, with an easy living lifestyle, renowned for uncongested cities and a crime rate that runs 62% behind the national average.

For **free, confidential** site selection information, call Bob Henningsen at the Iowa Department of Economic Development: **1-800-245-IOWA.** In Iowa, call **1-515-281-3000.** Or, write to 200 East Grand Avenue, Des Moines, Iowa 50309.

IOWA
THE TIME IS RIGHT

the customer. If you need a tooth filled, you cannot simply request the dentist to ship you a filling via UPS.

A second key location factor is raw materials. If the raw materials are very heavy, the company will tend to locate near them. For example, steel mills have located in the Pittsburgh area because the coal needed to process the iron ore is near there. The same is true of perishable raw materials. For example, fruit and vegetable canneries must locate near the fields and fish canneries near the harbors.

Producers who need a large or specialized trained labor force may locate near the labor supply. For example, high-tech firms have tended to set up business in California's Silicon Valley, in the Boston area, or around Austin, Texas, because these areas are sources of engineers and scientists. It is easier to attract these well-educated technical people by moving into their area than it is to try to persuade them to move across the country. In order to attract workers, many businesses locate in or near a community that is pleasant to live in. Businesses look for an environment that will provide their employees with good educational, cultural, religious, and medical facilities.

Other location considerations include proximity to sources of power and water, the availability of transportation facilities, and the rules and policies of the community. If the operation draws heavily on power and water, the company may decide to locate near those resources. For example, companies that make chemical fertilizers need to be near abundant, cheap sources of power. Paper companies locate near rivers because of the tremendous amount of water needed to produce paper.

Transportation is another location factor that must be considered. Companies depend on transportation facilities to ship raw materials to the plant and finished goods to customers. When many sources of transportation are available, the competition between them is likely to keep prices down. Even a company with its own trucks needs to consider whether it has easy access to highways. Businesses that provide services try to locate near parking facilities and public transportation.

The rules and policies of various communities also influence the location decision. Zoning ordinances restrict where commercial, industrial and service firms such as a bar or a movie theatre may operate. Some cities or townships have policies discouraging growth. However, the vast majority of cities and states have tried to attract businesses. Sometimes the government offers to let the business pay low (or even no) taxes for a period of time to help finance the operation. The government may even provide free or very inexpensive land for the facility. With all communities and states interested in creating jobs, the location alternatives are becoming increasingly attractive.

1. What are three factors that should be considered in locating a facility?
2. What considerations might apply more specifically to service businesses?

CHECK ✔ POINT

Layout of the Facility

Layout of the facility is important to service operations. For example, a bank needs some departments open and accessible to customers and others closed and private. Also, a key to successful retailing is to arrange the store's shelving and aisles to accommodate and control traffic patterns and security. Most attention, however, has been given to the layout of manufacturing facilities. The layout depends on the type and sequence of manufacturing processes used and determines the flows that the goods take through the plant.

Manufacturing Processes

In determining an appropriate plant layout, the operations manager considers how the goods are to be produced. The two most common manufacturing processes are analytic and synthetic.

Analytic Process   An **analytic manufacturing process** is one that reduces a raw material to its component parts for the purpose of obtaining one or

Analytic manufacturing process
A process that reduces a raw material to its component parts for the purpose of obtaining one or more products.

FIGURE 9.5
The Analytic Process: Crude Oil and Its Products

Crude Oil

more products. Texaco, Phillips Petroleum, Exxon, and other big oil refiners use an analytic process in converting crude oil into gasoline and a host of other oil-related products. "Cracking" the crude, as shown in Figure 9.5, produces a number of by-products. The same type of process is used in meat-packing firms such as Iowa Beef Processors, where cattle are slaughtered for food. The company obtains animal hides, which can be used for making clothing and sporting goods (baseball gloves, for example), as well as hooves and horns, which can be used for making glue. Mining firms also employ an analytic production process to separate ore from dirt and other useless materials.

Synthetic Process   A second manufacturing process relevant to how the plant is laid out is the **synthetic manufacturing process.** This process converts a number of raw materials or parts into a finished product. It often uses fabrication or modification. **Fabrication** is the combining of materials or parts in order to form or assemble them into a finished product. A Chevrolet assembly plant uses fabrication when it takes the components shown in Figure 9.6 and creates a finished car. **Modification** is the process of changing raw materials into a product. An example is when USX takes iron ore and changes it into steel rods or pipes.

Production Sequences

In addition to the manufacturing processes, efficient plant layout also depends on the sequence in which the production activities are carried out. For example, the product being built may move along a conveyor belt to the workers, or it may stay in one place while the workers move. Each sequence requires a different type of layout. The two most common types of production sequences are continuous and intermittent.

Continuous Production   Firms producing a standardized, high-volume good use **continuous production,** which is the steady, constant flow of

Synthetic manufacturing process
A process that converts a number of raw materials or parts into a finished product.

Fabrication Combining materials or parts in order to form or assemble them into a finished product.

Modification The process of changing raw materials into a product.

Continuous production
A production sequence in which the flow of materials is steady and constant.

FIGURE 9.6
The Synthetic Process: Auto Assembly

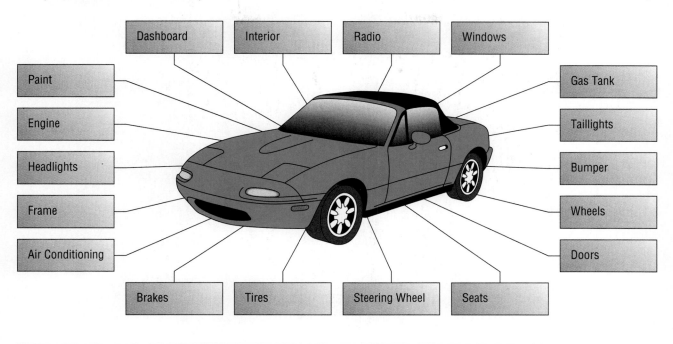

materials. The automobile production line is perhaps the best example. In these plants, autos just keep coming down the line, hour after hour, day after day. Many General Electric plants use the same production process in producing consumer products such as washing machines. White Consolidated uses this process in turning out refrigerators. Companies use this production sequence when producing for immediate demand or when warehousing the goods to meet future demand.

Intermittent Production   In the second type of sequence, **intermittent production,** the flow of materials is noncontinuous. This production sequence is used for making one-of-a-kind products or small batches of output. A one-of-a-kind item would be a communications satellite that is specially designed to handle certain types of communication transmissions. An example of small batches is production of ten locomotives designed to haul freight. The intermittent production sequence is used for handling specific customer orders.

Materials Flow
After operations management determines the production processes and sequences, they lay out the flow the materials will take. There are two major possibilities, downward processing and horizontal flow.

Downward Processing   In **downward processing,** different parts of the same product are produced on different levels or floors of the facility. Where

Intermittent production
A production sequence in which the flow of materials is noncontinuous.

Downward processing
A materials flow in which different parts of the same product are produced on different floors.

A Cooper Industries employee checks Crouse-Hinds® high-volume circuit breakers being assembled as they move along a conveyor. This continuous production process is suitable for producing a large volume of goods of consistent size, shape, quality, and quantity.

Source: Courtesy of Cooper Industries, Inc./ Tom Watson Photography, Skaneateles, NY.

possible, the lightest parts of the product are assembled first at the top level, and the heavier parts are added as the unit moves closer to the ground floor. This makes it easier to transport the unit from one level to the next. The unit is then shipped out from the ground floor.

Horizontal flow   A materials flow in which all production takes place on the same floor.

Horizontal Flow   In a **horizontal flow,** all production takes place on the same floor. The specific movement of the goods varies. Some firms use an I flow, in which goods move from one end of the factory directly to the other end. If the building is L-shaped, the production flow often follows this pattern. Sometimes companies use a U flow, in which the raw materials and parts come in one end of the building and the finished goods are shipped out from the same end. Which form of horizontal materials flow the company uses will depend on the type of product and the space available.

Common Forms of Layout

In planning the layout, operations management considers the ways of combining movements of workers and products. The result is generally one of three common forms of layout: process, product, or static.

Process layout   A production layout that groups machines and equipment on the basis of function.

The company can group machines and equipment on the basis of function. This is called a **process layout.** A company using this layout might place welding machines in one area, lathe machines in another, and painting equipment in another. Under a process layout, the goods being produced move around the factory to the machines and equipment that will be used for the various operations. Job shops that produce small-batch orders often use a process layout because it gives them the greatest flexibility.

In a **product layout,** all machines are set up along a product-flow line, and the units to be manufactured move down this line. The auto assembly plant is a good example. As the auto frame moves down the line, workers attach parts to it until it reaches the end of the line as a completed car.

Under a **static layout,** the product stays in one place and the workers come to the product. Sometimes called fixed position layout, this approach is common when the product is extremely heavy or bulky. For example, in building a large aircraft or a locomotive, it is easier to move the workers than the product.

1. What do managers consider in laying out a plant?
2. What are three forms of plant layout?

Product layout A production layout in which all machines are set up along a product-flow line, and the units to be manufactured move down this line.

Static layout A production layout in which the product stays in one place and the workers come to the product.

CHECK ✓ POINT

The Automatic Factory

The procedures discussed so far have enabled managers to operate production facilities efficiently. Now, however, as in all areas of business, procedures are rapidly changing. A good example is emergence of **concurrent engineering,** a process in which people involved in designing new products work together as a group to create the final product.[12] This approach results in a more effective manufacturing process because the designers, engineers, production planners, and marketing specialists in the group can identify problems and prevent them before the product gets into manufacturing. The emphasis is on avoiding mistakes rather than on correcting them after they occur.

Additionally, over the past 10 years a technological revolution has taken place in American factories.[13] New manufacturing systems and ideas are enabling the production of better-quality goods faster and at lower cost. Unfortunately, this does not necessarily lead to the creation of new jobs or to improvement in the factory environment for workers. The new automated jobs often involve big adjustments for both managers and workers. Managers often feel threatened about relinquishing their power, and among operating employees problem solving, analytical skills, and teamwork are in high demand and short supply. The managers and workers are sometimes just not prepared for this workplace revolution.[14]

Despite such problems, however, the use of robotics and flexible and computer-integrated manufacturing are having an impact on production and have arrived.

Concurrent engineering A process in which people involved in designing new products work together as a group to create the final product.

Robotics

When most people think of the automatic factory, they envision characters such as R2D2 or C3PO from the movie *Star Wars* making cars on the assembly line, but robots come in many shapes and forms. In general, **robots** are machines capable of doing a variety of tasks based on computer-programmed manipulations of materials and tools.

Robot A machine capable of doing a variety of tasks based on computer-programmed manipulations of materials and tools.

Robots and humans work side by side in this Navistar plant, as they do in many factories across the country. Successful manufacturers combine the best available technology with an effective workforce.

Source: Courtesy of Navistar International Corporation.

Industrial robots are programmed to perform specific motions. The robot's computer "brain" allows it to remember what motions have been programmed in order to perform a job. The programs can be changed to have the robot perform a variety of tasks. What is most important, the robots' arms never get tired or make a mistake, they are not distracted by the heat or noise, and they never have any problems at home or with the supervisor.

The use of robots in American industry is falling short of earlier predictions. Going into the 1990s, Japanese firms had over 200,000 industrial robots installed in their factories compared to about 37,000 in the United States.[15] Moreover, the Japanese are adding more than 37,000 new robots every year.

Why have the robots not caught on in the United States? One reason is that there are often more productive ways of doing the work. Some manufacturers like Deere & Company have found that it takes far too long to program robots to handle all of the activities associated with painting tractor chassis. Humans can do the job more efficiently. To date, Deere uses robots primarily for boring, repetitive jobs with a high degree of human error such as to torque a series of identical cap screws on tractor transmissions. Whirlpool has also discovered that robots are not as productive as other forms of automation in performing certain production function jobs, so it has limited their use.

Why then are robots so widely used in Japan? One reason is that the country has a labor shortage and without robots this work would have to be shipped offshore or given to immigrants. The government wants to keep production at home and maintain high employment, so robots are used. A second reason is that many of their robots are designed and built by Japanese firms for use in their own plants. The focus is on boosting competitiveness and quality; profits are a secondary issue. Matsushita Electric, for example, uses robots to wind wire a little thinner than a human hair 16 times through a pinhole in a VCR video head and then solder it. The company's 530 robots work five times faster and more reliably than humans, and the machines even inspect their own work. These robots give Matsushita a strong competitive edge in the marketplace.[16] A third reason is that the cost of robots is going down while the cost of labor in Japan is rising. So an investment in robots in Japan is viewed as a long-run, money-saving decision. In the United States,

CLOSE-UP / *Innovation*

Here Comes Robodoc

Companies that make robots are finding that their market is not limited to the factory floor. Surgeons are coming to rely more and more on these machines to help provide critical assistance during operations such as hip-replacement surgery, where it is critical for the surgeon to whittle the shape of the bone cavity to fit the implant. The better the fit of the implant to the cavity, the faster and more successful the patient's recovery. Today some orthopedic surgeons use a robot connected to a computer that provides imaging data to depict the patient's bones, enabling the surgeon to map out a strategy for creating the necessary cavity. During the surgery the physician will cut through the soft tissue and use the robot to mill the bone.

Another example of how robots are being used in surgery is the making of tiny, precise incisions at exact locations. Once the surgeon has lined up the incision, the robot can take over and carefully cut away a brain tumor or the small amount of bone in the middle ear that is preventing the patient from hearing properly. At the University of Bristol in England, researchers are currently developing a robot that can drill a hole a mere 2.5 millimeters deep into the interfering bone, thus opening up the passage for a tiny device that will help restore hearing. At the Imperial College in London, robots are being similarly used in prostate cancer surgery.

The future may see even greater use of robodocs (robot doctors) because of the many benefits they bring to the operating room. They are precise and always perform the function for which they are programmed. Unlike a physician who may make a mistake because of fatigue or mental lapse, the machines are accurate and tireless. Of course, the surgeon remains on hand to override the computer as happens when a tumor's location shifts between the time it is pinpointed with imaging tools and the time the surgery begins. The future will undoubtedly see more of a blending of doctor and robot, with the physician carefully directing the operation and overseeing the robot carrying out orders precisely and efficiently.

Source: Elizabeth Corcoran, "Robots for the Operating Room," *New York Times,* July 19, 1992, Section F, p. 9.

robots are not given as much attention as in Japan, but they are certainly not being ignored. They are even being used in operating rooms. The accompanying Innovation Close-Up (Here Comes Robodoc) provides an illustration.

Flexible Manufacturing Systems

While robots are not as widely used as once predicted, other features of the automated factory such as computers in general and electronically controlled industrial machinery in particular are widely used by companies today. For example, a **flexible manufacturing system (FMS)** involves the use of computer-controlled machining centers that produce complicated metal parts at high speed. These systems are created by firms such as Giddings & Lewis, a Wisconsin machine-tool maker that has developed clusters of automated machines that simultaneously perform multiple operations on products.[17]

The greatest benefit of a flexible manufacturing system is its ability to produce small quantities of goods at low prices. Before the use of FMSs, a small batch of goods would cost more per unit to produce than a large batch because the setup costs would have to be spread over fewer units. FMS allows firms to manufacture a few units or a few thousand units at the same basic cost per unit. This is good news for manufacturing firms, because a majority of all machined parts are produced in batches of 50 or fewer.

FMS also allows companies to change from producing one part to another quickly. For example, Caterpillar flexible manufacturing systems mill, bore, tap, deburr, and ream crude steel from the foundry at three-and-a-half times the speed of more conventional machines because the new units can

Flexible manufacturing system (FMS) A manufacturing system in which computer-controlled machining centers produce complicated parts at high speed.

TABLE 9.1
Contrasting Traditional and Flexible
Manufacturing Systems

The Traditional Style	The Flexible Style
Profitable only when making large batches.	Can be profitable making small batches of products.
The process is designed after the product has been designed.	The product and the process for making it are designed concurrently.
The fat inventory turns over slowly.	The lean inventory turns over fast.
Suppliers are kept at arm's length.	Suppliers are helped, informed, and kept close.
Engineers are insular, don't welcome outside ideas.	Engineers search widely for ideas and technology.
Employees are compartmentalized.	Employees learn several skills, work well in teams.
The company looks for the big break-throughs.	The company stresses continuous small improvements.
The system pushes products through to the customers.	The customers' orders pull the products through the factory.

Source: Jeremy Main, "Manufacturing the Right Way," *Fortune*, May 21, 1990, 60.

switch quickly from one operation to another. At C&J Industries computer-driven machines now enable the company to design a new product in 4 days, down from 12 weeks previously.[18] These developments are helping American manufacturers improve their production techniques and move from their old rigid system to a lean flexible system. Table 9.1 contrasts the traditional, rigid manufacturing system with the now increasingly used lexible system.

Few firms can afford to spend the millions of dollars needed to completely change over to a flexible manufacturing system. However, they can introduce FMS gradually. For example, IBM, General Electric, Ford Motor, and General Motors have revitalized parts of conventional plants by installing flexible manufacturing systems where they will do the most good.

Computer-Integrated Manufacturing

Computer-integrated manufacturing (CIM)
A manufacturing system that automates all of the factory functions and links them with company headquarters.

Closely related to robotics and FMS is **computer-integrated manufacturing (CIM),** which automates all of the factory functions and links them with company headquarters so that both groups are working as a team. At the present time, CIM is still being implemented. Some of the things it can do include:

- Conceive new products on a computer-aided design (CAD) system.
- Pass information on to a computer-aided engineering system to verify that the design will do the intended job.
- Take the information needed to make the product and send it directly to the automated equipment on the shop floor, where it will be produced.
- Coordinate all of the information with a computerized inventory control system, which ensures that all the necessary parts and materials are available.

A CIM factory allows the company to switch from manufacturing one product to another automatically. It also drastically cuts labor costs. General Electric has invested $1 billion to automate 14 appliance plants. Other large manufacturers are doing the same. Clearly, American manufacturing facilities have undergone dramatic changes in recent years.[19]

1. What are two ways in which businesses are automating factories?
2. What are two benefits of flexible manufacturing systems?

Purchasing and Inventory Control

Some companies find a more efficient alternative to producing parts or materials internally; they find that the time and cost involved make it wiser to buy from an outside supplier. In deciding whether to make or buy, the firm considers the costs and benefits of each alternative. Companies that buy from the outside are carrying out the purchasing function of production and operations.

Purchasing is the process of buying inventory and other assets. In most business organizations, managers of individual departments can directly buy whatever they need up to some limit, such as $200. Anything over this stated amount is handled through a central purchasing department. There are two reasons for this. One is that when buying large amounts of goods, the company often can get a quantity discount from the supplier. For example, Dunkin Donuts uses centralized purchasing to benefit its franchises. By centralizing the purchases, the firm ensures that it is able to get quantity discounts. Another reason is that management is better able to coordinate and control what is going on if all large orders come through one central unit. Company management can better monitor costs and quality and build relations with suppliers and vendors.

Purchasing The process of buying inventory and other assets.

The purchasing department buys the needed equipment and inventories and then, along with operations management, controls the inventory costs and makes sure the right amount of inventory is on hand.

Equipment Purchasing

An organization occasionally needs to purchase equipment, from office equipment such as laser printers, personal computers, and photocopiers to production equipment such as lathes, welding equipment, and robots. In most cases, the purchases are handled through the central purchasing unit. For example, Domino's Pizza Distribution Company purchases the dough makers and other equipment for their numerous franchises in order to obtain better prices and control the large expenses. Also, centralizing results in better records on the reliability of the vendors and the quality of their products.

Inventory Purchasing

The business must also purchase inventory when supplies begin to run low. For a manufacturer, this means keeping a supply of parts and raw materials; for a wholesaler or retailer, this means keeping a supply of the goods or services it sells. Most companies monitor their stock through the use of perpetual and physical inventory techniques.

Perpetual inventory A system for keeping track of inventory by subtracting what the company uses up or sells and adding what the company purchases.

The **perpetual inventory** technique involves keeping track of the amount of inventory by subtracting whatever the company uses up or sells and adding whatever the company purchases. This technique is called "perpetual" because inventory records are updated as changes occur.

At a company using perpetual inventory, items are reordered whenever stocks hit a predetermined level. For example, if a company buys 100 units of a part that will be installed in product A and estimates that two units will be installed each day, the company will be out of this inventory in 50 working days. Under a perpetual inventory system, it will set a reorder level of, say, 20 units. When inventory reaches this level, the purchasing agent will reorder 100 more. If the reorder point is correct, the new units will arrive before current inventory is depleted, but not so soon that the company will spend a lot to store the extra inventory.

Physical inventory The process of counting the amount of inventory on hand.

The **physical inventory** technique involves counting how many units are on hand. Small firms conduct this process by literally sending someone to the storeroom or warehouse to count the inventory. Larger companies and many retail stores use a computer in this process. An example would be the local supermarket, where the clerk rings up groceries via an optical scanner that sends a computer information about what has been sold. The computer keeps track of the exact number of units on hand at any given moment. At some point, however, these firms supplement the computer information with a physical count of inventory. This procedure enables the store to adjust for errors that result from pilferage from shoplifters or employees and for items that the clerks charged without using the scanner or let slip by.

Controlling Inventory Costs

Order costs The expenses associated with ordering inventory.

Carrying costs The expenses associated with keeping inventory on hand.

Maintaining an inventory constitutes an expense for businesses. Inventory expenses fall into two categories: order costs and carrying costs. **Order costs** are the expenses associated with ordering inventory. This includes typing up the order, mailing it, filing a copy, checking to see that the delivered inventory matches the order, and cutting a check for payment to the seller. **Carrying costs** are the expenses associated with keeping the inventory on hand. This includes the costs of storing or warehousing the goods; insuring them against theft, fire, and damage; and any losses associated with obsolescence.

In controlling these two usually significant costs, the company must take into account that order costs are greatest with frequent ordering, while carrying costs are greatest with infrequent ordering. Thus, there is a trade-off involved. For example, if a law firm were to order enough office supplies to last an entire year, its order cost would be very low but its carrying cost would be very high. Conversely, if it ordered every day, the order costs would go up and the carrying costs would go down; the company would also run the risk that a delivery would be late and the firm would run out of supplies.

Maintaining the Right Amount of Inventory

Economic order quantity (EOQ) model An inventory-ordering model that balances order and carrying costs and reduces the likelihood of running out of inventory.

What is the right amount of inventory to carry? The answer must weigh the costs of carrying the inventory against the risks of running out. Purchasing agents have traditionally done this by using quantitative methods such as the **economic order quantity (EOQ) model.** These methods maintain the right amount of inventory by estimating the probability of running out at various levels.

The raw materials inventory of Campbell Soup Company includes large amounts of perishable produce such as tomatoes. This means that careful planning is a crucial part of inventory control. The company cannot keep crates of tomatoes around for months while it builds production capacity or demand for tomato soup.

Source: Courtesy of Campbell Soup Company.

Although such quantitative approaches have been effective, the success of Japanese manufacturers with carrying very small, if any, supply inventories has led many American firms to begin reexamining their approach to inventory control. Many have arrived at a solution that allows them to carry very small amounts of inventory and thus reduce their costs. They restock continuously. This system of receiving inventory just before it is needed in the production process is called **just-in-time (JIT) inventory.**

Small firms are just beginning to make use of JIT, but the big manufacturers are widely using the approach. The Big Three automakers (General Motors, Ford, and Chrysler) all use just-in-time inventory on the assembly line. For example, the Chrysler Windsor plant receives sheet metal parts almost hourly from nearby plants; engines come from as far away as Mexico and Japan twice a week and sometimes every day; and, depending on their sizes and quantities, trim parts are received hourly to weekly. Thanks to JIT inventory, the plant has been able to cut hundreds of millions of dollars from its costs.

The JIT system shifts a lot of the problems and pressures onto the suppliers, who have been forced to carry more inventory and be more responsive to the automakers' demands. Those suppliers who are unable to provide the necessary parts when needed, where needed, and with an acceptable quality level are quickly dropped in favor of those who can. In Japan the relationship between suppliers and manufacturers is sometimes so strong that the firm has only one supplier for a particular material. Moreover, rather than count the units when they are delivered, the manufacturer pays based on how many are in the products coming off the assembly line.[20]

Just-in-time (JIT) inventory
A system of receiving inventory just before it is needed in the production process.

1. What activities are involved in the purchasing function?
2. How are companies benefiting from using the just-in-time (JIT) approach to inventory?

CHECK ✓ POINT

Quality Control

Quality control The process of ensuring that goods and services are produced or provided within predetermined specifications.

Besides controlling costs, operations managers must control quality. **Quality control** is the process of ensuring that goods and services are produced or provided within predetermined specifications.

Many firms today are concerned about the quality of their products and services. In the words of W. Edwards Deming, the quality-control expert who has been credited with teaching the Japanese about quality, "Improve quality and you automatically improve productivity. You capture the market with lower price and better quality. You stay in business and you provide jobs. It's so simple."[21] Companies have traditionally controlled quality through simple inspection and sampling techniques.

Inspection Techniques

Inspection takes place in service as well as manufacturing industries. For service businesses, inspection is an easy, practical way of checking on quality. For example, in many restaurants the owner comes around to the tables and asks the patrons whether everything is satisfactory. This is one way of ensuring that quality is up to standards. Another way is to examine the amount of repeat business in the establishment. If customers come back again, this is an indication that the quality is good. If few ever return, this indicates that something is wrong. Restaurants also closely monitor product quality. For example, McDonald's has strict quality standards such as the requirement that unsold Big Macs must be discarded after 10 minutes and french fries after 7 minutes so the products are always fresh.

In manufacturing, managers want to conduct an inspection before the products are out in the marketplace. For example, a firm does not want to find out after the fact that the product has a safety problem. For this reason, quality-control inspection is often carried out in the factory. If relatively few units are being produced, the company may inspect every one of them. For example, at Perdue Farms, inspectors are at work at every stage of production. This company believes that because customers inspect chickens one at a time, the company should do it that way, too.

Sampling Techniques

Sampling The process of inspecting some of the goods and using the results to judge the overall quality of all the goods.

For companies manufacturing in large quantities, inspection can be very costly. These companies often rely on sampling techniques. Applied to quality control, **sampling** is the process of inspecting some of the goods and using the results to judge the overall quality of all the goods. For example, at General Electric it is too expensive to test every light bulb coming off the line. However, the firm takes a sample and tests it in order to generalize the results to the whole batch. For example, if the firm has found that it is cheaper to allow one defective unit per 100, it will take no action if 1 percent or less of these units are defective. If more than 1 percent are defective, the company looks for the problem and corrects it.

Sampling is an important part of quality control because it helps the firm stay within the limits that it has established as "acceptable." However, with pressure from customers now demanding "zero defects" from products and some Japanese companies often reaching this level of quality, many American firms are making a new commitment to improve the quality of their products and services.[22]

Quality-Control Circles

Managers and engineers do not have all, nor necessarily the best, answers on ways to improve product quality. Effective managers try to draw on the insights of their front-line workers. One way they do this is by forming formal groups and giving them a voice in how to improve the quality of goods and services. For example, at Weaver Popcorn quality control has been pushed right down the line so that everyone is responsible for product quality. As one of the workers put it, "Quality is in our hands." Today the firm holds 60 percent of the Japanese popcorn market and its domestic share is growing 7 percent annually.[23] This participative technique often benefits the company by improving products and production processes.[24]

Total Quality Management (TQM)

Today's managers realize that while special techniques are important to quality control, management commitment to quality is the real key. This has led to total quality management (TQM). The TQM approach treats quality as a strategic objective for the entire organization and becomes the dominant cultural value. Importantly, under TQM, quality is not delegated to the quality control department, but is championed by senior and middle managers alike who live the quality message with passion, persistence and, above all, consistency.[25] The head of Campbell Soup Company remarked, "Above all, we've got to teach our people to focus on quality first, cost second."[26]

GTE Telephone Operations focuses on quality by maintaining Trouble Analysis Centers like this one in Los Angeles. The centers scan the network to identify problems before they are noticed and reported by customers.

Source: © 1989 Jeff Smith.

Focus on TQM in Manufacturing Whole industries in America have recently taken up the quality challenge. Autos, high-tech, textiles, steel and major appliance industries are heavily committed to improving quality. In the computer industry, for example, the quality of the machines has improved so greatly that computer maintenance firms are finding it hard to survive.[27] Manufacturing firms in these industries are not just talking about quality or putting out catchy slogans such as Ford's "Quality Is Job One" for advertising purposes. They are training their workers to be quality conscious and to "do it right the first time." However, there is still quite a way to go. A recent survey of chief executive officers (CEOs) of large industrial firms and services companies found that, when compared to their global competitors, U.S. auto manufacturers were rated the poorest.[28] On the other hand, as seen in the accompanying International Close-Up (The Recall Record), the quality challenge is not confined to the U.S. firms.

How do the successful manufacturers actually implement a quality focus? At Kawasaki Motors in Lincoln, Nebraska, production workers on the line making jet skis have the authority to request help or to stop the assembly line. When they get behind, they push a yellow button to get help so no sloppy work goes through. When they spot a defect, they push a red button to stop the line so that the problem can be fixed on the spot. Traditionally in American industrial plants, no one would ever dare stop the line. It would be considered sabotage, and the worker would be fired. But companies such as Kawasaki put quality ahead of quantity.

Firms such as Motorola have improved quality so much in recent years that output in some product areas is now at the "sigma six" level. This means that, statistically speaking, the products are virtually free of error. This has helped Motorola win the very prestigious Baldrige award created by Con-

CLOSE-UP / *International*

The Recall Record

Mention product quality and many people immediately think of Japanese manufacturers — with good reason. When a group of CEOs was asked to name the major advantage that top-notch Japanese producers had, over 60 percent said it was manufacturing. Moreover, although the quality of American manufacturers has greatly improved over the past decade, so has that of Japan. In autos, neither American nor European manufacturers for that matter, can match the quality record of the Japanese. On the other hand, Japanese quality is now coming under question in some circles because of a relatively large number of product recalls. Here are some examples:

Company/Product	Problem
Toyota Lexus automobiles	cruise control, brake light
Mitsubishi Motors Pajero wagon	accelerator
Isuzu trucks	loose belt
Fuji Heavy Rex minicars	clutch contact
Yamaha Virago motorcycles	fuel leak
Honda Horizon motorcycles	transmission cog
Seiko Epson laptop computers	circuit soldering
Toshiba TVs	high-voltage circuits
Pioneer Electric TVs	circuit soldering
Matsushita TVs	transformer insulation
Sony TVs	high-voltage circuits

TV manufacturers Matsushita, Sony, Pioneer, and Toshiba have had to recall dozens of makes because they smoked or caused fires. Seiko pulled in 100,000 of its laptop computers because they smoked, and Toyota's Lexus sedan had to go back to the dealer when brake light and cruise control problems were discovered.

Is Japan losing its quality edge? Most observers say it is not, although there are many customers who now refuse to buy Japanese electronic components because of quality problems. The major culprit appears to be high-tech design and engineering. Sadao Maeda, a management consultant at Kansai Productivity Center, has noted, "Product engineers are operating at a more sophisticated level, but their quality control lags that of factory workers." Other factors that are cited include design problems, lack of skilled workers, and the use of offshore suppliers to build components.

How is Japan responding? Both the government and business are cracking down hard on quality and demanding that production units correct these problems immediately. If they can accomplish this feat, "made in Japan" will continue to give a product a competitive edge.

Source: Robert Neff, Neil Gross, and William J. Holstein, "Now Japan Is Getting Jumpy about Quality," *Business Week*, March 5, 1990, 40–41; and Terence P. Pare, "Why Some Do It the Wrong Way," *Fortune*, May 21, 1990, 75–76.

---

gress and given only to those firms judged annually to be the most outstanding. In addition to Motorola, Xerox, Milliken, Cadillac, and Westinghouse have won the Baldrige. One of the primary areas of excellence is quality.[29] Table 9.2 sets forth six lessons that Westinghouse learned in winning the award. These lessons help explain the reason why quality is such a great challenge.

Focus on TQM in the Service Industry   The commitment to quality exists not only in manufacturing but also in the mushrooming service industry.[30] In fact, some experts are proclaiming that we now live in a new economy, a service economy, where service and white collar productivity are becoming more important than the production of physical goods. One observer noted that "McDonald's has more employees than U.S. Steel. Golden Arches, not blast furnaces, symbolize the American economy."[31]

TABLE 9.2
Lessons about Quality That
Westinghouse Learned in Winning
the Baldrige Award

1. Quality is a matter of survival. We have divested over 70 businesses in the past several years, and it's a question whether we would have divested all 70 if they had embraced quality 10 years ago. If you are really the best in your business, you're going to survive.

2. Total quality requires a cultural change, and I believe that you cannot make a cultural change without an emotional experience. It can be a positive experience, but mostly it's going to be negative, like "The plant's going to be closed."

3. It's going to take time. If you don't have the time to do it, don't start it. We began our total quality program 10 years ago.

4. You've really got to have top management pay attention. If you're talking corporate, I've got to pay attention. If you're talking division, the division manager must pay attention.

5. You have to have a scoreboard because if you don't want to win, why keep score? Here's where you create the objectives, the recognition, the pay for performance.

6. Everybody — *everybody* — has to be involved. You just can't have one person doing it. This is how you get the contribution from the guy who knows his job better than you'll ever know it and therefore knows how to improve it better than anybody else.

Source: Jeremy Main, "How to Win the Baldrige Award," *Fortune*, April 23, 1990, 104.

The commitment to "quality service," currently a popular phrase in the business world, becomes especially important when it is realized that the average American firm may lose up to one third of its customers every year because of poor quality service.[32] At Target stores customer service assistants roam the aisles and help shoppers. Assistants go out of their way to provide quality customer service.[33]

At MBNA America, a Baltimore-based credit card operation, the company puts its focus on maintaining customers. Most credit card companies lose 12 percent of their customers every year but MBNA holds this loss to 5 percent. In this business it costs $100 to get a new customer and a company will earn an average profit of $100 a year thereafter. So customer retention is critical. In an effort to encourage customer service, MBNA has a sign above each doorway that reads, "Think of Yourself as a Customer."[34]

At the American Savings Bank, customer service representatives have had their salaries raised by 75 percent and their positions have been elevated to the highest nonmanagerial level. At the same time, new computer equipment has been installed so that, when a customer calls, waiting time has been reduced to an average of 28 seconds instead of the previous 2 to 3 minutes.

Amica Mutual Insurance, a top-rated small insurance company based in Providence, Rhode Island, focuses on quality customer care. Amica does no advertising and uses only company-employed agents, adjusters, and underwriters. It prides itself on answering all customer mail within one day of receipt and responds to claims in the same speedy manner. When one policyholder was unable to get any government agency to remove a 10-ton tree that had fallen onto her house from a hurricane, she called Amica, and an adjuster came out the same day and arranged for a construction company to haul the tree away.

At Target stores, where quality service is emphasized, customer service specialists roam the aisles in order to be accessible to customers who need help.

Source: Copyright Dayton Hudson Corporation/ Steve Niedorf, 1989.

This quality service delivery by these successful firms does not just happen by accident. To obtain its premier quality position on products and service, Motorola spends considerable time and money on human resource training, with 40 percent of the expenditures going directly toward building the skills that lead to high-quality products and prompt, efficient, courteous service.[35] The Unisys Corporation has developed a comprehensive skills program to help customer support personnel continually update their skills. The program uses videotapes and interactive personal computer software to provide this customer service training.[36]

CHECK ✓ POINT

1. What are two ways in which operations managers control quality?
2. How can managers demonstrate a commitment to quality?

Closing Comments

Operations management underlies the efficient functioning of most manufacturing firms and, as this chapter indicated, is also part of running a service business. Operations managers plan how to make products and offer services. They schedule work and make sure the necessary materials and equipment are available. Operations involves increasingly sophisticated computerization techniques, but in the end still comes down to people (who can produce quality products or deliver quality service) and ideas (such as just-in-time inventory in a manufacturing plant or calling back new customers the next day to get feedback on what could be done better in a service business).

VIDEO CASE / *It's All a Matter of Breaking Even*

Book manufacturing requires a large investment in plant and equipment. A correspondingly large volume of business is needed in order to make money. This is a major reason R.R. Donnelley & Sons, the largest U.S. book printer, is so successful. Most of the major textbook publishers, from The Dryden Press to McGraw-Hill, contract with Donnelley to print at least some of their product offerings.

Unfortunately, an increasing number of firms in other industries have not been as successful as Donnelley; they have not had enough business to break even. Hotels are a good example. In 1979, there were approximately 2 million hotel rooms in the United States, breakeven was around 1.4 million rooms, and occupancy was around 1.45 million. In other words, the industry occupancy as a whole was above the breakeven point. However, during the 1980s, the number of hotel rooms rose

to almost 3 million and today is well over 3 million. Breakeven, which is approximately 70 percent of occupancy, is now around 2.4 million, but occupied rooms are less than this. Many hotels are losing money because of this overbuilding and they are now looking for ways to break even. This can be done by reducing costs or increasing revenues through higher occupancy rates.

One way hotel managers have tried to cut costs is to turn over more functions to computers and thus become more efficient. They have tried to increase occupancy through selective discounting and more competitive pricing. This has worked fairly well in recent times because many in the business community are insisting that their people stay at less expensive hotels. This development is putting strong pressure on the upper to mid-priced hotels, which are finding themselves

having to cut costs and improve services in order to prevent customers from looking for less expensive alternatives. The luxury hotels are also taking steps to keep their clientele. For example, some luxury hotels have installed fax machines in the rooms, so that customers' correspondence need not pass through the hands of hotel personnel. Additionally, almost all hotel chains have implemented "frequent stayer" plans (such as the airlines have used for years) that entitle regular customers to special benefits and to accumulate points for free rooms.

The years ahead are likely to see major increases in productivity and service in the hotel industry. Unlike R.R. Donnelley, which dominates its industry in the United States and because of its tremendous volume has no trouble breaking even, other companies and even entire industries are having trouble doing so.

Source: Philip S. Gutis, "After a Decade of Growth, Far Too Much Room at the Inn," *New York Times*, April 8, 1990, Sec. F, 8.

Case Questions

1. Using Figure 9.2 as your point of reference, how does the breakeven point of R.R. Donnelley compare to that of the average hotel?

2. If the hotel industry hopes to break even, what are some things that they will have to do differently? Again, use Figure 9.2 as your point of reference.

3. How important do you think purchasing and inventory control is to R.R. Donnelley? To a hotel? What conclusions can you draw regarding these forms of control and why Donnelley is profitable but many hotels are not? Include a discussion of service in your answer.

Learning Objectives Revisited

1. **Describe the operations system.** The operations system has three components: an input, which is any resource needed to produce a desired good or service; a transformation process, which changes the inputs into the desired outputs; and an output, which is the finished good or service.

2. **Examine the specifics of operations planning and scheduling.** Operations planning involves determining the most profitable way to produce the goods and services the company will sell. A major planning technique is breakeven analysis, which identifies the level of production at which total revenues equal total expenses. Another part of planning is product design, or deciding the specific physical dimensions of the good or service to be produced. Operations scheduling is based on the master schedule, which coordinates all of the raw materials, parts, equipment, manufacturing processes, and assembly operations. Two techniques for this are Gantt charts and PERT analysis.

3. **Identify the important factors of facility location and layout.** The key factors for location are proximity to customers, raw materials, a labor supply, power and water, and transportation. Location should also take into consideration community regulations and quality of life. The plant layout depends in part on the type of manufacturing process used. An analytic manufacturing process reduces a raw material to its component parts in order to obtain one or more products. A synthetic manufacturing process converts a number of raw materials or parts into a finished product. Plant layout also depends on the direction of material flow. In downward processing, different parts of the same product are produced on different floors of the factory. In horizontal flow, all production takes place on the same floor, and the material often flows in the shape of an I, L, or U.

4. **Discuss the automatic factory.** The automatic factory uses robots, machines capable of doing a variety of tasks based on computer-programmed manipulations of materials and tools. Another feature of the automatic factory is a flexible manufacturing system (FMS), in which computer-controlled machining centers produce complicated metal parts at high speed. Still another feature is computer-integrated manufacturing (CIM), which automates and links together all of the factory functions with company headquarters, so that factory and headquarters are working as a team. Although CIM is much more sophisticated and costly than an FMS, it enables the company to slash labor costs and to switch from one product to another automatically.

5. **Explain the important dimensions of purchasing and inventory control.** Purchasing is the process of buying equipment and inventory. Perpetual inventory is a system that calls for reordering inventory whenever stocks hit a predetermined level. Physical inventory involves counting how many units are on hand. Every firm does this occasionally to ensure that its inventory on the books is in line with the actual inventory in the warehouse. Quantitative techniques such as the economic order quantity (EOQ) model have been helpful to operations managers in deciding what is the right amount of inventory to carry. However, based on the experience of Japanese firms, companies have been moving to innovative techniques such as just-in-time (JIT) inventory.

6. **Discuss quality control in both manufacturing and service industries.** Quality control is the process of ensuring that goods and services are produced or provided within predetermined specifications. Manufacturing and service businesses have traditionally used inspection, an easy, practical technique of

checking on quality. Some companies require that every product be inspected, but companies that produce large numbers of goods find it too expensive to check every item. These firms use the technique of sampling, in which only a small number of units per batch are inspected. If the quality is sufficient, the firm assumes that the rest of the uninspected units are also acceptable. In recent times, however, consumer demand for "zero defects" and "quality service" has resulted in a commitment to total quality management or TQM. This approach treats quality as a strategic objective and it becomes part of the corporate culture.

Key Terms Reviewed

Review each of the following terms. For any that you do not know or are unsure of, look up the definitions and see how they were used in the chapter.

operations
input
transformation process
output
operations planning
breakeven point
product design
value engineering
value analysis
master production schedule
Gantt chart
program evaluation and review
 technique (PERT)
critical path
analytic manufacturing process

synthetic manufacturing process
fabrication
modification
continuous production
intermittent production
downward processing
horizontal flow
process layout
product layout
static layout
concurrent engineering
robot
flexible manufacturing system
 (FMS)

computer-integrated manufacturing
 (CIM)
purchasing
perpetual inventory
physical inventory
order costs
carrying costs
economic order quantity (EOQ)
 model
just-in-time (JIT) inventory
quality control
sampling

Review Questions

1. Identify the input, transformation process, and output for each of the following: a pickle factory, a movie theater, and a writer of mysteries.
2. How can operations people improve the design of products?
3. You are an operations manager for a company that makes washing machines. To schedule production, would you use a Gantt chart or a PERT network? Explain your choice.
4. In deciding where to locate a plant, what factors are important?
5. Miracle Processors Inc. is a company that makes sweet-and-sour sauce, puts it into small plastic packets, and sells it to Chinese restaurants to give out with egg rolls. Does this company use continuous production or intermittent production? Explain.

6. Blue Streak Boat Company has just leased a three-story factory. The operations manager wants to take advantage of the factory's height to use downward processing. In laying out the factory, where should the manager try to have the heaviest parts of the boats installed?
7. How does a process layout differ from a static layout? For what products would each layout be most suitable?
8. How can a small company automate its factory? Would it be too expensive?
9. What is computer-integrated manufacturing? How can companies benefit from using it?
10. Why would a store want to conduct both a perpetual inventory and a physical inventory?
11. Because Ted's Drive-In-and-Thru uses just-in-time inventory, it has on hand a minimal supply of

menu items and risks running out if many more customers show up than expected. Why do you think Ted doesn't order a lot of these items so that he can be sure not to run out?

12. What is the difference between inspection and sampling? What are the advantages of each?
13. How do firms such as Westinghouse demonstrate a commitment to quality? What can small firms learn from these ideas?

Applied Exercise

The Wymuth Corporation is looking into manufacturing circuits for use in electronic products. The Namin Company has offered to buy 400,000 circuits from Wymuth at $4 each. In order to produce these circuits, Wymuth must buy two machines at a cost of $280,000 each. The cost to produce each circuit is $2.65 and the firm would like to make a profit of $100,000 on the contract. Should Wymuth produce the circuits or pass up the contract? Would it make any difference if Namin ordered 500,000 circuits? Explain.

YOU BE THE ADVISER / *From the Bottom Up*

Pedro Ramirez has run a small factory for over 15 years. Recently he decided to expand his operation and to start bidding on more subcontracting work. To ensure that his factory is as up-to-date as possible, Pedro has decided to build a new facility from the bottom up. He plans on a one-story building that will be highly automated and will be capable of handling both small- and large-batch orders.

Some of the work he will be doing will call for receiving finished parts, assembling them into finished goods, and then shipping everything to the major contractor. Most of the work, however, will require Pedro's company to take raw material and convert it into the finished products. In either event, all of these jobs will involve making various kinds of small and intermediate-sized industrial equipment.

Right now Pedro is in the process of looking over all of the production-related activities that will be handled in the factory and completing plans for plant layout and operations. His local banker has promised to lend him all of the necessary money, and Pedro is determined to build the most efficient plant possible.

In the interim, Pedro is thinking of bidding on a contract to provide machine parts to a large farm equipment manufacturer. The cost of the machinery for producing the parts is $15,000 and each part will cost $4.18. The equipment manufacturer will pay $60,000 for 10,000 parts.

Your Advice

1. What should Pedro do?
   ___ a. Bid on the contract in its current form.
   ___ b. Accept the contract but only for 5,000 parts.
   ___ c. Decide against bidding.
2. What type of materials flow in the new plant would you suggest to Pedro? Why?
3. What type of plant layout (process, product, or static) would you recommend? Why?
4. What advice would you give Pedro regarding inventory control? Be as complete as possible in your answer.

COMPUTER PEOPLE KNOW HIM

Mention the name Michael Dell and most people won't know who he is. However, those in the computer industry know Michael quite well. He is president of Dell Computer Corporation, a major direct-marketing firm that sells computers to buyers all over the world. Dell's strategy is simple: By eliminating the wholesaler and the retailer, his company is able to slash prices and provide a highly competitive product in an industry that is undergoing dramatic change.

Five years ago most knowledgeable people in the computer industry would have argued

Managing Information and Computer Technology

10

Chapter Learning Objectives

- Explain how information systems help managers make decisions.

- Describe the evolution of computer technology.

- Identify the hardware and software components of computer technology.

- Define the basic types of computers.

- Discuss how businesspeople evaluate the merits of computers.

- Present the basic applications of computer technology to business.

that Michael Dell's direct-marketing approach could not work because customers want to see the computer and buy it from a salesperson who can explain and demonstrate the features of the machine. However, many people have now become so knowledgeable about computers that they know what they want and can describe it over the phone, and they shop on the basis of price. Moreover, home computers are now aimed at a much larger market. Several years ago, many home computers were bought by people who were simply going to use them to play computer games or for personal budgeting and

letter writing. Today, the primary reason for buying a home computer is to handle work that is brought home from the office. Another major reason for purchasing a home computer is to do schoolwork. Personal uses of home computers such as balancing the checkbook or carrying out financial planning rank far down the list.

Michael Dell's company has also been successful because computer customers are changing their purchasing habits. Five years ago, as in the auto industry, retail dealers licensed by the manufacturers dominated the computer industry. Today, such dealers account for less

than half of all computer sales. Other retailers such as Sears and Tandy, and specialty stores that assemble systems, account for 35 percent of sales. Direct-marketing firms such as Dell Computer make up 5 percent of the market, but they are likely to grow the fastest. The computer market is becoming highly competitive and retailers are finding that their profit margins are being driven lower and lower. As a result, Michael Dell's firm is likely to reach a billion in sales by the end of the decade.

Photo source: Reprinted with permission, *Inc.* Magazine, January 1990. Copyright © 1990, by Goldhirsh Group, Inc. 38 Commercial Wharf, Boston, MA 02110.

Introduction

We have already moved into the second generation of the Information Age. The first was characterized by automated data processing. Now the emphasis is on managing information and computer technology in order to accomplish business goals. As one executive noted, "Speed, scope, quality, adaptability, flexibility, and globalization — organizations use a variety of terms to describe their goals for achieving greater efficiency and effectiveness. And top managers are starting to appreciate the critical role of information technology in attaining each of them."[1] This chapter begins by describing what information systems are and some ways in which businesses use them. It then focuses on computers: their evolution, how they work, some benefits and disadvantages of using computers, and basic applications of computer technology in business.

Information Systems

Today's and tomorrow's businesses depend on the effective management of information. Most of the functions of business today are directly involved in producing information. This is true in both the manufacturing and the service sectors. Accountants, managers, and secretaries in production firms generate and use information; so, too, do lawyers, doctors, and tellers in service firms. Getting or sending data often requires some form of information technology, and in recent years this technology has increased dramatically. From communication satellites to supercomputers to cellular phones to laptop computers, new forms of information technology have emerged.[2] Years ago managers used to complain that they did not have all the information they needed for decision making. Today the challenge is to manage the information explosion through the use of well-designed information systems.

Management Information Systems

Few businesses have a shortage of data. Most are swamped by daily inpouring of sales literature, news stories, press releases, customer comments, and internally generated production, sales, and financial reports. As one observer put it, "Managers are inundated with data, but starved for information." The decision maker's problem, therefore, has become not one of how to get data, but how to sift through it and make sense of it. This process consists of turning data into information, that is, data relevant to the decision maker.

To turn data into information, businesses use some form of a **management information system (MIS),** a method for collecting, analyzing, and disseminating timely information to support decision making. The MIS determines what information each decision maker needs, finds a source of that information, and reports the information to the decision maker.

Management information system (MIS) A method for collecting, analyzing, and disseminating timely information to support decision making.

Elements of Information Systems

A company's MIS provides management decision makers with information about both internal operations and external events. It applies to a wide variety of activities. For example, marketing research, used to gather data on the goods and services desired by customers, is a vital part of a company's infor-

FIGURE 10.1
Elements of a Management Information System for a Manufacturer

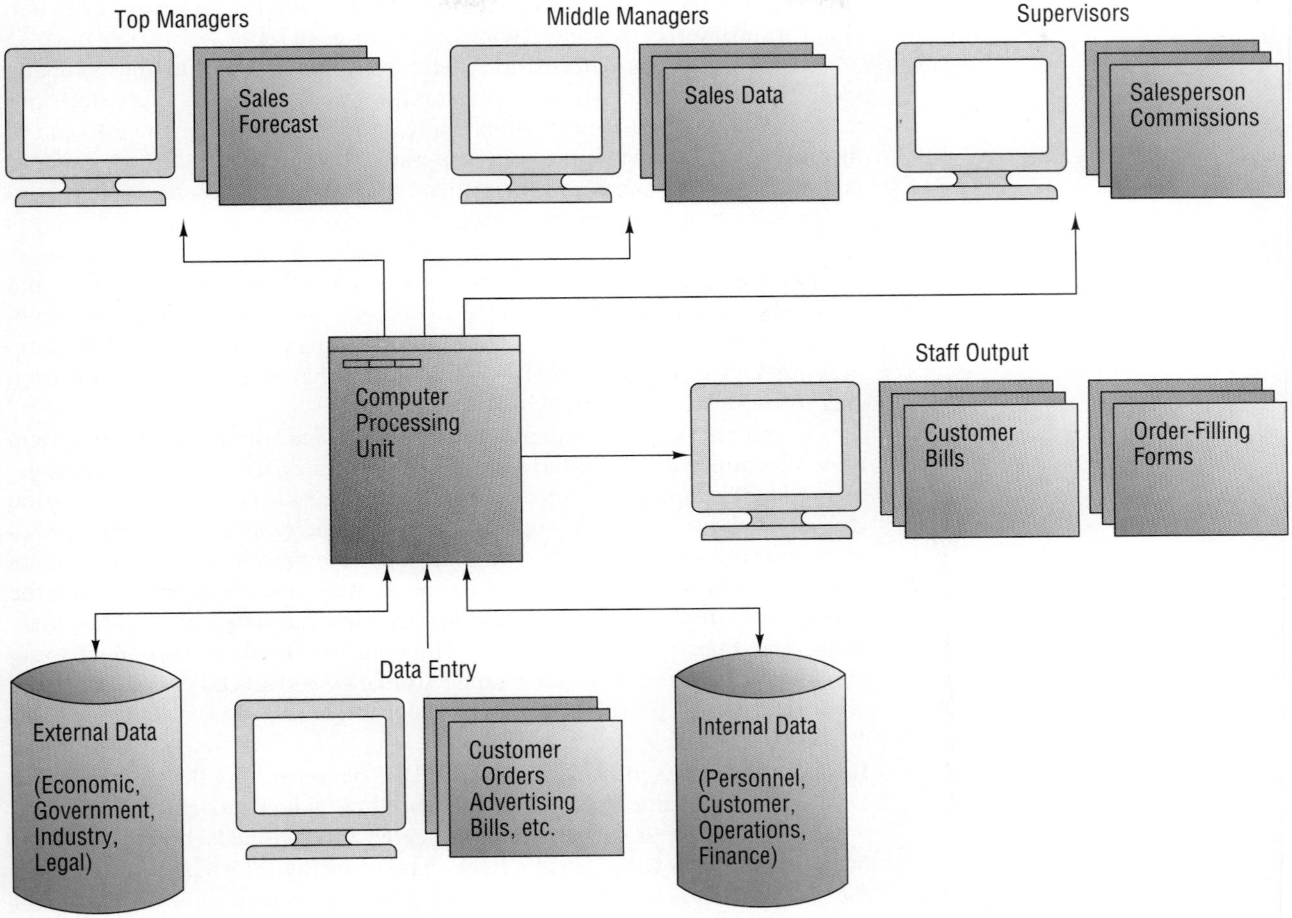

Top Managers — Sales Forecast

Middle Managers — Sales Data

Supervisors — Salesperson Commissions

Computer Processing Unit

Staff Output — Customer Bills — Order-Filling Forms

External Data (Economic, Government, Industry, Legal)

Data Entry — Customer Orders Advertising Bills, etc.

Internal Data (Personnel, Customer, Operations, Finance)

Source: J. Daniel Couger and Fred R. McFadden, *First Course in Data Processing*, 2d ed. (New York: Wiley, 1984), 401.

mation system. Tying these data into the company's overall information system helps keep marketing activities in line with overall company objectives. The same is true of other areas of the business. While each MIS is adapted to meet needs, all of these systems have the same basic components. These are information sources, users, information, and equipment. Figure 10.1 illustrates these elements for a typical manufacturing company.

Information Sources   The information in an MIS comes from a variety of sources inside and outside the firm. One outside source consists of federal, state, and local governments, which provide data on regional and national economic trends, information on industry regulations and tax laws, demographic data, and much more. The bank and other organizations that help finance the business may also provide information on economic trends, and, especially for small businesses, advice on financial matters. The business's customers can provide information on their experiences with the company's and competitors' products. Vendors are often a good source of information about industry trends and activities.

Many important information sources are located within the company itself. Virtually every department conducts activities that affect decisions made in other departments. For example, when various departments request the purchasing department to buy supplies and equipment, they are generating information about where the company is spending its money. This information affects accounting and budgeting decisions.

Users   The users of the information system are all the decision makers and those who support them (thus the term decision support system is sometimes used instead of MIS). This includes line managers as well as staff back-up personnel. A well-planned MIS should ensure that each type of information gets to those who need it, when they need it.

To get the right information to the right users, the information system must accommodate the different needs of users at different levels of management. For example, first-line managers are more likely to seek information that affects how to run daily operations in their particular area. They tend to be most interested in how they can influence the present and the immediate future. Middle managers, on the other hand, may look for information on the appropriate strategies for contributing to corporate objectives. They may focus more on the next year or two. Top managers tend to focus on information that helps them plan long-range strategies and overall policies for the organization.

Information   The information in an MIS is data that have been organized in a way that is useful to decision makers and those who support them. Increasingly, the data are organized for rapid search and retrieval; this type of organization of data is called a **data base.** The resulting information often takes the shape of reports and forms. For example, an organization may transmit information through purchase orders, inventory reports, tax forms, and reports of earnings projections, among other means.

Data base An organization of data for rapid search and retrieval.

Equipment   Companies used to store all their information in file cabinets and disseminate it <u>m</u>anually by filling out forms and typing reports. Today, however, most companies rely on computers that are programmed to speed up the process of retrieving and disseminating information. Companies can more than halve the time it takes to respond to problems, because pulling files together in an information system is much faster than obtaining them from file drawers. For example, one study found that a big insurance company cut the time it took to resolve complex claims from 6 months to 10 days and a manufacturing company cut the parts reordering process from an average of 20 minutes to 3 minutes.[3] An increasing number of companies are hiring MIS experts to help design and set up such systems for their particular needs. The accompanying International Close-Up (Apple is Catching on in Japan) provides examples of how Apple Computer is building and marketing equipment worldwide.

C L O S E - U P / *International*

Apple is Catching on in Japan

Mention the name Apple Computer and most people think of an American company that became famous for pioneering microcomputers. However, Apple has become more than just an American-based firm. In recent years Apple has realized that in order to be competitive and even survive in the global economy, it is necessary to become an international player. As a result, Apple has expanded into Europe and the hotbed of microcomputers — Japan.

In 1988 Apple had virtually no sales in Japan. However, by 1992 the company was selling over 150,000 units annually, and if it continues this growth rate, Apple will edge past IBM Japan and become one of that country's top five personal computer sellers.

How has Apple managed to do so well? The primary answer is that the firm has begun creating strategic alliances with Japanese manufacturers. As a result, Sony now manufactures Apple's smallest laptop, the PowerBook 100; Sharp Electronics makes Newton, Apple's brand-new electronic organizer; and it is likely that Toshiba will manufacture a new, portable, color or multimedia Macintosh that combines video, text, and sound. These deals are helping Apple gain a competitive leg up on major trends in the industry.

Apple is also making major headway in some Japanese universities. The Nagoya University of Commerce and Business recently placed an order for 1,200 Apple notebook computers. Meanwhile, Apple is continuing to push its product hard at the primary and secondary school levels. Over the next five years the Education Ministry will be putting 400,000 computers into schools across Japan, and Apple hopes to get a big share of this with its user-friendly Macintosh. If Apple can keep up this pace, it will be as big a player in the international arena as it is back home.

Source: Neil Gross and Kathy Rebello, ''Apple? Japan Can't Say No,'' *Business Week*, June 29, 1992, pp. 32–33.

Applications for MIS

Although it is obvious that decision makers and those who support them in all departments of a business need information, the specific needs of some major MIS users bear a closer look. Examples of those that rely heavily on information systems are sales, production, and top-level and middle-level managers.

Information Systems for Sales   Top sales managers need to know what the sales forecast is for the next couple of years, what products the company will sell, and which areas of the country are projected as having the greatest sales potential. These managers also need to know how well each sales region is doing relative to its sales forecast. They review general sales information that is designed to provide an overall picture of expectations and progress.

Middle- and lower-level sales managers need to know the sales quotas and goals for their regions and whether they are meeting these objectives. The information they receive tends to be specific (sales revenue by area, number sold of each product, and so forth) and provides a basis for measuring how well they are doing in each area of their overall sales territory. Those in the field calling on customers also need product information for making sales and for follow-up service.

Information Systems for Production   Top production managers are interested in the number of units being manufactured each week and how this compares to the forecast. These managers need information related to the overall production picture.

Middle- and lower-level production managers are interested in day-to-day operations, such as machine downtime and repairs, quality problems and

International Technology Corporation (IT) employees collect samples of soil at an air force base for environmental evaluation. The company created database software to process and store information from soil samples and other environmental data. The IT Environmental Database Management System™ increases the company's efficiency in issuing reports, retrieving regulatory information, and managing field and analytical data.

Source: Courtesy of International Technology Corporation.

the reject rate, and worker tardiness, absenteeism, and turnover. This information helps the managers and supervisors resolve specific problems and clear up bottlenecks that affect production.

Information Systems for Top- and Middle-Level Management   Top-level executives use information systems for planning the organization's overall direction and measuring results quarterly, semiannually, and annually. To this end, they are interested in information related to strategic planning and policy decisions.

Middle- and lower-level managers use information systems for planning their department's direction and measuring results daily, weekly, and monthly. These managers are most interested in information related to controlling and operating decisions. For example, manufacturing supervisors receive timely reports from quality control on the number of defects and from the human resource information system (HRIS) concerning their subordinates' training, compensation, and benefits.[4]

CHECK ✓ POINT

1. What are the elements of an information system?
2. How do managers' information needs vary by their level in the organization?

Computer Technology

As noted in Chapter 1, technology is the application of knowledge to production, physical equipment, and machinery. In the business world, information has been most affected by computer technology. The first modern computers were large, cumbersome, and slow. In fact, the popular personal computers of today hold more data and operate faster than any of the early computers, which were much larger and more expensive. To arrive at this modern stage, the computer has moved through four recognized generations.

Computer Generations

The first generation of computers, built from 1944 to 1959, operated with vacuum tubes. The machines were extremely heavy, took up a lot of space, and contained a large number of tubes. For example, the pioneering ENIAC weighed 30 tons and held 18,000 vacuum tubes. During the second generation (1959 to 1964), computer makers replaced the vacuum tubes with more reliable transistors, and high-speed card readers and printers were introduced to speed up input and output. From 1964 to 1974, the introduction of integrated circuits brought in the third generation of computers. An **integrated circuit** is a network of dozens of tiny transistors etched onto a silicon wafer. The result was a smaller, faster computer that required less electricity and provided greater storage. During this generation, remote terminals were also introduced so that users could gain access to the computer from various locales and at all levels and functions of the organization.

The mid-1970s saw the emergence of large-scale integrated circuits, which some people call "superchips." These silicon-wafer chips can fit in the palm of one's hand, but they can accommodate millions of integrated circuits and perform multiple applications, such as payroll, inventory, and economic forecasts. This miniaturization of the computer chip revolutionized the industry. With mass production of the chip, its price plummeted and the market for home microcomputers opened up. Consumers could now buy a small computer that performed more functions, worked faster, and cost much less than the large computers of the previous decade.

Artificial Intelligence

Researchers continue to work on new computer technology. For example, computers are now being trial-tested in operating electronic navigation systems in autos,[5] playing chess,[6] and being used to make trillions of calculations in a mere second.[7] The efforts are ushering in another computer generation: **artificial intelligence (AI).** Sometimes called the fifth generation, this technology involves developing computers that can mimic human logic and allow the user to interact with the computer in English rather than "computerese."[8] Chess is a good practical example. Some of the latest computer programs are so sophisticated that they have beaten grand master chess players. While the very best players can still win, some experts predict that by the year 2000 the computer will be able to defeat even them.[9]

Another good example of AI is the creation of "what if" simulations that allow the user to create and examine situations before actually investing money or proceeding with action. For example, Autodesk of Sausalito, California, has developed a computer program that allows the user to see 3-D images on the computer screen and to manipulate the objects that are being observed. If this technology can be expanded, it may be possible for architects and clients to take a 3-D tour through a newly designed building and move walls and doorways before committing the architectural design to paper. It may even be possible for a surgeon to practice scalpel techniques by

Integrated circuit A network of dozens of tiny transistors etched onto a silicon wafer.

Artificial intelligence (AI) Information technology for developing computers that can mimic human logic and allow the user to interact with the computer in English rather than a computer language.

Technicians at Mead Corporation check webs of paper for imperfections that could cause a web to break. In order to prevent imperfections in the paper, Mead is experimenting with a form of artificial intelligence (AI) called the expert system. It uses computers that can mimic human logic. The expert system at Mead captures the knowledge of some of the company's skilled papermakers and technicians to analyze where and why problems occur.

Source: © William Taufic for Mead Corporation.

"operating" on a computer-generated human body.[10] In other cases computers are being used to simulate past events such as airline crashes and to help explain how the people involved in the crash acted.[11] This information could be of great value in designing safer airplanes.

Another example of the application of AI is American Express's "expert system," called "Laurel's Brain." This AI system is named after Laurel Miller, a credit authorization manager. Her decision-making expertise was programmed into the computer system to screen out bad credit risks among the company's millions of cardholders. American Express has reaped increased productivity and profits from this application of artificial intelligence, and Laurel says, "There's no question it can do as good a job as I can."[12]

Other programs for AI and closely related "expert systems" are being developed for use in sales work, inventory control, and financial planning. In every case, the approach is the same — the programmer teaches the computer to think like a human. Some of the latest approaches involve teaching the computers to create their own solutions to problems.

CHECK ✓ POINT

1. What are the identifiable generations of computer technology so far?
2. How does an "expert system" work and how could one help a small business?

How Computers Work

Computers receive, manipulate, and store data based on the instructions they receive. The machinery and physical components of the computer that perform the tasks are called computer **hardware.** The series of instructions, or programming, that tells the computer what to do is called **software.** These instructions may be built into the computer or stored separately.

Basic Hardware Components

Although the design and capabilities of computers vary substantially, the basic components of computers fall into the following categories: input units, central processing units (CPUs), secondary storage devices, and output units. These components are interrelated, in that the input unit passes data to the CPU, where the information is processed. The results then go to the output unit to be available to the user. The results also are usually stored. Meanwhile, the control unit of the CPU continuously monitors operations. Figure 10.2 diagrams the components and shows how they are linked.

Software: Programming the Computer

The most sophisticated computer hardware in the world cannot meet the business's information needs without instructions directing it what to do. The software that gives the machine its instructions comes in the form of computer programs. A **computer program** is a series of coded instructions that tell the computer what to do. Software quality is important because, except for some recent systems dealing with artificial intelligence, computers generally do what they are told to do — no more, no less. Therefore, if "garbage" (incorrect or useless information) is programmed into the com-

Hardware The machinery and physical components of a computer.

Software The series of instructions, or programming, that tells the computer what to do.

Computer program A series of coded instructions that tells the computer what to do.

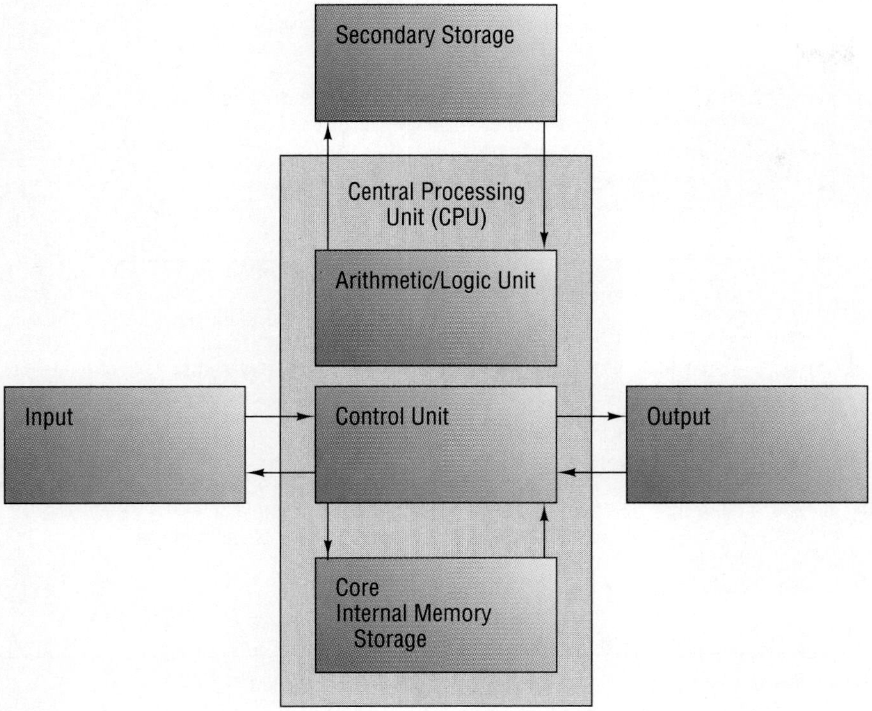

FIGURE 10.2
Basic Components of a Computer

Figure content:
- Secondary Storage
- Central Processing Unit (CPU)
- Arithmetic/Logic Unit
- Input
- Control Unit
- Output
- Core Internal Memory Storage

puter, then "garbage" will be the output. This observation is commonly summarized as GIGO: garbage in, garbage out.

For most businesspeople, learning how to program a computer is no more necessary to operating one than learning the intricacies of the internal combustion engine is to driving a car. Businesspeople can hire computer programmers to create software for the company or to modify existing software, or they can buy ready-made computer programs. Figure 10.3 shows the basic logic of simple programming that could be used in a bank. Such a **user-friendly** program is one that is easy to understand and master. The dynamic growth of personal computers has done a great deal to stimulate the development of user-friendly programs. The development of computer graphics, the translation of print concepts to video, is helping this process. For example, instead of tediously wading through numerical data bases on, say, medical information, the graphic software might create a form of a human body to speed the search. The user could glide over the model, magnifying specific organs and pushing a key to read data about a precise location. Such computer graphics are so user friendly that it is almost like playing a video game.[13] However, it should be remembered that graphics are not meant to totally replace numerical presentations. As one software expert noted, "Data tables add another dimension of clarity; they're the hardest to lie with."[14]

User-friendly program
A computer program that is easy to understand and master.

FIGURE 10.3
A New Way to Write Programs

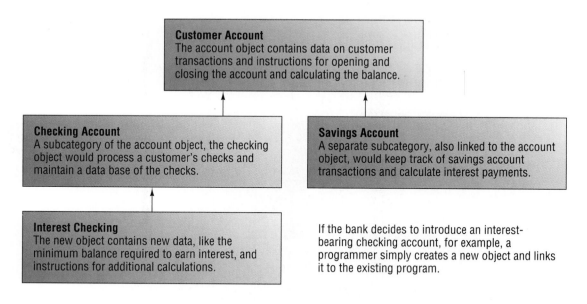

Customer Account
The account object contains data on customer transactions and instructions for opening and closing the account and calculating the balance.

Checking Account
A subcategory of the account object, the checking object would process a customer's checks and maintain a data base of the checks.

Savings Account
A separate subcategory, also linked to the account object, would keep track of savings account transactions and calculate interest payments.

Interest Checking
The new object contains new data, like the minimum balance required to earn interest, and instructions for additional calculations.

If the bank decides to introduce an interest-bearing checking account, for example, a programmer simply creates a new object and links it to the existing program.

Source: *New York Times*, April 23, 1990, C1.

CHECK ✓ POINT

1. What are the basic types of computer hardware?
2. How do most businesspeople go about obtaining software for their computers?

Types of Modern Computers

Today's computers provide a striking contrast to the large, cumbersome early machines. In addition, computers cost much less and offer versatility in size and power. Today, there are two basic categories of computers: mainframe computers and microcomputers.

Mainframe Computers

Mainframe computer A large computer system with considerable storage capacity and fast processing capability.

A **mainframe computer** is a large computer system with considerable storage capacity. It offers faster processing than smaller systems and may tie together a network of terminals.[15] For example, a large chain of retail stores could have each of its units tied in directly to the mainframe at corporate headquarters. Each of the stores, via terminals, could feed expense and revenue information into the mainframe computer at headquarters and get back financial reports and other operating data that help the store manager make important on-site decisions. Large enterprises need a large central computer to coordinate data and provide a primary source of operating information. A mainframe computer performs this function.

Microcomputers

A **microcomputer** is a small desktop computer that relies on a microprocessor. A **microprocessor** is an integrated circuit on one chip that is the equivalent of the central processing unit in a larger computer. The microprocessor was developed in 1971, and since then it has spawned a major market for computers: the personal computer (PC). In recent years, PCs have largely replaced **minicomputers** (medium-sized computers in terms of physical dimensions and storage capacity) and are beginning even to replace mainframes.[16]

The personal computer has become very popular because of its size (it takes up little office space), processing power, and price. In recent years, the price of a PC has dropped to less than half of what it was a few years ago. Depending on its features, it can range from a few hundred to a few thousand dollars. Another attractive feature is that PCs can be tied to one another via a network in an office complex. Microcomputers allow small businesses to use computerized information to manage operations in the way that large companies do.

The basic components required to operate a PC system are a system unit and a keyboard. In addition, the user adds other components, depending on the needs the computer is designed to fill. These components usually include diskettes, a video monitor (screen), and some type of printer, and sometimes a modem, a mouse, or extra storage devices. Figure 10.4 illustrates the components of a typical personal computer system.

1. What are the differences between a mainframe computer and a microcomputer?
2. What is a microprocessor, and what role does it play in a personal computer?

Microcomputer A small desktop computer that relies on a microprocessor.

Microprocessor An integrated circuit on one chip that is the equivalent of the central processing unit in a larger computer.

Minicomputer A medium-sized computer in terms of physical dimensions and storage capacity.

CHECK ✓ POINT

Evaluating Computer Technology

Although computers offer many benefits, businesspeople must also consider their shortcomings in determining how computers can help meet the company's information-processing needs. Generally, evaluating computers boils down to weighing the efficiency they provide against the costs and risks they create.

Advantages to Business

Businesspeople can use computers when they want to make a job faster, easier, and even more interesting.

Speed Computers are fast; they can make calculations in a fraction of the time it would take an individual. In fact, the person feeding the information into the computer is typically the slowest link in the process. The machine itself can carry out billions of instructions per second. For example, the Cray-3 supercomputer is capable of 16 billion computations a second. Within a decade, Cray expects to achieve a mind-boggling 60 billion computations a second[17] by using computers in parallel (using many processors linked together so they can share the load, each working on a different piece of a

FIGURE 10.4
A Typical Personal Computer System

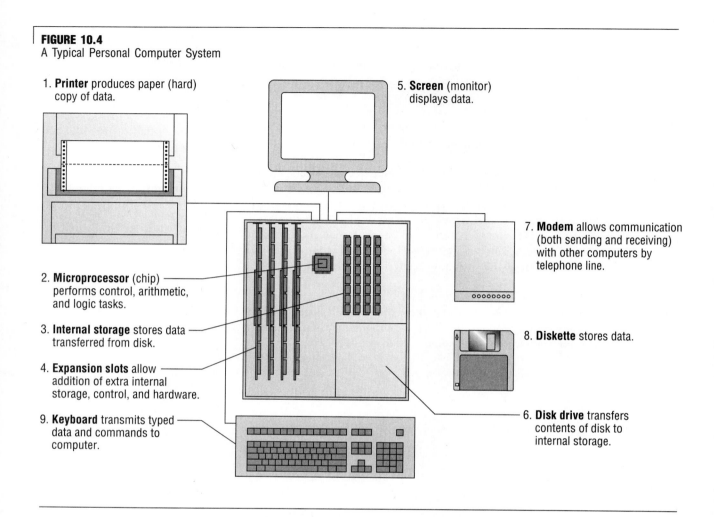

1. **Printer** produces paper (hard) copy of data.

5. **Screen** (monitor) displays data.

2. **Microprocessor** (chip) performs control, arithmetic, and logic tasks.

3. **Internal storage** stores data transferred from disk.

4. **Expansion slots** allow addition of extra internal storage, control, and hardware.

9. **Keyboard** transmits typed data and commands to computer.

7. **Modem** allows communication (both sending and receiving) with other computers by telephone line.

8. **Diskette** stores data.

6. **Disk drive** transfers contents of disk to internal storage.

problem at the same time). Computer scientists have achieved speedups of problem solving by 2,000 times faster than a single processor from the same system. Figure 10.5 shows the relative speeds of the various types of computers. Although the PC appears relatively slow compared to the more powerful and expensive machines, PCs have more than enough speed and capacity for business, if not scientific, needs.

Accuracy Properly programmed computers are accurate, because, as noted earlier, computers do as they are programmed to do. If the machine is told to add 100, 200, 225, 406, and 911, the answer will be 1,842 every time. People get tired; computers do not. Some experts like to point out that "computers are too dumb to make mistakes," which means that mistakes typically result from improper programming, not machine errors.

Large Capacity Computers are capable of storing huge amounts of information. The amount of a computer's memory is measured in terms of a unit

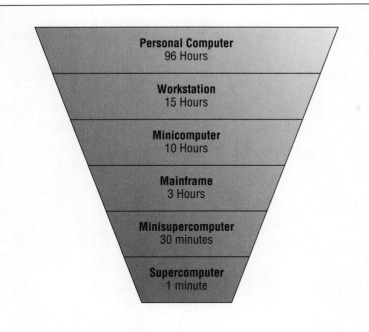

FIGURE 10.5
The Relative Time Needed to Complete a Scientific Calculation with Various Types of Computers

Source: John W. Veritz, "Supercomputers," *Business Week,* April 30, 1990, 83.

called a byte. A **byte** is a character of data, such as 6, A, or +. For example, the word *help* takes up four bytes. Because most memories are so large, the common units are Kbytes (1,024 bytes) and Mbytes (1,048,576 bytes). You may find it useful to think of Kbytes as roughly a thousand bytes and Mbytes as roughly a million bytes. Most personal computers today have a minimum of 640K of memory. The cost to add memory to a PC is minimal. Also the development of technologically superior chips already underway by the major manufacturers such as Toshiba, Mitsubishi, and Texas Instruments will greatly increase the memory capacities of PCs in the near future.[18]

Byte A character of data.

Assumption of the Boring and Routine   Many businesspeople appreciate computers because they handle boring tasks such as adding numbers, re-arranging data, and performing routine computations. The computer performs these tasks quickly and accurately, thus freeing employees to devote their time to more creative work. As one computer firm put it, "Computers do the busy work and free people up to do the think work."

Increased Efficiency   Finally, computers can greatly help organizations increase their efficiency. They do so in a number of ways. The last section of this chapter will provide the details of how computers help managers at all levels and all types of organizations become more efficient. However, first the major disadvantages and potential problems are recognized.

Disadvantages to Business
Some of the problems of today's organizations are blamed on computer technology.[19] Specifically, the real and potential drawbacks to computers are that

A training coordinator at Merck Sharpe & Dohme, a major manufacturer of prescription drugs, shows a company sales representative how to use an interactive video program to learn about the physiological process of heart disease. Using computers for some routine training tasks frees trainers to improve content and presentation. It also allows the reps to learn at their own pace.

Source: Courtesy of Merck & Co., Inc., 1989 Annual Report.

they can be expensive, can lead to mistakes, can be relied on too much, seem to be antipeople, and can be a security risk.

Expense Unfortunately, computers can be expensive, especially if the organization does not know how to use them efficiently. Managers must weigh the benefits a computer can provide against its cost. A manager who buys out of awe at a computer's capabilities may purchase much more computer memory or power than is necessary. Some managers may blindly buy whatever their competitors are purchasing. The desire to have the best equipment or do exactly as the others do can override such down-to-earth criteria as profitability and efficiency. However, careful consideration of benefits may render even a high price worthwhile.

Mistakes   Another potential pitfall of computers is that they may lead to errors. Computers do only what they are programmed to do; thus, programmers and operators can cause mistakes. And when an error is made, it often turns out to be a big one. As one critic lightheartedly remarked, "In a few minutes, a computer can make a mistake so great that it would take many men many months to equal it." For example, not long ago, a computer operator called up the wrong mailing list and sent out a letter to businesspeople all over the country, thanking them for staying at the company's hotel. In reality, few, if any, had stayed at the hotel. Unfortunately, many of the managers' spouses read the letter and wanted to know what was going on at that hotel. The president of the hotel chain wrote a personal letter of apology to everyone who called to complain, including one complainer who said, "If you don't straighten out this problem immediately, my marriage is on the rocks!"

Vulnerability to Overreliance   Computers also cause problems when managers overrely on them. A research study found this is especially true of managers with little or no computer experience. If they had little computer experience, their decision making was greatly influenced by the mere fact that the data were generated by a computer.[20] Other studies have found that even when computerized printouts contain erroneous data, the manager tends to accept the information. This overreliance is dangerous and shows that many managers use computers to make decisions, as opposed to using the machines to help them analyze the information on which to base their decisions.

People Problems   Computers are sometimes viewed as "antipeople." One reason is that they simply do as they are told without taking into account what the ramifications might be. For example, some people have received computerized bills for goods either that they have not purchased or for which they have already submitted payment. In either case, every time they indicate this information on their computer bill, it is ignored and they receive increasingly more urgent letters demanding that they pay up or else. Their inability to get a human to intervene in the process makes it all the worse.

A second people problem is technological unemployment, which occurs when computerization leads to elimination of workers' jobs. For example, in the auto industry, welders and other assembly-line workers are being replaced by robots. These high-speed, sophisticated machines can do some types of work faster, cheaper, and more efficiently than humans. Computerization also can affect white-collar jobs, in that computers can collect and analyze data more quickly and cheaply than staff personnel.

Security Risks   The use of computers also raises the issue of security. In recent years, students have managed to gain access to computers at the government weapons research laboratory in Los Alamos, New Mexico, and the Sloan-Kettering Cancer Center in New York City. In another case, a student so-called "hacker" introduced a "virus" into a national computer system and managed to destroy a great deal of stored data. A **computer virus** is a small

Computer virus A small piece of computer code that can automatically hide duplicates of itself inside legitimate programs and when activated can destroy data and software.

piece of computer code that can automatically hide duplicates of itself inside legitimate programs. When it is activated, the virus can destroy data and software.[21] These stories made headlines. What have not made headlines are the bank computer thefts carried out by computer whizzes who know the correct codes to use to enter accounts in order to steal or manipulate money. Industry experts estimate that computer theft runs into the hundreds of millions of dollars each year.

Societal Implications of Computers

Besides the implications that computers have for business, computers also affect society at large. For example, many people fear that computers can result in an invasion of their privacy. Many businesses keep their payroll and personnel files on computers. Anyone with access to the company computer can easily obtain private information on the firm's personnel. Additionally, anyone who has used a credit card in the last year is in a computer file somewhere. If such a person were to apply for a home mortgage, the bank would have a credit agency carry out a credit check on the person. This agency would have little trouble getting the individual's outstanding credit card balances and other personal financial information. Most people, whether they know it or not, could have their privacy invaded by an individual with access to their computer file. If the file contains a mistake, the problems could be even worse.

In an effort to prevent these abuses, many organizations are establishing tighter security measures. Some companies continually change the computer access code so that only those who are supposed to know the code can get into the files. Another approach is to install a "callback" unit, which checks to make sure that the person attempting to reach the computer through a telephone is calling from a company's authorized telephone number. The company may limit access to certain computer files to certain times of the day, thus preventing people from getting into these files when no one is around. The system might also alert security people if someone is trying to gain computer access.

Another issue relating to privacy concerns the monitoring of employees in the workplace.[22] A report released by the Congressional Office of Technology Assessment indicates that more than 7 million employees have their daily work monitored by computers. At present, computer monitoring mostly affects clerical workers in areas such as computer data entry and insurance claims processing who sit at a computer work station. Activities being monitored include job production, use of telephones, presence at the workstation, customer service calls, and frequency of errors. Besides the invasion of privacy issue, there is some evidence that computer monitoring leads to job stress and more frequent illness. Computer monitoring also seems to be spreading to those doing more complicated tasks. Critics are concerned that this is another example that the United States is becoming a "surveillance society" and that those companies that use computers to monitor their employees have become "electronic sweatshops."

CHECK ✓ POINT

1. What are two major advantages and two disadvantages of computers?
2. What societal issues must businesspeople consider when setting up and using a computer system?

Information and Computer Technology in the Business World

Businesses today use information systems to handle a multitude of tasks. Some of these, such as handling deposits and withdrawals or booking airline reservations, are unique to a particular industry. But most businesses use information technology in one or more basic functions: word processing, desktop publishing and video, spreadsheets, data base management, telecommunications, electronic mail, facsimile machines, and networking.

Word Processing

An application that has revolutionized business offices across the country is **word processing,** a system to store, retrieve, edit, and print text. Typically, the operator enters a report, letter, or other text by typing it on the keyboard or retrieving it from a file. Then the operator makes any changes desired and prints or saves the revised text. The two biggest advantages of word processing are that it reduces the time needed to revise documents and that it cuts back on the amount of storage space required for filing them.

Word processing A system to store, retrieve, edit, and print text.

Word processing offers many features that vary somewhat from program to program. However, most word processing programs offer the following:

- *Ease in correcting errors.* The operator can back up and type over characters or delete words by pressing a few keys.

- *Assistance in catching errors.* A "spell check" in the program can compare every word in the document with a dictionary file to make sure the words are correctly spelled. However, one problem is that a word in the document may match a word in the dictionary while not being the correct word for that context. For example, the operator may have typed *the* instead of *they*.

- *Ease in making revisions.* Word processing programs allow the user to move text around. If users want to insert new material in the middle of a paragraph, they merely type it in the desired location, and the program automatically adjusts the text that follows it. This means that the operator can make a change without having to retype an entire page or report.

- *Flexibility in creating a format.* The operator can specify margins, spacing, and usually type size. Depending on the printer's capabilities, the word processing program allows the operator to specify that some text be in boldface, italics, uppercase, or underlined. Special commands can also center text or align it at the right margin.

- *Capability for reusing text.* The ability to save and retrieve files of information enables the operator to save time spent retyping the same information. For example, the user could retrieve files containing report formats or standard closing paragraphs, rather than retype them each time a report or letter called for them.

- *Special features.* Some programs can make an index out of words that the operator flags. Others can sort data alphabetically or numerically. Some programs make graphs out of quantitative data. Most word processing programs contain some of these features plus a wide variety of others.

These features make word processing useful for a variety of tasks, from typing letters and memos to creating reports, invoices, and other documents. The manuscript for this book was prepared on a word processor.

Desktop Publishing and Desktop Video

Desktop publishing A computer system that allows companies to publish newsletters, charts, brochures, and other printed material in-house.

A recent development that has taken word processing one step further is called **desktop publishing.** This allows companies to create and produce newsletters, charts, brochures, and other printed material in-house. What used to be sent out to professional publishers and printers can now be done on a desktop computer system consisting of a computer, laser printer, and software package. At present, such systems run about $7,500 to $10,000, and the costs for producing printed materials can be 50 to 65 percent below that charged by outside printing firms. Those familiar with word processing can learn the system with little effort. Desktop publishing offers great potential for the future. Industry experts estimate that within a few years most companies will have such a system in place, enabling them to create high-quality printed material at a low cost and with little lead time.

Desktop video (DTV) A new technology that combines both audio and visual effects to create sales or financial analysis in the form of an animated video.

Another emerging development is **desktop video (DTV)** presentations that combine both audio and visual effects. This new technology allows salespeople, forecasters, analysts, and others to create their presentations in the form of an animated video that costs less to produce than the average slide presentation. Pie charts and graphs can be created on screen and then made to explode off the screen. Economic business cycles can be made to move from left to right, thus communicating their change over time. It is even possible to overlay computer graphic images on video images; and material on the screen can be made to spin, flop, break up, and even zoom out at the audience.[23] The creative features of DTV are so great that many companies are now looking into it as a replacement or complement to the standard presentation.[24]

Spreadsheets

Spreadsheets Data arranged in tables of rows and columns.

While word processing programs help businesspeople manage and present information in the form of text, decision makers also work with information in the form of numbers. For help with this quantitative information, they turn to **spreadsheets,** which are simply tables, such as the one shown in Table 10.1. Of course, it's possible to create such a table with a pen or typewriter, but spreadsheet software makes the job simpler and more flexible.

The user of a spreadsheet program labels the columns and rows that will contain information. The user can also identify which amounts are calculated from other amounts, specifying how to calculate them. For example, in Table 10.1, the user would have the computer add the quarterly amounts in each row to find the total for each row. Also, he or she would specify that income for each column is the difference between sales and total expenses. When the user enters the amounts for sales and expenses, the computer automatically calculates the total for each item, total expenses, and income.

Spreadsheets have a variety of applications. A spreadsheet along the lines of the one shown in Table 10.1 might be useful for financial statements or in preparing a budget. Managers might use a spreadsheet for their department's budget. A related use would be to compare planned revenues and expenses with actual ones. The company could also use spreadsheets for

	First Quarter	Second Quarter	Third Quarter	Fourth Quarter	Total	**TABLE 10.1** Sample Spreadsheet
Sales	$101.2	$93.6	$75.3	$162.1	$432.2	
Expenses						
Cost of Goods Sold	54.5	47.8	39.2	72.0	213.5	
Salaries	10.2	10.2	10.2	10.2	40.8	
Rent	5.0	5.0	5.0	5.0	20.0	
Other Expenses	3.3	3.0	3.0	3.5	12.8	
Total Expenses	$ 73.0	$66.0	$57.4	$ 90.7	$287.1	
Income	$ 28.2	$27.6	$17.9	$ 71.4	$145.1	

preparing payroll. The spreadsheet could contain wage rates, hours worked, and deductions, and use this information to compute each worker's total pay automatically. Other uses of spreadsheets are for bank transactions and balances and for estimating the financial impact of proposed new projects. In fact, the application of spreadsheets is limited only by the user's imagination.

Data Base Management

As you learned earlier in this chapter, management information systems often store data in the form of a data base for easy retrieval. Computer programs called data base management software automate this task. Data base management programs store information labeled according to category. For example, in a customer list, the file may identify the customer's name, telephone number, address, zip code, and product purchased. The company can then use the computer to search the file for specific characteristics in any of these categories. For example, the company may want to send a mailing to everyone who bought a certain product or who lives in a certain area (identified by a range of zip codes). Using the computer to generate a mailing list and print out the mailing labels is far simpler than searching through piles of receipts and hand typing mailing labels.

Data base management systems have other applications besides mailing lists. The company could use this software to keep track of marketing research information, such as reports on the company's various products. If the company has a library, it might want to keep its records on such a system. This software is also useful for preparing directories, glossaries, or other information that the user wants sorted alphabetically. In general, data base management programs are helpful for information that users want to organize, reorganize, and retrieve swiftly.

Telecommunicating

Besides help in interpreting information, businesspeople use information systems for communication — the sending and receiving of information. The basis for communicating is software designed for **telecommunicating,** or using a modem to send information between two computers or between a terminal and a processing unit. A court ruling allowing the seven regional Bell companies to use their telephone network to carry information services

Petaks Caterers of Wall Street serves its customers with the help of a fax machine. Busy customers avoid waiting by faxing their orders ahead of time.

Source: © Gregory Heisler for Nynex Corporation.

Telecommunicating Using a modem to send information between two computers or between a terminal and a processing unit.

CLOSE-UP / *Innovation*

Going Cellular

An important part of today's information technology is the cellular phone. The cost of these units is declining rapidly. Just a few years ago, a cellular phone cost $3,000. Today some of them can be purchased for less than $600. So when businesspeople are away from the office and unable to use a computer to link themselves to company operations, many now rely on their portable, cellular phone to keep them in touch.

The latest units are so lightweight and small that they can be carried around in a purse or a jacket pocket. Moreover, thanks to rapidly improving technology, cellular technology has dramatically increased and many units now offer the same high resonance as do conventional phones.

The biggest problem perhaps is that of overreliance, which can drive the monthly phone bill sky-high. This is because the rate per minute is steep when compared to conventional phones. In many locales the cost is 40 to 60 cents a minute plus a monthly service charge. A person paying 50 cents a minute for 100 minutes a month and a monthly charge of $50 will have an annual cellular bill of $1,200. In encouraging people to go cel-

lular, however, some communication firms that are providing this service are making the cost of the phone very attractive and are offering a reduced monthly charge in hopes of increasing the number of customers and the amount of phone use. For example, the firm will sell the phone for $500 and offer a monthly charge of only $25 to all customers who use the phone over 120 minutes a month. All other subscribers pay a monthly charge of $50 a month.

How attractive are these phones for handling the communication needs of today's business firms? Research shows that in the United States in the past 5 years demand has climbed dramatically, and an increasing number of competitors are entering the field. Major markets exist in Europe and Japan, and some Third World countries are also beginning to go cellular. Mexico, Thailand, Pakistan, and Indonesia, in particular, are feeling the boom, and this is only the beginning. As Eastern Europe becomes more industrialized and China and India start building cellular systems, the worldwide market will produce revenues in excess of $100 billion annually. Quite clearly, businesspeople are relying more and more heavily on information, and cellular phones are one way they are getting it.

Source: Robert D. Hof, "For Cellular, Freedom Has Its Place," *Business Week*, March 26, 1990, 36–37; Christine Forbes, "Entrepreneur's Guide to Cellular Phones," *Entrepreneur*, April 1990, 74–77; and Stephen Baker, Sally Gelston, and Jonathan Kapstein, "The Third World Is Getting Cellular Fever," *Business Week*, April 16, 1990, 80–81.

greatly expands the availability and ease of using telecommunication. Everyone with a phone can now tap into the growing number of information services, ranging from voice mail (recording and sending out telephone messages) to pay-for-view cable TV.

Telecommunicating is an efficient way to send long or complex information. A company might telecommunicate with its sales force in the field by sending customer requests and feedback from managers, while the sales people could send sales reports and customer orders. Many decision makers use telecommunicating to link up with data bases produced by other companies. For example, a manager might telephone a data base service and look up information on stock prices or the latest research in a particular field. However, because telecommunication is more expensive for short messages than sending a letter or placing a phone call, businesspeople have to establish which means of communication is most appropriate for a particular situation. In some cases, as seen in the accompanying Innovation Close-Up (Going Cellular), this means relying on cellular technology.

Telecommunicating is changing the nature of the workplace by allowing employees, ranging from clerical workers to staff specialists to top-level managers, to work at home while remaining in touch with the office through a

A person whose office is at home, whether he or she is an entrepreneur or a telecommuting employee, is likely to need a computer modem and a fax machine. Both of them use telephone lines to transmit messages. Telephone companies like US West offer work-at-home customers an array of services that enable them to work efficiently.

Source: © John Blaustein 1990.

computer hookup. Companies that adopt this approach with clerical workers can save themselves office space. Those employees who use this approach are given the opportunity to work on their own schedule. Parents who want to be home for their children in the afternoon are able to be there. These "telecommuting" employees must complete a minimum amount of work; in many cases, they actually end up doing much more than employees who commute to the office.

Electronic Mail and Facsimile Machines

Another relatively new application of communication by computer technology is **electronic mail,** or E-mail. This is a system for sending and receiving messages through computers. The process is quite simple. The sender normally types the message into the computer and tells the machine who is to receive it. The computer sends the message as soon as it can contact the recipient's computer. That computer saves the message in a special file. When people in the electronic mail system turn on their computer, they can ask the machine whether they have any messages. If they do, the computer then displays their mail on the screen. Many firms have found that they need 2 to 3 days to distribute a regular paper memo; with electronic mail, the same process takes only seconds. It also avoids the annoyance and wasted time of "telephone tag" — calling someone who is unavailable and who finds you unavailable when trying to return the call. With electronic mail, the entire message waits in the computer file until the recipient is free to read it.[25]

If a copy of a letter or document must be transmitted, a **facsimile machine (fax)** is typically used. This machine conveys images over telephone lines. In most cases, the document is first fed into a fax machine and sent by phone to the other party's fax machine. On the receiving end a printer produces the copy. In some cases, the sender or the receiver in a fax transmission

Electronic mail A system for sending and receiving messages through computers.

Facsimile machine (fax) A machine that transmits and receives documents via telephone lines.

FIGURE 10.6

A Value-Added Network (VAN) for Auto Manufacturing

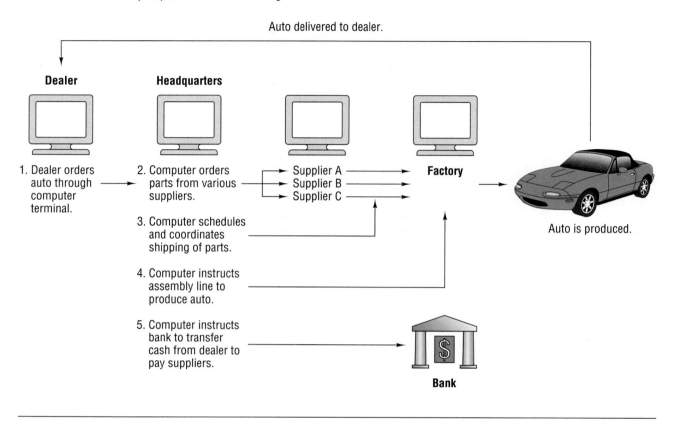

Source: Joel Dreyfuss, "Networking: Japan's Latest Computer Craze," *Fortune,* July 7, 1986, 95.

may be a computer. Sharp Corporation of Japan has also developed a machine for full-color facsimiles. Faxes eliminate postal costs and of course eliminate delivery time, although the cost of transmitting documents long distances can result in fairly substantial phone bills.[26]

Computer Networking

Computer network A system that allows for multiple users and multiple activities.

Especially if they use several of the applications described previously, companies with several users often have a comprehensive **computer network.** This is a system that allows for multiple users and multiple activities. A number of people can use the system simultaneously, and they can all be doing different things. Some may be communicating through the computer; others may be ordering the computer to print a letter or file, while still others are analyzing spreadsheet data. Each of these users, communicating with his or her computer or terminal, is able to draw on the computer's power.

Value-added network (VAN) A system providing electronic links between an organization and outside personnel.

In the future, this idea may expand into what is sometimes called value-added networks. A **value-added network (VAN)** is a system providing electronic links between an organization and outside personnel. Figure 10.6 illustrates how this would work for an auto manufacturer. The VAN electronically links the dealer, company headquarters, and suppliers.

An increasing number of companies are using VANs to communicate over long distances, thereby linking manufacturers, suppliers, and customers. As a result, goods are produced faster and more cheaply and are brought to market in record time.

1. What are two major computer applications in business?
2. Which applications would be suitable for a small manufacturing firm? For a large insurance company?

CHECK ✓ POINT

Closing Comments

This chapter examined how information systems and computer technology help businesspeople generate, transmit, analyze, and use information. As numerous organizations have discovered, managing the flow and accuracy of information is crucial to making well-informed, effective decisions. With careful data entry and programming, computer technology can be an immense help in the task of managing information. The use of computers will no doubt grow as they continue to become more powerful and versatile, thanks to hardware and software developments. In turn, this will open up many new uses, complementing or even replacing those that were discussed in this chapter.

If information systems and computer technology have as big an impact on business in the next 15 years as they have had in the past 15 years, students and practitioners of business must be knowledgeable about what they can expect. To address that need, this chapter explained what types of information systems and computer technology are available and the basic functions they perform in helping businesspeople make better decisions.

VIDEO CASE / *Microcomputers for Everyone*

Dell Computer is a good example of a firm that has grown rapidly. The owner, Michael Dell, born in 1965, has created a major direct-marketing firm with sales of over $500 million, and if the computer industry continues to be inundated with competitors, Dell Computer will likely gain further market share. The reason is simple: As more and more computer firms offer home computers, the market will become glutted with models that are forced to compete on price. Because the Dell company sells through direct marketing, it eliminates the middle person and can pass the savings along to the

customer, thus making it very price competitive.

Michael Dell's strategy is effective because of the wide range of offerings for home computers that are now available. These include: (1) Atari's 1040 STE, popularly tabbed as the poor man's Macintosh, which uses a Motorola 6800 chip and sells for about $699; (2) the Tandy 1000 RL, which uses the Intel 8086 chip, comes with 24 software programs, and sells in the range of $750 to $1,299; (3) the Apple Macintosh, which has been dramatically slashed in price and now sells in the $1,500 range; (4) the IBM PS/1, which uses the Intel

80286 microchip, comes with business programs and on-line help from IBM, and sells in the $1,500 range; (5) the Laser Computer Pal, which is one of dozens of IBM clones, contains a hard disk drive and a modem, and sells for about $1,500; and (6) the Packard Bell, an 80286-based clone, which comes with in-home service for one year and sells for around $1,400.

Many computer makers are concerned about the number of competitors and the impending price war. However, the picture has a bright side. At the beginning of the decade approximately 4 million Americans had home

PCs. By 1994, this number is projected to be twice as big, up to 8 million. The projected growth is good news for firms such as Dell Computer.

Source: Diedre Depke, "Home Computers," *Business Week*, September 10, 1990, 64–74.

Case Questions

1. Which type of computers is Dell Computer selling: mainframes or micros?
2. What benefits do personal home computers have for the customers? Identify and discuss two of them.
3. Why is it likely that firms such as Dell Computer will continue to do well in the future?

Learning Objectives Revisited

1. **Explain how information systems help managers make decisions.** A management information system (MIS) is a method for collecting, analyzing, and disseminating timely information to support decision making. This system typically uses computers to link information sources with users, directing the appropriate types of information to each user. Managers at upper levels of an organization need general information to help them formulate the enterprise's overall goals and long-range strategy. Middle managers look for information that helps them contribute to corporate objectives in the near future. First-line managers need more specific information for help in running day-to-day operations.

2. **Describe the evolution of computer technology.** The first generation of computers relied on vacuum tubes and were large, heavy, and expensive to operate. The second generation replaced tubes with smaller and more reliable transistors. The introduction of the integrated circuit ushered in the third generation, making computers smaller and faster. The fourth generation uses microprocessors containing millions of integrated circuits. This generation has brought computer power into the home as well as the business. The next generation is still in the development stage; one direction receiving attention is artificial intelligence, programming that would enable computers to mimic human thinking and logical reasoning.

3. **Identify the hardware and software components of computer technology.** Hardware is the machinery and physical components of the computer. These components consist of input, processing, secondary storage, and output units. Software is the series of instructions, or programming, that tells the machine what to do. Most businesspeople buy ready-made software designed to do specific tasks rather than write or commission their own programs.

4. **Define the basic types of computers.** The basic types of computers are mainframe computers and microcomputers. A mainframe is a large computer system that offers tremendous storage capacity and rapid processing of information. A microcomputer, or personal computer, is a small, but increasingly powerful, desktop computer that relies on a microprocessor. These have largely replaced the medium-sized minicomputers. The microcomputer typically includes a system unit, keyboard, video screen, and printer. Some systems also have a modem, a mouse, or extra storage devices.

5. **Discuss how businesspeople evaluate the merits of computers.** Businesspeople weigh business advantages and disadvantages of computer technology, as well as societal implications. Some of the major advantages include speed, accuracy, large capacity, assumption of boring tasks, and increased efficiency. Some of the major disadvantages are expense, consequences of mistakes, vulnerability to overreliance, people problems, and security risks.

6. **Present the basic applications of computer technology to business.** Basic applications to business include word processing, desktop publishing and video, spreadsheets, data base management, telecommunications, electronic mail and facsimile machines, and networking. Many programs combine these applications to meet specific business needs such as payroll processing and inventory control.

Key Terms Reviewed

Review the following terms. For any that you do not know or are unsure of, look up the definitions and see how they were used in the chapter

management information system (MIS)	user-friendly program	desktop publishing
	mainframe computer	desktop video (DTV)
data base	microcomputer	spreadsheets
integrated circuit	microprocessor	telecommunicating
artificial intelligence (AI)	minicomputer	electronic mail
hardware	byte	facsimile machine
software	computer virus	computer network
computer program	word processing	value-added network (VAN)

Review Questions

1. Most businesses are inundated with information. Why doesn't this influx eliminate their need for a management information system?

2. Can a management information system exist without computers? Explain. What benefits do computers bring to an MIS?

3. What kinds of information might each of the following need? Give some specific examples. What would be a possible source for each type of information?
   a. The supervisor of a telemarketing staff for a company that sells magazine subscriptions
   b. The marketing manager of the company that sells magazine subscriptions
   c. A certified public accountant whose clients are primarily small businesses
   d. The president of a large chain of hair salon franchises

4. Clara Wilson is in the process of buying a computer. She is first going to decide the software she will need and will then choose the hardware. Is her approach correct or is she doing things in reverse order?

5. What hardware components would be appropriate for performing each of the following tasks? Give an example for each, being as specific as you can.
   a. Performing statistical calculations
   b. Distributing a memo to department heads
   c. Entering research data into the computer

6. Pablo Gutierrez needs to purchase software for controlling his inventory. Which approach do you think he should use?

7. What type of computer would you recommend for each of the following situations? Explain your reasoning.
   a. A research company that processes large quantities of data but has a limited budget
   b. A major bank that keeps records on thousands of accounts and investments, as well as conducts internal accounting and reporting
   c. A small manufacturing company that wants to make its office work more efficiently

8. Frank Whitney depends on his computer to perform all of the necessary spreadsheet calculations accurately. What more does Frank need to be concerned about?

9. Pete Gardner is thinking of buying a billing system for his health clinic. The system will cost roughly $8,000 for hardware and software. How might Pete go about deciding whether this expense is worthwhile?

10. Joan Barkley is in the process of introducing computers into her retail operation. What are some personnel-related problems she is likely to encounter? How can she address these problems?

11. What are the basic applications of computers to business? What does each type of software do?

12. LaDonna Finch is trying to decide whether to add a third shift in her fiberglass manufacturing company. How can spreadsheet software help LaDonna to make this decision?

13. What are some ways in which businesspeople can use computers to communicate information?

Applied Exercise

How much do you know about information systems and computer technology? Read each of these statements and indicate whether it is basically true or false as of the current time. The answers are based on data provided by experts in the field.

	Basically True	Basically False
1. Computers are now smaller and more powerful than ever before.	_____	_____
2. Computer simulations are now able to help doctors identify and prevent patient cancer.	_____	_____
3. Computers are being used to design buildings and airplanes.	_____	_____
4. Cellular phones are less expensive to own and operate than are conventional phones.	_____	_____
5. It is possible to use computer data searches to eliminate the need to go to the library and find desired materials.	_____	_____
6. Facsimile machines are resulting in a tremendous loss of income to the post office.	_____	_____
7. Computer programs can now integrate text, quantitative data, and graphs.	_____	_____
8. Computers have resulted in massive unemployment in many industries.	_____	_____
9. Many firms are using desktop publishing to totally eliminate their photocopying expenses.	_____	_____
10. Textbook publishers have linked computers into their production process and eliminated a lot of the time previously needed for typesetting.	_____	_____

Eileen Crespo owns an auto supply store. She bought the store 6 months ago, just after she quit her job with a large oil company. While with the oil company for 5 years, Eileen had sold auto supplies to service stations and other retail outlets. During this time, she became familiar with the field and concluded that it has the potential for high profit. In particular, Eileen believes that over the next decade more and more people are going to begin servicing their own cars. "A growing number of people want to save money on their cars," she recently told a friend. "It's going to be a lot like the home repair business in the mid-1980s."

When Eileen learned that Tony Rezazzo was looking to sell his auto supply store, Eileen went to talk to him. Within 2 days, they had struck a deal, and within a month, Eileen had taken over.

One of the first things she has done is to make a complete count of the inventory. She currently has $203,000 of auto supplies, including batteries, hoses, spark plugs, mufflers, windshield wipers, and various parts. Eileen believes that the key to success in this business is a small inventory that turns over rapidly. However, she is concerned that if the inventory is too small, she will continually be out of stock and will lose customers. Last week she had a visit from a computer salesperson. He suggested that Eileen purchase a microcomputer and accompanying software for $2,500 to maintain her financial records and control inventory. The idea sounds fine to Eileen, but she wonders whether the computerized information system approach is really necessary. It might be just as easy to control inventory by adding and subtracting the units purchased and sold from her physical count of how much she has. This would provide a running total of her inventory. When Eileen begins to run low on some products, she can reorder them.

Your Advice

1. What should Eileen do?
    ___ a. Eileen should forget about the computer system and use a physical inventory to keep track of units on hand.
    ___ b. Eileen should buy the computer, learn how to use it for inventory control, and rely on it to help minimize costs.
    ___ c. Eileen should hire an outside firm to keep computer records on her inventory and to advise her appropriately.
2. What kinds of information does Eileen need? How can a computer help her manage this information?
3. Could Eileen control inventory manually? How would this compare to using a computer?
4. Would you recommend that Eileen buy a microcomputer? Why or why not? Be sure to consider the advantages and disadvantages.

Career Opportunities in Business

A large number of management opportunities exist in today's business organizations. Entry level positions can be found at the supervisory (first level) and middle management ranks. As the manager gains experience over the years, all kinds of opportunities become available. The following examines some representative jobs that offer challenging career opportunities.

First Line Supervisor

A first line supervisor is the lowest level manager in an organization. This important position is management's direct interface with operating employees in all types of organizations.

Job Description. The first line supervisor is responsible for directing the activities of operating personnel by telling them what has to be done and making sure the work is completed correctly. Supervisors ensure that goods and services are being produced according to specifications and that quality standards are being met. Supervisors also plan employees' activities, teach safe work habits, enforce regulations, demonstrate time-saving techniques, and ensure that workers are properly trained.

Employment Outlook and Earnings. Every organization of any size employs first line supervisors. They work in a wide variety of organizations including con-struction, manufacturing, wholesale and retail trade, restaurants, public utilities, hotels, transportation, and government agencies. Earnings vary widely depending on the industry and the amount of experience. The first line supervisor with a bachelor's degree can expect a starting salary between $22,000 and $26,000 depending on prior experience and the amount of responsibility.

Purchasing Agent

A purchasing agent, sometimes called an industrial buyer or a procurement manager, will secure the inputs that a company needs for its operation.

Job Description. A purchasing agent is responsible for obtaining raw materials, component parts, and supplies needed by the firm to turn out the goods and services it sells. The agent works closely with in-house personnel who need these materials and determines precise specifications and quantities so that the order meets these needs. The purchasing agent also works closely with outside vendors who provide the necessary goods and tries to acquire the best possible deal. This typically involves comparing vendor offerings on the basis of price, quality, delivery, and payment.

Employment Outlook and Earnings. Today there are close to one-half million purchasing agents in the United States and there should be a general increase in this number during the years ahead. Most college graduates would start out as an assistant purchasing manager and work their way up. Senior-level management positions in purchasing include director of purchasing, director of procurement, vice president for purchasing, or vice president for materials management. The beginning salary in private industry is around $25,000 and in the public sector it is approximately $22,000. Senior-level managers often make three times this amount.

Systems Analyst

A systems analyst develops or improves information systems (usually computer-based) for the organization.

Job Description. A systems analyst identifies the information needed to support management decision making and determines how best to obtain and provide this information. The analyst presents a plan to management and, once approval is obtained, develops a management information system with the assistance of computer programmers. The analyst will then help maintain and update the system.

Employment Outlook and Earnings. This is one of the fastest growing career opportunities. Today entry-level information systems experts can expect to start at around $25,000 and the average software developer makes $30,000 to $40,000. Experienced, senior-level analysts make $50,000 and up.

Computer Programmer

A computer programmer carries out the instructions of a systems analyst. The programmer is important in the development, implementation, and maintenance of information systems.

Job Description. Working within the system analyst's overall plan, a computer programmer helps develop software that provides the needed information. After these programs have been tested and verified, the programmer will turn them over to the computer operating personnel.

Employment Outlook and Earnings. Beginning programmers are typically assigned to basic tasks, while experienced experts will work on more sophisticated, complex assignments. As is true for other jobs, experience is a critical factor in both employment and earnings. Entry-level computer personnel can expect salaries in the $20,000 to $25,000 range. More experienced programmers earn up to $40,000 and, if the current trend continues, these salaries should increase much faster than inflation over the next 5 years.

1-800-DENTIST
© 1989 Futuredontics, Inc.℠

RELAXING THEIR EMPLOYEES

Most organizations have a fairly strict
set of operating procedures, rules,
and regulations that everyone is
expected to abide by. However, an
increasing number of companies are
finding that a personalized work
environment, where employees feel
relaxed and confident, motivates them
to perform effectively. An example is
1-800-Dentist. Staff members trying
to help customers who are in pain are
likely to feel relatively great stress

Motivation and Leadership

11

Chapter Learning Objectives

- Describe how the major approaches to the directing function have changed over the years.

- Discuss approaches to understanding motivation.

- Present some techniques for motivating employees by improving the work environment.

- Describe the techniques managers use to motivate individual employees.

- Identify some basic leadership styles.

- Explain how leaders can choose an effective style.

---

and tension themselves. They need a relaxing organizational climate in which to do their jobs.

The 1-800-Dentist group helps clients find and link up with practicing dentists. This can fill an important consumer need because someone who does not have a regular dentist may have a dental problem that requires attention right away. The company is genuinely interested in helping these clients but is equally concerned about its employees. In addition to the usual birthday parties, company picnics, and softball games, once a week every staff member is treated to a 10- to 15-minute massage. In an industry where high stress is common (dentists report higher stress levels than almost any other professional group), 1-800-Dentist works to relieve the tension of its employees and keep them relaxed so that they can do a better job.

How do the people at 1-800-Dentist feel about management's approach? They love it. When someone calls 1-800-Dentist and asks for help with a dental problem, staff members want the client to feel as good as they do. The result is that morale is high, demand for the service is increasing, and the company is undergoing a major expansion.

Photo source: Courtesy of Futuredontics.

Introduction

Most management research and effective practicing managers say that employees are a business's most important asset. They are the key to every successful enterprise. Support for this idea comes from Sam Walton, who is worth several billion dollars and is the founder of the successful Wal-Mart chain of stores. Describing the basis for his success in business, Walton said, "It can be summarized in one word — people." This chapter focuses on the directing function of management. It describes how managers motivate and lead employees to achieve organizational and individual goals.

The Directing Function of Modern Management

Directing function
A management approach that brings employees and the organization together to achieve the objectives of both.

Chapter 8 introduced directing (along with planning, organizing, and controlling) as a function of modern management. Through the **directing function** managers can bring employees and the organization together in a way that achieves the objectives of both. For example, if employees find that by working hard they can meet their own objectives of earning more or feeling proud of their work, they will put forth extra effort. This effort helps the organization meet its objectives for productivity and profits.

The directing function of management has evolved through several stages. First there was the scientific management movement. This was followed by early behavioral management that has now become best known as the human resource management approach. After briefly giving background on these stages, the chapter focuses on the two major dimensions of the directing function: motivation and leadership.

Scientific Management

Scientific management
An approach started around 1900 that used engineering techniques such as time-and-motion analysis to increase plant efficiency by establishing the one best method for each task.

About 100 years ago, America was in the throes of the Industrial Revolution. Huge factories, each employing hundreds or thousands of workers, were springing up across the country, and managers primarily focused on how to get workers and machines to operate as efficiently as possible. Around the beginning of the century, companies began using **scientific management,** which was an approach that used engineering techniques such as time and motion analysis to increase plant efficiency. Pioneering scientific managers helped solve such problems as laying out the plant efficiently, determining the best machine speed, and figuring out how employees could work most productively and quickly. Some of the basic beliefs of the scientific managers during this time period are summarized in the first column of Figure 11.1

The founding father of scientific management was Frederick W. Taylor, who analyzed tasks and conducted time-and-motion studies to determine the "best way" to perform a job. Scientific managers such as Taylor divided jobs into elementary movements, then discarded the nonessential ones. They determined the most efficient way of performing each essential movement; and then they prepared written instructions for how to perform a job, down to the minute details. Workers were to follow these instructions without deviation.

For example, through scientific analysis, Taylor was able to almost quadruple the output of pig-iron handlers (those who loaded slabs of iron weighing about 92 pounds that were shaped somewhat like a pig) and shovel-

FIGURE 11.1
Management Approaches through the Years

	Elements of Scientific Management	Elements of Early Behavioral Management	Elements of Human Resources Management
Treatment of Employees	Supervise and control workers closely. Treat them as a factor of production.	Make employees feel that they are important. Give them fringe benefits and good working conditions.	Try to tap each employee's full potential by giving increased responsibility and challenging work.
Employee Relationship to Work	Reduce all work into simple repetitive processes. Use scientific method.	Give employees some self-direction and self-control over their work.	Encourage subordinates to participate in decision making.
Employee Role in a Firm	Make sure employees follow the rules. There is no room for flexibility or initiative.	Keep subordinates informed about what is going on. Make them feel like they are insiders.	Keep in mind that employees are the enterprise's most important asset.
Motivation of Employees	Money motivates.	Money and a friendly work environment are the two most important motivators.	Interesting and challenging work and good wages motivate most people.

Contributions in Relation to Time			
		Labor unions and personnel departments gain strength.	
	Frederick W. Taylor applies scientific management in steel plants successfully.	Hawthorne studies provide new insights into human behavior.	Human relations provides good wages and working conditions.	World competition and recognition that human resources are the key to increased productivity.

```
1880   1890   1900   1910   1920   1930   1940   1950   1960   1970   1980   1990   Present
```

ers at steel plants. Scientific managers also planned the sequence of machines used and the route the materials followed. Under this approach, the company's managers were responsible for seeing that the work was carried out in accordance with the scientific managers' instructions.

Although these efforts enabled companies to improve their efficiency and productivity, other problems arose. Managers and workers resisted the loss of autonomy in deciding how they did their jobs. Although sophisticated wage incentives were used, advocates of scientific management generally regarded the worker more as a machine than as a thinking, feeling person.

Early Behavioral Management

Beginning in the late 1920s and early 1930s, the approach to managing people began to change. The labor union movement was gaining momentum, forcing companies to consider the interests of workers. As a result, companies began to form personnel departments. Management experts were also learning more about workers. They looked beyond the job itself to the person holding the job.

Hawthorne studies Pioneering research studies on worker behavior and motivation.

The Hawthorne Studies One famous examination of the dynamics of human behavior at work was a series of pioneering studies conducted between 1924 and 1932 at the Hawthorne works of the Western Electric Company. The **Hawthorne studies** provided important insights into worker motivation and behavior. The initial phase of the studies was intended to determine whether the level of illumination affected worker productivity. In the experiment, the researchers increased the illumination level for workers who were doing simple assembly tasks. As expected, productivity increased. Then the researchers *decreased* the level of light. To their bafflement, the performance increased again. The researchers decreased the illumination again until it was comparable to that of moonlight, and still the workers' productivity improved.

Clearly, something besides the level of light was influencing performance. As further studies showed, this "additional influence" was the human element. The workers put forth extra effort in part because they saw the research as a sign of management's interest in them.[1] In another phase of the Hawthorne studies, the informal work group was shown to have considerable influence on individual workers. The Hawthorne workers needed to be accepted by their work group, to be able to talk to their boss, and to feel that the company in general and managers in particular cared about them. The researchers concluded that workers are more complicated than just another factor of production and that aspects of the work setting other than the job itself influence worker behavior.

A More Humanistic Approach As a result of the Hawthorne studies and a growing body of other research, management began to adopt a more humanistic approach. Companies still valued scientific management's emphasis on efficiency, but came to appreciate an additional element of management: the way in which managers attempt to motivate and lead their employees. Cleveland-based Lincoln Electric, the world's largest manufacturer of welding machines and electrodes, was one of the first firms to implement a lifetime employment policy, promotion from within, performance appraisals, pay-for-performance incentive systems, an employee stock ownership plan (employees currently own about half of the company's stock), pensions and extensive fringe benefits (a company cafeteria serves meals at about 60 percent of usual costs), and employee participation in decision making. The second column in Figure 11.1 summarizes this behavioral management approach.

Just as scientific management led to some dramatic increases in productivity and profits, so did the early behavioral management approach. For instance, at Lincoln Electric, profits and productivity grew rapidly. Between 1934 and 1941, productivity per employee at this innovative company more than doubled.

Human Resource Management
Beginning in the 1970s, a newer approach to managing employees developed. Today's effective managers regard their employees as important resources —

"human resources" — having a great deal of untapped potential. Under human resource management, the manager's job is to create an environment in which employees can unleash their considerable potential and use it for the good of both the organization and themselves. Instead of trying to structure jobs rigidly and monitor employees' behavior closely (as under scientific management) or trying to make employees feel that they are all part of one big, happy family (early behavioral management), the human resource approach recognizes the importance of people to organizational performance and seeks to provide them with the opportunity to develop their full potential. Today this takes such forms as employee involvement and empowerment. It is estimated that 50 to 60 percent of large U.S. corporations now use quality circles, problem-solving groups, and other ways to get employee suggestions. Another 5 to 10 percent have work teams that allow the workers themselves to make decisions about hiring, firing, and pay.[2]

Besides involvement and empowerment, the human resource approach takes many other forms, ranging from recruiting, selecting, training, and developing personnel to motivating and leading them. For example, the Sherwin-Williams Paint Company instituted a human resource approach in its Richmond, Kentucky, plant. It hires only those who would enjoy working on challenging and important tasks, then it groups the employees into teams. These teams have complete autonomy to determine where members work, what work they do, and how to train a newcomer. The teams are also responsible for the results, and pay is based on performance.

Like scientific management and the early behavioral approaches, the human resource approach has had considerable success. At the Richmond Sherwin-Williams plant, absenteeism is much lower than at the company's other plants, and productivity is greater. Recent research has found that firms with effective human resource management practices tend to be more profitable than those with less effective practices.[3]

The human resource approach to management is the basis for and the term used for the modern function of personnel management and will be covered in Chapter 12. This human resource perspective, however, is also the foundation for the broader based modern directing function. All managers of people (whether in production, marketing, or finance, or even in non-business organizations) need an understanding of how to motivate and lead their people. In particular, motivating and leading human resources has become recognized as a, if not the, key management challenge for business success and international competitiveness in the critical years ahead.[4]

CHECK ✓ POINT

1. What approaches to management have preceded the development of modern human resource management?
2. What have managers learned from each of these management approaches?

Understanding Motivation

To gain a competitive advantage and survive in the global economy, managers must motivate their employees. **Motivation** is a complex psychological process in which needs or wants lead to drives (behavior intended to satisfy a

Motivation The process through which needs or wants lead to drives aimed at goals or incentives.

FIGURE 11.2
The Process of Motivation

need) aimed at goals or incentives. As shown in Figure 11.2, the needs are really the mainspring of the motivation. For example, if you have a need for achievement, your behavior aimed at satisfying that need (that is, your drive) may be to study hard. Your goal might be straight A's. If you get straight A's, your drive may be less intense and your need satisfied or you may raise your goals to, say, graduate number one in your class. Another possibility is that, after final exams, your need for rest might seem more important than your need for achievement.

To know what motivates employees, managers must look at the world the way they do. One representative survey asked managers to rank the rewards that workers desired from their jobs and then asked the workers to rank the things that motivated them. It was found that the three factors the supervisors rated lowest were rated highest by the workers. This finding shows that many managers really do not know what motivates their employees. Furthermore, one recent survey found that 38 percent of American workers feel that their bosses rarely or never recognize or praise their accomplishments.[5] Another recent survey of 400 managers discovered that one-third of them distrust their boss and 55 percent of them do not believe top management.[6]

Needs and Motivation

Employees may be motivated by challenging work, good wages and salaries, increased responsibility, or fringe benefits (a company car, free life insurance, or low-cost health insurance). Each employee will seek to satisfy personal needs. A person with a strong need for job security may gravitate into a government bureaucracy, where lifetime employment is common. An individual with a high need for achievement may seek a job in sales, where progress is largely up to the individual and security is less important. The influence of motivational needs helps explain employee behavior.

Primary needs Physiological needs such as food, water, sex, sleep, clothing, and shelter.

Secondary needs Psychological needs such as friendship, recognition, power, and achievement.

Primary and Secondary Needs   People have two major types of needs, primary and secondary. **Primary needs** are physiological; they include the needs for food, water, sex, sleep, clothing, and shelter. Students who work part-time at the library to cover living expenses do so to fulfill some of these primary needs. **Secondary needs** are psychological; they include the needs for friendship, recognition, control or power, and achievement. Students who join a fraternity, sorority, or social club or run for an office do so to fulfill some of these secondary needs.

The two kinds of needs have different sources. Primary needs are innate, meaning that people are born with them. Secondary needs are learned, meaning that people acquire these needs from parents, friends, and society as they grow up and mature.

FIGURE 11.3
Maslow's Hierarchy of Needs

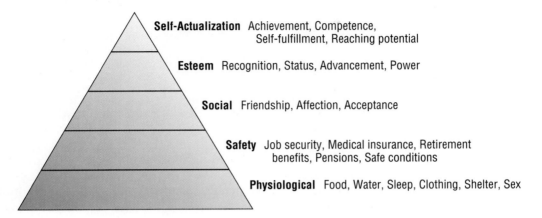

Self-Actualization Achievement, Competence, Self-fulfillment, Reaching potential

Esteem Recognition, Status, Advancement, Power

Social Friendship, Affection, Acceptance

Safety Job security, Medical insurance, Retirement benefits, Pensions, Safe conditions

Physiological Food, Water, Sleep, Clothing, Shelter, Sex

Maslow's Hierarchy of Needs   The best-known explanation of motivation based on needs is that of the famous humanistic psychologist Abraham Maslow. He described a five-step hierarchy of needs people strive to attain:

- Physiological needs — the primary needs for survival: food, water, clothing, shelter, sex, and sleep
- Safety needs — the need to protect yourself from physical and financial risks
- Social needs — the needs for friendship, affection, and acceptance
- Esteem needs — the need to be recognized and to have status and power
- Self-actualization needs — the need to reach your potential, to be the best you can be

Figure 11.3 summarizes and gives examples of Maslow's hierarchy of human needs.

Once a person fulfills a particular level of need, it no longer serves to motivate. The next level of need then serves to motivate the individual. For example, suppose Mary Smith has just been laid off and has no money saved up. Her primary concern is how to buy groceries and pay the rent; she is motivated by physiological needs. Then Mary starts receiving unemployment compensation, so she knows she can satisfy her basic physiological needs. Now she is interested in a job that will offer her safe working conditions, health insurance, and job security; these are safety needs.

If Mary finds such a job, she will probably start devoting more energy to fulfilling social and esteem needs — spending more time with family, friends, and coworkers, and seeking a promotion and recognition at work. If she doesn't feel like part of the group at work, she might start looking for another job. Finally, Mary hopes that someday she will be free to devote more energy to attaining her full potential. This motivation to achieve self-actualization may lead to accomplishments in areas as diverse as career advancement, body building, child rearing, and charity work.

FIGURE 11.4
Herzberg's Two-Factor Theory

Motivators Work Itself Recognition Responsibility Advancement Achievement	**Hygiene Factors** Money Job Security Working Conditions Technical Supervision Company Policies
These result in workers feeling satisfied.	**Absence of these results in workers feeling dissatisfied.**

Maslow's approach to motivation is useful in helping identify the types of needs people have and the role of the manager and the organization in motivating employees. Maslow's theory points out that the sources of motivation are diverse. It explains why some workers may be unmotivated in an organization that pays good wages, offers fringe benefits, and has excellent working conditions. The company is taking care of the lower level needs, but not the higher level needs for esteem and self-actualization.

In order to fulfill their need to realize their potential, some employees may feel forced to leave a company and become entrepreneurs. However, as Chapter 7 pointed out, companies can appeal to their employees' need for self-actualization, and reap benefits from their increased motivation, by encouraging and creating a climate of intrapreneurship. Employees are thus able to fulfill their need for self-actualization on the job through intrapreneuring, and both the individuals and the company benefit.

Two-Factor Theory of Work Motivation

Although Maslow provides a beginning for understanding work motivation, Frederick Herzberg has developed an even more relevant theory: the two-factor theory of work motivation. Whereas Maslow never tested his theory in the workplace, Herzberg based his theory on industrial research. Herzberg and his research associates asked two basic questions of employees: What makes you feel exceptionally good about your job? What makes you feel exceptionally bad about your job? Figure 11.4 illustrates the specific factors that workers mentioned.

Motivator factors Job characteristics that make people feel exceptionally good about their jobs, including challenge, recognition, and responsibility.

Herzberg termed as **motivator factors** those job characteristics that make people feel exceptionally good about their jobs. These include the challenge of the work, recognition for doing a good job, the responsibility associated with the work, prospects for advancement, and a sense of achievement. According to Herzberg, these factors lead to job satisfaction and motivate employees.

Hygiene factors Job characteristics that do not motivate people but that cause dissatisfaction when absent, including money, working conditions, and job security.

He called **hygiene factors** those job characteristics that do not directly motivate workers but that cause dissatisfaction when they are absent. These factors include money, job security, working conditions, technical supervision, and company policies. By giving people competitive salaries, good working conditions, and job security, managers can prevent dissatisfaction. However, to create satisfaction, managers also must provide motivator fac-

Company/Chief Executive Officer	Total Compensation	TABLE 11.1 Compensation for Chief Executive Officers
Coca Cola/Roberta Goizueta	$10,814,000	
Wal-Mart Stores/David Glass	6,759,000	
Philip Morris Cos./Hamish Maxwell	6,453,000	
Federal National Mortgage/D. O. Maxwell	4,782,000	
Texaco/James W. Kinnear	3,943,000	
ITT/Rand Araskog	3,932,000	
General Electric/John Welch	3,566,000	
American Express/James D. Robinson	3,537,000	
Hewlett-Packard/John Young	3,161,000	
Westinghouse/John C. Marcus	3,147,000	

Source: Steve Kichen, "Pay Preview," *Forbes*, May 14, 1990, 91.

tors. Surveys indicate that today's workers want such satisfaction more than the hygiene factors, and this holds throughout the world.[7]

For example, at a branch office of AT&T, the computer operators were well paid and had good fringe benefits and working conditions, but they were not satisfied with their jobs. Absenteeism was high, and quality of work was low. The operators simply did their assigned pile of work every day and then passed it on, whether it was correct or not. If they didn't feel like working they stayed home, because someone would cover for them. To motivate the employees, AT&T tried assigning each computer operator a specific area of responsibility, such as payroll or billing. In other words, the operators received the motivator factors of responsibility, recognition, and opportunity for growth and achievement. As a result, the operators became more satisfied with their jobs. Absenteeism and the quality of work improved dramatically.

CHECK ✓ POINT

1. How do Maslow's hierarchy and Herzberg's two-factor theory explain motivation?
2. How can companies use these theories to motivate their employees?

Techniques for Motivating Employees

Maslow's and Herzberg's models provide some understanding of what motivates employees. For example, both models demonstrate that money is important to one's physiological needs (Maslow's first level) and to prevent dissatisfaction (Herzberg's hygiene factors). As seen in Table 11.1, monetary compensation is obviously important for attracting and retaining chief executive officers,[8] although such financial compensation alone certainly does not guarantee increased performance of the firm.[9] Maslow's and Herzberg's models also point out that an employer can expect that if money satisfies physiological needs, they next should try to meet the employees' safety needs by providing safe working conditions and insurance and retirement benefits.

The tasks of lab technicians at TRW Electronic Systems Group who assemble and test advanced gallium arsenide components have been expanded to include planning and controlling the work flow. Added responsibility and opportunities for achievement — two of Herzberg's motivators — improve the technicians' work environment.

Source: Courtesy of TRW Inc.

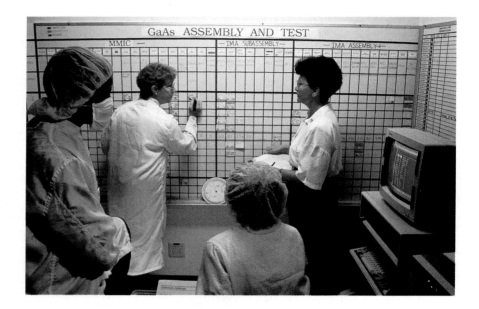

But as Herzberg's model shows, money, fringe benefits, and safe conditions may only prevent dissatisfaction; these factors may not motivate employees. Workers also look for the motivator factors (recognition and responsibility) that help them meet their higher level needs (esteem and self-actualization).

Employers' efforts to motivate employees take many forms. One way is through commonsense, yet innovative approaches such as discussed in the accompanying Innovation Close-Up (Lean and Mean or Lifetime Employment?). Another way is by improving the overall work environment.

Improving the Work Environment

One of the most important concerns affecting employee motivation is the dramatically changing technological environment of work. Increasingly sophisticated technology has simplified many jobs but, by the same token, has made many other jobs more sophisticated and demanding. For example, at Swift Textiles, a maintenance worker used to lug a 30-pound tool belt to manually repair broken looms. Today this same worker has shed the heavy belt for a hand-sized terminal that can diagnose 100 different problems on new computer-driven equipment. At CUNA Mutual Insurance clerks used to spend the workday typing stacks of claims checks, but today they talk with customers and decide how claims will be settled.[10]

The problem of today's workplace, both in manufacturing and in the service industries, is that the workers and managers either have been stripped of any meaningful work or they are unprepared for the sudden demands placed on them. The company in general and their supervisors in particular do not seem to care about them or their ideas on how to improve productivity. To overcome these feelings of being left out and at the same time make the job more interesting and rewarding, many firms are developing quality of work life programs, which are often based on feedback from the workers and managers themselves regarding what they like and dislike about their jobs.[11]

CLOSE-UP / *Innovation*

Lean and Mean or Lifetime Employment?

The effective organizations of today are trying to come up with innovative solutions for preventing employee layoffs. In recent years, in order to become efficient and compete in international markets, an increasing number of companies have begun to downsize, cut their work forces, and flatten their organization structures. The objective has been to make themselves "lean and mean." The downside of this strategy is that the remaining employees become insecure, lose their loyalty and commitment, and wonder about their own future with the company. Too often the results of downsizing have been that the reduced work force has been unable or unwilling to pick up the slack left by the cutbacks, leaving the firm no more productive than it was before. This is why the well known Japanese firms and innovative American companies such as Dow Chemical, Ford, and 3M try to avoid layoffs. These companies believe that a strategy of offering lifetime employment strengthens employee motivation and commitment and results in greater productivity and higher profits.

Taking a lead from the excellent firms that have used a lifetime employment policy, some recession-hit firms are trying to implement strategies designed to protect the jobs of full-time employees. A common approach is to simply put a freeze on hiring. As employees leave through natural attrition, their work is distributed among the remaining workers, who are encouraged to use their creativity in thinking up ways to their jobs more efficiently. A second approach is to restrict overtime in order to protect the work of as many full-time employees as possible. Still another approach is the retraining and redeployment of people where they can be most productive. If things continue to go badly, some companies encourage and provide incentives for early retirement.

The companies that are implementing these approaches are determined to implement layoffs only as a last resort — and this strategy really pays off. The CEO of Dow Chemical recently explained the logic behind the strategy this way, "When you lay people off, you lose all the loyalty you've busted your butt to build. The quality of work you get from motivated people is literally light-years ahead of what you get from people who aren't well motivated." Even when profits at Dow dropped 62 percent over a recent two-year period, not one person was laid off. Dow knows that the economy will bounce back, and if the firm maintains its highly qualified, motivated, and committed work force, it will be in an excellent position to take advantage of the upturn.

Source: Edmund Faltermayer, "Is This Layoff Necessary?" *Fortune*, June 1, 1992, pp. 71–86.

Quality of work life (QWL) refers to efforts to improve the job environment and make work life more enjoyable and meaningful. Such efforts may extend beyond the job site and include providing day care centers and recreational activities. The idea is to create a total supportive, quality environment for the employees. Some of the most widely recognized specific techniques associated with QWL at the workplace are job enrichment, quality-control circles, self-managed teams, flextime, and job sharing.

Quality of work life (QWL)
Efforts to improve the job environment and make work life more enjoyable and meaningful.

Job Enrichment   Management can use the Herzberg two-factor theory to improve employee performance by adding motivators to the job design. This approach has been termed **job enrichment.** Managers can add motivators in a variety of ways:[12]

Job enrichment A technique for motivating employees by adding motivator factors to their jobs.

- Varying the work so that employees are able to use more of their skills and abilities
- Giving employees a chance to complete a whole or identifiable piece of work, as opposed to doing just one small task in a large project
- Making workers aware of how important their jobs are

Campbell Soup Company has established quality-control circles like the one shown here at facilities worldwide. Production and office employees discuss ways to improve quality and keep costs down. Their input helps move the company ahead in an increasingly competitive environment.

Source: Courtesy of Campbell Soup Company.

- Giving employees more autonomy, freedom, and responsibility to do the job their own way
- Providing employees with immediate feedback so they know how they are doing

Many employees have tried job enrichment approaches. Sherwin-Williams, mentioned earlier, has combined a well-designed work layout with the use of autonomous work groups that set their own pace. When the company instituted this arrangement, the cost per gallon of paint declined, productivity rose, product quality hit an all-time high, and work time lost through accidents was virtually eliminated. In another case, a major insurance company gave its workers greater control over their work and used their ideas to redesign the jobs. Work output rose significantly. Examples such as these show that job enrichment can make the job more interesting and challenging for the employee, while simultaneously increasing productivity and lowering costs.

Quality-Control Circles and Self-Managed Teams   Companies also challenge employees and give recognition through the institution of quality-control circles and self-managed teams. A **quality-control circle** consists of a group of workers who meet regularly to discuss the way they do their jobs and to recommend changes. Quality-control (QC) circles have been popular in Japan. For example, Toyota has had QC circles for over 25 years and now has several hundred circles involving thousands of its employees. The circles have also gained wide use in the United States at firms such as General Foods, Weyerhaeuser, Heinz, Nabisco, Honeywell, and Lockheed.

Quality-control circles typically consist of 5 to 10 employees and a group leader. Membership is voluntary. The objective of each group is to study

Quality-control circle A group of workers who meet regularly to discuss the way they do their jobs and to recommend changes.

problems of production or service that fall within their scope of work, such as how to assemble more TVs per hour or reduce the number of defects per TV set. Quality-control circle participants are trained in how to identify areas that warrant consideration and how to work harmoniously with others in a group setting. The group usually meets for one or two hours a week to discuss projects it wants to undertake and changes it wants to make as a result of its investigations of current work procedures.

After the QC group has completed its study of a problem, it suggests what should be done to improve quality and productivity. In one case, a quality-control circle began by counting the number of defects at each of the stages of the production process covered by members of the group. The circle members then identified what was causing each of these defects (incorrect engineering specifications, a part produced improperly by one of the subcontractors, a defective processing machine, and so on) and suggested ways of correcting each problem. The group then reported its findings to management for action.

Closely related to QC groups are **self-managed teams.** These teams have no supervisor and manage themselves by determining their own approach to getting the job done and even hire their own members and sometimes determine their own pay. These are becoming increasingly popular in today's complex work environment. Here are a sampling of recent applications:

- At a cereal plant in Lodi, California, General Mills found that self-managed teams worked so effectively that the factory night shift now operates without managers.
- At Federal Express a team at a weekly meeting spotted and eventually solved a billing problem that was costing the firm $1.2 million annually.
- A team of mill workers at Chaparral Steel traveled the world to evaluate new production machinery that eventually led to their mill becoming one of the most efficient in the world.
- In one of its divisions the 3M Company created work teams that consisted of managers from a variety of different functional areas and, as a result, the number of new products produced by the division tripled.
- Aetna Life & Casualty organized its home office into superteams and was able to reduce the ratio of middle managers to workers from 1:7 down to 1:30 while, at the same time, improving customer service.[13]

Self-managed teams Employee teams that have no supervisor and manage themselves by determining their own approach to getting the job done and sometimes hire their own members and determine their own pay.

Flexible Work Schedules Companies also improve the work environment through the use of **flexible work schedules,** which allow workers to control their own work schedule within limitations established by the organization. Flexible schedules can take several forms including part-time employment; a compressed work week, month, or even the whole year; and work at home. However, the most popular arrangement is called **flextime.** The firm establishes **core hours,** which are the times when everyone must be on the job, say, from 10:00 a.m. to 3:00 p.m. (see Figure 11.5). In addition to these five core hours, everyone must put in an additional three hours, and these can be before or after the core hours. For example, if a mother or father has to drop the children at school at 8:30 a.m., the parent can start work at 9:00 a.m. and

Flexible work schedule An approach that allows workers to control their own schedule, within limitations established by the organization.

Flextime A flexible work schedule built around core hours.

Core hours Those times when everyone must be on the job under a flexible work schedule.

FIGURE 11.5
A Flexible Work Schedule

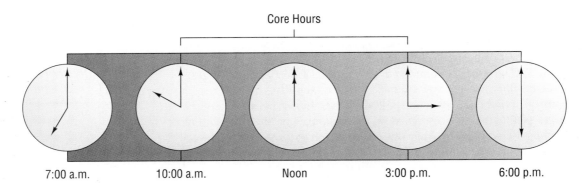

Core Hours

| 7:00 a.m. | 10:00 a.m. | Noon | 3:00 p.m. | 6:00 p.m. |

work until 5:00 p.m. Likewise, a person who wants to pursue a hobby or exercise after work can schedule the work day to start at 7:00 a.m. and work until 3:00 p.m. For example, at Hewlett-Packard, employees can start work at 6:00 a.m., 7:00 a.m., or 8:00 a.m.

A recent survey found the majority of firms sampled had some form of flexible scheduling and 42 percent had flextime.[14] For example, the State Street Bank of Boston was able to reduce its overtime cost and employee turnover. The Metropolitan Life Insurance Company reduced tardiness and improved employee morale. At Control Data, a 3-year study revealed that flextime had increased morale and productivity. At Quad/Graphics, productivity increased 20 percent when the company moved to its flextime work weeks.

Job Sharing   Another form of flexible scheduling and a way companies can enable employees to combine career and personal objectives is through job sharing. **Job sharing** consists of employing two or more part-time workers to fulfill the requirements of a single full-time position. Under this arrangement, a student can work part time while attending school, or a parent can have more time to be with the children. This enables the employee to earn some income and keep abreast of job developments while still meeting other obligations. The employer, in turn, benefits from not losing a valued employee who otherwise could not put in the hours required for a full-time position. Job sharing is not as common with companies as is flextime, but it may become more important as families attempt to strike more of a balance between work and family obligations on the part of both working mothers and fathers.[15]

Job sharing Employing two or more part-time workers to fulfill the requirements of a single full-time position.

Motivating Individual Employees
Besides modifying the work environment to motivate employees, another approach is to focus on the individual. The work motivation theories state

that both the individual employee and the context or environment in which the employee works are important to motivation. Although it is relatively easier to change and manage the environment, in the final analysis it is the individual worker who must feel motivated to perform. Fortunately, some effective techniques to motivate on the level of the individual have recently emerged. These include goal setting, stress management, and retraining.

Goal Setting   Employees want to know what their employer expects of them and to feel part of a team effort. Businesses can motivate employees to improve their performance by setting goals. Applied to work motivation, **goal setting** is the process of establishing specific objectives for an individual to pursue. Research has uncovered some important guidelines for effective goal setting:[16]

An employee's daughter visits her mother at Key Bank of Eastern New York. The bank has an optional 40-week work schedule that allows employees with school-age children to have summers free. The policy is part of an effort to help reduce turnover and improve the work environment.

Source: © William Taufic.

- Specific goals lead to more effective task performance than those that are vague or simply encourage employees to "do the best you can."
- Goals that are difficult but attainable lead to higher performance than do easy goals, as long as the employee accepts these goals.
- Employees tend to work harder in pursuing goals that they have helped set than those that have been assigned to them.
- Frequent feedback on how well an employee is doing typically generates higher performance from that employee.

Simply put, goal setting leads to better performance. One manager who experienced this is the successful general agent of an office of Mutual of Omaha who each quarter determined sales goals together with his agents *and* their spouses. Most sales managers find it effective to set goals for their sales force. However, this manager got even better performance because he allowed his sales agents to participate in the goal-setting process. By involving spouses, he obtained for his salespeople their families' support for their selling after hours and on weekends.

Goal setting The process of establishing specific objectives for an individual to pursue.

Stress Management   Businesses can also motivate employees to do their best by showing them how to manage stress. **Stress** is the body's response to an action or situation that places demands on a person. Life would be dull if you were never subject to any stress. However, intense or continuous stress can be harmful. In fact, some jobs put so much pressure on employees that they suffer **burnout,** which is mental and/or physical exhaustion caused by excess stress. People at particular risk for burnout include air traffic controllers, medical personnel, teachers, and stockbrokers. The accompanying International Close-Up (The Japanese Dream Factory Attacks Stress) shows how Nissan is trying to help reduce stress in its factories.

Researchers have tried to determine whether some characteristics make people especially susceptible to stress and burnout. Some evidence suggests that a certain type of personality is at risk. This personality, described in the left column of Table 11.2, is called a **Type A personality.** It includes a drive to get more and more done in less and less time. At first it was reported that Type A people wear themselves down and are even more likely to have heart attacks or other serious health problems than those with a so-called Type B

Stress The body's response to an action or situation that places demands on a person.

Burnout Mental and/or physical exhaustion caused by excess stress.

Type A personality
A personality characterized by a drive to get more and more done in less and less time.

CLOSE-UP / *International*

The Japanese Dream Factory Attacks Stress

Many auto manufacturers in Japan are finding it increasingly difficult to hire new people. Worse yet, the turnover rate in some factories runs as high as 50 percent annually. In explaining the reason for this turnover, many workers refer to the three K's: kiken (dangerous), kitsui (difficult), and kitanai (dirty). Young people, in particular, prefer the slower-paced world of office work where people where suits and ties, take leisurely lunch hours, and are not exhausted at the end of a long day.

In an effort to deal with this problem, Nissan Motor has just built a new factory that promises to be far less stressful on the workers than other factories. Company officials refer to it as a "dream factory", and claim that it is designed to reduce many of the pitfalls of previously built manufacturing plants. The traditional factory, for example, is characterized by the old conveyor belt from which cars are suspended. When the car reaches the workers, the employees scramble to install parts and complete their tasks as quickly as possible. This typically involves squatting on the floor, stretching across the seat or the hood, ducking under the car, or reaching across the top of the vehicle to install or tighten parts. If workers are unable to keep up with the line, the conveyor belt must be stopped until they catch up because all cars advance in lockstep. Nissan's new plant has done away with the conveyor belt. All cars are now placed on motor-driven dollies. These dollies can be raised or lowered so that the workers do not have to stretch or squat. Additionally, even if it takes longer than usual to complete a particular task, this creates no problem for the factory. The workers can simply scoot the dolly up to the next station as soon as they are finished.

Another difference between the Nissan plant and more conventional ones is that the work area at Nissan is brightly lit with natural sunlight filtering in through skylights. Additionally, the factory is air-conditioned to maintain a temperature of 77 degrees, in contrast to other auto plants where there is no air-conditioning. Another welcome feature is the use of robots to perform the dirtiest and most difficult jobs, such as painting and welding. And to reduce worker exhaustion, a large percentage of the actual assembly is carried out by robots. A huge robot arm, for example, grabs seats from an overhead rack and swings them into the car with a flick of its mechanical wrist. Then a small robot arm bolts the seat to the floor.

Nissan contends that this new plant will not only cut down on worker absenteeism and turnover, but that the factory will be 30 percent more efficient than that of the competition. While it is still too early to know if these estimates are correct, one thing is certain: The factory of the future will have to help reduce work stress and Nissan's new plant is a big step in that direction.

Source: Adapted from Andrew Pollack, "Assembly-Line Amenities for Japan's Auto Workers," *New York Times*, July 20, 1992, pp. A 1, C 5.

---

personality. Now the research is less clear. People who hold frustration in and keep their problems to themselves, get angry easily, and have demanding jobs with little freedom to make decisions may be more susceptible to serious health problems than Type A personalities per se.[17]

Many companies are beginning to help their personnel eliminate or cope with excess stress. For example, Johnson & Johnson and IBM have instituted comprehensive programs of health checkups, exercise, and lifestyle classes for stress management. In addition to encouraging employees to watch their diet and give up smoking, some business firms are providing on-site facilities for exercising. These programs — sometimes called wellness programs — are keeping personnel healthier, happier, and more productive. As a result of its wellness programs, New York Telephone estimates it saves at least $2.7 million on its health costs annually, and Lockheed estimates $1 million in sav-

Type A	Type B	**TABLE 11.2** Type A and Type B Personality Profiles
Is always moving	Is not concerned about time	
Walks rapidly	Is patient	
Eats rapidly	Doesn't brag	
Talks rapidly	Plays for fun, not to win	
Is impatient	Relaxes without guilt	
Does two things at once	Has no pressing deadlines	
Can't cope with leisure time	Is mild-mannered	
Is obsessed with numbers	Is never in a hurry	
Measures success by quantity		
Is aggressive		
Is competitive		
Constantly feels under time pressure		

ings on its life insurance premiums. These companies are also showing the workers that they actively promote the well-being of their employees.

Crosstraining   A particularly stressful situation is job insecurity caused by the threat of layoffs or new technological developments. When workers are worried about losing their jobs, they may not think it is worthwhile to do their best. They will not come forth with new ideas for fear it may eliminate their job or the jobs of their friends. Some workers may even turn to drugs or alcohol to dull their fears.

Companies can help workers cope with this problem more productively. Some companies have followed the lead of many Japanese companies by having a lifetime employment policy. Although lifetime employment for Japanese firms sometimes turns out to be a myth,[18] there are some American companies that do follow such a policy. For example, at Worthington Steel, once employees pass a rigid probationary period (they are voted on by their coworkers), they are guaranteed a job for life.

Another approach, which can be used alone or in conjunction with lifetime employment, is to crosstrain workers in skills the employer is more likely to need after cutbacks or technological changes. The federal government even has programs that will help employers pay for these training costs. Still another popular approach is to allow people to switch jobs and to train for things that they find more rewarding. For example, at GSI Transcomm Data Systems individuals who are bored with their current jobs can get the needed training and transfer to others. As a result, the firm's labor turnover has declined from 25 percent annually to less than 7 percent.[19] If employees see hope for their future and have a sense that management values them, they are more likely to respond to such programs and be motivated to perform.

1. What techniques are available to motivate today's employees?
2. How do improvements in the quality of work life enhance employees' performance?

Centel employees take a break from bicycling. Centel promotes employee well-being and fitness in a variety of ways: health club facilities, partial reimbursement of private health club membership, and rewards for reaching goals in self-paced, health-related programs.

Source: Bruce Davidson/Magnum Photos and Centel Corporation.

CHECK ✓ POINT

Leadership Styles

Leadership The process of influencing people to direct their efforts toward the achievement of particular objectives.

Along with motivation, the other major dimension of the directing function of management is leadership. A comprehensive definition of **leadership** is that it is the process of influencing people to direct their efforts toward the achievement of particular objectives. Although there are many different views and it is hard to pin down, both researchers and practitioners would agree that effective leadership is a major contributor to successful organizations and becomes particularly important in managing under the changing conditions faced by today's organizations.[20]

Every manager has a style of leadership or a particular way of using power to lead. These leadership styles fall into three broad categories: autocratic, democratic, and laissez-faire. In an autocratic style, the leader exercises the greatest amount of authority, leaving little freedom to the workers. A democratic leader shares authority with the workers. Laissez-faire leadership leaves a great deal of freedom to the workers, with the manager merely establishing some broad limits. (The term laissez-faire is a French expression that roughly translates as "leave it alone.") These leadership styles are not absolutes; they fall along a continuum, as illustrated in Figure 11.6

In evaluating how managers lead, researchers have developed several theories. These theories describe the assumptions that underlie a manager's choice of leadership style. They are known as Theories X, Y, and Z.

Theories X and Y

The pioneering human relations theorist Douglas McGregor recognized that leadership style is heavily influenced by leaders' assumptions about their subordinates. A manager who thinks employees are lazy and will cut corners whenever possible will adopt a much different leadership style than will a manager who believes employees generally work hard and are reliable. McGregor called these assumptions Theory X and Theory Y.

Theory X The assumption that people are basically lazy and have to be coerced or threatened before they will work.

Theory X assumes people are basically lazy and have to be threatened before they will work. Some specific assumptions of this theory include:

- People dislike work and will avoid it when possible.
- Employees have little ambition, shun responsibility, and like to be directed.
- Employees want security above all else and actually like to be told what to do.
- To get employees to attain organizational objectives, the leader must keep a close watch over them and use threats of punishment.

Based on these assumptions, a manager who adopts Theory X is likely to use a relatively autocratic management style.

Theory Y The assumption that people are creative and responsible and will work hard under the proper conditions.

Theory Y assumes people are creative and responsible and will work hard under the proper conditions. Some of the specific assumptions of this theory include:

- Work is as natural as play.
- If people are committed to objectives, they will exercise self-direction and self-control.

FIGURE 11.6
Leadership Styles

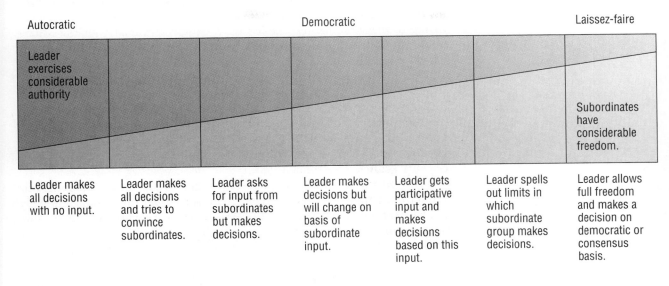

Autocratic			Democratic			Laissez-faire
Leader makes all decisions with no input.	Leader makes all decisions and tries to convince subordinates.	Leader asks for input from subordinates but makes decisions.	Leader makes decisions but will change on basis of subordinate input.	Leader gets participative input and makes decisions based on this input.	Leader spells out limits in which subordinate group makes decisions.	Leader allows full freedom and makes a decision on democratic or consensus basis.

Source: This continuum is based on the classic article by Robert Tannenbaum and Warren H. Schmidt, "How to Choose a Leadership Pattern," *Harvard Business Review,* March–April, 1958, 96.

- Commitment to objectives depends on the rewards associated with achieving the objectives.
- Under proper conditions, people will seek responsibility.
- People are highly creative.
- In industrial life, the intellectual potential of the average employee is only partially tapped.

A Theory Y manager is likely to choose a democratic or laissez-faire leadership style. Most successful leaders make Theory Y assumptions about people. They feel most subordinates will work hard if given the proper environment.

Theory Z

A third, more recent, theory of how managers should lead is Theory Z, proposed by UCLA professor William G. Ouchi. This is sometimes referred to as a Japanese approach, because it is based on a style of management found in typical Japanese companies. According to **Theory Z,** the key is to create a culture or climate that lends itself to openness, trust, and employee involvement. Managers who adhere to Theory Z try to make workers feel like family, involving them in decision making and seldom if ever laying off anyone. In addition, Theory Z companies provide employees with broad experience and crosstraining to avoid boredom and broaden career paths. They may also use the quality of work life techniques discussed earlier. Interestingly, there is recent evidence that many managers of U.S. firms bought by the Japanese report that leadership climate is better under their new owners.[21]

Theory Z The assumption that the key to productivity is to create a climate or culture of openness and trust that leads to increased employee involvement.

Choosing a Leadership Style

Choosing a style of leadership is a complicated process. Some leaders seem able to lead naturally. Research and experience concerning leadership styles have led to the conclusion that the best leadership style must consider the nature of the subordinates, the leaders themselves, and the situation. Some subordinates, such as inexperienced workers, may perform best when they are closely monitored; others, for example, scientists in a research laboratory, may do well when they have free rein. Some leaders operate more effectively when they exercise close control; others do better when they delegate a great deal of authority and let the subordinates set their own pace. Some situations require managers to monitor personnel with care because any mistake can be very costly (making heart pacemakers), while other situations allow for more general control because the work is basically simple and mistakes matter less (making shipping containers).

Because of these variables, modern managers often find they get the best results when they don't settle for one leadership style. Instead, they practice **contingency leadership,** which calls for using the style that will be the most effective in a specific situation. Specifically, research indicates that an autocratic style is most effective in two situations:[22]

1. A very favorable leadership situation, which includes a structured task, a great deal of formal power and authority, and respect and loyalty from subordinates. An example of such a very favorable situation would be that facing an airline pilot. The same is true of the situation faced by military commanders in combat. For example, in the Desert Storm campaign in the Middle East, Generals Powell and Schwarzkopf had a structured task, considerable power and authority, and respect and loyalty from their troops.[23] Contingency theory would suggest that a relatively autocratic style would be effective in this situation.

2. A very unfavorable leadership situation, which includes an unstructured task, no formal power or authority, and a reluctant, "volunteered" group of subordinates. An example of a leader in such a situation is the chairperson of the annual company picnic. A company having financial problems would be another example of an unfavorable leadership situation that may require autocratic leadership to turn things around. This was recently tried at the big insurer USF&G where an autocratic manager was brought in to try to rescue the firm.[24]

In contrast, a human-oriented style is most effective between these extremes, in moderately favorable or moderately unfavorable situations, which make up most modern jobs.[25] Thus, except in the few situations that are very favorable or very unfavorable, most managers would be better off using Theory Y or Theory Z styles.

Despite the general preference for a Theory Y or Z approach, a Theory X style may be more appropriate when economic or competitive times are tough. For example, the former head of E. F. Hutton did not make a change in leadership style, and this eventually led to the downfall of his company. His style was to take risks and make quick decisions. He considered traditional techniques such as budgets and organization charts a waste of time. During the boom of the 1970s this style worked. He assembled the best sales force on Wall Street, and Hutton's profits were the envy of the indus-

Contingency leadership The leadership technique of using the style that will be most effective in a specific situation.

A Theory Y style of leadership assumes that people are basically creative and responsible. Based on this assumption, the management of 3M had this building in Austin, Texas, designed to facilitate informal gatherings among research and marketing personnel. This environment stimulates the flow of ideas — and new, innovative products for 3M.

try. But when the securities industry entered a new competitive era in the 1980s, a new style of leadership was needed. Tighter controls and a more forceful, Theory X type of leadership was needed. He either couldn't or wouldn't make the transition to a new style of leadership, and as a result Hutton succumbed to a takeover by Shearson Lehman, and 5,000 Hutton employees lost their jobs.[26] In other words, managers have to be somewhat flexible and change their styles with the conditions they face.

Whatever style they choose, managers must avoid being inconsistent or vacillating between styles *within* a given situation.[27] The key is to be flexible in choosing the style to fit the situation and consistent within the identified situation. And the situation facing managers now and in the years ahead is certainly different than in the past. As the head of General Electric John Welch recently noted: "The pace of change in the Nineties will make the Eighties look like a picnic — a walk in the park. Competition will be relentless. The bar of excellence in everything we do will be raised every day."[28] This type of change will require effective leadership at all levels to get the job done.

1. What are some basic leadership styles?
2. When would you use a Theory X style? When would you use a Theory Y style?

CHECK ✓ POINT

Closing Comments

This chapter discussed what Sam Walton, one of the richest people in America and the founder of Wal-Mart, identified as the major single reason for his business success: people. The directing function of management takes many forms but mainly focuses on motivation and leadership. Motivation stems from formal reward systems, such as wages and promotions, and also from interesting and challenging work. Effective leadership balances a concern for getting the job done with a concern for the worker. From Exxon and Texaco to Bank of America and Chase Manhattan to Motorola and Hewlett-Packard, most major corporations in America spend millions of dollars annually training their managers to motivate and lead their employees more effectively.

VIDEO CASE / *Getting the Best of Their People*

The one thing that employees at 1-800-Dentist probably like best about their company is the leadership style of the management. Top management tries to create and maintain a relaxed environment in which to do potentially stressful work. The job of employees at this service firm is to respond to calls from clients who need help in locating a dental specialist, often on an emergency basis. Management uses a wide variety of activities such as softball games, birthday parties, weekend seminars, boating on the river, and even weekly massages to promote a relaxing environment.

Unfortunately, 1-800-Dentist seems to be the exception rather than the rule. Increasing evidence indicates that the level of job stress is high in most organizations today and that management is pushing employees harder and harder. For example, a Gallup poll of personnel and medical directors at 201 large and small corporations revealed that, on average, 25 percent of the employees suffered from anxiety or stress-related disorders. As a result, these people lost an estimated average of 16 working days a year. According to North Carolina's Research Triangle Institute, problems caused by stress in the workplace cost American industry $183 billion in lost productivity, job errors, and doctors' bills in one year.

Companies that are most vulnerable to the negative effects of pushing people too hard are those in labor-intensive industries. The 1-800-Dentist people fall into this category, but management has overcome stressful conditions there by creating a unique environment. Other examples of stressful jobs would be baggage handlers in airports, maids in hotels and motels, and food preparers in fast-food chains. A major contributor to the stress in these jobs is that there is never a letup in the work pace. Employees are under constant pressure with virtually no "down time." As a result, employee turnover is very high in such jobs. For example, in many hotels and motels, maids stay an average of 9 months and then move on to other lines of work. In the case of fast-food preparers at McDonald's, the average is 5 months. On the other hand, at 1-800-Dentist turnover is low. One reason is that, even though the work pace can be as hectic, efforts are made to create a climate that minimizes the amount of pressure. Employees are allowed to work at their own pace. The founders of the company still manage it and they believe in promoting a healthy environment. In addition to receiving weekly massages, employees are encouraged to engage in transcendental meditation and other mind-relaxing techniques.

Source: Thomas A. Stewart, "Do You Push Your People Too Hard?" *Fortune*, October 22, 1990, 121–128.

Case Questions

1. In what way can stress cause problems for employees?
2. Are the managers at 1-800-Dentist Theory X or Theory Y leaders? Explain your answer.
3. What do you think employees at 1-800-Dentist like most about their company?

Learning Objectives Revisited

1. **Describe how the major approaches to the directing function of management have changed over the years.** Beginning at the turn of the century, the scientific management era focused on achieving increased efficiency through the application of scientific procedures in the workplace. Workers were treated as if they were merely factors of production. During the early behavioral management era, which began about 1920, management came to realize that treating workers as thinking, feeling human beings both motivated them and improved productivity. Finally, the human resource management era emerged around 1970. Management has realized the importance of employees to organizational performance and has begun providing them with the opportunity to use their full potential and ability.

2. **Discuss approaches to understanding motivation.** Maslow's hierarchy of needs explains that people are motivated, in turn, by physiological, safety, social, esteem, and self-actualization needs. The two-factor theory proposed by Herzberg holds that work motivation and resulting employee satisfaction has two dimensions: hygiene factors and motivator factors. Hygiene factors such as money and working conditions can help prevent employee dissatisfaction, but only the motivator factors—responsibility, recognition, and opportunities for achievement—motivate employees directly and lead to satisfaction. To improve performance and satisfaction, managers need to offer motivator factors as well as hygiene factors.

3. **Present some techniques for motivating employees by improving the work environment.** Quality of work life (QWL) programs are used to manage the dramatically changing environment of the workplace. Some QWL techniques are job enrichment, quality-control circles, self-managed teams, flextime, and job sharing. Job enrichment redesigns jobs, building in psychological motivators such as increased responsibility. A quality-control circle is a group of workers who meet regularly to discuss and recommend changes in the way their jobs are being done. Self-managed teams have no supervisors and make their own decisions. With flextime, workers may set their own work hours as long as everyone is on the job during specific core hours. Job sharing means employing two or more part-time workers for one full-time position.

4. **Describe the techniques managers use to motivate individual employees.** Techniques to motivate today's employees include goal setting, stress management, and crosstraining. Goal setting is the process of helping employees to set clear, specific, and difficult but attainable performance goals, and providing them with feedback on progress. Stress management techniques help employees find constructive ways to respond to the demands placed on them. Crosstraining equips employees with the skills the employer is more likely to need after cutbacks or technological changes.

5. **Identify some basic leadership styles.** Broadly stated, a leader's style can range from autocratic to demo-

cratic to laissez-faire. Some theories describe the assumptions underlying the way a manager leads. Theory X managers assume workers are basically lazy and have to be threatened. Theory Y managers assume people are creative and responsible and will work hard under the proper conditions. Theory Z managers assume that creating an open, trusting climate or culture will lead to increased employee involvement and improved performance.

6. **Explain how leaders can choose an effective style.** The best leadership style depends on the nature of the subordinates, the leaders themselves, and the situation. Contingency leadership calls for using the style that will be most effective in a specific situation. An autocratic style is most effective in very favorable or very unfavorable leadership situations. In most situations, however, a human-oriented style is most effective.

Key Terms Reviewed

Review each of the following terms. For any that you do not know or are unsure of, look up the definitions and see how they were used in the chapter.

directing function
scientific management
Hawthorne studies
motivation
primary needs
secondary needs
motivator factors
hygiene factors
quality of work life (QWL)

job enrichment
quality-control circle
self-managed teams
flexible work schedule
flextime
core hours
job sharing
goal setting

stress
burnout
Type A personality
leadership
Theory X
Theory Y
Theory Z
contingency leadership

Review Questions

1. Do managers today use the scientific management ideas of Frederick Taylor? Why or why not?
2. Claire Daniels owns a small advertising agency. What lesson from the Hawthorne studies can help her be more effective in motivating her staff?
3. What beliefs about workers and motivation underlie the human resource approach to management?
4. Give an example of how a company can enable an employee to meet each of the types of needs in Maslow's hierarchy. Give one example for each type of need.
5. Bob Crunch, president of a manufacturing company, called the personnel director into his office. "You're the expert on employees," said Bob, "so please explain to me why our turnover is so high and our quality is so low, when our salaries are above industry average and we have one of the safest, cleanest plants in the country. Our people just don't seem motivated." Based on your reading of the two-factor theory of motivation, offer a possible explanation for the high turnover and low quality at this company.

6. Charles Blackburn owns a manufacturing firm that employs 750 people. What techniques might he use in improving the quality of work life of his people?
7. How can employers and employees benefit from flextime?
8. Every year, Martha Moore gives each member of her staff a list of goals for the year. At the end of the year, Martha sits down with each worker to discuss the achievements for the year. To Martha's dismay, she finds that staff members often fall short of the goals, even though she makes them easier every year. What principles of goal setting has Martha failed to take into account? How could she better use goal setting to motivate her staff?
9. Is all stress harmful? Write a short description of totally stress-free living.
10. The sales manager for Wonder Washers prefers to let his salespeople use whatever style works for them. He helps them set sales goals, and then he leaves them alone unless they ask for assistance. The salespeople send in weekly sales reports but set their own hours and decide which customers in

their territory to call on. What is the sales manager's leadership style?

11. In general, what kind of leadership style would a Theory X manager adopt? A Theory Y manager?

12. How do Theory Z managers motivate and lead their employees?

13. Which leadership approach is usually more suitable — Theory X or Theory Y? Explain.

14. Pat Petro tries to use contingency leadership. Every morning when she plans her day, Pat decides what management style will be most appropriate for achieving the day's goals. What may be wrong with this approach to leadership?

Applied Exercise

Read each of the following pairs of statements. In each pair indicate your beliefs by assigning a weight from 0 to 10. For example, in the first pair of statements, if you totally agree with the first one and totally disagree with the second, give the first a 10 and the second a zero; if you believe equally in both statements, give each a 5; and so on.

1. Most people are fairly creative but they usually do not have a chance to use this creativity on the job. _____ (a)

   Most people are not at all creative, but that is all right because their jobs do not lend themselves to creativity. _____ (b)

2. If people are given enough money, this will offset their desire for challenging, meaningful work. _____ (c)

   If people are given challenging, meaningful work, they are less likely to complain about money and fringe benefits. _____ (d)

3. When workers are allowed to set their own goals, they tend to set them higher than management would. _____ (e)

   When workers are allowed to set their own goals, they tend to set them lower than management would. _____ (f)

4. Employees want freedom to work the way they believe is right. _____ (g)

   Employees like to be told what to do. _____ (h)

5. The better an employee knows his or her job, the more likely it is that the individual will try to do just enough to get by. _____ (i)

   The better an employee knows his or her job, the more likely it is that the individual will try to produce at least as much as the average worker. _____ (j)

6. Most employees do not have the intellectual potential to do their jobs. _____ (k)

   Most employees have more than sufficient intellectual potential to do their jobs. _____ (l)

7. Most employees dislike work, and if given the chance they will goof off. _____ (m)

   Most employees like work, especially if it is interesting and challenging. _____ (n)

8. Most employees work best under loose control. _____ (o)

   Most employees work best under close control. _____ (p)

9. Most of all, employees want job security. _____ (q)

   While employees want job security, this is only one of many desires and it seldom ranks first on their list. _____ (r)

10. If a manager admits that he or she made a mistake, this increases the individual's prestige. _____ (s)

    If a manager admits that he or she made a mistake, this decreases the individual's prestige. _____ (t)

This graph will be used to interpret your results from the exercise.

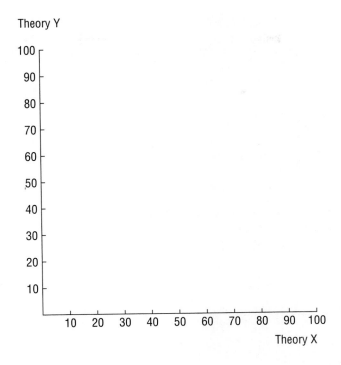

Theory Y

Theory X

As the Lorek Company expanded, it began filling many of its new supervisory positions with people from inside the firm. That is how Howard Iznek got his promotion. Howard has been with the firm for 3 years and has continually been evaluated as one of the highest performers in his department. Based on this performance, the company decided to promote him into the management ranks.

Howard is in charge of nine assemblers, each of whom puts together a hand-held calculator. The workers are expected to assemble 15 calculators an hour. Before Howard took over the unit, the average worker was assembling 13.5 calculators per hour. Management asked Howard to get the number up to 15, but it appears that just the reverse has occurred. Since Howard took command, the average workers' output has fallen to 11.7 an hour.

Howard is not the only new supervisor having productivity problems. As a result, management decided to investigate why. To date, the company has interviewed the supervisors and the workers and put together a general picture of Howard's leadership approach. It also gave Howard and the workers a questionnaire to fill out. Howard's questionnaire asked him to describe his leadership style; the workers' ques-

tionnaire asked each of them to describe Howard's leadership style. In both cases, the answers were the same: Howard has an autocratic style.

Your Advice

1. What should Howard do?
   ___ a. Discuss with the workers why he is an autocratic leader and ask them to accept him as he is.
   ___ b. Discuss with the workers the type of leadership they would like and work to adapt his style to this situation.
   ___ c. Use a laissez-faire leadership style and let the workers manage themselves.

2. If you were advising Howard on how he could improve worker output, what would you tell him about motivation and leadership?

3. What type of motivation techniques and leadership style would you recommend that Howard use? Why?

4. How would you suggest that Howard change to or maintain the recommended leadership style? Be as specific as you can.

AGGRESSIVE HOSPITALITY

Lakeway Resort & Conference Center is located 18 miles northwest of Austin, Texas. Built in the 1960s as a tennis and golf resort, it attracted a local clientele but did not have national appeal. This changed in the late 1980s when the resort was bought by Rothschild Property Investors of New York and managed by the Dolce Company and millions of dollars were spent to expand and modernize the facilities. New guest rooms were added, a dining room and a game room were built, and a

Human Resource Management

12

Chapter Learning Objectives

- Describe human resource management.

- Explain the processes of human resource planning and staffing.

- Discuss employee training and development.

- Define and analyze the techniques for performance appraisal.

- Present the ways compensation and benefits maintain employees.

- Identify the important issues surrounding employee rights.

---

corporate meeting space for groups of up to 325 people, as well as 24 other meeting rooms and workshop suites, were added. The overall strategy was to upgrade the resort and distinguish it from the competition.

A major part of Lakeway's strategy focused on human resource management. Lakeway management realized that in order to attract new business it would have to provide better quality service than the competition. Lakeway managers understand that employees, not advertising slogans, deliver quality

service. They carefully selected and trained staff members and encouraged them to follow a philosophy of "aggressive hospitality" — that is, to go out of their way to make a guest's stay as enjoyable as possible. If a guest is carrying boxes from a car to a meeting site, for example, a staff member will step forward, take the boxes, and carry them.

Aggressive hospitality means that guests should not have to ask for help. If something goes wrong, staff members take whatever action is necessary to correct the problem. For

example, if a piece of audiovisual equipment is found to be defective prior to a business meeting, another unit will be brought from storage immediately. If none is available, a staff member will rent whatever is needed to ensure that the meeting can start on time and will proceed smoothly.

Photo source: Courtesy of Lakeway Resort & Conference Center.

Introduction

For motivating and leading to bring results, employees must also be qualified and well trained. This chapter moves beyond the general directing functions of motivation and leadership, discussed in the last chapter, to the more specialized human resource management function of businesses. The chapter examines the specific activities involved: human resource planning, staffing, training and developing, appraising performance, and maintaining staff with compensation and benefits. The last section of the chapter explores the recently emerging issues surrounding employee rights. Another responsibility of human resource management — union–management relations — is so important that it will receive separate attention in Chapter 13.

The Nature of Human Resource Management

Human resource management
The process of planning personnel needs; staffing the organization; and training, developing, appraising, and maintaining an organization's personnel.

The process of planning personnel needs, staffing the organization, and training, developing, appraising, and maintaining an organization's personnel is called **human resource management.** The terms personnel management and human resource management refer to the same basic organizational function. The newer of these terms — human resource management — recognizes that employees are not merely an expense but a resource of the firm, just as capital and equipment are resources.

Human resource management takes place on two levels. On one level, *all* managers, whether in the production, marketing, finance, or personnel departments, are human resource managers as long as they manage others. These managers provide their staff with assistance, counseling, guidance, and training, no matter what their technical specialty. The last chapter examined this responsibility. It is an important responsibility for overall effective management but one that managers often neglect. Many managers get so caught up in their technical specialties that they forget they have a human resource role as well.

Personnel managers   Human resource managers.

Human resource managers
Managers responsible for staffing the organization and training, developing, appraising, and maintaining its employees.

Human resource management is also a specialized area of the organization. Specialized managers, traditionally called **personnel managers,** but now commonly called **human resource managers,** are responsible for staffing the organization and training, developing, appraising, and maintaining its employees. Figure 12.1 illustrates the responsibilities typically associated with modern human resource management. This chapter focuses on the organizational level of human resource management, beginning with its historical background and present status.

Historical Background

Over the last several decades, the personnel or human resource department has evolved greatly. At the beginning of the century, although there were a few companies such as NCR and Ford that had departments handling personnel matters, foremen and supervisors largely took care of hiring, firing, and paying their own employees. The Great Depression in the 1930s brought legalization and power to trade unions through labor laws. To handle this more complex situation, companies created personnel departments. Personnel managers became responsible for hiring, firing, wage and salary

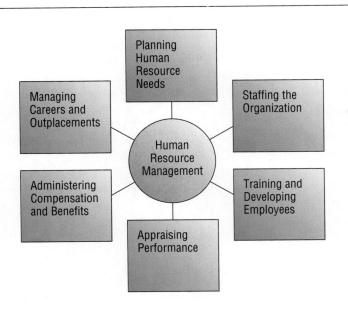

FIGURE 12.1
The Activities of Human Resource Management

administration, handling discipline problems, and administering benefit plans. They also handled employee relations and the negotiation and administration of union contracts.

The Current Status of Human Resource Management

Today, human resource managers carry ever-greater responsibilities. The human resource function is now being recognized as making a valuable contribution to the goals of businesses. In particular, many large firms rely heavily on their human resource departments to help plan for human resource needs and to advise top management in such areas as product quality and productivity improvement[1] and even mergers and acquisitions. At General Electric, Ford, General Motors, IBM, Mobil, Chase Manhattan, and many other large corporations, the head of the human resource department reports directly to the chief executive officer. From this vantage point, the human resource manager helps influence the overall direction of the company.

CHECK ✓ POINT

1. What activities are involved in human resource management?
2. How has the management of human resources changed since the 1930s?

Human Resource Planning

The many activities included in the human resource function start with **human resource planning (HRP),** the process of forecasting personnel needs and developing the necessary strategies for meeting those needs. This information helps managers in several ways:

Human resource planning The process of forecasting personnel needs and developing the necessary strategies for meeting those needs.

- Managers can anticipate personnel shortages or vacancies and act to create or fill jobs before problems arise.
- Managers can anticipate the types of training and development the personnel will need.
- Managers can identify the particular skills and abilities of the present employees to help develop effective career paths for them.
- Managers can evaluate the effect of human resource decisions and make any necessary changes.

Forecasting Human Resource Needs

Effective HRP starts with a forecast. The human resource forecast estimates the number and types of employees the organization will need over the next one to two years. The forecast also predicts the supply of employees to fill these needs. In predicting supply, the human resource manager considers internal sources, or employees who could be promoted or shifted into the vacant positions, as well as external sources: people currently in school, working for another company, or actively seeking employment.

For the owner of a small company, a forecast may be the only information needed to plan for human resource needs. The owner usually has a good idea of the kind of person who would fill the needs of a new position. But in a larger, more complex organization, the human resource manager cannot possibly keep track of all the requirements for employees doing many different kinds of work. In these cases, HRP has a second step, job analysis.

Job Analysis

Job analysis is a comprehensive step in HRP that involves creating job descriptions and job specifications. First, an analysis is made of the jobs in the organization, with particular attention given to the tasks and skills involved in performing them. This list of the specific duties of a particular job is called a job description. The human resource manager next lists the qualifications for each of these duties — the education, abilities, and experience required of the person who fills the position. This list of qualifications is called the job specification. Often, a job description and a job specification appear together on a single form and are referred to jointly as a job description.

CHECK ✓ POINT

1. What activities are involved in human resource planning?
2. What is involved in job analysis?

Staffing the Organization

A major function of human resource managers is making sure that the company has the staff it needs. This staffing function involves more than simply hiring personnel. In some cases firms may even rent a replacement until an appropriate person is hired full-time. Such temporary workers are becoming increasingly common at the operating levels of organizations, but now this is also happening at the manager levels. For example, USCJ, a mortgage service firm, hired a temporary executive as director of corporate development for $2,250 a day. Two-thirds of this goes to the executive and one-third to the placement firm.[2] While this is a great deal of money, USCJ is able to have

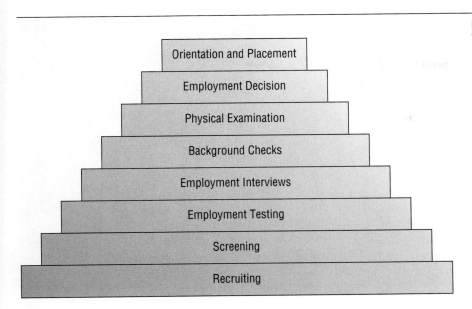

FIGURE 12.2
The Staffing Process

corporate development covered while it continues the search for a full-time executive. There are also special and unique staffing procedures for overseas operations that are receiving increased attention as firms enter the global economy.[3] However, normal staffing contains several phases: recruiting, screening, testing, interviewing, conducting background checks, overseeing physical examinations, making employment decisions, and administering orientation and placement. Figure 12.2 illustrates this process.

Recruiting

The recruiting process involves locating and attracting qualified job applicants. Managers can find candidates both inside and outside the company.

Hiring from Within Most organizations prefer to recruit existing employees and promote them when possible. This policy helps motivate present employees because they realize that, if they do a good job, the organization will reward them with a promotion. Promoting from within also eliminates the cost of placing employment ads in newspapers and trade journals, sending recruiters out to interview, and paying private employment agencies and executive search firms.

Outside Sources A firm that recruits on the outside has many potential sources of employees. Some of the most common sources include private and public employment agencies and educational institutions. An often overlooked source of leads is present employees. Some companies even pay employees for their recommendations. For example, Baxter Travenol pays $350 to $500 to employees if a person they recommend is eventually hired.

Most organizations find that certain sources of recruits are more likely than others to provide them with qualified applicants for their particular

Compaq Computer Corporation tries to attract people who will thrive in an environment that fosters teamwork but recognizes individual contributions. Compaq's culture encourages employees to make recommendations and suggest alternatives. The company's recruiters seek candidates who are not afraid to speak up.

Source: Courtesy of Compaq Computer Corporation.

needs. For example, insurance and high-tech firms have found university and college recruitment to be extremely effective. Most personnel managers, however, seem to prefer using newspaper ads and private employment agencies. The Bureau of National Affairs reports that community agencies and referrals are the best sources for locating minority and handicapped workers, and advertising is the best way to attract female applicants. To recruit married candidates from out of the area, an attractive approach is often to help their spouses find work.

Legal Climate   Throughout the recruiting process and the employment steps that follow, the organization must take care to adhere to the letter and the spirit of legislation designed to regulate hiring practices. Firms have to avoid possible charges of discrimination on the basis of race, color, sex, or national origin. Table 12.1 summarizes some of the most important statutes pertaining to the employment process.

After a number of court cases in which firms were tried and convicted of discriminatory hiring practices, many firms shied away and even dropped some of their procedures for systematically recruiting and selecting new employees. However, this reaction was not really justified or warranted. The courts and the general public never intended for companies to drop all recruitment and selection procedures, only those that discriminate on the basis of race, color, sex, age, or national origin. More recent prohibitions extend to discrimination against Vietnam-era veterans, women who are pregnant or new mothers,[4] and those with disabilities. The intent of these laws is to secure equal employment opportunities for everyone.

The years ahead are going to be characterized by an extremely diverse workforce. The number of minorities and women will increase as the number of white males entering the workforce is declining.[5] In the 1990s projections are that over 80 percent of new entrants in the U.S. labor force will be African-Americans, Hispanics, recent immigrants, and women. By the year

TABLE 12.1
Important Laws Regulating Hiring

Law	What It Requires
Title VII of the Civil Rights Act of 1964 (as amended by the Equal Employment Opportunity Act of 1972)	Prohibits discrimination in employment for employers with 15 or more employees on the basis of race, color, religion, sex, or national origin. Includes discrimination in hiring, firing, wages, benefits, classifying, referring, assigning, promoting, training, or apprenticeships.
Age Discrimination in Employment Act of 1968 (as amended)	Prohibits discrimination in employment for employers with 20 or more employees against any person 40 years of age or over in hiring, firing, compensating, or any other conditions of employment.
Executive Order 11246 (1965)	Prohibits employment discrimination based on sex, race, color, religion, or national origin by federal contractors or subcontractors with $10,000 or more in contracts and on federally assisted construction contracts.
Equal Pay Act of 1963	Requires equal pay for men and women who work in the same establishment and whose jobs require equal skill, effort, and responsibility.
Rehabilitation Act of 1973	Requires employers to take affirmative action to employ and promote qualified handicapped individuals.
Pregnancy Discrimination Act (1978)	Requires businesses with more than 15 employees to treat pregnant women and new mothers the same as other employees for all employment-related purposes, including receipt of benefits under fringe benefits programs.
Vietnam Era Veterans Readjustment Assistance Act of 1974	Requires government contractors and subcontractors to take affirmative action to employ disabled veterans.
Americans with Disabilities Act of 1990	Prohibits discrimination against disabled persons in hiring or firing and requires employers to provide reasonable accommodations to the disabled.

2000, women employed full-time will constitute 65 percent of all new labor force entrants and 47 percent of the entire workforce.[6] A major human resource challenge in the years ahead will be to manage and provide an equal opportunity climate for this diverse workforce. Forward-thinking firms such as Goodyear and Hewlett-Packard are already hiring and training managers who can meet this challenge. As an executive at Hewlett-Packard put it, "Managing diversity has given affirmative action a new vitality, new objectives, and new language."[7] The impact of this growing work force is further described in the Diversity Close-Up (Immigrants Strengthening the New Work Force).

308   Part Four Managing People

C L O S E - U P / *Diversity*

Immigrants Strengthening the New Work Force

A few citizens are fearful that opening up U.S. employment to immigrants will weaken companies and eventually lead to economic decline. However, the argument can be made that immigrants are actually helping to strengthen and revitalize the economy. Support for this statement can start with education. Many immigrants have more education than that of native-born Americans. In recent years the average education of employed immigrants from India, the Philippines, China, and Korea is over 13 years, the average for Americans. Moreover, over a fourth of recent immigrants are college graduates, which is more than that for native-born Americans.

 Even immigrants with less education are contributing to

the economy as workers, consumers, business owners, and tax-payers. At the present time, there are over 11 million immigrants. They are earning over $240 billion and paying $90 billion in taxes. Immigrants are coming into the country fast enough to account for an increasing share of the total population growth. Of these newly arrived people, around 35 percent come from Asia and 24 percent from Mexico. Europe, which used to be the major source of immigration, now accounts for only 12 percent.

 The conclusion to be drawn from these statistics seems obvious: Immigrants are an integral part of America and they will continue being so. This is why so many companies are working hard to recruit and retain non-Anglo employees. They realize that the makeup of the work force is changing; and if they are to succeed, they must depend on and gain strength from a diverse work force. The big challenge will be learning how to effectively manage this diversity.

Source: Michael J. Mandel *et al.*, "The Immigrants," *Business Week*, July 13, 1992, pp. 114–122.

Screening

After recruitment, the human resource staff begins the selection process. This starts with screening, or eliminating applicants who are unlikely to succeed on the job.[8] Screening takes place in a number of ways. One is to have job seekers fill out an application form. The recruiter compares the information from the application with the minimum training and experience specified in the job description for the position. For example, a life insurance company may strive to hire salespeople with college degrees. Applicants without a degree would therefore be screened out.

 Another source of information for screening is resumés. Job seekers often prefer resumés over application forms because they have more control over the format; they can arrange the information in the most flattering way. However, human resource managers are often inundated with resumés and may feel that they all look alike after a while. Some job seekers have responded to this by looking for ways to make their resumés stand out, such as enclosing a short videotape of themselves being interviewed.

Employment Testing

For the applicants who pass the initial screening, the next step in the selection process is often some form of employment testing. Whereas the screening determines whether applicants have the necessary background to do the job, the testing helps determine whether they can really meet the demands of the job.

Types of Tests   For jobs that depend on specific, measurable skills, the staff of the human resource department tries to assess whether applicants possess those skills. For example, does the applicant for the job of computer programmer have knowledge of the relevant computer languages? Can the machinist applicants operate a lathe properly? Can the proofreading applicants spell accurately? The tests that answer these questions are skill or competency tests. A large survey of companies of all sizes found that 39 percent used such testing with job applicants.[9]

For other jobs, skill in performing specific tasks is less important than the applicant's potential and personality. Aptitude and personality tests try to measure characteristics such as interests, attitudes, and feelings. Companies often use such tests for sales and managerial positions, where the skills of interacting with and leading people are important to job success, but evidence suggests that a growing number of firms are using them for entry-level, blue-collar jobs as well. Most U.S. firms give about an hour-long test for entry-level, blue-collar workers, and candidates for top-management jobs take personality tests requiring a day or less. Some companies such as Honeywell and Manufacturers Financial Group also use brief tests for measuring drive and desire to do things.[10]

Validity and Reliability No matter what the purpose of an employment test, it must be both valid and reliable. A **valid test** measures what it is intended to measure. For example, if an applicant for the job of executive secretary is given a typing test for speed and accuracy, this would validly demonstrate typing skills. The test measures what the company wants it to measure. If the applicant takes a personality test and is turned down for the job because the results show characteristics that the firm considers inappropriate for a good secretary, the test is not valid unless the company can prove that these personality characteristics are required for the position and that the test really measures them.

A **reliable test** must have consistent and accurate results. For a test of dexterity to be reliable, an applicant for an assembler's job who scores poorly should score poorly again if he or she repeated the test. A test must be reliable in order to be valid. However, a test may be reliable but not valid. In that case, the test is consistently and accurately measuring the wrong thing.

Most employment tests are reliable, and the ones used to determine specific skills, such as typing or hand-eye coordination, are also valid. The challenge facing human resource management is to develop and use valid and reliable tests for assessing leadership, personality, and certain complex abilities such as selling. Valid tests in these areas are needed not only to counter charges of discrimination in court but, more important, to enable effective selection — getting the best person to fill the job.

Employment Interviews

After the initial screening and testing, the next step in the selection process is usually to interview the remaining applicants (although some companies conduct interviews before testing). The employment interview enables the interviewer to size up the applicant in person.

The interview may be structured or semistructured. A **structured interview** is one in which the interviewer follows a prepared format that consists of a series of direct questions. These questions specifically request

Valid test Test that measures what it is intended to measure.

Reliable test Test that gives consistent and accurate results.

Structured interview An interview that follows a prepared format that consists of a series of direct questions.

Semistructured interview
An interview that consists of prepared questions to direct the interview but that allows the interviewee to develop ideas that seem important.

desired information; for example, "Why did you leave your last job?" or "How did you find out about this current opening?"

In contrast, a **semistructured interview** is one in which the interviewer uses prepared questions to direct the interview but allows the interviewee to develop ideas that seem important. This interviewing style uses indirect questions such as "What do you expect of the company?" or "What can you contribute to the company?" to try to find out whether the individual seems interested in the job, has the right temperament to fit in with the existing personnel, and meets the job requirements. Some companies are beginning to use computer-assisted interviews to gather this type of information.[11] Others also use behavioral questions that require the candidate to explain how he or she would handle a particular situation, such as "How would you reprimand an employee? Give me an example of how you have done it and what the result was." Johnson Wax and Radisson Hotels have found that these types of specific questions help them more effectively evaluate applicants.[12]

Regardless of the method, however, the interviewer must avoid questions that are considered discriminatory. For example, even if the company needs to know the applicant's marital status for insurance purposes, the interviewer must wait until after the individual is hired to obtain this information. Table 12.2 shows guidelines as to which questions are considered fair to ask and which are considered unfair.[13]

Background and Reference Checks

After the initial screening, tests, and interviews, the human resource staff conducts background and reference checks of candidates still under consideration. Because of the employee's rights of privacy (discussed more fully in a later section), an increasing number of employers are unwilling to answer questions related to a former employee's education, overall character, safety record, union activity, or family background.[14] Nevertheless, the personnel staff usually should still verify the basic information on the application blank. If an applicant has lied about anything, most firms will automatically drop the individual from further consideration.

Physical Examination

Many enterprises require job applicants to take a physical examination. One reason is that the firm wants to ensure that the individual is physically able to perform the job. An incoming top executive who is found to have a serious heart ailment may not be able to stand up to the pressures of the job. A loading-dock laborer with a slipped disk may not be able to carry anything weighing more than 10 pounds.

A special case in recent years has been AIDS victims. If coworkers find out that a new employee has this dreaded disease, they may protest. Besides the obvious problem of getting along with coworkers, the afflicted person will also cost the company a great deal of money in disability payments and/or insurance premiums. However, the legal decisions so far have interpreted AIDS as a disability and have generally protected the rights of people with AIDS to keep working. Business will have to contribute to the effort to better educate people about how AIDS is transmitted and help in the fight against this recognized major problem.

TABLE 12.2
Pre-employment Inquiries: Guidelines for Fairness

Topic	Fair Inquiry	Unfair Inquiry
Name	Have you ever worked for this company before under a different name?	Your name is Polish (or any other ethnic reference) isn't it? Do you use Miss, Mrs., or Ms.?
Age	Are you the minimum legal age?	How old are you? (Any inquiry that implies a preference for candidates under 40 years of age.)
Citizenship	Are you prevented from being lawfully employed in this country because of a lack of a visa or because of your immigration status? Are you a citizen?	Are you a naturalized citizen? What country did your parents come from?
Family	Will you have any problems meeting our work schedules? We start at 7 a.m. every work day, you know.	Does your spouse work? How much does he (or she) make? How many children do you have? What types of arrangements have you made for taking care of your children while you are at work?
Pregnancy	None.	Are you pregnant? Do you plan on having (more) children?
Disabilities	Do you have any disabilities that would prevent you from doing this job?	Do you have any disabilities?
Marital Status	None.	Are you single, married, or divorced?
Military Record	What type of work experience did you gain in the military?	What type of military discharge did you receive? Can I see your records?
Criminal Record	Have you had any convictions that relate to the job requirements?	Have you been arrested?
Religion	None.	To what church do you belong? Are there any specific religious holidays that you observe?
Organizational Memberships	Are you a member of any professional or technical organizations?	What political party do you belong to? Are you a member of any voluntary organizations or clubs? Are you a member of a union?
Residence	What is your current address?	Do you own or rent your home? What are your previous addresses?
Auto	Do you have the use of a reliable vehicle?	Do you own an automobile? Is your car paid for?

Source: Some of these questions are drawn from Elliot H. Shaller, "Avoid Pitfalls in Hiring, Firing," *Nation's Business*, February 1991, 51–54. Remember that these are only guidelines to help prevent legal problems and would be judged on a case-by-case basis.

Employment Decision

The final step in the employment process is the actual decision to hire. This final decision is usually made by the manager in the department in which the individual will work. Staff in the human resource department usually take care of the preliminary steps and then recommend a candidate. The supervisor for whom the applicant will work reviews this recommendation, may conduct another interview with the candidate, and then decides either to hire the candidate or to ask for another recommendation.

All newly employed people become part of the in-house pool of talent that serves as a source for future internal recruiting. Today, more and more companies are keeping track of this pool of talent by maintaining records of employees in specially designed computer programs.[15] For example, a company's records could contain evaluations of all workers. When vacancies occur, managers can scan the evaluations to identify the ones that indicate supervisory potential or the best performance. The records can also contain special credentials, such as ability to speak French or experience with personal computers. When the company needs a person with such credentials, the computer can search the files and retrieve the appropriate records.[16]

Orientation and Placement

Staffing the modern organization continues beyond selecting employees and includes orienting them and placing them in their new jobs. Orientation is the process of introducing a new employee to the job and creating a basis for the employee to cooperate with the work unit as part of a team. Orientation is extremely popular,[17] and a good orientation offers a number of important advantages. One is that well-oriented workers tend to get off on the right foot. They learn the "ropes to skip and the ropes to know" in order to get along and be productive. Also, the orientation helps reduce anxiety associated with a new job and frees supervisors and coworkers from having to take time to answer questions or explain why things are being done in a particular manner.

Orientation Techniques   In small companies, orientation often takes place informally. The new employee's boss or someone from the human resource department takes the employee around the facilities and introduces him or her to everyone. Then the direct supervisor fills in the newcomer on company procedures. In larger companies, the orientation process is often much more formal. A new employee receives a briefing and usually a booklet from the human resource department regarding company policies, rules, benefits, services, and other information.

Traditionally, companies presented such orientations in glowing terms, saying that this is the greatest job in the greatest company in the world. Now, research findings have led many companies to adopt what are called **realistic job previews,** which attempt to tell the full story about the job instead of creating false expectations. Considerable evidence suggests that realistic orientations significantly reduce turnover.[18]

Realistic job previews
Orientations that attempt to tell the full story about the job instead of creating false expectations.

Placement Decision   After the company has oriented the new employee, it places that person into the new job. This first assignment, and who the new employee works with and for, can affect this person's career and long-run contribution to the organization. This step will be crucial to the new employee in learning the proper values of the company. For example, is customer service just a slogan or a reality? Are people who take a risk and try something new rewarded? Human resource management often slights placement, but increasing evidence shows that this activity is as important as the preceding steps in the staffing process.

CHECK ✓ POINT

1. What are the steps in staffing an organization?
2. Describe two ways managers can ensure they follow fair employment practices during the staffing process.

These dealers from West Texas are participating in Pump School, the hands-on product and sales training program of Gould Pumps Inc. The company provides training for dealers and distributors as well as employees, believing that training is one of the best investments it can make.

Source: Courtesy of Goulds Pumps, Inc.

Training and Developing

To treat the company's employees as resources, managers cannot simply hire the necessary staff and call their job finished. Rather, managers need to help employees fulfill their potential by learning new skills and developing their abilities. Managers accomplish this through training and development.

Training is the process of teaching employees the procedures and techniques to do their job efficiently. A great deal of training takes place at the lower and intermediate levels of organizations. Examples include teaching employees to fill out a new cost-control report, run a simple program on the computer, process a customer order, or operate a machine or specialized piece of equipment.

A broader approach than training, development is the process of helping people gain the necessary skills and experiences they need to become or remain successful in their jobs. Whereas training is aimed more at lower level operating employees, development takes place at the middle and upper levels of the organization. Examples include programs designed to help managers manage their time more effectively, build teamwork among their subordinates, and cope with stress.

Human resource managers have a variety of choices in selecting training and development programs. For 1990 alone, $44.4 billion was budgeted for formal training programs in U.S. organizations with 100 or more employees.[19] This seems like a staggering amount until it is realized that Japan spends relatively much more on training and development than do U.S. organizations.[20]

Types of Employee Training Programs

The most common training approach is **on-the-job training,** which is informal instruction conducted at the job site. In the actual job environment, the trainee mainly learns by doing the job, with help provided by an experienced partner. Another traditional training approach used with operating employees is **apprentice training,** an approach that is similar to but more formal than on-the-job training. The employee learns a job by spending a relatively long time working directly with a more experienced employee, who teaches procedures, rules, and techniques.

A newer, less traditional approach to training is called mentoring. Specifically, a **mentor** is an experienced employee who coaches and counsels a less experienced employee in the latter's training and development. Mentors take the person "under their wing" or act as sponsors. A new salesperson may start out by teaming up with a mentor to make calls on customers and prospects. During the calls, the new employee watches how the experienced mentor handles questions and closes sales; after a while, the mentor may have the new employee do more of the talking. The mentor will also provide guidance on how to get along with important managers and customers, and can transmit the cultural values of the organization. Women and members of other groups that have traditionally experienced discrimination have successfully used mentors to get ahead in organizations. A recently recognized problem, however, is when the relationship does not work out or when the protege passes up the mentor. As one expert on mentoring recently noted, "When these relationships work, they're fabulous, but when they don't work, they can be terribly destructive."[21]

Types of Employee Development Programs

Chapter 11 discussed allowing people to change or rotate jobs and crosstrain for other jobs as a motivational technique. This can also be thought of as a developmental technique. To provide broader experience, companies may use **job rotation,** which involves moving an employee from one job to another. Although the approach is commonly used with operating employees to reduce boredom, it is becoming an increasingly popular approach to management development. This is especially true when the person not only moves from one routine job to another, as in traditional job rotation, but also learns new jobs requiring different skills or perspectives. This expanded version of job rotation is called **cross training** and in management ranks might involve moving an engineering manager into a short assignment in customer service and then on to a stint in sales. This provides managers with a broad understanding of how the overall business functions.

Most companies also provide or encourage participation in off-the-job programs, formal training and development that takes place away from the job site. Such a program may be conducted by company trainers at a local motel or at corporate headquarters located in another city. Other programs are presented by professional training organizations such as the American Management Association or the American Society for Training and Development (ASTD), or by local colleges and universities that sponsor one-day training workshops and longer comprehensive programs. Examples might be a stress management workshop sponsored by ASTD held at a local hotel or a

On-the-job training Informal instruction conducted at the job site.

Apprentice training Training a new employee by assigning a more experienced employee to teach procedures, rules, and techniques over a relatively long period.

Mentor An experienced employee who coaches and counsels a less experienced employee in the latter's training and development.

Job rotation Development of broad experience by moving an employee from one job to another.

Cross training An expanded version of job rotation, in which the employee learns different skills or perspectives.

short course on personal computers given at the local college. A Penn State study found that almost 25 percent of major companies require upper-middle and senior executives to participate in such continuing education programs.[22]

1. What are two ways companies train employees and two ways they develop employees?
2. How do managers decide on the kinds of training the company should offer?

Performance Appraisal

Once employees are in place and learning new skills, managers need to keep track of how the employees are doing. Human resource managers take responsibility for this activity by making sure the company has an effective means of performance appraisal. Performance appraisal is the systematic observation and evaluation of worker behavior. Managers use these evaluations to make decisions about promotion and compensation, as well as to uncover needs for training and development and to identify employees who have potential for advancement.

Types of Appraisals

Performance appraisals take many forms. The most common is an evaluation by the supervisor. A **supervisory appraisal** is when the immediate superior evaluates the performance of a subordinate. Sometimes the human resource department supplements the supervisory appraisal with other forms of performance appraisal, such as peer ratings, subordinate ratings, and self-rating. A **peer rating** is one in which the workers all rate each other. The company sometimes uses this approach when it wants to give an award to the best worker in each unit and is interested in the workers' opinions about who should get the award. This peer approach may also be used in the increasingly popular self-managed team approach[23] discussed in the last chapter. A **subordinate rating** is one in which the workers evaluate their superior. This reverse appraisal is particularly useful when the organization wants feedback on how workers view their boss's leadership style. A **self-rating** is one in which the employees evaluate themselves. This rating is useful when management wants to compare how people see themselves against how their bosses see them. The evaluations indicate areas where disagreements exist.

Supervisory appraisal
A performance appraisal in which the immediate supervisor evaluates the performance of a subordinate.

Peer rating A performance appraisal in which the workers all rate each other.

Subordinate rating
A performance appraisal in which the workers evaluate their superior.

Self-rating A performance appraisal in which the employees evaluate themselves.

Common Rating Errors

In conducting performance appraisals, managers must be careful to avoid making rating errors. One common error is the **halo effect,** which is the tendency to allow an overall positive evaluation of the person to influence the specific characteristics being rated. For example, the supervisor likes Bob because he is so friendly and cooperative. The halo effect leads Bob's supervisor to automatically rate him high on all evaluation factors, including work quality and quantity as well as his ability to get along with the other members of the unit.

Another rating problem is the **severity error,** which occurs when a manager rates all of the subordinates lower than they deserve. For example, a

Halo effect The tendency to allow an overall positive evaluation of a person to influence the specific characteristics being rated.

Severity error A rating error in which a manager rates all of the subordinates lower than they deserve.

The job performance of these Pacific Gas and Electric linemen in Santa Cruz, California, is measured against factors established jointly by the company and the union.

Source: Courtesy of Pacific Gas and Electric Company.

Leniency error A rating error in which a manager rates most employees above average or excellent.

Central tendency error A rating error in which a manager tends to rate all employees as average regardless of how well or poorly they performed.

CHECK ✓ POINT

supervisor may believe that no one in the department ever deserves an outstanding rating and therefore gives mostly average and poor ratings. This severity error may be punishing relatively good subordinates.

The opposite kind of error is the **leniency error,** which occurs when a manager rates most employees as above average or excellent. If a supervisor rates 75 percent of the employees as outstanding and the rest as good, the supervisor is probably making leniency errors. Just as the severity error punishes good employees, so does the leniency error. The supervisor who is too lenient penalizes the best performers by preventing them from building performance records that are clearly superior to those of the average performers.

A final kind of error is the **central tendency error.** The manager tends to rate everyone as average. Very few are rated either high or low, which means that good performers may be penalized and poor performers are not identified. This can have a deteriorating effect on employee morale. Employees know that no matter how hard they work or how much they contribute they still will get only an average evaluation.[24]

1. What are two ways of appraising an employee's performance?
2. What are two ways in which supervisors can make errors in appraising performance?

Maintaining Human Resources: Compensation and Benefits

Human resource managers know that to retain their good employees, they must reward them fairly for their time and effort. The formal reward system takes the form of compensation and benefits. Supervisors use informal rewards such as increased responsibility and other techniques discussed in Chapter 11, and they often also make decisions concerning what to pay individual employees. The human resource department, on the other hand, is responsible for managing the overall package of compensation and benefits that the company offers.

Compensation Management

Compensation serves as both a payment to employees for their past efforts and an incentive for future performance. The payment for past efforts may take the form of wages (payment per hour worked) or salaries (payment at a flat monthly or annual rate). Incentive pay is usually tied to performance.

To assemble a compensation package, human resource managers weigh wage and salary levels for the industry and geographic area against the firm's ability to pay. Most companies pay about what the competition is paying. If they pay less, they may have trouble attracting and keeping good workers. If they pay more, they may have a hard time keeping the prices they must charge for their goods or services competitive. This wage differential between the United States and undeveloped countries in the Far East has been a major reason why American companies have had a tough time in those markets in recent years.[25]

If management determines that it is overpaying an individual or type of job, the company can freeze the pay at that level until the market catches up. If the company is underpaying, it can increase the compensation until it eliminates the difference. There are a number of important current issues related to this compensation process.

Equal Pay for Equal Work   The Equal Pay Act of 1963 and the Civil Rights Act of 1964 require employers to pay employees equally for doing the same job (see Table 12.1). Although the act does allow for differences in seniority, merit or shift differentials, if these things are equal a female accounting clerk must be paid the same as a male accounting clerk in the same office. Likewise, an African-American or Hispanic welder with 2 years' experience must receive the same pay as a white welder with 2 years' experience.

Comparable Worth   A controversial issue facing compensation management is whether employers should pay equally for different jobs that have comparable worth to the company. Some people argue that jobs requiring equal amounts of skill and responsibility are of **comparable worth** to an employer, and that employees performing jobs of comparable worth should receive equal pay. Some state and local government agencies have explored and in a few cases implemented policies based on equal pay for comparable worth. The city of Colorado Springs, for example, determined that it was paying less for jobs held primarily by female workers, such as clerical work,

Comparable worth   The idea that jobs requiring equal amounts of skill and responsibility are of equal value to the employer and therefore should receive equal pay.

Colorado Springs was the first city in the United States to adopt a policy of comparable worth. For example, city officials analyzed the responsibilities, skills, and job difficulty of a senior accounting clerk and an on-site carpentry foreman and determined they were doing jobs of comparable worth. The city then accelerated salary increases for the accounting clerk, who was the lower paid of the two, until she was getting at least 80 percent of the amount paid to the carpenter.

Source: © John Lawlor/The Stock Market; © Craig Hammel/The Stock Market.

than it was for jobs requiring a similar degree of responsibility (comparable worth) but filled primarily by male workers. The city then planned a way to bring the salaries more closely into line. It increased the salaries of the jobs held primarily by women faster than the salaries of the jobs held predominantly by men. Four years later, the differences were minimal. In Canada, the Ontario government recently enacted legislation that requires all public sector and private organizations with 500 or more workers to have equity pay plans in place that ensure all personnel are paid based on the value of their work.[26] For example, in a Canadian publishing company a female-dominated librarian job received about a $3,000 annual wage increase in order to obtain equity with a truck loader job that was judged to be comparable.

In the United States, organizations have resisted the idea of comparable worth. Those who object to this policy argue about the difficulty and subjectivity involved in attempting to calculate the worth of different jobs. They also note that market forces influence compensation. For example, if there are a large number of applicants for a particular job (a large supply) and/or if there are very few openings (low demand) for a particular job, this market situation will affect the wages paid for the job. Thus, if there is an oversupply of, say, clerical workers, it is very difficult for a company to justify paying higher wages when there are plenty of people who will work for lower wages. Nevertheless, some companies, including AT&T, are moving toward paying equally for work of comparable worth.

Individual incentive payment plan Compensation that rewards a specific worker for high performance.

Straight piecework A compensation plan in which employees are paid in direct relation to their output.

Performance-Based Compensation   Besides paying wages and salaries, many companies offer their employees the incentive of performance-based compensation. During the past decade, pay linked to performance has become increasingly popular.[27]

The compensation may reward individual or group performance. An **individual incentive payment plan** rewards a specific worker for high performance. The most popular such plan is **straight piecework,** in which employees are paid in direct relation to their output. For example, a plan that pays 40 cents per item will pay $4 to a worker who produces 10 items and $6 to a worker who produces 15 items. Besides piecework, which is associated with production workers, individual incentive plans can also be designed for salaried employees. For example, at General Motors they moved to a pay-for-performance plan. Under the old system, all salaried employees received about the same pay increases. Under the new plan, employees who are evaluated to have performed well receive big increases and those who performed poorly receive little or nothing.[28] Another example is investment bankers who earn about half their pay from individual bonuses. Because of a slump in business in 1990, their bonuses dropped by an average of 40 percent from the previous year.[29]

In addition to individual plans, a number of **group incentive plans** are in operation today. These plans are designed to provide incentive pay to units, departments, and sometimes the entire organization when they meet or exceed a goal. For example, at Borden Inc. some 28,000 workers at 180 different plants can earn bonuses ranging from $250 to $800 each, depending on how their individual plants performed,[30] and at DuPont's Fibers Department employees share in the profits when the department's earnings objectives are exceeded.[31] Group incentives promote working for and with the group instead of against the group. That result is especially important in jobs requiring group cooperation and teamwork. For example, construction crews, many manufacturing jobs, and the newly forming self-managed teams depend on collective efforts and would benefit from group incentive programs.

Group incentive plan
Compensation to units, departments, and sometimes the entire organization for meeting or exceeding a goal.

Benefits and Services

Besides compensating employees, most companies offer employee benefits and services. Although during tight economic times some companies will cut back on benefits, most still offer a wide variety. Besides those required by law, the major categories of benefits are pensions, insurance, paid vacations and leave time, and employee services. Going into the 1990s, the average cost of benefits per full-time employee stood at $11,527. This represented 37.6 percent of payroll.[32]

Legally Required Benefits   Some benefits are required by law. The most important ones protect employees who are injured, disabled, retired, or between jobs:

- **Workers' compensation** provides compensation to those who suffer job-related injuries or illnesses.
- **Social security** provides disability payments, old-age benefits, and survivors' benefits.
- **Unemployment insurance** provides subsistence payments to employees who have been laid off.

Workers' compensation
A legally required benefit that provides compensation to those who suffer job-related injuries or illnesses.

Social security A legally required benefit that provides disability payments, old-age benefits, and survivors' benefits.

Unemployment insurance
A legally required benefit that provides subsistence payments to employees who have been laid off.

Pension Programs   Many companies also offer pension programs, which are designed to provide employees with income for their retirement years. Today, about two-thirds of all hourly and salaried workers in the United States are covered by pension plans. In some cases, the employer makes the entire contribution; in other cases, the employer and the employee both contribute to the plan. Either way, the objective is to help the employee build up savings for retirement.

TABLE 12.3
The 10 Most Popular Executive Perks

1. Physical exam
2. Company car
3. Financial counseling
4. Use of company plane
5. Income tax preparation
6. First-class air travel
7. Country club membership
8. Luncheon-club membership
9. Estate planning
10. Personal liability insurance

Source: *The Wall Street Journal,* April 18, 1990, R25.

Insurance benefit programs
Benefits designed to provide various forms of coverage against accident, illness, or death.

Flex benefits approach
An employee benefit arrangement that allows each worker to tailor his or her own benefit package.

CHECK ✓ POINT

Insurance Programs   Another major benefit is **insurance benefit programs.** Companies offer these programs to supplement government programs so that their employees have a sense of well-being and security. These programs provide various forms of coverage against accident, illness, or death. One of the most common insurance benefits is life insurance, which provides a stated benefit (for example, $25,000) if the person dies while the policy is in force.

Another common form of coverage is health insurance. Most firms provide their employees with at least basic coverage, which pays (partially or totally) hospital-related expenses, surgical expenses, and physicians' expenses. Some firms offer insurance that covers dental care, alcoholism treatment, drug abuse treatment, and vision care. The costs of health care insurance have skyrocketed in recent years and a major challenge for human resource managers is to contain these costs and still provide necessary benefits.[33]

Other Benefits and Services   In addition to pensions and insurance, companies offer many other benefits, often called "fringe benefits." They include payment for time not worked, such as paid vacation, paid sick leave, payment for holidays not worked, and payment for time lost due to a death in the family.

Other fringe benefits are employee services. These include a variety of monetary and nonmonetary benefits, such as tuition assistance, company-provided cars, credit unions, financial counseling, and day-care centers. Table 12.3 lists the most popular perquisites (perks) that top executives receive. Today, however, employees at all levels are getting an increasing number of interesting benefits. For example, almost one-third of Polaroid's employees take tuition-free courses for personal development on company time. Employees of Zale Corporation in Dallas can eat lunch with their young children at the company's on-site day-care center. America West Airlines screens babysitters and their homes for its Home Caregivers program and reserves spaces for employees' children at a 24-hour facility.

Flexible Benefits   Because so many options are available, companies often give employees some benefits and allow them to choose others up to a particular limit. This **flex benefits approach** allows each worker to tailor his or her own benefit package. For example, in addition to basic life and health insurance, employees may pick certain other benefits worth up to a maximum dollar amount, such as $5,000 annually. They may select benefits that are of most value to them. Going into the 1990s a small minority of companies use a flexible, sometimes called cafeteria, approach to their benefit package, but all indications are that this will become more popular in the years ahead.[34]

1. What are the basic components of compensation and benefits?
2. Why do some companies offer group rather than individual incentives?

Issues Concerning Employee Rights

In recent years, employee rights have become a major area of concern in human resource management. Most attention has focused on three areas: sexual harassment, disability, and privacy.

Sexual Harassment

Any unwelcome sexual advance or hostile environment is considered **sexual harassment.** A typical incident might involve a supervisor promising a subordinate a more desirable task assignment or a positive evaluation in return for sexual favors. Harassment can also consist of unwelcome hugs, pats or body language, gestures, and suggestive verbal interactions. Although usually thought of as a problem for women in the workplace, some men are also experiencing harassment.

Title VII of the Civil Rights Act specifically outlaws sexual harassment. In recent years, a number of lawsuits have been filed by employees who charged that they were sexually harassed. The court decisions that followed have been instrumental in shaping company policies regarding how to handle complaints of sexual harassment. For example, in one case the court held that the employer is liable for the acts of its personnel. The only way for the firm to avoid being responsible is for it to have a written policy that specifically prohibits sexual discrimination and harassment and to show that the employee who violated the policy was aware of it. In another case, the court held that a company is responsible if it fails to investigate complaints of sexual discrimination or harassment.

What can organizations do to prevent or stop sexual harassment? The many possible measures include:

- Formulating and communicating an effective policy that defines what sexual harassment is and states that it will not be tolerated.
- Establishing a grievance procedure that employees can follow if they want to lodge a complaint.
- Investigating all complaints thoroughly and objectively.
- Making a decision regarding the offender based on the facts and following up to ensure that the decision is being carried out.

Disability

Armed with a new law, the Americans with Disabilities Act of 1990 (ADA), disabled people have specific rights in the workplace.[35] Under the law, the "disabled" are those with physical or mental impairments that substantially limit one or more of the major activities of life, such as walking or talking. The term also applies to people with a record of such an impairment, such as someone who has recovered from cancer, as well as people "regarded" as having a disability, such as a person with a disfiguring injury.

Under the law, employers may *not*:

1. Discriminate against disabled persons qualified for a job, in hiring or firing.
2. Inquire whether an applicant has a disability, but may ask about ability to perform a job.
3. Limit advancement opportunity or job classifications.
4. Use tests or job requirements that tend to screen out the disabled.
5. Participate in contractual arrangements that discriminate against the disabled.
6. Deny opportunity to anyone in a relationship with a disabled person.

Sexual harassment Any unwelcome sexual advance or hostile environment.

An employee of General Foods picks up a few of the 1,000 or so items stocked at the General Foods USA Company Store, where prices are 20 percent to 50 percent below retail. The store is one of the benefits provided to employees and retirees.

Source: John Olson for Philip Morris Globe.

In addition, employers must provide "reasonable accommodations" to the disabled such as:

1. Making existing facilities accessible.
2. Providing special equipment and training.
3. Arranging part-time or modified work schedules.
4. Providing readers for the blind.

The estimated 43 million people covered by ADA now are protected against discrimination in employment. Activists in disability rights compare their movement to the African-Americans' struggle for equality.[36] First came the effort to integrate the schools ("mainstreaming" in the language of the disabled movement), next the desegregation of public facilities ("you've got to get into the buildings to work") and, finally, equal opportunity in employment. McDonald's and DuPont are cited by the activists as "islands of excellence" in their recruiting and hiring of the disabled.[37] In view of the fact that two-thirds of the working age disabled were unemployed at the beginning of the decade, the challenge for human resource management becomes clear.

Companies have found that employees challenged with a disability are excellent workers. A poll of 921 companies found that 88 percent of the department heads responded that disabled workers do a "good" or "excellent" job.[38] Research also shows that disabled workers often turn out to be more intelligent, more motivated, better qualified, and better educated than those without a disability. They also have lower accident rates.[39] Hiring people challenged by a disability is indeed good business.

Privacy

Another important employee right is that of privacy. The federal government's Privacy Act of 1974 guarantees employees of federal agencies some degree of privacy with regard to information available to potential employers who are checking references. The act allows employees to determine which records the company collects, uses, and keeps. Since the 1974 law, there has been a great deal of interest in and legislation about employee privacy. Some states have enacted privacy laws, which allow employees to examine their personnel records.

Many companies are beginning to give more attention to employee privacy. For example, Cummins Engine's privacy policy extends to the desk files that supervisors keep on their subordinates. All performance review notes are discarded, and all disciplinary reviews are thrown out after the disciplinary period is over. At Northrop, a major government contractor, information gathered for federal clearances is kept separate from ordinary personnel records in order to maintain employees' privacy. Chase Manhattan Bank has a formal privacy policy that assures that an employee's file will be seen only by those who need to know the information in it. Except for confirming employment dates, the bank will release other employee data to outsiders only after that individual has given permission.

Employment at Will

Fired employees often wonder whether the company had a right to force them to leave. "It wasn't fair!" they often exclaim. In fact, employers can usually fire anyone, unless the firing is based on unlawful discrimination or

CLOSE-UP / *Diversity*

Opportunities for Immigrants

The employment at will concept is bothersome to some new immigrants in the U.S. work force because they think it gives the right to an employer to get rid of them at any time. In truth, this concept cannot be applied indiscriminately; and many successful firms go out of their way to make opportunities for immigrants and try to encourage them to stay and grow with the company. Some high tech firms in the Silicon Valley provide good examples of how immigrants have found opportunities and been successful.

Today, approximately one-third of the engineers in Silicon Valley firms are of Asian descent. In fact, the design of Intel Corporation's latest microprocessor, which will run a new generation of personal computers, was managed by an East Indian and a Taiwanese-born vice-president. Many of the valley's best known entrepreneurs are also foreign-born. Andrew Grove, chief executive officer of Intel, escaped from Hungary and has now built his company into the largest chipmaker in the United States. Philippe Kahn from France founded Borland International, one of the world's largest software companies. Winston Chen of Taiwan brought a 50 percent interest in the Solectron Company in 1979 when the firm was going bankrupt. And since then, he has built the circuit-board assembler into a multimillion dollar firm, which in 1991 won the prestigious Malcolm Baldridge National Quality Award, given annually to but a handful of firms that are judged to have the highest quality goods and services.

Although these are the most highly visible success stories, many new immigrants are finding jobs and opportunities both as employees and managers. Of course, there obviously remains some degree of prejudice among those who believe that immigrants cannot be good managers. However, one observer of American business recently noted that concrete steps are being taken to open up the managerial ranks to new immigrants:

In many companies, managers routinely take courses on "managing diversity." Some companies offer immigrants classes on American idioms and business culture. In the highly competitive electronics business, more and more companies are finding it pays to tap the cultural backgrounds, financial contacts, and entrepreneurial drive of the new immigrants.

Source: Robert D. Hof, "High Tech's Huddled Masses: Making a Mark in Silicon Valley," *Business Week*, July 13, 1992, p. 120.

in retaliation for union activities[40] or for reporting unlawful behavior on the part of the company (whistle-blowing). The courts have long upheld the principle of **employment at will,** which means that the employer can retain or dismiss personnel as it wishes. If employees do not perform up to expectations, the employer may dismiss them.

However, in recent years, the courts have weakened this employer right. In particular, the courts ruled that companies must act in good faith.[41] For example, if a manager tells an employee, "We never fire anyone without giving a second chance," then the company may not fire this employee for making only one mistake. Likewise, the courts have held that employees cannot be fired to prevent them from collecting a sales bonus or to stop them from qualifying for the company's retirement program. As of 1986, the right of companies to force personnel to retire on the basis of age is illegal.[42]

Some companies on their own initiative exchanged the principle of employment at will for no-layoff policies.[43] Others are simply happy to keep anyone around who does a good job. The accompanying Diversity Close-Up (Opportunities for Immigrants) provides an example.

Employment at will The principle that the employer can retain or dismiss personnel as it wishes.

CHECK ✓ POINT

1. What are two ways in which companies can minimize sexual harassment?
2. Why do companies try to hire and accommodate workers challenged with a disability?

Closing Comments

This chapter explored the dimensions of human resource management. This function extends beyond hiring to planning, staffing, training, appraising performance, and administering benefits. In addition, many interesting and relevant issues face the human resource manager, including avoiding charges of discrimination and respecting employee rights.

VIDEO CASE / *Gaining a Competitive Edge*

Lakeway Resort & Conference Center outside Austin, Texas, has about 250 employees. This may not sound like enough people to attend to dining, business meeting, banquet, and guest rooms, and recreational facilities for golf, tennis, swimming, sculling, skiing, paddle boating, jogging, biking, and horseback riding. However, because of careful screening, selecting, and training of personnel, Lakeway is able to provide high-quality service to its guests. Lakeway managers try to hire people with enthusiasm and assign them where they will be most effective. They want people who are confident, can maintain eye contact, and who are naturally outgoing to work at the reception desk and in areas where they are likely to come in frequent contact with the guests. Individuals who are more introverted are assigned to other jobs.

Training varies by department. Employees in the food and beverage department are taught to understand the wine list and learn how to sell the various types of wine. Those assigned to the front desk are trained to sell rooms and upgrades to suites.

Lakeway also teaches its employees to implement a philosophy of aggressive hospitality — that is, they should anticipate needs rather than wait for guests to ask for help. Aggressive hospitality is considered to be so important to the success of the resort that it is discussed at the monthly council meetings of employee representatives. Every month an employee of the month award and an aggressive hospitality award are presented to those who have exhibited especially outstanding customer quality service.

Lakeway management believes that there are only a few great resorts that are able to span the gap between average and outstanding quality service. Lakeway strives to be one of these. In the words of one Lakeway manager, "The only way to become great is to understand and satisfy the needs of our guests better than anyone else. We are committed to doing whatever is necessary to achieve that goal."

Case Questions
1. Why do Lakeway managers want to hire people who believe in aggressive hospitality?
2. In what way does Lakeway try to match personal characteristics with the job?
3. How important is training to the Lakeway Resort & Conference Center? Why?

Learning Objectives Revisited

1. **Describe human resource management.** Human resource management is the process of planning for, staffing, training, developing, appraising, and maintaining an organization's personnel. Supervisors used to handle this function, but since the 1930s, personnel and now human resource departments bear that responsibility. Today the human resource department also formulates human resource plans and even advises top management in areas such as productivity improvement and acquisitions and mergers.

2. **Explain the processes of human resource planning and staffing.** Human resource planning begins with a forecast of the number and kinds of employees needed to run the operation over the next year or two. If additional positions must be filled, the plan addresses sources of recruits and ways to attract them. Planning also includes preparation of job descriptions and specifications. Staffing begins where the plan leaves off. It involves recruiting, screening, testing, and interviewing job applicants and orienting and placing newly hired employees. The new employees come from the pool of job applicants that survive the selection process. The actual hiring decision is usually made by the manager to whom the individual will directly report.

3. **Discuss employee training and development.** The most common types of employee training are on-the-job training and apprentice training. Mentors, experienced employees who act as sponsors for the new employees, can also be used in certain situations. Other types of training and development programs include job rotation, cross training, and the use of outside workshops and programs.

4. **Define and analyze the techniques for performance appraisal.** Performance appraisal is the systematic observation and evaluation of worker behavior. Some of the most commonly used types of appraisal are supervisory appraisals, in which the immediate superior evaluates subordinates; peer ratings, in which workers rate each other; subordinate ratings, in which the workers evaluate their superior; and self-ratings, in which workers evaluate themselves. Some common rating errors that cause problems in performance appraisals are the halo effect, severity and leniency errors, and central tendency.

5. **Present the ways compensation and benefits maintain employees.** Compensation management combines wages and salaries with performance-based compensation. The wage and salary levels are usually tied to what other firms in the industry pay. Performance-based compensation includes individual incentive plans, such as straight piecework, and group incentive plans. In addition, companies provide benefits and services. Legally required benefits are workers' compensation, social security, and unemployment insurance. Other benefits include pension programs, insurance programs, and a variety of so-called fringe benefits.

6. **Identify the important issues surrounding employee rights.** Some of the most important areas that human resource managers must consider in their efforts to protect employee rights are preventing sexual harassment, hiring and maintaining employees challenged by a disability, ensuring employee privacy, and understanding the concept of employment at will.

Key Terms Reviewed

Review each of the following terms. For any that you do not know or are unsure of, look up the definitions and see how they were used in the chapter.

human resource management	job rotation	straight piecework
personnel managers	cross training	group incentive plan
human resource managers	supervisory appraisal	workers' compensation
human resource planning	peer rating	social security
valid test	subordinate rating	unemployment insurance
reliable test	self-rating	insurance benefit programs
structured interview	halo effect	flex benefits approach
semistructured interview	severity error	sexual harassment
realistic job previews	leniency error	employment at will
on-the-job training	central tendency error	
apprentice training	comparable worth	
mentor	individual incentive payment plan	

Review Questions

1. How would the activities of the human resource department of IBM have changed over the past 50 years? Give two examples.

2. Why would human resource planning be important to a company such as Ford Motor? Would this planning also be of value to a small manufacturing firm?

3. The owner of a fictional manufacturing company believes that minority workers are less productive than other workers. He will hire them, but he pays them less than other workers and refuses to "waste my good money" on putting them through the training programs available for other employees. This owner claims, "I'm well within the law, because I'm providing equal employment opportunity. I hire them just like I have to." Is this owner in fact abiding by the fair employment laws? Explain.

4. Clarissa Lee, president of You Wreck–We Fix Auto Body, is considering using a personality test in selecting workers for her chain of automobile body shops. "Well," said a human resource management consultant, "the information would be interesting. But you should know that while the test you're considering is reliable, it's not really valid for your purposes." What does the consultant mean by this?

5. James Hampton is head teller at Great National Bank. When orienting new employees, he likes to get them off to a positive start by giving them a glowing description of life as a teller at Great National. What's wrong with this approach? What should James do instead?

6. Because Stephanie Grant can't be at both of her flower shops at the same time, she instituted a system of performance appraisals. The manager of each shop rates the employees who work at that shop. In reviewing the appraisal forms, she noticed that the employees at the downtown shop consistently received higher scores than the employees at the shopping center store. Does this mean she has better employees at the downtown shop? Explain.

7. What is the difference between equal pay for equal work and equal pay for jobs of comparable worth? Why is the latter concept controversial?

8. How can human resource managers tie compensation to performance?

9. Acme Insurance is a medium-sized firm that has been growing rapidly. How can Acme ensure that there is no sexual harassment in the firm? Would the steps be the same as those taken by a much larger insurance company?

10. Adapting the work environment to make it accessible to those with a disability can be an expense to a company. Why would companies do it?

11. Doug Sanderson's boss fired him because they didn't get along very well. In Doug's opinion he always did a good job; his only problem was a personality clash with the boss. Did Doug's company have a right to dismiss him? Explain.

Applied Exercise

Each of the following is a statement commonly asked during a job interview. Some are fair questions and can be asked; others are unfair and should be avoided (even if the person asking them has no intention of deliberately discriminating against the job applicant). Place an *F* next to those that are fair and a *U* next to those that are unfair.

___ 1. How old are you?

___ 2. Do you have any disabilities that would prevent you from doing this job?

___ 3. Are you a naturalized citizen?

___ 4. Have you ever been arrested?

___ 5. Will you have any problems meeting our work time schedules?

___ 6. Are you a member of a labor union?

___ 7. What type of military discharge did you receive?

___ 8. What type of work experience did you gain in the military?

___ 9. To what church do you belong?

___ 10. Have you ever worked in this company under a different name?

Business has been so good at the Waxler Corporation that the board of directors has decided to open a new plant. The company manufactures and wholesales small appliances designed for the do-it-yourself home repairer. This market has grown so much over the past 5 years, largely due to franchising, that Waxler has seen its business mushroom. In particular, the high quality of the firm's products and its ability to meet delivery deadlines have helped it increase market share.

The board would like to see the company take over and refurbish the facilities of a plant that has gone out of business. This will eliminate the time delay associated with building a facility from the ground up. Then the company will have to recruit a workforce of approximately 325 blue-collar workers and 125 managers and other white-collar workers. A site selection committee has been formed and hopes to make a final decision within 30 days. The head of the human resource department, Pat de Vries, has been charged with recruiting the necessary personnel.

The president would like Pat to get started immediately by drawing up a proposed plan of action. "Put together a plan that can be implemented the moment we have made our final decision about where we are going to set up the new plant," the president told Pat. "Then as the refurbishing is going on,

you can be making progress toward getting the workforce put together. I want to start using those facilities at the earliest possible moment. Let's see if we can't hit the ground running." Pat has 30 days in which to work up an overall plan.

Your Advice

1. What should Pat do first?
   ___ a. Determine the specific number and type of employees that will be needed.
   ___ b. Establish the salary schedule of wages to be paid.
   ___ c. Decide how to go about screening the new job applicants.
2. If you were advising Pat, what would you suggest about recruiting people for this new plant? Offer at least two practical recommendations.
3. What steps will Pat have to take in screening job applicants? What should the plan include at this stage?
4. If the president also wanted these new hires to have some training and development within the first 6 months after the plant opened, what should the plan include? Be as specific as possible in your recommendations.

Union–Management Relations

13

Chapter Learning Objectives

- Explain what a union is and why employees join unions.

- Discuss the history of the labor movement in the United States.

- Describe union structures and functions.

- Present the dimensions of the collective bargaining process.

- Identify ways unions and management resolve disputes.

- Relate the major challenges facing unions.

the more traditional one- or two-year contracts because they decrease the number of negotiation battles and increase stability. Still another example that things are looking up for some unions is their ability to negotiate a type of signing bonus similar to that given to pro athletes. When an agreement is signed under this provision, each of the union members receives a lump sum payment. This becomes an attractive bonus for the workers, in addition to their annual wage increase negotiated by the union.

Despite these examples, things are not always rosy for the American labor movement. In many cases,

management is digging in its heels and openly fighting on wage, benefit, and security issues, even though it may face strikes or walkouts. However, there is evidence that confrontation with the union seldom results in a satisfactory solution for the company. For example, one researcher examined 56 unionized manufacturers that either were able to eliminate their unions or develop cooperative, positive relationships with them ten or more years ago. The research revealed that those companies that tried to cooperate with the unions and work out their differences reported a 19 percent increase in value added to the

company over a 10-year period. On the other hand, those companies that tried to bust the unions had a 15 percent decrease in value added.

The lessons from this type of finding seem quite clear. A confrontational union–management relationship not only leads to stress and strain for all parties, but more important may have a deteriorating effect on the organization's financial performance. By the same token, a positive, cooperative union–management relationship will benefit not only workers, but may also enhance the bottom-line profitability and value of the firm.

Photo source: © Jim Richardson/ Westlight.

Introduction

In many organizations, a large part of managing human resources involves union–management relations. Management's relationship with unions is often crucial to the success of modern business firms. If a company has a good relationship with its employees in general and the union in particular, operations are likely to move smoothly and both groups can prosper. Understanding unions and how to work with them helps managers avoid problems. This chapter begins by discussing the overall nature of union–management relations and summarizing the history of the labor movement. The rest of the chapter describes union structure and function, including the union-organizing campaign, grievance handling, collective bargaining, dispute settlements, and the challenges confronting unions today.

Nature and Importance of Union–Management Relations

Union An organization of workers who have joined forces to achieve common goals, such as higher wages and improved working conditions.

A **union** is an organization of workers who have joined forces to achieve common goals, such as higher wages and improved working conditions. The underlying assumption is that if workers speak with one voice through union representatives, they will have greater power relative to management.

Extent of Unionization

In the United States today, over 17 million workers belong to a union; this number represents a little less than one out of every five members of the workforce.[1] The graph in Figure 13.1 shows that union membership has dramatically declined in recent years. In certain industries, such as the railroad, automobile, primary metals, and transportation equipment industries, a majority of employees belong to a union. But even in manufacturing in general, the stronghold of unions, there has been a slight decline. Going into the 1990s fewer than 25 percent of all manufacturing employees are unionized.[2] In other industries, such as retail trade, insurance, and banking, fewer than 10 percent of employees are union members. Unions have had a difficult time breaking into the high-tech and service industries, and only a small percentage of the white-collar work force has become unionized. Nevertheless, unions are still an important group in the business arena.

Why Employees Join Unions

The working conditions we take for granted were only a dream a hundred years ago during the Industrial Revolution. Employees worked from sunup to sundown, typically 60 hours, sometimes even 84 hours a week (seven 12-hour days). Conditions were often unsafe, and many factory laborers were children. Workers found that by joining together, they had more influence over management policies and public opinion and could gradually improve working conditions. Today, it is a rare manager who would propose returning to the conditions of the Industrial Revolution. Even though conditions and wages are far removed from the Industrial Revolution, many workers still join unions for a number of reasons.

FIGURE 13.1
Union Growth and Decline

Number of Union Members (in Millions)

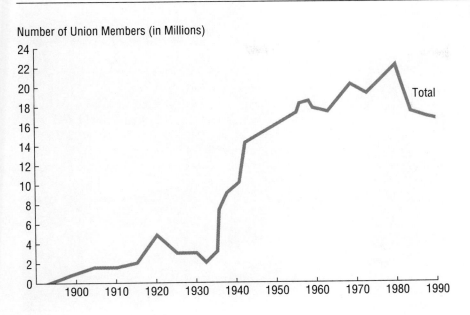

Wages, Benefits, and Security   The primary reason employees join a union is very simple: They believe the union can help secure them higher wages, better benefits, and greater job security. Most union members feel that their union is aggressively pursuing these objectives for them. The facts are that despite some slight shrinking of the wage gap in a few industries, union members, on average, still make 15 to 20 percent more than their nonunion counterparts.[3]

Power and Influence   Workers want to make their voices heard and to know that the company will listen. For an individual worker, especially in a large company, this is unlikely to happen. One way employees can counter the power of management is to join together in a union. Membership offers strength in numbers.

The union contract gives the workers specific rights and restricts management action. For example, when the union wins a 6 percent annual wage increase, it is exercising its influence over management. The union also exercises its power by challenging management's interpretation of the contract and demanding that any disagreements be settled through a prearranged grievance procedure.

Social Reasons   Besides the obvious economic and political advantages of joining unions, workers also join for purely social reasons. Joining a union gives employees a common bond of friendship and draws them closer together. They become part of a social group as well as an economic and power group. This component of fellowship and good interpersonal relations helps sustain members' support of the union.

A robotics class is offered to General Motors employees through the United Auto Workers-General Motors Human Resource Center, which was established as one of the benefits under the 1984 UAW-GM national contract. The center provides training in technical skills, basic education, communications, and safety, plus job placement, assessment, and retraining services.

Source: Courtesy of General Motors Corporation.

CHECK ✓ POINT

Limited Choice In some cases, workers join a union because they must if they want to work for a specific company or in a specific trade. Some states allow unions to require that all workers at a particular company be made members of the union. Workers who practice a trade such as carpentry or plumbing may find it difficult or impossible to get work without a union card. Some of these workers may not feel that the benefits of the union are worth the dues they pay, but they join to secure their livelihood.

1. What is the extent of unionization in the United States?
2. What are three reasons employees join unions?

History of the Labor Movement

The earliest unions in the United States were groups of printers and shoe-makers in Philadelphia and New York in the 18th century. Both managers and the courts were hostile to these early unions. In a celebrated 1806 case, a union of Philadelphia cordwainers (shoemakers) that went on strike for higher pay was found guilty of criminal conspiracy to restrain trade.

Courts issued similar rulings for other strikes, and they also determined that boycotts, where union members or sympathizers refuse to buy or handle products of a targeted company, constituted illegal restraint of trade. To combat unions, companies used so-called "yellow-dog contracts," documents in which workers stated that as a condition of employment they would not join a union. Unions that tried to organize these workers were then found guilty of inducing breach of contract. Recurring economic depressions also took their toll in terms of unemployment and lowered wages. Despite these setbacks, workers continued to organize.

At the turn of the century children like these water boys worked in factories and shops across America. The Knights of Labor had called for an end to child labor in the 1870s, but by 1900 only 28 states had laws regulating child labor. The first federal legislation was not passed until 1916. In 1900 about three million children—almost 20 percent of children aged 5 to 15 — held full-time or part-time jobs.

Source: Helena Frost Associates, Ltd.

The Knights of Labor

In 1869 a group of tailors met and secretly founded the Noble and Holy Order of the Knights of Labor. The **Knights of Labor,** which included unskilled as well as skilled workers, was the most important federation of unions of its time. By 1879, membership had reached 10,000, and the Knights ended the secrecy. By 1886, the federation had 700,000 members. However, rapid turnover in membership, lack of experienced leadership, lost strikes, and union violence that led to public disapproval brought about a rapid demise of the Knights. By 1890, membership had shrunk to less than 100,000. The organization finally disbanded in 1917.

Knights of Labor The most important federation of unions for skilled and unskilled workers in the years following the Civil War.

The American Federation of Labor (AFL)

Many of the craft unions looked for an alternative to the Knights of Labor. In 1881, under the leadership of Samuel Gompers, they formed the Federation of Organized Trades and Labor Union. Later they changed the name to the **American Federation of Labor (AFL),** the most important craft union federation in the United States.

The AFL organized only skilled trade or craft workers and focused on specific practical gains. Each union developed its own constitution and collective bargaining approach while remaining a member of the central AFL. This arrangement helped the AFL rapidly become a major force on the labor scene.

American Federation of Labor (AFL) The most important craft union federation in the United States.

A Changing Climate

During the early part of the 20th century, employers continued to resist unionization. At the same time, they began to develop a new concern for the

TABLE 13.1
Major Legislation Affecting Union–Management Relations

Law	Date	Major Provisions
Railway Labor Act	1926	Gave railroad workers the right to unionize without fear of reprisal by the employer. Created the National Mediation Board to resolve disputes in the railroad industry.
Norris–La Guardia Act	1932	Prohibited courts from restraining nonviolent union activities. Outlawed yellow-dog contracts and contracts forbidding union activities.
National Labor Relations Act (Wagner Act)	1935	Gave workers the right to choose their own union and to engage in collective bargaining with the employer. Set forth unfair management practices. Created the National Labor Relations Board (NLRB).
Labor Management Relations Act (Taft–Hartley Act)	1947	Set forth unfair labor union practices such as the closed shop, which had required workers to be union members as a condition of employment. Swung the pendulum of labor regulation back to a more promanagement position.
Labor–Management Reporting and Disclosure Act (Landrum–Griffin Act)	1959	Regulated internal union activities. Provided a bill of rights for union members.
Executive Order 10988	1962	Encouraged public sector bargaining. Followed by state laws giving employees of local and state governments the right to bargain.
Civil Service Reform Act	1978	Set up the system for federal employee unionization, bargaining, and impasse resolution.

welfare of their employees. Often, this concern for improved employee relations was intended to reduce the likelihood of their employees joining a union.

Congress also began to demonstrate concern for workers. In 1926, Congress passed the Railway Labor Act, the first law guaranteeing the right of workers to bargain collectively as a union. During the Depression of the 1930s, public attitudes and the backing of the Roosevelt administration led to the passage of laws favorable to unions. Notable among these was the National Labor Relations Act (known as the Wagner Act), which established the National Labor Relations Board. This federal agency hears worker complaints of unfair labor practices and oversees the elections in which workers vote whether to have a particular union represent them. After World War II, the Taft–Hartley Act spelled out the rights of employers as well as those of unions. Table 13.1 describes these and other major laws affecting union–management relations.

The Congress of Industrial Organizations (CIO)

In the more favorable climate beginning in the 1930s, union membership grew rapidly. Notably, as mass-production and mining operations began to grow, unionization in these industries met with considerable success. These unions organized workers industrywide, rather than by specific skill or craft. The industrial unions initially formed a coalition called the Committee for Industrial Organizations within the AFL. However, the AFL was unsympathetic to union organization on an industrial basis; so, in 1938, led by John L. Lewis of the United Mine Workers of America, the industrial unions left to form their own union federation, the **Congress of Industrial Organizations (CIO).** This became the most important industrial union federation in the United States. The CIO quickly became a major union force by organizing unskilled as well as skilled workers in the giant mining, steel, automobile, and rubber industries.

Congress of Industrial Organizations (CIO) The most important industrial union federation in the United States.

AFL-CIO Merger

In 1955 the AFL and the CIO took their own philosophy of strength in numbers to heart, set aside their differences, and merged under the leadership of George Meany. At that time the two groups collectively represented more than 16 million workers. Today the AFL–CIO is a confederation of semiautonomous labor unions representing over three-quarters of all union members. The confederation contains 100 national unions, including almost all the large unions in the United States. Even the large Teamsters Union (founded to represent truck drivers), which had not been a member for many years, rejoined the AFL–CIO in late 1987..

CHECK ✓ POINT

1. Name three major pieces of labor legislation. What impact did these laws have on the labor movement?
2. How has the attitude of business toward unions changed during the 20th century?

Union Structure

An angry worker marching in a picket line carrying a sign demanding higher wages is the vision that many people have of what a union is all about. Although strikes, defiance, picket lines, and demands are part of unionism, it also must be remembered that there is an extensive organizational structure that backs up every union member. Employees at the local factory, professional athletes, the workers on the construction project across campus, or perhaps even some of your instructors are members of national and international unions that provide them with various types of support. However, it all begins at the local level.

Local Unions

The **local union** (the local) is the basic unit of the union structure, representing members in a limited area. Local unions usually operate democratically, that is, each dues-paying member has one vote and can participate in electing officials to run the union. Small local unions typically have a president, a secretary-treasurer, and an executive board. Larger locals also have a business agent, a negotiating committee, and a grievance committee.

Regardless of their size, all locals have a number of stewards. A **steward** is an on-site union representative whose job is to protect the rights of members. For example, if a supervisor and one of the workers were to dispute

Local union The basic unit of the union structure, representing members in a limited area.

Steward An on-site union representative whose job is to protect the rights of members.

schedules of pay rates, the worker could quickly contact the shop steward. The steward would then contact the supervisor and try to work out the problem. Usually they can reach an agreement but if not, the contract spells out steps for resolving the dispute.

National Unions

National union The parent organization for local unions, which focuses on long-range considerations that affect all of the locals.

The **national union** (or international union if it has branches or locals in other countries) is the parent organization for the locals. While the local is concerned with day-to-day matters, the national union focuses on long-range considerations such as lobbying for favorable legislation that affect all of the locals. In addition, the national provides a host of specific services to the locals, including:

- Providing data on comparable wage and cost-of-living changes
- Training local leaders in contract negotiations and grievance handling
- Familiarizing local leaders with how to administer their union efficiently

At the national level, elected officials often consist of a president, secretary-treasurer, and several vice presidents. These national officers constitute the top policy-making board for the union. For specialized assistance, they often appoint experts such as lawyers, economists, statisticians, and public relations personnel.

CHECK ✓ POINT

1. What is the relationship between a local union and a national union?
2. How does a steward protect the rights of union members?

The Organizing Campaign

The national union is actively involved at the start of union–management relations during the organizing campaign. This campaign persuades workers in a company to join the union and to allow the union to represent them in bargaining over wages, hours, and conditions of employment.

Initial Efforts

The union strategy in organizing a firm starts with some quiet contacts. Union organizers contact a few selected employees at the work site and try to find out who is interested in unionizing and who is willing to help in the campaign. The union uses these volunteers to help recruit others. This initial activity may occur secretly.

Authorization card A request that the union represent the workers.

Next, the organizers try to get the employees to sign an authorization card. An **authorization card** is a request that the union represent the workers. If 30 percent of the employees sign this card, the union may petition the employer to become the bargaining representative or may petition the National Labor Relations Board (NLRB) for an election. However, to be assured of winning, most unions wait until they get at least 50 percent of the workers to sign these cards before asking for official recognition as the representative of the employees. If the NLRB is brought in, it determines whether the union has met all the requirements. If they have been met, an election will be held.

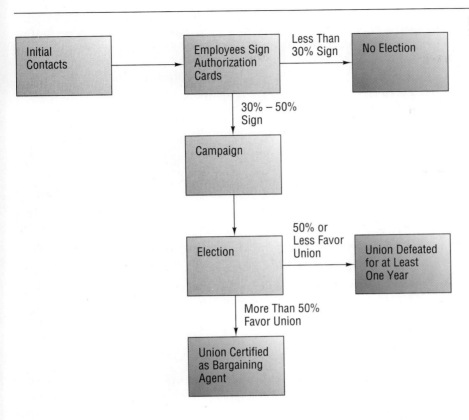

FIGURE 13.2
The Union Organizing Process

Campaign and Election

Before the election date, management and the union usually campaign vigorously. The preelection period usually lasts 30 to 60 days. During this time, both sides bring up a number of campaign issues. For example, management may stress points such as these:

- Improvements in wages and job security do not depend on unionization.
- The cost of union dues far outweighs the benefits members will receive.
- If the union succeeds in the election, workers may lose benefits or have to go on strike.

The union may focus on the following issues:

- The union will bring more job security and better wages and benefits.
- The union will give employees a voice with management.
- The union will set up grievance and seniority systems.

The NLRB conducts the election. If more than half of the workers vote for union representation, the union will be certified by the NLRB and will become the official bargaining agent for the workers. If only half or less of the workers vote for union representation, the union is defeated and may not try again for at least one year. Figure 13.2 illustrates this process. Over the past several years, unions have been losing more elections than they have been winning. For example, manufacturing sector unions won just 40 percent of the 1,066 elections in 1990. This is down from 54 percent of 4,361 elections won 20 years earlier.[4]

Decertification The process of dropping a union as the bargaining agent for the workers.

There also has been an increase in **decertification,** the process of dropping a union as the bargaining agent for the workers. For decertification to take place, three criteria must be met:

1. At least half of the employees in the bargaining unit must ask for the union to be decertified.
2. The workers must file the petition at least one year after the union was certified.
3. The workers must file the petition within the time period established by law, which in most cases is 60 to 90 days before the current labor contract expires.

In recent years in firms like Nordstrom, the giant retailer, employees have sought to decertify the union as their representative in collective bargaining.[5]

CHECK ✓ POINT

1. What agency supervises an organizing election?
2. What steps are involved in a union-organizing campaign?

Collective Bargaining

Collective bargaining The process in which management and employees, represented by the union of their choice, negotiate over wages, hours, and conditions of employment.

Picture a smoke-filled room with union members on one side of a big oak table and managers on the other, glaring at each other and pounding their fists on the table. Is this collective bargaining? The answer is yes and no. **Collective bargaining** is a process in which management and employees, represented by the union of their choice, negotiate over the wages, hours, and conditions of employment. Collective bargaining often involves tough negotiations between unions and management, and it often takes place in smoke-filled rooms with hostility on both sides. But there is also much more to collective bargaining. There are many basic issues that need to be resolved and many different bargaining strategies and techniques.

Union Security and Management Prerogatives
In the collective bargaining process, both the union and management stick up for and often fight for their rights. In particular, the union strives for the most secure position possible and managers try to protect and clarify their rights to run the business as they see fit.

Union Security Unions try to gain the security of being the sole bargaining agent for their members. Unions want to ensure that they will survive and prosper. To obtain such security, unions would ideally like to have closed shops, which would require that workers be union members in order to be considered for employment. Although the Taft–Hartley Act made closed shops illegal, the states are allowed to rule on other forms of union security. Thus, unions seek contract provisions for union or agency shops, maintenance of membership, and the checkoff.

Union shop A company at which all employees, as a condition of employment, must join the union after a predetermined time period.

A **union shop** is a company at which all employees, as a condition of employment, must join the union after a predetermined time period, usually

30 days. If employees fail to join within this time period, the company must let them go.

A **maintenance-of-membership provision** states that those who join the union must remain members. There is, however, a brief escape period just before the contract runs out (usually 10 to 15 days), during which members may leave the union. Additionally, those who are not members are not required to join.

An **agency shop** is one in which employees do not have to join the union but nevertheless have to pay union dues. The courts have ruled it is legal to assess dues for both union and nonunion members because members and nonmembers alike benefit from the services provided by the union.

The **checkoff** is a process by which the company deducts union dues directly from each member's paycheck and pays them to the union. The Taft–Hartley Act requires that employees sign a form authorizing the company to do this; the union may not demand that the company do this automatically.

These provisions are common in union strongholds in the industrialized Northeast, Midwest, and Far West. Many other states require an **open shop,** in which the workers do not have to join a union or pay union dues. Open shops exist in Sun Belt and agriculturally oriented midwestern states that have **right-to-work laws,** which prohibit union shops and other such union security arrangements. However, they do allow for the checkoff. Figure 13.3 shows which states have right-to-work laws.

Management Rights   While unions strive to maintain their security, management tries to protect its own rights. Any rights not given to the union in the contract are usually assumed to belong to management. These are called management prerogatives. In an effort to protect these prerogatives more formally, management often tries to spell them out in the contract. In particular, the company tries to protect its right to set production schedules, assign jobs, schedule work, impose disciplinary penalties, and subcontract work outside the facility.

Especially in recent years, to become more competitive in the international marketplace, businesses have become increasingly concerned with the motivation and productivity of their workers, and they are demanding more flexibility. For example, going into the 1990s the Big Three automakers in the United States made manufacturing flexibility — specifically a reduction in the number of job classifications and the expanded use of the team concept on plant floors — a major bargaining issue with the United Auto Workers. Because union membership has been declining and some of the companies that are unionized are struggling even to survive, management has been able to expand its prerogatives.

Bargaining Issues

The most important bargaining issues vary from one industry to another and from one contract period to another. Some issues raised during collective bargaining are simply invented to wring concessions from the other side. However, most of the bargaining issues are substantive. The most common across industries are job security, working conditions, compensation and benefits.

Maintenance-of-membership provision   A requirement that those who join the union must remain members.

Agency shop   A company at which the employees do not have to join the union but nevertheless have to pay union dues.

Checkoff   Deducting union dues directly from each member's paycheck.

Open shop   A company at which the workers do not have to join a union or pay union dues.

Right-to-work laws   State laws that prohibit union shops and other such union security arrangements.

As president, Gene Upshaw oversaw the change in status of the National Football League Players Association, from a union to a player association over the issue of free agency. With the complete support of the NFL players, Upshaw ended the NFLPA's role as a bargaining agent. By decertifying the union, members hope to win the right to sell their services to the highest bidding team.

Source: © Katharine Lambert Photography.

FIGURE 13.3
Right-to-Work States

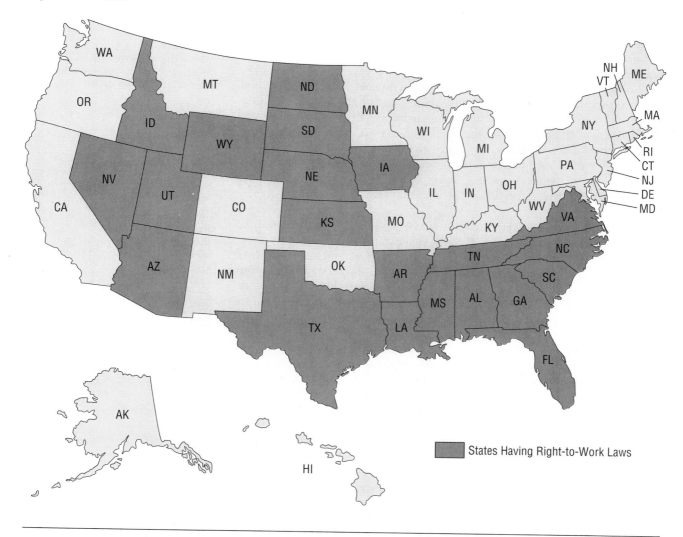

States Having Right-to-Work Laws

Job Security Going into the 1990s, job security has probably become the major bargaining issue. This is because the traditionally strong unionized industries such as steel and autos have been hit hard in recent years. For example, U.S. Steel, now USX, slashed its unionized workforce from some 50,000 in 1982 to about 18,000 in 1991[6], and the United Auto Workers membership has dwindled by a third since the early 1980s. If the steel and auto companies and others struggling against domestic and foreign competition must cut back, who will be let go? Many contracts call for a "last hired, first fired" or seniority approach specifying that the newest employees are laid off first. Some contracts also allow for **bumping,** which means that employees laid off from one department may transfer to another department in the company and replace someone there who has less seniority.

Bumping An arrangement permitting employees laid off from one department to go to another department in the company and replace, or bump, someone there who has less seniority.

Working Conditions   Union negotiators also try to obtain agreements that will promote safe and pleasant working conditions for union members. These agreements may include safety standards for employees working with video-display terminals or with heavy machinery in factories. They may prevent the company from expecting workers to work faster than a mutually agreed-upon standard.

In addition, work rules specify what tasks a particular employee may perform. For example, in some situations, a company may only require a welder to do welding; no one else may perform the job, and the welder may not perform other jobs. However, managers at many companies have complained that such restrictions seriously hurt efficiency, and unions have recently made concessions in this area. For example, firms such as Sun Oil, H.J. Heinz, and Colgate-Palmolive have negotiated the elimination of many such rules and, in the process of becoming more productive, been able to ensure continued employment for their workers.[7]

Compensation and Benefits   While allowing workers to play an increasing role in the design of work, management still carefully negotiates the wage package. The reason is that labor is a major cost in most organizations. The wage bill in today's firms often ranges from 30 to 90 percent of total costs, depending on the industry. This includes across-the-board wages, cost-of-living adjustments, and various wage incentives. Some firms such as American Airlines, Lockheed, and Northwest Airlines have even gone to a two-tier wage scale: New hires receive a much lower rate of pay than those already on the payroll. However, the popularity of this two-tiered approach is now declining.[8]

Besides wages, benefits such as pensions, health care, life insurance, and supplemental unemployment benefits are also an important bargaining issue. For example, veteran United Auto Workers laid off in 1991 were able to receive about 85 percent of their regular take-home pay for up to three years because of a contract signed with GM in 1990.[9] Obviously, such benefits are important to both the union and management. The dramatically rising health-care costs in particular have become an important bargaining issue. Unions are trying to keep what they have and management is trying to reduce its escalating costs by reducing coverage and/or proposing copayments from employees. Companies such as General Motors are saying they have to cut back because they are now spending $622 per car in health-care costs for hourly workers.[10]

The Negotiation Process

To negotiate the bargaining issues, management and the union each puts together a negotiating team. The management team usually consists of key executives, a lawyer, and members of the human resource or labor relations department. If management expects bargaining to be difficult or if the firm is very large, it may also bring in an outside specialist in labor law and a professional negotiator.

The union team usually consists of the local union president, other members of the local leadership, and a representative from the national union. If the union anticipates problems or if it is bargaining with a big company, its team may also include a lawyer and a specialist from the national union.

Once each side has assembled its negotiation teams, the bargaining process begins. Traditionally, this process has followed an "us against them" approach. However, this combative relationship has been slowly changing.

Preparation and Initial Demands   Both sides begin the negotiation process by gathering as much information and relevant data as possible. The union wants to find out what its membership wants to see in the next contract and what terms are in new contract agreements in the industry as a whole. By looking at other settlements, the union can gauge how far it can go in demanding wages, salaries, and benefits. Management checks with relevant personnel (such as first-line supervisors and specialists in the human resource department) to determine what changes these people would like to see in the new contract. Managers also examine the newly negotiated contracts of other firms in the industry. Both sides review the language of the current contract to see what clauses they want amended, modified, or removed.

Based on this pool of information, the two groups set forth their initial demands. These demands give each party an idea of the direction in which the other party will be moving. The initial demands also set the overall tone for the bargaining that will follow.

New Bargaining Strategies   Over the years, the predominant bargaining strategy has been a relatively combative give and take bargaining approach. In recent years, more cooperative strategies have emerged. These approaches include concessionary and continuous bargaining strategies.

A struggling company may be able to persuade the union to engage in concessionary bargaining, in which unions agree to give back some of the previously won gains. For example, managers of some companies have been able to convince labor to accept reduced benefits or even wage cuts. In recent years, companies in the auto and airline industries have used concessionary bargaining to help them survive, and wage and benefit concessions have become common throughout the meat-packing industry.

In combination with any of the preceding strategies, labor and management may conduct continuous bargaining, which involves regularly scheduled meetings between their negotiators. Rather than wait for the contract period to roll around, commonly up to 3 to 4 years, the two sides discuss and attempt to overcome problems on an ongoing basis. As a result, a more cooperative relationship evolves, and bargaining becomes a less adversarial undertaking, free from the pressure of deadlines. In some cases, however, as seen in the International Close-Up (A Strategic Retreat for German Unions?) companies are still prepared to be confrontational.

Resolution Methods

Despite the variety of negotiating techniques available, unions and management cannot always reach an agreement. Nevertheless, it is still in the best interests of both sides to resolve differences harmoniously. **Resolution methods** are approaches used to overcome union–management disagreements. The two most commonly used methods of resolving these disputes are mediation and arbitration.

Mediation   When the parties use **mediation,** a neutral third party helps both sides reach a settlement. A mediator has no formal authority to order

Resolution methods   Approaches used to overcome union–management disagreements.

Mediation   A resolution method in which a neutral third party with no formal authority helps both sides reach a settlement.

CLOSE-UP / *International*

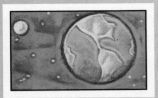

A Strategic Retreat for German Unions?

While cooperative management-union relations are recognized as being important to success in today's competitive environment, some business firms are still taking a get-tough approach. IBM Deutschland is an example. The company's management has decided to pull 17,500 of its 24,500 workers out of the national labor contract with IG Metall, Germany's most powerful union. The firm has created four operating companies, but only one, the 7,000-employee manufacturing unit, will remain under the union contract.

A primary reason given for this action is that labor costs in Germany are soaring. Manufacturing labor costs run about $28 an hour, and there are strict work rules which greatly limit management's flexibility. IBM feels that this arrangement is too confining and limits the company's ability to reward performance and results. IBM currently pays more than union scale, but because it must spread 90 percent of all pay hikes across the entire work force, there is little opportunity to individually reward productive workers. Moreover, union moves to shrink the industry work week from 37 to 35 hours will make the problem even worse.

Because of industrial democracy in Germany, IBM is still required to negotiate with the workers' council. However, this is no guarantee that the metalworkers will be able to keep IBM in line; and if the company is successful in combating the union, there are a lot of other German firms that will try the same strategy. Additionally, many large manufacturers are finding that it is too costly to produce goods in Germany, and they are beginning to set up operations in overseas markets. As a result, it may prove more difficult than ever for unions to obtain or even maintain high wages and restrictive work rules. Many observers of German labor relations believe that the unions should attempt to formulate a more conciliatory negotiating strategy because the tide is beginning to turn against high-cost labor. With Germany facing tough economic conditions; with European free trade on the horizon; and global competition becoming more intense every day, it may be time for German unions to consider a strategic retreat. However, given its past successes, powerful IG Metall and other German unions may chose to hold the line and let the chips fall where they may.

Source: John Templeman and Ann Hollifield, ''IBM Drops a Bomb on Labor,'' *Business Week*, July 13, 1992, p. 45.

either side to do anything, but instead recommends solutions in an effort to bring the parties together. Most mediators try to reduce the problems by first instructing both sides to identify their differences. Then each side is required to focus on these actual differences and make counterproposals for dealing with the demands of the other side. Each party is encouraged to accept reasonable accommodations by the other and to compromise. This no-nonsense approach that emphasizes compromise often resolves the dispute to the satisfaction of both parties.

Arbitration   In some cases, a neutral third party listens to both sides and then directs each side in what to do. This process is called **arbitration.** Under **binding arbitration,** both parties agree to follow the decision of the third party (the arbitrator). Under final-offer arbitration, both sides make their final offers, and the arbitrator chooses one.

Arbitration has a number of benefits:

- It may save time and money.
- The parties in the dispute do not have to resort to drastic actions, and both can save face.
- The resolution is rendered by an impartial, qualified third party, so it is as fair as possible for both union and management.

1. What are three major bargaining issues?
2. How can union and management reach an agreement when bargaining alone is not enough?

Arbitration A resolution method in which a neutral third party listens to both sides and then directs each side in what to do.

Binding arbitration Arbitration in which both parties agree to follow the arbitrator's decision.

CHECK ✓ POINT

Grievance Handling

Jim Adams was told by his supervisor the first day on the job at Purity Ice Cream Company that so many employees had been stealing boxes of novelty products to take home to their kids that the company had just passed a strict rule that the first time anyone was caught stealing he or she would be docked a day's pay, and the second time would be fired. Jim noticed that when his coworkers took breaks they would grab a couple of ice cream bars off the line and eat them in the lounge. The first time Jim ate an ice cream bar during the break, his supervisor ran up to him and said, "Jim, you know the rule about stealing. Since this is the first time, you will be docked a day's pay, but if I catch you again, you're fired!" Jim was shaken. He did not consider this stealing and filed a grievance with his union steward.

The contract that results from collective bargaining generally contains procedures for handling complaints brought by employees such as Jim who believe they have been treated improperly. These complaints are called **grievances.** Most labor contracts spell out the specific steps to follow if an employee files a grievance. The specific steps in the grievance procedure vary from contract to contract. Typically, the steps would be as follows:

Grievance A complaint brought by an employee who feels that he or she has been treated improperly.

1. An employee who has a grievance simply tells the supervisor. If the supervisor does not resolve it on the spot, the employee then informs the union steward, who contacts the supervisor. If this does not resolve the grievance to the satisfaction of both parties, then the grievance moves to the next step.
2. The department head or the industrial relations manager and the steward, supported by a union official such as the president or the business agent, try to reach a compromise. Often they work out a solution at this point to prevent the process from going to the next level.
3. If not resolved, the plant or division manager or the human resource director reviews the grievance. The local negotiating committee, supported by top local officials and in some cases a representative from the national union, will represent the union. Grievances that reach this step may have far-reaching implications for union–management relations and may be costly. Only rarely would the grievance go beyond this step.
4. In the final step of the procedure a neutral arbitrator reviews the evidence on both sides and renders a decision that is binding on both parties.

CHECK ✓ POINT

1. What is a grievance?
2. What are the steps in a typical grievance procedure?

Responses to a Breakdown in Negotiations

Although minor grievances are settled according to a specified procedure, other major disputes, especially those occurring during negotiations over wages or job security may lead the union and management to take drastic action against each other.

Union Actions

Strike A collective refusal to work until a dispute is resolved.

When the union cannot resolve a major problem with management, it may resort to a strike. A **strike** is a collective refusal to work until a dispute is

West Virginia State Police take a United Mine Workers of America member into custody when some UMWA members and supporters blocked a bridge leading to the non-union Elk Run Coal Company in Prenter, West Virginia.

Source: AP/Wide World Photos.

resolved. Strikes occur only as a last resort and are usually damaging to both parties, the local economy, and sometimes even the nation as a whole. Some strikes, such as an airline strike, inconvenience the public at large. Others drag out and become violent, as happens periodically in the meat-packing industry. The Pittston Coal Group strike lasted 10 months, during which the company lost an estimated $60 million in operating profits.[11]

Workers may combine a strike with a picket. A **picket** is an assembly of workers stationed outside the premises for the purpose of calling attention to their grievances. Often the picketers carry signs or posters describing the reason for their actions. Sometimes union picketers will attempt to prevent nonunion workers from entering a company that is being struck. Members of other unions generally respect the striking unions and do not cross their picket line.

Another union technique is the **boycott,** which is an organized effort to convince people to refrain from buying goods or services from a targeted business. Unions have organized boycotts against clothing manufacturers such as Farrah and J. P. Stevens. When the union urges its members not to do business with a company, the action is a primary boycott and is legal. However, if the union attempts to influence others to boycott the company's goods, the action is a secondary boycott, which is illegal under the provisions of the Taft–Hartley Act.

Still another union action is a **work slowdown,** in which the workers cut back their efforts and do only the minimum amount of work required. Employees at a General Motors plant recently used this approach and within 15 months plant productivity had fallen almost 20 percent.[12]

Picket An assembly of workers stationed outside the premises for the purpose of calling attention to their grievances.

Boycott An organized effort to convince people to refrain from buying goods or services from a targeted business.

Work slowdown A union action in which workers cut back their efforts and do only the minimum amount of work required.

When unionized Greyhound bus drivers went on strike, company executives immediately hired nonunion, permanent replacements. Some buses became snipers' targets, causing injury to several passengers. The union disavowed the shootings, but the incidents generated bad publicity for the union cause.

Source: UPI/Bettmann.

Unions can also bring pressure on an employer through their influence on others. They can stir public pressure by providing information to and making appearances in the mass media. They also can use some of their financial resources to support the campaigns of political candidates who take prounion positions. Under pressure from public opinion and government officials, the company may give in to union demands.

Management Actions

Management also has techniques that it can use in countering the union. Under certain conditions, a company will resort to a **lockout,** which is a refusal to allow workers to enter a facility. For example, if wage negotiations break down because management feels that the union is making unreasonable demands, management may lock out the employees. For this to be legal, the contract must have expired and the company must not interfere with the rights of its employees or their union activities. Ravenswood Aluminum recently locked out 1,700 Steelworkers Union members whom it felt were making unreasonable demands.[13] In combination with a lockout, managers may try to run the company on their own.

If management wants to counter a union strike without the financial risk of a lockout, it may try to get a court order that directs the strikers to return to work. In some cases, such as a business whose operation is vital to national security, a judge may issue such an order in an attempt to get the parties back together.

If all attempts at settling a strike fail, management may eventually turn to the use of **strikebreakers,** nonunion workers hired to do the jobs of striking union employees. Strikebreakers are called "scabs" by the union members. In recent years some companies have refused to rehire union members

Lockout A company's refusal to allow workers to enter a facility.

Strikebreaker A nonunion worker hired to do the job of a striking union employee.

who have gone on strike and not reported for work. For example, International Paper replaced striking workers at its paper mill in Jay, Maine, and Greyhound threatened to replace all striking workers permanently.[14] The U.S. General Accounting Office found that such permanent replacements were hired in about one-third of all strikes in recent years.[15] As a result, management has found that, if there is a ready supply of replacements, this can be a very effective tool for minimizing the effects of strikers.

To counter the unions' influence in the social and political arenas, companies can also use **employer associations.** These are employer-sponsored lobbying and public relations organizations primarily designed to promote promanagement legislation.

1. What are two actions unions can take when collective bargaining breaks down?
2. What are two ways management can respond?

Employer associations
Employer-sponsored lobbying and public relations organizations primarily designed to promote promanagement legislation.

CHECK ✓ POINT

Challenges Facing Unions

Unions face tremendous challenges in managing the present and planning for the future. In recent years, they have been struggling. For over 40 years, union membership as a percentage of the nonfarm workforce has been declining. Over the past decade, there has been about a 20 percent plunge in union ranks. At about 17 percent of the workforce currently, union membership is projected to be under 14 percent by the year 2000. This section explores some of the major reasons for this decline of the union movement.

Loss of Unionized Jobs
One reason for the decline in union membership are the job losses being experienced in heavily unionized industries, such as the steel and automobile industries, and an increase in employment in the traditionally nonunionized service sector.[16] Over the years unions have mainly appealed to blue-collar workers, and this segment of the workforce has seen the greatest decline in employment in recent years.

The employment decline has stemmed from a number of sources. Some companies have found that it is cheaper to have work done overseas. Thus, they may transfer some or all operations to developing countries such as Thailand, where wages are lower and union activity virtually nonexistent. Others have had to shut down plants because they have let them become old and inefficient. In some cases, a merger or acquisition may mean that the company can continue operations more efficiently with fewer employees. Or the company may install robots to replace workers or discontinue producing a product that no longer has sufficient demand. Whatever the reason for cutbacks, plant shutdowns, and so-called downsizing, unions face the challenge of stemming the loss of existing members' jobs.

Declining Public Image
Many Americans have lost confidence in unions. While they may still admit that unions can improve wages and working conditions, they have reservations regarding their overall value. For example, one recent public opinion survey found that:

Nurse Teresa Yates (left) and union activist Gayle Fleming prepare to bargain for the first union contract at Dickenson County (Virginia) Medical Center. Yates and a dozen coworkers led a successful campaign to unionize, and now the United Mine Workers of America is certified as their union. The health care industry employs twice as many people as the auto and steel industries combined, often in low-wage positions, and is therefore an important target for unionization.

Source: © Mildred Deel.

CLOSE-UP / *Ethics*

The Unions May Have a Friend in Washington After All

Ever since the Reagan administration busted the air traffic controllers strike, unions have felt that the federal government has not been very supportive. However, one recent event may turn this perception around. The landmark National Labor Relations Act of 1935 prohibited employers from unfairly interfering with union activities. A major purpose of this law was to discourage employer-dominated unions that would be obligated to the company rather than to the rank-and-file members. Because of this law, companies have traditionally been very careful to distance themselves from union matters. For example, if an organization's disgruntled employees were to ask the company how they could go about decertifying the union, they would be quickly rebuffed and told to seek assistance elsewhere. No company wants to face a charge of attempting to influence union decisions.

Despite the traditional hands-off policy, some companies may have inadvertently crossed the line set by the National Labor Relations Act. The National Labor Relations Board (NLRB) general counsel has announced that DuPont was guilty of such action, and the company has been brought up before an NLRB administrative judge. What is particularly interesting about the charge is that it stemmed from efforts to promote job safety. To encourage safety awareness, DuPont's labor/management safety committee at the New Jersey Chamber Works passed out T-shirts, coolers, and driving gloves to employees in early 1990. The NLRB counsel now charges that the company broke the law because handing out gifts "changed the terms and conditions of employment" at the plant. DuPont has responded that these efforts were nothing more than safety-driven concerns that are encouraged by another arm of the government, the Occupational Safety & Health Administration (OSHA).

If the government is successful in this case, many of the employee involvement programs that companies all around the country have established in recent years to promote quality, productivity, and safety could also be declared illegal. This is why corporate lawyers are now heatedly arguing that these worker involvement programs are a far cry from the company unions that the law was designed to outlaw. On the other hand, many unions are arguing that these recent efforts involving employee groups do indeed violate the law, claiming that the only reason that they have not been ruled illegal is that the government has failed to do its job.

Even if the unions do not win this challenge, they still have something to smile about. While they have been steadily losing members and political influence, they may have one friend left in Washington: the National Labor Relations Board.

Source: Janet Novack, "Make Them All Form Unions," *Forbes*, May 11, 1992, p. 174.

- 50 percent of the respondents felt that if private sector employees go on strike, they should not be guaranteed their jobs.
- 40 percent said they felt that labor unions had too much power.
- 22 percent said that workers no longer needed unions.[17]

Unions are aware of these image problems and are taking steps to solve them. One way is to push out the old guard and replace them with younger, fresher leadership as is being done in unions like the Teamsters, where new candidates are continuing to win election to union offices.[18] A second way is to take opinion polls among the rank and file to learn more about what the membership really wants. Many unions are finding that their people are concerned about losing their jobs to what they see as unfair trade practices of Japan and other countries. Unions are responding to such feedback by demanding that the government act to restrict imports.

The Need to Attract Women and White-Collar Service Workers

Women are a particularly important target of the union movement because of their growing number in the workforce and the fact that many are underpaid and, in some cases, still discriminated against. White-collar workers in service industries are another important target because they constitute a large segment of the workforce. To date, unions have had only moderate success in their efforts to organize service workers and the college educated. When it is realized that the service sector will continue to dominate in the years ahead, and jobs requiring a college degree will rise from the present 22 percent of the total to 30 percent by 2000,[19] the challenge facing unions is clear.

Unions must meet the important challenges of stemming the loss of unionized jobs, enhancing their public image, and organizing women, service workers, and those with a higher education if the union movement is to remain a viable force in the economy and in American society. There are a few encouraging signs that this may be happening as seen in the Ethics Close-Up (The Unions May Have a Friend in Washington After All). Unions have reason to be optimistic for the future largely because their members have already taken most of their lumps.[20] Also, unions have negotiated some very lucrative contracts with firms such as Xerox, Bethlehem Steel, and AT&T[21]; and the National Labor Relations Board has adopted regulations that will make it easier for unions to organize areas such as hospital employees.[22]

CHECK ✓ POINT

1. What are three major challenges facing unions today?
2. How are unions trying to rebuild their declining membership?

Closing Comments

Most business managers either attempt to work with the union if their workforce is organized or attempt to keep the union out if it has not yet gained a foothold. By understanding the background and structure of unions and the various dimensions of collective bargaining, managers can build a harmonious and constructive relationship with unions or with employee groups in nonunionized organizations.[23] In such a relationship, workers and management can both be winners and can accomplish two goals of one of the union movement's pioneering leaders, Samuel Gompers: "more" for the employees and "profits" for the employers.

VIDEO CASE / *Moderate, Cooperative Beats Macho*

When union–management relations break down, each side has several options. In 1935, the passage of the National Labor Relations Act, better known as the Wagner Act, provided unions with the necessary legal ammunition to fight their battles. Then in 1947, the Taft-Hartley Act gave management the right to use countermeasures, and both sides settled into a confrontational relationship in the ensuing years.

This period was characterized by a great deal of mutual distrust. Negotiation sessions often ended up with one side trying to muscle the other into accepting certain contract terms. However, each side has begun to realize the uselessness of this combative stance, and a positive, cooperative relationship is becoming more common.

This transition to a cooperative relationship took time, and even now some unions and management are still fighting tooth and nail. However both sides seem to have learned important lessons during the 1980s. The decade opened with President Reagan breaking the air traffic controllers' strike by replacing the strikers with nonunion controllers. This widely publicized event was followed a few years later by Frank Lorenzo's anti-union strategy at both Eastern and Continental Airlines. In both of these cases, Lorenzo used hardball tactics and cut labor costs to the bone. In the case of Continental, employees eventually crossed the picket lines and went back to work.

By the late 1980s, however, things were changing. Unions and management were becoming much more cooperative, and attempts by companies to pressure unions into line were vigorously resisted. In 1989, Lorenzo again adopted a get-tough stance with Eastern Airlines, but this time it failed. The unions were ready, and the pilots and machinists joined forces to fight a common enemy. The fight became so personal that many employees were willing to lose their jobs rather than let Lorenzo win. In the final outcome, the airline was sold and Lorenzo lost.

Other companies that adopted a confrontational strategy during the 1980s and early 1990s suffered similar fates. Greyhound Lines, for example, allegedly violated labor laws in an effort to oust the union. Recently, the company has been having financial difficulties. More recently, the *Daily News*, New York City's picture newspaper, fared little better despite management's attempt to prepare for the worst. When the paper's unions went on strike, the *Daily News* management hired and trained nonunion drivers and brought in security guards to protect the employees and the property. However, management overlooked one key element in the distribution chain: the news vendors. More than 80 percent of the daily circulation was handled by newsstands, and the unions convinced

stand owners not to carry the *News*. As circulation collapsed, advertisers began pulling their business, and the company was soon losing $750,000 daily. The paper was finally sold to Robert Maxwell, the British media baron, who promised to work with the union in resolving their differences.

Other companies that have used a cooperative, positive stance relating to their unions have done better. For example, the major competitor of the *News*, the *New York Post*, received life-saving concessions from the same unions that fought the *News*. In one week, the *Post* unions gave up 20 percent in wage cuts in order to keep the paper afloat. Ford Motor and Cummins Engine also successfully undertook a cooperative relationship with the union in an effort to boost productivity and hold down costs. In other cases, companies have voluntarily agreed to cooperate with the union. Japan's Bridgestone Corporation, which bought Firestone Tire & Rubber in 1988, accepted the United Rubber Workers at the Warren County, Tennessee plant after a majority of the plant's 150 hourly workers said they wanted a union. Bridgestone

management said it saw an advantage to having the union as a partner in the facility.

Not everyone would agree with Bridgestone's decision, but there is growing evidence that the most profitable firms are those that work with the union to resolve their differences. As one labor economist at the Conference Board put it, "What gets the headlines is macho behavior with high testosterone levels. But over the long haul, moderate behavior is probably more efficient."

Source: Aaron Bernstein, "Busting Unions Can Backfire on the Bottom Line," *Business Week*, March 18, 1991, 108.

Case Questions

1. What types of issues are most important to unions? To management? Identify and describe two such issues for each.
2. If there is a breakdown in negotiations, what actions are available to unions? To management?
3. What does this case illustrate about the need for union–management cooperation? Based on your answer, what can you conclude regarding union–management relations during the 1990s? Why?

Learning Objectives Revisited

1. **Explain what a union is and why employees join unions.** Unions are organizations of workers who have joined forces to achieve common goals. Employees join unions because they believe the union can improve their wages, benefits, and job security; give them a more influential voice with management; and promote friendship and good relations among members. Sometimes workers join unions because it is their only real choice.

2. **Discuss the history of the labor movement in the United States.** Unions have existed in the United States since the 18th century. As the labor movement began to grow in the 1800s, many unions were hampered in their efforts to organize. The courts often ruled them to be illegal conspiracies acting in restraint of trade. Nevertheless, during the 1880s the Knights of Labor had membership of 700,000. Although this early federation of unions had a

rapid demise, it was soon replaced by the American Federation of Labor (AFL), which brought together craft unions from all over the nation. Legislation passed in the 1930s that was favorable to labor helped spur union membership. One result was that the Congress of Industrial Organizations (CIO) became the largest industrial union federation in the nation. In the 1950s, the AFL and CIO merged; today most of the large unions are part of the AFL–CIO.

3. **Describe union structures and functions.** Each union member may vote for those who will run the local, typically the president, secretary-treasurer, and executive board. Large locals also have a business agent, a negotiating committee, and a grievance committee. The union negotiates and administers the labor contract. The worker's day-to-day contact with the union occurs through the steward.

The locals are members of large national unions, which in turn may be members of the AFL–CIO.

4. **Present the dimensions of the collective bargaining process.** Before collective bargaining occurs, the firm must be organized. If at least 30 percent of the workers sign authorization cards calling for a vote, the NLRB reviews the cards and schedules an election. If over half of the workers vote to unionize, the union becomes the workers' bargaining agent. During collective bargaining, management and the union negotiate over wages, hours, and conditions of employment and administering the labor contract. The most commonly used strategy is to have a give and take between management and the union and is combative in nature; some newer approaches are concessionary and continuous bargaining. When the parties need help in reaching an agreement, they may turn to mediation and arbitration.

5. **Identify ways union and management resolve disputes.** The contract provides for a specified procedure for minor grievances. Typically, the first step is for the supervisor and union member, along with the union steward, to resolve the problem. If this fails, the grievance then moves to the department head or industrial relations manager and the local union president or business agent. If necessary, top management and union officials become involved. If the grievance still is not settled, a neutral arbitrator issues a decision. With major unresolved disputes, labor may resort to striking, picketing, boycotting, or slowdowns. Management may use lockouts, court orders, strikebreakers, or simply permanently replace the strikers. Both sides may attempt to influence public opinion and government policy through lobbying and public relations efforts.

6. **Relate the major challenges facing unions.** The major challenges facing unions are stemming the loss of union jobs; enhancing a declining public image; and organizing nonunionized segments of the workforce, particularly women, service workers, and those with a higher education.

Key Terms Reviewed

Review each of the following terms. For any that you do not know or are unsure of, look up the definitions and see how they were used in the chapter.

union	collective bargaining	arbitration
Knights of Labor	union shop	binding arbitration
American Federation of	maintenance-of-membership	grievance
Labor (AFL)	provision	strike
Congress of Industrial	agency shop	picket
Organizations (CIO)	checkoff	boycott
local union	open shop	work slowdown
steward	right-to-work laws	lockout
national union	bumping	strikebreaker
authorization card	resolution methods	employer associations
decertification	mediation	

Review Questions

1. Why would college instructors join a union? Give three reasons.
2. How has the legal climate for unionizing changed since the early part of the 20th century? In your answer, identify specific laws where possible.
3. What is the role of the union steward?
4. What are the usual responsibilities of a national union?
5. A union wants to organize the salesclerks at a local chain of supermarkets. What steps should the union plan to take?
6. What are some arguments the union in Question 5 could make in its organizing campaign? What are some arguments that the store owners could make?
7. How do unions try to maintain security for themselves? Give two examples.

8. How do unions try to improve working conditions? Give two examples.

9. Central States Steel Company did not make a profit last year and is attempting to increase work efficiency. What bargaining strategy should the company adopt? Explain how this strategy works.

10. Do you think a union should seek to engage in concessionary bargaining? Why or why not?

11. What is the difference between mediation and arbitration?

12 When Alice Hiller was returning from lunch, the vice president stopped her in the parking lot to ask her how things were going in her department. Consequently, Alice was late getting back to her desk, and her supervisor docked her for an afternoon's pay. Alice thinks her supervisor's action was unfair. As a union member, what can she do?

13. The union contract has expired at Blue Sky Aviation Company, and management has announced that it will not negotiate. "We are in a holding pattern around here; you can have what you had last time — take it or leave it," said the personnel manager to the union business agent. What actions can the union resort to? Why should Blue Sky try to avoid such a scenario?

14. What challenges currently face unions? Add any you can think of to those described in the chapter.

Applied Exercise

The following are some strategies that might be used by a company that is trying to head off unionization and/or deal with it. Read each of the strategies and put an *L* next to those that are legal and an *I* next to those that are illegal.

In preventing unionization

___ 1. Point out to the employees that if they join the union they may have to pay union dues out of their paycheck, so their take-home pay will be reduced.

___ 2. Offer the workers a 10 percent raise across-the-board if they call off their union drive.

___ 3. Conduct an investigation into the union's past history, note some of the mistakes the union has made, and call these to the attention of the workers.

___ 4. Identify those individuals who are the strongest union supporters and lay them off or fire them as soon as possible.

If the union wins

___ 5. Refuse to bargain with them, thus making it impossible for the union representatives to hammer out a contract.

___ 6. Provide legal advice to any members who are displeased and are looking to vote for decertification of the union.

YOU BE THE ADVISER / *Getting Prepared*

The Rivers Company has been a family-run operation for over 15 years. The company was extremely profitable until around 6 years ago, when industry competition increased dramatically and profits hit an all-time low. Since then, Joe Rivers, the president, has been cutting the budget to the bone. In the process, wages and benefits have dropped below what competitors offer.

Last week Joe learned that a union is trying to organize his workers. While he believes that this would be a mistake for the workers, he is equally certain that the union will win the election. Joe estimates that the organizers will be in a position to call for an election within 30 days. Rather than wait, he has decided to start planning for the labor contract negotiations. He has spoken with the head of the accounting department and the company lawyer. Both of them will join him on the management negotiating team. The heads of production and marketing will round out the group.

When asked why he was in such a hurry to get organized, Joe explained, "I'm just getting prepared for the inevitable. I know that the union is going to win, and if they get their way, they'll bankrupt us in the process. The only way to fight back is to have a strong negotiating team in place and have our strategy worked out ahead of time. In this way, we can save ourselves from getting steamrolled by the union." Joe then proceeded to assign tasks to everyone on the team. The group agreed to meet again in one week to begin hammering out their strategy.

Your Advice

1. What should Joe do?
   ___ a. Have his committee evaluate industry conditions and the company's financial position and work up an initial negotiating position.
   ___ b. Have the committee arrive at a contract offer that can be offered to the union on a "take it or leave it" basis.
   ___ c. Have as many meetings as the union wants, but agree to nothing so that it becomes impossible to hammer out a final labor contract.

2. What types of issues do you think the management team should be prepared to deal with? Identify and describe three.

3. What would you recommend that the management team include on their list of objectives? Identify and describe three items. What will the union want? Identify and describe three items.

4. If the bargaining reaches an impasse, what would you recommend that Joe do? Why?

Career Opportunities in Business

Those whose interests lean toward the human rather than the technical side of management may want to explore career opportunities in human resource management and labor relations. Organizations try to hire, train, and retain the best people, and human resource managers play an important role in this effort. Labor relations specialists deal with unions and various aspects of labor agreements. This section examines the nature of some of the employment opportunities available in these areas.

Human Resource Specialist

Human resource managers (or personnel managers) traditionally were almost solely concerned with interviewing job applicants and helping identify those the company should hire. Today their job has greatly expanded into other areas such as human resource planning, compensation and benefits, and training.

Job Description. The jobs performed by human resource specialists include: (a) recruiting; (b) testing and reference checking; (c) wage and salary administration; (d) the development and administration of pension, benefit, and employee assistance programs; (e) exami-

nation of company policies and practices to ensure compliance with equal employment opportunity laws; and (f) investigation and resolution of grievances arising from alleged violations of employment laws.

Employment Outlook and Earnings. The human resource specialist typically has a college degree and has majored in human resource management. At present approximately 150,000 people work in this field and opportunities should grow at the same rate as the economy in general. Salaries depend on the organization and its geographic location. Those with no experience can expect to earn approximately $20,000 to $25,000. Many human resource directors earn approximately $60,000 and those who are vice presidents of human resources at large corporations can make in excess of $100,000.

Training Specialist

A training specialist provides training and development programs to employees. With training becoming increasingly important in today's organizations, this job promises important career opportunities.

Job Description. A training specialist develops courses, workshops, and other programs tailored to the training and development needs of employees at all levels. Trainers consult with managers and supervisors about specific needs, develop manuals and other materials for use in training and development sessions, and inform employees about training and development opportunities. Trainers may also be responsible for conducting orientation sessions and for coordinating and facilitating on-the-job training for new employees.

Employment Outlook and Earnings. At present there are approximately 60,000 training specialists in industry and government. Most have college degrees in business administration with a specialization in human resource management, organizational behavior, education, or psychology. Starting salaries are in the $20,000 to $25,000 range and experienced trainers earn $40,000 and higher.

Labor Relations Specialist

A labor relations specialist deals with all aspects of labor-management relations. For example, this specialist may help management in negotiations with the union.

Job Description. The labor relations specialist is knowledgeable in labor law and collective bargaining. Those holding this job are often called upon to help management interpret the labor contract, identify employee and union rights and obligations, and make decisions in areas such as changing work assignments, adjusting pay, and terminating employees. During contract negotiations with the union, this person may be called upon to help management on both technical and legal matters. Once a labor contract is signed, the labor relations specialist helps management ensure that the union lives up to both the letter and the spirit of the agreement.

Employment and Earnings. Although union membership as a whole is slowly declining, in many areas unions are still quite strong. There is likely to be moderate growth in demand for labor relations specialists during the years ahead. The starting salaries for those in labor relations with undergraduate degrees are in the $15,000 to $20,000 range. Senior-level labor relations directors at large organizations make $50,000 and up.

The Forgotten Woman

LEXINGTON AVENUE, NEW YORK
ROCKEFELLER CENTER, NEW YORK
MANHASSET, NEW YORK
FORT LEE, NEW JERSEY
BEVERLY HILLS, CALIFORNIA
SPRINGS, CALIFORNIA
CALIFORNIA
ORNIA

WASHINGTON, D.C.
BOCA RATON, FLORIDA
FORT LAUDERDALE, FLORIDA
NORTH PALM BEACH, FLORIDA
FORT MYERS, FLORIDA
CHICAGO, ILLINOIS
DALLAS, TEXAS
HOUSTON, TEXAS
BOSTON, MASSACHUSETTS
TA, GEORGIA
OUISIANA

REMEMBERING THE FORGOTTEN MARKETS

"Find a market niche and exploit it." This guideline is a key to business success, many marketing experts believe. Countless businesspeople can verify that it is good advice.

Take the case of Nancye Radmin, founder and owner of the Forgotten Woman. Although glamour magazines and TV fashion shows use very thin, sleek women to model the latest designs and styles, most women do not look like this. In fact, a study by the National Center for Health Statistics estimates that 27 percent of American women are overweight. This represents a sizable market niche for full-cut, larger sized clothes. Traditionally, clothing designers did

Marketing Functions and Strategies

Chapter Learning Objectives

- Define the overall nature of marketing.

- Describe the basic functions of marketing.

- Discuss the nature and importance of marketing research.

- Present the various types of market segmentation.

- Explain how a marketing manager identifies a target market.

- Identify the four Ps of marketing.

---

not focus on this market because they felt it was unfashionable. In 1977, when Nancye Radmin went out to buy clothes after the birth of her second child, she was unable to find anything stylish in size 14 and above. This is when she hit on the idea of opening a retail store that catered to "the forgotten woman." Today, her Forgotten Woman is a well-established $40 million large-size specialty store chain with plans to add about 40 outlets in the next five years. Although Nancye had no previous business experience, her timing could not have been better. The 1990s are seeing the emergence of tough customers who know what they want and won't settle for anything less.

Business firms are finding that they need to identify a market niche and build that market. For example, to expand her market, Nancye Radmin has entered into upper-end market boutiques that sell very expensive dresses to the larger woman. She uses well-known designers such as Oscar de la Renta and Bob Mackie, and the prices range from $2,000 to $10,000; as compared with the $50 to $3,000 bracket for the labels in the Forgotten Woman stores. The manager of the boutique operations notes that it has been an adventure. "There are some things we avoided — anything terribly fitted, bare arms, backless, and of course in some cases, skirt length. You can go

to Bergdorf Goodman — and I have tremendous respect for Bergdorf Goodman — but they won't even special order a size 18. That woman is hurting."

Today's successful companies offer goods and services that have higher quality and more market appeal because they have been designed with the customer in mind. Nancye Radmin of the Forgotten Woman is a good example of the marketing adage of knowing the importance of finding a market niche and exploiting it.

Photo source: © 1991 Benning Photographic Works.

Introduction

It used to be that businesses rarely had any trouble selling what they produced. Consumers had a pent-up demand for goods and services, and they pretty much bought whatever business could supply. Production ruled supreme. But the production experts did their job almost too well. Business inventories began to build up, and managers began to wonder, "How will we get rid of this stuff?" Enter the marketing function.

This chapter defines the overall nature of the marketing concept and process and then examines the marketing functions. It ends by discussing how marketing managers obtain information and use it to formulate a marketing strategy.

The Nature of Marketing

American business has come to recognize the customer as king. Although Henry Ford himself may not have recognized this, the current chairman of Ford Motor observed, "If we aren't customer-driven, our cars won't be either."[1] Serving the customer is the basis of the marketing function of the modern business firm. More specifically, **marketing** is the process of identifying the goods and services the customer needs and providing them at the right price, place, and time.

Marketing Identifying the goods and services the customer needs and providing them at the right price, place, and time.

The Modern Marketing Concept

Over the past 50 years, the marketing concept in American business has changed significantly. In particular, the emphasis has shifted from production-oriented marketing to consumer-oriented marketing.

Production-Oriented Marketing Fifty years ago, companies typically engaged in **production-oriented marketing.** This approach to the marketing concept is based on the belief that a good product or service will sell itself. This belief certainly has merit and has worked for many companies. For example, when Edwin Land first introduced the Polaroid camera, he was convinced that people would buy it once they saw that it could produce instant pictures. He was right. However, success from production-oriented marketing has turned out to be more the exception than the rule.

Production-oriented marketing A marketing concept based on the belief that a good product or service will sell itself.

The goal of production-oriented marketing has been to "build a better mousetrap." The business must always have the best product, so it will sell itself. Some time ago, a company called Woodstream actually built a better mousetrap. In contrast to the typical, cheap wooden trap, which the user could throw out with the mouse, this one was made of metal and could be cleaned and reused. The trap was more efficient and easy to set. Although it cost more than the wooden version, it was more economical because it could be continually reused. The company shipped thousands of these traps to hardware stores across the country — and there they sat, gathering dust. Why? People were unwilling to take the dead mouse out of the trap. The metal trap may have been a better designed product than its wooden competitor, but there was no demand for it.[2] Thus, the old adage may need to be rephrased: American consumers may not always *buy* the better mousetrap.

Had Woodstream's managers depended on a consumer-oriented marketing concept, they would not have been stuck with thousands of technologically superior but unsalable mousetraps.

Consumer-Oriented Marketing   In contrast to the production-oriented approach **consumer-oriented marketing,** sometimes called total marketing, is based on the belief that a company must find out what the customer needs before providing a good or service. This approach underlies the modern marketing concept and holds that the consumer is the most important part of the business.[3]

McDonald's Corporation is an excellent example of effective consumer-oriented marketing. Every year, McDonald's tries out a host of new products to see which ones customers like. Those that prove popular are added to their menu; those that receive little acceptance are dropped. For example, the company had little success with a pork sandwich, but had considerable success with salad, chicken, decaf coffee, and sausage on a biscuit. The standard McDonald's menu has 25 percent more items than 10 years ago and is most recently going into pizza.[4] Nor is McDonald's alone. Customer surveys rank American Express as one of the most consumer-oriented firms in the financial service business; and Wal-Mart, 3M, and American Airlines are other leaders in their respective industries because they are customer-driven.[5]

The Role of Quality and Price

The quality and price of the products also play a key role in modern marketing. Some companies focus more heavily on one of these than the other, although most consider both product characteristics. For example, every year, the Harris Corporation sells millions of dollars in sophisticated computer equipment to the federal government. The government is more interested in the performance of this equipment than in getting the lowest possible price. For this reason, Harris uses a marketing approach that emphasizes product quality. Other high-tech firms employ the same approach. For example, when selling to business, IBM and Hewlett-Packard both emphasize what their machines can do to help the company operate more efficiently.

In contrast, many firms emphasize price. Although J.C. Penney's is well known for the quality of its merchandise, most people shop there because of its competitive prices. They feel they get more "bang for the buck" at Penney's than at, for example, Lord & Taylor, a store with a reputation for high-quality, expensive merchandise. The same is true for K mart and Wal-Mart, which most often attract customers on the basis of their prices. For example, much of the success of Wal-Mart is attributed to its being known for "everyday low prices."

Business executives often fly first class because they need the extra seating space and comfort for doing their work en route, for relaxing, and for knowing that someone will take care of all their needs (a cup of coffee, a cocktail, an attractive meal, a newspaper, or a magazine). Northwest Airlines has recently added extra attendants to ensure faster in-flight service.[6] Quality ground transportation and lodgings are also important to business executives. Often, senior-level executives have a limousine take them to the hotel, where they have reservations for first-class accommodations.

Consumer-oriented marketing
A marketing concept based on the belief that a company must find out what the customer needs before providing a good or service.

FIGURE 14.1
Marketing Functions

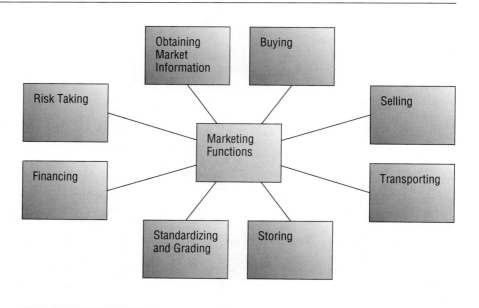

On the other hand, most consumers are neither interested in nor willing to pay the price for first-class service. They would rather fly coach and put up with some inconvenience than pay a higher price. In fact, the airlines have found that many travelers, especially vacationers, will bear the inconvenience of flying at off-peak hours or in the middle of the week for cut-rate fares. When they arrive at the airport, they will often be willing to wait for the hotel minibus or public transportation to take them to the hotel, and they will have reservations for comfortable, clean, but not lavish, accommodations.

CHECK ✓ POINT

1. How is production-oriented marketing different from consumer-oriented marketing?
2. What roles do quality and price play in modern marketing?

Marketing Functions

Marketing involves more than just selling. The marketing process involves eight basic functions: buying, selling, transporting, storing, standardizing and grading, financing, risk taking, and obtaining marketing information. Figure 14.1 illustrates these marketing functions. Some firms use all of them, but most carry out only some.

Buying

Buying Deciding the type and amount of goods to be purchased.

When applied to marketing, the purchasing function is called **buying** and involves deciding the type and amount of goods to be purchased. Managers typically base such decisions on a forecast of consumer demand. In the case of giant retailers such as Macy's in New York, Bullock's in Los Angeles, or

CLOSE-UP / *International*

Tapping the European Market

Europeans drink more beer per capita than do Americans. So in recent years, American brewers have been trying hard to establish a foothold in the European market. The effort has not been easy because many of the marketing strategies that work well in the United States are less useful in Europe. For example, many Europeans are fiercely loyal to their local breweries. They will not buy beer produced by others, regardless of promotion efforts. Big European brewers such as Heineken and Guinness have long been aware of this and to increase their share of the market they have made a concentrated effort to buy out local breweries. The big American brewers such as Anheuser-Busch, Miller, and Coors are now following suit — and none too soon. Recent marketing research indicates that these three firms combined earn less than 5 percent of their revenue from inter-national sales. In contrast, the Netherlands' Heineken earns 85 percent of its sales revenue internationally, and Britain's Guinness earns 65 percent outside the country.

Another marketing strategy being carried out by the American brewers is to go after markets where there has been a weak beer tradition. So instead of focusing exclusively on Germany and the Netherlands, which have strong markets, they are putting marketing muscle into wine drinking countries such as Spain and Italy.

The U.S. brewers are also finding that in some regions of Europe changing tastes are helping create a demand for their products. For example, in England there is now a shift from traditional ales and bitters to the kinds of lagers that American brewers make. Additionally, as the battle of the beers picks up speed, there is going to be more and more money spent on sophisticated marketing. This is an area in which the American brewers know a lot more than their European competitors. As a result, during the years ahead it is likely that American beer makers will find themselves tapping the European market for an increasing percentage of their revenues.

Source: Adapted from Julia Flynn Siler, Patrick Oster, and Mark Maremont, "Wooing Jacques and Fritz Six-Pack," *Business Week*, February 4, 1991, pp. 92–93.

Rich's in Atlanta, buying involves thousands of merchandise orders that vary in quality and quantity. In the case of a small boutique in a college town, the decision is much more limited and is likely to involve purchases that are but a fraction of those made by a giant retailer.

Selling

The selling function is probably most closely associated with marketing and really is its central activity. **Selling** includes identifying buyers, developing a promotional campaign to attract their business, and concluding the sale. An example would be when Coca-Cola sold Burger King on the idea of dropping Pepsi in favor of its own product because of Coke's technical and marketing assistance.[7] And in the luxury car market BMW is trying to bolster sales with an aggressive sales campaign that goes well beyond getting people into the showroom.[8] Notice that the selling process involves much more than simply handing over the merchandise and ringing up the sale. In fact, marketers usually spend more time and effort identifying potential buyers and figuring out how to entice them to seek out the company's goods and services than they do giving a sales pitch and then closing the sale. This is why many firms first focus on selling more or new merchandise to current customers before they direct their sales efforts to new customers.[9] They already have a good idea of how to sell to their present buyers. Then they start looking for new customers. The following International Close-Up (Tapping the European Market) shows how this is being done by the large American brewers.

Selling Identifying buyers, developing a promotion campaign to attract their business, and concluding the sale.

At Boston's Legal Sea Foods live lobsters are packed for overnight shipment to customers around the country via Federal Express. Sophisticated transportation networks like that of Federal Express permit local businesses to grow into national ones.

Source: Jeff Smith.

Transporting Moving goods from where they were manufactured or purchased to where they are needed.

Transporting

For selling to take place, the company must also engage in **transporting,** the process of moving goods from where they were manufactured or purchased to where they are needed. In many instances, the manufacturer performs this function by shipping the goods to wholesalers. The wholesaler, in turn, breaks up the shipment into smaller lots and transports them to retailers. Customers then visit the retail store to purchase the merchandise.

Although the manufacturer-wholesaler-retailer sequence is the most common, it is not the only way to carry out the transportation function. For example, some wholesalers buy in large quantities from the manufacturer and then sell directly to customers, while some manufacturers ship directly to retailers. Increasingly, apparel manufacturers own and operate direct retail outlets. For example, Pendleton has a direct factory outlet for its fine woolen apparel at Bemidji, Minnesota. Some companies, such as L. L. Bean and Domino's Pizza, take orders through the mail or over the phone and then transport goods directly to the customers. However the business does it, transportation is an important marketing function because it gets the goods or services to a location where customers buy them.

Storing Warehousing goods.

Storing

Following transporting comes the process of **storing,** or warehousing, goods. Few firms operate hand to mouth; instead, most firms store goods until they are demanded. Even small retail stores have large back rooms where they keep additional merchandise. If they need more room, they rent space from a public storage company. Large firms typically have their own warehouses, although they also rent or purchase storage space if they run out of room. While companies that sell services rarely can keep an inventory, they might address this need by hiring more workers for busy periods.

Because storing goods is expensive, the trend is to store or warehouse as little as possible. Although Wal-Mart has huge warehouses, the individual stores often take merchandise right from the truck to the shelves. Managers have to weigh the benefits of having the goods on hand against the expense. The procedures are similar to the ones described in Chapter 9 for managing inventories of raw materials.

Standardizing and Grading

When you go to a hardware store to buy 100-watt light bulbs, you don't want to bother with testing each bulb until you find enough 100-watt bulbs. Likewise, if you need a shirt, you don't want to try on every shirt in the store looking for one that fits. Companies meet this need by standardizing. **Standardizing** is establishing specifications or categories for products. For example, when General Electric makes a light bulb, the company makes it to certain specifications, such as 100 watts. Clothing manufacturers make shirts to certain size specifications. The company then labels the product with this information. Standardization is important in helping customers identify the specific characteristics they are looking for — such as size, weight, height, texture, ingredients, or color.

Standardizing Establishing specifications or categories for products.

Closely related to standardizing is **grading,** which involves sorting goods into classes on the basis of quality. For example, eggs and dairy products are graded. Meat, fruit, and farm produce are also sorted by quality. Grading goods make it much easier for the consumer to decide what to buy.

Grading Sorting goods into classes based on quality.

Financing in Marketing

As a marketing function, financing is paying for merchandise to sell and arranging for credit to buyers. Part Six of this text covers all aspects of financing. Applied to marketing, this process has two major parts: financing the purchase of the goods and financing the sale of the goods.

Many marketers pay for their merchandise at the end of the month. When this time rolls around, they issue a check to the seller. If the marketers cannot afford to pay for the goods out of current revenues, they will typically arrange for a short-term loan with the local bank and draw on these funds. When marketers sell goods, they sometimes offer financing terms to buyers. For example, large firms such as General Motors, Ford Motor, General Electric, and Sears all offer their customers financing arrangements.

If consumers buy a General Motors automobile, they can arrange financing for it through General Motors Acceptance Corporation (GMAC). The buyer can pay the bill in monthly installments. In recent years, this has been an important marketing approach for the automobile industry.

Many manufacturers and wholesalers also provide financing arrangements to the businesses that purchase their merchandise. This ranges from giving the buyer 30 days to pay for the goods (in essence, a month of free credit) to allowing the buyer to pay for it over an extended period of time. A good example of the latter occurs when the manufacturer has a great deal of inventory and is willing to ship it to the seller under an arrangement whereby the customer pays for it as it is sold. This agreement permits both sides to come out ahead.

Risk Taking in Marketing

As a marketing function, risk taking is the process of assuming potential liability. When marketers take possession of merchandise, they run the risk that the goods will be destroyed by fire, be stolen, or (perhaps worst of all) have no market demand and not be sold. Some marketers reduce this risk by purchasing insurance against such calamities as fire and theft. (Chapter 22 covers risk management.) Others limit their risk by assuming ownership of no more merchandise than they believe they can sell over the next 30 days. Still others, like brokers, never take possession of goods. They simply try to identify buyers and sellers, and then bring the two groups together. In this case, the risk is that of losing a lot of time trying to put together a deal that eventually falls through. For virtually all businesses, risk taking is an inherent part of the marketing function. In this sense, marketing resembles entre- or intrapreneurship (discussed in Chapter 7).

Obtaining Market Information

Market information helps businesses identify and address consumer needs. Businesses need answers to many types of questions, from how consumers behave to what the most effective advertising is to where to sell the merchandise. Large companies spend millions of dollars each year obtaining market information. AT&T wants to know how well it is providing telephone service and what additional services customers would like. Swanson's wants to know if there are a growing number of vegetarians, so they can develop new frozen dinners. American Express wants to know what new services they can offer their customers. To a large degree, then, marketing effectiveness is based on accurate information. For example, there is recent evidence that an increasing number of people prefer to buy a car from a saleswoman rather than a salesman, hence a number of dealers in recent years have hired women to sell their cars.[10]

CHECK ✓ POINT

1. What are three functions of marketing?
2. How do businesses use financing to make it easier for customers to buy their products?

Understanding Markets

Applying the eight functions of marketing is a complex process. Each company's situation requires a unique approach. To make the marketing functions part of a successful strategy, marketing managers must prepare themselves by developing an understanding of the market to which they must appeal.

A **market** consists of a group of customers who have the money and desire to purchase goods and services. There are two basic types of markets: industrial and consumer. Goods and services that are used to produce still other goods are called **industrial goods or services.** For example, a chain saw in a lumber camp is an industrial good because it is used to produce other goods. However, if a consumer bought a chain saw to cut firewood on his or her acreage, the saw would not be considered an industrial good. In other words, it is the use to which a good is put rather than any intrinsic qualities

Market A group of customers who have the money and desire to purchase goods and services.

Industrial good or service A good or service used to produce still other goods or services.

that classifies it. Temporary secretarial help is another example of an industrial service. The primary purpose of hiring temporary help is to produce some other output. Other common examples are tools, personal services, office equipment, supplies such as chemicals and building materials, and raw materials such as coal and iron.

Goods and services destined to be used by consumers are **consumer goods or services.** The chain saw used by a homeowner to cut firewood is a consumer good. There are many examples; for purposes of clarity, they can be categorized into the following four groups:

1. A *convenience good or service* is one that consumers tend to purchase quickly and with a minimum of effort. Typically low-priced items, convenience goods include newspapers, bread, milk, chewing gum, candy, and toothpaste. A service such as a shoeshine could also be considered in this category. The success of convenience stores such as 7-Eleven and Kwik Shops attests to the market that exists for these goods. The stores have become extremely popular in recent years as consumers have become less patient and society has grown increasingly fast paced.

2. A *shopping good or service* is one that consumers buy only after comparing the various models or approaches. In this process, they consider price, style, quality, service, and so forth. Examples include automobiles, furniture, refrigerators, microwave ovens, and TVs. Services such as photo finishing or hairstyling could also be included.

3. A *specialty good or service* is one that consumers are willing to spend extra effort to locate and buy. Consumers often buy these goods on the basis of brand name and/or quality. A good example is provided by Hill's Pet Products, a subsidiary of Colgate-Palmolive.[11] Hill's has two main product lines: Science Diet for healthy dogs and Prescription Diet for dogs under dietary supervision. Both goods are sold only through veterinarians. Hill's Pet currently holds over 20 percent of the $1 billion market even though its products retail for more than twice that of similar pet foods sold in supermarkets. Simply put, Hill's dog food is a specialty good for which customers are willing to pay.

4. An *unsought good or service* is one that customers do not initially want or are unaware that they can afford or practically use. Examples of the first category often include encyclopedias, life insurance, and cemetery plots. Examples of the second category might be products such as a riding lawn mower or a satellite dish. Travel packages to exotic places would be an example of a service in this category.

1. What are the two basic types of markets?
2. What are some examples of consumer goods?

Consumer good or service
A good or service destined to be used by a consumer.

CHECK ✓ POINT

Consumer Behavior

Whether they are selling industrial or consumer goods and services, marketers need to understand how buyers behave. For example, why do some consumers say they are concerned about price but then buy an expensive brand of shampoo that cleans hair no better than a generic brand? Why do some people go to college upon graduating from high school, while others

FIGURE 14.2
How a Consumer Makes a Purchase Decision

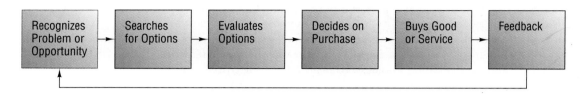

---

begin full-time jobs to buy cars and compact disc players? Possible answers to such questions come from an understanding of the nature of consumer behavior.

Consumer behavior The way consumers go about making their purchase decisions.

The way consumers go about making their purchase decisions is referred to as **consumer behavior.** This complex psychological process typically follows the steps shown in Figure 14.2. First, the prospective buyer or customer recognizes a problem or opportunity. For example, a young mother may conclude that she needs to place her 3-year-old son in a day-care center if she wants to get a good job and contribute income to her family. The buyer searches the available options and evaluates each one of them. The mother might visit the various day-care centers and compare programs, meals, facilities, and costs. Based on the evaluation, the consumer decides whether and what to buy and enters into a transaction. The mother might decide to enroll her child in one of the centers on a trial basis. The experience with this center provides feedback. She might decide this center isn't for her child, or she might decide that she likes it so much she will enroll him and take a full-time job. Thus, the feedback from a transaction influences future decisions.

Buying Motives

The consumer's ultimate decision depends on a variety of motives. Family and friends may encourage certain decisions; for example, parents or friends who value nutrition highly may encourage their children or friends to buy certain types of foods. The consumer's own attitudes and beliefs also influence a buying decision. For example, a consumer who values projecting an image of being wealthy will buy a different car than one who values saving money.

Conscious motives The reasons for buying that people are willing to express.

Consumers are more aware of some of these motives than others. Applied to consumer behavior, **conscious motives** are the reasons for buying that people are willing to express. For example, consumers may consciously decide that they prefer MCI long-distance service over that of AT&T because they feel MCI is less expensive and provides better quality service.

Suppressed motives The reasons for buying that people are unwilling to express.

People are often unwilling to express some of the reasons they have for buying. These reasons are called **suppressed motives.** For example, many consumers buy products that give them prestige, such as an expensive car (a Cadillac, Mercedes, or BMW) or a Rolex watch. They often explain such a purchase in terms of the performance of the automobile, the quality of the watch, or the fact that both are likely to hold their resale value. They do not want to say, "I'm trying to impress people."

People also buy in response to **unconscious motives,** reasons they are unaware of. Many people are influenced by advertising but do not know it. When they go to the supermarket, they may purchase some products without giving their choices a second thought. Sometimes this undetected influence comes from family, friends, or coworkers. For example, a young man whose favorite uncle drives a sports car may also buy one without realizing that he is emulating his uncle. He may explain the purchase in terms of sale price or car performance, but his real reason is that he wants to be like his uncle.

Unconscious motives The reasons for buying that people are unaware of.

Reasons for Understanding Consumer Behavior

To effectively sell goods and services, marketers have to know *why* people buy their products or can be influenced to buy them.[12] However, marketers have come to realize that what people say is not always a reliable indicator of what they will do. For example, a number of years ago, a farm equipment firm researched the behavior of its potential consumers and found out that farmers liked multicolored machinery. However, the company's dealers reported that the farmers resisted buying machinery that had bright, eye-appealing colors. Apparently, the farmers liked the eye-appealing machinery, but were unwilling to admit it.

The company overcame the problem by successfully tying the bright color scheme to product safety and ease of operation. The company painted red any parts of the machine that tended to get hot and were never to be touched without wearing gloves, yellow parts were for operating the machine, and so forth. Once farmers heard this explanation, they consciously accepted what they unconsciously wanted. This example shows how understanding consumer behavior can help marketers develop products and sales messages that will appeal to buyers' real needs and wants.

1. What are three types of motives that buyers may have?
2. Why is understanding consumer behavior important to marketers?

CHECK ✓ POINT

Marketing Research

To move beyond general principles and apply them to specific situations, companies conduct **marketing research.** This is the process of investigating marketing problems and identifying market opportunities.

Marketing research has many applications. It typically addresses questions such as the following:

- Why do customers buy our products? (Or why don't they?)
- How good is our quality vis-à-vis that of our competitors?
- What do people like most (or least) about our advertising campaign?
- Would people buy more of our products if we lowered our price?
- What effect would a price increase have on the demand?
- What do our customers want that we are not currently providing?

One important objective of marketing research is to find out why some consumers are buying the company's products and others are not. A firm

Marketing research Investigating marketing problems and identifying market opportunities.

Marketing research helps Kraft General Foods evaluate how advertising and promotions influence purchases of its products like Maxwell House coffee. By collecting data from stores in 50 U.S. markets, Nielsen Marketing Research provides KGF with data on sales, retail prices, and market shares, as well as promotion information.

often learns as much from those who are not buying as from those who are. For example, new salespeople often learn that when a customer says, "I don't want the product," the correct response is to ask "Why not?" By listening to potential customers explain why the product will not meet their needs, the salesperson can identify important information that the company can use in redesigning or improving the product. Many large makers of office equipment, including NCR, Xerox, and IBM, make extensive use of this approach.

The marketing department gathers information in a variety of ways. These techniques involve using existing internal company data or going outside the firm for secondary and primary sources of data.

Company Data

Internal research Collecting and analyzing information contained in company records.

The marketing research effort typically begins with gathering information currently contained in company records. Collecting and analyzing this information is called **internal research.** Many firms have data from questionnaire cards accompanying their product that instruct the buyer to fill out and mail back the card. Such cards typically ask the buyer's occupation, age, income level, and reason for buying the product. This information helps marketing researchers identify who buys the product and why.

Secondary Research

Researchers also conduct **secondary research,** information gathered from external sources such as newspapers, books, magazines, and government reports. This information often provides a better understanding of the market and the customer. For example, market researchers in the home appliance industry are particularly interested in numbers of new-housing starts. People building or buying new homes are likely to want new appliances; therefore, this is a major source of product demand in the appliance industry. Other information available from secondary research includes economic trends, plans and activities of competitors, new technology that might be applicable to the company's products, and changes in customer needs. A pet store might want to change its offerings if it learns that homeowners are becoming concerned about thefts in their area of town, and a travel agency might want to shift its emphasis in packages if it learns that the local population is aging.

Marketing managers often find it most efficient to begin research with an investigation of information that already exists within the company and in outside publications. This is because the company can save a lot of money by building on existing information rather than duplicating it unnecessarily.

Secondary research Gathering information from sources such as newspapers, books, magazines, and government reports.

Primary Research

Sometimes the marketing department also conducts **primary research,** which is research conducted to gather information for the first time. Interviewers who conduct surveys in person, over the phone, or by mailed questionnaires are doing primary research. Another approach is observing behavior. For example, a new automated system called Shopper Trak uses a hidden optical eye that, when placed in a store, can give an accurate picture of how many shoppers came in, where they went, and why they bought the things they bought.[13]

Primary research is generally not the most important source of information, but many companies spend the money because it is most adaptable to specific information needs. While large companies, especially consumer product firms, often have their own in-house marketing staff do primary research, many firms hire outside marketing research firms to collect information for them. Other market research firms conduct research and then sell the information to interested businesses.

Primary research Obtaining information for the first time through interviews or direct observation.

Uses of Marketing Research

Small firms tend to rely most heavily on internal research and possibly also on secondary research. Large companies use all three techniques. For example, while the Big Three automakers (General Motors, Ford, and Chrysler) all conduct internal and external research on car buying, they also read and study published reports in the area. One such report is the *Power Report on Automotive Marketing*, published annually by J.D. Power & Associates, an independent automotive marketing research firm. The company ranks new car quality and consumer satisfaction and also provides insights into automobile-purchasing trends. Table 14.1 describes some of the major categories of car buyers Power & Associates has identified through their research.

1. What are the three sources of data used in marketing research?
2. How can marketing research be used by marketers?

CHECK ✓ POINT

TABLE 14.1
Categories of Car Buyers

Buyer Category	Percentage of the Market	Description	Type of Car Owned
Autophiles	24%	Know a lot about cars and enjoy working on them	Dodge, Pontiac
Sensible centrists	20	Prize practicality	Volvo, AMC
Comfort-seekers	17	Favor options and luxury	Jaguar, Mercedes, Lincoln
Auto-cynics	14	View cars as appliances	Porsche
Necessity drivers	13	Prefer an alternative way of traveling	AMC
Autophobes	12	Care most about safety	Oldsmobile, Mercury

Source: John Holusha, "A Noted Voice on Car Buying," *New York Times*, January 21, 1986, p. 29.

Market Segmentation

Market segmentation Dividing markets into groups that have similar characteristics.

Marketing research and an understanding of consumer behavior helps marketers conduct **market segmentation,** the process of dividing markets into groups that have similar characteristics. Market segmentation gives marketers a clearer picture of the kinds of buyers that constitute a market and what they are looking for.[14]

Marketers divide up markets in several ways. The most common are demographic, geographic, psychographic, and benefit segmentation. Figure 14.3 gives some examples of these.

Demographic Segmentation

Demographic segmentation Dividing up a market on the basis of socioeconomic characteristics.

Under **demographic segmentation,** the company segments the market on the basis of socioeconomic characteristics. These characteristics, such as age, income, sex, education, and occupation, describe a person's place in society and in the economy. These characteristics are the subject of demographics, the statistical study of populations.

Marketers of toys, for example, are interested in demographic information such as the birthrate, the number of children in each age category, and income level of parents. This helps the marketers determine the size of the market and what parents can afford to buy. They also try to learn what kinds of toys parents and children in the different groups tend to like. By comparing preferences to the demographic information, they are able to segment the toy market. This helps them decide what types of toys are most popular and why.[15] From here, the marketer can develop the appropriate strategy to appeal to its chosen segments.

Marketers select demographic segments according to various criteria. Some marketers attempt to appeal to certain income groups. Others focus on different age groups. For example, Petticord Swimwear sells a line of swimwear specifically for women between the ages of 25 and 45. Levi Strauss markets one line of jeans to adults by advertising how the jeans are made to

FIGURE 14.3
Market Segmentation: Some Examples

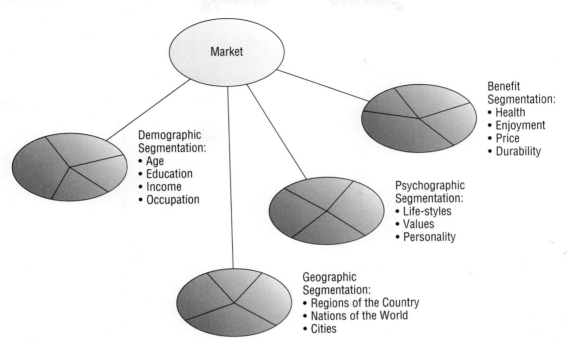

give a little extra room where it is needed. Marketing research has also found that 13- and 14-year-olds may have considerable influence on the purchase decision for high-priced items such as VCRs, TVs, computers, and boats.

Geographic Segmentation

Dividing up a market on the basis of where people live is called **geographic segmentation.** Over the past 20 years, the population of the United States has shifted. Between now and the turn of the century, this shift will continue, with the Sun Belt (Florida, Texas, and Arizona in particular) and western states (for example, Nevada) gaining population and other states, such as Iowa and West Virginia, losing population.

Geographic segmentation often takes into account more than population concentration and state boundaries. In the example in Figure 14.4 the geographic segments are determined by criteria such as ethnic composition and economic status. These data help firms determine what to sell and where to sell it.

Geographic segmentation helps marketers refine their product lines. For example, a clothing manufacturer will sell warmer clothing in the North than in the South. Given the population trend toward the Sun Belt, the company may be well advised to focus on lighter clothing. For auto manufacturers, a car heater is more important to northern customers than to southern customers. On the West Coast, buyers are accustomed to purchasing fully loaded

Geographic segmentation
Dividing up a market on the basis of where people live.

FIGURE 14.4
Market Segments by Geographic Area

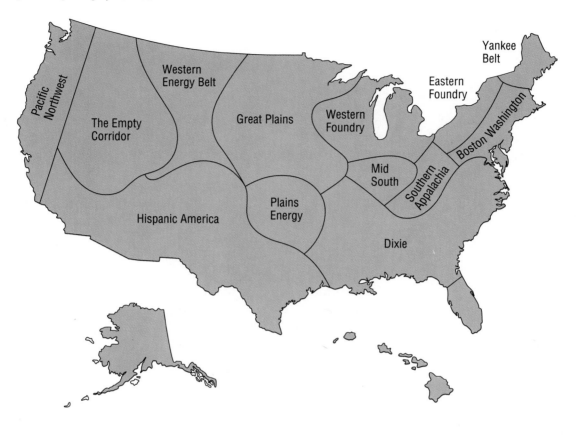

automobiles, because this is how the Japanese automakers tend to ship them in. Consequently, American manufacturers tend to put extra features on the cars they market there.

Psychographic Segmentation

Psychographic segmentation
Dividing up a market on the basis of the customer's lifestyle, values, or personality.

Another way to divide the market is by **psychographic segmentation,** which is segmentation on the basis of the customer's lifestyle, values, or personality. Based on an understanding of consumer behavior, the objective of this type of segmentation is to understand how the buyer's lifestyle influences overall purchasing habits. For example, college-educated people are more likely to buy encyclopedias for their children than are people with less education. Why? Because education is part of their lifestyle. Overall, Yuppies (well-educated, young people) are more likely than most other people to buy goods based on lifestyle than on physical needs.

Marketers find many applications for psychographic data. For example, people with children are more likely to purchase cable TV because it provides more channels for the children's enjoyment. Medical doctors tend to purchase large, expensive cars if only to maintain an image of success and let

TABLE 14.2
Benefit Segmentation

Product or Service	Benefit Promoted	Target Market
Gleem toothpaste	Reduces cavities and keeps your teeth white	Parents and young people
Certs mints	Keeps your breath smelling fresh	Adolescents and young adults
All Bran cereal	Provides the daily fiber needed to keep you healthy	Middle-aged and older people
One-a-Day vitamins	Gives all the vitamins you need for a healthy body	Active young people
The Wall Street Journal	Gives timely business information you need to keep up with trends in your industry	Young executives and those in the investment business
Long-distance phone service	Provides reliable phone service anywhere in the country	Businesses and households

their clients know that they are in good hands. Miller and Budweiser beers attempt to attract the working person with their commercials. McDonald's targets children with its commercials because hamburgers have now become a part of many kids' regular diets. It's part of their lifestyle. Psychographic segmentation is becoming more popular today because it goes further than many other types of segmentation in identifying and appealing to specific consumer tastes.

Benefit Segmentation

Under **benefit segmentation,** the market is divided up on the basis of the benefits that people seek. A company will identify the reasons why certain people would want to buy their product or service — how they would benefit from it — and they try to target this group. For example, for years Jergens hand lotion had been marketed to older people. The company then applied benefit segmentation by pointing out that the product also helped protect the skin of young people. The advertising showed young people using the lotion to soften their skin from the weather and make them more attractive. In short, the hand lotion was beneficial to everyone, not just older people. The result: Jergens' revenues rose as young people began buying the product. Table 14.2 provides other examples of benefit segmentation.

Benefit segmentation Dividing up a market on the basis of the benefits that people seek.

Segmenting Industrial Markets

The types of segmentation described so far apply not only to consumers but also to the buyers of industrial products. For example, when selling oil-drilling equipment, manufacturers use geographic segmentation. They note the areas where drilling is to occur and design their equipment to handle that type of terrain. The equipment needed in a Texas oil field must meet different specifications than that employed in the Gulf of Mexico or in Saudi Arabia.

FIGURE 14.5
Formulating Marketing Strategy

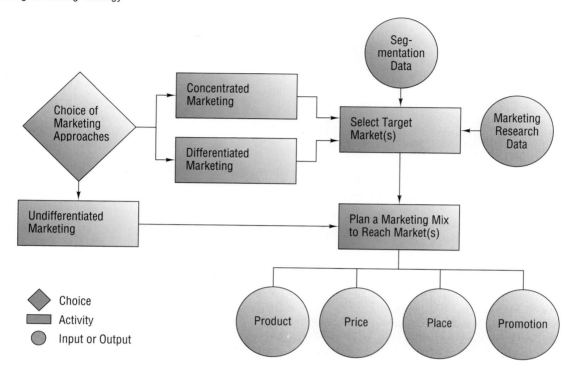

Virtually all industrial marketers use benefit segmentation. They continually ask themselves, "How can our product meet the customer's need?" A good example is provided in the case of a major Miami boat builder. This builder's craft were well known for their sleekness and speed, so drug dealers were buying his boats and outrunning the Coast Guard's slower boats. Then the builder started designing and building even faster craft for the government so that its people could catch up with the drug runners. This is marketing in action!

CHECK ✓ POINT

1. What are three kinds of market segmentation?
2. How can segmentation be used in industrial markets?

Formulating a Marketing Strategy

Based on the information gathered through marketing research and market segmentation, as well as general knowledge of consumer behavior, the marketing manager formulates a marketing strategy. The variables and steps involved are shown in Figure 14.5. First, the manager determines whether the company should sell to the entire market or target certain groups. Then the manager decides which segments of the market the company can serve most effectively. Based on this information, the manager puts together a marketing mix, which brings together strategies for product, price, place, and promotion. A discussion of the steps in this process follows.

Basic Approaches

As shown in Figure 14.5, before the marketing manager can devise a strategy, he or she must select one of three basic marketing approaches:

1. **Concentrated marketing** occurs when a firm focuses on a single market segment. The Limited clothing stores are a good example. The company directs its marketing effort toward teenage girls and young women who want trend-setting clothes.
2. **Differentiated marketing** involves selling a range of related products to specific market segments. For example, Coca-Cola offers Classic Coke, Diet Coke, and other brands. Many people drink one of these products but not the others. A differentiated marketing approach allows a firm to appeal to many parts of the overall market.
3. **Undifferentiated marketing** involves selling a single product to all customers. Dry cleaning is a good example. This service is appealing to consumers regardless of age, income, sex, or geographic locale. Most dry-cleaning establishments offer the same basic service to all customers.

Concentrated marketing
Focusing marketing efforts on a single market segment.

Differentiated marketing
Selling a range of related products to specific market segments.

Undifferentiated marketing
Selling a single product to all customers.

Target Markets

If the manager decides to use concentrated or differentiated marketing, the next step is to identify target markets. A **target market** is a group of customers who are likely to buy a company's goods or services. For example, a target market for health clubs is young professionals in the 25 to 45 age bracket; a target market for home-cleaning services is families with two working spouses.

Determining a target is more complex than simply identifying the business the company is in. Each business has certain strengths and advantages. A business that produces a high-quality, state-of-the-art product tries to determine which market segments value such a product. A business that manufactures products in large quantities and at a low price targets segments that value low price. A tax preparation company with many outlets may try to identify customers who value convenience. A competitor with a famous, respected name may try to identify customers who want the reassurance of dealing with a familiar and trusted business. In every case, the business determines its target markets by analyzing its particular areas of strength. The manager uses the available research and information on market segments to select the appropriate markets to target. Those markets selected should be ones the company can serve profitably.[16]

Target market A group of customers who are likely to buy a company's goods and services.

The Marketing Mix

When the marketing department has a clear picture of whom it is selling to — its target market — it is ready to complete its strategy by planning a marketing mix that will effectively reach the target market. The **marketing mix** is the combination of a firm's strategies for product, price, place, and promotion. Figure 14.6 depicts these four elements, often referred to as the four Ps.

Marketing mix The combination of a firm's strategies for product, price, place, and promotion.

FIGURE 14.6
The Four Ps

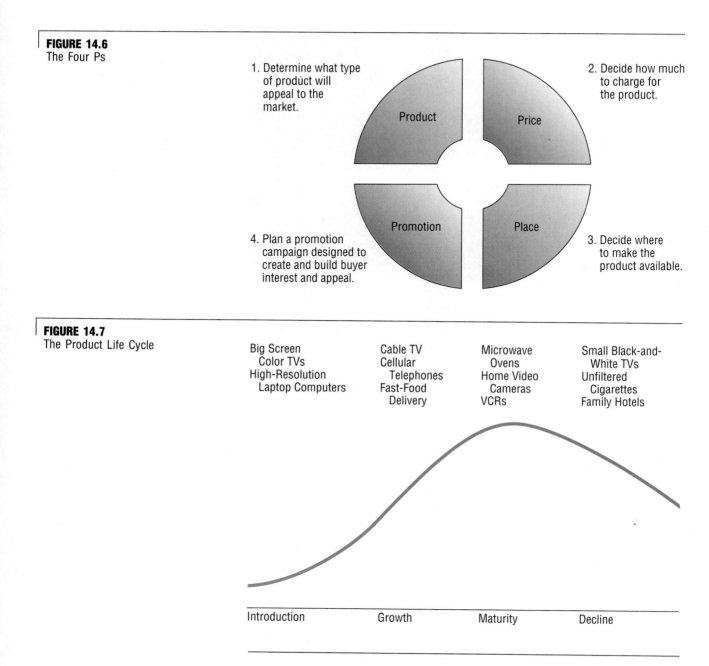

1. Determine what type of product will appeal to the market.

2. Decide how much to charge for the product.

Product

Price

Promotion

Place

4. Plan a promotion campaign designed to create and build buyer interest and appeal.

3. Decide where to make the product available.

FIGURE 14.7
The Product Life Cycle

| Big Screen Color TVs High-Resolution Laptop Computers | Cable TV Cellular Telephones Fast-Food Delivery | Microwave Ovens Home Video Cameras VCRs | Small Black-and-White TVs Unfiltered Cigarettes Family Hotels |

| Introduction | Growth | Maturity | Decline |

Product Any good or service that the firm offers to the customer.

Product In determining the optimal marketing mix, the marketing manager starts with the **product,** the good or service that the firm offers to the customer. The company may sell an existing product, modify it, or develop a new product. One example is Motorola's new line of powerful multi-user business computers.[17] Another example is Burger King's BK Broiler chicken sandwich. This successful entry into the fast food market took advantage of the health-food craze.[18] Interestingly, research shows that for every 100 new

Employees of Primerica Corporation, a financial services company, examine direct mail materials used to generate new loan customers. The mailings are sent to selected people — with good payment records and likely to need loans — who live in zip code areas surrounding Primerica branch offices. The mailing lists are made up using demographic data from both in-house and external sources.

Source: © Jose L. PeLaez/The Stock Market

product ideas, only two ever become products, and only one succeeds. Coca-Cola learned this the hard way with its failure of New Coke in the mid-1980s.[19] Yet it is important for business firms to continue developing new goods and services because most become obsolete in less than 10 years. Many of the electronic products on the local retailer's shelf were not there a decade ago. Those that are may be obsolete before the end of this century.

This reflects the fact that products go through a life cycle. A typical cycle begins with the introduction of the product, followed by growth, maturity, and decline. The home video rental business, for example, which was in the growth stage in the mid-1980s, is now entering the maturity stage and decline is likely to follow.[20] In some cases, companies have been able to stave off this eventuality by taking a product that is in the mature stage of its life cycle and finding new uses for it. For example, DuPont initially made nylon for parachutes. When the company found additional uses for nylon, such as in stockings, the product returned to the growth stage and continued to generate revenues and profits for the big chemical company. Figure 14.7 provides some examples of products at different stages of their life cycles.

Price The second component of the marketing mix is **price,** which is the cost of the product or service to the purchaser. In the case of manufacturers, price is the charge to the wholesaler or retailer. In the case of a retail store, it is the charge to the final customer.

Price strategy typically depends on industry and company practices. At the industry level, for example, businesses often give discounts to customers

Price The cost of the product or service to the purchaser.

C L O S E - U P / *Ethics*

Missing the Boat

For a long time many retailers have not focused a great deal of attention on minority shoppers. However, that is now beginning to change. One reason is because African-Americans, Hispanics, and Asians have total purchasing power of $400 billion and many retailers are beginning to realize that they have been overlooking a huge market. Moreover, African-Americans and Hispanics who visit shopping centers and malls make more visits each year than do Anglos and they spend more. The average African-American shopper spends $2,000 annually and the average Hispanic shopper spends $2,200 at shopping centers. Both totals are higher than the average $1,900 spent by Anglo shoppers. And while Asians spend only $1,600 per year at shopping centers, they have more money to spend than any other ethnic group.

These statistics may not seem very significant until we realize that over 80 percent of all sales at shopping centers are made to Anglo customers. Relatively few minorities spend their money at these locations, and retailers are now looking for ways to attract them.

Woolworth, which has long been interested in selling to minorities, has 45 percent of its stores located in minority neighborhoods. Sears and Nordstrom also have a large number of units in the inner city, where many minorities live. Many other retailers are now scurrying to get on the bandwagon. A $100 million Concourse Plaza Shopping Center opened in New York's South Bronx, smaller shopping malls are springing up in the Watts section of Los Angeles, and the first phase of Chicago's Grand Boulevard Plaza is in operation.

Does this mean that more and more minorities will be shopping in malls? Based on current developments, the answer seems yes. But this is not good news to everyone. The president of Woolworth pointed out that most shopping malls are fighting it out in the suburbs, while those in the inner city, in many cases, are doing a tremendous business. He noted with some glee that these retail chains were ignoring opportunities and expressed the hope that "they keep missing the boat."

Source: Greg Krikorian, "The Minority Community's Shopping-Mall Hard Sell," *New York Times*, May 20, 1990, Sec. F, 5.

---

who pay their bills within 10 days of receipt. However, in some industries, such as auto supplies, it is equally common to find firms taking the discount even when they pay 30 days later. The practice is so widespread that auto supply companies have learned to accept the discounted payment.

At the individual consumer level, many stores, such as supermarkets, refuse to discount. Their advertised or posted price is their final price. The same is true among some types of specialized distributors.[21] However, among many small businesses and stores such as those selling jewelry, furniture, or autos, there is almost always room for price negotiation.[22] Additionally, regardless of its initial pricing strategy, just about every firm makes a point of meeting the advertised prices of their competitors.

Place The location where a good or service is available for purchase.

Place The third ingredient in the marketing mix is **place,** which is the location to which customers go to buy a particular good or service. Most consumers know where to find goods that have been on the market for some time. For example, they get their hamburgers at a fast-food franchise, their medicine at a drugstore, and the latest best-selling novel at a bookstore. In recent years, however, place strategy has gained in importance because businesses have been changing their approach to providing goods and services and making them more convenient for shoppers. One of the primary areas of emphasis, as seen in the accompanying Ethics Close-Up (Missing The Boat), is minority neighborhoods that have long been ignored by retail stores.

A decade ago, a person with a toothache went to a local dentist's office. Today, large dentist offices, such as Dental Land, are located in shopping malls all around the country. The facilities are larger, a number of dentists are on hand to provide both general and specialized services, and the price is often less than that charged by the traditional dentist. These new locations, often referred to as McDentists, are having a major impact on the field. So are small medical offices set up to provide such services as general physical examinations and minor surgical procedures. These offices are competing vigorously with hospitals for the high-profit, easy-to-handle outpatient business. Popularly known as "Doc in the Box," they usually locate in suburban areas and eliminate the need for people to drive a distance to the hospital.

Place is also an important strategy for businesses trying to break into a market or gain market share. For example, Coca-Cola and Pepsi have long dominated the supermarket soft-drink shelf. Because space is limited other soft drink brands such as Shasta and Diet-Rite have had a difficult time getting on the shelf, a major problem that has stifled their opportunity for growth.

However, a change in place strategy can backfire. If people are unaccustomed to going to a particular locale to buy a product, it may be impossible to lure them to it. For example, when IBM entered the personal computer market and saw how popular its IBM PC was, it decided to open IBM Service Centers through which it could sell them. However, the firm was unable to dislodge the computer stores that were already selling the product. Most people were accustomed to going to stores like ComputerLand and Computer World to look for a personal computer. IBM also lacked the sales staff to deal directly with the noncommercial consumer. As a result, its place strategy proved to be ineffective, and IBM sold the service centers to NYNEX.

Promotion   The final component of the marketing mix is **promotion,** the process of stimulating demand for a company's goods and services. Advertising and personal selling are the most common techniques used by companies. Other promotional techniques include packaging, branding, point-of-purchase displays, coupons, and premiums. Chapter 17 provides an in-depth examination of promotional techniques and strategies.

A company develops a promotional strategy for one of two reasons: to maintain or to increase its share of the market. IBM entered the personal computer market and then spent a considerable amount on advertising its PCs because it wanted to maintain its share of the total computer market. Although the market for computers had been growing annually, IBM's share had been slowly declining. Once it saw Apple take off in the personal computer market, IBM knew it had to enter this market and effectively promote its product or lose more overall share. And as PC sales have taken off, manufacturers have sought to target their promotion to specific markets such as professional women, who have long been ignored as potential PC users.[23]

In other cases, firms want to increase their market share. For example, Kraft General Foods has been increasing its advertising of Maxwell House coffee in order to regain market share lost when it stopped advertising the brand a few years ago. Promotion has also been important in the beer business. Thanks to promotion, in recent years Budweiser, Miller, Coors, and Pabst have been increasing their market shares, while Stroh's and other

In 1985 Kraft's *Cheez Whiz* pasteurized processed cheese spread was in the decline phase of the product life cycle. Sales were flat to declining previously. In 1986 Kraft repositioned *Cheez Whiz* as a microwaveable cheese sauce with an advertising and promotional campaign that boosted sales 40 percent over two years.

Source: KRAFT and CHEEZ WHIZ are registered trademarks of Kraft General Foods, Inc. Reproduced with permission.

Promotion   The process of stimulating demand for a company's goods and services.

domestic brewers have been losing share. Imports have also declined in the face of this competition.[24] So promotion is very important in the beer industry.

The Marketing Mix in Action   The marketing mix will vary depending on the product's life cycle. For example, when a product is first introduced, the company often sets a high price. The firm will want to recover quickly some of the costs of getting the product launched. Later, as other firms enter the market, it will lower the price to meet the competition. Price strategy will change as the good moves along its life cycle.

The same is true for place strategy. Initially, the company may offer the product only in certain locales. However, as the item enters its growth and maturity stages, the firm will offer it in any store where it can generate sales. When the product reaches the decline phase, distribution will again be selective as the company phases out unprofitable outlets.

Promotional strategy follows a similar pattern. Initial advertising, for example, will be aimed at early adopters, those who first buy a product. However, as the product enters the growth phase, the ads will be focused on making the mass market aware of the item's benefits. By the time the product enters the decline phase, the firm will have switched to an ad strategy that emphasizes low price.

CHECK ✓ POINT

1.   What are the four Ps?
2.   How do marketing managers formulate a marketing strategy?

Closing Comments

Successful managers know that marketing involves more than just selling and more than just intuition regarding what will sell. Managers also must conduct marketing research and, where possible, segment the market. Based on knowledge of the target market, the manager formulates the marketing mix — the combination of strategies for product, price, place, and promotion. The remaining chapters in this part examine these four Ps in more depth.

VIDEO CASE / *The Customer Is King*

Nancye Radmin has been very successful with her Forgotten Woman stores and her high-fashion boutiques. How did Nancye do it? By identifying what the customer wanted, in this case clothing for large women, and then going out and catering to this market. For many women who carry more than the ideal weight, the Forgotten Woman and the high-fashion boutiques meet a critical need. Now the heavier woman can look as stylish as many of the models they see in the glamour magazines and TV fashion shows.

Nancye Radmin had an advantage over owners or managers of many larger firms because she was her own best customer. Even though she gained considerable weight after giving birth to her children, she knew the types of clothes she still wanted to buy, and she also knew that there were many women who fit into this same category. One way in which companies try to identify markets is by getting feedback from their customers regarding what they like and perhaps, equally important, what they dislike about the goods and

services being offered. For example, Cadillac has an 800 number that customers can call for 24-hour roadside service. The firm has also used information received from this toll-free line in its decision to eliminate deductibles on warranties and to make other changes that keep customers coming back. They are not alone. Colgate-Palmolive uses its 800 toll-free line to listen to complaints from customers and then ask if they would evaluate new product offerings. This valuable feedback information is used to help the company improve its current offerings and design and market new ones.

Food manufacturers are also finding that markets now and in the future will be won by those who are best able to adjust to consumer demands. For example, an increasing number of consumers want to hold down the cholesterol, fat, and calories in their foods. During the past 10 years the consumption of eggs, bacon, and sausage fell by about a third and beef consumption dropped by over a fourth. On the other hand, turkey consumption rose 43 percent and fresh fruit went up 18 percent. This trend toward lean cuisine did not go unnoticed by firms such as Entenmann's, a division of General Foods.

The company introduced 30-odd varieties of cookies, pastries, and cakes that are low in sodium and free of artificial sweeteners. Sales for their fat-free line during the first 9 months were in excess of $160 million. In contrast, companies that stayed with their rich desserts and high calorie foods consistently lost market share. These developments indicate that the old cliché, "the customer is king," is going to become more true during the current decade than at any time during the past. Firms such as Nancye Radmin's the Forgotten Woman that recognize this and develop their products and services to meet their customers' needs are going to be successful.

Source: Faye Rice, "How to Deal with Tougher Customers," *Fortune*, December 3, 1990, 39–48.

Case Questions

1. When women buy clothes at the Forgotten Woman, what type of buying motives are they fulfilling?
2. In what way do 800 telephone numbers help companies with their marketing research efforts?
3. In what way are firms such as the Forgotten Woman, Cadillac, and Entenmann's using psychographic segmentation to help them with their marketing strategies?

Learning Objectives Revisited

1. **Define the overall nature of marketing.** Marketing is the process of identifying what goods and services the customer needs and providing them at the right price, place, and time. A production-oriented approach to marketing assumes that, if a firm provides a good product or service, it will basically sell itself. A consumer-oriented approach assumes that a company must find out what the consumer needs before deciding what to provide. Marketing can emphasize two dimensions of a product, quality and price. Most firms emphasize a combination of the two, although they tend to favor one.

2. **Describe the basic functions of marketing.** The major functions of marketing are buying, or deciding the type and amount of goods to be purchased; selling, or identifying buyers, developing a promotional campaign, and closing the sale; transporting, or moving the goods to where they are needed; storing, or warehousing the goods; standardizing and grading, or establishing specifications or categories for the goods and sorting them into classes based on quality; financing, or paying for the merchandise and arranging for credit; risk taking, or assuming potential liability; and obtaining market information, or gathering information on the customer's needs.

3. **Discuss the nature and importance of marketing research.** Marketing research lies at the very heart of formulating marketing strategy. It involves gathering information to help managers investigate marketing problems and identify market opportunities. This research can draw on internal, secondary, and primary sources. Most large firms rely on all three sources; many small firms use just the first two.

4. **Present the various types of market segmentation.** Market segmentation is the process of dividing markets into groups that have similar characteristics. Some of the most common forms of segmentation include: demographic segmentation, which divides the market on the basis of socioeconomic characteristics; geographic segmentation, which divides the market on the basis of where people live; psychographic segmentation, which divides the market on the basis of the customer's lifestyle; and benefit segmentation, which divides the market on the basis of the benefits people seek from products or services.

5. **Explain how a marketing manager identifies a target market.** When the manager has decided to engage in concentrated (a single market segment) or differentiated (range of related products to specific market segments) marketing rather than undifferentiated (single product to all consumers) marketing, the first step is to review information gathered from marketing research and segmentation. Based on this information and an assessment of the company's strengths, the manager selects a target market the company can profitably satisfy.

6. **Identify the four Ps of marketing.** The four Ps of marketing are product, the good or service that the firm offers to the customer; price, the cost of the product or service to the customer; place, the location where the product or service is available for purchase; and promotion, the process of stimulating demand for the good or service. The company uses all four Ps in developing an overall marketing strategy.

Key Terms Reviewed

Review each of the following terms. For any that you do not know or are unsure of, look up the definitions and see how they were used in the chapter.

marketing
production-oriented marketing
consumer-oriented marketing
buying
selling
transporting
storing
standardizing
grading
market
industrial good or service
consumer good or service

consumer behavior
conscious motives
suppressed motives
unconscious motives
marketing research
internal research
secondary research
primary research
market segmentation
demographic segmentation
geographic segmentation

psychographic segmentation
benefit segmentation
concentrated marketing
differentiated marketing
undifferentiated marketing
target market
marketing mix
product
price
place
promotion

Review Questions

1. How does production-oriented marketing differ from consumer-oriented marketing? What approach is used by your college or university? Is a company guaranteed to succeed if it has the best version of a product? Explain.

2. Sea Sweets Inc. makes salt-water taffy. The company mails out bright-colored catalogs showing the various flavors of taffy and the attractive gift packages they come in. Buyers can mail in an order or call a toll-free number, and Sea Sweets will ship out the order via UPS or, for an extra charge, Express Mail. The company accepts MasterCard and Visa. Based on this description, what marketing functions does Sea Sweets engage in?

3. Rivera Funeral Home sells cemetery plots. What marketing functions would be especially important to this business? Why?

4. How do consumers make buying decisions? If Ron Hall receives information stating the advantages of resort condominiums, but doesn't think owning resort property is an opportunity or the solution to a problem, how will this information affect his decision of whether to buy?

5. Phil Victor is a marketing consultant. One of his clients, Lucy Green, called him in to investigate the market potential of the new line of diet doughnut shops she was thinking of opening. "I'm eager to get started," said Lucy. "Let's get going on a survey." What type of marketing research do surveys fall under? If you were Phil, what would you do next?

6. What are some ways in which a marketer such as General Motors would divide the market into segments?

7. How do marketing managers formulate a marketing strategy? Use Burger King's BK Broiler as an example.

8. What might be an appropriate target market for each of the following businesses? Explain your choice.
   a. A chain of law offices that specializes in handling routine documents and legal matters
   b. A passenger railroad company
   c. A maker of high-fashion but inexpensive sportswear

9. What are the elements of the marketing mix? Describe each in terms of the following products:
   a. televisions
   b. cars
   c. airline travel

10. How do marketing managers adapt the marketing mix to the product's stage in the product life cycle?

Applied Exercise

Identify the specific type of segmentation that is being used in the introduction of each of these products by employing the following designation:

B = Benefit segmentation
G = Geographic segmentation
P = Psychographic segmentation

___ 1. No-calorie food for overweight people.
___ 2. A high performance sports car.
___ 3. Snow shoes for Arctic wear.
___ 4. A cable television channel carrying only Shakespearian plays and classical opera.
___ 5. Car heaters designed to warm an auto in less than 3 minutes.
___ 6. Specially designed shoes for marathon runners.

YOU BE THE ADVISER / *Branching Out*

Phil Krantz was a computer programmer for 7 years before he broke away last year to start his own business. Phil has been writing software for three large insurance companies that want special programs designed to meet their needs. They have been pleased with Phil's efforts, and it looks as if he will be able to keep them as customers for at least another 2 years. However, Phil would also like to branch out and start writing software for other customers.

Recently, Phil has been toying with the idea of writing educational software. In particular, he believes that there could be a massive market for software teaching mathematics and science. Over the past 3 months he has developed a science package designed to help students tutor themselves in high school physics. The program contains a number of different subject areas. Phil was able to identify these areas by reviewing the ten leading high school physics books in the country. For each subject area, he wrote a module that presents information and then tests the student on it. If the student enters a wrong answer, the program gives him or her a chance to try again or to simply ask for the right answer and the explanation. In either case, the program explains the correct answer before moving on. At the end of the module, the program gives the student a score based on the number of right answers the student gave on the first try.

Phil has shown the program to a number of teachers in the local high school system, as well as to the head of the board of education. Everyone appears interested in the project, and Phil believes it will be worth his time to pursue the marketing and sale of this product.

Your Advice
1. What should Phil do?
   ___ a. Continue developing the current program, refine it, and use it as a basis for other programs.
   ___ b. Now break into nonscience areas such as history, English, and foreign languages.
   ___ c. Quickly expand into other science subjects such as chemistry and biology.
2. Is Phil production oriented or consumer oriented? Based on your answer, what advice would you give to him regarding how to proceed?
3. What types of market information does Phil still need to gather? What would you recommend? Explain your answer.
4. How can market segmentation help Phil develop a strategy? What approach would you suggest? Why?

CREATIVE CHOCOLATES

Hoffman's Chocolate Shoppe and Gardens, headquartered in Greenacres City, Florida, is not a large company. After several years in the business, Paul and Theresa Hoffman opened the Greenacres facility in late 1989, and in its first full year the south Florida attraction had $2 million in sales. Hoffman has managed to make a very successful living thanks to his product planning. Not only does Paul design his own candies, but he grows many of the ingredients in the lush, tropical garden containing the plants and trees that surround the shop. In this way,

Product Planning and Pricing

15

Chapter Learning Objectives

- Describe the steps involved in development of new products.

- Explain how businesses use product analysis.

- Discuss the use of brands and trademarks.

- Describe the value of packaging and labeling.

- Present the dimensions of product-pricing strategies.

- Identify product-pricing techniques.

---

nearby area so that he can control the input of materials that are being used in the process.

Paul continually creates new recipes for different types of chocolate candies, and he has added a chocolate-covered ice cream offering. Why does Hoffman Chocolates do so well? One reason is the high quality of the ingredients. Only creamy, fresh chocolate is used and the production process is continually monitored to ensure that the ingredients are first rate. A second reason accounting for Paul's success is his ability to develop new products to supplement the old standbys that sell

year in and year out — chocolate and pecan candies. A third is Paul's experience in the food business. He has been working in kitchens since he was 12 years old so he knows how to cook, and he has the creativity needed to mix up batches of new chocolate offerings to see how well they are accepted by the customers. Finally, Paul insists that his products be made in full view of the customers so they can see the candy being created. Paul notes that, "We're going to continue to do it this way because people love to see things done the old-fashioned way." Viewing the process has become a tourist attraction and

gives buyers a feeling of confidence in and firsthand knowledge about the product, thus contributing to demand.

When Paul started out, his goal was to make enough money in the business to survive. Today, he has a flourishing enterprise consisting of not only the production facility and retail outlet at Greenacres, but also several other company-owned stores and a franchise program. Hoffman has been able to deliver quality products and create new ones that keep the customers coming back for more.

Photo source: Courtesy of Hoffman's Chocolate Shoppe and Gardens.

Introduction

From the neighborhood grocer to the big automakers, businesses depend for their survival on having appealing goods and services to sell. To survive and grow, companies must plan what to sell and at what price. This effort is part of the marketing function, described in Chapter 14. Chapter 15 takes a closer look at the product and pricing aspects of marketing. It begins by examining the various product strategies, including branding and packaging, employed in today's successful marketing efforts. The chapter ends with a discussion of pricing strategies and techniques.

New-Product Development

In the 1960s, people played music on "record players"; a decade later, music lovers found their new stereos to be a big improvement. Today, most music fans think that CDs (compact discs) and digital audio tapes have made records obsolete.[1] Whereas young people of previous generations talked about their 45s, today most young people do not even know that 45s are small records that play at a speed of 45 rpm.

Customer wants, needs, and expectations are continually changing, so marketers must keep up. The typical life cycle is only 5 to 10 years. Unless a company develops new products, it may find its total sales declining. Large and small companies avoid this problem by making new product development an important part of their marketing effort. New products help companies achieve sales growth, meet competition, and round out the product line.

The Development Process

Companies can add new products in two ways. The easiest way is to acquire them from another firm and simply add them to the existing product line. A company's product line is the group or line of products that it offers. In recent years, many companies have done this through acquisitions or mergers. For example, when R. J. Reynolds merged with Nabisco, it acquired Oreo cookies, Ritz crackers, and many other products.

The other way to add new products is to develop them from the ground up, which is how greeting card companies such as Hallmark[2] and clothes designers such as Nicole Miller do it.[3] The process of developing new products typically involves six steps, shown in Figure 15.1. Management reviews the idea at each step of the process and may terminate the project at any time.

Idea Generation   New-product development begins with the formulation of an idea that can be translated into a new product. Marketers primarily formulate ideas in two ways. The most popular is to gather suggestions from customers, salespeople, and in-house personnel who have knowledge of the market. The marketer supplements this information by reviewing what the competition is doing.

The other approach is to develop the entire idea in-house. This commonly takes place in firms that are committed to research and development. These companies are usually part of industries in which new technology is an

FIGURE 15.1
The Process of New-Product
Development

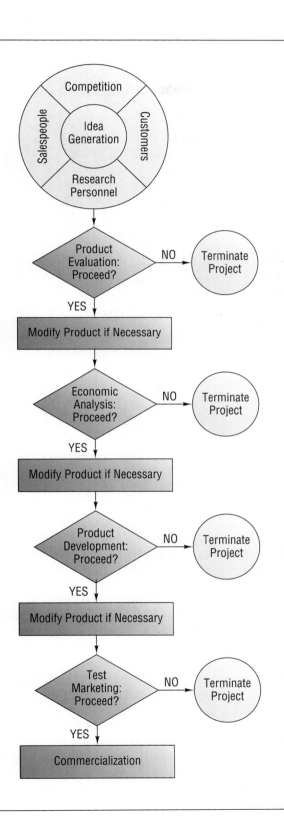

At Nike, the sport research lab investigates sport and fitness problems and evaluates ideas generated by the product engineering department. Their work on a new cushioning system led to the innovative Air 180.

Source: Courtesy of NIKE, Inc. Photographer, Philip Newton.

important advantage. For example, the success of the so-called "smart weapons" in the Persian Gulf war stimulated further research and development on sophisticated weapons systems by military contractors such as LTV, Lockheed, General Dynamics, and Martin Marietta.[4] The accompanying Innovation Close-Up (Information at Your Fingertips) describes some new products that are likely to gain market share during the years ahead.

Product Evaluation   The purpose of the next stage, product evaluation, is to determine whether the product fits with the company's long-term objectives. Will the proposed product be compatible with the current product line? Can the firm promote it using existing promotion efforts? Can the company produce it with its existing production facilities? Can the company distribute it through existing channels? Sometimes a firm will find that a proposed product is likely to be successful but does not fit with the company's image or the firm's ability to manufacture and market it.

Economic Analysis   The next stage is economic analysis. At this stage, the manager evaluates the overall profitability of the product. How much demand will there be for it? How much will it cost to produce? What is the likely selling price? The answers to such questions will help the manager evaluate how profitable the product is likely to be and decide whether to proceed. General Electric, for example, is evaluating the ways in which it can apply its technological expertise in the area of plastics by developing high strength plastic-based products.[5]

CLOSE-UP / *Innovation*

Providing a Trillion Instructions per Second to the Market

The computer industry is becoming increasingly competitive. As a result, companies such as IBM are working harder than ever to develop new ideas and bring them to fruition. One of the areas in which IBM is focusing considerable attention on is supercomputing. IBM is quietly becoming a major player in this end of the market. The company has assembled the broadest array of technical computing gear in the industry, ranging from speedy workstations to $20 million souped-up mainframes that compete favorably with all but the fastest Cray Computers, still the market leader in supercomputers.

IBM is interested in building ultrapowerful machines because research indicates this is going to be a growing market niche. In particular, the line between commercial and scientific computing is beginning to blur. Whereas these two groups used to have different needs, both are now finding themselves interested in computers that can process millions of bits of information in a matter of seconds.

IBM has had a great deal of experience building large computers and believes it can develop the necessary technology to become the premier firm in the supercomputer field. This will mean developing massive parallel processing (MPP), which calls for linking together dozens and dozens of inexpensive, powerful microprocessors to attack large computing problems en masse. For example, the Argonne National Laboratory, a government research lab, has tapped IBM to supply a giant MPP system as the heart of a proposed supercomputing research center. Current plans call for IBM to install its first MPP system at Argonne by 1994 and then follow on with a production-level machine that will be able to perform 400 billion instructions per second, while connected to an array of disk drives storing 6 trillion characters of information. A year later IBM will be expected to provide a machine that can perform an unbelievable 1 trillion instructions per second.

Even for IBMers, this is pretty heady stuff. IBM currently holds the lead in MPP and has sufficient resources to fund a variety of different efforts for maintaining and increasing their lead. Now it is a matter of taking the ideas that are being generated by the engineers and turning them into products that will increase computer performance, while simultaneously driving down the cost of doing this. If IBM can meet the challenge, it will be able to translate its market leadership into bottomline profits.

Source: Adapted from John W. Verity and Julie Flynn, "Call It Superbig Blue," *Business Week,* June 29, 1992, pp. 74–75.

Product Development   The fourth stage, product development, involves building a model, mock-up, or prototype. Many manufacturers have production design engineers to do this. Figure 15.2 shows the mock-up of Gillette's new razor that was developed by a team of 40 engineers and scientists at an estimated cost of $300 million.[6] In a small concern, this process might be much simpler. For example, a restaurant's chef might try out a new type of soup or an exotic dessert. The value of a prototype is that it helps everyone understand what the product will be like. The accompanying Innovation Close-Up (Providing a Trillion Instructions per Second to the Market) describes some new products that IBM is currently developing.

Test Marketing   Test marketing involves taking the product into the marketplace to see how selected customers respond to it. A national company often chooses one or two cities in which to sell the product. Based on consumer response, the company decides whether to go forward with the product in its current form, make changes in it, or drop the idea. Coke II is a good example of a product that is developing from test marketing.[7] Another is Procter & Gamble's Downy liquid fabric softener that has been test marketed in a concentrated form.[8] So are the new products continually being tested by fast-food franchises, which are always looking to replace slow-moving items with new product offerings.[9]

FIGURE 15.2
A Mock-Up, or Prototype, of
Gillette's Sensor Razor

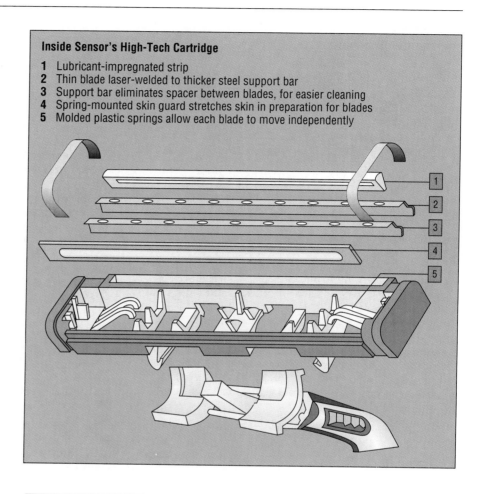

Inside Sensor's High-Tech Cartridge

1 Lubricant-impregnated strip
2 Thin blade laser-welded to thicker steel support bar
3 Support bar eliminates spacer between blades, for easier cleaning
4 Spring-mounted skin guard stretches skin in preparation for blades
5 Molded plastic springs allow each blade to move independently

Source: Reprinted from January 29, 1990 issue of *Business Week*, p. 62, by special permission, copyright
© 1990 by McGraw-Hill, Inc.

Commercialization   At the final stage, commercialization, the company
makes the product available to the entire target market. Large companies
selling consumer goods usually sell the good in one particular region or to one
target group and then expand coverage to the national market. For example,
during the mid-1990s General Motors will begin installing General Electric
high-intensity discharge lamps on their higher-priced models and, eventually, put them on bottom-of-the-line cars as well.[10] Motorola is aiming its
new line of multi-user business computers at larger firms but plans to come
out eventually with lower-priced models for smaller firms.[11] Smaller companies usually start with local distribution and gradually expand to a regional
market. In any event, the firm starts small and seeks to identify the sales
strategies that work best. Then, as the company increases distribution, it can
better handle any marketing problems that happen to arise.

An auto insurance claims adjuster estimates repair costs using a new hand-held computer system from Automatic Data Processing Inc. This adjuster is participating in the test marketing of the computer. ADP, like other companies, tests a new product before making it generally available.

Source: © 1990 Vickers & Beechler.

Why Products Fail

Using the stages of new-product development helps ensure successful new products, but most new products still fail. A number of reasons account for this. Three of the most common have been found to be inadequate market analysis, ineffective sales effort, and problems or defects in the product.[12] Research has also found that product quality often has more to do with a new product's success or failure than does price.[13] This is particularly true for high-tech goods such as computers and cameras and for luxury products such as automobiles. For example, after brisk initial sales, Kodak withdrew its disc cameras because of the fatal flaw with its minuscule negatives, which tended to produce grainy snapshots. This defect became even more glaring with the arrival of simple and inexpensive 35mm cameras.

Another important reason why new products fail is that it costs too much to produce them. Detroit automakers have been wrestling with this problem for years and seem to be finally getting costs under control. As a result, cars of the 1990s are going to be different from those of the 1980s. By using new materials such as ultra-high-strength plastics, aluminum, and electrogalvanized steel, manufacturers will be able to build more durable and cheaper-to-produce automobiles.

Besides cost, another critical variable is how long it takes to get a new product developed. For example, Hewlett-Packard surprised many desktop publishing firms when it brought to market a laser printer priced under $1,000. No one expected such a product so soon and Hewlett-Packard's low price helped it garner market share while forcing competitors to drop their prices.[14]

1. What are the steps in the process of new-product development?
2. Why do some products fail?

CHECK ✓ POINT

FIGURE 15.3
Matrix for Portfolio Analysis

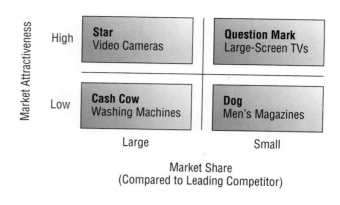

Product Analysis

Once a company develops a product and makes it available, the marketing manager must decide how to price, package, distribute, and promote it. One way of planning these strategies is to analyze an existing product's current performance or the potential of a new product. Is it or could it be a market leader? Is it just barely paying its own way? Or is it losing money? The results of product analysis determine what follow-up strategy to develop.

Portfolio Analysis

Portfolio analysis   A method for developing a product strategy based on the attractiveness of a market and the product's share of that market.

Many firms use an approach to product analysis called **portfolio analysis.** This is a method for developing a product strategy based on the attractiveness of a market and the product's share of that market. The attractiveness of a given market depends on the degree of consumer demand, the amount of existing competition from other firms, and the potential for growth in the coming years. The widely used technique for portfolio analysis is the four-cell matrix developed by the Boston Consulting Group and illustrated in Figure 15.3.

A manager using this matrix considers two factors: the attractiveness of the market and the market share currently held by the product. Depending on these factors, the manager places the product into one of the four cells in Figure 15.3. The appropriate strategy depends on the cell into which the product fits. In general, companies using portfolio analysis employ a strategy that cultivates the stars, pushes the question marks, milks the cows, and drops the dogs. Of course, this is just a general guideline; companies try to take into account the unique characteristics of each product and market.

Life Cycle Approach to Product Analysis

Not all firms use portfolio analysis. Some look at the product's place in its life cycle and develop a strategy based on this. Chapter 14 introduced the concept of the product life cycle. Table 15.1 shows the strategies that apply at each stage.

TABLE 15.1
The Product Life Cycle: Characteristics and Product Strategies

	Introduction	**Growth**	**Maturity**	**Decline**
Characteristics				
Sales	Low	Increasing rapidly	Increasing slowly	Declining
Profits	Negligible or very low	Very high	Starting to decline	Low or negative
Customers	Early adopters	Mass-market adopters	Mass-market adopters	Loyal adopters
Competitors	Few	Increasing number	Many	Declining number
Product Strategies				
Objectives	Expand the market	Penetrate the market	Defend market share	Keep expenses down
Marketing expenditures	High	High but declining	Declining	Low
Marketing emphasis	Product awareness	Brand preference	Brand loyalty	Hold on to die-hard customers
Distribution	Selective	Many outlets	Many outlets	Selective outlets
Price	High	Lower	Lowest	Going back up

The strategy is tied to the characteristics of the life cycle stage. When a product is in the introduction stage, sales tend to be low and profits are negligible. The firm's objective at this stage is to expand the market and make people aware of the product.

Unless the firm wants to gain entry to the market through a low-price strategy, it sets the initial price fairly high. This was the strategy when Sharp Corporation introduced a new desktop facsimile machine that could transmit photography-like full-color images. This new product carried an initial price of $23,500.[15] As more and more people buy the product and it enters a growth stage, the company lowers the price and begins to seek greater market share. This is what happened in the cellular phone business.[16] When the product enters the maturity stage, the firm tries to defend its market by lowering the price or developing persuasive promotional techniques. Cigarette firms are now relying heavily on such a defensive strategy.[17] Finally, when the product enters the decline stage, the company tries to cut its expenses and remain profitable as long as it can. Sometimes the company can combat a decline in sales by modifying existing products or introducing a new mix of products. Nike's "Pump" basketball shoes are a good example.[18] The accompanying Innovation Close-Up (Marketing Down from Jordan and McEnroe) provides more insights into how Nike has done this. So are the light and fat-free dietary offerings developed by the fast food franchises[19] and the food companies.[20] The Bentley automobile is an especially good example because its new turbo-charged engine is being marketed as a hybrid Italian sports car *and* British sedan.[21] Still another example is liquor firms that are trying to deal with the current trend away from alcoholic beverages.

CHECK ✓ POINT

1. What are two techniques for conducting product analysis?
2. What kind of product strategy would be appropriate for a growing market?

CLOSE-UP / *Innovation*

Marketing Down From Jordan and McEnroe

Nike is one of the best-known names in sportswear and athletic shoes today and the company commands a dominant market share. However, a few years ago Nike began having marketing problems. Its products were not selling as well as expected. An analysis of the situation revealed that many of their best products had limited market appeal. The Air Jordan sneaker is a good example. For the first two years after the product launch, Air Jordans were a dominant market offering. Then the product began to falter. A market investigation revealed that there were many people to whom Air Jordans did not appeal. These individuals could not visualize themselves as Michael Jordan: and even if they were excellent players, they did not have Michael's style of play. Result: Nike developed additional offerings to appeal to other segments of the basketball market.

By slicing up the market this way, the company developed two new segments and products for each. One is Force shoes,

represented by NBA superstars David Robinson and Charles Barkley. These shoes are more stable than Air Jordans and are designed for the aggressive, muscular style of play represented by Robinson and Barkley. The other product is the Flight shoe, represented by Jordan's teammate Scottie Pippin. These shoes are more flexible and lighter weight. They work best for players with a quick, high-flying style like Pippin's. How well has the company done by creating three product lines in lieu of one? Of the top five basketball shoes on the market today, these hold first, second, and fourth place.

Nike has used a similar strategy of slicing up the market to help it hold a large share of the tennis shoe market. The firm initially built its Challenge Court Collection around the flamboyant personalities of John McEnroe and Andre Agassi and the product soon dominated the market. However, more conservative players shied away from these shoes, which were considered too flashy. So Nike developed a second type of shoe called the Supreme Court, which is more toned down and conservative. As with its basketball offerings, Nike has again been able to maintain market dominance by slicing up the market niche and not putting all of its eggs in one basket.

Source: Adapted from Geraldine E. Willigan, ''High Performance Marketing: An Interview with Nike's Phil Knight,'' *Harvard Business Review*, July-August 1992, pp. 96, 98.

Brands and Trademarks

Brand A name, term, symbol, or combination of these used to identify a firm's products and differentiate them from competing products.

For products at all stages of the life cycle, marketers are interested in finding ways to make their products stand out from competitor's offerings. One way is to use brands and trademarks. A **brand** is a name, term, symbol, or combination thereof used to identify a firm's products and differentiate them from competing products. Brands can include names such as Levi's, Jiffy Lube, and Xerox.[22] They can also incorporate visual symbols such as NBC's peacock and McDonald's golden arches.

Marketers try to build sales and market share by developing a positive association between a brand and a product benefit. McDonald's hopes that hungry travelers will stop when they see the golden arches. Levi Strauss hopes that people shopping for jeans will look for the Levi's label. Two products for which branding has been particularly successful are Coca-Cola and Pepsi. In blind taste tests, cola drinkers generally have trouble telling the two apart; nevertheless, most consumers are very loyal to one brand or the other.

The owner of the brand may be the manufacturer or the retailer of the product. For example, Chrysler, General Electric, Westinghouse, AT&T,

General Mills increased sales of its Yoplait® brand by offering yogurt products in snack-sized containers and by introducing Yoplait Light.

Source: Parallel Productions Inc.

and Goodyear all manufacture products bearing their own brand names. In contrast, Sears purchases appliances from many manufacturers and markets them under the Kenmore brand. A&P, the giant supermarket chain, buys canned goods, jams, jellies, household cleaning products, and an assortment of other commodities and offers them for sale under the Ann Page, A&P, and Jane Parker brand names.

Types of Brands

Marketers can use a number of different types of brands. Figure 15.4 illustrates the major ones. They are:

- **Private brands,** which are owned by the retailer. An example is Sears's Craftsman brand for tools.
- **National brands,** which are owned by the manufacturer. Ford and Nike are examples.
- **Family brands,** which are used with all of the products a firm sells. For example, all of Kellogg's, Post, Nabisco, or Keebler products carry the brand name. These companies hope that by building a good reputation for their names, they can persuade buyers of one of its products to look for its name when buying other products.
- **Individual brands,** which are used exclusively for one of the products a firm sells. For example, General Motors manufactures the Chevrolet, Pontiac, Oldsmobile, Buick, Cadillac, and Saturn brands of automobiles. Companies use individual brand names when customers prefer a

Private brand A brand owned by a retailer.

National brand A brand owned by a manufacturer.

Family brand A brand used with all of the products a firm sells.

Individual brand A brand used exclusively for one of the products a firm sells.

FIGURE 15.4
Types of Brands

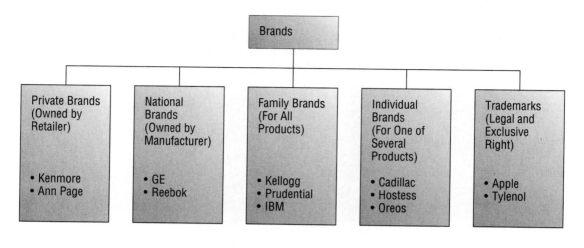

particular product or product line rather than just any one manufactured by that corporation. This preference may be based on differences in price, quality, style, prestige, or other features.

Trademarks

A **trademark** is a brand that the owner has the legal and exclusive right to use. Trademarks are registered with the U.S. Patent Trademark Office. Common examples include the Prudential rock, the NBC peacock, and names such as 7-Up, Buick, and Memorex.

The owner of a trademark must protect its rights to the trademark,[23] or it may become a generic term, unprotected by law. In that case, competitors can trade on a company's brand name by using a similar one. For example, a few years ago, a firm offered a board game called Anti-Monopoly. Parker Brothers, owners of the trademark Monopoly, which identified their own board game, sued. The court held that because the name of the Parker Brothers board game had passed into common usage, it had become a generic name and was no longer protected by the law. Thus, manufacturers of the Anti-Monopoly game were free to market their product. Nestlé's Toll House cookies have met a similar fate. The courts have ruled that this is another generic name, and the company no longer has an exclusive right to its use.

One way in which companies protect their trademarks is by advertising the special status of these words and symbols. Companies also print the symbol ® next to the name to show that it is a registered trademark. If a company believes its trademark has been violated, it can take court action. For example, a judge granted a request to block the sale of actress Elizabeth Taylor's perfume called Passion to large department stores because a French firm has a fragrance by the same name.

Branding Alternatives

In recent years, a special form of branding has become popular: licensing. Under this arrangement, a company pays the creator of a character for the right to use that character to help promote the company's products. For example, if a movie or TV character becomes popular, manufacturers try to license the name of the character and use it to sell toys, food, clothing, or whatever products the name might be associated with. Popular movie characters, such as Dick Tracy, have been used in this way in promoting clothes.

Some marketers avoid branding altogether in favor of generic products. A **generic product** is one with no brand and simple packaging. Many generics are on the market today. Most supermarkets, including national chains

Generic product A product with no brand and simple packaging.

such as Jewel, A&P, and Safeway, stock generic paper towels, facial tissues, bleaches, coffee creamers, plastic bags, cooking oil, ice cream, and a host of other products. Even generic alcoholic beverages simply labeled "beer," "vodka," "bourbon," and so on are available.

Generics have grabbed a large share of the market among products that do not vary much by quality. For example, most people feel that paper towels are all basically the same, and generics have done well in this market niche. However, many consumers believe that when it comes to food, the quality of the generics is sometimes below par, and branded foods are more reliable. As a result, generic foods have done poorly compared to other generic products. The same is true for drugs, where the generics have run into trouble in recent years.[24]

CHECK ✓ POINT

1. What are some different types of brands? Give an example of each.
2. How does a trademark differ from a brand?

Product Packages and Labels

One place a product's brand appears is on the product's package. Marketers have found that labeling and the packages themselves can be important marketing tools.

Objectives for Packaging

Over the past 25 years, packaging has begun to play a greater role in the marketing process. As a result, packaging has become one of the largest industries in the country, accounting for annual sales exceeding those of either steel or textiles. Besides using attention-getting colors, by designing convenient and safe packaging, marketers can make the package a product benefit. Marketers can also evaluate and try to minimize the effects of packaging on the environment.

Convenience If you bought a dozen unpackaged eggs and carried them home in a paper bag, you would have a mess before long, because some of the eggs would inevitably break and leak all over. An egg carton makes it easy to transport them. Likewise, carrying home a large jar of liquid laundry detergent might be a burden. However, today you can buy detergent in a lightweight plastic container with a convenient handle that makes it easy to carry. Frozen dinners are another product for which the package provides benefits. Until a few years ago, they were all packaged in aluminum wrap in order to keep the food fresh. With the advent of the microwave oven, manufacturers are now offering frozen food packaged in a special cardboard and plastic wrap that still keeps the product fresh, but can be put right into a microwave. Other examples include calculators for left-handed people, garden tools shaped for the hand, and lamps that can be shaped into any configuration.[25] W. R. Grace's cement bags don't even need to be opened. They can be tossed into the mixer where they quickly dissolve.[26]

Safety Besides offering convenience, packaging helps preserve and protect products such as foods and pharmaceuticals. In the case of food, it prevents

The "tin" can may just be the world's perfect container. It's made of durable, high-grade steel that is completely recyclable.* It saves energy because it requires no refrigeration. And the can is made, shipped and stored more economically than other packages. So the dollars you spend go more to the food you eat than the package that contains it. The steel can. Precious little could be done to improve it. **FOOD FOR THOUGHT**

*Del Monte supports recycling. Please call 1-800-453-2589 for more information on steel can recycling.

As the environmental impact of packaging becomes an issue with consumers, marketers are promoting better management of resources. Del Monte created this ad informing the public that "tin" cans (actually made of steel) are recyclable. The company also provides information to consumers on steel can recycling.

contamination. In the case of drugs (and some food products), it provides protection from tampering. In computers and other electronic goods, packaging can prevent damage to the products during transit.

Pollution Control   A drawback of packaging is that it is often a source of pollution. For example, common plastics cannot be recycled and are not biodegradable. In fact, some emit dangerous gases when burned. In addition, glass and plastic bottles and aluminum cans litter the streets and countryside and create millions of tons of garbage each year. Some makers of glass bottles recycle their products and urge retailers to stock their products because glass-packaged goods usually have a longer shelf life than other packaged products. However, aluminum and plastic-packaged goods are usually easier to stock, and more of them can fit into the same space. Some states have enacted — often over industry protests — laws in which customers are charged a deposit (typically 5 cents) on all soft drink and sometimes beer products that is refundable only when the empty bottles or cans are returned to the store. However, because the states with such laws are few, and because both bottles and cans are still widely used, pollution will continue to remain a major area of social concern to marketers and package designers.

Most marketers now realize that having their packaging compatible with the environment makes good business sense. For example, a survey found that 77 percent of Americans say a company's environmental reputation affects what they buy.[27] Firms such as Procter & Gamble are taking up the challenge. They have reduced excess packaging by doing things such as redesigning Crisco oil bottles to use 28 percent less plastic, having their detergents in 15 percent less packaging, and will soon be using up to 80 million recycled milk, water, and soft drink bottles a year.[28]

Labeling

Label The part of a package that presents information about its contents.

Most packages contain labels. A **label** is the part of a package that presents information about its contents. The label may include a wide variety of information including the following:

- *Brand name and logo.* This helps distinguish products from competing offerings. Putting the company's name on the product also tells consumers that the company is putting its reputation on the line for the product's quality.

- *Registered trademark symbol (®).* This symbol indicates that the company has exclusive rights to its trademark. This is one way a company can protect its trademark rights.

- *Package size.* This information helps buyers make informed decisions on the price they are paying for a given amount.

- *Materials or ingredients.* The buyer may be attracted to a product based on its materials or ingredients. The purchaser of a shirt may like the comfort of cotton or the easy care of polyester. The buyer of cereal may look for high calcium or fiber content. In recent years detailed labeling has become more common, thus helping consumers identify product content. In fact, most packaged goods will soon be required to carry nutrition labels.[29]

- *Directions for using the product.* A buyer who can't figure out how to use a product will be disappointed with it. Consequently, many labels contain directions.

- *Safety precautions.* Companies include safety precautions for the same reasons they include directions. In addition, their social responsibility and their fear of lawsuits lead them to include this information.

- *Name and address of the manufacturer.* Some manufacturers include their name, address, and a toll-free phone number to encourage questions or comments from customers.

Today most products sold in the United States include universal product codes (UPCs) on their labels. At the checkout counter, an electronic scanner reads this bar code to identify the product and ring up the price. This enables the store to automatically keep track of inventory and speed up the checkout process.

Today, the uses of UPCs extend far beyond the grocery or department store checkout counter. As technology continues to develop, these systems are becoming cheaper and more flexible. Libraries use bar codes to keep track of their books. Clinical laboratories put the codes on containers of blood and urine samples for accurate identification. Airlines use them to keep track of luggage.

FIGURE 15.5
Supply, Demand, and Price for Shirts

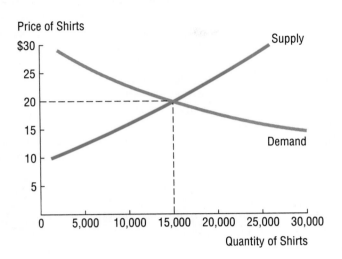

Price of Shirts

Quantity of Shirts

CHECK ✓ POINT

1. What objectives do marketers aim for in designing a package?
2. What kinds of information are found on food labels?

Pricing Strategies

While most everyone associates product strategies with marketing, they less often think of pricing strategies as a marketing approach. Yet understanding and using an effective pricing strategy can give a company a distinct advantage in the marketplace.[30]

Businesses use many different pricing strategies in their marketing efforts. The best strategy depends on the customers. For example, research has shown that at one time, personal computers that sold for *less* than $1,000 encountered market resistance. Customers believed that the machines were not powerful and sophisticated enough to do "real" computer work. The market viewed them as merely low-quality, expensive toys. On the other hand, personal computers priced above $3,000 also ran into market resistance, because consumers believed these machines were too sophisticated and expensive for the intended use.

Marketers can't predict exactly how each customer will respond to a given price. Consequently, in determining the best pricing strategy, they consider the economic environment and the company's profitability objectives.

The Economic Implications for Pricing

Chapter 2 discussed the important role that supply and demand plays in a competitive economy. To remind you, supply is the amount of a good provided at a particular price, and demand is the amount of a good purchased at a particular price. Supply is greatest at high prices, while demand is greatest at low prices. Between these extremes is the equilibrium, or market price, where supply and demand are equal — $20 in Figure 15.5. What supply and

Price level   The price being
charged in the industry.

demand and equilibrium mean for marketers is that in a competitive market
they must set a price at the overall **price level,** the price being charged in the
industry. All other things being equal (for example, service, convenience,
reputation, and so forth), a company that charges more than the equilibrium
price may lose customers to competitors who charge less. A company that
charges less than the equilibrium price may shortchange itself; in a competitive market, that doesn't make good business sense. Yet, there is considerable
evidence that businesses do not always make rational pricing decisions.[31]

Sometimes, marketers may seem to violate this pricing arrangement by
trying to shift the price downward. For example, a gas-station owner might
try undercutting a competitor across the street. Soon the competitor cuts
prices to match, and price wars rage for a while. But this cuts into profits,
and before long the prices creep back up to the equilibrium point.

Sometimes, companies seem to be charging different prices for the same
product. For example, different stores may charge different prices for the
same merchandise. But when customers buy something at a store, they are
buying more than just the item itself. Recall the discussion in Chapter 14 of
the trade-offs customers may use when buying a product or service. The
store may be making the product available in a convenient location at convenient times. In addition, some stores offer more services than others. For
example, some shoppers may derive greater enjoyment from shopping in the
quiet, carpeted aisles of Nieman-Marcus, where they can easily obtain sales
assistance, than they do from shopping for the same products at K mart, and
they are willing to pay more for this additional benefit.

Profitability

Most businesses have profit goals. Therefore, marketers must consider how
the price of the product will enable the company to earn a profit. To determine profitability, or in less competitive environments, to set the price, the
manager computes costs, then adds a markup to reach profit goals. Only in
the short run can the seller afford to sell below cost in the hopes of creating a
loyal customer base or, perhaps, driving out the competition.

The major issue for the seller is how far above its costs it can price the
product. For example, many car dealers will sell to customers on the basis of
dealer's invoice (their cost) plus an agreed-upon amount. The size of this
amount depends on the degree to which customers will be influenced by
price. In general, if customers can easily find the same thing somewhere else,
the seller is limited to a small markup. If the product is difficult to obtain or
is prestigious, the markup can be larger.

Quality and Price

Traditionally, the price a company charged depended on whether it chose to
please a few quality-conscious customers by emphasizing quality or to sell a
lot of a product by emphasizing low price. Today, there is increasing evidence that a growing segment of the marketplace is demanding high-quality
products and services.[32] This quality-conscious American consumer is tired
of things that don't work and the hassles of trying to get things fixed or
returned. Japanese companies have been so successful in the American marketplace largely because of the quality (not the price) of their products. Qual-

ity drives profits, mainly through repeat business. Companies such as Xerox, Motorola, and Rubbermaid have turned to a quality focus and have become quite successful. For example, Motorola's profits soared 44 percent because, by emphasizing quality the company nearly eliminated its rework and repair costs and built a loyal customer following for its products such as cellular phones.

This does not mean that price is no longer important. Prices still dominate the largest segment of most markets. Consider an example. Häagen-Dazs charges an above-average price for its ice cream, because some customers are willing to pay extra for the quality ingredients. In contrast, Sealtest — which doesn't boast of the same quality, but costs less than premium brands like Häagen-Dazs — sells a lot more ice cream.

The key for the years ahead is to give emphasis to both quality and price. Even companies with low-price strategies must provide quality service to their customers. An increasing number of companies are guaranteeing customer satisfaction. For example, Hampton Inns tell guests that if they are not satisfied they don't have to pay. In the first year under this policy 7,000 guests have stayed free, costing the company $350,000 in lost revenues. However, management says they are happy with the policy because 99 percent of those who use the guarantee say they will come back and over half already have.[33]

1. What basic concerns do marketers consider in setting a price strategy?
2. What would be a suitable price strategy for a small bookstore?

CHECK ✓ POINT

Pricing Techniques

Based on the product's breakeven point (discussed in Chapter 9) and the pricing strategy adopted, the manager selects pricing techniques from a variety of options. The major kinds of techniques are traditional pricing, discounts, and special techniques to stimulate sales.

Traditional Pricing

Pricing starts with the **list price.** This is the price announced for a product. At a supermarket, the list price is usually found on the product itself and on the shelf. At an auto dealership, the list price is found on the sticker attached to the car window. In a college bookstore, it is often on a label attached to the cover or stamped on the inside cover of each book. The list price of clothing appears on tags attached to it.

The traditional approach is to sell only at the list price. Under this **fixed-price technique,** the marketer sells at the announced price. In the supermarket, for example, if one can of tuna is priced at 60 cents, then two cans will cost $1.20 and three cans will cost $1.80. The seller does not negotiate. Restaurants and retail stores like Dillards or K mart also use a fixed-price strategy. So does Jan Bell Marketing, a Florida-based jewelry distributor.[34] Hair stylists charge twice as much for two haircuts as they do for one, and the price is set in advance.

List price The price announced for a product.

Fixed-price technique A pricing technique in which the marketer sells at the announced price.

FIGURE 15.6
Types of Discounts

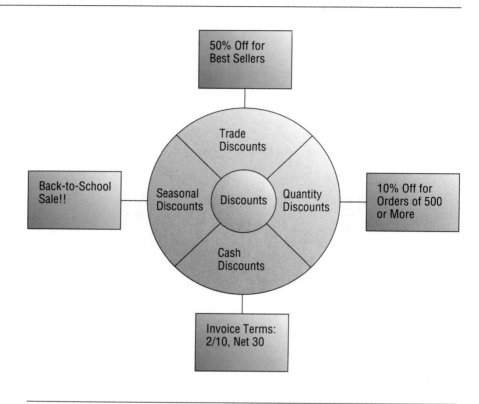

Discounts

Many businesses find that they can profitably boost sales by deviating from the fixed-price technique. Managers at these companies have strategically chosen or have been forced by the competition to use discounting. A **discount** is an amount subtracted from the list price. As illustrated in Figure 15.6, some common forms include trade, quantity, cash, and seasonal discounts.

Some businesses sell below list price to merchants in the distribution channel. Such a price reduction is called a **trade discount.** Manufacturers often give wholesalers a trade discount. In turn, wholesalers give retailers a discount. In publishing, bookstores such as Waldenbooks and B. Dalton, the two largest in the industry, typically pay half of list price for a best seller. They, in turn, may pass on some of the discount to customers. Sellers also may give a price reduction to buyers who place larger-than-average orders. This price reduction is a **quantity discount.** Such discounts are typically based on the number of units purchased. The larger the order, the greater the discount.

Some businesses reward their customers for paying their bills on time. A **cash discount** is a price reduction given for paying a bill within a predetermined time period. One common cash-discount term is "2/10, net 30," pronounced "two ten, net thirty." This means that, if the buyer pays the bill

Discount An amount subtracted from the list price.

Trade discount A discount given to merchants in the distribution channel.

Quantity discount A discount given to buyers who place larger-than-average orders.

Cash discount A discount given for paying a bill within a predetermined time period.

within 10 days, the seller grants a 2 percent discount, but in any case the bill must be paid in 30 days. Under these terms, a buyer who gets a bill for $100 can settle it for $98 by paying within 10 days; otherwise, the entire $100 is due in 30 days.

Finally, a seller that wants to stimulate buying before or after peak periods may offer a **seasonal discount.** This is a price reduction given during particular times of the year. For example, swimsuit manufacturers offer discounts to retailers in the Midwest for buying before the peak summer months. Most bathing suits are sold between May and August, so manufacturers offer seasonal discounts in March and April. These discounts do more than help the manufacturer increase sales. They also save the company the cost of warehousing the inventory.

Seasonal discount A discount given during particular times of the year.

Many retailers also offer seasonal discounts. Using the same example, swimsuits are heavily discounted in the late summer and early fall. By this time, the retailer knows that anyone who needs a bathing suit for the summer already has one; the only way to get buyers to consider another is with a sale. Many merchandisers also have post-holiday sales, marking down candy on February 15 and Christmas decorations, cards, and wrapping paper during the last week of December. In an effort to generate even higher sales, some retailers have begun changing these holiday sale periods and offering discounts *before* the holiday. Christmas sales on the Friday and Saturday after Thanksgiving have, to the distress of many people, become the norm.

Other Pricing Techniques

Although discounts stimulate sales, they are not the only pricing techniques that businesses use. Other popular approaches include loss leaders, odd pricing, and flexible pricing.

Loss Leaders A **loss leader** is a product that is priced below cost. This pricing method is designed to attract people into the store, where, the retailer hopes, they will buy other goods as well. To ensure that the first group of customers to arrive doesn't buy up all the loss leaders, most stores limit purchases, such as "one to a customer."

Loss leader A product that is priced below cost to attract people into a store.

Examples of loss leaders appear in the newspaper every week. Many supermarkets, for example, run ads for loss leaders such as coffee, soft drinks, and toothpaste in an effort to generate heavier-than-usual traffic. The pizzeria that placed the ad in Figure 15.7 will take a loss on Crazy Bread®, but this popular product appeals to many customers and should build traffic. Also, note that two large pizzas are priced differently than the medium pizzas on special. The store managers may be hoping that many customers will decide that medium pizzas are not enough and will switch to the higher-priced large size. Department stores often run sales featuring loss leaders on weekends in order to attract customers at the time of the week when they are most likely to go shopping.

Odd Pricing A second pricing method is **odd pricing,** which is setting a price just below a round number for psychological reasons. An item may be priced at $98.95 instead of $100, or $2,995 rather than $3,000. This type of pricing is often referred to as psychological pricing, because it tends to get

Odd pricing Setting a price just below a round number for psychological reasons.

people's attention and to suggest they are getting a good deal. At first glance, a price of $98.95 may seem to be a lot less than $100. More important, people feel that they are getting a bargain at $98.95 instead of $100. Odd pricing is an old technique that probably still works on many buyers.

A possibly mythical story involving Marshall Field suggests another basis for odd pricing. The founder of the well-known department store suspected that some cashiers were pocketing money from customers rather than putting it into the cash register. That was relatively easy to do when sales were for round amounts, such as $2. By changing to odd pricing, Field forced cashiers to ring up the sale in order to open the cash register, deposit the money, and give the customer back some change. According to this story, the store's receipts increased after Field instituted odd pricing.

Flexible Pricing An increasing number of sellers are willing to negotiate on price.[35] These sellers use **flexible pricing,** in which the price of a product is negotiable. For example, flexible pricing is in effect on Saturdays at the farmers' market in Detroit. Especially toward the end of the day, when the choice produce is gone and the farmers are eager to return home, buyers haggle with sellers over the prices of the goods for sale. Many farmers will cut prices in order to sell off what they have. Some haggling also takes place at flea markets and garage sales around the country.

Auto dealers are also known for flexible pricing. They typically set the initial price as high as they can, figuring in every cost they possibly can. Their hope is that customers will be more likely to make a purchase when they see the price come down than they would if the price were fixed. If you've ever tried to sell your car to a dealer for cash, you might have found that the amount offered is considerably less than the dealer would offer for the same car as a trade-in allowance. That's because a generous trade-in allowance is one way dealers bring down the price of the car they are selling; it isn't necessarily based on the value of your car.

1. Name two kinds of discounts marketers use.
2. What two pricing techniques do marketers often consider when introducing a new product?

Flexible pricing Selling a product at a price that is negotiable.

CHECK ✓ POINT

Closing Comments

This chapter examined some of the basics of product planning and pricing. In general, marketing managers develop a product strategy plan using techniques such as portfolio analysis and life cycle analysis. They also consider proper branding, packaging, and labeling. These elements often spell the difference between success and failure. In addition, marketing success depends on pricing strategies and techniques. The price depends on the economic environment, the company's profit goals, and consumer expectations.

VIDEO CASE / *New Product Offerings*

Hoffman Chocolates is known for the delicious, quality products Paul Hoffman creates. Year after year people buy his newest chocolate offerings as well as the old standbys. Paul is unflagging in his efforts to offer products that will keep people coming back and he is not alone. Every year numerous new products and services from all types of industries hit the market and prove to be big winners. Many of them are introduced by large companies that find they are unable to maintain their mar-

ket position without new product offerings. Some are introduced by small firms that are seeking to establish themselves and become the success stories of tomorrow.

One example is Windows 3.0 by Microsoft. This software allows IBM PCs to work in much the same graphic, easy-to-use way as Apple's friendly Macintosh. Within a year of its introduction, Windows sold almost 1.5 million copies. Another example is Panasonic's PV-40 Palmcorder for

home videos. It uses a digital antijiggle technology system that provides a steadier picture. The camera is so small that it can fit in the hand. A third high-tech offering is the notebook computer from a number of different companies. Intel's 386 SL microprocessor enabled those companies to increase the power of small computers while also reducing the size of the machine.

Other new product offerings have been geared toward the general public. For example, ConAgra has developed a microwaveable line of meals that produce sales of over $225 million annually. This is the most successful new food product line in the past 5 years. And for those who feel that they are eating too much and need some exercise, there is Rollerblades, the most popular form of transportation since the skateboard. These skates have four wheels that are lined in a single row rather than two in the front and two in the back. They have proven so popular that sales are over $150 million. Finally, for those who are exhausted from skating, new television programs offer ongoing entertainment.

One of the biggest hits of recent years was Public TV's 11-hour documentary, *The Civil War*. Over the 5 nights it was aired, the program had an average viewing audience of 12 million a night. The program also generated a book that provides the same information and a lot more. Priced at a steep $50, the book still managed to become one of the major best sellers of the year. Like Paul Hoffman's delicious chocolates, quality education is a product that also has market appeal.

Source: Joshua Mendes, "Products of the Year," *Fortune*, December 17, 1990, 72–82; and "The New Products Best," *Business Week*, January 14, 1991, 124–128.

Case Questions

1. Why are so many new products high tech in nature?
2. How does Hoffman Chocolates manage to maintain its market, given that the firm is not high tech in focus?
3. How important is pricing to the success of a new product? How do you explain the fact that the Civil War book described in this case retailed for $50 and still managed to garner major sales?

Key Terms Reviewed

Review each of the following terms. For any that you do not know or are unsure of, look up the definitions and see how they were used in the chapter.

portfolio analysis	generic product	quantity discount
brand	label	cash discount
private brand	price level	seasonal discount
national brand	list price	loss leader
family brand	fixed-price technique	odd pricing
individual brand	discount	flexible pricing
trademark	trade discount	

Learning Objectives Revisited

1. **Describe the steps involved in development of new products.** New-product development involves six steps: idea generation, coming up with ideas and concepts that can be turned into new products; production evaluation, looking over the proposed products to see whether they fit with the firm's long-range objectives; economic analysis, evaluation of the project's overall profitability; product development, the construction of a model, mock-up, or prototype of the product; test marketing, taking the product into the marketplace to see how well it does; and commercialization, making the product available to the market at large.

2. **Explain how businesses use product analysis.** To decide on a strategy for pricing, distributing, and promoting a product, the company analyzes the product's performance. Two common ways of doing this are portfolio analysis and analysis of the product's life cycle stage. Portfolio analysis bases product strategy on market attractiveness and market share. Companies generally promote their stars, push their question marks in hopes of making them stars, milk their cows, and get rid of their dogs. Life cycle analysis bases product strategy on the product's current life cycle stage. For a product in the introduction stage, the company focuses on achieving product awareness and expanding the market. During this stage, the company sets the price and marketing expenditures high. When a product reaches the growth stage, the focus shifts

to achieving brand preference and increasing market share. In the maturity stage, the firm focuses on brand loyalty and keeping its present market share. Finally, when the product enters the decline stage, the firm focuses on holding on to the product's most loyal customers and keeping its expenses down.

3. **Discuss the use of brands and trademarks.** A brand is a name, term, symbol, or combination of these used to identify a firm's products and differentiate them from those of the competition. A trademark is a brand that the owner has the legal and exclusive right to use. Businesses use brand names and trademarks in advertising and packaging so that the consumer will identify a particular type of product with their brand.

4. **Describe the value of packaging and labeling.** Packaging is of value in marketing products because it often is part of the product itself. Effective packaging makes a product convenient and safe to use. Labeling tells what is in the product, provides informa-

tion related to the product's use, and often carries an advertising message as well.

5. **Present the dimensions of product-pricing strategies.** In competitive markets, businesses must sell at the equilibrium price. In a less competitive environment, a company may be able to set a price that covers costs plus a markup. In recent years quality of products and service has become relatively more important to customers and to the profits of companies. The key for the future is to develop effective quality and price strategies.

6. **Identify product-pricing techniques.** Some companies accept only their list price, but many offer trade, quantity, cash, or seasonal discounts. Store owners may use loss leaders, which are goods priced below cost in an effort to draw customers. Another technique is odd pricing, which attempts to attract customers by setting a price just below a round number, say, $19.95 rather than $20.00. Some sellers use flexible pricing, in which the price of a product is negotiable.

Review Questions

1. Why do companies need to be concerned about developing new products? Use IBM as an example.
2. Louise Radcliffe is president of a company that produces paper products. So far, her company has made only familiar products such as cups, plates, and napkins, but Louise thinks that it is time the company set up a formal process for developing new products. What activities should Louise plan for?
3. Identify each of the following products as a star, a question mark, a cash cow, or a dog. Explain why you chose each category. What implications does the product's category have for the way the company should market it?
   a. Reynolds Wrap aluminum foil
   b. VHS videocassette recorders
   c. A locally owned health club
   d. Adler manual typewriters
4. For each of the products in Question 3, identify the product's stage in its life cycle. What does this tell you about how each product should be marketed?
5. What is the difference between a brand and a trademark? Which of the following terms are trademarks? (If you aren't sure, try consulting a recent edition of a dictionary.)
   a. Kleenex
   b. Toll House cookies
   c. Ping-Pong
   d. Vaseline
6. For the items in Question 5 that are trademarks, how can the owner protect its rights to the trademark? What will happen if the company fails to do so?
7. Why do you think marketers spend money on improving packaging? Isn't it the product inside the package that counts? In improving packaging, what concerns do marketers take into account?
8. What information would you recommend go on the label of each of the following products? Why would you include each item?
   a. A bag of corn chips
   b. A portable power drill

c. A paperback novel (*Hint:* What functions as the label on a paperback?)

d. A winter coat

9. In a competitive market, what can a marketer do if the company can't afford to produce at a low enough cost to sell at the equilibrium price?

10. Why do companies that focus on either quality or price achieve the greatest profitability?

11. What pricing techniques might help the owner of a bookstore build business?

12. What pricing techniques do companies typically use for introducing new products such as large-screen TV sets?

Applied Exercise

Identify each of these pricing strategies by using the following designation:

T = Trade discount
Q = Quantity discount
C = Cash discount
S = Seasonal discount
L = Loss leader
O = Odd pricing

___ 1. $24.99
___ 2. 2/15, net 30
___ 3. 25 percent off after September 1
___ 4. 30 percent price cut given to wholesalers
___ 5. a price 15 percent below cost
___ 6. $1 each; a dozen for $10
___ 7. $99.95
___ 8. 20 percent off if payment is made by check rather than credit card
___ 9. 15 percent off if purchased before November 10
___ 10. a price 5 percent below cost
___ 11. 10 percent off for the purchase of a second unit
___ 12. 20 percent price cut given to retailers

YOU BE THE ADVISER / *Helping Them Do It*

Product Concepts, a small company located on the East Coast, has done extremely well over the past 5 years. The company is a research and development firm that investigates, researches, develops, and sells new products to large, national firms, which in turn market them. Over the past 3 years, Product Concepts has begun marketing some of its own discoveries, although only in the New England area.

Recently, the firm's product development scientists have told the president that they have discovered what might be a revolutionary product. It is a process that will allow a ballpoint pen to be used for 5 to 7 years. The process involves a new method for generating ink so that, as ink is used, it is replaced within the cartridge.

The president believes that this idea could change the entire ballpoint pen industry. In particular, he is thinking about developing and marketing the pen with a 5-year guarantee. If at any time during this period the pen runs out of ink, the company will replace it free.

As far as the president is concerned, the new product idea merits serious consideration. However, the firm has never entered an industry in direct competition with major,

well-entrenched firms. Because this new venture will be risky and require a large investment, the president would like to examine the situation closely and be sure that the company is not biting off more than it can chew.

Your Advice

1. What should the president do?
   ___ a. Proceed as quickly as possible into production.
   ___ b. Test market the idea and get some feedback.
   ___ c. Forget about developing the product; sell it to a large, national firm.
2. What steps would you recommend that the president take in developing this product? Identify and describe what to do at each step.
3. If the company introduces a 5-year ballpoint pen, what pricing strategy and techniques would you recommend that the president use when it is first introduced? Explain your reasoning. Would you recommend a change in pricing if the product enters a growth phase? Why or why not?
4. Does this product idea seem to have a good chance of success? Why or why not?

A STONEWASH LAUNDROMAT

When Cesar Viramontes opened his laundromat, his goal was to eventually expand and have nine more units around the El Paso area. Then Cesar found that his laundry facilities were of value to others besides the people looking for a place to wash their clothes. Manufacturers like Levi Strauss needed someone to stonewash, press, sort, tag, package, and ship their jeans. As a result, Economy Laundry built a $5 million jeans washing plant that employs 400 people. Not only did Cesar create a lot of new jobs for his community,

Wholesaling, Retailing, and Physical Distribution

16

Chapter Learning Objectives

- Define the nature and types of channels of distribution.

- Explain the benefits of using wholesalers.

- Identify the types of wholesalers.

- Describe the types of retailers.

- Discuss the nature and functions of physical distribution.

- Present the major modes of transportation.

---

but the undrinkable, brackish water the plant uses for laundering is treated and used to irrigate adjacent land growing alfalfa.

Economy Laundry has become part of the marketing path or channel that extends from the Levi factory to the retail stores where the jeans are sold. Economy Laundry stone washes 90,000 pairs of denim jeans every week and then packages and sends them on.

The company prides itself on quality service — the work is done right and it is done on time. Levi Strauss benefits from this handling and packaging assistance in getting stone-washed jeans to the stores.

In recent years, retail stores are having a difficult time surviving because of rising costs and resulting shrinking profits. In fact, the gap between the most successful retailers and those that are just surviving is beginning to become ever wider. There are many reasons for the troubles facing the retail industry. For example, some discount retailers have trouble getting certain types of goods because the manufacturer, not wanting its merchandise to be sold cut rate, refuses to sell to low-priced retail outlets. Another problem that retailers have had in recent years is that they have confused their customers. For example, J.C. Penney has been able to maintain its image with its clientele, but Sears may have confused customers in terms of the quality of merchandise being sold. In the future, retailers as well as manufacturers may have to take advantage of unusual services offered by companies such as Cesar Viramontes's Economy Laundry as a way to cut their costs.

Photo source: Courtesy of Economy Laundry.

Introduction

When businesspeople think of distribution, they often focus on products — and how they are moved from where they are produced to where they are sold to the customer. This is only a part of the distribution process. Marketers of a product decide what kind of help they need from outside the company in the form of wholesalers, retailers, modes of transportation, and even storage facilities. Providers of services also make distribution decisions; for example, medical professionals may establish a drop-in clinic. This chapter examines these paths or channels of distribution.

Placement or Distribution: Making Products Available

Marketing adds utility to products by making them available at convenient times and in convenient locations and by providing a way for customers to obtain ownership of them. A marketer's efforts to do this constitute one of the four Ps in the marketing mix: placement, also called distribution. Thus, when Wendy's arranges for franchisees to sell its hamburgers at conveniently located outlets, it is fulfilling its distribution function. When Wendy's sets up a test project to let customers in selected locations pay for their hamburgers with electronic banking cards, it is also carrying out this function.

Channels of Distribution

Channel of distribution The path a product follows from production to final sale.

Wholesaler An intermediary that normally purchases goods and sells them to buyers for the purpose of resale.

Retailer An intermediary that sells goods and services to the final consumer.

The path a product follows from production to final sale is the **channel of distribution** for that product. Besides the manufacturer and the ultimate user, the channel may contain one or more intermediaries: wholesalers and retailers. A **wholesaler** is an intermediary that normally purchases goods and sells them to buyers for the purpose of resale. A **retailer** is an intermediary that sells goods and services to the final consumer.

Consumers sometimes complain that intermediaries increase the price of the products. However, despite the often-heard cry to "eliminate the middleperson" (another term for an intermediary), intermediaries serve an important role in business. They simplify and make more efficient the exchange process between buyer and seller.

Figure 16.1 shows a simple example of how this works. Suppose an apple grower, a baker, a butcher, and a dairy farmer want to sell their products to four households. Without intermediaries, the sales would require 16 (four times four) exchanges. To buy their groceries, the households would have to chase around from seller to seller. But with a grocer acting as intermediary, only eight exchanges are required. With more sellers and buyers, the use of intermediaries becomes considerably more important.

Today, enormous variety in the types of intermediaries brings great diversity to marketing channels. Customers may buy from tiny boutiques, giant department stores, sidewalk vendors, factory outlets, warehouses, hypermarkets, catalogs, and more. But the basic patterns of the channels are more limited. The choices available depend on whether the marketer is selling industrial or consumer goods.

FIGURE 16.1
The Role of Intermediaries

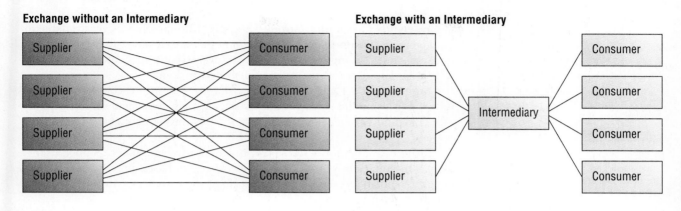

Exchange without an Intermediary

Exchange with an Intermediary

Channels for Industrial Goods   Industrial goods, as defined in Chapter 14, are those used in the production of other products. Machinery and office supplies are examples. Businesses commonly purchase them for use in operations or in providing goods and services to their own customers. Figure 16.2 shows the two common types of distribution channels used for industrial goods.

Most often, marketers of industrial goods use a **direct channel,** which bypasses all intermediaries. The company that produces the product sends out salespeople or catalogs to sell it. For example, a company that builds custom machinery might receive an order for a particular type of lathe, build it to customer specifications, and then ship it directly to the buyer. Most aircraft manufacturers use a direct channel. For example, if United Airlines orders 50 aircraft from Boeing, the latter will manufacture and deliver the planes directly to the airline. Heavy machinery and equipment are also handled through a direct channel. Buses, trucks, locomotives, mainframe computers, and hydroelectric generators are other examples.

Besides selling directly to the customer, the manufacturer may use a wholesaler to distribute the product. This is common when the producer

Direct channel A distribution channel that bypasses all intermediaries.

FIGURE 16.2
Distribution Channels for Industrial Goods

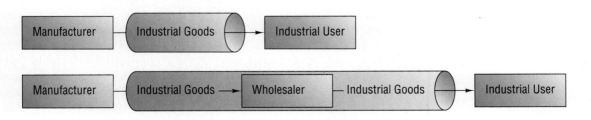

A Carlon technician checks one of the company's plastic sewer pipes, which are used primarily by contractors working on sewer projects and by industrial and residential developers. Most manufacturers of industrial products sell directly to users but some, like Carlon, distribute through a wholesaler.

Source: Courtesy of the Lamson & Sessions Co.

does not want to go through the bother of building a sales force or is just getting into the business and has, at best, only a few customers. The manufacturer needs someone to sell the product and turns to a wholesaler.

Channels for Consumer Goods Slightly different choices are available to marketers of consumer goods — products that are destined to be sold to the final consumer. In moving from manufacturer to consumer, these goods typically take one of the three routes illustrated in Figure 16.3.

Some manufacturers use a direct channel, selling to consumers themselves. For example, some producers set up their own retail outlets. Goodyear Tire and Rubber sometimes sells its tires through company-owned tire outlets.

Other manufacturers sell to consumers through a retailer. A good example is a discount chain such as Wal-Mart that purchases directly from manufacturers and then passes the savings along to customers. Auto dealers also buy from manufacturers.

Some situations call for a more complex channel: manufacturer to wholesaler to retailer to consumer. Many retailers use this channel because they cannot afford to buy in large quantities from the manufacturer. They have to rely on a wholesaler to supply them with smaller shipments as well as other services. Companies that sell their product through many different stores also find wholesalers helpful.

Many businesses use more than one channel. Magazine publishers use routes such as selling to subscribers through direct channels (subscriptions) and to single-copy buyers through retailers (over-the-counter sales). Large general-merchandise retailers such as Sears and J.C. Penney use different forms of a direct channel: mail-order catalogs and retail outlets. General Motors sells cars directly to the government and to rental car companies (Hertz, Avis, National, and Budget), while using its dealers to handle retail sales to the average single-car buyer.

Channel Strategies

Why do some companies use one type of channel, while others use a different channel or a combination of channels? The answer depends on the company's strategy. Marketers develop a strategy by considering the nature of the product and customers and the extent of the company's resources.

Product Considerations Companies that make complex products for which quality and service are important tend to use the shortest channels. For example, a consulting firm will sell its services directly to clients, so that company representatives can discuss how the firm can meet the client's specific needs. A company that sells computers may choose a direct channel because customers will expect the company to service the products and answer questions. The closeness to the customer provided by a direct channel gives the manufacturer more control over service accompanying the product.

If they use an intermediary, companies that sell expensive and complex products may allow only one intermediary to distribute the product in a given area. This approach is called **exclusive distribution.** For example, General Motors arranges for Buick, Cadillac, and Chevrolet dealers to sell these products exclusively in one area. This allows each dealer to sell an

Exclusive distribution A channel strategy in which only one intermediary distributes a product in a given area.

FIGURE 16.3
Distribution Channels for Consumer Goods

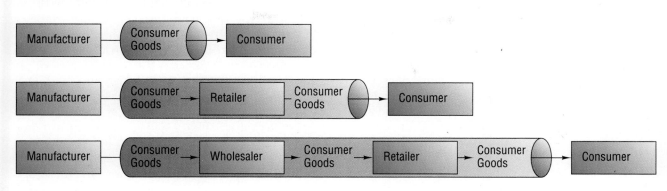

acceptable number of cars without cutting into another dealer's sales. Limiting the number of distributors is another way the manufacturer can keep more control over distribution and maintain its reputation for quality.

For products that are less complex but that do have quality and style differences, companies use distribution channels that help them set the product apart. Companies that want to differentiate their products also limit the number of intermediaries that handle their product. As an example, until recently ice cream shops licensed to use the Häagen Dazs ice cream name could sell the entire line of flavors while grocery stores were limited to only a few flavors. Allowing only a few intermediaries to distribute a product is called **selective distribution.**

In the case of products of standard quality, customers look for convenience as well as low price. Customers will not travel to the other side of town to buy a particular brand of milk or paper clips. For these products, companies use **intensive distribution,** in which the producer sells its goods through every available outlet. Milk is available in grocery stores, convenience stores, service stations, and vending machines. Paper clips can be purchased in office-supply stores, drugstores, department stores, hardware stores, and through catalogs. Companies using intensive distribution often depend heavily on wholesalers to get their products into these various outlets. In fact, the company may use several wholesalers.

Companies that produce services instead of goods usually employ direct channels. The reason is because the customer must be present when services are produced.

Customer Considerations The nature of their customers also gives marketers some clues about the most appropriate distribution channel. For example, if a company's customers are clustered geographically, the company may use a direct channel. If the customers are widely dispersed, intermediaries become more important. Likewise, companies with several target markets may use several channels, while companies with one specific target market will more likely use a single, possibly direct channel.

Selective distribution A channel strategy in which only a few intermediaries distribute a product.

Intensive distribution A channel strategy in which the producer sells its product through every available outlet.

Changes in markets lead companies to take a new look at their marketing channels. For example, households today are less likely to have someone home during business hours than was the case 30 years ago. Fuller Brush Company traditionally sold its brushes and home-cleaning products through door-to-door salespeople. However, it has responded to the change in customer habits by opening test stores in Texas. The company also sells its products through direct-mail catalogs. Another trend is that American incomes increasingly can be classified into extremes of high and low. This means that stores with a reputation for low prices, such as Wal-Mart or K mart, and high-status retailers, such as Neiman-Marcus or Lord & Taylor, currently tend to prosper at the expense of more midlevel department stores such as Macy's, which has had troubles in recent years[1] and general merchandisers, such as Sears, which had a significant drop in earnings in 1990 and cut 33,000 jobs by the end of 1991.[2] Manufacturers often find they must choose a strategy that is either very selective or very broad.

Company Considerations   In selecting a distribution channel, the company also has to consider its own strengths and limitations. A large manufacturer may find that selling directly to retailers or through its own stores enables it to pass along to customers the savings gained in bypassing a wholesaler. In contrast, small or young companies are often unable to afford the sales force necessary to get the product to all interested buyers.

A well-known brand name is another company strength. One reason that Fuller Brush has done well with catalogs is that many consumers already recognize and trust the name. In contrast, a buyer might be reluctant to order an unknown brand sight unseen from a catalog. In that case, the name of a reputable distributor might be helpful.

Vertical Marketing Systems

In the past, most marketing channels evolved over time and were basically unplanned. As producers and intermediaries realized the need to open a more direct channel to have more control over distribution or to expand volume they took a more proactive approach and changed the marketing channel. In recent years, however, some managers have established planned distribution systems in which all levels are brought under unified control. Such a system is called a **vertical marketing system (VMS).** The producer of the product may own the distributors in the VMS (an example would be Firestone), or it may establish contractual agreements with channel members (an example would be a franchisor such as Burger King or a wholesaler-sponsored chain of retail stores such as Western Auto).

1. What is a channel of distribution?
2. What do companies consider when deciding what intermediaries to include in a channel of distribution?

Vertical marketing system (VMS) A planned distribution system in which all levels are brought under unified control.

CHECK ✔ POINT

Wholesalers

When most people think of wholesalers, they think of the intermediaries that provide a link between producers and retailers. However, wholesalers may also sell to industrial users or to other wholesalers. The nation's 322,000 wholesalers[3] are an important part of the marketing function because of the benefits they provide to manufacturers and to the intermediaries (mostly retailers) that follow them in the marketing channel.

Benefits of Wholesalers

Producers or manufacturers use wholesalers because they perform functions that the producers cannot perform as efficiently or at all. The producer may turn to the wholesaler for help with some or all of the following activities:

- *Carrying inventory.* Wholesalers buy inventory, which they in turn sell to retailers or other customers. Without wholesalers, manufacturers would bear the burden and, more important, the expense of keeping all of this inventory on hand.

- *Providing a sales force.* Wholesalers can serve as the manufacturer's sales force. This frees the manufacturer from the substantial time and effort required to recruit, train, and maintain salespeople.

- *Providing marketing information and support.* Wholesalers deal with hundreds of retailers and generally have a clear idea of what the marketplace wants. By feeding this information back to the producers, wholesalers help producers decide what to produce and in what quantities. Wholesalers also assist producers in the marketing effort. They may design store displays or advertise the product.

Retailers and industrial customers often would rather buy from wholesalers than from producers. The reason is that they, too, benefit from some of the services wholesalers provide. Wholesalers' customers turn to them for some of the following services:

- *Breaking bulk.* Wholesalers can help both large- and small-volume retailers by breaking large shipments into smaller ones that meet each retailer's particular demand. For example, a paper company might ship out pallets stacked with 10-ream cartons of copier paper. A wholesaler could buy a few pallets and then sell offices a single carton or even a few reams.

- *Providing credit.* Wholesalers often give their retail customers better credit terms than they could get if they purchased directly from the manufacturer. They keep closer tabs on the retailer and are thus willing to take higher risks. Small retailers, in particular, often need this break in order to survive.

- *Providing marketing information.* Wholesalers, thanks to their contacts with competitive retailers, often know what is selling and what to stock for the upcoming season. These insights are extremely valuable to retailers, many of whom have limited access to such sources of information.

Choosing a Wholesaler

Producers that decide to include wholesalers in their channels of distribution need to consider which wholesaler services they require and which services will be important to their customers. Different wholesalers provide different combinations of services, such as breaking bulk or providing marketing information. This means that a producer can select a wholesaler based on marketing objectives. However, industry tradition sometimes makes it harder for a producer to choose a type of wholesaler. To ease this problem, Wal-Mart

FIGURE 16.4
Common Types of Wholesalers

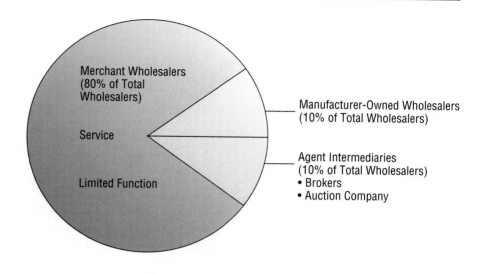

Corporation has created Sam's Warehouse Clubs (named after the founder, Sam Walton), to serve as an intermediary for small retail merchants. Small retailers can shop at Sam's Warehouses and take advantage of buying a small amount of merchandise at a relatively low price. Also, because the Wal-Mart buyers know what will be in high demand, the small retailer can also take advantage of this marketing knowledge when shopping at a Sam's Warehouse. However, clothing manufacturers have typically not used this method of wholesaling, and whether it will be successful remains to be seen.

To make informed choices, marketers need to be aware of the major types of wholesalers. These fall into three general categories: merchant wholesalers, manufacturer-owned wholesalers, and agent intermediaries. Figure 16.4 illustrates these categories.

Merchant Wholesalers   The largest group of wholesalers, accounting for approximately 80 percent of all wholesale business, are **merchant wholesalers.** These intermediaries actually buy, or take title to, goods. After purchasing merchandise, the merchant wholesaler sells it to retailers. Producers usually prefer this approach because a wholesaler that buys the merchandise is assuming risks of ownership and immediately owes money to the producer.

Some merchant wholesalers provide a wide variety of services to customers. Typical services include storing the goods and then delivering them to the customer as needed, restocking the shelves as required, and providing financial assistance in helping the retailer pay for the goods. Other merchant wholesalers carry out only some of the wholesaling functions. For example, many do not offer financial arrangements to the buyer. Others may own the goods but never physically take possession of them.

Manufacturer-Owned Wholesalers   Some manufacturers prefer the control of owning their own wholesaler. While manufacturer-owned wholesalers account for only 10 percent of wholesale business, they are common among

Merchant wholesalers
Intermediaries that take title to the goods they distribute.

some of the largest corporations in America. For example, rather than have an independent wholesaler handle their output, the major automakers each have their own wholesale arm. So do most of the large companies in the chemical and petroleum products industries.

While owning a wholesale operation means that the company must incur the effort and risks of the wholesale business, some companies are large enough to cut distribution costs this way and pass the savings along to their customers. Manufacturer-owned wholesalers are also advantageous to companies selling a product for which service is important. Construction and farm equipment producers are examples. These firms often find that their own outlets provide faster and more reliable service to customers. In addition, if customers need technical assistance or advice, the manufacturer can provide it better than anyone else.

Agent Intermediaries   Some wholesalers do not take title to (do not own) the goods they exchange. Although the producer would like to sell to the intermediary and thus reduce risk, this is not always possible. Such a wholesaler, called an **agent intermediary,** provides other services to the buyer or seller, in exchange for which this intermediary receives a commission or fee.

A common type of agent intermediary is the **broker,** who brings buyers and sellers together. In the real estate business, brokers help people buy and sell houses. Not all salespeople in real estate are brokers; only brokers have the necessary license to buy and sell. Brokers also work in the financial securities markets, where they buy and sell stock for customers. In some cases, brokers receive their commission from the buyer, as in the case of a businessperson who uses a broker to purchase some used machinery. In other cases, the broker receives a commission from the seller, as in the case of a couple who use a real estate broker to sell their house.

Agent intermediaries can take many forms. Some represent several noncompeting manufacturers, while others specialize in, say, grocery products. Some agent intermediaries handle the company's entire marketing job in a particular geographic area, from pricing to advertising to selling the product. Sellers of tobacco, livestock, used cars, and art often turn to auction companies, which provide a common place for buyers and sellers to come together. Companies that do not have a salesperson in a particular locale to handle a transaction there may turn to an agent intermediary that sells goods on commission. Thus, even companies with limited means can usually find a suitable wholesaler.

Agent intermediaries
Wholesalers that do not take title to the goods they distribute.

Broker   An agent intermediary that brings buyers and sellers together.

1. What are the three broad categories of wholesalers?
2. What are three ways in which wholesalers benefit producers?

CHECK ✓ POINT

Retailers

Producers of consumer products often rely on retailers to make their products available at convenient times and locations. Table 16.1 provides a list of the most admired retailers in America as compiled by *Fortune* according to criteria such as quality of management, financial soundness, and innovativeness.[4] Besides these large and well-known firms, many small retail outlets

TABLE 16.1
Fortune's Most Admired
Retailers in America

Rank	Company	Average Score on Attributes
1.	Wal-Mart Stores	8.35
2.	Dayton Hudson	6.99
3.	J.C. Penney	6.53
4.	May Department Stores	6.45
5.	Kroger	5.68
6.	Great Atlantic & Pacific Tea	5.62
7.	American Stores	5.58
8.	Safeway	5.42
9.	K mart	5.19
10.	Sears Roebuck	4.34

Source: Alison L. Sprout, "America's Most Admired Corporations," *Fortune*, February 11, 1991. 75.

provide opportunities for people interested in sales, management, and entrepreneurship.

Choosing a Retailer

Companies that decide to channel their goods through retailers must answer some seemingly basic questions that are becoming increasingly complicated. Managers of goods-producing firms must decide whether to sell through stores, nonstore retailing, or both. Then they must decide which stores will make their products convenient enough, maintain the desired image, and sell at the right price. Choosing stores is also complicated by changes resulting from scrambled merchandising and strategy shifts.

Scrambled merchandising
Diversifying the store's selection of products in order to increase sales volume.

Scrambled Merchandising Years ago, producers had an easier time identifying the right retailer for their product. People bought groceries at grocery stores, fabric at dry-goods stores, and medicine at pharmacies. However, this has changed over the past two decades because of scrambled merchandising. **Scrambled merchandising** consists of diversifying the store's selection of products in order to increase sales volume. For example, grocery stores became supermarkets, and many now offer a variety of drugs, toiletries, alcoholic beverages, small appliances, and more. This one-stop shopping concept has revitalized supermarket sales.[5] Today's average supermarket shopper is exposed to thousands of products, and large department stores sell not only clothing, appliances, and auto supplies but also services such as optical exams, hair styling, dry cleaning, and photocopying.

Strategy Shifts Besides adding merchandise, stores often adjust their marketing strategies over time. Like other businesses, many stores start out by attempting to establish a foothold with a low-price strategy. However, as they encounter competition and the market matures, these stores begin offering more services and upgraded products. For example, K mart originally

Modern supermarkets scramble merchandise by offering services and products unheard of a few years ago — banking, post office, video rental, photo lab, flowers, prescription drugs, shoe repair, and dry cleaning. Supermarket retailers are attempting to find the right combination of services, groceries, and non-food products to satisfy customers' demands for convenience and service and to increase sales volume.

Source: Courtesy of Wetterau Incorporated.

started as a low-price outlet, but in recent years has tried to upgrade its image and set itself apart from other low-price retailers by changing the decor of its stores.[6] In other cases, stores use special promotional strategies to differentiate their units from those of the competition. For example, Burger King stresses "having it your way" in their ads to differentiate their burgers from those of McDonald's. Another recent trend of retailers is to stress quality service. For example, some retailers have introduced computer robots that can help customers locate goods throughout the store while others have emphasized greatly improved personal service from their salesclerks.[7] Table 16.2 identifies some of the major customer turnoffs that service workers too often exhibit and that must be eliminated by a quality service strategy.

Types of Retail Stores

Not only is retailing changeable, but there are a wide variety of stores. Sometimes the types of stores overlap and the distinctions may be blurry. One way to understand the different types of retail stores is to divide them into categories by what they offer consumers: variety, specialty, and low price. Figure 16.5 illustrates the types of stores in each category.

Stores Offering Variety Some stores offer a variety of food and personal-care items; other stores offer a variety of more expensive goods. The broad selection attracts many customers from all walks of life. This makes the stores important for producers with a mass-merchandising strategy.

Most common today are **department stores,** which are relatively large and offer a wide variety of merchandise grouped into departments, such as housewares, electronic equipment, men's clothing, and cosmetics. These stores are popular because they allow the customer to do a great deal of shopping under one roof. Consequently, developers of shopping centers or malls try to get at least one department store such as J.C. Penney or Dillards to locate there and draw customers.

Department store A large store that offers a wide variety of merchandise grouped into departments.

TABLE 16.2
Customer Turnoffs Exhibited by
Service Workers

Apathy   This is an attitude that tells the customer the employee could not care less. One distinguishing feature is what comedian George Carlin calls the DILLIGAD look: the one that says, "Do I Look Like I Give A Damn?"

Brush-Off   This involves trying to get rid of the customer by brushing off his or her problem. The company tries to "slam dunk" the customer with some standard procedure that doesn't solve the problem but lets the employee off the hook for doing anything special.

Coldness   This is characterized by hostility, curtness, unfriendliness, thoughtlessness — any behavior that says to the customer, "You're a nuisance; please go away."

Condescension   This is a patronizing attitude toward the customer. Nurses, for instance, are notorious for this. They call the physician "Dr. Jones," but they call patients by their first names and talk to them as if they were 4 years old. They check the patient's blood pressure but don't believe he or she is intelligent or mature enough to be told the result: "Dr. Jones will tell you if he thinks you need to know."

Robotism   This is the unfocused stare, the pasted-on smile that tells you nobody's home upstairs. The employee puts every customer through the same routine, with no trace of warmth or individuality: "Thank-you-for-shopping-with-us-have-a-nice-day. Next."

Rulebook   In this case the employee is trapped by (or hiding behind) a set of company policies that leave no room for discretion in the name of customer satisfaction or even common sense. Any customer problem with more than one moving part confounds the system.

Runaround   "Sorry, you'll have to talk to so-and-so. We don't handle that here." This is the "not my job syndrome." The airlines have turned it into an art form. The ticket agent tells you the gate people will take care of it; the gate people tell you to see the ticket agent when you get to your destination; the agent at your destination tells you to talk to your travel agent.

Source: Ronald Zemke and Karl Albrecht, "Service Workers from You-Know-Where," *Training*, February 1990, 30.

Supermarket A large store that sells a wide variety of food products as well as some nonfood offerings.

Impulse items Goods that consumers buy on the spur of the moment.

People who want variety in food offerings shop at **supermarkets,** large stores that sell a wide variety of food products as well as some nonfood items. Unlike the original grocery stores, supermarkets operate on a self-service basis. They emphasize low price and customer convenience. Because the markup on food is so low, many have added nonfood items that have large markups, especially **impulse items,** which are goods that consumers buy on the spur of the moment, such as magazines, razor blades, and gum. One marketing research firm concludes that almost two-thirds of supermarket purchases are unplanned.[8] In recent years, supermarket managers have found that some of the most profitable products are those that offer freshness and convenience, so they have set up in-store bakeries, delis, and seafood counters.

Competition among supermarkets has become fierce. In response, some supermarkets try to differentiate themselves from their competitors by offering gourmet foods, check-cashing services, extended hours of operation, and free carryout service. In St. Louis, for example, Dierbergs Markets offer FTD florists, full-service banks, post offices, and videocassette rentals. The grocery chain was the first to provide motorized shopping carts for the handicapped. The store's managers have found that educating shoppers about food increases sales, so several of the stores have home economists on the premises

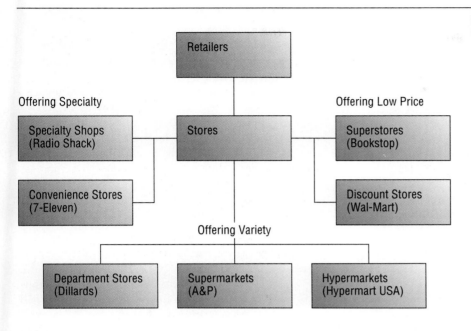

FIGURE 16.5
Major Types of Store Retailers

to answer shoppers' questions. Dierbergs also provides information through a quarterly newsletter titled "Customer Club News," demonstrations of recipes featuring in-season produce, and five cooking schools. According to Dierbergs' consumer services director, people who learn quick and easy methods of cooking will eat at home more.[9]

Taking the expansion of supermarkets one step further are **hypermarkets,** giant stores selling a combination of grocery items and general merchandise, from fresh shrimp to CDs. These stores, which originated in Europe a quarter-century ago, emphasize convenience because they offer so much under one roof. They are also able to offer low prices because their enormous size gives them bargaining leverage with suppliers. One French-based chain, Carrefour, even sells insurance through a subsidiary and other financial services as well. Wal-Mart has launched into the hypermarket concept, sometimes called "malls without walls." Their Hypermart USA is a combination discount store and supermarket in 200,000 or more square feet.

Stores Offering Specialty   Some stores target specific market segments by offering specialized goods or services such as high-fashion shoes, quality sound systems, or fast service. The targeted approach of these stores often makes them appropriate outlets for producers that want to maintain a quality image or reach customers with special interests.

An example of a retail outlet that specializes in fast service is a **convenience store.** Many of these stores sell only fast-moving merchandise such as bread, beer, milk, cigarettes, and snack foods. 7-Eleven and Kwik Shops are good examples. In recent years, gasoline retailers have begun to copy this approach by setting up stations that sell fast-moving grocery products in

Hypermarket A giant store selling a combination of groceries and general merchandise at low prices.

Convenience store A limited-line store that specializes in fast service.

addition to gasoline. This has led to trouble for traditional convenience store chains such as 7-Eleven and Circle K. However, others such as Stop N Go have met the challenge by changing the image of the convenience store using bright lights and decorative wooden shelves stuffed with trendy products such as fresh pasta, expensive wine, and Bart Simpson T-shirts.[10]

Many find specialty retailing an attractive way to start a business because it is suitable for small stores. However, to compete with the broad appeal of stores offering variety, specialized stores often have to use ingenuity to attract customers. Sunglass Huts, for example, locates its kiosks (a type of open booth) in the busy aisles of shopping malls or under mall escalators. Specially trained salespeople convince shoppers of the benefits of Sunglass Huts' quality sunglasses, which cost from $35 to $80 a pair. This strategy has paid off: At the oldest outlet, sales have run $5,200 per square foot — a retailing record.[11]

Stores Offering Low Prices   As you learned in Chapter 15, many companies adopt a marketing strategy emphasizing low price. This strategy is not limited to manufacturers; a variety of retail outlets feature a low-price strategy. Such stores are particularly suitable for products targeted to a broad segment of the population: customers interested in prices.

While many kinds of retailers can keep prices down, discount stores and catalog stores really focus on low price. A **discount store** is an outlet that offers lower prices and fewer customer services than other retail stores. When these stores first emerged, they limited their offerings to hard goods, such as radios, TVs, cameras, and typewriters. Today, they offer a wide variety of merchandise, including clothing, toys, sporting goods, office supplies, and home and garden supplies. K mart, Wal-Mart, and Home Depot, the very fast growing do-it-yourself home repair chain,[12] for example, offer a variety of products at low prices. Retailers such as the Texas-based Bookstop Inc. bookstore chain, an example of what are being called superstores, carry large inventories (Bookstop stores have three times the industry average) and feature low prices (all books are discounted up to 45 percent).[13]

Some stores keep prices down by storing most of their merchandise in a backroom warehouse, with only one sample of each item displayed in the showroom. Customers look through a catalog they receive in the mail or find in the showroom. They fill out an order form for the items they want, and employees fill the order from the backroom warehouse. This type of retail store is called a catalog showroom. These stores — such as Best Products and Service Merchandise — attract buyers willing to make a little extra effort in their shopping in exchange for lower prices.

Nonstore Retailing

Although most people associate retailing with stores, many retailers have found other effective ways to sell the consumers. Through mail, telephones, television, and other means, such retailers are able to reach consumers in their homes and workplaces. In many cases, nonstore retailing enables companies to focus their efforts on those consumers most likely to buy a particular product. Figure 16.6 shows the types and some examples of nonstore retailers.

Discount store   A retail store that offers lower prices and fewer customer services than other retailers.

Convenience stores like this SuperAmerica store in Lexington, Kentucky, stock grocery, delicatessen, and snack foods. SuperAmerica differentiates itself from competitors by offering a larger, broader mix of items and tailoring each store's inventory to local buying habits.

Source: Courtesy of Ashland Oil Inc.

A company can achieve a personal touch by using **door-to-door retailers,** salespeople who sell products house to house. While this used to be a popular retail channel, the high costs associated with direct selling have led many companies such as Fuller Brush to look for alternatives. However, door-to-door retailers still sell vacuum cleaners and encyclopedias in this fashion, and go into people's homes to sell Avon and Amway products and Tupperware.

Many companies find that selling through the mail is a more efficient way to approach customers. A **mail-order house** is a merchandiser that sells goods through a mail-order catalog. Sears is still the leading mail-order retailer in the United States. Others such as Lands' End, which became very popular in the 1980s because of their quality and service, have recently showed signs of some problems.[14] For companies that also operate stores, items in catalogs generally carry lower prices than the same merchandise sold in the company's store. Mail-order retailing is a popular way to start retail selling, because the seller avoids the expense of setting up a store. Taking the lead of mail-order merchandisers, even some banks such as Bank of America and insurance companies are beginning to use catalogs to sell their financial services. The approach is also being used, as seen in the accompanying International Close-Up (Cracking the Japanese Market), to enter overseas markets.

Companies selling impulse items often use **vending machines,** mechanical retail outlets that store products and dispense them directly to customers. The vending machine makes products conveniently available to customers at a low cost to the seller. Typical vended goods include candy, cigarettes, coffee, and stamps. Some units are even dispensing videos, fresh-cooked French fries, capuccino, and pizza. Jukeboxes, pinball machines, and automatic teller machines are vending machines that dispense services. Vending machines are located in facilities such as hotel lobbies, airports, service stations, and company cafeterias.

A relatively new approach to nonstore retailing involves selling products by displaying them on cable television, along with a toll-free number for viewers to call and place an order. This type of retailing, called home shopping or teleshopping, combines the convenience of door-to-door selling with the great efficiency of catalog selling. One of the major teleshopping retailers is Home Shopping Network (HSN), which sends out a wide variety of merchandise from liquidators and overseas manufacturers at tantalizing prices. Lured by HSN's success, operators of traditional retail stores, such as J.C. Penney and Sears, are getting involved in the home-shopping trend.

Trends in Retailing

A number of trends reflect retailer efforts to differentiate themselves, as seen in the Innovation Close-Up (Holding Their Own with the Retailing Giants). These developments include citylike complexes, vertical shopping malls, theme plazas, drop-in professional clinics, and greater use of direct channels.

Citylike Complexes Consumers have traditionally traveled some distance from their home to get to work and to go shopping. However, they now have a new alternative with the emergence of citylike complexes, which typically contain apartments and condominiums, business offices, and facilities for shopping and entertainment. Today these complexes exist in all parts of the

Door-to-door retailer
A salesperson who sells products house to house.

Mail-order house A retailer that sells goods through a mail-order catalog.

Vending machine A mechanical retail outlet that stores products and dispenses them directly to customers.

FIGURE 16.6
Major Types of Nonstore Retailers

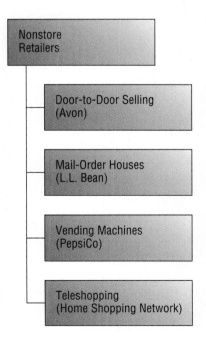

CLOSE-UP / *International*

Cracking the Japanese Market

Many U.S. retailers are finding it hard to break into the Japanese market. However, Vernon Fraenkel of Shop America Ltd. has discovered a way around some of the significant barriers to entry. In particular, he has put together a Japanese-language mail-order catalog that will be distributed through 7-Eleven Japan Co. This is a good place to have his catalogs because there are 4 million customers who visit 7-Eleven's 4,000 stores daily in Japan. But will the Japanese buy from Fraenkel's catalogs? One of the major reasons why they are likely to do so is that Fraenkel's catalog prices are much lower than that of the average Tokyo retail store. Examples shown on the right.

This is not the first time that someone has tried to invade the Japanese market with a mail-order catalog strategy; and there are a number of problems that have to be resolved. A major one is that of making timely delivery. Fraenkel's strategy is to have 7-Eleven clerks send orders directly from the store to his company's home office in New York by simply waving a scanner over bar codes in the catalog. In turn, Shop America will have the goods shipped directly to Japan. Initial plans call for delivery of merchandise within 2 weeks, and this has been a problem

Product	Average Tokyo Retail Price	Catalog Price
Audio cassette	$11–14	$6–8
Auto-Reverse Walkman	70	50
Canon Autoboy camera	260	180
Chanel No. 5 (½ oz.) perfume	153	85
Lady Remington shaver	86	46
Rolex watch	4,857	3,078

for many firms that have attempted to break into the Japanese market with a mail-order strategy.

A second problem will be getting Japanese customers to buy high-priced items through a mail-order catalog. For example, how much demand will there be for a Rolex watch? Are the customers who have an interest in these expensive watches the same ones who frequent 7-Eleven stores? The answers to these types of questions will help determine the success of Fraenkel's strategy. Yet, whatever happens, it is likely that mail-order retailers will continue to try to crack the huge, largely untapped, Japanese market.

Source: Ted Holden, "Can This Catalog Company Crack the Japanese Marketing Maze?" *Business Week*, March 19, 1990, 60.

country. They allow residents to meet most of their needs within one high-rise building or series of large interconnected buildings. Examples include the Renaissance Center in Detroit, the Broadway Plaza in Los Angeles, the Crown Center in Kansas City, and the Venetia in Miami.

Vertical Shopping Malls With land becoming more expensive, some developers are building shopping malls tall rather than wide. In some cases, they are including these malls in the citylike complexes just described. Sometimes, vertical malls are built into landmark buildings, such as the Jax brewery in New Orleans.

Theme Plazas Small, outdoor shopping centers often take on themes. Rather than lease the units to anyone who is willing to pay the rent, developers can match the businesses with a central theme. In one plaza, there may be a certain ethnic theme such as Hispanic or Greek that features restaurants, food, and clothing stores. In another, there may be a wellness theme featuring a health-food store, a spa, a sporting goods store, and an exercise equipment retailer. As seen in the Innovation Close-Up (Pulling Them In), Tyson's Corner has been very successful with this type of strategy.

CLOSE-UP / *Innovation*

Holding Their Own with the Retailing Giants

Large retailers such as Sears, K-Mart, and Wal-Mart can offer vigorous competition to small companies and, in many cases, drive them from the marketplace. However, successful regional retailers are learning that they can hold their own against these giants if they follow some basic retailing strategies. One approach that has been successful for small retailers has been to look closely at what the large competitors are doing, and searching for a weak link or opening where the big chains are vulnerable.

After doing this, Family Dollar Stores of North Carolina felt that they could beat the big retailers in the area of convenience to local customers. Family Dollar's units are typically within three miles of shoppers' homes. In contrast, many of the giant retailers such as K-Mart and Wal-Mart like to set up stores on the outskirts of a town where land for building giant facilities is cheap and they can draw from a large geographic area. Most of Family Dollar's customers are local people who do not have cars or do not like to travel very far to shop. A nearby store is attractive to them. Additionally, the average household income of Dollar's customers is under $25,000, so their stores emphasize low price.

Another good example of regional retailing strategy is provided by ShopKo, a discount chain with over 100 stores from Michigan to Washington. ShopKo went after some market voids, by becoming one of the first discounters to offer eye exams and to sell eyeglasses. ShopKo was also one of the first retailers to start filling prescriptions. Today, optical and pharmaceutical services account for more than 15 percent of ShopKo's revenues and 30 percent of its earnings.

Still another example is provided by Venture, a midwest discounter that used to be part of the May Department Stores chain. Venture created for itself a market identification with higher-margin, soft-line items. Today, 40 percent of Venture's sales come from fashion-oriented merchandise at low prices. The large discounters do not try to attract this end of the market, so Venture is able to sidestep competitors who have not pursued this market niche.

As Wal Mart and other giants of the retail industry continue to grow rapidly and increase market share, more and more regional and smaller retailers are going to come under attack. However, those who carefully follow retailing trends will find that they are able to hold their own by continually sidestepping direct competition with the giants.

Source: Mary Beth Grover, "Tornado Watch," *Forbes*, June 22, 1992, pp. 66–73.

Convenient Professional Services Drop-in professional clinics, where no appointment is necessary, are becoming popular. These facilities may bring together lawyers, accountants, and financial planners to handle basic financial and legal matters, such as planning a retirement fund or drawing up a will. In medical facilities, dentists and doctors of various specialties can conduct tests and carry out minor surgery within a few hours and without an appointment. The cost of these services is often lower than in a traditional office, because the professionals share expenses for the facility and administrative work.

Direct Channels More and more manufacturing firms are opening their own retail outlets. By eliminating the expenses of intermediaries, the manufacturer may be able to pass some cost savings on to the consumer and reap greater profits. In recent years, Tandy, Xerox, and Texas Instruments have done this. Other manufacturers, especially in the clothing business, are opening factory outlet stores. These factory outlets are usually located in smaller towns a short distance from large cities so they do not directly compete with their regular retailers. For example, Formfit Rogers has a factory outlet selling women's intimate apparel and sportswear in Nebraska City, Nebraska (located between Omaha and Kansas City). The cities of Freeport, Maine (a couple of hours north of Boston), and Reading, Pennsylvania (a few

A new concept from Pearle is EyeBuys stores, which offer a huge selection of eyeglass frames. For some time Pearle Vision Centers and competitors have offered complete eye care products and services on a drop-in basis. They were forerunners of the new drop-in professional clinics of physicians, dentists, lawyers, and accountants.

Source: Reproduced by permission of Grand Metropolitan PLC.

hours outside of Philadelphia), each have numerous factory outlets. The outlets do not advertise in the media (again, so they do not appear to compete with their retailers), but tell you upon entering that the merchandise is highly discounted.

CHECK ✓ POINT

1. Name three types of retail stores.
2. How can retailers sell products without opening a store?

Physical Distribution

When they have decided on distribution channels, marketers of tangible products still have to figure out how to move the goods physically through the channels to the users. The activities necessary to move goods from the producer to the final user are known collectively as **physical distribution.** These activities, illustrated in Figure 16.7, are order processing, inventory management, packaging and materials handling, warehousing, and transporting.

Physical distribution The activities necessary to move goods from the producer to the final user.

Order Processing

Before the company can ship goods to customers, it must be determined what they want. Therefore, the manager sets up a system for **order processing.** This involves taking sales orders, checking them, and then seeing that the product is shipped to the customer. Employees accomplish these tasks through some combination of face-to-face communication, telephone conversations, memos, and letters. For example, employees at L. L. Bean, the highly successful general store that specializes in outdoor clothing and equipment, process mail-order forms worth millions per year and take thousands of telephone orders a day. These employees ensure that each order is filled and shipped as specified. To prepare them for this important task, L. L. Bean provides 40 hours of training before the employees take their first order. Many firms rely increasingly on computers to help them carry out this order processing function.

Order processing Taking sales orders, checking them, and then seeing that the product is shipped to the customer.

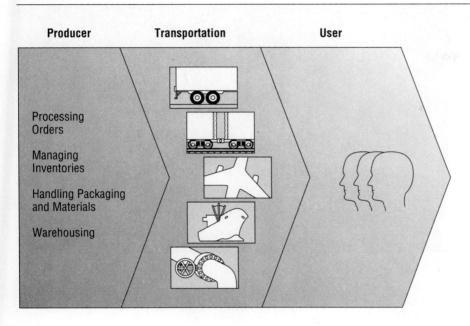

FIGURE 16.7
Physical Distribution

Inventory Management

To be able to fill orders, the company needs an inventory of finished goods. However, carrying extra inventory may be unnecessarily expensive. To resolve this conflict, effective firms use **inventory management,** which involves efficiently balancing inventory with sales orders. Ideally, the company should have a lot of inventory on hand just before its peak selling season and little on hand during its slowest selling season. This requires that inventory managers study previous consumer buying habits, evaluate the firm's current promotional efforts, and forecast economic conditions.

Inventory management
Efficiently balancing inventory with sales orders.

Packaging and Materials Handling

Whether or not the order was processed and filled promptly, the customer will be upset if it arrives damaged. Such mistakes are costly to the seller and the buyer. Therefore, physical distribution also involves ensuring the goods are properly packaged so that they are not damaged in the warehouse or in transit. Packaging experts decide what materials the package should be made of and whether the goods should be placed in individual packages, large boxes, or sealed containers.

Protecting the goods also involves **materials handling,** overseeing the movement of goods within the company's facilities. This includes moving finished goods directly from the production line to the shipping dock or to the warehouse and then, at some later time, to the shipping dock.

Materials handling Overseeing the movement of goods within the company's facilities.

Warehousing

While the company theoretically could avoid inventory costs by transporting goods directly to the customer, this is often impossible or impractical. To get

Airborne Express, in the business of providing overnight, before-noon delivery of customers' packages, has added a warehousing service to speed up deliveries even further. Airborne customers can keep inventories of fast-moving items in a new distribution center adjacent to the Airborne hub at Wilmington, Ohio, for immediate dispatch anywhere in the world. Airborne manages the process, ensuring that sufficient inventory is on hand.

Source: Courtesy of Airborne Express.

Warehousing Storing goods until they are ready to be shipped.

Private warehouse A storage facility owned or leased by the company whose goods it stores.

Public warehouse A public storage facility whose owner is not the company storing goods there.

a head start on meeting orders, most companies produce goods in advance. They warehouse the products, make arrangements for shipment, and send the goods so that they reach the customer on the desired delivery date. The storing of goods until they are ready to be shipped is called **warehousing.**

A company's size influences its choice of a warehouse. Large firms use a **private warehouse,** which is a storage facility owned or leased by the company. If the amount of inventory is too great or the firm has no private warehouse, it typically rents space in a **public warehouse,** which is a public storage facility owned by someone outside the company.

Transporting Goods

The transportation of goods from the warehouse to the customer lies at the heart of physical distribution. Transportation is the largest single expense associated with the distribution of most goods. Managing the transportation of goods starts with selecting a carrier. To do this, the manager must match the company's needs and resources with the types of carriers and modes of transportation available.

Common carrier
A transportation company that performs services within a particular line of business for the general public.

Companies that need relatively few special services and want to minimize cost often use a **common carrier.** This type of transportation company performs transportation services within a particular line of business for the general public. For example, United Airlines flies people and certain types of freight on its many routes. The Union Pacific Railroad carries freight along its rails. These companies follow timetables, so a company that wants to use them must have the goods ready on time. Similarly, a trucker for a common carrier starts out with a list of stops. The company wanting to transport goods must wait for the trucker to come around.

Contract carrier
A transportation company that performs services called for by an individual contract.

Companies that prefer to pay for special service might turn to a **contract carrier.** Such a company performs transportation services called for by an individual contract. The carrier works exclusively for a particular customer; when the contract is completed, the carrier moves on to another job. Most contract carriers are in the trucking business, where the truckers may own their own rig and work on a "for hire" basis.

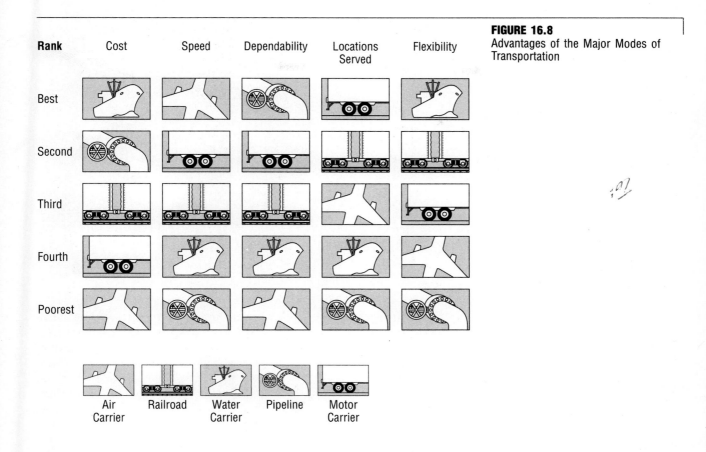

FIGURE 16.8
Advantages of the Major Modes of Transportation

Sometimes a company ships in such volume that it finds a **private carrier** to be most efficient. This type of carrier is owned by the company whose goods it transports. For example, Exxon owns oil tankers, and Safeway owns delivery trucks. This arrangement requires a substantial investment in equipment and wages but gives companies the greatest control over transportation practices.

Companies with small shipments may turn to a **freight forwarder.** This is a common carrier that leases or contracts space from other carriers and resells it to small-volume shippers. Freight forwarders do not own any of the transportation equipment that hauls the merchandise. They simply pick up the goods from the shipper, see that these goods are loaded on the carrier and transported to their destination, and take care of all the billing involved. Freight forwarders help small shippers by selling them space on common carriers such as ships or airplanes. They also help common carriers by taking care of all the minor details associated with small shipments.

Private carrier A transportation company owned by the company whose goods it transports.

Freight forwarder A common carrier that leases or contracts space from other carriers and resells it to small-volume shippers.

Transportation Modes

Managers must also select an appropriate mode of transportation. The options include railroads, trucks, water carriers, pipelines, and air carriers. Figure 16.8 compares the advantages of these five modes.

FIGURE 16.9
Domestic Freight Traffic by Major
Carriers (in billions of ton-miles)

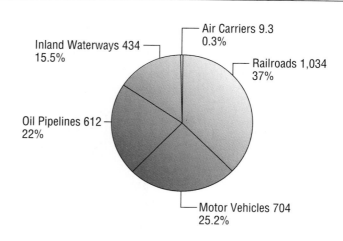

The two biggest questions marketers must answer in deciding what transportation modes to use are how quickly must the goods be delivered, and how much will it cost. After balancing the time and expense involved, the company selects the modes it will use.

Railroads   As shown in Figure 16.9, the railroads carry more freight than any other transportation mode. They are particularly cost-effective in transporting bulk commodities over long distances. In recent years, the railroads have responded to vigorous competition from motor carriers by introducing a number of new services, including the following:

Piggyback service The shipment of a fully loaded truck trailer on a specially designed railroad flatcar.

- **Piggyback service,** which involves the shipment of a fully loaded truck trailer on a specially designed flatcar. The merchandise does not have to be taken out of the truck, loaded into a railroad car, and then reloaded into a truck at the final destination. The simplicity of this arrangement greatly reduces shipping costs.

Fast freight The rapid conveyance of perishable goods by train.

- **Fast freight,** which is the rapid conveyance of perishable goods. The train bypasses congested freight yards, stays on the main track, and races great distances in delivering the goods rapidly. This gives railroad companies an edge in competing for business when speed is important.

In-transit privileges Permission to stop a train shipment along the way in order to perform a function and then continue the shipment.

- **In-transit privileges,** which allow shippers to stop a shipment along the way in order to perform a function such as an assembly task on the product being transported and then continue the shipment.

Motor Carriers   Motor carriers—almost always trucks—account for about a quarter of all domestically shipped freight. These vehicles are efficient for moving small shipments over short distances. Trucks are flexible and can operate anywhere there is a road. For shipments traveling less than a few hundred miles, trucks are almost always cheaper than the railroad.

Economic and political forces are keeping trucking rates down. In recent years, the trucking industry has been deregulated. This, combined with the

The *S.S. Maui* approaches Honolulu harbor carrying containerized cargo such as construction materials, dry and refrigerated foodstuffs, and paper products. Matson Navigation Company, which owns the *Maui,* is the principal carrier of containerized goods and automobiles from West Coast ports to Hawaii. The State of Hawaii relies on ocean transportation to bring many goods that can be delivered by truck or train to other states.

Source: Alexander & Baldwin, Inc., 1989 annual report.

fact that many of the common carriers are independents who own their own rig and trailer, means that prices have become extremely competitive. Some firms have further cut costs by using truck transportation to cut out intermediaries by delivering goods directly to the final consumer.

Water Transportation Transporting by water is an inexpensive way of shipping goods. However, it is also a slow way of getting the goods to their destination. The two most common forms of water carriers are inland or barge lines and deep-water, ocean-going vessels. Barges work the Great Lakes, major rivers, and inland canals across the country. Ocean-going vessels also operate on the Great Lakes and between port cities of the United States and other nations.

Pipelines Transportation via pipelines is primarily used to carry oil and natural gas. A good example is the Alaskan pipeline, which carries crude oil from the north slope of Alaska to the southern Alaskan city of Valdez, where it is loaded on tankers and transported to oil refineries. Pipelines are one of the lowest-cost forms of transportation, but can handle only limited types of products.

Air Carriers Air transportation is the fastest mode now available. It is also the most expensive. Therefore, companies tend to use air carriers only when speed far outweighs cost considerations. For example, air carriers transport millions of tons of mail that must be delivered overnight or within a few days. However, as Figure 16.9 shows, air carriers handle less than 1 percent of all freight.

Combined Modes Not all products are distributed by a single mode of transportation. Often a company uses two or more modes. For example, Alaskan crude oil is carried by pipeline and then by oil tanker to the refinery. Goods arriving at a seaport are typically transferred to a motor carrier and then, perhaps, to a railroad. Trains may deliver goods to the buyer's factory, but often a motor carrier picks up the freight at a railroad terminal and delivers it to the buyer. In fact, some railroads have their own trucking line. Motor carriers complement air carriers in a similar fashion. The ability to combine transportation modes gives marketers great flexibility in moving goods to their customers.

CHECK ✓ POINT

1. What are the five basic modes of transportation?
2. Besides transportation, what do marketers have to plan for in arranging physical distribution?

Closing Comments

The way a company distributes its product can make the difference between marketing success and failure. This chapter explained how companies manage this important function, from choosing marketing channels to planning a means of physical distribution. Often producers turn to intermediaries — wholesalers and retailers — for help in carrying out these activities. Consequently, wholesaling and retailing are an important and growing part of American business.

VIDEO CASE / Big Winners, Big Losers

Some of the most profitable firms in America are those that move manufactured products through the marketing channel. Cesar Viramontes's Economy Laundry is a good example. This $13-million-a-year business draws the bulk of its revenue from stone washing jeans for Levi Strauss and then removing stains, pressing, sorting by size, tagging, packaging, and shipping the goods to retailers.

Another success story is Home Depot, the largest chain selling do-it-yourself products for the home. The salespeople in the stores are well versed in how to use the products. For example, if a customer is thinking of putting up a stockade fence in his or her yard, a Home Depot salesperson can explain how many sections to order, the kinds of posts that will be needed for the fence, and even the size of nails to use. There are people in every store that can guide the customer through the project before he or she ever digs a hole or drives a nail. Besides helpful salespeople, Home Depot also offers low prices.

Perhaps the major reason Home Depot is doing so well, however, is that it has not been tempted to get into a variety of product lines. It focuses on do-it-yourself home-related products.

Even though more than half of the 50,000 people who walk through Home Depot stores every week are women, the chain refuses to sell pantyhose. Nor will it offer food or toys, because management believes this will confuse the Home Depot image in the mind of the customer. It has not fallen into the trap that Sears did during the 1980s and for which it paid dearly in terms of customer loyalty. A major reason people no longer shop as often at Sears seems to be because they do not understand the type of merchandise the company is carrying; product lines became too diverse and changed too often. How well has Home Depot's retail strategy paid off? The company has gone from $22 million in sales to over $3 billion in 10 years.

Another success story is that of J.C. Penney, one of the few old-line firms still doing well in the retail industry. The company has upgraded its merchandise and now carries high-grade, national brand apparel. In addition, it has turned to high tech to keep its stores up-to-date on merchandise offerings. Several times a week buyers in all of its metropolitan stores can tune into direct satellite broadcasts from headquarters in Dallas. If merchandise managers see a product offering that they think will sell well, they can order up a few samples from manufacturers and show that selection via satellite to buyers throughout the country. The buyers can then place their orders and have the merchandise in the store within days. When Sears was starting to limp along with anemic profits, J.C. Penney going into the 1990s was reporting annual profits of over $800 million on sales of $16.4 billion. Like successful upstarts such as Viramontes's Economy Laundry, old-line companies such as J.C. Penney realize that the times require a strategy that is highly marketing focused.

Source: Susan Caminiti, "The New Champs of Retailing," *Fortune*, September 24, 1990, 85–100.

Case Questions

1. What type of physical distribution services does Economy Laundry perform? Why does Levi Strauss not do this itself?
2. Why has J.C. Penney done so well in recent years while its major competitor, Sears, has not? How has J.C. Penney sidestepped some of the major retailing pitfalls?

Learning Objectives Revisited

1. **Define the nature and types of channels of distribution.** The channel of distribution is the route that goods take in moving from producer to user. Different channels are used for industrial goods and consumer goods. Industrial goods commonly move through direct channels or through wholesalers. Consumer goods take one of three different routes: through direct channels, through retailers, or through both wholesalers and retailers.

2. **Explain the benefits of using wholesalers.** Manufacturers benefit because wholesalers can take inventory off the producer's hands, assume the risk associated with carrying inventory, provide a sales force, and provide marketing information and support. Retailers and industrial customers benefit because wholesalers can break bulk for them, provide better credit terms, and provide marketing information.

3. **Identify the types of wholesalers.** Merchant wholesalers are intermediaries that take title to the goods. These wholesalers may provide a variety of services or carry out only some of them. Manufacturer-owned wholesalers handle the wholesale function for the parent company. Agent intermediaries are wholesalers that do not take title to the goods. For example, brokers specialize in bringing together buyers and sellers.

4. **Describe the types of retailers.** Retail stores that offer variety include department stores, supermarkets, and hypermarkets. Stores that offer specialization include convenience stores. Stores offering low price include discount stores and catalog showrooms. Nonstore retailing includes door-to-door retailers, mail-order houses, vending machines, and teleshopping.

5. **Discuss the nature and functions of physical distribution.** Physical distribution consists of the activities necessary to move goods from the producer to the final user: order processing (taking sales orders, checking them, and seeing that the product is shipped to the customer); inventory management (the efficient balancing of inventory with sales orders); packaging and materials handling (packaging the goods properly and moving them within the company's facilities); warehousing (storing the goods until they are ready to be shipped); and transporting goods (moving the goods from the company's warehouse to the customer).

6. **Present the major modes of transportation.** The five major modes of transportation used to convey goods through the distribution channel are railroads, motor carriers, water carriers, pipelines, and air carriers. Railroads are particularly cost effective when shipping goods long distances and offer many special privileges, such as piggyback service, to shippers. Motor carriers are often the most efficient mode when shipping goods short distances. Water carriers are an inexpensive, but slow, way to move goods over great distances. Pipelines are highly efficient in transporting certain products, such as petroleum. Air carriers are a good choice when speed, not cost, is of the essence.

Key Terms Reviewed

Review each of the following terms. For any that you do not know or are unsure of, look up the definitions and see how they were used in the chapter.

channel of distribution
wholesaler
retailer
direct channel
exclusive distribution
selective distribution
intensive distribution
vertical marketing system
  (VMS)
merchant wholesalers
agent intermediaries
broker

scrambled merchandising
department store
supermarket
impulse items
hypermarket
convenience store
discount store
door-to-door retailer
mail-order house
vending machine
physical distribution
order processing

inventory management
materials handling
warehousing
private warehouse
public warehouse
common carrier
contract carrier
private carrier
freight forwarder
piggyback service
fast freight
in-transit privileges

Review Questions

1. What is a channel of distribution? How would the channel used to sell mainframe computers be different from the one used to sell personal computers?
2. What do producers consider when deciding on the appropriate type of distribution channel?
3. What is a vertical marketing system? Why would some companies use this system?
4. Sam Tobias is setting up a new company, Tobias Restaurant Supply, which will sell huge ovens and refrigerators to restaurants. Sam figures he can keep more of the profits if he doesn't use wholesalers, but he wonders whether wholesalers might benefit him in the long run. How might wholesalers benefit Sam's business?
5. What type of wholesaler provides the widest variety of services?
6. Francine Quinn wants to sell a parcel of land to a developer. She thinks it is in an ideal location for development as a shopping mall. What kind of wholesaler will be interested in helping Francine sell the land? Describe this type of intermediary.
7. Why are retailers hard to classify?
8. Identify and describe types of retailers that appeal to a broad cross-section of consumers. Why did you select each?
9. What kind of retail outlets would a publisher of college textbooks use? Why?
10. How are some retail outlets able to offer consistently lower prices?
11. What are some ways in which retailers sell to consumers without using a store?
12. Green Lawn Mowers sells its products through hardware stores nationwide. What physical distribution activities does this involve? Briefly describe each.
13. Which modes of transportation do you think would be most appropriate for Green Lawn Mowers (Question 12)? Why?
14. Why do you think United Parcel Service (UPS) owns its own trucks, while some manufacturers ship through common carriers?

Applied Exercise

For each of the following 10 situations, one mode of transportation is preferable or should be the primary choice. Indicate which one by entering the appropriate letter from this list:

A = Air carrier
M = Motor carrier
P = Pipeline
R = Railroad
W = Water carrier

___ 1. Gas must be transported as dependably as possible over a distance of 1,300 miles.
___ 2. Four giant grain combines must be shipped from Chicago to Omaha.
___ 3. Speed is of the essence because an organ for a transplant must be delivered to a hospital 250 miles away, but all air flights have been grounded due to bad weather.
___ 4. A large volume of coal must be shipped from Minnesota to Louisiana as cheaply as possible.
___ 5. A package must be shipped across country within 24 hours.
___ 6. Ten thousand new cars must be shipped to Europe within the next 2 weeks.
___ 7. Five hundred tons of iron ore must be transported from Duluth, Minnesota, to Gary, Indiana.
___ 8. One box of toys must be delivered to each of 15 different locales within a 10-mile radius before the close of business today.
___ 9. A small gift purchased in New York City must be delivered in Anchorage, Alaska, by late tomorrow afternoon.
___ 10. A large quantity of crude oil must be shipped from the coast to a refinery 1,000 miles in the interior.

A large company headquartered in the central United States is famous for its high-quality industrial machinery. The firm manufactures this machinery on a to-order basis. This means that when a customer places an order, the firm builds the machine to the client's specifications.

Over the past 5 years, the company has concluded that it needs to expand its customer base and start selling more products. As a result, it bought a firm that makes gourmet foods and another that manufactures pastas, sauces, and related products. The company then acquired a firm that produces snack foods. Next, it purchased a company that makes office equipment, including file cabinets, metal desks and chairs, and related accessories. More recently, it acquired a firm that manufactures high-quality electric lawn mowers (both riding and nonriding types). At the same time, the corporation has decided to complement its to-order approach to producing machinery by manufacturing and selling some selected types of machinery through a newly created sales force. These latest developments promise to make the firm twice as large as it was 5 years ago.

The president of the company would like to attain some coordination among these new acquisitions in terms of distribution channels. For example, where possible he would like to use the same channels to move goods to the customer. "If we are selling a number of different types of food, we have a host of different market niches, but we can reach these people by using the same distribution channel. The same is true of other products we ship to our customers," he explained to one of his major stockholders. "For example, our gourmet foods, pastas, and snack foods all use the same channel. So despite the fact that we have a number of different product lines, distribution channels for many of them will be the same."

Your Advice

1. What should the president do?
    ___ a. Forget the idea of looking for similar distribution channels because the products are too diverse.
    ___ b. Focus on the current objective of looking for marketing channel similarities and try to spin these off into money-saving decisions.
    ___ c. Allow each product line to use its current distribution channels, but negotiate hard with the carriers in order to get the lowest possible price.
2. Through what marketing channels would you recommend the company market its gourmet foods? Its pasta products? Its snack foods? In each case, explain your answer.
3. What marketing channels would you recommend for the office equipment line? The lawn mowers? Why?
4. How would you recommend that the firm market the industrial machinery that it is going to sell through its newly created sales force? Why?

AN AUTHENTIC ITALIAN RESTAURANT WHERE NO ONE'S BEEN SHOT.

YET

Positano
250 Park Avenue South
NYC
212 777 6211

A COUPLE OF WILD AND CRAZY GUYS

The number of advertising agencies has been increasing. A reason for this growth is that young, creative advertising people are breaking away from the large, established firms and starting their own agencies. Unshackled by years of doing things in one particular way, these upstart advertising experts are often able to offer their clients more creative approaches to promote products and services.

A good example of a new, young ad agency is Kirshenbaum & Bond (K&B). When they started their

Promotional Strategies

Chapter Learning Objectives

- Define advertising and its basic types.

- Identify the various advertising media.

- Explain how marketers analyze the effectiveness of advertising.

- Describe the types and process of personal selling.

- Discuss the basic techniques of sales promotion.

- Relate the roles that publicity and public relations play in promotion.

agency a few years ago, Richard Kirshenbaum was 24 years old and Jonathan Bond was 28. Hiring other young, talented, and highly creative people (one skateboarding employee smacked into a visiting client), K&B managed to garner over $25 million in billings within the first 3 years. The two founders are so young and brash that they are known as "ad brats" by some of their older, more experienced competitors. This doesn't bother Richard and Jonathan, who believe that their fresh approach to advertising is just what is needed. A typical Kirshenbaum piece of work is

an ad for an Italian restaurant riddled with mock bullet holes. They have already won Clio awards for their advertising, and have attracted large accounts such as Hennessy Cognac which indicates that they are on the right track.

K&B still has a long way to go if it hopes to match the billings of advertising giants such as Saatchi & Saatchi, which has worldwide offices and billings in excess of $16.1 billion, or the network of Interpublic Agencies with $10 billion in billings. However, for the moment K&B is content to remain small and pick its

clients carefully. It gives each client personal attention and plays an active role in identifying and developing the promotional strategy. Clients like to be able to talk directly to the top people in an agency and spell out their ideas regarding who will buy their product or service and how they would like it portrayed in an advertising campaign. Not only do clients like the personal involvement, but it also provides some direction and sense to Richard and Jonathan's "wild and crazy" ideas.

Photo source: Courtesy of Kirshenbaum & Bond.

Introduction

Unless customers know about a product and its benefits, all of the product design and pricing strategies in the world would go to waste. Consequently, this chapter focuses on promotional strategy as part of the marketing mix. Applied to marketing, the term promotion means moving or selling products and services. Promotion may involve a variety of marketing activities, ranging from selling products face-to-face (personal selling) to nonpersonal efforts such as advertising and publicity.

Overall Strategy

Before a company starts promoting a product or service, the managers must decide on an overall strategy for doing so. They consider what they want the promotion to accomplish, whom they want to reach, and the nature of the product or service they are selling. They also evaluate the various methods of promotion in order to decide which will best accomplish their objectives.

Objectives for Promotion

Promotion is not an end in itself; it is used as a tool to achieve marketing and company objectives. If the company has an effective procedure for setting goals, the manager will have a clear sense of what the promotion is intended to achieve. (Chapter 11 described procedures for goal setting.) Typical goals are achieving a certain profit level or attaining a particular market share (the percentage of all product buyers that buys the company's product).

In deciding how to achieve goals, the marketer takes into account the nature of the product or service. If it is radically new, the promotion will probably have to explain to potential buyers what it is and why they would want it. If the product or service has many competitors, the promotion will have to give potential buyers reasons to prefer the company's brand or approach to a service. For a complex product, buyers may need visual information to help them understand it. Buyers of an expensive product or service may be hesitant to make a commitment without the influence of a personalized approach.

Likewise, marketers consider the nature of the target market. Approaches that are suitable for a consumer market may be ineffective with an industrial market. For example, the percentage of people viewing the evening news who might buy an industrial robot would be very small; thus a TV ad would be an expensive way to reach customers of industrial robots. By the same token, private banks have recently learned that direct mail and magazine advertising are effective ways to draw in customers.[1]

Sometimes marketers promote to an industrial market consisting of their wholesalers or retailers. In this case, they are using a pushing strategy — they are trying to make wholesalers and retailers want to sell their product and therefore push consumers to buy it. For example, when GM offers special quantity discounts to its dealers, this is a push strategy.

Marketers can also use the opposite approach: they can convince consumers to ask retailers to stock the product. This strategy, called a pulling

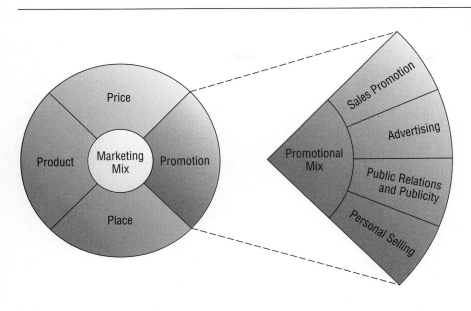

FIGURE 17.1
The Promotional Mix

strategy, is intended to get retailers to order more of the product. When GM announces a rebate to customers on new car purchases, this is a pull strategy to get the dealers to order more inventory to meet their customer demand.

Marketers also need to know whether people in their target market read a lot and, if so, what publications. Do they watch television a lot? Do they drive to work or ride public transit? Do they buy on the basis of facts or the way the product makes them feel? Answers to such questions help marketers decide what to say and what methods to use.

The Promotional Mix

When marketers select the methods through which they promote their products or services, they are planning a promotional mix. This mix consists of the types of promotion available to marketers. Figure 17.1 illustrates the elements of the promotional mix and the relationship of the promotional mix to the marketing mix.

The elements of the promotional mix are advertising, personal selling, sales promotion, and publicity and public relations. The marketer selects which elements to use based on how well they help the company achieve its objectives. Most companies use sales promotion, publicity, and public relations to supplement their advertising and personal selling efforts. The rest of this chapter describes some of the information marketers consider in developing an overall strategy and implementing specific promotional techniques.

CHECK ✓ POINT

1. What is the difference between a pushing promotional strategy and a pulling strategy?
2. What are the elements of the promotional mix?

TABLE 17.1
Ten Leading Advertisers

		U.S. Ad Spending in 1989 (millions)	U.S. Sales/Ad Dollar
1	Philip Morris	$2,072.0	$15.07
2	Procter & Gamble	1,779.3	8.41
3	Sears, Roebuck	1,432.1	37.56
4	General Motors	1,363.8	68.84
5	Grand Metropolitan	823.3	7.57
6	PepsiCo	786.1	15.93
7	McDonald's	774.4	5.07
8	Eastman Kodak	718.8	15.12
9	RJR Nabisco	703.5	N/A
10	Kellogg	611.6	4.81

Advertising Age, Special Edition: 100 Leading National Advertisers 1989 Edition, September 26, 1990, 6.

Advertising

Advertising   A nonpersonal form of promotion in which a firm attempts to persuade someone to a particular point of view.

For most companies, the focus of the promotional effort is **advertising,** which is used both to maintain[2] and to increase market share.[3] Advertising can be defined as a nonpersonal form of promotion in which a firm attempts to persuade someone to a particular point of view. It is so much a part of our culture that it literally affects the way we think and talk. For example, as a result of product advertising, just about every American understands and associates an image with the following words: Pepsi, Mickey Mouse, Pontiac, and Xerox. Some brands are even part of the vocabulary of foreign countries. In South America, for example, Raton Miqueto (Mickey Mouse) is familiar to every child. Table 17.1 shows America's 10 leading advertisers; Table 17.2 shows annual advertising spending in various industries.

Types of Advertising

Advertising can take many different forms. One of the most common in modern times is a TV ad designed to persuade customers to buy a particular product. Another is a newspaper ad announcing a giant sale at a local retail store. The form a marketer selects depends on the promotional strategy.

Regardless of the form advertising takes, its ultimate objective is to sell more goods and services. To do this, the ad may introduce a new product or encourage people to buy the good or service more often. Sometimes companies use ads that attempt to create a positive image of the firm, in the hope that customers will be more inclined to buy from a company they admire.

Primary-demand advertising
Advertising designed to increase the total demand for a good or service, rather than for a particular brand.

Primary-Demand Advertising   Some advertising is designed to increase the total demand for a good or service, rather than for a particular brand. This is called **primary-demand advertising.** Associations often use this approach to promote their members' products. For example, the American Dairy Association promotes the healthfulness of milk and the benefits of real

TABLE 17.2
Advertising Expenditures by Industry

Rank	Industry	Total Ad Spending in 1989 (millions)
1	Retail	$6,028.7
2	Automotive	5,519.9
3	Food	3,897.5
4	Business and consumer services	3,891.4
5	Entertainment	2,753.2
6	Toiletries, cosmetics	2,212.2
7	Travel, hotels	2,133.1
8	Drugs and remedies	1,604.9
9	Beer, wine, and liquor	1,184.6
10	Direct response companies	1,150.9

Advertising Age, Special Edition: 100 Leading National Advertisers 1989 Edition, September 26, 1990, 8.

butter. The American Dental Association encourages proper dental care (including, of course, regular checkups). An ad for wool clothing is another example of primary-demand advertising.

Selective Advertising   More typically, advertisements are designed to increase the demand for a particular brand of product. Advertising with this objective is called **selective advertising,** or sometimes called brand advertising. Most advertising fits into this category, and more money is spent on selective advertising than on any other type.

Selective advertising attempts to set the advertiser's product apart from the competition. When Visa says, "It's everywhere you want to be," the company is suggesting that other credit cards might be less widely recognized. When AT&T calls itself "the right choice," it is implying that other long-distance carriers might not be such a good choice. Similarly, using Michael Jordan to market basketball shoes for Nike or Michael J. Fox for Diet Pepsi, the advertisers are trying to establish a particular identity for their product or service. A problem with this strategy is that so many celebrities pitch products that the buying public may get confused as to who is selling what.[4] The ads must also be compatible with world events. For example, after the outbreak of war in the Persian Gulf, RJR Nabisco dropped an ad claiming that Chips Ahoy cookies are "richer than an OPEC nation" and NYNEX stopped airing a TV spot of a Marine Corps drill team dancing to rock 'n' roll music.[5] In addition, as firms go international, their selective advertising strategies may have to change. The accompanying International Close-Up (The Dream Team Sells) provides an example of an international strategy for selective advertising of a series of new products.

Institutional Advertising   Companies also use advertising to create goodwill and build a desired company image. Such advertising is called **institutional advertising.** This advertising includes ads that tell of a company's

Selective advertising
Advertising designed to increase the demand for a particular brand of product.

Institutional advertising
Advertising designed to create goodwill and build a desired company image.

The Beef Industry Council and Beef Board created this primary-demand ad for beef. It suggests serving sizes, provides nutrition information, and urges healthy eating habits. The ad encourages overall demand for beef, not a particular company's product.

Source: Reprinted by permission of the Beef Industry Council and Beef Board.

concern for quality or dedication to environmental protection. A company may sponsor cultural programming on TV or radio and even buy print ads promoting that fact. For example, Mobil Oil has underwritten the costs of producing Masterpiece Theater on public television for years.

Companies use institutional ads so that people will think positively of the firm when they are looking for products that the company offers. For example, if someone who wants to buy a car thinks favorably of General Motors, GM's institutional advertising has done its job. Institutional advertising can also help keep people informed about changes that the company is making

CLOSE-UP / *International*

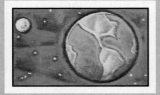

The Dream Team Sells

The Olympics are truly an international event. At the 1992 games, the hottest tickets were those for the Dream Team: 11 NBA All-Star pros and one top college player. From the beginning, advertisers realized that this was the greatest basketball team ever assembled, and they hurried to hitch their wagon to these stars. For example, Kraft USA spent several million dollars advertising its role in feeding the team, running a sales promotion for Olympic basketball caps and posters, and offering retailers a life-size, diecut display if they would feature Kraft products prominently. Nike, which had signed Michael Jordan and a host of other members of the dream team to a lucrative contract, aired a commercial wishing these players good luck as they flew off to Barcelona to compete for the gold. Champion spent heavily to advertise its role as the official tailor of USA Basketball's uniform, cleverly referring to its work as "the common thread that binds them all together."

USA Basketball, the governing body for basketball in the United States, including the Olympic team, designated NBA Properties to handle its marketing chores. This group has some of the savviest marketers in professional sports, and they proved it in the way they lined up advertisers and licensees for the Olympic event. At the same time, USA Basketball bought the rights to the team-qualifying tournament and staged the event in Portland, Oregon. All the commercial time on all of the game broadcasts were sold exclusively to tournament sponsors. These sponsorships went for $1 million and up. One sponsor, SkyBox International, which markets basketball playing cards, spent a total of $7 million for the sponsorship package and the media advertising campaign.

Were the advertisers pleased with their investment? Since the Dream Team handily won every game in what was by far the most popular televised event of the Olympics, they felt that their money was very well spent. The next Olympics games will be in 1996 in Atlanta, Georgia, and if the United States again puts together an NBA-staffed team, it is likely that advertisers will again rush to buy advertising time and sponsorships. Given the large market audience that can be reached during these events, for advertisers this is truly a dream team.

Source: Joshua Levine, "Slam Dunk," *Forbes,* July 20, 1992, pp. 92, 96.

---

that will result in better goods and services. Some companies promote themselves in business publications. They may hope that creating a better corporate image will help them raise funds from lenders or potential investors if needed and attract and keep management talent.

Cooperative Advertising   Sometimes manufacturers and retailers share the costs of a joint advertising campaign. This is called **cooperative advertising.** This approach encourages customers to buy a product, while also encouraging merchants to push the product. Large manufacturers often use cooperative advertising when they introduce a new product or want to stimulate sales. At the present time, companies spend billions annually for cooperative advertising.

Typical examples of cooperative advertising are arrangements between auto manufacturers and local dealers, computer makers and local outlets, and cosmetics firms and department stores. Franchises also use a form of cooperative advertising. The local franchisees pay a fee to the franchisor, who uses part of these funds for advertisements that complement the promotion efforts of the local operators.

Cooperative advertising
Advertising for a product in which the manufacturer and merchant share the costs.

FIGURE 17.2
Distribution of Advertising Expenditures

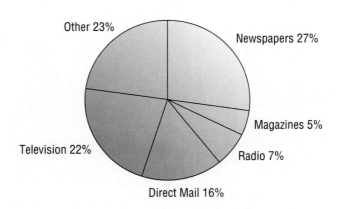

Advertising Media

In deciding where to place their promotional messages, advertisers can select from among an ever-growing variety of advertising media. Figure 17.2 shows how U.S. advertising expenditures are distributed among the media. The most popular media today are newspapers, magazines, radio, TV, and direct mail. Table 17.3 summarizes the major advantages and disadvantages of these media.

Newspapers Marketers spend more money on newspaper advertising than on any other medium. One reason is that newspapers reach so many people. With total daily circulation exceeding 60 million, newspapers reach about two-thirds of American adults during the week and almost three-quarters on Sundays.

Because the circulation of most newspapers is geographically concentrated, marketers find newspapers an effective way to target local markets. Stores advertise sales, and movie theaters announce their current offerings. A restaurant or hairdresser in a particular suburb can take out an ad in the suburban newspaper. Marketers can also target geographically by buying an ad in certain editions of a newspaper that serves a relatively wide geographic area. For example, the suburban restaurant or hairdresser can place ads in the suburban edition of the city newspaper. It wouldn't make sense for these businesses to spend the money to reach a national audience, because people visit restaurants and hairdressers that are reasonably close to home.

One disadvantage of newspaper advertising is that people usually throw away the newspaper once they have read it. This means that they are unlikely to see an ad more than once. They also are unlikely to pass the newspaper along to someone else who would also see the ad.

Magazines Millions of Americans read magazines, and ads are an integral part of each issue. Subscriptions and counter sales do not begin to cover the expenses of producing most magazines. To make money and even to stay in business, publishers need to generate ad revenue.

TABLE 17.3
Advantages and Disadvantages of the Major Advertising Media

Medium	Advantages	Disadvantages
Newspapers	Reaches many people Geographically concentrated to target local markets Can place ads to catch the eye of those not looking for ads Can place ads in classified section for those wanting to buy	Read only once Not passed on to others Poorer quality paper than magazines
Magazines	Can generate considerable revenue for publisher Reach a large audience Can reach target markets Relative permanence of message because people keep and pass on to others	Needs advance preparation High cost
Radio	Can be targeted to specific location Can be targeted to specific audience Effective with products where sound is as or more important than appearance	Cannot see the product or service Short life of message Not passed on to others
Television	Reaches a large audience Can be targeted to specific location Can be targeted to specific audience Allows the product or service to be shown and demonstrated Allows creative input for big impact	Very expensive Short life of message Needs advance preparation
Direct Mail	Covers a wide territory Can focus on a particular market	Can be expensive to deliver Difficulty in obtaining relevant mailing list Consumer resistance

Many companies rely heavily on magazine advertising because of the large audiences these publications serve. General-interest publications such as *Time* and *People* reach millions of readers nationwide. This makes these publications suitable for advertising products with a broad appeal, such as lawn mowers, automobiles, and insurance.

Magazines also allow advertisers to reach target markets effectively. Like newspapers, many magazines offer regional editions for targeting geographically. The subject matter of magazines also enables advertisers to target groups with special interests and needs. For example, a marketer of makeup and high-fashion clothing might advertise in *Cosmopolitan*, while a marketer of software for IBM-compatible personal computers could reach the owners of such computers by advertising in *PC Magazine*.

Another advantage of magazine advertising is that people tend to keep magazines around for some time before throwing them away. They also pass them along to family members and friends, which increases the chance of the ads being read many times.

Besides the relatively high cost, another major disadvantage of magazine advertising is that ads usually have to be submitted 6 to 8 weeks before publication. Current events or business conditions may change, making the ad less relevant by the time it is seen by the buying public. Another problem is the type of ads carried by a magazine. Many advertisers complain that

This institutional ad is for the cable television series *Invention* on the Discovery Channel. As the ad indicates, DuPont is a major underwriter of the series. Such sponsorship generates good will and associates DuPont with invention, a vital component of modern business.

unique ads with peel-off stickers, holograms, or pull-up tabs reduce the chances of their ads being seen. Those without the gimmicks do not want to advertise in the same issue.[6]

Radio   Contrary to popular belief, advertisers are increasingly turning to radio advertising. One of its biggest advantages is that it lets the advertiser choose both the territory and the market to which the message is directed. Multicultural cities are a good example. In Miami, Florida, businesses selling to the Cuban-American market can advertise over Spanish-language stations. The same is true when selling to Mexican-Americans in Los Angeles or Puerto Ricans in New York.

Within a particular radio station's overall market, business can also target specific audiences. For example, those selling to teenagers or young adults can advertise on stations that feature the latest in rock music. Those selling to business people can run their ads during commuting times in large urban centers. Those selling to retired persons can advertise on programs that appeal to this particular audience. In recent years major companies such as Burger King, Volkswagen, and Procter & Gamble have begun using radio to target narrow, specific audiences. And when compared to newspapers, magazines, and television, their cost per listener/reader is markedly lower.[7]

As with newspaper ads, a major disadvantage of radio advertising is that the message is short-lived and not passed on to others. Another drawback is that the audience cannot see the product being advertised. This means that

The Canon Color Laser Copier 200
could do a lot for your business. And
Digital Image Processing is the reason.
Now copies from graphics, slides and
photos look more lifelike while text stays
pure black. Reproduction is comparable to
professional printing with 256 gradations
per color and 400 dots per inch resolution.

And with 50% to 400% zoom and
advanced editing, as well as automatic
feeding and sorting functions and a quick
20 black-and-white copies per minute,
it's one color copier that's all business.
To find out more, call 1-800-OK-
CANON, or write us at Canon USA
Inc., P.O. Box 3900, Peoria, IL 61614.

Imagine what a Canon Color Laser Copier could do with a pie chart.

Canon COLOR LASER COPIER **200**
The Digital Difference.

This ad for a Canon color copier, directed to a business audience, ran in business magazines like *Fortune* and also in general interest magazines like *Time*.

those who produce the ads must use their creative talent to draw on the listener's imagination. For example, 7-Up ran a series of commercials in which the fizzy, gurgly sound of the drink being poured into a glass was used to demonstrate 7-Up's refreshing nature. Also, radio advertising is effective in promoting products for which sound is more important than appearance. These products include CDs, concerts, cassette tapes, and car stereos.

Television Over the past decade, TV advertising has increased dramatically. Perhaps a major reason is that TV advertising allows for an actual demonstration of a product or service, along with delivery of the advertising message. Because it combines sight, sound, and motion, television offers great opportunities for advertisers to make a big impact.[8] In terms of disadvantages, TV ads are very expensive with cost varying by time of day and the type of show on which they are aired. Also, ads have a short life and need considerable lead time to prepare.

TV advertising varies according to the breadth of the audience. There are three basic types of advertisements: network, spot, and local. A TV ad directed at a major audience around the country is a **network ad.** A common example is an ad carried during network evening news. Everyone watching NBC *Evening News* will see the same national ads at the same time. The same is true of ads carried during a blockbuster miniseries or a major sports event such as the Super Bowl.[9] These programs are seen by a big portion of the national TV audience, so they are very expensive, as shown in Figure 17.3. However, the cost per viewer may actually be similar to that of other shows,

Network ad A television ad directed at a major audience around the country.

Arby's network TV campaign poking good-natured fun at McDonald's, Burger King, and Wendy's caught the public's attention. National newspapers then printed positive articles about the series of ads, further heightening customers' awareness and image of Arby's.

Source: Courtesy of Arby's.

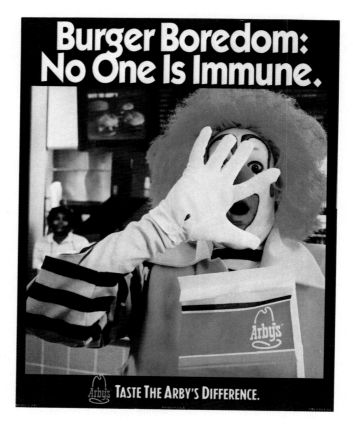

and to reduce costs network ads in general are moving from 30 to 15 seconds in length.[10]

Spot ad A television ad broadcast over one or more stations at various times.

A **spot ad** is a message broadcast over one or more stations at various times. An example would be a short commercial for Godfather's Pizza that is run on station breaks over several stations in the Midwest. Each station sends out the ad separately. Advertisers who use spot ads can choose the station, program, and time for their message.

Local ad A television ad carried only in the immediate area.

A **local ad** is a message carried only in the immediate area. These are popular among local merchants. For example, the local furniture store may be running a big sale on TVs and appliances, so it advertises during the broadcast of local news.

Direct Mail When consumers and businesspeople collect their mail, they usually find direct-mail advertisements among their letters and bills. This type of advertising ranges from circulars put out by the local grocery store to letters offering a credit card or magazine subscription to brochures describing the latest machine tool or VCR. Doctors receive information on drugs, salespeople receive literature on training and motivation cassettes, and computer owners receive a stream of offers for supplies and software. People in all lines of work get direct-mail ads for related books and magazines.

One of the major advantages of direct mail is that it helps the marketer cover a wide territory while simultaneously focusing on a particular target

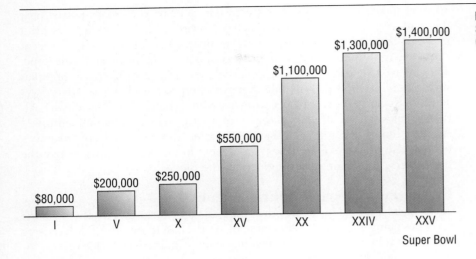

FIGURE 17.3
Super Bowl Advertising Rates for
60-Second TV Commercials

market. Marketers can buy mailing lists that contain the names and addresses of people whom they have identified as likely to purchase their product. These may consist of people who subscribe to a certain magazine, support some charity, buy from a particular catalog, or belong to a trade or professional association. Selecting the right mailing lists is central to the success of direct-mail advertising.

One of the major drawbacks of direct mail is that this type of advertising can be expensive compared to other forms of promotion. Much of the expense comes from the labor costs associated with hand-delivering circulars or the postage expense associated with mailing the materials. Also, many people throw away this type of mail without even opening it. One way advertisers try to overcome this problem is by designing the piece to look like a personal letter, a telegram, or, more recently, a Federal Express package or letter. These look-alikes attract attention and may at least get opened. Of course, the ethics of this misrepresentation may be called into question.

Other Media Besides the major advertising media, marketers look for other ways to get their message across. One way is with outdoor advertising such as billboards and signs. These ads must be simple because viewers seldom have much time to take in the message, but they can be useful for reinforcing awareness of a product. Marketers of cigarettes and liquor are heavy users of billboards because they have few ways to reach nonreaders; the law forbids them from advertising on radio and television. Radio stations also use this approach to advertise themselves. They post ads along heavily traveled routes, in the hope that commuters who see the ads will tune in the station on their car radio right away. Public transit systems often sell signs on the outside and inside of buses, trains, and stations. These have the advantage of advertising to a captive audience. Advertisers can reach target markets by choosing stations and routes in selected neighborhoods.

Advertisers are always on the lookout for new ways to advertise their products. They have tried skywriting, neon signs, and the Yellow Pages.

San Antonio Spurs fans watch instant replays on JumboTron. This giant display system from Sony serves as an advertising medium, getting company logos and products — including Sony's — before the public.

Source: Sony Corporation of America, 1989 annual report.

Consumer pretest   A test of advertising effectiveness that asks people to examine ads and rank them on their ability to capture and retain interest.

Readership report   A test of advertising effectiveness that asks people to look at ads that have appeared in publications and identify those that they recognize and those that they have read.

People-meter   An electronic instrument attached to a TV that records the channel to which the set is tuned.

Visitors to sports stadiums may see corporate or product logos posted near the field as well as ads on electronic scoreboards. Electronic displays print messages to people standing in line at post offices and supermarkets. A recent approach is the video magazine that combines both print and videotape. These video magazines have original articles covering a wide variety of topics such as sailing, golf, music, and games. The newer videos use advertisers such as Revlon and Coca-Cola to help reduce the costs to the buyer. Although sales started off poorly, they now appear to be gaining momentum.[11] Another innovative approach that is becoming an increasingly popular way to advertise products is to have them appear in movies. Companies pay the filmmakers to include their products in the movie.

Evaluating Advertising Effectiveness

Advertisers want to know whether their ads are working. Are the business revenues being generated sufficient to offset the cost of the ads?[12] Advertisers also try to minimize the risk of spending money on ineffective ads. To do so, they evaluate ideas before running the ads. To evaluate print ads, many advertisers use consumer pretests. A **consumer pretest** asks people to examine ads and rank them on their ability to capture and retain interest. Advertisers use this method in deciding which of several ads to run.

To test print ads they are already using, advertisers use readership reports. A **readership report** asks people to look at ads that have appeared in publications and to identify those that they recognize and those that they have read. Marketers want to prepare ads that readers will read as well as notice.

Similar tests rate TV ads. For example, every year Video Storyboard conducts interviews that ask consumers to name the most outstanding commercials they have watched. Table 17.4 shows the results of a recent Video Storyboard survey of 24,000 viewers who indicated the most popular commercials.[13] They have found that while the average person sees over 2,000 ads during this time period, one-third of the respondents are unable to identify even one.

The Video Storyboard research does not merely indicate which ads are the best-remembered. It also computes how much the advertiser spent for every 1,000 people who remembered the ad. The lower this number, the greater the ad's overall efficiency, because the advertiser was able to receive more attention for less money.

Another method used to test the effectiveness of radio and TV advertising is to call people's homes at random and ask them what channel they are watching or what station they are listening to. Advertisers assume that if people are watching or listening to a program, they are also watching or listening to the advertising that accompanies it.

The A.C. Nielsen Company took this idea a step further with the use of people-meters installed in TV viewers' homes. The **people-meter** is a complex electronic instrument that records who is watching which television programs. These ratings tell the networks and local stations how popular their programs are and help them decide how much to charge for a TV ad. In recent years Nielsen has reported that TV viewing has declined and the major networks have challenged these data. As a result, ABC, NBC, and Fox have modified the use of this information in determining TV ad rates.[14]

TABLE 17.4
The Most Popular TV Commercials of 1990

Brand	Ad Agency
1. Pepsi/Diet Pepsi	BBDO
2. Nike	Wieden & Kennedy
3. Energizer	Chiat/Day/Mojo
4. Coca-Cola	McCann-Erickson
5. McDonald's	Leo Burnett
6. Little Caesars	Cliff Freeman & Partners
7. Miller Lite	Backer Spielvogel Bates
8. California Raisins	Foote, Cone & Belding
9. Budweiser	DMB&B
10. Infiniti	Hill, Holliday, Connors, Cosmopulos

Source: Thomas King, "Top Spots of '90 Reflect Marketers Turn to Caution," *The Wall Street Journal*, January 22, 1991, B1.

These TV ratings certainly will continue to be an area of interest and concern for both the networks and the advertisers. For example, the networks used the results of viewer studies to show advertisers that relatively few people thought advertisers were doing something wrong by buying air time during coverage of the war in the Persian Gulf.[15]

Criticisms of Advertising

Many people profit from advertising. Consumers use it to learn about goods and services. Businesses use it to create, build, and sustain demand for their products. The general public benefits by getting free radio and television programming and reduced prices for newspapers and magazines. Yet some important criticisms have been launched against advertising. Chapter 6 identified advertising abuses such as the "bait and switch" tactic as a consumerism issue. Other common criticisms are that advertising is misleading,[16] increases the price of a product, and encourages materialistic values.

Is advertising misleading? Opinion polls continue to report that consumers think so. Also competing companies accuse one another of misleading advertising. For example, MCI sued AT&T for false and misleading advertising[17] and Gillette charged Wilkinson Sword Blade with false, exaggerated, and unsubstantiated ads.[18]

Over the years, the Federal Trade Commission (FTC) has forced advertisers to modify or drop many ads. For example, the FTC made a baking company admit in its ads that about as many calories were in a loaf of their diet bread as in regular bread. The major difference was that the so-called diet bread was sliced thinner and thus had fewer calories per slice. The FTC also ruled that a Kraft General Foods ad campaign exaggerated the calcium content of its Singles cheese slices and barred Kraft from making misleading nutritional claims.[19] In an effort to prevent children from being misled, the FTC also carefully watches ads directed at this impressionable market. The accompanying Ethics Close-Up (Outlandish Claims) discusses other recent ad developments that have resulted in criticism.

C L O S E - U P / *Ethics*

Outlandish Claims

In many areas of the country, a consumer revolt against advertising appears to be taking shape. One of the primary reasons is that advertising claims are being challenged as untrue or misleading. After complaints from consumer advocates, Mobil Chemical dropped a claim that its Hefty garbage bags are biodegradable. Faced with a storm of protest from both health care people and minorities, RJR Nabisco canceled the Uptown cigarette brand that it planned to market to African-Americans. Meanwhile, in movie theaters audiences are demanding that commercials be removed from the screen. However, the biggest attacks seem to be directed at health care food claims. As one observer noted, "Cereal boxes proclaim that a bowl a day will help ward off cancer and heart disease. Vegetable oils vow to keep your arteries free of unhealthy deposits. Orange juice with added calcium aims to prevent brittle bones."

One example are the so-called "light" foods that are touted as guilt-free pleasures, but which may not reduce caloric intake. For example, Klondike Lite ice cream bars are adver-

tised to have half the calories and fat of the original bars. However, the Lite bars are only half the size of the original, and so eating two Lite bars is the same as eating one original. Another example is oat bran, which all the food companies have unqualifiedly claimed can reduce cholesterol and the risk of heart attack, but some in the medical community dispute this.

In dealing with these advertising claims, the federal government and state agencies are taking action. For example, the Federal Trade Commission has gone after Fibre Trim, a diet product, and toy maker Lewis Galoob Toys Inc. for making false or deceptive claims. Nine states have persuaded Carnation Company to stop claiming that its Good Start formula is hypoallergenic; and state officials have been successful in getting Campbell Soup to curb broad ads that promote its soups as sources of calcium and fiber. Meanwhile Texas sued Quaker Oats over a claim that some of its cereals significantly lower the risk of heart attack. To settle, Quaker admitted no wrongdoing but agreed to donate $75,000 worth of food to the hungry in Texas.

Source: Mark Landler and Walecia Konrad, "Consumers Are Getting Mad, Mad, Mad, Mad at Mad Ave," *Business Week,* April 30, 1990, 70–72; James S. Hirsch, "As 'Light' Foods Multiply on Shelves, Critics Contend Health Claims Are Thin," *The Wall Street Journal,* March 28, 1990, B1; Joanne Lipman, "Some Food Marketers May Shelve Outlandish Health Claims," *The Wall Street Journal,* January 29, 1990, B1; and "Suddenly, Green Marketers Are Seeing Red Flags," *Business Week,* February 25, 1991, 74.

Besides being misleading, many people argue that advertising merely runs up the price of a product. After all, if a firm spends $50,000 in advertising to sell 50,000 units, the sales price must somewhere reflect this $1 per unit. Thus, consumers pay for the advertising costs in the form of higher prices. Additionally, critics contend, advertising does nothing more than switch buyers from one product to another. The final result is that prices go up but no one is really any better off as a result of advertising.

Another criticism of advertising is that it creates materialistic values. It makes people want what is being advertised, affecting their purchasing habits and, in the process, altering their lifestyles. For example, many people today feel compelled to buy brand-name merchandise and to have the latest model car. This, decry the critics, is a result of advertising, which in the final analysis traps and imprisons people. It creates expectations for material possessions that, especially for poorer people, can never be met. The result is frustration, despair, and possibly crime. Advertisers also attempt to influence consumers to purchase products such as cigarettes and alcohol, which most would agree are hazardous to the users' health.[20]

How accurate are the criticisms of advertising? On the one hand, there is undoubtedly some truth in them.[21] On the other hand, advertising also has value for business and the society at large. It not only helps generate a demand for goods and services, but also informs buyers and helps them make more intelligent purchasing decisions.

1. What are the five major advertising media?
2. How do companies measure the effectiveness of their advertising?

Personal Selling

For some products and services, advertising alone is not enough to persuade people to buy. Few people buy cars or insurance on the basis of an advertisement, and institutional buyers are equally reluctant to order major equipment or expensive services such as corporate tax-preparation assistance based on an ad. In these cases, marketers turn to personal selling.

The mix of advertising and personal selling depends on the marketing strategy. For example, it takes considerable effort to persuade many buyers that they would be better off with a new car. Rather than pay a salesperson to make repeated calls on each potential buyer, Chrysler runs advertising to stir interest. Then salespeople at the dealership close the sale on a particular car with particular options. In contrast, Mary Kay Corporation relies entirely on personal selling for its cosmetics. It may take only one selling effort to persuade a customer of the desirability of a new shade of lipstick, and the decision to buy is typically more emotional and less dependent on gathering information about the product or on comparing prices.

Types of Personal Selling

Depending on the nature of the product and the customer's needs, the salesperson may engage in order taking, missionary selling, or creative selling. Most salespeople do each of these at least occasionally.

Order Taking   The simplest type of personal selling is **order taking,** which involves processing orders from customers who have decided they want to buy. This is the major portion of the job of many retail store salespeople. It also is the task of salespeople who call on retailers, checking the store's inventory and finding out what additional products the store wants to order to replenish its shelves.

The selling function comes in when the salesperson suggests some other item to go along with the order. For example, after you have placed your order while driving through a fast-food establishment, the order taker asks, "Would you like some fries to go with that?" or "How about a hot apple pie to go with that?" Research has shown that this "suggestive selling" can greatly increase sales.[22] In addition, the salesperson can build repeat business by being courteous and helpful.[23]

Order taking   Processing orders from customers who have decided they want to buy.

Missionary Selling   Salespeople also can engage in **missionary selling,** which is a type of personal selling in which one salesperson supports the sales efforts of others. The objective of missionary selling is to win over supporters for the product or service; the supporters then buy it from other salespeople or encourage others to do so. Missionary selling is the primary activity of pharmaceutical salespeople who make calls on doctors. Such a salesperson

Missionary selling   A type of personal selling in which one salesperson supports the sales efforts of others.

explains the benefits of the company's medications and encourages the doctor to prescribe them. The salesperson also provides the physician with free samples. At the same time, other salespeople are calling on pharmacies to convince them to stock the medicine. The success of the missionary salesperson helps generate sales at the retail level; if doctors prescribe a certain brand, pharmacies will have to carry it. Similarly, a computer salesperson who tells a customer about the benefits of having the machine serviced at the company's store is generating future sales for the service department.

Creative selling Determining the buyer's needs and matching them with the products for sale.

Creative Selling The most complex type of selling is **creative selling,** which involves determining the buyer's needs and matching them with the products. For example, many buyers of computers are uncertain what to ask for. A creative salesperson starts by asking, "What do you want to do with the computer?" and then suggests a system that can handle those tasks.

Sometimes creative selling involves steering buyers from their current request to a substitute that the firm has on hand. If someone comes into a store to buy a shirt or blouse and the requested style or size is not in stock, the salesperson may say, "Let me show you what we have" or "Have you thought about this style? It is very popular." In this way, the salesperson is persuading the buyer to accept a substitute. Such creative personal selling is a large part of an effective salesperson's job.

The Process of Personal Selling

Salespeople can improve their performance by making sure they are proficient at each of the six steps of the personal selling process: prospecting, approaching, presenting, handling objections, closing, and follow-up. Figure 17.4 illustrates each step in sequence.

Prospecting Researching potential buyers and choosing those who are the most likely customers.

Prospecting Personal selling begins with **prospecting,** which involves researching potential buyers and choosing those who are the most likely customers. A salesperson in a department store may try to spot shoppers who seem to want help. Brokerage houses such as Merrill Lynch and Lehman Brothers identify high-income people, such as physicians, dentists, and other professionals, who are likely to have money to invest or need financial planning. The company prepares a financial program and presents it in such a way that it will appeal to the potential client's needs. Insurance firms such as New York Life and Prudential do the same. In many cases, salespeople identify current customers as prospects for additional company products.

A Saturn team member and a member of the Kennametal tool management team check items in a Saturn tool crib. More than 50 companies vied to furnish Saturn Corporation, a subsidiary of General Motors, with the cutting tools required for powertrain manufacturing at its new, fully integrated Saturn plant at Spring Hill, Tennessee. Kennametal Inc., using creative selling to present itself as a full-service supplier, won the contract. It will supply both its own products and products it purchases from other tool manufacturers.

Source: Courtesy of Kennametal Inc. and Saturn Corporation.

Approaching the Prospect Armed with background information, the salesperson approaches the prospective customer. A salesperson in a retail store simply walks up to a customer who looks interested and asks, "May I help you?" Sometimes, approaching the customer is much more difficult. For example, salespeople at brokerage and insurance firms, who typically identify prospects by telephoning, may have to make repeated phone calls before getting through to the prospect. If the prospect initially shows little interest, the salesperson may have to call back several more times before being able to set up an appointment to make a presentation. Technological developments such as cellular phones have made some salespeople more effective at this and other stages of the selling process.

FIGURE 17.4
The Personal Selling Process

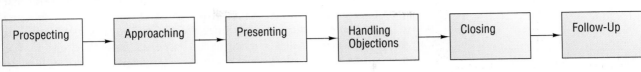

Making the Presentation   If the prospect is interested, the salesperson then makes the presentation. The nature of the presentation depends on the good or service. In the case of financial planning, the salesperson will describe the past performance of various investments and show the prospect why it is wise to begin a particular investment program immediately. The retail salesperson will let the customer examine the product and can demonstrate how it works and discuss its attractiveness or value. An automobile salesperson will suggest that the prospect take a test drive.

To present complex and expensive products, the salesperson may rely on the support of various presentation aids. For example, insurance is an abstract concept, so a salesperson often uses charts, graphs, and even photos illustrating the benefits of insurance. To convince a prospective client to buy consulting services, a consultant brings a proposal, often bound in a handsome binder, describing what the company intends to do and what its qualifications are. To convince a group to hold a convention in its city, representatives from the city government may show the convention committee slides or a videotape describing the city's features and try to convince the group that this is the place to hold the convention.

Handling Objections   Usually the salesperson handles objections after making the sales presentation. This forces the customer to focus on the presentation and leaves the salesperson in charge of the situation. If the customer interrupts the salesperson every few seconds with questions, the rhythm of the presentation is lost. Ideally, it addresses and resolves commonly raised objections or questions before the prospect can raise them.

Closing   After handling objections, the salesperson is ready to close the sale. Closing involves asking the prospect for the order. This is the key to any sale; everything else is preliminary. Salespeople have a number of ways of closing. One is simply to ask for the sale. For example, a salesperson may ask the customer, "Would you like to buy this TV?" A second approach is to offer a choice: "Would you like to take it with you or have it delivered?" This approach implies that the customer has already decided to buy and sometimes serves as a final nudge in helping the buyer make the purchase. Often, salespeople who are reluctant to make a closing simply start writing up the order. If the individual does not object, the sale is completed. This can be a difficult step, because the salesperson walks a fine line between losing the sale by being pushy and making the sale by being assertive.

Following Up   Once a sale is completed, the salesperson must follow up on the order and ensure that the customer is satisfied. This includes making sure that delivery was on time, the goods were in proper condition, and the customer had no problem in using the purchase. The follow-up lets the customer know that the salesperson is interested in the buyer's satisfaction. It also gives the salesperson a chance to reinforce the buyer's decision. For example, successful car salespeople know that a key ingredient is to follow up by calls and mail to make sure the new owner is satisfied. This also helps generate future sales. This is important because the effort and cost of selling most products and services to previous satisfied customers is much less than that of selling to new ones.[24]

1.   What are the types of personal selling?
2.   What steps must a salesperson take before closing a sale?

Sales Promotion

Sales promotion   Promotional activities other than advertising and personal selling that stimulate consumer purchasing and dealer effectiveness.

For prospects who need a nudge to make up their minds, many companies supplement advertising and personal selling with sales promotion techniques. **Sales promotion** consists of promotional activities, other than advertising and personal selling, that stimulate consumer purchasing and dealer effectiveness. This definition, drawn from the American Marketing Association, shows that sales promotion is open-ended, comprising a variety of techniques from trade shows to coupons to free samples.

Attention-Getting Techniques

One way in which marketers use sales promotion to stimulate sales is to get customers' attention. The customer may notice the product at a trade fair or on a special display. In addition, a contest or a novelty item may attract a customer to a product.

Trade Shows, Fairs, and Conventions   One popular approach to sales promotion is the use of trade shows, fairs, and conventions. Often an industry organizes trade fairs in conjunction with its conventions. The industry group invites producers to display their products so that potential customers can see what is available. For example, at computer conventions, hardware and software manufacturers rent booths and display their products. At academic conventions, textbook firms display their latest offerings for professors to examine for adoption in their classes. Restaurant and food-service conventions are filled with the smells of the new products that company representatives are cooking and passing out to attendees. The companies displaying their products also send their salespeople to the convention, where they are able to make contacts with potential customers.

Point-of-purchase (POP) displays   In-store displays of a product that draw attention to it.

Point-of-Purchase Displays   Marketers enlist the help of retailers to promote products by using **point-of-purchase (POP) displays.** These are in-store displays of a product that draw attention by setting the product apart and putting it in an eye-catching holder. For example, Hanes displays L'eggs pantyhose on 7-foot egg-shaped units placed in supermarkets and drugstores.

Publishers often design POP displays for books that they expect to become best-sellers. These cardboard stands typically use bright graphics and attention-getting headlines. POP is particularly effective in promoting unplanned purchases. Research shows that people make almost two-thirds of their buying decisions for consumer goods when in the store.

Contests Firms also generate interest in their products with contests. One of the best known is the Publishers Clearing House Sweepstakes. Another is the Reader's Digest Sweepstakes. Both of these contests offer thousands of dollars worth of prizes and prize money.

Many radio stations have their own versions of contests, sometimes sponsored by companies that provide the winners with their products. A typical contest might have someone on the air, four times a day, ask listeners to call in with the answer to a particular question, and the 10th caller with the right answer will win a prize. In other cases, the contest calls for members of the audience to send their name to the station. At various intervals during the day, a name drawn from among those sent in is announced on the air, and if that person calls the station within a predetermined time period, such as 10 minutes, he or she gets all of the money in the jackpot. If there is no winner, the station adds a certain amount to the jackpot, and the contest continues. The higher the jackpot goes, the greater the number of people who stay tuned, listening for their name.

Specialties Marketers also create awareness by giving away specialties, useful items on which the company's name is imprinted. Typical specialties are pens, hats, T-shirts, drinking glasses, coffee cups, notepads, and calculators. Specialties such as buttons and bumper stickers are usually part of the promotion effort for political candidates. In some cases, certain items have become popular enough that the company sells them rather than giving them away. When the recipient uses the specialty, it serves as a reminder of the product or service and generates goodwill or, in the case of bumper stickers, publicity for the company.

Discounts and Giveaways

Marketers can also interest customers by making their product look like a good deal. A customer considering a product might be swayed by the savings from a coupon, rebate, or premium. A free sample might entice the customer to give the product a try.

Couponing Marketers sometimes use **couponing,** a sales promotion technique that offers buyers a specified discount if they redeem a coupon. Going into the 1990s, manufacturers distributed almost 3,000 coupons per household that averaged about 50 cents, but less than 3 percent of them were redeemed.[25] However, their use is increasing and can be useful for persuading buyers to try a new product. It also can help build and maintain market share and ward off the competition. Customers who see two brands as similar are more likely to buy the brand for which they have a coupon. Coupons are most commonly distributed in newspapers, magazines, and direct mailings. Another technique is to print the coupon on the package of the product.

Couponing A sales promotion technique that offers buyers a specified discount if they redeem a coupon.

Some companies avoid using coupons because they have found that the cost of printing and processing them can be extremely high. Additionally, coupon fraud has been on the rise in recent years. In one case, federal agents arrested supermarket employees who were submitting cents-off coupons, without ever having sold the products, and keeping the refunds for themselves.

Refunds and Rebates   Some manufacturers find that refunds or rebates are an effective way of promoting their products. One of the most common approaches is a money-back offer, such as $1 for five proofs of purchase of a certain product. On big-ticket items such as automobiles, some manufacturers have offered rebates of $500 to $1,000. These rebates have become so common that many auto buyers now seem to expect a rebate and refuse to buy a car until one is offered. To avoid such situations, marketers must use rebates with care. If the rebate becomes a customer expectation, then it is no longer an effective way to promote the product.

Samples   Still another form of sales promotion is the use of samples that the company gives away to customers or sells for nominal prices. Typically, the sample is a smaller version of the regular-sized good. If it is toothpaste, the tube is perhaps 20 percent of the size of a regular tube; if it is a candy bar, it is a miniature of the average size. In the case of a newspaper, magazine, or textbook, the company offers a sample in the hope that the recipient will buy a subscription or adopt the textbook for a class. Often, the company mails the samples to customers or distributes them at the store where the product is being offered.

Premiums   Goods offered to potential customers as an incentive to purchase a product.

Premiums   Companies can also give away **premiums.** These are goods offered to potential customers as an incentive to purchase a product. A common example is a bank that gives a free coffee percolator or toaster on all new accounts of $2,000 or more. Manufacturers and retailers of personal computers may give away certain software with the purchase of a machine so that the buyer can begin using the computer immediately.

CHECK ✓ POINT

1.   What are two ways in which marketers use sales promotion to get attention?
2.   What are two ways in which marketers use sales promotion to make products or services seem more affordable?

Publicity and Public Relations

Seldom can a company convince the public that it is a responsible organization producing a fine product just by saying so. Most organizations find it necessary to cultivate good relations with the general public and persuade other sources to spread positive messages about the company. Consequently, companies make publicity and public relations part of their promotional strategy.

Publicity

Although advertising and publicity closely resemble one another, there are major differences between them. Both are messages about a company or its products communicated by the mass media. However, **publicity** is product- or company-related information that the firm does not pay the media to carry and that the firm does not control. When new fat substitutes came on the market, the popular press compared and contrasted NutraSweet Company's Simplesse product with Procter & Gamble's Olestra. The writers of the news stories, not the companies, controlled what was said about each product.

In an effort to get as much favorable publicity as possible, most large firms provide the media with news releases. These releases are typically a page or two long and describe some new development or decision by the firm. For example, a local newspaper recently ran a half-page story and accompanying picture about the very successful game Pictionary. As the head of the firm that promotes the game noted in the news story, "The thing that really got this game going was publicity."[26] All the stores in town sold out of the game after the story ran.

Publicity is especially important to small, local firms. Typically, the business's owner or a top manager makes a personal telephone call to the business editor's desk at the local paper or radio station and relates what the firm is doing and why it is newsworthy. Small firms need to take more advantage of publicity than most of them do.

One challenge of generating publicity is that most media outlets are inundated with press releases. Marketers cannot hope that every new product or promotion will receive television or newspaper coverage. Consequently, marketers try to stage events that will draw attention. For example, Austin, Minnesota, drew national attention when it celebrated the 50th year of Spam. Events in the town, where Spam was first canned, include a "hog jog," a Spam cook-off, and a parade. It is also important to remember that negative publicity can hurt sales. For example, as Sears marketing strategy ran into trouble recently, negative publicity in the newspapers and business magazines hurt the firm's ability to attract more customers.[27]

Publicity Product- or company-related information that the firm does not pay the media to carry and that the firm does not control.

Public Relations

Another way in which a company indirectly communicates information about itself is through **public relations,** which comprises all activities directed toward creating and maintaining a favorable public image. Public relations activities include sponsoring events, handling consumer and press inquiries, and supporting charities. Unlike publicity, the company does have direct control over its public relations efforts.

Sponsoring charitable events is a popular method of public relations. Coca-Cola, for example, often provides free soft drinks to charities that are attempting to raise money for worthwhile causes. Tony Roma's, a national chain of spareribs restaurants, donates all of the food for the annual Miami Spinal Cord Research picnic.

Other firms sponsor sports or cultural events, or public television or radio programs. The objective of these activities is to provide enjoyment and assistance to the community at large. At the same time, the company gets its

Public relations All activities directed toward creating and maintaining a favorable public image.

name and, in turn, its products in front of the public and is associated with being a responsible member of the community.

| CHECK ✓ POINT |

1. What is publicity?
2. What are two common public relations techniques?

Closing Comments

This chapter examined the elements of the promotional mix: advertising, personal selling, sales promotion, and publicity and public relations. Companies combine the use of these according to the nature of their product or service and the market for it. A successful businessperson observed: "I know half of my promotional dollars are wasted, but since I don't know which half, I'm not willing to cut back on my expenditures." A major challenge for marketing managers is to make sure the company is getting its money's worth out of the promotional effort. But whether or not marketers have a dependable way to do so, they know that a promotion strategy and specific techniques are necessary to make buyers aware of the products or services that are available.

VIDEO CASE / *Big versus Small*

Not all successful advertising agencies are large. A number of small agencies specialize in certain types of promotions and do not intend to grow very large; others have been started in recent years and are on their way up. Kirshenbaum & Bond (K&B) is an example of a small, upstart ad agency. K&B has no research department or substantial media department to plan and buy broadcast time. However, to counteract the lack of such services provided by the big agencies, the personnel at K&B tend to be fairly young (in their 20s and 30s) and take accounts that require an innovative, fresh approach. For example, K&B created an ad that ridiculed exiled Philippine first lady Imelda Marcos's overstuffed closet of shoes for their Kenneth Cole shoes account. The larger, well-established agencies do not always work this way. In fact, a number of large agencies have done quite well by not emphasizing creativity. An example is Interpublic, which is made up of a large number of agencies that all work under one corporate umbrella. Three of the biggest groups under the Interpublic umbrella

are McCann-Erickson, the Lintas Group, and the Lowe Group.

McCann has major clients such as Coca-Cola and Brooks Brothers, for which less creative ads seem to do quite well. As one observer put it, "If you are advertising a product all over the world, you have to find an ad that appeals to everyone and one over which the client has control. So you need a more sedate approach." Lintas has the Chevrolet account and developed the pulsating "Heartbeat of America" campaign, a somewhat creative approach that was aimed at selling automobiles to young people in America. The Lowe Group has the Heineken beer account and in that international market the degree of creativity is particularly important.

The problem for some of these large agencies such as McCann is that clients today want more than just advertising. They want a fully coordinated promotional approach that includes public relations, marketing research, direct marketing, and events marketing. Quite often clients find that small agencies are better able to provide

these services than large ones. In the case of Sony Corporation of America, for example, the firm recently took $20 million in billings away from McCann and gave it to smaller agencies because the smaller ones could give more personal attention and provide a comprehensive promotional effort.

Source: Randall Rothenberg, "Fixing a Mad Mad Ave. World," *New York Times*, September 30, 1990, Sec. 3, 1, 6; and Randall Rothenberg, "Madison Ave. 'Bad Boys' Grow Up in a Downturn," *New York Times*, January 23, 1991, C1, C3.

Case Questions
1. What are some of the benefits of using a small, upstart advertising agency such as Kirshenbaum & Bond versus a big, well-established agency?
2. Why would a business firm choose Kirshenbaum & Bond rather than McCann-Erickson?
3. When would a large firm such as McCann-Erickson be of more value to a business firm than would a small ad agency?

Learning Objectives Revisited

1. **Define advertising and its basic types.** Advertising is a nonpersonal form of promotion designed to persuade someone to a particular point of view. Primary-demand advertising is designed to increase total demand for a particular good or service. Selective advertising is designed to increase the demand for a particular brand of product. Institutional advertising is designed to create goodwill and to build a desired image for the company. Cooperative advertising jointly promotes manufacturers and merchants, who share the advertising costs.

2. **Identify the various advertising media.** The five most common types of advertising media are newspapers, which continue to be the most popular form; magazines, which provide the opportunity for both national and regional coverage; radio, which helps advertisers target their market audience; TV, which allows advertisers to describe and demonstrate the product; and direct mail, which allows advertisers to cover a wide territory while focusing on a particular target market.

3. **Explain how marketers analyze the effectiveness of advertising.** To analyze the effectiveness of advertising, marketers use aids such as consumer pretests, which ask people to examine and rank ads based on their ability to capture and retain interest; readership reports, which ask people to look at ads that have been run and to identify those they recognize and have read; and the Nielsen people-meter, which records the channel to which the viewer's TV is tuned.

4. **Describe the types and process of personal selling** The three basic types of personal selling are creative selling, which is determining the buyer's needs and matching them with the products for sale; missionary selling, which is personal selling in support of the sales efforts of others; and order taking, which is the processing of orders from customers who have decided what they want to buy. Personal selling involves prospecting, approaching the prospect, making the presentation, handling objections, closing the sale, and following up on the sale to ensure that the customer is satisfied.

5. **Discuss the basic techniques of sales promotion.** The basic techniques of sales promotion include attention-getting techniques such as trade-show and convention displays, point-of-purchase (POP) displays, contests, specialty items, and discounts and giveaways such as coupons, refunds, samples, and premiums.

6. **Relate the roles that publicity and public relations play in promotion.** Publicity is product- or company-related information that the company does not control and does not pay the mass media to carry. Companies rely on publicity to help keep their name in front of the public and to create a positive image. Public relations comprises all activities whose objective is to create and maintain a favorable public image. Business firms do this in many ways, such as sponsoring sports and cultural events, public television, and so forth. Along with bringing the company's name and products to the public's attention, these activities provide enjoyment and assistance to the community at large and show the company to be a responsible member of society.

Key Terms Reviewed

Review each of the following terms. For any that you do not know or are unsure of, look up the definitions and see how they are used in the chapter.

advertising
primary-demand advertising
selective advertising
institutional advertising
cooperative advertising
network ad
spot ad
local ad

consumer pretest
readership report
people-meter
order taking
missionary selling
creative selling
prospecting

sales promotion
point-of-purchase (POP)
  displays
couponing
premiums
publicity
public relations

Review Questions

1. Downhill Skier, a new manufacturer of snow skis, wants to reach the $5 million sales mark before the end of its third year of business. To whom should the firm promote the product, retailers or consumers?
2. Of the basic types (not media) of advertising, which is used most? Why do you think it is?
3. Which kind of advertising do you think the Florida Citrus Commission would use most? Why?
4. If stories about a car's defects were hurting the reputation of its maker, which kind of advertising do you think it would use? Why?
5. Ultimate Bike Company has just introduced a programmable bicycle. How should the company's advertising message change as the product moves through its life cycle?
6. Which media would you use for advertising each of the following products? Explain your choices.
   a. Used cars
   b. Xerox copiers
   c. The latest concert series at the local auditorium
   d. Diet Pepsi
7. Fred Forsythe is a small retailer selling home electronics goods. Most of Fred's advertising is done through the local newspaper. What are some of the benefits of this form of advertising that make it ideal for Fred's business?
8. If you were targeting a local market, would television advertising ever be appropriate? If so, explain what circumstances would make it appropriate.
9. How do advertisers evaluate print ads? How do they evaluate broadcast ads?
10. American Brands spends millions of dollars every year advertising its cigarettes. Why do some consumers object to this type of advertising? Are they right?
11. Roger Mills sells business forms. His employer prints and sells standardized forms or will print forms to the client's specifications. What type of selling should Roger engage in?
12. Eloise Churchman thinks that because she only sells dresses in a clothing store, she doesn't need to bother with presenting the product. However, sales in her department are not meeting expectations. How can Eloise use the presentation step in the personal selling process to boost sales?
13. What sales promotion techniques would you recommend for each of the following situations? Explain your choices.
   a. A recording company wants to boost sales of a CD by a popular rock group.
   b. A small Mexican restaurant in a suburb of a large city wants to build business among neighborhood residents.
   c. A national food company wants to introduce a new line of tea.
14. Henrietta Rogardine has developed a new bicycle that is more comfortable and stylish than that of the competition. How might she go about getting publicity for her new product?
15. Would Henrietta's company benefit from public relations? What form might this take? Give two examples.

Applied Exercise

Many advertising slogans and messages are heard on a daily basis. Twelve such slogans are presented here as well as the company that uses each. Match the company and its advertising message.

Company	Advertising message
1. United Parcel Service	___ a. Quality is job 1
2. Pan American Airlines	___ b. All we make are great copiers
3. Burger King	___ c. We run the tightest ship in the shipping business
4. Ford Motor	___ d. Where imagination becomes reality
5. Allstate Insurance	___ e. You're in good hands
6. United Airlines	___ f. We're flying better than ever
7. New York Life Insurance	___ g. I love what you do for me
8. Toyota	___ h. A car you can believe in
9. Mita	___ i. Sometimes you gotta break the rules
10. Okidata	___ j. The company you keep
11. Volvo	___ k. We put business on paper
12. Ricoh	___ l. Come fly the friendly skies

YOU BE THE ADVISER / *Helping Bill Get Started*

Bill Hartack is in the process of opening a hardware store. Bill has had 20 years of experience in this business, most of it working for a large hardware chain in the Northeast. Last year, for health reasons, Bill moved to a southwestern state. Drawing on his early-retirement income and his savings, Bill has more than enough money to start a store of his own.

Bill's location is on the west side of town. This area is not densely settled, but the rent is quite low and if Bill can attract a clientele drawn from throughout the town, he can make the operation profitable. Bill will have four salespeople working with him, and two others will staff the back office.

Right now Bill is in the process of doing two things. First, he is trying to write interesting, effective ads that will attract customers and acquaint the community with his store. Second, he has to train the salespeople in selling techniques, because none of them has had much experience in this area.

Bill has 3 weeks before his store is scheduled to open. During this time, he intends to devote his efforts to the advertising and personal selling activities. The biggest problems confronting him are that he has no experience in writing ads and that, although he feels he knows a lot about selling, he has never received formal instruction on how to sell. Nevertheless, Bill is determined to deal with these two issues.

Your Advice

1. What should Bill do in handling his advertising?
   ___ a. Focus on writing institutional ads.
   ___ b. Write primary-demand ads.
   ___ c. Write selective ads.
2. What type of advertising media would you recommend that Bill use? Why?
3. How can Bill determine the effectiveness of his advertising efforts? What would you suggest that he do? Explain.
4. What type of training in personal selling would you recommend that Bill give to his people? What do they need to know? Briefly describe what Bill should teach his sales staff.

Career Opportunities in Business

Marketing is one of the most exciting areas of business. No enterprise can afford to operate without a well-formulated marketing strategy that identifies consumer needs and then addresses these desires through a carefully implemented plan of action. The many career opportunities in marketing range from selling to advertising to marketing analysis. The following are some of the most rewarding.

Wholesale Salesperson

A wholesale salesperson helps move goods from the manufacturer to the consumer. In so doing, the individual works closely with both producers and retailers.

Job Description. A wholesale salesperson often calls on retail stores, industrial firms, and institutions such as hospitals and schools, shows these potential customers the company's products, and attempts to generate sales. This salesperson usually brings along samples or catalogs of the goods the company sells. Besides selling, this job often requires the individual to perform services for the retailer such as checking the store's stock, showing how to reorder, and providing assistance in advertising, pricing, and creating window and counter displays.

Employment Outlook and Earnings. Employment typically depends on the product line and market. Complex products require technical backgrounds. For example, drug wholesale salespeople typically have college degrees in chemistry, biology, or pharmacy. A nontechnical salesperson is often a graduate with a major in marketing or business administration. At present, over a million people work in this career field and the number of jobs is expected to increase faster than the average of all occupations. Newcomers can expect to earn in the range of $20,000 to $30,000 annually, while experienced salespeople earn $50,000 or more.

Retail Salesperson

A retail salesperson is the link between the wholesaler and the final consumer. This individual is responsible for a wide range of activities ranging from personal selling to taking orders to ensuring that the company is aware of customer needs and desires.

Job Description. The typical responsibilities of a retail salesperson include not only showing and selling merchandise to customers but also ringing up orders, making out sales slips, receiving cash payments, giving change and receipts, handling returns and exchanges, helping stock racks and shelves, marking price tags, taking inventory, and preparing displays.

Employment Outlook and Earnings. The field of retail sales is growing. Currently about 4 million people in the United States are retail salespeople. These individuals are employed, in the main, in department stores; general merchandise stores; apparel and accessories stores; food, drug, and furniture stores; and car dealerships. Employment is expected to grow about as fast as the average for all workers. Most full-time retail salespeople earn between $12,000 and $25,000, although salespeople whose earnings are tied directly to sales can make $40,000 and up.

Travel Agent

A travel agent is a type of marketing specialist who uses his or her information and training to provide the best possible travel arrangements within each client's tastes and budgets.

Job Description. A travel agent consults a variety of sources of information on air and land transportation in arranging a client's itinerary. In the case of international travel, the agent may provide information on customs regulations, required papers (passports, visas, and certificates of vaccination), and the most recent currency exchange rates. The agent may also do considerable promotion work on putting together travel tours and making special arrangements with hotels, airlines, and car-rental firms.

Employment Outlook and Earnings. Many travel agents are self-employed and secure contracts with companies to be their exclusive agent for all travel arrangements. However, before going into business for themselves, most will have worked in travel agencies and gained important job-related experience. No particular educational background is required to secure a job in this business, but a business degree or diploma in hotel and restaurant management can be useful. The travel agency business is expected to grow much faster than the average for all occupations through the mid-1990s. While earnings will depend on dollar volume, most travel agents make between $15,000 and $50,000 annually, not counting all of the extra benefits that are provided to them including free or discounted travel and lodging.

Marketing Research Analyst

A marketing research analyst tries to answer the question, What goods and services will the customer buy? The analyst also works to identify the steps that a company might take to improve a market offering to make it even more attractive.

Job Description. A marketing research analyst uses a variety of techniques to determine consumer perceptions and interests. These techniques include surveys, personal interviews, and market testing. Statistical analysis may also be utilized. In the process, the analyst learns about the consumer's needs, the types of goods and services that the individual would be prepared to purchase, and how the consumer would use the merchandise. This awareness is critical to the proper production and promotion of products and services. These findings are then reported to the marketing executives for use in product development and promotion.

Employment Outlook and Earnings. Approximately 30,000 marketing research analysts are employed in the United States. Entry-level jobs typically include data collection and statistical analysis. However, once an individual is established as a market research analyst, he or she will work on specific projects and may be assigned to a supervisory position. If the person remains in this field, he or she may ultimately become director of marketing research. Entry-level positions usually require an undergraduate degree in business, marketing, or statistics and pay around $20,000 to $25,000. Senior marketing research analysts make between $33,000 and $40,000. Marketing research directors command $50,000 to $75,000.

Buyer

A buyer is responsible for choosing the merchandise that his or her store offers to the customer. This function is carried out by all retail stores, in one form or another, and helps determine the store's reputation and market success.

Job Description. The buyer must stay abreast of the latest trends in consumer preferences. Quite often the buyer must anticipate the market and make purchasing decisions that reflect changes in typical customer habits. The buyer must also be aware of special discounts that are offered by manufacturers and distributors and take advantage of these price breaks. At the same time, the buyer must interact with the salespeople, learn about such market developments as changing customer preferences, and incorporate this information into the buying decision. The individual must also be able to make decisions months ahead of the selling season so that the store has merchandise in stock to meet demand.

Employment Outlook and Earnings. At the present time there are over 200,000 buyers in the wholesale and retail fields. New employees generally start as assistant buyers with a salary range of $15,000 to $20,000. Top buyers for large organizations can expect to make $50,000 and more. Earnings are a reflection of the nature, size, and location of the store or corporation, as well as the incentive compensation plan that is in effect.

PART

Six

Financing the Enterprise

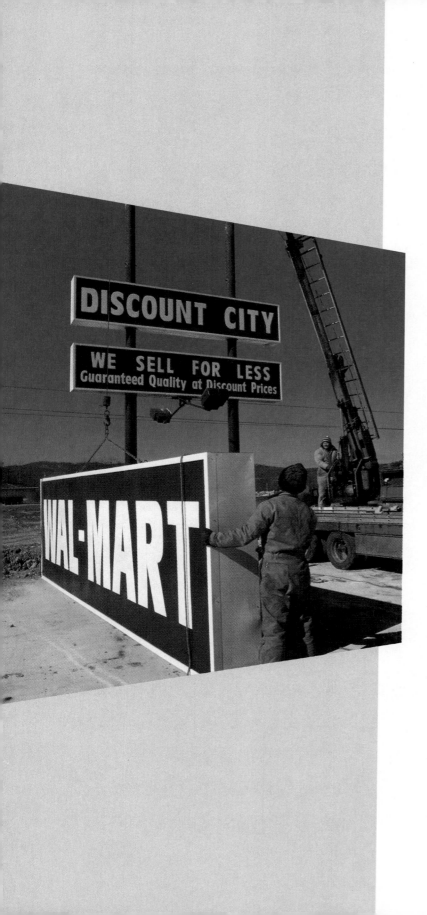

CUSTOMER IS THE BOSS, BUT ACCOUNTING CONTROLS FURTHER WAL-MART'S SUCCESS

Who is the biggest retailer in America? Most people would say Sears Roebuck. However, they would be wrong. The biggest retailer is Wal-Mart, which surpassed Sears in early 1991. The Arkansas-based retailer has seen growth of over 25 percent for each of the last 20 years.

How has Wal-Mart managed to accomplish this phenomenal growth? Although its "Customer Is the Boss" orientation, human resources management, and marketing

Accounting for Financial Control

18

Chapter Learning Objectives

- Define accounting and the types of accountants.

- Discuss the nature and types of budgets.

- Explain the accounting equation and double-entry bookkeeping.

- Describe the balance sheet.

- Present the income statement and the statement of cash flows.

- Identify ratios used to analyze financial statements.

---

approaches are widely acclaimed, of equal importance to founder Sam Walton are careful accounting controls. The giant retailer closely monitors all expenses and pays particular attention to warehouse and shipping costs. Thanks to high technology, the company can monitor the sales of every store and resupply them on a 24-hour basis. This is no simple feat, given the rapid growth of Wal-Mart stores. In 1981 the company had 491 stores; in 1991 there were 1,925, and the retailer

plans for a lot more in the years ahead.

How well has the company been able to control the operations of this growing empire? Sales increased from $2.4 billion in 1981 to an estimated $40 billion in 1991, yet the firm's net profit margin rose from 3.4 percent to 3.9 percent. Most firms find that their margins decline as they increase sales, but Wal-Mart's are going up. Additionally, financial forecasters are predicting that during the early 1990s Wal-Mart's margins will increase to

around 4.2 percent. This ability to manage growth and maintain high profit margins has convinced the management of Wal-Mart that it can continue to grow at a rapid rate. Sam Walton has predicted that by the year 2000 the company will have greater gross revenues than General Motors. Given Wal-Mart's outstanding track record, there are few who doubt his prediction.

Photo source: Courtesy of Wal-Mart Stores, Inc.

Introduction

Traditionally, managers used accounting information almost solely to control unit costs. Now, in order to be competitive in the global economy, successful firms recognize that accounting must play a broader role.[1] Accounting tools and the information generated by accountants are used to control the financial side of the enterprise and assist managers in making more effective decisions. This chapter, after presenting an overview of the accounting profession and the budgeting process, describes the major accounting statements: the balance sheet, the income statement, and the statement of cash flows. It then discusses the most common ways to analyze them.

Accounting and the Accounting Profession

Accounting The process of measuring, interpreting, evaluating, and communicating financial information for the purpose of financial control and effective decision making.

The process of measuring, interpreting, evaluating, and communicating financial information for the purpose of financial control and effective decision making is called **accounting.** The role of accounting in business firms has changed considerably over the past few decades. Years ago, a bookkeeper systematically entered the company's financial transactions in a ledger book. For example, if the company bought a new piece of equipment, the bookkeeper would see that the purchase was correctly entered on the books.

Today's accountants provide services that go far beyond mere bookkeeping. Financial accountants measure and analyze financial data for legal purposes. The focus of financial accounting is to provide accounting information to users outside the firm such as lenders, investors, and the government. Managerial accountants, on the other hand, provide information for internal purposes. Managerial accounting data makes an important contribution to financial control and decision making. Both financial and managerial accountants help management to analyze and evaluate the firm's financial position and plan for the future.

These accountants, collectively called private accountants, are generally employed by large companies. Small firms seldom employ a full-time accountant. They use a bookkeeper to handle the day-to-day financial activities and periodically hire an outside public accountant to balance the books, provide financial statements that reflect the financial condition of the firm, and prepare the tax returns. Large companies, on the other hand, employ a full-time, in-house accounting staff to carry out these activities. They too may use public accounting firms, often specifically to examine the company's books and provide information about the company's performance to stockholders, the government, and others who are interested.

The major responsibilities of both public and private accountants are summarized in Figure 18.1. Sometimes the ethics of how these responsibilities are carried out is called into question. For example, the practices of several large public accounting firms are being questioned and some of them are even facing damage suits over the collapse of institutions in the savings and loan industry.[2] Table 18.1 summarizes some of the pending suits brought by the Federal Deposit Insurance Corporation (FDIC). These major public accounting firms are being accused of fraud, negligence, or other professional misconduct. In other ways the conduct of smaller firms and of

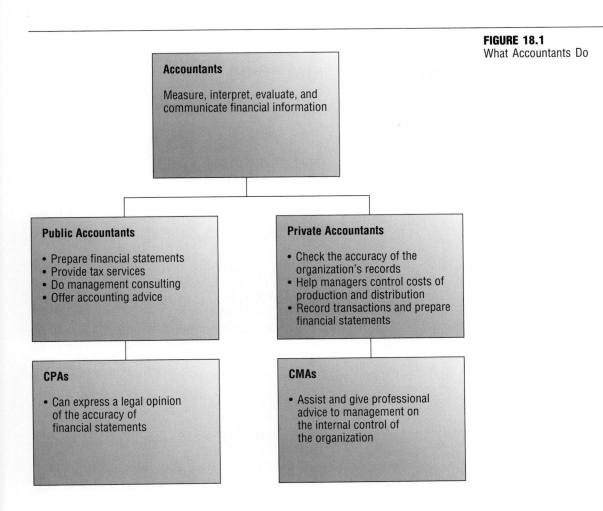

FIGURE 18.1
What Accountants Do

individual accountants is also being questioned. For example, tax-related malpractice suits by upset clients have more than doubled in the past four years and are now the number one cause of legal action against accountants.[3] Besides tax problems, the accompanying Ethics Close-Up (Cooking the Books) gives a detailed look at the role accountants have played in fraudulent or at least questionable business practices.

Public Accountants

Public accountants are employed by public accounting firms. They are independent of the organizations for which they provide financial services. They are expected to be objective and follow generally accepted accounting principles (GAAP) in evaluating a company's financial statements.[4] The importance of objectivity has led public accountants to set and follow professional standards, such as refusing to be paid a fee based on the company's profits and limiting advertising by members of their profession.[5]

TABLE 18.1

Examples of Damages Sought by the F.D.I.C. from Major Accounting Firms in the Collapse of Some Savings and Loan Institutions

Public Accounting Firm*	Savings and Loan	Damages Sought
Coopers & Lybrand	First Federal Savings and Loan (Shawnee, Okla.)	$ 7,000,000
Arthur Young	Imperial Savings (San Diego)	26,000,000
Ernst & Young	Western Savings (Dallas)	500,000,000
Deloitte, Haskins & Sells	Sunrise Savings and Loan (Boynton Beach, Fla.)	250,000,000
	Commonwealth Federal (Fort Lauderdale, Fla.)	50,000,000
	Aspen Savings Bank (Aspen, Colo.)	Subject to compensatory damages
	Royal Palm Federal (West Palm Beach, Fla.)	Not specified
Touche, Ross	Beverly Hills Savings and Loan (Beverly Hills, Calif.)	300,000,000
	Midwest Federal (Minneapolis)	100,000,000
	Westwood Savings and Loan (Los Angeles)	100,000,000
	Peoples Federal (Bartlesville, Okla.)	460,000
	Lee Savings and Loan (Gidding, Tex.)	38,500
Peat Marwick	Duval Federal (Jacksonville, Fla.)	16,500,000

*Arthur Young has merged with Ernst & Whinney to become Ernst & Young. Deloitte, Haskins & Sells has merged with Touche, Ross.
Source: Alison Leigh Cowan, "S. & L. Backlash Against Accountants," *The New York Times*, July 31, 1990, C1.

Certified public accountant (CPA) A public accountant who has met state certification requirements of education and job experience and has passed a comprehensive examination.

Many public accountants have become certified. A **certified public accountant (CPA)** has met the state certification requirements of education and job experience and has passed a comprehensive examination. In recent years, most states have been increasing the requirements for the CPA. For example, some states now require 5 years of accounting education and 2 more of practice, in addition to passing a rigorous CPA exam.

CPAs have professional status in their field the same way that physicians or attorneys do within their respective fields. In recent years CPAs have expanded into areas such as financial planning and advice for individual investors, but this has not proved to be as attractive as once thought.[6] CPAs are still mainly concerned with traditional accounting matters, and there are some activities only they can perform. For example, only CPAs may officially express an opinion on whether a firm's financial statements are accurate and have been reported fairly. The annual reports of firms that have had their accounts reviewed by a CPA contain a statement from the accounting firm that reads something like this:

CLOSE-UP / *Ethics*

Cooking the Books

The task of a public accountant who examines the books and provides information on the company's financial performance is not always easy. It is especially difficult when the company's managers are "cooking the books" by entering fictitious or erroneous information in the ledgers. Regina Company, best known for its vacuum cleaners, provides a good example.

Don Sheelen became Regina's chief executive officer after leading a buyout from the previous owner and then taking control himself. A year after the buyout, the company issued stock and announced a number of new products. Things looked very good for Regina and many stockbrokers recommended that their clients buy the stock. Within 2½ years, the stock had risen from $5.25 to $27.50 a share. To keep the price high and protect his own large investment, Sheelen had to generate higher and higher sales. However, this was not happening. Not only were sales sluggish but some of the new products that the firm brought to market were defective and needed repairs. In an effort to prevent this bad news from driving down the stock price, Sheelen allegedly ordered his chief financial officer to juggle the figures and to report higher sales and profits.

Despite the phony bookkeeping entries, the outside accountants did not pick up the problem until Regina finally announced that it would have a quarterly loss. At that time, the public accounting firm withdrew its unqualified opinion about the accuracy of Regina's financial statements and the stock quickly plummeted to a new low. The investors became very upset because they put their money in the stock based on the belief that the company was doing well. As a result, they brought legal action against the accounting firm.

In another recent case, the government brought action against three public accounting firms, charging that they knew of certain accounting irregularities in their client's books and ignored them. In still another case, an administrative judge imposed sanctions on the public accountants for failing to uncover wrongdoing at U.S. Surgical Corporation.

The accused accounting firms contend that there has been no unethical behavior and they never deliberately overlooked errors in the books or allowed their large fees to blind them to client problems. They hold that it is very difficult to uncover fraud when a company's financial officer starts cooking the books. They further point out that outside accountants are often unable to uncover carefully hatched schemes designed to hide the truth and make a company look much stronger than it is. However, despite these arguments, it appears likely that the government and the stockholders will continue to hold accounting firms responsible for failure to uncover deliberate fraud and will question whether personal relationships between public accountants and clients sometimes result in a willingness to overlook fraudulent or questionable practices.

Source: Allison Leigh Cowan, "Audit Firm: Victim or Accomplice?" *New York Times*, July 17, 1990, C6; and John A. Byrne, "How Don Sheelen Made a Mess that Regina Couldn't Clean Up," *Business Week*, February 12, 1990, 46–50.

In our opinion, the consolidated financial statements that appear in this report present fairly the financial position of [company's name]. Our examinations of these statements were made in accordance with generally accepted auditing standards and accordingly included such tests of the accounting records and other auditing procedures as we considered necessary in the circumstances.

The CPAs who work for public accounting firms can provide a wide range of services for their clients, including tax services and professional accounting advice. Because of the increasing number of fraud cases, like the one discussed in the Close-Up, and an increase in the number of malpractice suits against accounting firms, a new service specializing in detecting fraud is in high demand. One of these so-called forensic (as in crime detection) accountants describes his job as follows: "When the death of a company occurs under mysterious circumstances, forensic accountants are essential. Other accountants look at the charts. But forensic accountants actually dig into the body."[7]

Most of the corporations listed on the New York and American Stock Exchanges have their books examined by one of the "Big Six" public accounting firms. These prestigious firms are Arthur Andersen & Company; Coopers & Lybrand; Ernst & Young; Deloitte, Touche & Company; KPMG-Peat Marwick & Company; and Price Waterhouse.

Private Accountants

Private accountants may be involved with either financial accounting or managerial accounting, as mentioned earlier. In recent years, managerial accountants have been increasingly used by successful firms to help control costs and, even more important, provide useful information for more effective management decision making. Similar to their counterparts in public accounting, some of these managerial accountants have gone through a certification process. A **certified management accountant (CMA)** has met certain educational and professional requirements and has also passed a series of exams from the National Association of Accountants. These exams are comparable in length and difficulty to the CPA exam. The CMA was created in 1972, and today thousands of private accountants hold this certification. Although holding the CMA does not give any special privileges, it does designate a level of competency and professionalism for private accountants.

Some companies also use in-house accountants to perform the same type of function as do the public accountants. Called **internal auditors,** they check the accuracy of the organization's records and accounting methods.

The Budgeting Process   Accountants often help managers through the budgeting process that is a part of the planning function discussed in Chapter 8. A **budget** is a financial plan that specifies revenues and expenses for a given time period. Budgeting puts financial data into management planning. Most budgets are for one year, and many are revised quarterly (every three months). Effective managers, especially in large firms, use budgets to make sure that the goals of the various divisions are in harmony. The budget is also an excellent method of controlling the operation (discussed in Chapters 8 and 9). However, managers must also be careful that budgets do not become ends in themselves; budgets must not become inflexible "straitjackets," that restrain them from making changes and innovations needed in today's competitive environment.[8]

Most supervisors and managers provide information for preparing the budget and work with the accountant or someone familiar with the accounting process. Managers will require different types of budgets depending on their needs. Most companies must plan for and control sales income, production costs, and cash requirements. Consequently, the most common budgets are these:

- *Sales budget.* Predicts sales revenue based on a forecast of unit sales and selling price.
- *Production budget.* Forecasts the number of units to be manufactured in order to meet sales demand and desired ending inventory levels.
- *Cost of goods sold budget.* Estimates the cost of materials, labor, and overhead expenses that will be used in manufacturing the goods.

Certified management accountant (CMA)   A private accountant who has met certain education and professional requirements and has passed a series of exams.

Internal auditor   In-house accountant who checks the accuracy of the organization's records and accounting methods.

Budget   A financial plan that specifies revenues and expenses for a given time period.

Audit teams such as this one from Ernst & Young, one of the Big Six accounting firms, often work in client offices for weeks at a time. They carefully examine records to make sure they accurately represent the company's financial position.

Source: Arnold Zahn © 1987.

- *Cash budget*. Forecasts cash receipts and disbursements. The purpose of this forecast is to prevent the company from running out of daily operating funds. It usually covers a period of 30 to 60 days.

1. How do public accountants differ from private accountants?
2. What kinds of budgets do managers use?

Foundation for Accounting

Although different accountants specialize in different activities, modern accounting is built on a common set of principles and procedures. Understanding them is the basis for applying accounting information to financial control and more effective management decisions.

The Accounting Equation

A basic concern of a company's owners (whether proprietors, partners, or stockholders in a corporation) is the worth of their investment. How much do they own, and how much does the company owe to others? To get a picture of this, businesspeople use the **accounting equation:**

$$\text{Assets} = \text{Liabilities} + \text{Owners' Equity}$$

Accounting equation   The relationship stating that assets equal liabilities plus owners' equity.

Everything of value owned by the enterprise is classified as its **assets.** Examples include cash, accounts receivable (money due to the company), inventory, and machinery. **Liabilities** are creditors' claims on the enterprise's assets. These claims may be for credit purchases, wages, salaries, taxes that are as yet unpaid, and long-term debt. **Owners' equity** is the owners' claim on the assets of the enterprise. This is often referred to as a "residual" claim because it consists of whatever is left over after the liabilities have been satisfied.

Assets   Everything of value owned by an enterprise.

Liabilities   Creditors' claims on an enterprise's assets.

Owners' equity   The owners' claim on the assets of an enterprise.

If you can determine any two of the numbers in the accounting equation, you can compute the third. For example, if the company has assets of $1,000,000 and liabilities of $700,000, then owners' equity is $300,000. Similarly, if the company has liabilities of $400,000 and owners' equity of $200,000, then assets are worth $600,000.

Double-Entry Bookkeeping

From the accounting equation, you can see that a change in one category means that the same or some other category must change to keep the equation balanced. For example, if an asset increases, then another asset must decrease or liabilities and/or owners' equity must increase by the same amount. To maintain this balance, accountants use **double-entry bookkeeping,** or the use of two entries for every transaction.

Double-entry bookkeeping   The use of two entries for every transaction.

The actual entries start by recording a financial transaction in a journal. These are chronologically listed and represent changes in account balances. These journal entries are then transferred to a ledger that contains separate accounts for items such as accounts receivable, inventory, salaries, and sales. The data from these ledgers are then used to prepare the financial statements. Traditionally, this process was done by hand by bookkeepers. Today, much of this process is done by computers. For example, when a sale is made or an

Employees of Loral Corporation test an infrared system for protecting aircraft. This laser and other equipment are assets of the company. The obligation to pay the workers is a liability. The difference between the company's assets and its liabilities constitutes the owner's equity in Loral.

Source: Courtesy of Loral Corporation.

item is taken from or added to inventory, this information is put into the computer and stored until called on for calculating financial statements.

As an example of double-entry bookkeeping, if a company buys $7,500 of computer equipment, it has increased its assets by that amount. However, it also has acquired the obligation to pay for the purchase within 30 days. This is a liability called "accounts payable." The two changes to the equation are as follows:

$$\text{Assets} = \text{Liabilities} + \text{Owners' Equity}$$
$$\underset{\text{(equipment)}}{\$7,500} = \underset{\text{(accounts payable)}}{\$7,500} + \$0$$

As shown, assets increase by $7,500 and this is counterbalanced by liabilities increasing by $7,500. Owner's equity is not affected.

Under double-entry bookkeeping every transaction requires two entries. Sometimes these involve a change in each side of the accounting equation; in other cases, they affect only one side. For example, if one of the assets increases, then one of the following occurs:

- Another asset decreases by an equal amount. For example, the company could sell some machinery (decrease in assets) in exchange for cash (increase in assets).

- Liability or owners' equity increases by an equal amount. For example, the company could sell some stock (increase in owners' equity) in exchange for cash (increase in assets).
- Some combination of the two above will occur. For example, the company could buy a new facility (increase in assets) in exchange for a cash down payment (decrease in assets) plus an agreement to pay the balance in monthly installments (increase in liabilities).

In this way, the accounting equation remains in balance.

Accounting Statements
Over the years, accountants have developed basic formats for accounting statements. These formats give managers and others a basis for comparing the financial positions of different departments or companies. The accounting statements most commonly used for measuring a company's current profits and position for earning future profits are the balance sheet, the income statement, and the relatively new statement of cash flows.

1. What is the accounting equation?
2. How does double-entry bookkeeping work?

CHECK ✓ POINT

Balance Sheet

The accounting equation serves as the basis for the **balance sheet,** which is a financial statement showing the position of a firm as of a particular date. It is akin to a snapshot of the enterprise. The balance sheet is commonly prepared as of the close of business on December 31. This makes it possible to compare how the balance sheet has changed from year to year. For example, how much has cash gone up over the last year or how much have accounts payable declined?

In some cases, organizations use a different **fiscal year,** which is the 12 months that constitute their annual operation. Some companies, and many governmental bodies, operate on a fiscal year from June 1 to May 31. The federal government's fiscal year runs from October 1 to September 30. Regardless of the specific 12 months involved, the annual balance sheet reflects the organization's financial position as of the end of the fiscal year.

The balance sheet describes the three elements of the accounting equation: assets, liabilities, and owners' equity. Each category contains a number of accounts. In examining these accounts, we will use the balance sheet of a fictitious company, Sunrise Manufacturing Corporation, which appears in Table 18.2. The first column of data is taken from the ledger categories; the second column represents the totals for the categories (for example, there is $80,000 in cash assets); and the third column is the totals for assets, liabilities, owners' equity, and the grand total ($880,000).

Balance sheet A financial statement showing the position of a firm as of a particular date.

Fiscal year The 12 months that constitute an organization's annual operation.

Assets
The balance sheet usually divides the company's assets into three separate categories: current, fixed, and intangible assets.

TABLE 18.2

SUNRISE MANUFACTURING CORPORATION
Balance Sheet
December 31, 19XX

Assets

Current Assets			
Cash		$ 80,000	
Marketable securities		10,000	
Accounts receivable	$170,000		
Less: Allowance for doubtful accounts	10,000	160,000	
Notes receivable		15,000	
Inventory		210,000	
Prepaid expenses		5,000	
Total current assets			$480,000
Fixed Assets			
Machinery and equipment	$310,000		
Less: Accumulated depreciation	50,000	$260,000	
Office furniture and equipment	$ 30,000		
Less: Accumulated depreciation	10,000	20,000	
Building	$ 70,000		
Less: Accumulated depreciation	20,000	50,000	
Land		30,000	
Total fixed assets			$360,000
Intangible Assets			
Patents	$ 30,000		
Goodwill	10,000		
Total intangible assets			$ 40,000
Total Assets			$880,000

Liabilities and Owners' Equity

Current Liabilities			
Accounts payable	$ 80,000		
Notes payable	20,000		
Payroll and benefits payable	40,000		
Accrued taxes	70,000		
Accrued interest	40,000		
Total current liabilities		$250,000	
Long-Term Liabilities			
Mortgage payable	$ 70,000		
Notes payable	20,000		
Long-term bonds outstanding	100,000		
Total long-term liabilities		190,000	
Total liabilities			$440,000
Owners' Equity			
Common stock (120,000 shares)		$120,000	
Retained earnings		320,000	
Total owners' equity			440,000
Total Liabilities and Owners' Equity			$880,000

Current assets Assets that the company will use or convert into cash within the year.

Current Assets Management often needs to know which assets will be used or converted into cash within the next year. This gives an indication of the company's ability to generate cash. Therefore, balance sheets separate out these assets, called **current assets.** For Sunrise Manufacturing, these include:

- *Cash.* Funds that are on hand in the company or are in bank deposits and can be withdrawn as needed.
- *Marketable securities.* Temporary investments of surplus funds in forms that can be quickly converted to cash when the need arises. Examples are stocks and bonds, described in Chapters 20 and 21.
- *Accounts receivable.* Money due from customers who purchased goods and have not yet paid for them. In some cases, such as bills that are long overdue, managers expect that they will never be paid. To correct for this expectation, they subtract, or write off, the debt through an allowance for doubtful accounts ($10,000 for Sunrise).
- *Notes receivable.* Money owed to the firm by someone who has been given funds and, in turn, signed a written document acknowledging the debt. An example is a loan made to a major supplier who wants to expand operations and provide better service to the company.
- *Inventory.* Merchandise on hand, usually in the warehouse or out on the sales floor, which is available for sale, as well as raw materials, component parts, and goods that are in the manufacturing process.
- *Prepaid expenses.* Goods and services that the company has paid for but not yet received or used. Examples include insurance premiums that are paid before the coverage goes into effect and supplies that are paid for before delivery.

Fixed Assets   The remaining tangible assets are **fixed assets,** which are assets that the company intends to keep for more than one year. These assets are used in the operation of the business. Examples of fixed assets include machinery, equipment, furniture, fixtures, buildings, and land.

Machines, furniture, and other fixed assets are listed at the purchase price, but they lose value from year to year because they gradually wear out. To account for this, each year the accountant subtracts a percentage of the initial cost of an asset. This deduction is called **depreciation.** The specific procedure for calculating depreciation varies and depends on federal laws that frequently change. In general, the company either selects an equation or uses a table that indicates the percentage of the total value to subtract in a given year. The company usually depreciates all fixed assets except land. Land is not depreciable because it is not considered to wear out and in fact it often increases in value.

Intangible Assets   Sometimes a firm owns assets that do not have physical presence. If it does not, then this category will not be included in the balance sheet. These **intangible assets** include patents and goodwill. Goodwill represents the firm's reputation and is generally entered on the company's books only if the firm buys another company and, in the process, pays for the goodwill. In other words, the buyer is willing to pay for the intangible asset of the other company's excellent reputation.

Liabilities
Liabilities usually appear on the balance sheet in the order in which they will come due. Specifically, current liabilities are followed by long-term liabilities.

Fixed assets   Assets that the company intends to keep for more than one year and use in the operation of the business.

Depreciation   A deduction from the value of a fixed asset to account for its gradual wearing out.

Intangible assets   Assets such as patents or goodwill that do not have physical presence.

A deliveryman for Dreyer's Grand Ice Cream holds some of the other products the company distributes. Distribution rights are intangible assets and thus are listed on Dreyer's balance sheet.

Source: Courtesy of Dreyer's Grand Ice Cream, Inc.

Current liabilities   Financial obligations that will fall due within the year.

Current Liabilities   Financial obligations that will fall due within the next year are **current liabilities.** Table 18.2 shows typical liability accounts:

- *Accounts payable.* Amounts that the firm owes to its suppliers and others who have extended it credit.
- *Notes payable.* Loans due in one year or less to be paid by the firm. The firm has signed a written document or a note acknowledging the debt. An example would be a loan from a bank or a supplier.
- *Payroll and benefits payable.* Money owed to employees plus contributions to be made to the health insurance and retirement programs.
- *Accrued taxes.* Taxes the company owes but has not yet paid.
- *Accrued interest.* The amount of interest owed on outstanding loans.

Long-term liabilities   Debts that will be due one or more years in the future.

Long-Term Liabilities   After current liabilities, the balance sheet lists **long-term liabilities,** debts that will be due one or more years after the balance sheet is drawn up. Table 18.2 provides some typical examples:

- *Mortgage payable*. The outstanding real estate loan on the enterprise's land and buildings.
- *Notes payable*. Loans that will come due in more than a year (usually 2 to 5 years).
- *Long-term bonds outstanding*. Financial obligations that carry a fixed rate of interest and come due on a stipulated maturity date.

Owners' Equity

The difference between total assets and total liabilities is the owners' equity in the company. The last part of the balance sheet shows the different accounts that make up owners' equity. For corporations, such as Sunrise Manufacturing, this includes common stock and retained earnings. **Common stock** is the most basic type of stock ownership. It represents an ownership share in the corporation. This stock is described in detail in Chapters 20 and 21. **Retained earnings** are profits that have been reinvested in the corporation. When the firm has a profit at the end of the year and decides to use these funds to expand operations, the retained earnings account will increase by this amount. Conversely, if the corporation suffers an operating loss, retained earnings will decline by the amount of the loss.

For unincorporated businesses (proprietorships and partnerships), the owners' equity section will contain the direct investment of the owner or each partner in a capital account. This capital account includes the initial investment, subsequent additional investments, withdrawals, and retention of earnings. Unlike the corporate equity section, which lists common stock and retained earnings in separate accounts, the unincorporated business has everything combined into the single account. By looking at this section of the balance sheet the reader can determine the type of company ownership.

Common stock An ownership share in a corporation.

Retained earnings Profits that have been reinvested in the company.

The Balance Sheet as a Management Tool

The balance sheet is an important financial statement for controlling operations and helping management make effective decisions. It reveals whether the firm is solvent (i.e., current assets are greater than current liabilities, the firm can pay its bills and wages) by providing a breakdown of all assets, liabilities, and owners' equity. It allows managers to compare balance sheets from one year to the next to see changes in assets, liabilities, and owners' equity. By analyzing the data in the balance sheet and comparing it with previous years, managers can identify trends and pinpoint potential problem areas.

The balance sheet and the other financial statements of publicly held firms are printed in the annual report and are thus available to everyone. There is a trend to make annual reports slimmer and easier for stockholders to read, and some firms, such as London's Burton Group (a fashion retailer), use the report as a marketing tool. Burton's report looks like a fashion magazine, with the required accounting figures squeezed in among lavish photos of fun-loving models wearing stylish clothes.[9] Except for these innovative uses, management depends on the balance sheet as a financial statement to help lenders analyze the firm as a credit risk. Managers also compare their company's balance sheet with those of their competitors in order to identify their company's relative strengths and weaknesses.

A Boise Cascade nurseryman checks 2-year-old seedlings set for transplant in the company's timberlands. The cost of raising these Douglas fir and ponderosa pine trees from seed to maturity is included in cost of goods sold on the balance sheet.

Source: Courtesy of Boise Cascade Corporation.

CHECK ✓ POINT

1. What are the three major categories of accounts on the balance sheet?
2. What are two uses for the balance sheet?

Income Statement

Income statement A financial statement that summarizes the firm's operations for a given period of time, usually one year.

Managers want to know more than whether the company has sufficient resources; they also want to know whether the company is using those resources successfully. For this accounting information, they turn to the income statement. An **income statement** is a financial statement that summarizes the firm's operations for a given period of time, usually one calendar or fiscal year. The income statement indicates whether the company made a profit or a loss (the famous "bottom line" of business). This bottom line determines the very survival of business firms in a free-enterprise, market economy.

Contents of the Income Statement

Like the balance sheet, the income statement is based on an equation. This equation is:

$$\text{Revenues} - \text{Expenses} = \text{Profit}$$

Table 18.3 shows an income statement for the Oakland A's baseball team. Notice that even though the A's pay star players such as Jose Canseco, Dave Stewart, and Rickey Henderson millions of dollars,[10] the owner, Walter Haas, still made about a million himself. This healthy profit picture makes the A's, which Haas reluctantly bought for $12.75 million 10 years ago, worth an estimated $100 million today.[11]

TABLE 18.3
Simplified Income Statement for the
Oakland A's

Revenues		
Attendance	$21,340,000	
Advertising	6,095,000	
Royalties, promotions, and other concessions	5,910,000	
TV and radio	17,200,000	
Other	40,000	$50,585,000
Expenses		
Interest and depreciation	$ 1,700,000	
Scouting	2,870,000	
Stadium	4,210,000	
Marketing	5,950,000	
Administration	6,340,000	
Minor-league payroll	3,770,000	
Major-league payroll	24,800,000	$49,640,000
Net Income		$ 945,000

Source: "How the Oakland A's Make (Almost) a Million," *Fortune*, August 13, 1990, 98.

TABLE 18.4

SUNRISE MANUFACTURING CORPORATION
Income Statement
Year Ended December 31, 19XX

Revenue from Sales	$2,820,000	
Less: Sales returns and allowances	20,000	
Net Sales		$2,800,000
Cost of Goods Sold		
Beginning inventory	$ 230,000	
Cost of goods manufactured	1,900,000	
Total goods available for sale	$2,130,000	
Less: Ending inventory	210,000	
Total cost of goods sold		1,920,000
Gross margin		$ 880,000
Operating Expenses		
Selling expenses	$ 180,000	
Administrative expenses	220,000	
General expenses	120,000	
Total expenses		520,000
Net Income from Operations		$ 360,000
Less: Interest expense		40,000
Net Income before Taxes		$ 320,000
Less: Taxes		80,000
Net Income		$ 240,000

A more detailed income statement, for Sunrise Manufacturing Corporation, is presented in Table 18.4. As this table shows, income statements include four categories: revenues, cost of goods sold, operating expenses, and net income.

FIGURE 18.2

Calculating Cost of Goods Sold for a Wholesaler or Retailer

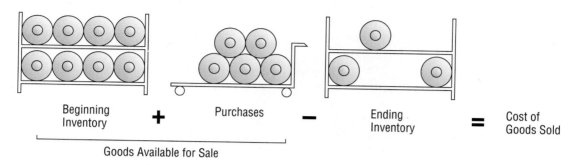

Beginning Inventory **+** Purchases **−** Ending Inventory **=** Cost of Goods Sold

Goods Available for Sale

Revenues The income statement begins by listing the company's revenues. This entry shows all the money the company earned during the year. Normally this is from sales, but in a professional service such as a doctor's office revenues will come from fees. Sometimes this entry is called "gross sales" or simply "sales." If the firm allows customers to return merchandise because the goods are damaged or do not meet quality standards, the accountant deducts these returns from the overall revenue to arrive at a net sales figure. Sunrise Manufacturing deducted $20,000 from total revenue for this reason.

Cost of Goods Sold The next section of the income statement describes the first of two kinds of expenses: cost of goods sold. The **cost of goods sold** consists of the costs involved in producing or acquiring a product to sell. For a manufacturing firm, the cost of goods sold primarily consists of expenses for production employees and raw materials. For a wholesaler or retailer, the cost of goods sold includes the money spent to acquire and stock the inventory it has sold.

To calculate the cost of goods sold, the accountant measures how the inventory changed from the beginning to the end of the year. The first step is to ascertain beginning inventory (often from the previous year's income statement). To this amount, the accountant adds cost of goods manufactured for a manufacturing firm or purchases for a wholesaler or retailer for the year; the sum is the total cost of goods available for sale during the year. This amount minus the ending inventory gives the total costs of the goods actually sold. Figure 18.2 illustrates this calculation for a wholesaler or retailer. In some cases, the financial statement does not show these calculations, but merely contains an entry for cost of goods sold.

Subtracting the cost of goods sold from net sales gives the gross margin. Managers are interested in this figure because it gives them information on evaluating performance and, when compared to previous years, identifies trends that help in controlling the firm and making effective decisions.

Operating Expenses Besides spending money to produce what it sells, the company incurs other expenses to keep running and to sell its products.

Cost of goods sold The costs involved in producing or acquiring a product to sell.

These operating expenses can be selling expenses, administrative expenses, or general expenses:

- *Selling expenses*. All costs directly related to the selling of goods and services. Examples include advertising, salaries and commissions paid to salespeople, sales supplies, delivery expenses, and other sales-related costs.
- *Administrative expenses*. Costs incurred by the management and office personnel in running the company's operation. Examples are management salaries, secretarial wages, and rent.
- *General expenses*. All costs not charged directly to one department or unit because it is too difficult or time-consuming to determine their proper allocation. For example, property taxes, insurance, and utilities often fall into this category.

Usually these expenses are deducted from revenues in order to determine taxable income. However, in some states, such as California, business entertainment expenses (dues, meals, or other costs) that are incurred at social clubs that discriminate on the basis of sex, race, religion, or ancestry are not deductible.[12]

Depreciation Expense   Companies that own fixed assets include a special kind of expense on their income statements: depreciation. Although the company does not actually spend any money on depreciation, this deduction is advantageous when calculating income for tax purposes. By using depreciation to reduce income, the accountant reduces the amount of taxes the company owes. This is the government's way of encouraging companies to invest in new facilities and equipment. In other situations, such as reporting the company's financial strengths to shareholders, the accountant tries to report as little depreciation as possible. Thus, within the guidelines of the law, which changes from time to time, accountants may consider the audience for their reports when selecting a method of calculating depreciation.

Net Income   The last part of the income statement shows the computation of net income. Accountants specify income from operations and income before taxes to gain more information for effective decisions and to use in further analysis. First the accountant subtracts total expenses from gross margin to arrive at net income from continuing operations. Then the accountant deducts the interest expense on outstanding loans to arrive at net income before taxes. The interest expense is separated out from the other expenses to show the cost of borrowing and financing the operation. Finally, by deducting taxes, the accountant arrives at net income.

Income Statement Decisions

The income statement is more than just a series of numbers added and subtracted to arrive at net income. Accountants must exercise judgment in deciding how to present and evaluate various kinds of information. An example of how calculations can have ethical implications is seen in the accompanying Ethics Close-Up (A Movie Blockbuster That Lost Money). An especially "gray" area is how depreciation is calculated. Earlier it was pointed out that

CLOSE-UP / *Ethics*

A Movie Blockbuster That Lost Money

One of the biggest box-office hits of recent years, *Coming to America,* had total worldwide receipts in the triple-digit millions. However, the film's major claim to fame may not be its popularity or the star Eddie Murphy, but the accounting-related lawsuit that it spawned.

The suit was filed by Art Buchwald, the noted newspaper columnist, and an associate. The two had offered a story idea, which they called *King for a Day,* to Paramount Pictures. Buchwald and friend were told by Paramount that their idea was not very good and they signed over the rights for a small amount. However, when *"Coming to America"* was released they sued Paramount on the grounds that the successful film was based on their story and they should have their old contract voided. The court agreed and awarded Buchwald and his associate a share of the film's profits. Unfortunately for Buchwald, Paramount accountants reported that the movie lost money. Shown here in the table at the right is the bookkeeping (in millions of dollars) that was used to support this finding.

Paramount's position is that Buchwald and his associate cannot be paid a share of the profits because there were none. Moreover, according to Paramount accountants many blockbuster films — including *Fatal Attraction* and *Batman* — have not made a profit. This may be a reason that many big stars take a hefty fee up front (Jack Nicholson was paid $10 million to play the Joker in *Batman*) rather than gamble on a percentage of the profits. They are aware that the breakeven point is not easy to pin down.

Revenue (excludes uncollected billings and some home video revenues)	$125.3
Expenses	
Up-front salaries to the film's superstar, Eddie Murphy, and the director	11
Development of the film and production and overhead costs	47.5
Paramount's distribution fees	42.3
Paramount's distribution costs	36.2
Paramount's charge for interest on the money used to make the film	6.4
	$143.4
Net Income (Loss)	($ 18.1)

Many people in the industry feel that the deductions used by film producers are unethical because they amount to unjustified expenses. For example, Paramount took a fee of 30 percent ($42.3 million) for distributing the movie, which is standard for the industry, although the actual cost for this service is far less. Charging interest of $6.4 million is also regarded as questionable.

Buchwald and his associate decided to bring legal action against the accounting methods used by Paramount in an effort to revise the deductions, put *Coming to America* in the profit column, and generate some income for themselves. In the view of many, any other outcome would be unethical.

Source: Richard W. Stevens, "Tinsel Magic: 'Hit' Loses Millions," *New York Times,* April 13, 1990, C1–2 and Ronald Grover, "Curtains for Tinseltown Accounting?" *Business Week,* January 14, 1991, 35.

even though companies do not spend money on depreciation, the way it is calculated affects the amount of income the company reports. Other judgment calls involve ways of valuing inventory and handling inflation.

Valuing Inventory   Accountants have a choice in deciding how to value inventory. The reason for this is that it would be costly and difficult to keep track of exactly which costs are associated with the sale of which items. To take an extreme example, imagine a hardware store that sells nails the old-fashioned way, from bins. The last batch of number 10 common nails that the store bought cost 50 cents a pound; the store sells them for $1 a pound. These nails are popular, so the next month the store gets another shipment of nails at 60 cents a pound and dumps them in the bin with the nails left from

FIGURE 18.3
Inventory Valuation Systems: LIFO and FIFO

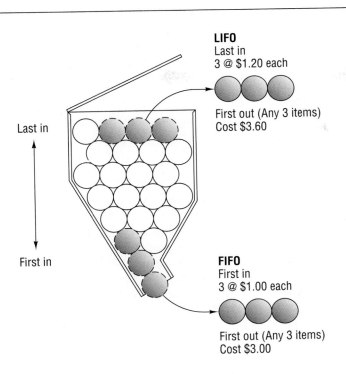

LIFO
Last in
3 @ $1.20 each

First out (Any 3 items)
Cost $3.60

Last in

First in

FIFO
First in
3 @ $1.00 each

First out (Any 3 items)
Cost $3.00

the preceding month. During the following week, customers come in and grab nails by the handful. Which nails are they buying: the 50-cent nails or the 60-cent nails?

Obviously, the company can't keep track, so it has its accountant make assumptions. Either the company assumes that it always sells the oldest nails it has, or it assumes that it always sells the nails that it bought most recently. If the accountant assumes that the last goods received are the first ones sold (Last In, First Out), the inventory system is called **LIFO.** If the accountant assumes the first goods received are the first ones sold (First In, First Out), the inventory system is called **FIFO.** Figure 18.3 illustrates the difference.

In times of rapid inflation, LIFO produces higher cost of goods sold (the last in goods cost more), a less valuable ending inventory, and lower profits. In contrast, FIFO brings about a lower cost of goods sold, a more valuable ending inventory, and greater profits. Many firms opt for LIFO in order to keep down their reported profits and, as a result, their cash payments for taxes. The choice of method is an important decision, because once set up, government approval is needed to change it. The financial statement should specify which method is used so that readers can take this into consideration in evaluating the firm's overall performance.

Handling Inflation   Besides having an impact on inventory values, inflation affects a company's bottom line in various ways. Inflation can enable a company to charge higher prices for its products, but it can also cause expenses to rise. For example, if a fast-food outlet that sells hamburgers for

LIFO An inventory valuation system under which the last goods produced or acquired are considered the first ones sold (Last In, First Out).

FIFO An inventory valuation system under which the first goods produced or acquired are considered the first ones sold (First In, First Out).

$1.20 finds that inflation enables it to raise prices to $1.30, it will receive 10 cents more for each hamburger it sells. If it sells 1,000 hamburgers a week, this increase comes to $100 more a week. However, the company may also find that it has to pay more for wages, ground beef, and heating the restaurant. Thus, revenues may increase, but not necessarily by as much as the expenses.

In evaluating an increase in revenues or even profits, readers of the income statement need to keep in mind whether the increase is the result of effective management or simply inflation. If the change reflects inflation, the company may run into serious problems when inflation slows.

Benefits of the Income Statement

Like the balance sheet, the income statement can be an important resource for effective financial control and management decision making. Most fundamentally, it tells managers whether the firm is operating at a profit. By comparing income statements from one period to another, the managers can see which expenses are rising too quickly and take steps to control them. The statement also allows banks and other financial institutions to evaluate the firm's creditworthiness. It shows whether the business is able to generate a profit with its resources.

CHECK ✓ POINT

1. What equation is the basis of the income statement?
2. How do accountants determine the cost of the goods the company sold?

Statement of Cash Flows

Statement of cash flows A financial statement that provides information regarding a firm's cash receipts and cash payments.

Besides a balance sheet and an income statement, accountants for most companies also prepare a **statement of cash flows.** This financial statement has most recently come on the scene and has replaced the funds statement or statement of changes in financial position. The older statement was mainly concerned with changes in working capital (current assets minus current liabilities). This newly accepted financial statement of cash flows provides information regarding a firm's cash receipts and cash payments. It does so by an **activity format,** which classifies cash inflows and outflows in terms of operating, investing, and financing activities.

Activity format A financial statement format that classifies cash inflows and outflows in terms of operating, investing, and financing activities.

Operating activities relate to a firm's main revenue-generating activities; the cash flows from operating activities. Cash inflows from customer collections would be the major one. Investing activities include lending money, say, to a supplier, and collecting on those loans. Another example reflecting the outflow of cash would be purchases of equipment and the inflow would be the sale of equipment. Financing activities would include borrowing and repaying money from creditors, obtaining funds from owners, and paying dividends to stockholders. Table 18.5 shows an example of a statement of cash flows. This financial statement helps management better control and manage cash flows, which are vital to the company's solvency.

CHECK ✓ POINT

1. What is measured by the statement of cash flows?
2. What are the three major activities involved in the cash flow?

TABLE 18.5

SUNRISE MANUFACTURING CORPORATION
Statement of Cash Flows
Year Ended December 31, 19XX

Cash flows from operating activities:		
Operations: net income	$ 240,000	
Add (deduct) items not affecting cash:		
Depreciation expense	40,000	
Increase in accounts receivable (net)	(10,000)	
Decrease in inventory	20,000	
Decrease in accounts payable	(5,000)	
Net cash provided by operating activities		$ 285,000
Cash flows from investing activities:		
Sale of equipment	10,000	
Purchase of machinery	(100,000)	
Net cash used by investing activities		(90,000)
Cash flows from financing activities:		
Retirement of mortgage payable	(100,000)	
Dividends	(50,000)	
Net cash used by financing activities		(150,000)
Net increase in cash		$ 45,000

Analysis of Financial Statements

Over the years, accountants and managers have developed standard techniques for evaluating the information contained in the various financial statements. Generally, they start by putting the statement into context. Then they use techniques based on a variety of ratios.

Putting the Statement in Context

When managers and others evaluate a company's performance and compare it to the performance of other companies, they must evaluate the context in which the accounting information appears. This requires an understanding of the environment in which the company has been operating. It also requires taking into account the various choices the accountant made.

A company's performance is colored by the economic environment. As already discussed, inflation can affect a business's profits. Likewise, companies typically suffer during an economic downturn. Some industries, such as real estate and oil, are particularly prone to business cycles. For example, in the fall of 1990, the Northeast part of the U.S. entered a recession with accompanying falling real estate prices and rising unemployment. By contrast, however, because of the crisis in the Middle East and the resulting increase in oil prices, the Southwest had an economic upturn.[13] To evaluate an individual company's performance without taking these differing circumstances into account would be misleading. If a company prospers during a time of growth or struggles during an economic decline, the evaluator must look for clues that indicate whether the performance reflects the position of the particular company or the nature of the economy in general.

AAR Corporation overhauls, buys, sells, and leases aircraft engines and components. Rather than keep track of each fan blade, for example, for purposes of determining profit, company accountants assume that the first one acquired is the first one sold. This system of inventory valuation is called FIFO (first in, first out).

Source: Courtesy of AAR Corporation.

The manager also needs to consider the accounting techniques used. As was already shown, how depreciation is calculated or the technique for valuing inventory affects the business's financial statements. The person using accounting information must determine whether a change in the financial statement reflects a change in the company's health or merely the adoption of a new accounting technique.

Analysis Using Ratios

Calculating ratios is a popular method of analyzing financial statements. Ratios are calculated by dividing one item on a financial statement by another item. The ratio shows relationships between financial variables. Managers who use ratio analysis can pinpoint where the firm is doing well and where it is doing poorly. When compared with previous years, the ratios identify trends. Many different types of ratios can be calculated to measure a company's short- and long-run position and profitability.

Ratios Measuring Short-Run Position   Ratios that measure the firm's short-run position investigate its liquidity. The short-run position is the firm's ability to pay currently maturing obligations, usually liabilities due within a year. **Liquidity** is the ease with which an asset can be converted into cash. For example, a firm with most of its assets in cash, stock, and accounts receivable is considered to be very liquid, because stocks are easy to sell and accounts receivable are likely to be paid before long. Conversely, a firm with most of its assets tied up in real estate and slow-moving inventory has very low liquidity. The two most common ratios that measure a firm's short-run position are the current ratio and the acid-test ratio.

Liquidity The ease with which an asset can be converted into cash.

The **current ratio,** the ratio of current assets to current liabilities, is a simple way to assess liquidity. For Sunrise Manufacturing (see Table 18.2), the current ratio is:

Current ratio The ratio of current assets to current liabilities.

$$\frac{\text{Total Current Assets}}{\text{Total Current Liabilities}} = \frac{\$480,000}{\$250,000} = 1.92 \text{ to } 1$$

This current ratio provides an indication of Sunrise's ability to meet its current liabilities.

Is 1.92 to 1 an adequate ratio? The answer will depend on the industry. Utilities have a lower current ratio than manufacturing firms. For a typical utility, 1 to 1 is adequate because the company has predictable sales, a high collection rate, and no product inventory. For most other kinds of firms, however, 2 to 1 or better is generally considered acceptable. Because Sunrise Manufacturing's current ratio is less than this, its managers may be a little concerned. On the other hand, they should withhold judgment until they compute the other liquidity ratio, the acid-test ratio.

Acid-test ratio The ratio of highly liquid assets to current liabilities.

The **acid-test ratio** (sometimes known as the quick ratio) compares highly liquid assets against current liabilities. While it resembles the current ratio, the acid-test ratio compares only highly liquid assets — cash, marketable securities, and accounts and notes receivable — against current liabilities. It does not take inventory into account because of the time it will take to convert this asset into cash. Thus, it is a more conservative ratio than the current ratio. The acid-test ratio gives increased information on a firm's ability to pay short-term debts. For Sunrise Manufacturing, the acid-test ratio is:

$$\frac{\text{Cash + Marketable Securities + Accounts Receivable + Notes Receivable}}{\text{Current Liabilities}}$$

$$= \frac{\$80,000 + \$10,000 + \$160,000 + \$15,000}{\$250,000} = \frac{\$265,000}{\$250,000} = 1.06 \text{ to } 1$$

A generally acceptable acid-test ratio is 1 to 1. If the manager doubts that marketable securities and accounts and notes receivable can be converted dollar for dollar, then 1.5 to 1 is acceptable. Sunrise Manufacturing meets the guideline, so it should have no trouble covering its current liabilities.

Ratios Measuring Long-Run Position   Managers who use financial statement analysis to control the firm are also interested in its long-run position. A representative ratio that measures long-run position is the debt-equity ratio.

To calculate the **debt-equity ratio,** the total debt is divided by total equity. For Sunrise Manufacturing, this calculation is:

Debt-equity ratio   The ratio of total debt to total equity.

$$\frac{\text{Total Debt}}{\text{Total Owners' Equity}} = \frac{\$440,000}{\$440,000} = 1 \text{ to } 1$$

This calculation indicates that the firm is being financed equally by debt and equity. Many lenders avoid lending a greater amount than the owners have in equity. A total debt-equity ratio of 1 to 1 is thus the maximum. In the future, it is likely that Sunrise will begin paying off this debt or increasing its equity by selling more stock and retaining more profits.

Income Statement Ratios   Businesspeople also calculate ratios from the data on the income statement. These ratios provide a measure of current operating performance and efficiency. A common income statement ratio is the net profit margin ratio.

The **net profit margin ratio** compares net income to net sales. For Sunrise Manufacturing, this calculation is:

Net profit margin ratio   The ratio of net income to net sales.

$$\frac{\text{Net Income}}{\text{Net Sales}} = \frac{\$240,000}{\$2,800,000} = 8.6\%$$

The net profit margin shows the company's overall profitability. By comparing this year's margin with those of the last 3 to 5 years, managers can see whether profitability is improving or declining. The 8.6 percent figure for Sunrise is fairly typical for modern firms. Profit margins are generally much lower than many people realize.

Combined Ratios   Businesspeople can gain additional insights from ratios that combine information from the balance sheet with information from the income statement. The most popular of these combined ratios are used to measure the level of activity known as the inventory turnover and to refine the profitability picture by analyzing the return on owners' equity and earnings per share in corporations.

The number of times that inventory is replaced during the year is the **inventory turnover.** Managers keep track of this because inventory that sits unsold on the shelf of a store or in a warehouse costs the firm money. It takes up space, may wear out or become dated, and ties up funds the company could have invested in something more profitable. Consequently, managers try to keep inventory turnover relatively high.

Inventory turnover The number of times that inventory is replaced during the year, expressed as the ratio of costs of goods sold to average inventory.

To compute inventory turnover, divide the cost of goods sold during the year by the average inventory. Average inventory is the average of beginning and ending inventory; it is computed by adding those amounts and dividing by 2. For Sunrise Manufacturing, average inventory is calculated this way:

$$\frac{\text{Beginning Inventory} + \text{Ending Inventory}}{2} = \frac{\$230,000 + \$210,000}{2} = \$220,000$$

Then average inventory is used to calculate inventory turnover:

$$\frac{\text{Cost of Goods Sold}}{\text{Average Inventory}} = \frac{\$1,920,000}{\$220,000} = 8.7$$

Sunrise is turning over its inventory 8.7 times a year. To determine the average number of days that inventory was on hand before being sold, divide 8.7 into 365, the number of days in a year.

$$\text{Average Number of Days to Turnover} = \frac{365}{8.7} = 42$$

To determine whether 8.7 is a good inventory turnover figure, Sunrise management would want to gather data on what competing firms are doing. If competitors have a turnover of 6.0, Sunrise is doing well. If the competition has a turnover of 11.3, Sunrise is doing poorly and must take steps to increase its turnover. This might involve dropping slow-moving lines or increasing sales on credit.

A more accurate financial picture of profitability requires a comparison of the income to the amount of investment that has been made. **Return on owners' investment** is the ratio of net income to total owners' equity. Commonly referred to as return on investment, or simply ROI, this ratio tells the stockholders the return the company earned on their investment. For Sunrise Manufacturing, the calculation is:

Return on owners' investment The ratio of net income to total owners' equity.

$$\frac{\text{Net Income}}{\text{Total Owners' Equity}} = \frac{\$240,000}{\$440,000} = 55\%$$

This return is extremely high. The owners could not possibly get this type of return on their money from a bank or a government note. Sunrise is doing extremely well, and the stockholders should be pleased.

As shown in Table 18.6, Wal-Mart's 42.16 percent average annual ROI over the past decade led *Fortune's* most admired corporations, and LTV's

TABLE 18.6
Return on Investment of *Fortune's* Most and Least Admired Corporations of 1980–1990

Most Admired Corporations		Least Admired Corporations	
Merck	23.62%	Goldome	N.A.
Rubbermaid	32.51	Great American Bank	N.A.
Procter & Gamble	22.18	CrossLand Savings	N.A.
Wal-Mart	42.16	Wang Laboratories	−18.06%
PepsiCo	27.62	Meritor Savings Bank	N.A.
Coca-Cola	28.96	Continental Airlines	−15.96
3M	15.82	Mack Trucks	N.A.
Johnson & Johnson	18.58	Unisys	−13.85
Boeing	16.95	LTV	−30.29
Eli Lilly	20.49	Control Data	−12.08

Source: Alison L. Sprout, "America's Most Admired Corporations," *Fortune*, February 11, 1991, 57.

−30.29 percent was the worst. Obviously, investors who held Wal-Mart stock during the past 10 years and then sold it would have made a lot of money. If they held stock of companies on the least admired list, they would have lost money on their investment.

A final profitability ratio is the **earnings per share.** This popular ratio shows the amount of income or profits earned for each share of common stock outstanding. Outside investors obviously are very interested in this ratio. Management uses it to decide on dividends to pay stockholders and as an important measure of performance of the firm. For Sunrise, it would be calculated as follows:

Earnings per share The ratio of net income to common stock shares outstanding.

$$\frac{\text{Net Income}}{\text{Common Stock Shares Outstanding}} = \frac{\$240,000}{120,000} = \$2.00$$

This $2.00 earnings per share can be compared to those of other years and to those of competitors in the same industry. Chapter 21 covers the topic of stocks in more detail.

Ratio Analysis in Perspective The ratios we have discussed are useful but, as was stated earlier, anyone evaluating the numbers must put them in the context of the company's practices and the economic environment. Sometimes a company's prospects are brighter or gloomier than the ratio numbers would suggest. So, while ratio analysis is a useful tool for helping make more effective decisions, managers must be careful not to let the numbers alone make the decision. On the other hand, these ratios are very useful from a financial control standpoint to pinpoint liquidity, inventory turnover, and profitability problems and suggest steps to correct them. These ratios also help managers make more effective investment and growth decisions that are aimed at increased profits, the bottom line. In short, as has been stated throughout, accounting information is extremely useful for financial control and effective management decision making.

CHECK ✓ POINT

1. Define two ratios managers use to interpret a company's financial position.
2. How do businesspeople decide whether the company is earning an adequate return on its assets or owners' equity?

Closing Comments

This chapter has launched a discussion of the financial side of the enterprise. The particular focus of attention was on the generation and analysis of accounting information. Accountants construct the firm's financial statements and often participate in analyzing them to help managers control the firm and make informed decisions. Managers inside the firm and other businesspeople on the outside analyze financial information by determining how much of revenues covers expenses and how much goes to income, as well as by calculating a variety of ratios.

VIDEO CASE / *Sam's Success*

Over the past decade, the fastest growing retail chain in America has been Wal-Mart Stores, Inc., of Bentonville, Arkansas, which was founded in the 1950s by Sam Walton. Most of Wal-Mart's initial chain of stores are in the central and southern regions of the United States, but the company is now expanding into other parts of the country. The stores offer general merchandise at discount prices. In addition, Wal-Mart has wholesale clubs, discount drug outlets, and hypermarts.

Bankers and investors alike agree that Wal-Mart is a phenomenal success story. Its financial statements show rapid sales and profit growth (see the following balance sheet and income statement), and its stock price has risen so sharply over the years that many of the employees and stockholders who bought stock in the 1970s and held on to it are millionaires today. Wal-Mart plans to be a $150 billion company by the year 2000. Given its annual rate of growth, this appears to be an achievable goal.

Wal-Mart Stores, Inc. and Subsidiaries
Balance Sheet, January 31, 1989 and 1990

Assets	1989	1990
	(amount in thousands)	
Current assets		
Cash and short-term market investments	$ 12,553	$ 12,790
Receivables	126,638	155,811
Recoverable costs from sales and leasebacks	114,653	78,727
Inventories	3,351,367	4,428,073
Prepaid expenses	25,776	37,215
Total current assets	$3,630,987	$4,712,616

Fixed assets

Property, plant, and equipment at cost	$2,277,384	$3,189,596
Less accumulated depreciation	520,318	711,763
Net property, plant, and equipment	1,757,066	2,477,833
Net property under capital leases	904,888	952,226
Goodwill	41,036	37,493
Other	25,691	18,316
Total assets	$6,359,668	$8,198,484

Liabilities and Owners' Equity

Current liabilities

Notes payable	$ 19,000	$ 184,774
Accounts payable	1,389,730	1,826,720
Accrued liabilities		
Salaries	126,661	157,216
Taxes, other than income	106,855	133,609
Other	281,156	340,068
Accrued federal and state taxes	121,158	179,049
Long-term debt due within one year	1,690	1,581
Obligations under capital leases due within one year	19,659	22,298
Total current liabilities	$2,065,909	$2,845,315

Long-term liabilities

Long-term debt	$ 184,439	$ 185,152
Long-term obligations under capital leases	1,009,046	1,087,403
Deferred income taxes	92,365	115,053
Common shareholders' equity		
Common stock	56,559	56,614
Capital in excess of par value	174,277	180,465
Retained earnings	2,777,073	3,728,482
Total liabilities and shareholders' equity	$6,359,668	$8,198,484

Wal-Mart Stores, Inc. and Subsidiaries
Income Sheet, January 31, 1989 and 1990

	1989	1990
	(amount in thousands)	
Revenues:		
Net sales	$20,649,001	$25,810,656
Rentals and other	136,867	174,644
Total revenues	$20,785,868	$25,985,300
Costs and expenses:		
Cost of sales	$16,056,856	$20,070,034
Operating, selling, and general and administrative expenses	3,267,864	4,069,695
Interest costs	135,681	138,071
Total costs and expenses	$19,460,401	$24,277,800
Income before income taxes	1,325,467	1,707,500
Provision for federal and state income taxes	488,246	631,600
Net income	$ 837,221	$ 1,075,900

Case Questions

1. What was Wal-Mart's working capital during the two years presented in the financial statements? What general conclusions can you draw as a result of your calculations?

2. What was Wal-Mart's net profit margin rate and return on investment (ROI) during the two years presented in the financial statements? What conclusions can you draw as a result of your calculations?

3. In addition to the financial calculations you have made already, what other accounting ratios would you compute in determining how well the firm is doing? Explain and give some examples.

Learning Objectives Revisited

1. **Define accounting and the types of accountants.** Accounting is the process of measuring, interpreting, evaluating, and communicating financial information for the purpose of financial control and more effective decision making. The two main types of accountants are public accountants and private accountants. Public accountants, who may be certified, are accountants who are independent of the business they serve. Private accountants work for a business other than a public accounting firm. They include internal auditors, financial accountants, and managerial accountants. The latter may also be certified.

2. **Discuss the nature and types of budgets.** A budget is a financial plan that specifies revenues and expenses for a given time period. The budget helps managers plan and control operations by identifying objectives and then providing feedback regarding how well the company is doing in meeting these targets. Some of the most popular budgets are the sales budget, the production budget, the cost of goods sold budget, and the cash budget.

3. **Explain the accounting equation and double-entry book-keeping.** The accounting equation is assets equal liabilities plus owners' equity. Assets are everything of value that the enterprise owns. Liabilities are creditors' claims on the enterprise's assets. Owners' equity is the owners' claim on the assets of the enterprise. To keep the equation in balance, accountants use double-entry bookkeeping, the use of two entries for every transaction. If the total on one side of the accounting equation changes, then the accountant must make an offsetting entry to keep the sides in balance.

4. **Describe the balance sheet.** The balance sheet describes the three components of the accounting equation: assets, liabilities, and owners' equity. The asset side of the balance sheet has two major categories: current assets and fixed assets. On the other side of the balance sheet are liabilities and owners' equity. The liabilities are current liabilities and long-term liabilities. The owners' equity section for a corporation lists stock and retained earnings and for an unincorporated business contains a single capital account.

5. **Present the income statement and the statement of cash flows.** An income statement summarizes the firm's operations for a given period of time. It reports the revenue from sales after deducting returns and allowances, as well as the cost of the goods that were sold, the operating expenses, and the net income. The statement of cash flows provides information on cash receipts and cash payments. Using an activity format, it classifies cash flows in terms of the operating, investing, and financing activities of the firm.

6. **Identify ratios used to analyze financial statements.** Some of the most important balance sheet ratios used in evaluating a firm's performance measure the company's short-run and long-run position. For the short run, these include the current ratio (current assets divided by current liabilities) and the acid-test ratio (liquid assets divided by current liabilities). For the long run, a representative ratio would be the debt-equity ratio (total debt divided by total owners' equity). An important income statement ratio used in evaluating a firm's performance is the net profit margin ratio (net income divided by net sales). Ratios that combine information from these statements are used to measure the level of activity such as the inventory turnover and refine the profitability picture by analyzing the return on investment or ROI (net income divided by owners' equity) and earnings per share.

Key Terms Reviewed

Review each of the following terms. For any that you do not know or are unsure of, look up the definitions and see how they were used in the chapter.

accounting	balance sheet	LIFO
certified public accountant (CPA)	fiscal year	FIFO
internal auditor	current assets	statement of cash flows
certified management accountant (CMA)	fixed assets	activity format
budget	depreciation	liquidity
accounting equation	intangible assets	current ratio
assets	current liabilities	acid-test ratio
liabilities	long-term liabilities	debt-equity ratio
owners' equity	common stock	net profit margin ratio
double-entry bookkeeping	retained earnings	inventory turnover
	income statement	return on owners' investment
	cost of goods sold	earnings per share

Review Questions

1. What is accounting? Why should anyone besides accountants be interested in this financial information?

2. Jose would like to be a certified public accountant (CPA). Barry would like to be a certified management accountant (CMA). How will their activities differ?

3. Ron Jacobs is business manager of a theater group that puts on plays in a small auditorium it owns downtown. In planning the group's finances for the upcoming season, what kinds of budgets should Ron use? What kinds of information should these budgets contain? Try to be specific.

4. What is the accounting equation? Describe how each of the following transactions would affect the elements of the accounting equation.
   a. A bakery sells doughnuts for cash.
   b. A car rental company acquires a new fleet of cars and agrees to pay for them within 90 days.
   c. An insurance company pays stockholders a dividend of $1 for every share of stock they own.
   d. A factory pays its workers their weekly wages.

5. What basic kinds of information appear on a balance sheet? Why are managers interested in this information?

6. Define the different categories of assets. Identify each of the following as a current, fixed, or intangible asset.
   a. A printing press
   b. The shoes in a shoe store
   c. The shoe store's reputation for quality
   d. The chairs in a doctor's waiting room

7. What is owners' equity? What forms does it take?

8. On what equation is the income statement based? What is the bottom line for a company that had total sales of $750,000 and spent $400,000 to produce the goods it sold and $200,000 on other expenses?

9. When Ann Wilson prepares the tax returns for Big T Manufacturing, she tries to depreciate the company's machinery as quickly as is legally possible. In other words, she tries to write off the maximum proportion of the total value in the first years of the machinery's life. Why would she want to do this? What effects does her approach have on the company's profits?

10. The Jackson Company values its inventory on a LIFO basis. The Horne Corporation uses FIFO. What is the difference between the two and how could it affect overall profit?

11. What is the statement of cash flows? What can business people learn from reading one?

12. What general procedures do businesspeople follow in analyzing financial statements?

13. Roberta Foster's business has a current ratio of 2.1 and an acid-test ratio of 1.2. June Wheatley's firm has a current ratio of 1.9 and an acid-test ratio of .6. Based on these data, what conclusions can you make regarding the liquidity of the two firms?

14. At the Thrill-A-Minute Amusement Park, total assets come to $5.5 million, total debts are $3 million, and owners' equity is $2.5 million. Compute a ratio that measures the company's long-run position. How can you tell whether such a ratio is favorable or not?

15. What ratio can a manager use to analyze the information on an income statement? Describe how it is calculated.

16. U-Stop Here had an inventory turnover of 9.7 last year. The company's major competitor had an inventory turnover of 6.1. Based on these data, what conclusion can you draw regarding U-Stop's performance in this area?

Applied Exercise

The Bratley Company is thinking of changing its inventory valuation from FIFO to LIFO. Sales for next month are projected at $100,000 (10,000 units at $10 each). Other expenses will be $30,000. Here is how long each unit has been on hand along with its cost:

On Hand	Number of Units	Cost per Unit
60 days	5,000	$5.50
40 days	4,000	6.00
20 days	2,000	6.50
10 days	1,000	7.00

If the company sells 10,000 units next month, what will be its profits using a FIFO valuation? A LIFO valuation? Why would the company prefer FIFO? LIFO? Explain.

YOU BE THE ADVISER / *The Proposed Expansion*

The Beldon Company is a large retail store that sells a wide variety of home appliances and convenience goods. Last year the company had a beginning inventory of $1 million, inventory purchases of $4 million, and an ending inventory of $1 million. The store sells its merchandise for double what it pays, and annual sales are approximately twice that of the competition. However, Beldon would like to expand.

For $2 million, the store will be able to double its warehouse and showroom floor space and, its managers hope, also double its annual sales. The competition currently turns its inventory over eight times a year, and Beldon would like to get its turnover up to ten times. At the present time, cash stands at $100,000, accounts receivable are $400,000, inventory is $1 million, and current liabilities are $2.5 million.

The president of Beldon believes that the company should expand operations as soon as possible. The accountant disagrees. She feels that, if anything, the firm should work on controlling inventory more closely.

Your Advice

1. What should Beldon do?
   ___ a. Expand vigorously, because it is doing so much better than the competition.
   ___ b. Analyze the financial statements and base the expansion decision on these results.
   ___ c. Be conservative and work on controlling operations rather than expanding.
2. From the information presented in the case, what is its present inventory turnover?
3. Based on your calculations in Question 2, which conclusions can you draw regarding inventory turnover? Explain.
4. Would you recommend following the president's desire to expand or the accountant's suggestion that the firm focus on controlling inventory? Explain your recommendation.

WINNING WITH FAST FOOD PROPERTIES

Most businesses could not survive without the services of banks or other financial institutions. In particular, companies have financial needs caused by cash flow shortages and expansion that require long-term loans; and this is where financial institutions enter the picture. One of the most unique, successful financial institutions in recent years has been the Franchise Finance Corporation of America (FFCA). FFCA primarily invests in fast food franchises and travel-related properties, areas that generally have been overlooked by most banks and other traditional financial institutions. FFCA has built an asset base of more than $1 billion by buying property and buildings and leasing them back to franchisees.

Money and Banking

Chapter Learning Objectives

- Explain the nature and purpose of money.

- Describe the money supply and its components.

- Present the major financial institutions.

- Discuss the Federal Reserve System.

- Explain how government agencies protect deposits.

- Identify recent developments in banking.

In fact, FFCA has more fast food franchises than any other company except McDonald's.

What is even more interesting than the phenomenal growth, is that FFCA has managed to remain highly profitable during an era when large banks and the entire savings and loan industry have been hard hit by losses. Although there are many reasons, most of the financial institutions that have lost money in recent years can point to real estate loans that have gone sour. For example, by the early 1990s real estate holdings in cities across the country had declined 10–30 percent from their peak values in the late 1980s. Big real estate owners such as Donald Trump suddenly found themselves in deep financial trouble.

They were unable to pay the interest on their loans and had to renegotiate loan agreements with their banks or S&Ls. In some cases they even had to relinquish or sell off some of their properties in order to meet their financial obligations. In fact, going into the 1990s things have gotten so bad in some areas of the country that banks and S&Ls have now stopped allowing borrowers to pledge real estate as collateral for loans because the value of these assets is shrinking, and perhaps even more important, the financial institutions do not want to end up with the questionable properties in their asset holdings.

Quite clearly, the U.S. money and banking system has undergone some fundamental changes, and traditional real estate holdings are no longer playing the major role in collateral and investment. The emphasis now is on lending money on safer collateral and investments. FFCA's fast food franchises have not gone the way of the traditional real estate investments such as downtown commercial properties, office complexes, shopping centers, apartments, condominiums and residential housing. FFCA's real estate investments have been safe and secure, which helps explain why it has been making money and expanding while its counterparts in banks and S&Ls have had big trouble in recent years.

Photo source: © 1991 Benning Photographic Works.

Introduction

If a big retailer wants to borrow several million dollars to build a new distribution center, the company president does not go through the phone book looking for people with extra money. This direct approach to financial transactions is usually much too inefficient. Instead, the suppliers and demanders of funds use intermediaries in the form of financial institutions. Consumers and organizations that have money to save or invest lend it to financial institutions in exchange for payments of interest. Borrowers — businesses, the government, and consumers — then pay the financial institution interest for the privilege of using money. This chapter begins a discussion of financing a business by considering the functions of money and banking.

The Nature and Purpose of Money

In a simpler world, if John has a loaf of bread and Mary has a gallon of milk, John might exchange half the loaf for half the milk so that they can both eat and drink. Such a transaction is called barter — the trading of goods and services. However, today's world is not so simple. To address this issue, the parties in most exchanges use **money** — anything a society generally accepts in payment for goods and services. In the past, societies have adopted many kinds of objects as money, including cattle, pepper, tobacco, animal hides, and, of course, gold and silver. Today, money usually takes the form of coins and specially printed pieces of paper.

Money Anything a society generally accepts in payment for goods and services.

The Functions of Money

Money is a medium of exchange. This means that a supplier of a product or service will accept money in exchange for the product or service, knowing that other suppliers will in turn accept that money for other products or services. For example, Attorney Mary Smith will accept money in exchange for drawing up a will, knowing that she can use the money to buy supplies for her law office and pay herself a salary for her personal needs.

Money is also a standard of value. In other words, it is a measure of the relative worth of goods and services. If a phone call costs 25 cents, a carton of yogurt costs 50 cents, and a dental checkup costs $25, then we know that a carton of yogurt is worth twice as much as a phone call and a checkup is worth 100 times as much as a phone call. This is easier to keep track of than remembering to bring 50 cartons of yogurt to the dental clinic.

Money also serves as a storehouse of value. If you don't need money right away, you can keep it or invest it until you are ready to use it. If you get paid twice a month, money enables you to spread out your expenditures from paycheck to paycheck and even into retirement.

Characteristics of Money

Money best performs these functions when it has certain characteristics: divisibility, portability, durability, stability, and security.

Divisibility To be flexible as a medium of exchange, money should be divisible into smaller units. Centuries ago, the Spanish government issued a gold doubloon. The coin was often carved into eight pieces, hence the term "pieces of eight." This allowed the owner of the coin to buy goods worth less than a doubloon.

Today, money is divisible in a symbolic sense; coins and bills are available in various denominations. The dollar is divided into pennies, the British pound into pence, and the German mark into *pfennigs*. If you buy a 25-cent newspaper with a 1-dollar bill, the seller can give you change.

Portability Money should also be easy to carry around. Imagine leading oxen or hauling silver ingots to the auto dealership at the other end of town. The bulkier or heavier the money, the more difficult it is to use. This is why governments eventually developed paper money. Bills with large denominations further increase portability. In the United States, bills have had denominations ranging from $1 to $100,000, but in recent years $100 is the largest bill issued.

Durability Money must be able to stand up to abuse and wear and tear; otherwise it will become worn out and useless. The importance of durability may explain the enduring popularity of precious metals as money. Over the centuries, gold coins have proved particularly effective in standing the test of time. Modern forms of money are less durable and thus are often replaced. New U.S. coins — pennies, nickels, dimes, and quarters — are issued every year, although they are in circulation 10 or more years. Paper money is replaced, on average, every 18 months.

Stability The value, or purchasing power, of money should remain relatively steady. This inspires confidence in the money and a willingness to continue using it as a medium of exchange. Governments pursue stability in the international arena. For example, the U.S. government tries to maintain a stable dollar vis-à-vis the currency of other countries.[1] Because stability is important, governments also try to keep inflation under control. Runaway inflation can rapidly erode the value of a country's money and lead people to look for other storehouses for their wealth. This happened in many South American countries such as Brazil which had an unbelievable 2,700 percent annual inflation rate a few years ago.[2]

Security To preserve the value of their money, governments must make it difficult to counterfeit. After all, if anyone could produce money on the nearest photocopier, the money wouldn't be worth much. When countries relied on gold coins as their major source of money, counterfeiting was a minor problem. The value of the currency was in the gold itself. The only way to undermine its value was to mint a coin with less gold and pass it off as having full value, and the color and standard weight of gold made this difficult to accomplish. However, with the issuance of paper money, the problem of counterfeiting became much more serious. Today, the paper on which U.S. money is printed has small red and blue threads embedded in it. While this makes effective counterfeiting extremely difficult, it is still a problem. Other nations have followed similar approaches in ensuring that their monetary system is not undermined by counterfeiters who flood the market with phony paper money.

For over 75 years Deluxe Corporation has been printing checks. Checks are the favorite method of payment in this country, which means that a large amount of money is kept in checking accounts. The federal government includes this amount in M1 when measuring the money supply.

Source: © Mark LaFavor/Parallel Productions, Inc.

The U.S. Money Supply

Stability and security are two of the concerns that lead the U.S. government to try to measure the supply of money. Changes in the supply that indicate instability might lead the government to attempt corrective actions.[3] Although economists and financial experts sometimes debate exactly what is included in the money supply, most refer to it as M1. **M1** is a measurement that usually consists of currency and demand deposits.[4]

Currency Coins and paper money make up **currency.** Coins are the small change of the money supply. At present, approximately 2 to 3 percent of the total U.S. money supply is in the form of coins. Paper money makes up approximately one-fourth of the money supply with about $200 billion of paper currency in circulation at any one time.

Demand Deposits The remainder of the money supply is made up of **demand deposits,** which consist of various types of checking accounts. A large percent of all financial transactions use a check. The reasons are quite simple:

M1 A measure of the money supply equal to currency and demand deposits.

Currency Coins and paper money.

Demand deposits Checking accounts.

- **Checks are versatile.** You can make a car payment of $223.42 with one check instead of coming up with the right combination of bills and change each month.
- **Checks reduce the possibility of theft.** You can specify who has a right to the money; this is especially important if you want to mail in a payment.
- **Checks provide a record of the transaction.** This simplifies bookkeeping and provides evidence if you need to prove a bill was paid or want to claim a tax deduction.

The most common type of demand deposit is **regular checking,** an account that pays no interest but allows the depositor to write checks on the funds. Most such accounts assess a monthly service charge based on the number of checks written or the average daily balance in the account. The more checks written or the lower the balance, the higher the fee.

An attractive type of demand deposit for those who are willing to forgo some privileges in exchange for earning a little money is the **negotiable order of withdrawal (NOW) account,** a checking account that pays interest. In recent years, the interest rate for NOW accounts has been about 5½ percent. However, these accounts are subject to some restrictions. In particular, the depositor sometimes may write only a limited number of checks in a stated period of time. In addition, the fees on NOW accounts sometimes exceed the interest paid. Depositors must therefore compare fees as well as interest when shopping for a checking account.

A special type of demand deposit is the **traveler's check,** which is a check that is sold with a preset value and is redeemable if lost. The price of the check is the value on the check plus a processing fee. The most popular brand is the American Express traveler's check, which is widely used by international travelers. As advertised, a buyer who loses one can often obtain a full refund within 24 hours.

Near Money: A Broader View of the Money Supply Sometimes observers of the economy want to measure not just the money supply in the strictest sense, but the total assets that owners can easily use to make purchases. As Chapter 18 pointed out, assets that can be converted into cash quickly are said to be liquid. Money itself, of course, is a liquid asset: if you have money during business hours, you can rush right to the store and convert the money to other assets by purchasing something. At the other extreme, real estate is not nearly as liquid; if your only asset is your house, you'd need a while to sell or mortgage it to pay your tuition.

To view this broader picture of the money supply, economists and financial experts measure **near money,** certain highly liquid assets that do not function as a medium of exchange. These assets consist of noncheckable savings and time deposits. These deposits are discussed next, but it should be noted that they do not function as a medium of exchange because, before you can use them, you have to go to the trouble and probable expense of converting them to money.

Savings Deposits There are several ways savers can keep their money. **Passbook savings accounts** are noncheckable interest-bearing accounts.

Regular checking An account that pays no interest but allows the depositor to write checks on the funds.

Negotiable order of withdrawal (NOW) account A checking account that pays interest.

Traveler's check A check that is sold with a preset value and is redeemable if lost.

Near money Certain highly liquid assets that do not function as a medium of exchange.

Passbook savings accounts Noncheckable interest-bearing accounts.

A small plane flies over the rain forest to land at a remote Costa Rican town and deliver an emergency refund of American Express traveler's checks. Because of the company's worldwide delivery program the stranded jungle traveler received his refund in 4 hours. This kind of worldwide service has made American Express the leading provider of traveler's checks.

Source: © Neil Selkirk.

These conservative investments tend to pay low interest rates. Years ago, they were popular because low inflation made the interest attractive and few alternatives were as readily available to small investors. Today, because of the higher interest rates available in other near-money investments, their popularity has waned. However, they are flexible and liquid, and their few restrictions appeal to small savers looking for a way to get started.

In recent years, depositors have been offered attractive alternatives to passbook savings accounts. One is the **money market mutual fund,** which consists of shares in mutual funds (pooled contributions of investors discussed in Chapter 21) that make short-term investments in securities of the federal government and major corporations. These investments expire on specified dates, at which time the mutual fund gets the invested money back and purchases other short-term investments. Because the rate of interest is usually higher than that on a savings account and has relatively low risk, these funds have become very popular over the past decade.

In 1982, Congress allowed financial institutions to start offering their own money market accounts, because many of their customers were withdrawing deposits and investing them in money market mutual funds. These **bank money market accounts** are short-term, special deposit accounts that offer competitive interest rates. Banks typically put these deposits into high-yield investments that allow them to pay high interest. Often, depositors can write checks against these accounts. If they can, then it no longer is classified as near money.

Time Deposits   Besides savings deposits, where depositors can withdraw money at any time, the other form of near money is time deposits. **Time deposits** are savings accounts that require the depositor to give notice before withdrawing funds or to pay a penalty for withdrawing funds before a speci-

Money market mutual funds
Shares in mutual funds that make short-term investments in securities of the federal government and major corporations.

Bank money market accounts
Short-term, special deposit accounts that offer competitive interest rates.

Time deposits   Savings accounts that require the depositor to give notice before withdrawing funds or to pay a penalty for withdrawing the funds before a specified date.

fied date. Because the restrictions mean that depositors are likely to leave their funds in the account longer, the financial institution usually pays more interest for these deposits.

For example, depositors can usually earn more interest on **certificates of deposit (CDs),** which are fixed-term accounts that pay a predetermined rate of interest. The longer their deposit term and the greater the investment, the higher will be the interest rate. Terms range from 90 days to 5 years or more, but the average CD depositor usually purchases a CD for a year or less. In the early 1980s, a small ($1,000 or less) one-year CD was paying around 14 percent. By 1987, inflation had slowed and the annual rate had dropped to around 7 or 8 percent, depending on the amount and term of the CD, and it has remained there in the early 1990s. Because of variable interest rates, some institutions are offering innovative techniques to attract long-term CDs. For example, to attract those saving for their children's college expenses, a New Jersey bank offers a CD with an interest rate tied to an annual index of higher education costs. As the chairman of the bank notes: "With us, families have shifted the risk of rising tuition and inflation from the household to the bank."[5] This is an instance of a family practicing risk management (discussed fully in Chapter 22).

Certificates of deposit (CDs) Fixed-term accounts that pay a predetermined rate of interest.

Credit Cards: Short-Term Loans   A comprehensive definition of money includes all near money, but it does *not* include credit cards, even though consumers use them to make purchases. A **credit card** is an instrument used for obtaining a short-term loan for a cash purchase. The term credit means these cards create loans that the borrower must repay with money; they are not money themselves. Visa and MasterCard are widely used credit cards.

Credit card   An instrument used for obtaining a short-term loan for a cash purchase.

Credit cards are enormously popular in the United States. Millions of the major cards are in circulation. For example, Citibank offers five different kinds of Visa and MasterCard products and has almost 36 million cards globally.[6] International firms are also getting into the credit card market as seen by the JCB card from Japan, which is held by over 70 million Japanese and is now being offered in the United States.[7] Coupled with charges to the hundreds of other cards issued by oil companies and other retailers, credit card purchases run into the hundreds of billions of dollars each year.

A less popular way to shop with plastic is to use a bank-issued **debit card,** which allows a merchant to deduct purchases directly from the buyer's bank account. Debit cards differ from credit cards in that they do not allow the holder to buy now and pay later; the amount is immediately withdrawn. Although consumers have preferred checks and credit cards for shopping, they do use the debit cards to obtain funds from **automatic teller machines (ATMs).** The user slides the card into the machine, types in an access code number assigned by the bank (which should be a secret to everyone except the user and the bank), and tells the ATM how much is to be deposited or withdrawn, and the machine takes care of the rest.

Debit card   An instrument that allows a merchant to deduct purchases directly from the buyer's bank account.

Automatic teller machine (ATM) A machine that takes bank customers' debit cards and secret access codes to automatically deposit or withdraw funds from their accounts.

In the case of withdrawals, the machine dispenses the money right on the spot. Typically, the financial institution sets a maximum for withdrawals at any one time (often $100 to $200) and during any 24-hour period ($200 in many locales). ATMs are spreading to many locations, including college campuses across the country. Whether used in ATMs or for shopping, debit cards are not part of the money supply; they merely move money in the

FIGURE 19.1
Financial Institutions as Intermediaries

customer's checking account, which has already been counted as part of the money supply.

Students without a credit history can get a credit card on their parents' account to cover them in emergencies. However, establishing your own credit is usually wise in the long run. Department stores and other retailers are usually the easiest sources of credit for those who are starting out. If you have a car, an oil company credit card is another possible way to begin. The companies that issue major credit cards traditionally were hesitant to establish an account until the applicant had worked for a year or two. However, in recent years, because of the increased competition among those institutions issuing cards, simply graduating from college and having a job may qualify you for a card. The key is to make payments on time, and pay other bills promptly, in order to get a good credit rating and keep your card.

CHECK ✓ POINT

1. What are the characteristics of money?
2. How does money differ from near money?

Types of Financial Institutions

In most cases, borrowers and lenders come together through some form of financial intermediary. These financial institutions typically pay interest on the money deposited by suppliers of funds; they then lend the funds to borrowers at a higher rate of interest. The difference between what the institution pays depositors and what it receives from borrowers goes to run the business and make a profit. Figure 19.1 shows how this works.

Several kinds of financial institutions provide money to borrowers. The major types of financial intermediaries in the United States are commercial banks, savings and loan associations, mutual savings banks, credit unions, and several kinds of nondeposit institutions. Some of these, such as commercial banks, lend the deposits they receive; others, such as life insurance companies and pension funds, invest money set aside to handle future contingencies such as death or retirement. Table 19.1 summarizes how each of these institutions serves as an intermediary. While the distinctions between them have blurred over the past decade because they have begun offering more similar services, all of these institutions continue to remain important.

TABLE 19.1
How Different Financial Institutions Serve as Intermediaries

Financial Institution	Major Sources of Funds	Most Common Forms of Investments	Services for Customers
Commercial banks	Customer deposits, interest from loans	Personal loans, business loans	Checking and savings accounts; ATMs; loans; credit cards; some brokerage, insurance, and financial/estate planning services
Savings and loan associations	Customer deposits, interest from loans	Home mortgages, construction loans	Checking and savings accounts; ATMs; loans; credit cards; some brokerage, insurance, and financial/estate planning services
Mutual savings banks	Customer deposits, interest from loans	Home mortgages, construction loans	Checking and savings accounts; ATMs; loans; credit cards; some brokerage, insurance, and financial/estate planning services
Credit unions	Member deposits, interest from loans	Second mortgages, auto loans, short-term member loans	Share draft account (like checking account); savings accounts; ATMs; loans; credit cards; large ones offer some brokerage, insurance, and financial estate planning services
Insurance companies	Policyholder premiums, earnings on investments	Government bonds, commercial real-estate mortgages, long-term loans	Savings plans; loans; insurance; some financial/estate planning services
Pension funds	Contributions by employers and/or employees, earnings on investments	Corporate securities, government bonds	Savings plans; some loans; insurance and financial/estate planning services
Commercial and consumer finance companies	Short-term borrowing, interest earned on loans	Short-term business loans, short-term consumer loans	Loans; some credit cards, insurance and financial planning services

Commercial Banks

The most common and readily identifiable financial institution is a **commercial bank.** This is a financial institution that accepts deposits and provides a wide array of financial services, from loans to checking accounts to safe-deposit boxes. Many of the largest financial institutions in the country are commercial banks.

Traditionally, the commercial banking industry has been strong. In recent years, however, there are signs of some trouble. Although the problems do not loom as large as those faced by the savings and loan industry (discussed in the next section), going into the 1990s banks around the country were writing off bad loans five times the amount of 10 years ago.[8] As shown in Figure 19.2, the number of problem banks is going down a little, but many experts feel the worst is yet ahead.[9] Only time will tell how seriously the banking industry is in trouble, but one way to move ahead is to become more competitive. The current banking scene is discussed in the accompanying Ethics Close-Up (Do Financial Institutions Finally Have Their House in Order?).

Commercial bank A financial institution that accepts deposits and provides a wide array of financial services.

CLOSE-UP / *Ethics*

Do Financial Institutions Finally Have Their House in Order?

A major social problem in recent years has been the near collapse of the banking industry. Whose fault is it? There is no question that many banks made poor loans. In many cases they were in too much of a hurry to beat out the competition in securing a loan or to close a deal because the interest rate was quite attractive. Unfortunately, it soon became clear that a large number of these loans were not only nonperforming, but were so bad that they simply had to be written off as uncollectible. Many banks were reluctant to write off the loans because of the effect this would have on their overall financial position. In some cases, the bank would need to raise additional capital in order to remain afloat because a writeoff of the delinquent loans would result in a dramatic decrease in the required equity capital.

Today, many of these reluctant banks have had to bite the bullet and write off their bad loans. In particular, many real estate loans and international loans have been acknowledged as uncollectible. However, circumstances may be getting better. Interest rates on savings accounts have fallen all the way to 2-3 percent, the lowest in many years. At the same time, the interest rates on mortgages, credit card loans, and business loans, where banks make their money, have dropped only slightly. This means that the margin between what banks are making and what they are paying has increased.

Despite some evidence for optimism, banks are not yet out of the woods. They still have a large number of nonperforming loans outstanding that must be turned around or written off. In fact, recent statistics show that approximately 5 percent of all loans are nonperforming, which is higher than the 2.2 percent in 1988. There are many home and office building mortgage loans that are greater than the assessed value of their properties. If borrowers default on these loans, banks will be unable to clear them by selling these properties.

In general, banking experts believe that the industry has turned the corner and the worst is now behind. However, from the standpoint of social responsibility, the banks must be more careful in evaluating borrowers and exercise greater prudence in the future. Perhaps they are learning the wisdom of J.P. Morgan who once commented that, "Sometimes a return *of* your investment is more important than a return *on* your investment."

Source: Gary Hector, "Banking Finally Hits the Bottom," *Fortune,* April 6, 1992, pp. 98–100.

FIGURE 19.2
Banks in Trouble: Federally Insured Banks Designated by Regulators as Problems

Source: John Meehan, "Banks: Is Big Trouble Brewing?" *Business Week,* July 16, 1990, 149.

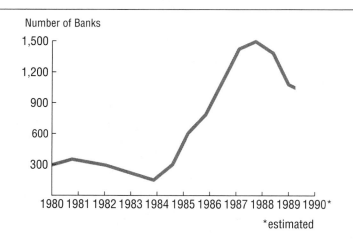

Number of Banks

*estimated

National banks Commercial banks chartered by the federal government.

A commercial bank may be a national bank or a state bank. A **national bank** is chartered by the federal government. The charter spells out the articles of incorporation under existing laws. About one-third of all commercial banks fall into this national bank category. These banks tend to be large,

(in millions)	1989	1988
Domestic:		
Commercial and Financial	$17,470	$17,243
Real Estate:		
Construction	2,756	3,131
Commercial Mortgages	4,122	3,601
Residential Mortgages	5,694	2,763
Consumer Expenditures	5,226	4,549
Lease Financing Receivables	510	616
Total Domestic	35,778	31,903
International	8,734	9,687
Total Loans	$44,512	$41,590

Chemical Bank is lead banker to New Jersey flag maker Annin & Co. Forty-one percent of all mid-sized businesses in this area have a banking relationship with Chemical. These relationships are reflected in Chemical Banking Corporation's loan portfolio (see chart), which shows that most of the corporation's lending is to commercial and financial borrowers.

Source: © Dana Duke 1991.

State banks Commercial banks chartered by individual states.

holding approximately 60 percent of all commercial bank deposits. A **state bank** is chartered by an individual state. There are about twice as many of these smaller state banks.

Commercial banks are often referred to as "full-service" banks. This is because they offer their customers a wide range of financial services, including checking and savings accounts, business and personal loans, bank credit cards, safe-deposit boxes, the electronic transfer of funds to other banks, traveler's checks, and financial counseling.[10] In addition, bank customers are increasingly using ATMs.

These services are not free. In one way or another, the bank charges for them, although many depositors are not always aware of it. For example, many banks assess a service fee if an account balance falls beneath a particular minimum, such as $200. Unless the depositor pays attention to the amount of interest earned and fees charged, the account can actually lose money. If the account is small enough, say, $50, the fees will eventually deplete the entire fund. Banks also charge a fee for overdrafts. If a depositor writes a check for $200 when only $180 is in the account, the bank may refuse to honor the check and impose a fee (often $5 to $10). Credit cards are another source of income for banks, because banks typically charge a fee of $20 to $35 a year per card in addition to charging interest on the balance. Borrowers also pay

Savings and loan association (S&L) Financial institution that emphasizes savings accounts and home mortgage loans.

Junk bonds High interest-bearing but very risky bonds that were mainly issued in the 1980s.

fees, usually based on the amount of the loan. Table 19.2 describes some of the specific services and fees charged by representative major banks.

Savings and Loan Associations

The original goal of **savings and loan associations (S&Ls)** was to encourage home ownership. These institutions originally used funds in families' savings accounts to make home mortgage loans. Today, S&Ls, sometimes called "thrifts," still emphasize this activity but also offer checking accounts, credit cards, and a variety of other types of loans and services.

Government regulations used to set the interest rates on S&L savings accounts slightly higher than comparable accounts at commercial banks. This enabled S&Ls to attract small savers who wanted to make the highest possible return without the risk of most investments. In turn, the S&L loaned these funds to home buyers at competitive rates. Because S&Ls specialized in home mortgages, they were often the first place people turned to when they wanted to finance a home.

In the 1980s all of this changed. Deregulation of the banking industry allowed banks and S&Ls to set interest rates freely, but banks matched the rates at S&Ls, thereby attracting depositors. At the same time, many S&Ls were stuck with mortgages paying relatively low interest while they had to pay higher rates to attract deposits.

In dealing with the situation, Congress gave S&Ls the freedom to seek creative ways of competing. These institutions were allowed to offer services that used to be the exclusive domain of the commercial banks. They were also free to invest in high-interest but very risky bonds — commonly known as **junk bonds** — and in real estate, hotels, motels, fast food franchises, and other relatively risky ventures.[11] In this climate of "wheeling and dealing" a few of the heads of S&Ls went so far as to, unethically, if not illegally, buy yachts and expensive paintings and to operate their institutions as if it were, in the words of one investigator, "a personal piggy bank."[12]

These highly questionable financial decisions in the 1980s eventually resulted in massive losses and hundreds of S&Ls found themselves insolvent. In 1989 alone, the industry lost $19.2 billion.[13] Congress has now begun working on a bailout plan that requires S&Ls to meet new capital standards that supposedly will ensure their survival.[14] Unfortunately, many S&Ls cannot meet these standards and will end up being sold off.[15] Some of these sales will help stem the losses, but in many cases the S&Ls that are in trouble are being sold very cheaply.[16] In fact, some people claim that the federal government's plan for handling the S&L bailout is actually making things worse.[17] In any event, the total loss, much of which is guaranteed to be made up by the federal government, is estimated to be in triple digit billions.[18] Only time will tell what the final price tag of the S&L bailout will be. Congress did appropriate $50 billion for bailout funds in 1990 and regulators asked for twice that amount for the following year.[19]

There has been and will continue to be tremendous political and financial fallout from the S&L crisis. Investigators are still seeking answers to how things could have got so far out of control. Going into the 1990s, however, most experts still treat the crisis in the S&L industry as a major setback rather than a death blow to this traditionally important financial intermediary.

TABLE 19.2
Examples of Specific Bank Services and Fees

Bank	Account	Features	Fees	Interest and Service
Bank One Columbus, Ohio	Blue Max	Checking Savings Credit card Money market	$2,500 balance or $10 a month	4.85% on checking; no annual fee for credit card; 500 free ATMs; debit card
Bank of America San Francisco	Alpha	Checking Savings Money market	$2,500 balance or $7 a month	4% on checking; 1,525 free ATMs; $300 automatic overdraft protection; monthly fee rises to $9 on 4/1/90
Barnett Banks Jacksonville, Florida	Senior Partners	Checking Savings Money market	$2,500 balance in money market, $11 a month, or $1,000 CD	4.25% interest on checking; 569 free ATMs; account holder must be at least 55; free copying service at most branches (useful for medical insurance forms)
Baybanks Boston	Interest Checking	Checking Savings Money market	$1,000 balance or $3.50 a month and 35 cents a transaction (including ATM)	5.25% on checking; 760 ATMs; bank card buys gasoline at the cash price
Citibank New York City	Citi-One	Checking Savings Credit card Money market	$5,000 average balance or $9.50 a month and 25 cents a withdrawal (including ATM)	5.5% on checking; 1,100 ATMs; 19.8% rate on credit card, but no first-year annual fee
First National Chicago	First Value	Checking	$250 balance or $7 a month	No interest on checking; credit cards available through subsidiaries; 150 free ATMs
NCNB Charlotte, North Carolina	Financial Connections	Checking Savings Credit card Auto loan	Balance rises monthly from $250 to $1,000, or $10 a month	No interest on checking; no annual fee for the first year of credit card; fees waived if customer borrows at least $6,000; 600 free ATMs; no fees on Plus System and Relay ATM networks
Norwest Minneapolis	Classic	Checking Savings Credit card Money market	$10,000 balance or $10 a month	5.37% on checking; 720 free ATMs; free children's checking accounts available if parents maintain higher balances; no first year annual fee on credit card
Security Pacific Los Angeles	ValuAdded	Checking Savings Credit card	$1,000 balance and $10 a month	4% on checking; credit card rate drops from 19.8% to 14.8% according to holder's number of accounts; no annual credit card fee; 1,601 free ATMs

*Rates are as of 1/10/90.

Mutual Savings Banks

Similar to savings and loan associations, but less common, are **mutual savings banks.** These are state-chartered banks that offer many of the same services as S&Ls. When these institutions were first formed in the early

Mutual savings bank State-chartered bank that offers many of the same services as S&Ls.

1800s in the Northeast, they were strictly savings banks; they encouraged savings by individual households and helped these groups meet their borrowing needs. The names of some of these institutions reflect their origins. Dime Savings Bank, Emigrant Savings Bank, and Seaman's Bank of Savings. With the changes in banking regulations, mutual savings banks have expanded their services. Today they offer NOW accounts, home mortgages, and other services that make them particularly competitive with S&Ls. However, because of relatively conservative state regulations, they can only make approved investments and thus have been spared some of the problems currently facing S&Ls.

Credit Unions

Sometimes the members of a group form a savings cooperative. They pool their funds and share ownership of the pool, each member in proportion to his or her investment. Representatives of the pool manage it for the group. A savings cooperative that lends money to its members is a **credit union.**

Credit union A savings cooperative that lends money to its members.

A typical credit union consists of members of a specific group, such as employees of a company or a university. Only those who belong to this group may join the credit union. Most credit unions require a minimum deposit such as $100 to join. In return for putting up the deposit, the members can earn interest on savings and apply for loans. In most cases, credit unions pay slightly higher interest rates than other financial institutions pay on similar accounts.

Like other financial institutions, credit unions have recently been expanding their financial services, offering life insurance and interest-bearing checking accounts. However, their ability to compete with other lending institutions is severely limited. For one thing, they accept deposits only from their members, which limits the funds they can accumulate. Also, they typically must limit the amount they can lend to any one person, making it extremely difficult for them to compete for large loans. Despite these limitations, in recent years the assets of the nation's approximately 15,000 credit unions have grown 50 percent but, similar to S&Ls, the annual number of credit union failures also continues to rise due to increased competition and poor management.[20]

Nondeposit Institutions

Unlike those discussed so far, some financial institutions do not get their money through deposits. Funds for "nondeposit" financial institutions come in three major forms: insurance premiums, contributions for retirement, and sale of bonds and short-term loans. Examples of such financial institutions include insurance companies, pension funds, and finance companies.

Insurance Companies   Besides protecting their customers against risk, as we will describe in Chapter 22, insurance companies act as financial institutions because they receive billions of dollars in premiums (payments for coverage) every year. When covered individuals die or have a theft or fire, the companies use some of these funds to pay claims. However, in any given year, most of the people covered with insurance have no claims and will continue to have none for decades. This leaves a substantial amount of funds from premiums for the company to invest so that they will grow large enough to cover future claims and generate a profit for the company.

Businesses with needs that may be too small or specialized to attract local banks or large financial institutions often take advantage of the services of commercial finance companies. Greyhound Financial Corporation, for example, seeks customers with experienced management like KMEL-FM, a leading pop radio station in San Francisco.

Source: Courtesy of Greyhound Financial Corporation, a Dial Corp company.

Pension Funds   The desire to prepare for retirement has led to the creation of another type of nondeposit financial institution: the **pension fund.** This is a pool of money set aside and invested to take care of retirement obligations. The money may come from employers, employees, or unions. In many organizations, employees are entitled to a pension based on how long they have worked there and how much they were paid annually. If the employee makes contributions, the size of this contribution may also affect the size of the pension. Often, pension funds are managed by professional pension fund managers. Preset rules specify the income that each person is entitled to receive upon retirement.

With assets in the range of $1 trillion, these funds are a significant source of financing. Typical investments include high-quality stocks and long-term mortgages on commercial properties. These investments provide funding to the corporations that issue the stock and to the developers of the real estate.

Finance Companies   Some nondeposit institutions, called finance companies, emphasize lending. They obtain funds to lend by borrowing themselves and by the sale of bonds. **Commercial finance companies** specialize in providing short-term, collateralized loans to businesses. A **collateralized loan** is backed with something of value that the lender can claim in case of default. **Consumer finance companies** do the same for individuals. The interest rate on these loans is generally higher than that charged by commercial banks. Because of this, borrowers usually turn to finance companies only

Pension fund A pool of money set aside and invested to take care of retirement obligations.

Commercial finance company Lending institution that provides short-term, collateralized loans to businesses.

Collateralized loan A loan that is backed with something of value that the lender can claim in case of default.

Consumer finance company Financial institution that makes short-term loans to individuals.

after they have been turned down by a bank. These borrowers are riskier because they are young or otherwise unable to meet the strict requirements of a commercial bank's lending policies. Commercial Credit and CIT Financial are two of the major commercial finance companies, and Beneficial Finance and Household Finance are examples of consumer finance companies. Big corporate-owned finance companies such as IBM Credit Corporation and General Motors Acceptance Corp. have greatly expanded their services. They make every type of loan, such as money for commercial real estate and corporate debt financing as well as offering credit cards and mortgage insurance. They are beginning to act like and compete against commercial banks.[21]

CHECK ✓ POINT

1. What are three major types of financial institutions?
2. You started a small word-processing business last year, and you want to borrow $2,000 to upgrade your computers. Two banks have turned you down. Where might you turn for financing?

Regulation and Control of Financial Institutions

Until this century, when one lending institution needed money, it would borrow from others with available funds. If it had more than enough funds to meet its obligations, the institution would seek to lend them to those with shortage of funds. This worked well as long as the amount that banks wanted to borrow approximated the amount available for lending. However, when too many banks needed funds at the same time, the shortage of funds often led to panics and the failure of some institutions.

To create greater stability, the federal government has over the years introduced various controls affecting all types of financial institutions. The major ones, which primarily involve banks and savings and loan associations, are the Federal Reserve System and agencies that insure deposits.

The Federal Reserve System

To oversee the thousands of banks throughout the nation, the government in 1913 created the **Federal Reserve System** (commonly called "the Fed"), a network of regional banks that regulates banking in America. The Fed is jointly owned by the government and its member banks.

As Figure 19.3 shows, at the top of the Federal Reserve System is the board of governors, seven people appointed by the president of the United States and confirmed by the Senate. To help keep the board free from political pressure, each board member serves a 14-year term, none may be nominated for a second term, and the terms are staggered so that one member is replaced every 2 years. (Despite this, in recent years there has been increased pressure to give Congress and the President greater influence on the Fed's operations.)[22] The board appoints a chairperson to a 4-year term. The board members come from the 12 different Federal Reserve districts.

Within each district is a regional bank called a Federal Reserve bank (Figure 19.4). These, in turn, operate 25 branch banks throughout the United States. Each of the 12 Federal Reserve banks is owned by member banks in that district, and each has its own governing board of directors

FIGURE 19.3
Organization Chart of the Federal Reserve System

Board of Governors
(7 Members, Each Appointed to a Single 14-Year Term)

12 Federal Reserve Banks
(Owned by Member Banks, Run by a 9-Member Board)

25 Branch Federal Reserve Banks
(Split among the 12 Federal Reserve Districts)

Member Banks
(Ultimate Owners of the Federal Reserve System)

FIGURE 19.4
Regions of the Federal Reserve System

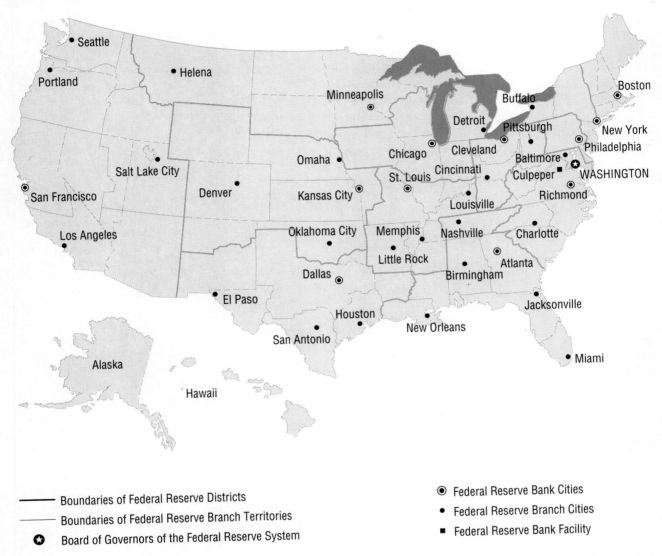

—— Boundaries of Federal Reserve Districts	◉ Federal Reserve Bank Cities
—— Boundaries of Federal Reserve Branch Territories	• Federal Reserve Branch Cities
✪ Board of Governors of the Federal Reserve System	■ Federal Reserve Bank Facility

consisting of nine people. Three are bankers and are elected by the member banks in the district. Three represent the borrowers and they also are elected by the district member banks. The final three are selected as representatives of the general public and they are chosen by the board of governors of the Fed.

All national banks must be members of the Federal Reserve System. State banks are not required to join, and most do not. Member banks have a number of important privileges, including the right to:

TABLE 19.3
The Federal Reserve System's Tools for Monetary Control

Tool	Fed Action	Effect on the Money Supply	Intended Effects on the Economy	
			Interest Rates	Economic Activity
Reserve requirement	Decrease the requirement	↑ (Increase)	↓	↑
	Increase the requirement	↓ (Decrease)	↑	↓
Open-market operations	Buy government securities	↑	↓	↑
	Sell government securities	↓	↑	↓
Discount rate	Lower the rate	↑	↓	↑
	Raise the rate	↓	↑	↓
Credit controls	Lower margin requirements	None	Purchases of securities increase; consumer buying increases	
	Raise margin requirements	None	Purchases of securities decrease; consumer buying decreases	

- Obtain funds by borrowing from their district reserve bank.
- Use a variety of services provided by the system.
- Obtain financial advice and assistance.
- Vote for six of the nine board members of the district bank.
- Receive a dividend on stock owned in the district bank.

The Fed carries out five basic functions, four of which are designed to control the money supply and keep the economy on an even keel: (1) establishing reserve requirements, (2) conducting open-market operations, (3) setting the discount rate, and (4) using credit controls. Table 19.3 summarizes how the Fed's monetary tools heat up or cool down the economy.[23] The fifth function of the Fed is check clearing.

Reserve requirement The percentage of all deposits that a bank must keep on hand at the bank or on deposit with the Fed.

Reserve Requirement The most powerful tool available to the Fed in controlling the money supply is the reserve requirement. The **reserve requirement** is the percentage of all deposits that a bank must keep on hand at the bank or on deposit with the Fed. The more the bank has on reserve, the less it has available to circulate through the economy by lending. If the Fed requires banks to keep 20 percent of all funds on deposit, then they can loan out the other 80 percent. Thus, if the banks in your city had $100 million in deposits, they could lend $80 million of it to individuals, who will buy more goods, and to businesses, which can use the funds to expand. If the Fed were to raise the reserve requirement to 25 percent, the banks would be able to lend only $75 million. Individuals and companies would have $5 million less for buying goods and expanding business.

These Fed actions can affect interest rates and economic activity. In basic supply-and-demand analysis, when the supply of something increases, its price falls, and vice versa. The price borrowers pay for the privilege of using money is the interest rate. Therefore, when the reserve requirement goes down, making more money available, interest rates fall. When the reserve requirement rises, less money is available and thus interest rates rise. When interest rates are high and money is hard to come by, businesses put off borrowing and expanding, and consumers put off borrowing and shopping. Economic activity slows down. When interest rates are low, the opposite occurs.

The reserve requirement also controls bank actions. For example, a bank with $10 million in checking accounts might have $1.5 million on hand at the Fed to meet a 15 percent reserve requirement. If the Fed raised the requirement to 20 percent, the bank would have to come up with another $500,000. This would mean calling in some loans and not making any new ones until it had met the reserve requirement.

During the late 1970s, the number of Fed member banks began to decline sharply. The reason was that in order to keep up with rapid inflation, banks wanted to earn as much interest as possible on their funds. Deposits at the district federal reserve banks do not earn interest. Banks began withdrawing from the system and putting these funds into interest-bearing investments. The government responded by requiring *all* banks and deposit institutions to keep a percentage of their deposits at the Fed, whether or not they are member institutions. As these changes have gone into effect, the distinction between member and nonmember banks has begun to fade.

Open-Market Operations   The Fed also controls the money supply through **open-market operations,** which consist of the buying and selling of government securities (bonds). When the Federal Open Market Committee buys government securities, it increases the money supply by putting more money into circulation. Conversely, when the committee sells government securities, it decreases the money supply by taking money out of circulation.

Open-market operations   The buying and selling of government securities by the Fed.

Open-market operations are easier to use for making small adjustments in the money supply. With these operations, the Fed can fine-tune the economy without shaking up the entire financial structure, which is what might happen if it continually announced changes in the reserve requirement.

Discount Rate   The Fed is sometimes referred to as "the banker's bank," because it lends money to member banks. The banks borrow from their district bank, which determines its own interest rate, subject to approval by the board of governors of the entire system. This rate — the rate the Fed charges — is called the **discount rate.**

When the Fed lowers the discount rate, member banks are more likely to borrow. When the rate goes up, they are less likely to do so. The banks, in turn, adjust the rates they charge their customers to cover what they pay the Fed. The amount of funds that commercial banks obtain through loans may be quite small, usually only about 3 to 4 percent of their total reserves. Nevertheless, the discount rate is an effective monetary tool because the Fed can use it to fine-tune the economy and influence the rate at which banks lend to their customers.

Discount rate   The interest rate that the Fed charges member banks for loans.

Credit Controls   The Fed also has the authority to use a series of selective credit controls. One of these is the power to establish the margin requirements on credit purchases of stocks and bonds. The margin is the percentage that credit customers must pay in advance. Before the stock market crash of 1929, this requirement was 10 percent. A person could buy stock worth $100 merely by putting down $10. If the stock started to drop into the low 90s, the stockbroker would ask for more money; if the buyer was unable to come up with it, the broker would sell the stock before it reached $90 and keep the balance due. The investor would lose most, or all, of the investment.

In recent years, the Fed has set the margin requirement on securities at 50 percent. Even so, in the stock market crash in 1987, many investors lost tremendous amounts of money when the stocks dropped dramatically and the brokerages called in their margin accounts. Chapter 21 will give more attention to this and other aspects of investing in the stock market.

The Fed also has the power to influence consumer credit purchases. It sets rules for the minimum down payment and the length of the repayment period. The Fed has not exercised this power in recent years, but if it did, it could have a dramatic impact. For example, most new-car loans have terms of 3 to 4 years and require a small down payment, usually 10 percent. If the Fed required a 20 percent minimum down payment and a loan term of no more than 2 years, many people would be unable to buy a new car. This restriction on credit would cripple consumers' purchasing power. As consumers bought less, the economy would slow down.

Check-Clearing Services   Besides its monetary functions, the Federal Reserve System also clears checks by moving them from the bank where they were deposited to the bank on which they are drawn. Figure 19.5 depicts how this works. The check travels electronically from the depositor's bank through the Federal Reserve bank in its district and the Federal Reserve bank in the district of the payer's bank to the payer's bank. Then the payer's bank sends the payment back through the same channel in the opposite direction. If a check is written and drawn on banks in the same Federal Reserve district, the Federal Reserve bank in that district handles the entire matter. For example, if a renter living in Manhattan writes a check to the landlord, who deposits it in a bank in Brooklyn, the Federal Reserve Bank of New York is the only Fed bank involved in clearing the check.

Insuring Deposits

The government is also involved in protecting deposits. During the depths of the Great Depression in the early 1930s, a run on a bank, in which masses of depositors demanded their money, was a common occurrence. In 1933 alone, almost 4,000 banks collapsed. To restore confidence in banks, Congress established the **Federal Deposit Insurance Corporation (FDIC)** in 1934. Until 1989, S&Ls were insured by their own agency called the Federal Savings and Loan Insurance Corporation (FSLIC). However, when the S&L industry got into serious trouble in the late 1980s, the FSLIC became insolvent. As part of the S&L bailout, Congress set up the **Resolution Trust Corporation (RTC)** to administer the sale of insolvent S&Ls and had the FDIC take over from the FSLIC to insure S&L deposits, like bank deposits, up to $100,000 in case of failure.

Federal Deposit Insurance Corporation (FDIC) A federal agency that insures, deposits up to $100,000 in case of bank, or more recently S&L failure.

Resolution Trust Corporation (RTC) A group set up by Congress in 1989 as part of the S&L bailout to administer the sale of failed S&Ls.

FIGURE 19.5
How the Federal Reserve System Clears Checks

What the Numbers Mean:

1. While on vacation, Mrs. Adele Johnson of Bangor, Maine, buys a western painting in Phoenix, Arizona, and pays with a check drawn on her hometown bank.

2. Joe Garcia, the artist, deposits the check in his Phoenix bank.

3. The Phoenix bank electronically transfers the check (the check does not physically travel through the Reserve system) for credit in its account at its district bank, the Federal Reserve Bank of San Francisco.

4. To collect the funds, the Federal Reserve Bank of San Francisco transfers the check to the district bank for Bangor, the Federal Reserve Bank of Boston.

5. The Federal Reserve Bank of Boston transfers the check to Mrs. Johnson's bank in Bangor, which deducts the amount of the check from her deposit account.

6. Mrs. Johnson's bank authorizes the Federal Reserve Bank of Boston to deduct the amount of the check from

its deposit account with the reserve bank.

7. The Federal Reserve Bank of Boston pays the Federal Reserve Bank of San Francisco the amount of the check.

8. The Federal Reserve Bank of San Francisco credits the Phoenix bank for the amount of the check.

9. The Phoenix bank credits Joe Garcia's account for the amount of the check.

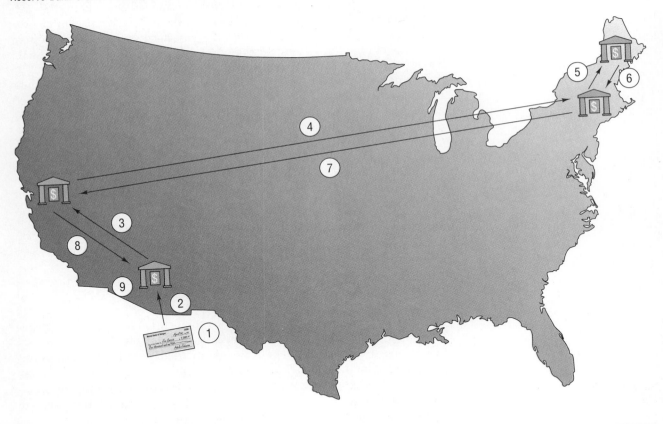

Going into the 1990s, the FDIC was insuring almost $4 trillion of bank and S&L deposits. This exposure, plus another about $3 trillion guarantees from agencies such as the Federal National Mortgage Association (known as Fannie Mae), Federal Home Loan Mortgage Corporation (known as Freddie Mac), and the Student Loan Marketing Association (known as Sallie Mae)

have many experts and members of the general public worried about what might happen in the future if things become as bad as they did in the S&L industry.[24] The first evidence of FDIC problems was in 1984 when the government rescued the Continental Illinois National Bank and Trust Company. That bailout cost $1.7 billion. Since then, deposit insurance has guaranteed the accounts of thousands of individuals who had their money in banks and S&Ls that went bankrupt. For example, the bailout of Bank of New England was estimated to cost the FDIC $2.3 billion.[25] Because of the enormous losses that have been generated by the S&L crisis and to a lesser degree banks, there is increasing pressure to change deposit insurance coverage and thus prevent the government and eventually taxpayers from having to pay more for bail outs.[26]

Besides the insurance, the FDIC also protects the public by requiring the banks and S&Ls it regulates to give customers, on request, information about asset quality (bad loans), capital, and earnings. This should prevent customers from doing business with banks and S&Ls that are in trouble. All commercial banks that are members of the Federal Reserve System pay for the insurance and are covered. Banks that are not members of the system may also join the FDIC, and most do. S&Ls that were under the old FSLIC are now part of the FDIC and must pay for the insurance.[27]

People who have more than $100,000 to deposit and want to be fully insured can establish a combination of accounts. For example, a married couple can open three accounts (two single and one joint), and each will be insured up to $100,000. Other combinations with children, grandchildren, or other relatives would have the same effect. Those who do not want to use joint accounts can open individual accounts in different S&Ls or banks. Using a little money management, a person can make sure that all deposits are insured. However, with all the problems in the financial industry in general and the FDIC in particular, this may all change in the near future.

> CHECK ✓ POINT

1. How does the Federal Reserve help control the money supply?
2. How does the government protect depositors?

Recent Developments in Banking

Technological developments and increased competition in the face of deregulation at home and the growth and power of Japanese and European banks[28] have changed the face of American banking. Managers of financial institutions are finding that today's environment requires more than financial expertise; they also must be able to use human relations, marketing, and computer techniques. In addition, they must be more skilled than ever in responding to the needs and concerns of the public.

Bank Technology

Banks and other financial institutions are using computer technology to help process billions of checks and keep records of a multitude of customer transactions. This technology is reducing the need for both individual customers or the financial institutions to carry large sums of money.

One developing area is the use of the **electronic funds transfer system,** which is a computerized system for depositing and withdrawing funds elec-

Electronic funds transfer system
A computerized system for depositing and withdrawing funds electronically.

tronically. One of the most popular ways of doing this is through the use of a push-button telephone. The user enters a personal identification number and presses other buttons to indicate what amounts the computer should transfer to pay certain bills (for example, the monthly car payment, the telephone bill, or the electric bill). The computer subtracts the amount from the customer's balance and adds it to the creditor's balance. The customer's monthly bank statement lists all of these telephone transactions, providing a record of what was paid and to whom that takes the place of canceled checks. Some bank customers have readily adopted this system, appreciating its convenience, while many others have been reluctant to give up the float (the time between the writing of a check and when it is withdrawn from the account) and tangibility of checks.

Another example of bank technology is the **point-of-sale terminal,** which allows a retail customer to pay for goods by using a computer terminal and a debit card to transfer funds from their bank account to that of the merchant. A number of companies are now using these cards, including Publix supermarkets in Florida, Atlantic Richfield gasoline stations, and some Montgomery Ward retail stores. The procedure for using these terminals is the same as that for debit cards, discussed earlier.

Point-of-sale terminal
A computer terminal that allows retail customers to use a debit card to transfer funds from their bank account to that of the merchant.

Deregulation and Competition

During the 1980s, the banking industry became less regulated, although some states still prohibit branch banking (where a bank will have a number of locations), holding companies (where a large bank will own several smaller banks), and similar developments. Nevertheless, this deregulation has stimulated mergers into regional banks, diversification efforts, and service competition. Unfortunately, deregulation has also been a major contributing factor in the dramatic increase in bank fraud and the increased failures of both banks and S&Ls noted in earlier discussion.[29] To date, the general public feels that banks and, to a lesser degree S&Ls, are still safe places for their money, but also believe that more careful monitoring of financial institutions is needed.[30]

Competitive Small Banks Many small banks are facing huge competitors by meeting them head on or by merging to form regional banks. These small banks combine expertise to serve local markets and are competing by finding a special need and meeting it. They may offer longer hours and special services. For example, University Bank and Trust of Palo Alto, California, makes twice the profit rate as larger banks because of what they call "endless service," including free shoeshines with deposits, helping customers balance their accounts, selling postage stamps at cost, and, if teller windows develop long lines of customers, having the bank president wait on customers.[31]

Some regional banks are also expanding into other areas of the country because growth in their own territory is being blocked. For example, KeyCorp, a regional bank located in Albany, New York, found that new legislation prevented it from entering Massachusetts and Connecticut. So the bank began buying a string of banks from Idaho to Alaska. Most of KeyCorp's holdings are in small communities where they have become highly competitive. The bank is often referred to as the "Wal-Mart of banking" because of its small-town approach. Also, similar to Wal-Mart, this

Indiana state banking laws changed in 1985 to allow the formation of bank holding companies. Since then INB Financial Corporation has expanded through the acquisition of ten banks in Indiana and one in Illinois.

Source: © 1990 Dick Spahr.

strategy has been very successful for KeyCorp and has resulted in dramatic increases in their earnings.[32]

Banks are also trying hard to be good corporate citizens and to see that they provide services to all members of the community. This strategy helps the community grow and the bank to prosper.

Diversification   A number of financial institutions have used deregulation as an opportunity to diversify. For example, many banks are providing brokerage services to help their customers invest their money. Before deregulation, the investor would have had to go through a brokerage house, but now a customer who wants to buy 100 shares of stock or sell a bond can do it through the bank. Banks are also providing financial counseling and helping people set up retirement accounts. Other institutions, too, are diversifying. As discussed earlier, finance companies are moving into every type of loan and are experimenting with credit cards and insurance, and most life insurance companies offer financial planning and a number of investment choices.

Service Competition   Many financial institutions are meeting the deregulation challenge by competing on the basis of service. The accompanying Innovation Close-Up (A "Win-Win" Bail Out Strategy) provides an illustration. One approach is to diversify and offer more services; another approach is to provide better customer service. Some banks have tried assigning each of their major customers to a "personal banker." If a customer has a problem or wants a question answered, he or she simply calls the personal banker, who gives the problem or question personal attention. At University Bank and Trust, cited earlier, a customer who needs something, even when the bank is closed, merely calls his or her personal banker.[33]

CLOSE-UP / *Innovation*

A "Win-Win" Bail Out Strategy

Ask practicing bankers to describe the biggest mistake that banks made during the 1980s and they are likely to say, "They loaned big businesses far too much money and then ended up with nonperforming loans." The statement is probably very accurate, and it is also a reason why many banks are now reluctant to make big loans to business. However, Chemical Bank of New York has developed an opposing strategy. In fact, Chemical is making a tidy profit by lending money to bankrupt firms that cannot survive without an additional inflow of capital.

The Chemical Bank strategy was developed and brought to fruition by Darla Moore, who is now head of the debtor-in-possession (DIP) department. The strategy used by Moore is direct and effective. Many companies that borrowed too much money during the 1980s are now finding themselves unable to repay their loans. If they do manage to get additional funds, it usually is from the bank that made the initial loan. However, since these lenders are now very nervous about losing even more money, they are often reluctant to increase these loans. This is where Moore's department at Chemical Bank comes into the picture.

After careful analysis, Chemical Bank may be willing to extend money to an applicant when other lenders will not. Borrowers include the bankrupt New York retailer Macy's, which recently received a $600 million loan; and the troubled jewelry store chain Zale's, which was loaned $510 million. Other borrowers in financial trouble include Carter Hawley Hale ($800 million), Columbia Gas ($875 million), and Allied Stores ($300 million). Why is Chemical bank willing to lend additional funds to companies that are unable to pay their current loans? One reason is that Chemical Bank believes these firms will eventually be able to turn around their operations and become healthy. Chemical Bank also receives priority on repayment. Chemical's loans move to the head of the list and are repaid before the old ones, lowering its risks significantly.

Why are other lenders willing to let Chemical go ahead of them on repayment? The answer is simply that the original lenders are currently unable to collect their money anyway and have little hope of ever doing so unless the borrower gets back on its feet. While the original lenders are unwilling to dig a deeper hole for themselves, they are willing to step aside and let Chemical go to the head of the line, if Chemical is willing to shoulder the risks. The arrangement is potentially a win-win situation for everyone involved, thanks to an innovative banking strategy.

Source: Gail Buchalter, "Debt Becomes Her," *Working Woman*, July 1992, pp. 52–61; 71.

CHECK ✓ POINT

1. What technological developments have recently affected banking?
2. How has deregulation influenced the banking industry?

Closing Comments

Every day, the banking system brings together suppliers and demanders of money, making possible a multitude of transactions — buying cars, building warehouses, earning interest. The financial institutions that make this possible include banks, savings and loan associations, mutual savings banks, credit unions, and nondeposit institutions. The government, too, plays a role. The Federal Reserve System regulates the money supply, and various agencies insure deposits. Together, financial institutions and the government try to ensure that a reliable supply of funds is available to meet the needs of business and consumers.

VIDEO CASE / *It's Crunch Time*

When Morton Fleischer started the Franchise Finance Corporation of America, he focused on a certain type of unique business funding. Specifically, FFCA finances fast food franchises and travel-related facilities. An example of the investments FFCA is now making in the travel plaza industry is the Flying J truck stop. Fleischer finances these businesses with cash rather than obtaining loans from banks. Combined with some safe real estate investments, this financial strategy has provided sizable returns to the owners of FFCA.

This is in sharp contrast to many of the large banks and S&Ls that have found themselves having to take big writeoffs in their loan portfolios in recent years. A good example is Citicorp, which recently had to cut its dividend from $1.78 to $1.00, let go 8,000 employees, and trim annual expenses by $800 million. What caused this huge bank's drastic action? One reason was the large number of "nonperforming loans," especially those in real estate. In 1980, Citicorp had outstanding loans to less developed countries of approximately $12 billion, about $200 million of which was in nonperforming loans. In 1990, the bank's outstanding loans to these countries were just under $10 billion, but almost $4 billion of these were nonperforming. Commercial real estate loans in the United States show an even bleaker picture than this international experience. In 1980, Citicorp had loans of approximately $2.2 billion for commercial real estate, and about $100 million of these loans were nonperforming. In 1990, the bank had $13 billion in commercial real estate loans, and $2.1 billion were nonperforming. Moreover in 1989–1990 alone, loans to highly leveraged American firms rose from almost $4.75 billion to $5.5 billion while nonperforming loans shot up from $250 million to $1 billion. Simply put, Citicorp, one of the nation's largest and most prestigious banks, was having major problems and was being forced to actively seek investors who could

provide them with additional capital to help cover losses and fund operations.

Citicorp is not alone. Many commercial banks and savings and loan institutions across the country, especially on the east coast and in the sun belt, have been having problems due to the sharp downturn in real estate prices in recent years.

The hardest hit area has been commercial real estate, where countless buildings around the country had vacancy rates that ran well over 15 percent at the beginning of the 1990s. For example, 1990 downtown office vacancy rates in Miami stood at 29 percent; Denver had 23 percent vacancy; Manhattan and Houston were 18 percent vacant; Atlanta was 17 percent vacant; and Los Angeles and Seattle had 16 percent vacancy rates. The national average was 17 percent, up sharply from 13 percent in 1983. What is even worse is that these rates are unlikely to drop a great deal in the coming years. Many industry experts believe that there are enough downtown office spaces to meet demand for at least the next 10–15 years without having to erect one more building.

Banks and S&Ls are not the only institutions getting caught in the real estate crunch. Insurance firms that have invested heavily in real estate have also been hurt; so have corporations that have used their own money to finance growth. A good example is Marriott:

Marriott . . . is also caught in the vise. Like other hotel chains, the company underwrote its own growth by developing hundreds of hotels and then selling them off to limited partnerships, retaining long-term management contracts on the properties. This led to a glut of hotel space over the past six years and a plethora of properties for sale. Says Stephen Brener, a New York City hotel industry consultant: 'The supply was built for resale at a time when the industry needed to take product off the market.' The company recently

announced that it is postponing construction starts of new hotels for at least a year. Capital expenditures are being cut in half to $650 million.

These developments affecting companies such as Marriott emphasize the problem banks are going to have with their nonperforming real estate loans. Specifically, if companies such as Marriott are slowing up their construction programs, it means that the market is soft. So the banks are likely to continue having trouble with their real estate loans and, if they end up having to take over the properties, they are likely to be unable to sell them for the face value of the loans.

Perhaps the major difference between FFCA and most banks, and especially S&Ls, is that FFCA has done a much better job of financial management. FFCA has made smaller, less risky investments per project and has stayed in an industry that it understands. As a result, while many banks and S&Ls in the 1990s will find their earnings eroded by writeoffs for bad loans, FFCA is continuing to generate profits for its investors.

Source: Carol J. Loomis, "Citicorp's World of Troubles," *Fortune*, January 14, 1991, 90–99; Bill Saporito, "Real Estate's Low-Rise Future," *Fortune*, January 28, 1991, 40–56; and William P. Barrett, "A Blank Check It Was Not," *Forbes*, April 29, 1991, 40–41.

Case Questions

1. What type of financial institution is FFCA? (Use Table 19.1 to help you answer this question.)
2. Why have commercial banks and savings and loan institutions run into trouble with mortgage loans, especially those for commercial real estate?
3. What is likely to be the result of many of these real estate loans? Why? What lesson can financial institutions learn from this experience?

Learning Objectives Revisited

1. **Explain the nature and purpose of money.** Money is anything generally accepted as payment. It serves as a medium of exchange, a standard of value, and a storehouse of value. Money best performs these functions when it is divisible, portable, durable, stable, and secure.

2. **Describe the money supply and its components.** The money supply is often defined as money and near money. Money includes currency and demand deposits. Currency consists of coins and paper money; demand deposits are checking accounts, including regular checking accounts, NOW accounts, and traveler's checks. Near money is certain highly liquid assets that do not function as a medium of exchange. These include savings accounts and time deposits such as money market mutual funds, bank money market accounts, and certificates of deposit. Unlike demand deposits, near money must be converted to money before you can use it.

3. **Present the major financial institutions.** The major financial institutions are commercial banks, savings and loan associations (S&Ls), mutual savings banks, credit unions, and nondeposit institutions. Nondeposit institutions include insurance companies, pension funds, and finance companies. In recent years, the differences between these institutions have become blurred. For example, like commercial banks, many S&Ls and mutual savings banks offer checking accounts, NOW accounts, savings accounts, and various forms of time deposits, and credit unions offer checking and savings accounts. Even finance companies offer many of the same types of loans and services as banks.

4. **Discuss the Federal Reserve System.** The Federal Reserve System (the Fed) is designed to control the nation's money supply and regulate the economy. A board of governors oversees 12 Federal Reserve districts, each of which has a Federal Reserve bank. The district banks operate 25 Federal Reserve branches. Each of the district banks is owned by the member banks in that district, and each has a governing board of directors. To regulate the economy, the Fed sets reserve requirements, conducts open-market operations to buy and sell government securities, determines the discount rate, and uses credit controls to increase or decrease the down payment needed to buy stocks, bonds, and consumer goods. The Fed also clears checks through the system.

5. **Explain how government agencies protect deposits.** For all banks that purchase its insurance, and now S&Ls that were under the old FSLIC, the Federal Deposit Insurance Corporation (FDIC) insures deposits up to $100,000. Only time will tell, but because of the problems faced by the financial industry in general and the FDIC in particular, there may be changes coming in the near future.

6. **Identify recent developments in banking.** Most current developments in the banking industry stem from new technological developments and deregulation. Electronic funds transfer systems and other computerized systems allow customers to receive financial services without ever coming into the bank. Less regulation and competition are resulting in a decrease in the distinctions between commercial banks, S&Ls, mutual savings banks, credit unions, and finance companies. To compete, institutions are merging, diversifying, and featuring personalized services to attract major accounts.

Key Terms Reviewed

Review each of the following terms. For any that you do not know or are unsure of, look up the definitions and see how they were used in the chapter.

money	near money	automatic teller machine (ATM)
M1	passbook savings accounts	commercial bank
currency	money market mutual funds	national bank
demand deposits	bank money market accounts	state bank
regular checking	time deposits	savings and loan association (S&L)
negotiable order of withdrawal (NOW) account	certificates of deposit (CDs)	junk bonds
traveler's check	credit card	
	debit card	

mutual savings bank
credit union
pension fund
commercial finance company
collateralized loan
consumer finance company

Federal Reserve System (Fed)
reserve requirement
open-market operations
discount rate
Federal Deposit Insurance
  Corporation (FDIC)

Resolution Trust Corporation
  (RTC)
electronic funds transfer
  system
point-of-sale terminal

Review Questions

1. What is the difference between money and currency?
2. People use credit cards to buy a wide variety of goods and services. Why aren't credit cards considered part of the money supply?
3. Mary and Frank Worthe would like to get a mortgage for a new house. Would they go to a commercial bank or a savings and loan?
4. Ralph Burgess just took a job with a company that has a credit union. Why might Ralph investigate switching his savings account from his S&L to the credit union?
5. Some financial institutions get their funds from sources other than deposits. What are these institutions, and where do they get their funds?
6. Which type of financial institution might be best suited for each of the following needs?
    a. The president of a company wants to set aside money for employees to retire on.
    b. A recent graduate wants a safe place to keep the earnings from her new job and a way to pay bills conveniently.
    c. A large and profitable corporation wants to sell stock to generate funds for expansion.
    d. A 20-year-old law firm with a steady flow of business wants to borrow funds to computerize its operations.

7. The Wyatt Professional Bank was founded 4 months ago by a group of local investors. What privileges would the bank gain by joining the Federal Reserve System?
8. Imagine that the economy is growing rapidly. Businesses are producing more and more, and consumer spending is keeping pace. Nevertheless, the members of the Fed's board of governors are worried. They fear that if the economy grows any faster, a dizzying inflation rate will result. How can they try to slow the pace of economic activity? Which approach or combination of approaches would you recommend? Why?
9. A sign in the window of Upright Savings and Loan Association reads "Deposits Insured by the FDIC." What does this mean?
10. Annette Blasedell is a commercial real estate broker. She is single and lives alone in a comfortable apartment near her parents' home. A stupendous deal has netted Annette an impressive $300,000 commission check. Until Annette decides what to do with the windfall, can she keep it all in an insured account?
11. How can a bank customer benefit from an electronic funds transfer system? Why are many bank customers reluctant to do their banking this way?

Applied Exercise

One of the primary ways the Federal Reserve controls the money supply is by increasing or decreasing the reserve requirement. For example, if the Fed reduced the reserve requirement from 22 percent to 20 percent, for every $100 of new deposits it received a bank could lend $80; and when this $80 was deposited in another bank, that institution could lend $64 (80 percent of $80), and so forth. If these transactions were continued until there was no money left to lend, the $100 would have generated a total of $400 in new loans. With this information in mind, answer these two questions:

1. How much money would be generated from a new $100 deposit if the Fed were to reduce the reserve requirement from 20 percent to 10 percent?

2. How much money would be generated from a new $100 deposit if the Fed were to raise the reserve requirement from 20 percent to 30 percent?

In making both sets of computations, use the format that follows; it provides the initial calculations for a new $100 deposit and a reserve requirement of 10 percent. When you have finished both sets of computations, answer this final question:

3. What impact would the Fed have on the economy if it lowered the reserve requirement by 10 percent as compared with raising it by 10 percent?

Bank	Acquired Deposit	Reserve Requirement	Amount That Bank Can Lend
1	$100.00	$10.00	$90.00
2	90.00	9.00	81.00
3	81.00	8.10	72.90

YOU BE THE ADVISER / *Profits and Problems*

When Tina Rodriguez was hired as president of the bank, it was in poor shape. Approximately 5 percent of its loans had been made to countries south of the border that were unable to pay, and another 10 percent were held by businesses in the agricultural sector of the economy and were judged to be "marginal" in terms of collectibility. Tina set to work straightening things out.

Over the past 3 years, she has managed to collect 70 percent of the foreign loans and has written off the rest as uncollectible. She has also managed to collect 80 percent of the marginal farm loans. At the same time, she has tightened up the borrowing policies of the bank and now lends only to those who are considered good risks and have the appropriate collateral. The board was afraid that if the loan policies were made more stringent, the bank would have trouble finding borrowers. Thanks to Tina's efforts, however, the bank has loaned just about as much money as it has available. In fact, just last week, one of the directors said he heard that the Fed was going to raise the reserve requirement. "How would you handle this situation?" he asked Tina. She said that she would look for additional deposits rather than try to call in any of the outstanding loans.

Despite its high profitability, the bank is not without its problems. An analysis of customer accounts shows that 20 percent of those who have checking accounts with the bank keep an average daily balance of less than $100. Even with the monthly service charge, these accounts cost the bank more than it collects. Tina has also had a visit from the local representatives of elderly people in the area. The spokesperson for the group has demanded that the bank do something about providing free financial services to all retired people over the age of 70. Tina has promised to look into the matter.

Earlier this morning, Tina told the board that quarterly profits would be at an all-time high and this should continue for the rest of the year. "My biggest concern," she said, "is to keep small accounts and free services from eating up all of our profits. We have to draw the line somewhere and start making people pay for what they're getting. After all, we're here to serve the community, but we are also a profit-making institution."

Your Advice

1. What would you recommend that Tina do?
   ___ a. Put in a minimum charge on all small accounts that covers the cost of these accounts.
   ___ b. Change the minimum charge for all new accounts, but let the old ones continue at the current rate.
   ___ c. Develop a two-tier system in which retired people or those over the age of 70 get free financial services, while everyone else pays a minimum charge that covers the expenses on all these accounts.
2. If the Fed does raise its reserve requirement, will this have any effect on Tina's bank?
3. If the Fed raises the reserve requirement, what would you recommend that Tina do?
4. What else might Tina do to help the bank increase its profitability?

LOANS ON THE BASIS OF DOLLS

Annalee dolls, now collectors' items, were not always so prized. The makers of the dolls have gone through some fairly tough financial times. At the beginning, a bank refused to lend the owners of the small family-run business even $100. However, the owners persevered and, through a developmental program of the state of New Hampshire, were able to get the capital they needed to expand.

Financial Management

Chapter Learning Objectives

- Define the role of financial management.

- Identify ways entrepreneurs can finance the start-up of their business.

- Present the various types of short-term financing.

- Discuss the use of loans for long-term financing.

- Describe the use of bonds for long-term financing.

- Explain how companies use stocks for long-term financing.

The attention that is given to detail on the dolls makes them interesting and endearing. Some people who bought them for $25 to $50 are now finding that they purchased more than a doll; they made a good investment. In recent years, Annalee dolls sell briskly at high prices, and banks are more than happy to do business with the company. If it were to run low on cash, the inventory could be used to back up a loan, because banks know that the dolls will eventually be sold at a handsome profit. Short-term financing problems have become a thing of the past.

Do the owners intend to borrow as much money as possible, expand the business, and take advantage of the opportunity to make millions? This is not likely. Family members seem happy just running the business and having fun. However, if they ever need additional funding, it will most likely be provided since financial institutions have categorized their corporate entity as risk free, noting their thirty years of consistent equity growth, management structure, and product evolution. As one of the owners put it, "It's a better investment than cash at Christmas."

Photo source: Margo Taussig Pinkerton for Annalee Dolls Inc.

Introduction

Money makes business transactions possible, and the banking system gets money from those who supply it to those who demand it. To make the most of this supply of funds, businesses require the help of experts in planning their needs and obtaining and investing money — the activities of financial management. This chapter begins by describing the role of financial management in modern business and the financing of a new business. The bulk of the chapter describes short-term and long-term financing of going businesses, with emphasis on sources of funds. These include various types of loans, bonds, and stock.

The Role of Financial Management in Modern Business

In the past, financial management was rarely a major concern for a business. The company treasurer would establish a working relationship with a local bank; in return for the business, the bank would give the company a loan when needed. If the bank thought the firm was becoming overextended, it would take action to protect itself, but this was considered a last resort. To a large degree, the bank handled the financing, and the company took care of producing and selling.

Today, this has changed. Although a few small, local firms still operate this way, few businesses of any size sit passively and let their banker decide what is best for them. They have their own financial people who work with lenders, negotiating terms, comparing rates among competing financial institutions, and matching resources to the company's needs as determined by its strategic plan.

Skillful management of finances is critical to the survival of a company and, if done effectively, can contribute greatly to its profits. Financial management begins with creation of a financial plan, which identifies the timing and amount of funding needs and sources. It also includes carrying out the plan, monitoring the flow of funds to make sure it is adequate, and adjusting the company's financial strategy as necessary. Successful financial management ensures that the company has adequate funding to meet company objectives for current operations and long-term growth.

The Financial Manager

Financial manager The person responsible for developing, implementing, and controlling the financial plan.

In intermediate-sized and large firms, the person charged with the management of finances is the **financial manager,** who is responsible for developing, implementing, and controlling the financial plan. This manager — who in large organizations heads a team of financial experts — generally has a formal education and practical experience in finance, accounting, and economics.

Today, financial managers often use personal computers to assist them with financial analysis and planning, employing popular computer programs such as Lotus 1-2-3® and Framework. This software is especially helpful in small businesses, where the owner-manager usually assumes the role of financial manager. Because the software is so easy to use, it can help a manager with limited financial experience get a feel for how various decisions will affect the business.

The Financial Management Process

An important goal of financial management is to maximize the wealth of the owners (stockholders in the case of corporations). To do this, financial managers must make sure that the company obtains, at the best possible price, the funding it needs to meet its strategic objectives. (The price of funds is measured in terms of interest rates.) Therefore, the financial manager's job starts and ends with the company's objectives. Figure 20.1 shows how the process of financial management works.

The financial manager begins by reviewing corporate objectives to determine the funding they require. Usually, the financial manager has participated with the other managers (such as those in personnel, operations, and marketing) in planning these objectives. The objectives should be familiar and financially achievable. The financial manager compares the expenses involved to the expected revenues. This information enables the financial manager to predict cash flow, the movement of funds illustrated in Figure 20.2. The available cash at any given time consists of beginning cash plus customer payments and funds from financing. This is the money available to the company for adding to its inventory and paying expenses.

The financial manager plans a strategy based on whether the ending cash is positive or negative. If cash inflows exceed cash outflows, the company will have cash to invest. The financial manager's job is to look for a reliable and flexible enough investment that will pay a satisfactory rate of interest. If cash outflows exceed cash inflows, the company will eventually run out of cash for operations. One solution is to find a way to reduce outflows. The manager may investigate a variety of options. Can the company pay bills more slowly or persuade customers to pay faster? Can the company trim expenses in some area, perhaps by keeping a smaller inventory? For answers to such questions, the financial manager must consult with the other managers and staff experts. In addition, the financial manager typically looks for outside sources of financing that offer an acceptable combination of flexibility, timing, and interest rate.

Varying circumstances guide the financial manager in examining avenues to use for obtaining funds. The choices include long-term and short-term financing techniques. The manager selects short-term techniques when flexibility is important or needs are limited. The manager selects long-term financing for extended needs; it is less flexible but typically less costly.

Periodically throughout the year and at the end of the fiscal year, the financial manager reviews the company's financial status to see whether the company is keeping to the financial plan and meeting corporate objectives. If it is not, the manager seeks ways to bring the company back on course. This activity helps the manager plan the next year's financial strategy.

Credit Policies

The best financing techniques in the world cannot save a company without paying customers. Consequently, establishing and following an effective credit policy should be part of financial management. Many firms overextend credit and find that some of their customers are unable to pay their bills. By

FIGURE 20.1
The Process of Financial Management

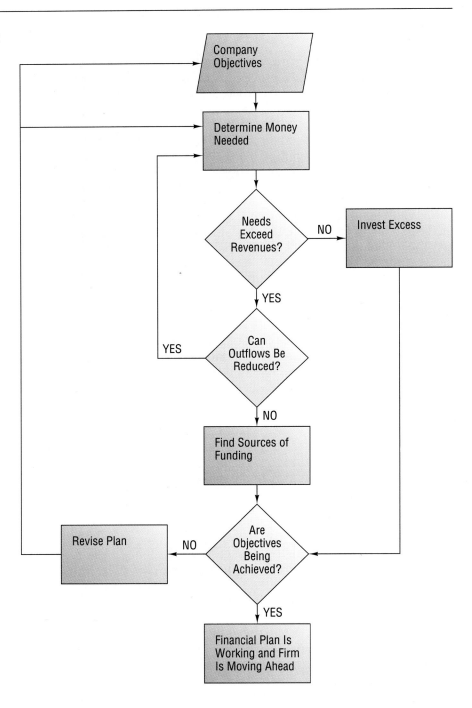

making credit too easy to obtain, the company ends up with uncollectible accounts. One way of reducing this problem is by investigating the credit rating of customers before allowing them to purchase on credit. Small firms do this in a number of different ways, including asking new customers for

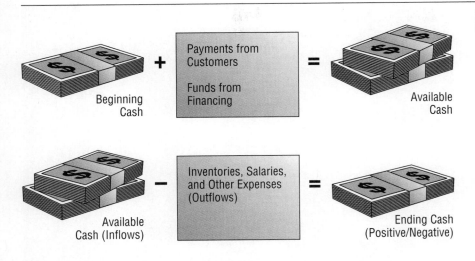

FIGURE 20.2
Simplified Cash Flow

credit references. The firm can check and find out how reliable the customer has been in the past. In recent years, a growing number of small businesses and practically all large firms have speeded up this process by combining computer credit checks at a local credit agency with computer verification of credit at a local bank.

1. What information is the basis of a financial plan?
2. What is the financial manager's role in a month when cash inflow exceeds cash outflow?

CHECK ✓ POINT

Start-Up Financing

Financial management starts from the beginning of the company. The entrepreneur must find sources of money that will last until revenue begins to exceed cash outflows. That time often comes much later than the owner initially anticipates, and as a result many new businesses fail. Most new small businesses draw heavily on the entrepreneur's own assets. In addition, start-up financing may come from friends and relatives or, for larger businesses, from venture capital investors.

Personal Assets

Most entrepreneurs invest personal assets in the start-up of their new small business. Other investors are understandably reluctant to put their money into a venture that an entrepreneur considers too risky for his or her own money. For example, small private investment firms made up of wealthy individuals and institutions insist that ventures they lend to have the management retain from 5 to 50 percent of the business. As a spokesman for one investment firm states, "It makes us feel we have some community of interest going forward."[1] Therefore, owners of new businesses spend money from their personal savings to cover business expenses, and they pledge assets such

The construction industry is made up of both large companies and small businesses. Small businesses typically have fewer credit relationships and hence a skimpier credit history on which to be judged when the owners attempt to establish new lines of credit. The likelihood of their being granted credit is greater when the owners have good personal credit histories. A source of this information is the Small Business Advisory Report from the TRW Business Credit Division.

Source: Courtesy of TRW Inc.

as a home or car as collateral when they borrow. If the new business goes bankrupt, the owner must sell these assets to meet the company's debts.

What types of personal assets can entrepreneurs use to help them raise funds for the business? One is their home. The value of the home that the owner has paid for is called the owner's equity in the home. By pledging this equity, the homeowner can obtain a second mortgage or a home equity loan. Many enterprising owners have borrowed all of the equity they have in their house and pumped it into their business. Managers who have been paying their original mortgage for 10 or more years have often been able to borrow $25,000 and up.

Another common source of start-up funding is a life insurance policy. Many policies build up what is called cash surrender value. This is money that the policyholder can borrow at low interest rates (typically 5 to 8 percent). If the borrower does not repay the loan, the amount is simply deducted from the overall face value of the policy.

Finally, for those who need more cash or lack some of these other assets, banks offer the variable-rate installment loan. This is a personal loan with an interest rate tied to government securities, the prime rate (the rate the institution charges its best customers), or some other index. When the index changes, the interest rate moves in the same direction. Lenders may be more willing to make a personal loan with a variable rate than a fixed rate. The reason is that the ability to change the interest rate reduces the risk of a money-losing loan in a changing economy.

Family and Friends

Family members and friends can be an excellent source of start-up funds. They tend to be most helpful for financing small businesses, which often need only a small amount of funds ($25,000 or less). Many people can afford to lend this amount of cash. These lenders are also often willing to lend at a low interest rate. However, if the lender charges no interest or an unusually low rate, the Internal Revenue Service may assess taxes as if the lender had charged more. Professional tax advice can avoid unpleasant surprises. Another concern is that important relationships may be jeopardized if the business flounders and the borrower cannot repay the loan. Entrepreneurs may conclude that the feelings of family and friends are too precious to risk.

Entrepreneurs who do decide to draw on the resources of family and friends may want to compensate them by sharing ownership of the business. The lender could become a partner or a shareholder in a corporation. Chapter 3 described the basic options available for sharing business ownership.

Venture Capital Firms

In some cases, new or young companies can receive funding from **venture capital firms.** These are financial intermediaries that specialize in funding ventures with special promise. Typically, venture capital firms invest in enterprises expected to generate high profits within 5 years. The businesses receiving funding have tended to be in high-tech industries, but venture capital firms have been broadening their base into areas such as health care. However, these companies typically finance only a small percentage of the projects they examine.

Venture capital firms Financial intermediaries that specialize in funding ventures with special promise.

Every week, new venture capital deals are put together. These funds are typically used for one of four types of financing: (1) seed money to get the company started, (2) funds for helping the venture grow and gain market share, (3) money for taking advantage of lucrative market opportunities, and (4) funds for buying out a business.

1. Where can an entrepreneur get money for starting a small business?
2. What kinds of companies are venture capital firms typically interested in funding?

CHECK ✓ POINT

Short-Term Financing

Once a business is under way, the financial manager must meet the company's needs for short-term and long-term financing. **Short-term financing** consists of raising funds to meet obligations that will come due within the next 12 months and investing funds that the company doesn't immediately need. Quite often a firm's receipt of funds does not directly match up with its outflow of funds. Firms can obtain short-term financing to fill the gap in a number of ways. The most popular sources of short-term funds include trade credit, loans from commercial banks, factors, sales finance companies, commercial paper, and government sources.

Short-term financing Raising funds to meet obligations that will come due within the next 12 months.

Trade Credit

The most popular source of short-term financing is **trade credit** — the purchase of merchandise on an open account. Under this arrangement, the seller lets the buyer use the goods immediately, and the buyer promises to pay at the end of a given time period, such as 30 days. A typical trade credit ar-

Trade credit The purchase of merchandise on an open account.

rangement is 2/10, net 30, which is a cash discount pricing technique described in Chapter 15, whereby if buyers pay within 10 days they get a 2 percent discount. The availability of this discount depends in part on industry practices.

A company that takes advantage of the trade credit can reap considerable savings that can be used as a source of short-term funds. For example, if the company purchases $1,000 of merchandise and pays within 10 days, it saves $20 on its bill. Assuming that it takes the same discount each month, the company is actually getting a 24 percent discount on an annual basis (2 percent × 12 months) for the purchase of $1,000 of goods. These terms are so favorable that many companies borrow the money from a bank (at, say, 10 to 15 percent) in order to take advantage of the trade discount.

Funding from Commercial Banks

Perhaps the most sought-after source of short-term funds is commercial banks. Although the number of bank loans have decreased in recent years, the reason does not appear to be that the banks are in trouble (as discussed in Chapter 19) and do not have money to lend, but because they are being more cautious than they have been in the past and are requiring sensible borrowers.[2] Business loans fall into three categories: unsecured loans, secured loans, and lines of credit.

Unsecured loan A loan that requires no collateral.

If the business doesn't put up collateral (does not back the loan with assets) when it borrows, the loan is an **unsecured loan.** An example would be a promissory note that is due within a short period of time. Banks usually restrict unsecured loans to customers with an excellent credit rating. Businesses usually apply these funds to inventory purchases and paying bills that will be coming due in the near future. They usually repay unsecured loans within a year's time.

Secured loan A loan backed up with collateral.

When the company wants to borrow a large amount of money or has an unsatisfactory credit rating, it pledges collateral to back up the loan. Such a loan is a **secured loan.** The business's managers sign an agreement to turn over pledged assets if they do not repay the loan. In the railroad business, for example, collateral often takes the form of rolling stock — railroad cars and locomotives. Manufacturing firms use their plant and equipment to secure the loan. In retailing, accounts receivable and inventory often serve as collateral.

Line of credit A stated cash reserve available whenever the business wants to draw on it.

A particularly flexible lending instrument is a **line of credit,** which is a stated cash reserve available whenever the business wants to draw on it. Companies with a solid financial position prefer lines of credit to normal loans for a number of reasons. One is that a bank charges interest on the entire loan from the day it turns over the funds to the company. However, on a line of credit, the bank charges interest only on the amount of money the company has borrowed. Lines of credit also tend to be open-ended. When the firm needs cash, it draws on its line of credit; when it has extra cash, it repays part or all of the outstanding balance. Moreover, as the company gets larger, it usually can have the bank increase the credit line, ensuring an adequate source of short-term funds.

Factors

Factor A financial institution that purchases accounts receivable.

Less widely known than commercial banks are factors. A **factor** is a financial institution that purchases accounts receivable. A business with a large

Arctco, Inc., maker of recreational Arctic Cat snowmobiles, establishes revolving charge accounts for its customers with the help of Household Retail Services Inc. HRSI is the country's second largest issuer of private label retail credit cards. It manages client's credit operations and develops credit marketing programs to promote use of the cards.

Source: Courtesy of Arctco, Inc.

amount of accounts receivable may find itself in a cash bind until customers pay the amounts due. Selling these receivables gives the business cash for continuing its operations. The factor buys the right to collect the money due; because collection is uncertain, the factor pays only a percentage of the amount due.

The percentage that the factor pays depends on the quality of the receivables and the conditions under which they are sold. The quality depends on how long the receivables have been outstanding and who owes them. In examining the length of time the receivables have been outstanding, the factor considers the terms under which the goods were sold. If the terms were 2/10, net 30, no receivables should be over 30 days old. The older the receivables, the higher the risk that they will not be paid and the less likely the factor will want to buy them.

Many industries use factoring, including the garment and furniture businesses, as well as small retailers in general. These firms sell on credit to generate high sales and then factor the accounts to get money.

Sales Finance Companies

For financing similar to that offered by factors, a firm may turn to a **sales finance company,** which is a financial institution that purchases installment sales contracts. Many merchants allow their customers to pay for purchases on a time payment schedule. For example, a consumer might buy a stereo and pay for it in 12 monthly installments. The merchant, in turn, can sell the

Sales finance company
A financial institution that purchases installment sales contracts.

installment contract to a sales finance company. The finance company may give the merchant the amount on the principal immediately, and then collect the interest and principal from the buyer. Merchants get their funds immediately, but considering that many installment loans cost 15 to 21 percent annually, the sales finance company can also benefit handsomely. In fact, profits have proved so lucrative that many large retailers have begun financing their own sales and profiting on both ends of the deal: the sale and the financing. For example, auto companies sell cars through dealers and finance the sales through General Motors Acceptance Corporation (GMAC), Ford Motor Credit, and Chrysler Financial. In recent years, these finance subsidiaries have been more profitable than the corporations as a whole.[3]

Commercial Paper

Commercial paper
An unsecured promissory note.

Some big firms obtain funds by selling **commercial paper,** which is a type of unsecured promissory note. Because commercial paper has no collateral behind it, only firms with a solid reputation, usually major corporations such as General Electric or Exxon, are able to sell it. Businesses known as commercial paper houses buy these notes from the issuing company and sell them to investors and other financial institutions.

Companies pay commercial paper obligations in the short term, typically 60 to 180 days. For major firms that need to raise working capital for day-to-day operations, commercial paper can be an important source of short-term financing. Conversely, for companies with idle cash, purchasing short-term paper is often a good investment because it usually provides a higher interest rate than is available elsewhere.

Government Sources

In special cases, a business may obtain short-term funds from the federal government. For example, the Small Business Administration (SBA), discussed in Chapter 4, lends directly to small businesses and works with banks to guarantee small-business loans. This assistance is available to small businesses that are unable to get financing any other way and can meet SBA loan requirements. In addition, the Department of Defense sometimes grants cash advances to firms engaged in defense-related work.

CHECK ✓ POINT

1. What are three sources of short-term funding?
2. Besides acquiring funds, how do financial managers handle short-term financing?

Long-Term Financing

Businesses that are expanding or upgrading facilities have long-term funding needs. Firms meet these needs by increasing the company's debt or its equity. Debt financing is taking out long-term loans or selling bonds. Equity financing involves the sale of stock. Figure 20.3 illustrates these alternatives.

Characteristics of Long-Term Debt

Whether loans or bonds, long-term debt instruments have a number of characteristics in common. The debt requires interest payments and provides the

FIGURE 20.3
Long-Term Financing Instruments

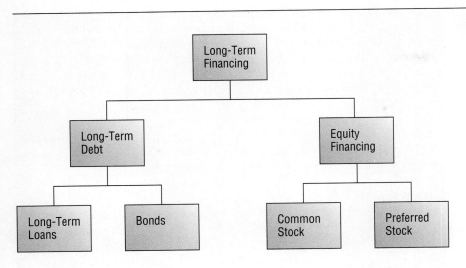

lender with a claim on assets. Both types of debt require repayment, and both offer tax advantages and leverage.

Interest   Most long-term debt instruments carry an interest rate. These rates vary based on risk and interest rates on other investments competing for lenders' funds. For example, during the early 1980s, bonds were considered to be a poor investment. Many of them with face value of $1,000 were selling at $300 to $500, reflecting the low interest at which they had been issued and the fact that many people felt other investments were much safer. By the early 1990s, the bond market had recovered quite a bit. The perception of investors was that bonds were not a high risk and were considered to be a good investment alternative. Annual returns were in the range of 9 to 10 percent, and bonds were once again proving to be an important avenue for raising long-term capital.

Claim on Assets   If a company declares bankruptcy, its assets will be sold to cover the debts. Under this arrangement, creditors are first in line for repayment. Unpaid vendors who have provided the firm with goods and services are often among the first to be paid. After these creditors, come the bondholders. This means that, in the case of bankruptcy, the bondholders may get only 10 to 50 percent of their money back. However, this is better than nothing; stockholders in most cases would end up getting nothing.

Repayment   At some time, long-term debts must be repaid. In the case of bonds, the company may set aside money in a special reserve fund. When the bonds reach maturity, the fund contains enough money to pay off the debt. The company can also refinance the entire long-term debt by obtaining a new loan or floating new bonds to replace the old ones. In this case, if the company had set up a fund for retirement of the debt, the company might use it for improvements such as new machinery, equipment, or facilities.

The Fantasy is one of Carnival Cruise Lines' newest liners. To pay for the construction of the ship, Carnival arranged a long-term loan of $141.8 million for a period of 8½ years.

Source: Courtesy of Carnival Cruise Lines.

Leverage   The use of borrowed funds to increase the return on equity.

Tax Advantages   Interest payments on loans and bonds are treated as expenses. This means that the company subtracts them from its revenues to find taxable income. The higher the interest expense, the lower the taxable income, and the lower the taxes that are paid.

Leverage   Long-term debt also provides a benefit that helps businesses grow: **leverage.** This is the use of borrowed funds to increase the return on the owner's own funds, or equity. Just as a mechanical lever lets users get more power out of their muscles, financial leverage enables users to get more financial power out of their cash. For example, if a firm can earn 15 percent on $10,000 of its own cash invested in a new piece of equipment, then the return is $1,500. But if it can borrow $30,000 at 10 percent in order to buy three more machines that also earn 15 percent, then it can realize an additional return of $1,500 ($4,500 return − $3,000 interest cost). Thus, by leveraging (using borrowed funds), the firm can greatly magnify its return. In other words, it takes money to make money. The key, of course, is that the cost of borrowing (the interest on the loan) must be less than the return realized. In other words, leveraging works best during good economic times.

However, low-leveraged firms (those with low debt) have a competitive advantage during an economic downturn. For example, they can buy equipment, facilities or whole divisions very cheaply from their cash-strapped competitors. In addition, they can still borrow money — something that their highly leveraged rivals can no longer do.[4] For this reason, many borrowers prefer to obtain long-term financing through equity rather than through debt.

	Market Value	Long-Term Debt	Net Worth	**TABLE 20.1** Some of Donald Trump's Financial Problems Going into the 1990s
	(in millions of dollars)			
Trump Plaza	$450	$273	$177	
Grand Hyatt (50% owned)	200	115	85	
Trump Tower	150	90	60	
Plaza Hotel	450	400	50	
Undeveloped Trump City (80% owned)	160	160	—	
Alexander's	65	68	−3	
Trump's Castle	324	335	−11	
Trump Shuttle	350	400	−50	

Source: Chris Welles, Gail De George, and Joseph Weber, "Welcome to the Nineties, Donald," *Business Week*, May 14, 1990, 120.

Long-Term Loans

A **long-term loan** is a loan that has a maturity of at least a year — typically one to ten years. During this time, the firm is required to pay interest on the debt and to abide by any other agreements associated with the loan. For example, the lender often protects its financial position by requiring that the company obtain the lender's permission before taking on any additional long-term debt. In addition, the lenders often require that the company either make periodic payments on the principal or establish a fund for paying off the loan in a lump sum at maturity. If the lender regards the loan as particularly risky, it may even require the firm to limit or eliminate dividends to stockholders. This increases the cash available for repaying the loan.

Whether the borrower will accept these conditions often depends on what funding options are available. If the lender's terms are stringent and the company can obtain funds elsewhere, it may turn to other sources. Companies that are in good financial shape can be more particular; other firms may have to accept the conditions laid down by the borrower. In any case, the borrower must pay the interest on the loan. In recent years, borrowers that run into financial difficulties, for example the retailer Macy's or Donald Trump, have had trouble making interest payments on long-term loans and had to try to negotiate a settlement.[5] Table 20.1 shows the market value of Trump's major holdings going into the 1990s and how much long-term debt he had against each. Notice that Alexander's, Trump's Castle, and the Shuttle had negative net worths.

Long-term loan A loan that has a term of at least one year.

Bonds

If the financial manager wants to use debt financing but wants a longer term and freedom from lenders' restrictions, the company might issue **bonds.** These are long-term debts with a maturity date 20 to 30 years in the future that are sold to raise funds. Federal, state, and local governments issue gov-

Bonds Long-term debts with a term of 20 to 30 years that are sold to raise funds.

FIGURE 20.4
A Sample Bond

Source: Courtesy of General Motors
Acceptance Corporation.

Debenture An unsecured bond.

ernment bonds. Corporations issue corporate bonds, which may be secured or unsecured. Figure 20.4 shows a typical corporate bond.

Whether the bond is secured or unsecured depends on the condition of the firm. When a company that has had financial problems wants to sell bonds, it often offers some collateral. For example, companies may sell mortgage bonds, which are backed by real or personal property, and firms in the transportation industry, such as the railroads or airlines, may secure their bond issues with rolling stock (their equipment). Without collateral, it is often difficult, if not impossible, to find investors who are willing to buy the bonds. Unsecured bonds, called **debentures,** have rarely been used in recent years. The corporations that have successfully used them in the past tended to be huge companies such as AT&T. But even AT&T now has problems because of the turmoil in the telephone industry, so debentures are seldom used.

Most bonds carry a face (sometimes called par) value of $1,000 and pay a predetermined interest rate, sometimes called the coupon rate. The rate is a percentage of the face value. The company pays this interest quarterly, semiannually, or annually, as agreed upon in advance.

Indenture agreement
A document that sets forth the terms of a bond issue.

The Indenture Agreement The terms of a bond issue are specified in an **indenture agreement.** For example, the indenture agreement may specify the amount and frequency of interest payments. It also may identify any assets that are pledged as collateral for the bonds.

Call provision A bond provision that allows the firm to repurchase the bonds before maturity.

Retiring Bonds Depending on the terms of the agreement, the issuer may retire bonds before they mature. If the indenture agreement contains a **call**

provision, the firm may repurchase the bonds before maturity. For example, if a firm issued 20-year $1,000 bonds at 10 percent in 1990, the company would redeem them in 2010 at $1,000 per bond. However, if by 1996 other companies were paying only 7 percent, the company might want to call in its 10 percent bonds and replace them with a 7 percent issue. When a firm exercises this option, it also pays the bondholders a **redemption premium,** a bonus paid for early redemption of bonds.

Another flexible feature in some indenture agreements is the **conversion privilege,** which allows bondholders to convert their investment into a stated number of shares of common stock. This privilege gives the bondholders some flexibility. For example, if the price of the company's common stock is going up, the investors can profit from conversion.

If the price of the stock remains steady or is going down, the investors can hang on to their bonds. Moreover, the investors know the price at which they may convert, so they can wait until the exchange is favorable to them. For example, if a bondholder paid $1,000 for the bond and can convert this to 100 shares of common stock, any rise in the stock above $10 makes conversion profitable. If the stock goes to $12 and levels off, the bondholder can convert or simply wait and see what happens. If the stock falls back, the bondholder has lost nothing; if the stock suddenly zooms to $20, he or she can convert and have an investment valued at $2,000. The main reason for offering convertibility is to make the bond issue more attractive to potential investors.

Bond Prices   Bonds do not always sell for their face value. Sometimes they sell at a **premium,** a price above face value. At other times, they sell at a **discount,** an amount below the bond's face value.

One determinant of a bond's actual selling price is its interest rate. If a newly issued bond pays the same interest rate as most bonds, it will probably sell for close to its face value. However, if interest rates begin to rise, bondholders can get more money by selling their bonds and investing in something else. As they begin to sell their bonds, the market price for them begins to drop. The result is that the effective interest rate on the bonds will rise. For example, if a bond that has a face value of $1,000 and pays $100 a year in interest sells for $900, it will provide the investor with an annual return of 11.1 percent ($100 ÷ $900). If the price were to drop to $800, the effective rate of return would go to 12.5 percent ($100 ÷ $800), because bondholders would now be earning $100 annually on an $800 investment. The accompanying Innovation Close-Up (Rebounding Junk Bonds) shows how bond yields for certain types of bonds have done extremely well in recent years.

Conversely, if interest rates on other investments started to drop, more people would begin buying bonds. This would cause the price to rise and the effective interest rate to drop. For example, if a $1,000 bond initially paid 10 percent a year and its price rose to $1,100, the effective interest rate would fall to 9.0 percent ($100 ÷ $1,100). As the price rose to $1,200, the effective interest rate would fall to 8.3 percent ($100 ÷ $1,200). The price of the bond would level off when the effective interest rate was equal to the rate investors could earn on investments with a similar risk.

Besides the interest rate, time until maturity causes a bond's price to fluctuate. If investors bought $1,000 bonds paying $100 annually for $800,

Redemption premium   A bonus the company pays bondholders for early redemption of bonds.

Conversion privilege
A provision permitting conversion of bonds into a stated number of shares of common stock.

Premium   The price paid for a bond above its face value.

Discount   The amount by which a bond's price is less than its face value.

C L O S E - U P / *Innovation*

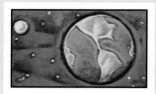

Rebounding Junk Bonds

With interest rates on savings accounts, certificates of deposit and traditional government and corporate bonds so low, investors are looking for innovative ways to get more "bang for their buck." They may have to look no further than the formerly disreputable junk bonds, although by the end of the 1980s, many investors were sorry they had bought junk bonds because some of the firms that had issued these securities were unable to pay the high yields that had been promised. Now, however, some junk bonds are making a recovery. Investors are finding that these securities can offer at least some degree of safety and a very high yield.

In January 1991, the average junk bond was selling for 65 cents on the dollar. By late 1992, this was up to 97 cents on the dollar and the average yield was over 12 percent. This yield was significantly higher than that on other bonds where an 8 percent return was typical, and it was much higher than the 2-3 percent being paid on savings accounts.

In the first five months of 1992, another $14 billion of these bonds were issued, compared to $10 billion for all of 1991. Part of this demand was a result of new bonds with lower interest rates replacing older ones issued during the 1980s and carrying much higher rates. Holders of these old bonds have found themselves recipients of a tidy windfall, since the provisions of the bonds require payment of a fee, typically around 3 percent, in the case of early repayment. For those who reinvested their funds in the new issues, this means that they received 3 percent and were able to obtain another 12 percent annually from the new junk bonds.

More daring investors believe that junk bonds will continue to be lucrative investments. Given that junk bonds have rates four to five points higher than that paid by U.S. Treasury bills, they will continue to attract investors willing to take a risk. In addition, junk bonds may offer more stability than that afforded by stocks. In any case, the junk bonds that were associated with problems a few years ago have seemed to rebound. At least for the time being, junk bonds are back in style for certain types of investors.

Source: Leah Nathans Spiro, "From Sensational to Pretty Darn Good," *Business Week*, June 22, 1992, p. 100.

they would be receiving an effective interest rate of 12.5 percent. However, this does not take into account the fact that upon maturity, the investors will receive $1,000, or $200 more than they paid for the bond. This increases the value of the bond, and the closer the bond is to maturity, the more the value rises. Therefore, as bonds get closer to maturity, their prices tend to move closer to the face value.

If the company is judged to be a poor risk, however, this may not happen. Investors will think that the firm is unable to redeem the bonds, and they will end up settling for less than the face value. In these cases, the bonds continue to sell at a discount.

Common Stock

Equity financing The sale of ownership in a firm.

Sometimes the company's managers want to avoid increasing the company's debt obligations. In that case, they turn to **equity financing,** the sale of ownership (or equity) in a firm. The two basic instruments of equity financing for corporations are common stock and preferred stock. For example, Tyson Foods, which had considerable debt from their purchase of Holly Farms, recently raised $94 million from the sale of common stock.[6] Chapter 3 described the rights and privileges of stock ownership, and Chapter 21 describes the market for stock. This section focuses on how stocks help the firm meet its needs for long-term funding.

TABLE 20.2
Some Firms That Have
Never Missed a Dividend
in Over a Century

Company	Year Dividend Payments Began
Bank of New York Company, Inc.	1784
Citicorp	1813
J. P. Morgan & Company, Inc.	1840
Chase Manhattan Corporation	1848
Continental Corporation	1853
Travelers Corporation	1866
American Express	1868
Cincinnati Bell, Inc.	1879

By far the most common form of equity financing is the sale of **common stock,** which is ownership shares in a corporation. Most people who own stock in a corporation hold common stock. (See Figure 3.3 in Chapter 3 for a sample common stock certificate.) Chapter 3 listed the technical rights of stockholders, but it can be simply said that most investors buy common stock because it gives them the right to share in the company's earnings.

Common stock Ownership shares in a corporation.

Share in the Earnings Common stockholders receive their share in the form of a **dividend,** which is a payment from earnings for each share of stock they own. Large firms usually pay dividends quarterly. Firms that declare minimum dividends, such as 25 cents per year, usually pay them annually.

As Table 20.2 shows, some companies have not missed a dividend in years. Most investors regard dividends as guaranteed payments. However, this is not really an accurate assumption. The board of directors declares a dividend based on the earnings and expected growth of the corporation. If the company runs into hard times, it may cut or eliminate the dividend. A firm may also use its profits for new-product development or to expand or upgrade its facilities, leaving little for dividends. For example, IBM has followed such a policy for many years. In the early 1990s, the firm was paying $4.84 annually, which represented a return of less than 5 percent on the value of the stock. IBM's philosophy is similar to that of many successful high-growth firms. Spending profits on research and development or on equipment and facilities may enhance the value of the company, benefiting the stockholders in the long run as the price of the stock rises to reflect the greater worth of the company.

Dividend A payment to stockholders from the corporation's earnings.

Voice in Management Common stockholders have the right to vote on certain corporate matters, including the election of the board of directors, as was discussed in Chapter 3. Consequently, financing through the sale of stock means that the original owners risk sacrificing control. That risk often influences the decision whether to finance with debt or equity. The accompanying Ethics Close-Up (The Stockholders Speak) provides some insights to the growing power of stockholders in gaining such a voice in management.

CLOSE-UP / *Ethics*

The Stockholders Speak

Over the past 5 years corporations are finding that stockholders are beginning to demand a greater voice in how things are done. One of the ways in which they are making their voices heard is through the use of shareholder proposals. These proposals are recommendations that are voted on by those who hold stock in the company. One popular proposal has been that of limiting the use of golden parachutes, which are arrangements that give managers a hefty bonus or stock option should a particular event occur. An example is a $250,000 payment that is awarded to a manager who voluntarily decides to leave the firm or is fired. Another example of a golden parachute might be a $250,000 payment if the company is acquired by another company through merger or acquisition. Many stockholders contend that these parachutes are too lucrative and it is unethical for management to set these up for themselves.

Golden parachute limitations or abolishment are only one of the many proposals that shareholders are putting forth. Others relate to doing business in South Africa or with companies that have a poor hiring record with minorities or women. Still others relate to company products that are judged to be bad for one's health — for example, cigarettes and liquor — or harmful to the environment. Stockholders may demand that management terminate these harmful products.

In most cases, shareholder proposals do not win because only a few strong voices are heard. However, the coming years are likely to see shareholders gaining more clout. One reason is because a large portion of the outstanding stock of giant corporations is held by the big institutional investors (pension plans, insurance companies, mutual companies) and these groups are now starting to flex their muscle. In particular, the institutions want to see companies become more responsive to shareholder concerns and to start replacing inside managers on the board of directors with outsiders. Surprisingly, many of the suggestions of the large institutional investors have gone unheeded. As one analyst recently noted, "Many institutional shareholders have complained that they have been ignored by corporations despite their enormous stock holdings, which now amount to more than half the shares of the nation's 50 largest companies."

The future is likely to see more stockholder involvement for a number of reasons. One is that shareholders are becoming more sophisticated and learning how to get management to respond appropriately. A second is that new proxy rules are being formulated by the Securities and Exchange Commission that will give the shareholders more power. A third is that recent trends show that stockholders are beginning to win more of their battles with management. As a result, the future is likely to see corporations being much more responsive to shareholder suggestions than they have in the past.

Source: Brett Duval Fromson, "The Big Owners Roar," *Fortune,* July 30, 1990, 66–78; and Leslie Wayne, "As Proxy Use Widens, New Rules Are Urged," *New York Times,* June 15, 1990, C1, 15.

Claim on Assets If the corporation dissolves or goes bankrupt, the common stockholders, as owners, have a claim on its assets. However, this claim is usually of little value, because the claims of so many others usually take priority over those of the common stockholders. The order of priority is determined by law. As noted earlier, those who come before common stockholders include creditors, lenders, bondholders, and preferred stockholders. As a result, if the corporation goes bankrupt, the common stockholders seldom receive much, if anything.

Permanent Ownership The corporations may not recall common stock. It can, however, get the stock back in two ways. One is to purchase it from the existing stockholders. Widely recognized firms such as Beatrice, Levi Strauss, and Denny's have bought back all their stock, an action called going private. For example, in Levi Strauss's case, going private allowed the firm the freedom it needed from outside interference to restructure operations and improve overall efficiency. As a result, net income increased 600 percent within four years.[7]

The other way of getting the stock back is to merge with another firm and trade the company's common stock for the merged firm's stock. For example, under this arrangement, stockholders in Company A will receive three shares of stock in Company B for every share of common stock they currently hold in Company A. When the exchange is complete, there is no longer any outstanding common stock in Company A; only Company B's stock remains in the marketplace. In recent years, many acquiring firms have swapped their stock for stock in the firm being purchased. For example, when USX took over Texas Oil and Gas, for every share of Texas Oil and Gas the shareholders received 0.633 of a share of USX.

Preferred Stock

Less often used than common stock in equity financing is **preferred stock,** which is stock that provides preferential treatment in the payment of dividends and the distribution of assets. Many people liken this form of stock to a combination of bonds and common stock, because it has characteristics of both. For example, preferred stock is like a bond in that it has a fixed dividend. However, it is unlike a bond because the board must declare the dividend, and it is paid before anything is distributed to the common stockholders. On the other hand, preferred stock is like common stock in that under specified conditions the preferred stockholder may have a voice in management. Although preferred stockholders may not vote for the board of directors, they may be able to vote on corporate matters when the corporation fails to pay the preferred dividends.

Another way in which preferred stockholders can obtain a voice in management is through the conversion privilege, which allows the investors to convert their holdings to common stock. This privilege has two advantages: it helps make the stock offering more attractive, and it gives the stockholders a chance to be heard by the board of directors.

After converting to common stock, the preferred stockholders can vote for the board of directors at the annual meeting. If the company has issued a large block of preferred stock and its owners convert a majority to common stock, they can hold a large percentage of the common stock. This, in turn, would ensure them a voice, and they may even obtain some seats on the board of directors. Aware of the consequences of such action, most board members try to see that the corporation is managed effectively, in order to prevent dissatisfaction among the preferred stockholders.

Preferred stock Stock that provides preferential treatment in the payment of dividends and the distribution of assets.

Help in Issuing Bonds and Stocks

Companies that want to issue bonds and stocks usually turn to financial intermediaries that help the company reach potential investors. The major intermediary for bond and stock sales is the **investment bank.** For example, if Consolidated Edison wanted to raise money by floating a $25 million bond issue, it would turn to investment banks. These firms, which include such prestigious names as Merrill Lynch, Morgan Stanley, Salomon Brothers, and Goldman Sachs will typically form a group or syndicate that agrees to sell the

Investment bank A financial intermediary that purchases and resells bonds and stocks.

TABLE 20.3
Bond Ratings

Ratings by Moody's Investor Service, Inc.	Meaning	Ratings by Standard & Poor Corporation	Meaning
Aaa	Prime quality	AAA	Highest grade
Aa	High grade	AA	High grade
A	Upper-medium grade	A	Upper-medium grade
Baa	Lower-medium grade or speculative	BBB	Medium grade
Ba	Lower-medium grade or speculative	BB	Lower-medium grade or speculative
B	Speculative	B	Speculative
Caa Ca C	Range from very speculative to in or near default	CCC CC C	Very speculative
		DDD DD D	In default; rating based on relative salvage value

bonds. For this service, these investment bankers receive a fee that depends on the interest rate the bonds will pay and the firm's credit rating at the time. The higher the company's credit rating, the lower the risk associated with repayment will be and the more likely that the investment bankers will be able to generate sales interest.

Organizations that analyze the financial shape of companies determine credit ratings for bond issuers. The two best-known ratings are those by Standard & Poor and the Moody's Investor Service. Table 20.3 shows their rating scales and describes what each rating means.

In the case of a stock issue, the arrangement with the investment banker is similar. The banks that form the syndicate will attempt to sell the stock to their clients or to other organizations such as retirement funds or investor groups that are looking to invest in the stock market. If the company issuing the stock is considered a good risk, the syndicate often agrees to take the issue at a discounted price, rather than charging a fee. For example, the banker may pay $9 million for 1 million shares of stock to be sold at $10 each. The $1 million profit is used to cover the expenses associated with reselling the stock, as well as the risk that the banker won't be able to sell all of the issue at the intended price and will have to hold on to it for a while or sell it for less.

CHECK ✓ POINT

1. What is the difference between long-term debt financing and equity financing?
2. Why are some managers reluctant to use equity financing?

This Upper Atmosphere Research Satellite being built by General Electric Astro Space will study the earth's ozone layer and atmospheric conditions. Like many companies, GE sometimes raises capital to fund its various projects by issuing bonds, notes, and/or preferred stock. These debt issues are rated by organizations like Moody's Investor Service and Standard & Poor, which provide to investors a consistent method of comparing the quality of such issues.

Source: © Joe McNally/The Image Bank.

Closing Comments

Financial management is a complex responsibility that begins with evaluating how funding will help the company achieve its objectives. The financial manager must ensure that the company has money for its short-term and long-term needs and that it makes wise use of the money on hand. Funding may come from trade credit, the sale of assets, the acquisition of debt, or the sale of stock. A well-designed financial plan is often necessary not only for profit and growth, but also for the firm's very survival.

VIDEO CASE / *The Nondeposit Bank*

Financial management is a major challenge for many businesses. In the case of Anna-Lee dolls, the early years were difficult, and the small family-run business often operated on a hand-to-mouth basis. Fortunately, the growing popularity of the dolls virtually guaranteed the success of the operation. Today, if the company needed money, its bank would be more than happy to provide the funds. Not all small businesses or individuals are in the same enviable situation. Yet, at one time or another, they need to borrow money from a bank.

Among bankers, Yvonne Scruggs-Leftwich is interesting and unique.

When she left public service a few years ago, she had outstanding credentials: Fulbright fellow, faculty member at the Wharton School, deputy assistant secretary of Housing and Urban Development, commissioner of the New York State Division of Housing, and deputy mayor of Philadelphia. Taking a job in investment banking, she found that she did not like the work. Yvonne decided to apply her financial management skills to working with people in the inner city in need of her help. She started a nondepository bank. In this kind of bank customers do not deposit money but, for a fee, are provided services that a deposit bank normally offers.

In Yvonne's bank, customers can cash checks, wire money, buy money orders and stamps, and pay their bills. In the latter case, her bank transfers the funds to the appropriate firm, such as the local utility company. Yvonne started out by staffing her offices with people from the local community. She hired people who would not have been able to find jobs otherwise, and they seized the opportunity and became outstanding employees. At the same time, more and more poor people learned about the financial services she was offering and flocked to her nondepository bank. She began letting local artists hang their works on the walls of her offices and neighborhood organizations began to use the offices for meetings after hours. The more her customers were made to feel welcome, the more she earned their loyalty and business.

Her first location, in Buffalo, soon turned a profit and she expanded into two other New York locales. Each of these offices services about 45,000 people a month and is proving profitable. When asked about her success, Yvonne said that the key to success is to look at financial areas in which banks are not doing anything or have pulled out of

that end of the business, and then figure out how to provide these financial services at a profit. Her nondeposit bank services are helping her attain two important objectives: making a profit and finding a way to help make other people's lives more enjoyable.

Source: "The People's Banker," *Success*, January–February 1991, 30.

Case Questions

1. What types of financial management services does a company like Anna-

Lee need? Identify and describe two.

2. What types of financial management services does Yvonne's nondeposit bank provide? Identify and describe two.

3. Who would be most interested in Yvonne's banking services? What does your answer reveal about emerging developments in the field of financial management?

Learning Objectives Revisited

1. **Define the role of financial management.** Financial management consists of creating a financial plan, carrying out the plan, monitoring the flow of funds, and making adjustments as needed. The financial plan identifies the timing, amount, and sources of funds needed to achieve company objectives. In a large company, the person charged with these responsibilities is the financial manager, who may head a team of financial experts.

2. **Identify ways entrepreneurs can finance the start-up of their business.** Entrepreneurs usually draw on their own assets to start up a small company. They may use money they have saved or pledge personal assets to obtain a loan. Sometimes an entrepreneur's friends and relatives are willing to invest their money in the company, in exchange for interest payments or perhaps part ownership. If the company has potential for rapid growth and large profits, venture capital firms may be willing to invest in it.

3. **Present the various types of short-term financing.** Short-term financing consists of raising funds to meet obligations that will come due within the next 12 months and investing funds that the company doesn't immediately need. Some of the most common ways of securing this type of financing include utilizing trade credit, commercial banks, factors, sales finance companies, and commercial paper. In some cases, a company may receive government assistance. When seeking investments for idle cash, the financial manager weighs the interest rate against the risks involved.

4. **Discuss the use of loans for long-term financing.** A long-term loan is a loan that has a maturity of at least a

year. It normally carries an annual interest rate and requires repayment at the end of a predetermined time. The company may make payments of principal and interest, or it may pay the interest in installments and the principal in a lump sum at the end of the loan's life.

5. **Describe the use of bonds for long-term financing.** A bond is a long-term debt instrument with a maturity date typically 20 to 30 years in the future that is sold to raise funds. Most bonds carry a face value of $1,000 and pay a predetermined interest rate. Some bonds include a call provision, which allows the firm to retire the bonds before their maturity, and a conversion privilege, which allows the bondholders to convert their investment into common stock.

6. **Explain how companies use stocks for long-term financing.** The company may issue common stock or preferred stock. Common stockholders are entitled to share in the company's earnings; they have the right to vote on corporate matters, including the election of the board of directors; in case of bankruptcy or liquidation, they have a claim on the assets; and their stock cannot be recalled by management. Preferred stock provides preferential treatment in the payment of dividends and the distribution of assets in the case of bankruptcy. Under certain conditions, preferred stockholders can have a voice in management. For help in selling stocks and bonds, companies turn to investment banks.

Key Terms Reviewed

Review each of the following terms. For any that you do not know or are unsure of, look up the definitions and see how they were used in the chapter.

financial manager
venture capital firms
short-term financing
trade credit
unsecured loan
secured loan
line of credit
factor
sales finance company

commercial paper
leverage
long-term loan
bonds
debenture
indenture agreement
call provision
redemption premium

conversion privilege
premium
discount
equity financing
common stock
dividend
preferred stock
investment bank

Review Questions

1. What does a financial manager do?
2. How does a credit policy serve as a financing technique? What are the risks of a liberal credit policy? What are the risks of a strict credit policy?
3. Bruce Russo is the financial manager for National Surgical Supply, a company that distributes surgical supplies, some of which it also manufactures. One of the company's objectives for next year is to increase sales 8 percent by adding several new products and increasing sales of current products. Based on this objective, what are some funding needs that Bruce might identify? List as many as you can think of.
4. Jane Rivera is a loan officer at National Bank. In reviewing a loan application from Greg Glasgow, who wants to start a photography studio, Jane observes that Greg wants to obtain all his start-up funds through an unsecured loan from National. When Jane suggests that Greg obtain part of the financing by taking out a home equity loan, Greg looks shocked. "No way!" he exclaims. "If the business doesn't work out like I hope it will, I could lose my home." Do you think Jane is likely to approve the loan request? Why or why not?
5. What kinds of companies typically are able to obtain funding from a venture capital firm?
6. How does trade credit serve as a source of funding?
7. John Fletcher, who owns a small business, would like to borrow $35,000 from his bank. Would the bank be likely to offer him a secured or an unsecured loan?
8. Linda Turner is the financial manager for a chain of coffee shops called Lucky Breaks. Last month, revenues exceeded expenses, and Linda expects this

pattern to continue for another month or two. Does this situation require action from Linda? Explain what Linda should do or why she need not act.
9. If the company looked like it might fail, would you rather be one of its bondholders, one of its stockholders, or one of its vendors? Why?
10. How does a long-term loan differ from a bond?
11. Why might a company want to include a call provision in a bond's indenture agreement? Why might it want to include a conversion privilege?
12. Golden Rent a Car is issuing $1,000 bonds, each paying $80. Most bonds on the market are currently providing a return of 9.25 percent. Do you think Golden's bonds will sell at a premium, at face value, or at a discount? Why?
13. Would an investor in a firm be better off buying common stock or preferred stock? Why?
14. Gradgrind Machining handles small, specialty machining jobs. Because of intense competition, the company has gone through some difficult times. The company's managers believe that their best chance for a rebound lies in careful investment in high-technology machinery and equipment, making the plant a model of efficiency. The company may have to sustain losses for several years, but ultimately it will be more profitable than ever. Do you think the company should finance this plan through the sale of stock? Why or why not? If you think equity financing is wise, would you recommend common or preferred stock? Explain.
15. Jill Glynn would like to sell 300,000 shares of the 1 million shares of stock in her firm. What role could an investment bank play in helping her do this?

Applied Exercise

Various financial needs of companies are given below. Strategies that can be used to meet these needs are listed in A–J. For each of the 10 needs, select the strategy that is best and fill in the letter.

A. commercial paper
B. trade credit
C. bonds
D. line of credit
E. long-term loan
F. venture capital firm
G. stock
H. sales finance company
I. factor
J. preferred stock

1. A company needs to raise $500,000, which it will repay within 5 years. _____
2. A business needs an immediate inflow of cash because too many of its assets are tied up in accounts receivable. _____
3. A firm wants to raise $12 million in exchange for giving the investors part ownership in the company. _____
4. A large business needs to raise $3 million but does not want to pledge any of its assets. _____
5. A company has a major cash shortage in December but by February has more cash than it needs. _____
6. A young, high-tech firm wants to raise money for expansion. _____
7. A business wants to raise $1 million in exchange for part ownership in the firm and is willing to pay a 6 percent fixed dividend on the investment. _____
8. A company wants to purchase merchandise today and pay for it at the beginning of next month. _____
9. A firm wants to sell its installment sales contracts in order to raise cash. _____
10. A business wants to raise $5 million that will be repaid at the end of 20 years. _____

Mike Sherral owns 14 fast-food outlets located in a 50-mile radius of Los Angeles. Mike opened his first one 3 years ago, and his restaurants have been extremely profitable from the beginning. Mike wants to keep expanding and sees only two avenues available: franchising or selling stock. Mike would like to retain control of the enterprise and believes that he can best accomplish this by selling stock and using the proceeds to expand.

He has put together two expansion proposals:

1. Issue 500,000 shares of common stock and sell 200,000 of them. A representative of a large investment banking firm has told Mike that the bank will take the shares off his hands at $9 each and will sell them for $10. To make the offer appealing, the investment bank wants Mike to declare an annual dividend of $1 payable quarterly.

2. Issue 300,000 shares of common stock and keep them all, and issue 20,000 shares of preferred stock. The investment bank is willing to buy these $100 par shares of preferred stock for $88 each. To make the offer appealing, the banker believes that Mike should pay a 7 percent dividend and allow the shares to be convertible at seven shares of common stock for each preferred share. The banker also feels that the stock should be callable with a 6 percent premium if the company exercises this option.

Both of these proposals are equally appealing to Mike, although he has continued to emphasize the importance of maintaining control of the firm. He also wants to ensure that if business continues to be as good or better, he can obtain more long-term funds for additional expansion. The investment banking people have told him that if his business continues to grow as it has in the past, this should be no problem. For the moment, however, the question is which of the two financing alternatives to pursue.

Your Advice

1. What should Mike do?
   ___ a. Issue 500,000 shares of common stock and sell 200,000 of them.
   ___ b. Issue 300,000 shares of common stock, keep them all, and issue 20,000 shares of preferred stock that will be sold.
   ___ c. Forgo the sale of stock and expand out of profits even though this will take much longer.
2. What are the benefits associated with issuing the common stock?
3. What are the benefits associated with issuing the preferred stock?
4. Which of the two alternatives would you recommend to Mike? Why? Defend your answer.
5. Is there any way for Mike to avoid sharing control with the stockholders?

When Iraq invaded Kuwait in August of 1990 the stock market took a major tumble. In the months that followed, the market bounced back after the early success of the Allied air attacks on Iraq, and it soared when Iraq was defeated. However, investors wanted to know why their stockbrokers did not warn them back in August of 1990 that the market was about to drop so drastically. If investors had learned about the impending invasion of Kuwait by Iraq, it is likely that they would have sold their holdings and stayed on the sidelines. However, most brokers did not know that Iraq would attack. Stock market experts believed what they were

Investments and the Stock Market

21

Chapter Learning Objectives

- Identify the types of investors and their major objectives.

- Describe securities exchanges.

- Relate the mechanics of buying and selling stock.

- Discuss how investors try to make money in the stock market.

- Explain how to read and understand financial news.

reading in the major newspapers such as the *New York Times* and *The Wall Street Journal*, which reported the Iraqis were threatening an invasion but that U.S. officials did not feel they would go through with it.

The same lack of prediction occurred when President Bush gave the order to bomb Iraq and begin the liberation of Kuwait. The common theme from stock market experts and the financial news was that once war broke out in the Middle East the market would take a nosedive and then, depending on how things went, would begin to recover. However, because of the tremendous success of the U.S. bombing on the first night of the war, and the glowing reports

seen on television, the stock market surged ahead the next day with the second highest one-day increase in history. Again, investors wanted to know why their stockbrokers didn't let them know this in advance.

These events in the Middle East illustrate how volatile stock markets have become in response to international developments. This was particularly evident in the case of oil. After Iraq took over Kuwait and diplomatic efforts failed to get them to leave and the U.S. embargo went into effect, the price shot up and eventually reached over $40 a barrel. However, as events unfolded before and after the war with Iraq, the price of oil was highly volatile and had a

big impact on investors. Those who succeeded in buying when the price was low and selling when it was high made a great deal of money. Others ended up losing money. On the other hand, there were many investors who sat on the sidelines and did not let the war affect their strategies. They simply invested in high-quality stocks and waited out the ups and downs of the stock market. These investors followed the old cliche, "Buy quality stocks and sit tight. You'll eventually be rich."

Photo source: © Peter Beck/The Stock Market.

563

Introduction

Businesses seeking funding need investors willing to buy stocks and bonds from them. Chapter 20 emphasized financial transactions from the operating business's point of view; this chapter focuses on financial transactions from the investor's standpoint. Because stock markets are the most visible and popular form of investment, they are the focus of attention. This chapter describes the marketplaces in which investors buy and sell stock and other investments, outlining the procedures involved in buying and selling stock. It then describes how investors try to make money in the stock market, a skill that depends on having enough knowledge of a given industry, a particular company, and economic changes.

Investors: Who and Why

Most of us are investors at some time in our lives; we spend money in ways that we hope will generate additional money. For example, a college education is in one sense an investment. When you spend money on tuition and books, you are increasing your eventual earning power. Statistics indicate that households headed by college graduates have median incomes over 50 percent greater than those of high school graduates. As this figure suggests, spending money for your education is a wise investment.

Most businesses depend on the goodwill of investors. When investors believe a company is strong, they will pay a higher price for its stock or accept a lower rate on its bond offerings. In this way, a firm's financial performance helps dictate its ability to raise additional funds. For example, if the price of the company's stock rises, investors will look forward to buying future stock issues. Businesspeople therefore need to understand investing and the markets for investments. This chapter focuses on the kind of investments that are easiest to exchange: **securities,** or evidence of ownership (stocks) or debt (bonds). In other words, securities can simply be thought of as stocks and bonds.

Securities Evidence of ownership (stocks) or debt (bonds).

Types of Investors

Investors may be organizations or individuals. Organizations that buy securities with their own funds or with funds held in trust for others, such as pension contributions or insurance premiums, are called **institutional investors.** Major institutional investors include insurance companies, pension funds, and university foundations. An insurance company wants its investments to generate profits and funds for paying future insurance claims. A pension fund wants to make money on its investments so that it can pay off pensioners. A university foundation is interested in making money so that it can draw on these funds to support research, erect buildings, and ensure the survival of the institution. Institutional investors undertake huge transactions, for example, buying or selling 10,000 shares of stock. In recent years, institutional investors have accounted for the large majority of all trading carried out on regulated stock exchanges.

Institutional investors Organizations that buy securities with their own funds or with funds held in trust for others.

The other type of investors, called **personal investors,** are individuals who trade securities for their own account. In fact, even though institutions

Personal investors Individuals who trade securities for their own account.

TABLE 21.1
Investment Objectives Related to
Type of Security

Type of Security	Investment Objectives: Opportunity For			
	Speculation	Growth	Income	Safety
Common stocks	Moderate	Very good	Moderate	Least
Preferred stocks	None	Very little	Steady	Moderate
Bonds	Very little	Very little	Very steady	High

carry out most of the volume on stock trades, individuals still control the majority of all stocks. Most personal investors have relatively small stock portfolios (collections of stock), usually valued at less than $50,000. They often use these funds as the down payment for major purchases such as a home, as supplemental retirement income, or as a source of cash should an emergency arise.

Objectives of Investors

Most institutional buyers are consistently conservative in their investment objectives. They want securities that will provide a predictable return. Personal investors have a wider range of investment objectives. While many personal investors are moderately conservative in their objectives, others are extremely conservative or much greater risk takers. The extremely conservative investors look for guaranteed income; the risk takers try to make a quick fortune. To be more precise, the objectives of investors can be identified in terms of speculation, growth, income, and safety. Table 21.1 summarizes how well the three major types of securities meet these investment objectives.

Speculation Most investors, especially institutional investors, prefer being fairly certain that their investment will make money or at least not lose money. Because the demand for risky investments is low, these investments pay a high return — when they succeed. Some investors set an objective of achieving big payoffs. They engage in **speculation,** or assuming large risks in the hope of large returns. Many investors made considerable sums of money speculating on stocks in the middle and late 1980s and in early 1991 when the market was on an upswing. Of course, they may also wind up with big losses. In the crash of the stock market in October 1987 and the rapid decline of stocks immediately following the 1990 Iraq invasion of Kuwait, many investors suffered big losses.

Speculators can pursue many different avenues. One is to purchase "penny stocks," highly speculative stocks that typically are shares in new ventures and sell for less than $5. The investor is hoping the price of the stock will rapidly soar. A $1 stock that is suddenly in great demand might quickly run up to $3, thus tripling the initial investment. On the other hand, few penny stocks actually see such a rapid rise. Speculators who make a killing in one of these stocks often lose it all when others they hold go down.

Speculation The assumption of large risks in the hope of large returns.

Reinvestment of company profits by American Airlines' management has helped the airline expand and refurbish its terminal at Chicago's O'Hare International Airport (shown), purchase TWA's Chicago–London route, and begin service from Chicago to Milan, Italy.

Source: Courtesy of American Airlines

Blue-chip stocks Stocks of large, high-quality companies with a proven track record.

Growth   More investors are interested in long-term growth in the value of their investment. When they cash in their securities, they want to have a sizable pool of funds. Although the stock market tends to be quite volatile, the track record for long-term growth returns has been impressive. For example, over the past 30 years the 500 stocks in the Standard & Poor's Index have returned an average of 11.2 percent annually.[1]

Investors interested in steady growth often choose blue-chip stocks. **Blue-chip stocks** are those of large, high-quality companies with a proven track record. Examples of such companies are IBM, General Electric, Wal-Mart, Coca-Cola, and American Express. Investors with a growth objective are typically interested in the long run and believe that regardless of what happens in the economy over the next 5 to 10 years, the firms they invest in will prosper. Often the dividend for blue-chip stocks is relatively low. This is because blue-chip firms such as Motorola or GE reinvest their profits in research and development in order to remain competitive and growing.

Income   Some investors rely on securities to provide them with income. A good example is a retired couple living on a small pension and social security. If the couple invests in the stock market, they probably will seek stocks that pay generous dividends.

Investors with income objectives are interested in a stock's yield. **Yield** is the percentage return from stock dividends, or the dividend divided by the selling price per share. Utility stocks (Commonwealth Edison or Kansas Power & Light) typically have higher yields than industrial stocks such as those of computer firms (IBM), manufacturing firms (General Electric), and financial service companies (American Express). The reason utility stocks have a high yield is that they have minimal risk. Also, because they are closely regulated and thus cannot rapidly grow, utility stocks must have a high yield in order to attract investors.

Yield   The percentage return from stock dividends, or the dividend divided by the selling price per share.

Safety   All investors have at least some interest in safety. They will take a risk but only within certain limits. Preferred stock is regarded as safer than common stock, because preferred stockholders receive dividends before any are paid to the common stockholders. In the case of common stock, utilities are considered safer than high-tech stocks. For example, Commonwealth Edison has paid quarterly dividends since 1890. However, even utilities have risks; today, especially, independent power producers are introducing competition, and nuclear power plants are causing problems related to costs and safety.

Government bonds are the safest type of security because they are backed by the government, but even corporate bonds offer the security of their face value. As Chapter 20 pointed out, no matter how low the price of the bond falls, the company will pay the face value upon maturity. Sometimes it is just a matter of holding on until the bond matures. Of course, if the company goes bankrupt, it may be unable to pay.

CHECK ✓ POINT

1. What are three major objectives of investors?
2. If you sat on a committee charged with investing $500,000 that had been willed to an orphanage, what types of stock would you recommend?

The Securities Exchanges

A **securities exchange** is a marketplace where securities such as stocks and bonds are bought and sold. It simplifies the selling process. Theoretically, if investors wanted to purchase 100 shares of AT&T stock, they could advertise in the newspaper for sellers. Similarly, if sellers wanted to get rid of 100 shares of AT&T, they could advertise for buyers. However, with a centralized marketplace, investors and their representatives know where to go to find interested buyers and sellers. It must be emphasized that securities exchanges do not buy and sell securities; they simply provide the location and services for the brokers who buy and sell through an auction process.

In most cases, personal investors use a stockbroker to handle stock transactions. A **stockbroker** is an individual who has demonstrated knowledge by passing a series of exams on buying and selling securities and who, for a fee, buys and sells securities for clients. Most stockbrokers are associated with a

Securities exchange
A marketplace where securities such as stocks and bonds are bought and sold.

Stockbroker   An individual who has demonstrated knowledge by passing a series of exams on buying and selling securities and who, for a fee, performs this function for clients.

Merrill Lynch

Shearson Lehman Brothers

Dean Witter Reynolds

Prudential Securities

Paine Webber

A.G. Edwards

Smith Barney, Harris Upham

Stock exchange An organization whose members provide a trading place for buying and selling securities for clients.

New York Stock Exchange (NYSE) The largest and best-known exchange in the United States.

American Stock Exchange (AMEX) The second-largest exchange in the United States.

brokerage house, the seven largest of which are listed in Table 21.2. Like other industries, the securities firms have undergone considerable consolidation and reorganization in recent years.[2]

Acting on the client's orders, the broker has the order executed at a stock exchange where the particular stock is traded. A **stock exchange** is an organization whose members provide a trading place for buying and selling securities for clients. Most stock exchanges are physical entities, and each of the larger ones occupies its own building. To trade on the exchange, a "seat" must be purchased on the exchange. There are only a limited number of seats, so the cost is highly variable. For example, in 1976 the high was $105,000 and the low was $40,000. In the fall of 1990, a seat on the New York Stock Exchange sold for $301,000. A seat is a membership; the members actually stand and move around to make contact with those interested in completing a transaction.

The members represent stockbrokers. When a stockbroker calls in an order to sell, the member representing that broker seeks a buyer at the price requested. When a broker calls in an order to buy, the exchange member seeks a buyer at the price offered. Often, the member keeps an inventory of certain stocks and may fill orders with that inventory if the price is right.

The New York Stock Exchange

The largest and best-known exchange in the United States is the **New York Stock Exchange (NYSE).** It is often referred to as the "Big Board" because of a large board on the stock exchange wall that was formerly used to summon brokers from the floor and relay messages to them. When the brokers were on the trading floor, they would continually look at the board to see if their number was showing. If it was, a message was waiting for them, and they would hurry to find out what orders were being sent over from their brokerage house. Today all of this is handled automatically by telecommunication technology (for example, linking computers at the brokerage with those at the exchange).

There are 1,366 seats on the NYSE. The record volume occurred on October 20, 1987, when over 600 million shares were traded. Securities on the NYSE represent 90 percent of the market value of all outstanding stocks in the United States.

Most of the stocks of major corporations are traded on the NYSE, including American Express, General Motors, General Electric, IBM, PepsiCo, McDonald's, and Xerox. In order to be listed on the NYSE, a firm has to meet certain requirements:

- Pretax earnings of at least $2.5 million in the previous year
- Tangible assets of at least $18 million
- At least 1.1 million shares of stock publicly held
- At least 2,000 shareholders who each own 100 or more shares of stock
- A minimum market value of publicly held shares of at least $18 million

The American Stock Exchange

The **American Stock Exchange (AMEX)** is the second-largest exchange in the United States. Located in downtown Manhattan, going into the 1990s it had 661 full members and 165 associate members. The AMEX operates in the same way as the NYSE, but smaller companies qualify for listing. Some of the firms whose stocks are listed on the AMEX include Atari, Cablevision, the *New York Times*, and Wang Computers. To be listed on the AMEX, a firm has to meet the following requirements:

- Pretax earnings of at least $750,000 in the previous year
- Shareholder equity of at least $4 million
- At least 500,000 shares of stock publicly held
- At least 800 public shareholders who each own 100 or more shares of stock or 400 who collectively hold at least 1 million shares
- A minimum market value of publicly held shares of at least $3 million
- An initial market price of at least $3

Other Stock Exchanges

Most people associate the stock market with the NYSE and possibly the AMEX. However, regional exchanges, the over-the-counter market, and foreign exchanges are also important for trading stocks.

Regional Exchanges The NYSE and the AMEX primarily trade in stocks of companies with national operations. Firms that serve regional markets usually trade on **regional stock exchanges.** Examples of these exchanges include the Midwest Exchange in Chicago, the Cincinnati Stock Exchange, the Pacific Coast Stock Exchange in San Francisco and Los Angeles, the Philadelphia Stock Exchange, the Boston Stock Exchange, and the Spokane Stock Exchange. In recent years, large national firms have had their stock listed on regional as well as national exchanges. If a broker in Chicago wants to buy 100 shares of USX for a customer, he or she might well purchase it at a regional exchange rather than send the order to the NYSE for execution.

Regional stock exchanges
Exchanges that trade the stocks of firms that serve regional markets.

Over-the-Counter Market One marketplace for stock is not located at a central location: The **over-the-counter (OTC) market** trades unlisted securities outside of the organized securities exchanges. The OTC market is difficult to pinpoint. The nearly 60,000 securities in this market are traded among about 5,000 brokers scattered throughout the country. They buy and sell unlisted stocks and bonds by phone and keep in regular contact with one another. A stockbroker wanting to buy an OTC stock for a customer will get in touch with a dealer firm that in essence acts as a securities wholesaler. If the dealer firm does not have an inventory of the desired stock, the broker will call around to find out who does and arrange for the transaction.

Over-the-counter (OTC) market A marketplace for unlisted securities that trade outside the organized securities exchanges.

Although being listed on the NYSE gives stock a certain credibility in the eyes of most investors, not all firms want their stocks so listed. Many firms prefer to be listed in the OTC market because these stocks are actively traded by brokers all across the country. In the minds of many investors, selling in multiple markets better reflects the real market price of stocks.

The prices of the OTC securities are established by supply and demand, just as they are in the major stock exchanges. Electronic screens located in the offices of brokerage firms display OTC transactions, so brokers can continually keep customers up-to-date on the latest prices. Some well-known stocks

Dun & Bradstreet Software aids foreign exchange by developing computer equipment in Japanese, as shown here through superimposed photos of a computer screen and keyboard.

Source: © 1991 Walter Biblikow.

traded over the counter included Apple Computer, Coors, MCI, Intel, and Safeco.

Foreign Exchanges International trading is growing in importance. Foreign exchanges are located in many of the major cities of the world, including Toronto, London, Paris, Hamburg, Hong Kong, and Tokyo. The October 1987 crash brought out the interdependence between these foreign markets and the U.S. markets. When stocks crashed in the United States, they did the same in these foreign markets. During the hectic days following the crash, American investors closely watched the foreign exchanges that opened earlier in the day to guide their buying or selling decisions for the coming day's session. In 1990 the Tokyo Stock Exchange lost over 25 percent of its overall value.[3] This was due in part to changes in that country's security regulation laws, the weakening of the Japanese yen, and the fact that stocks were overpriced in comparison with stocks on other exchanges.[4]

Major U.S. firms that do substantial business abroad often have their stock traded on the international exchanges. For example, IBM is traded on both the London and the Tokyo stock exchanges. Similarly, the stock of large foreign multinationals such as Sony (Japan) and Royal Dutch/Shell (the Netherlands) is traded on the NYSE. A recent development in international stock exchanges such as the London Stock Exchange is the replacement of face-to-face buying and selling of securities with telecommunication technology, especially computerization, paralleling what is happening in the U.S. OTC market.

Automation and the Stock Exchanges

Telecommunication is helping the OTC market. For instance, the National Association of Securities Dealers Automated Quotation (NASDAQ) has linked together the computers of the major OTC dealers into a nationwide electronic network that communicates OTC trades within 90 seconds of the time they take place. As a result, no matter where a share of Apple Computer stock is sold in the OTC market, it is in the electronic network in less than 2 minutes. Companies such as MCI, Intel, and Apple like the computerization of NASDAQ because it is directly in line with their own high-tech operating philosophy. The OTC market quotations (sometimes referred to as the NASDAQ national market quotations) appear in the daily stock sections of many national newspapers, including the *New York Times* and *The Wall Street Journal*.

Computerization has also had a major effect on the other stock exchanges. In recent years, all exchanges, including the NYSE and the AMEX, have spent millions to implement computerized information systems as discussed in Chapter 10. This eliminated the pencil-and-paper record keeping that they used for years. In the early 1960s the AMEX would have been unable to handle trading of 5 million shares a day without causing a monumental backlog of paperwork. By the mid-1980s computers were enabling the AMEX to handle volume in excess of 100 million shares a day. However, when the record volume of over 600 million shares occurred on October 20, 1987, there were backlogs of 2 hours on the NYSE and AMEX. Many brokers during that hectic time were uncertain whether the computers were registering their sell orders and so they just kept selling to make sure, and this fueled the plunge.

Some personal investors are also taking a lead from the stock exchanges and using computers to help them carry out their own stock transactions.[5] Both personal and institutional computerized selling greatly magnified the 1987 crash, and many experts attributed the extent and quickness of the plunge to automatic computer programs being triggered to sell in a type of domino effect. This stock crash led to an investigation and recommendations, as seen in the accompanying Ethics Closeup (Bringing Order Out of Chaos).

Markets for Other Securities

Besides the major marketplace for corporate stocks and bonds and government bonds, other specialized markets handle certain types of securities. For example, some trading involves financial instruments called options, described later in this chapter. Options are traded on the major stock exchanges and also on another important marketplace for options, the Chicago Board Options Exchange (CBOE).

Some businesspeople are interested in the prices of certain commodities, such as corn, soybeans, hogs, cattle, copper, and silver. They may trade contracts to buy or sell these commodities at a specified price in the future. These so-called futures contracts trade on commodities exchanges; one of the largest is the Chicago Board of Trade. The exchange members do not sell the actual commodities, but only the contracts for them. Businesspeople who buy the commodities for their company, such as food processors, watch prices on the commodities exchange to get an idea of their future expenses.

CHECK ✓ POINT

1. What are the two largest stock exchanges?
2. Who may conduct a transaction on a stock exchange?

CLOSE-UP / *Ethics*

Responsibility to Stakeholders

What responsibility do companies have to their various stakeholders? Are companies more responsible to their stockholders, customers, employees, or the community? Many investors frankly admit that they want to buy stock in companies where management's primary responsibility is to the stockholders. If this means keeping dividends high and placing short-term profits ahead of long-term growth, that is all right with these investors, who simply want to make their money and sell out.

Some companies, such as the H B. Fuller Company, believe that it is possible to maintain high stock prices without devoting primary responsibility to stockholders. When the firm's chief executive officer was recently asked about responsibility to his stakeholders, he said, "Customers are first, employees second, shareholders third, and the community fourth." Shareholders third? This sounds like heresy to many investors. However, the firm has returned almost 20 percent annually to its investors during each of the past ten years. So there must be something to the CEO's philosophy that if you worry about customers and employees, stock price will take care of itself.

H. B. Fuller makes glue. This does not sound like a very exciting product, but company sales have risen quickly and consistently. Today Fuller is one of the top 400 industrials in the United States and is quickly moving up the list. Part of this success has been the firm's ability to maintain permanent relationships with major customers. When the company wanted to land a major contract to make glue for Procter & Gamble's (P&G) disposable diapers in the United States, a top salesperson for Fuller was commissioned to study P&G's needs, and four chemists were assigned to create a moisture-resistant adhesive supple enough to replace the glue that P&G was using. Fuller than built a $17 million factory to handle production. Result: The company got P&G's business.

Fuller has also been very active in international expansion. Non-U.S. operations currently account for 46 percent of revenues and 63 percent of profits. However, these funds are not all repatriated. The company believes that it has an obligation to customers and citizens in the host locality. So, in Lima, Peru, for example, the company provides food to 10,000 children each day.

Due to its market-driven strategies, Fuller continues to be a high performing investment. The former head of international operations and now president of the company put it this way, "A company exists to make money for its shareholders, but if you have happy customers and employees who support its value system, the payoff to stockholders will work itself out."

Source: Patricia Sellers, "Who Cares About Shareholders?" *Fortune*, June 15, 1992, p. 122.

Buying and Selling Stocks

Many investors have traditionally put their money into stocks because they view them as a more attractive investment than bonds and safer and less trouble than dealing in real estate or precious metals. The Close-Up on Ethics (Responsibility to Stakeholders) provides an example of when this is true. However, there are risks involved in stock market investing. While stocks boomed during the mid-1980s, on October 19, 1987 the Dow Jones Industrial Average plummeted an astonishing 508.32 points, or 22.6 percent. In comparison, in the crash of 1929, which preceded the Great Depression of the 1930s, the market declined by 12.8 percent.

Almost all financial experts as well as the general public were puzzled by the dramatic turn of events. Amid lingering fears of inflation, rising interest rates, and a weakening dollar, and the facts that the United States had become the world's largest debtor nation and had a huge trade deficit, economic indicators were relatively strong. While stock prices tumbled, gold prices soared to their highest level in 5 years. The lessons to be learned are that history has a way of repeating itself and that all investments can be risky. As was pointed out in the opening vignette, five weeks before the August 1990 Iraq invasion of Kuwait many financial experts were predicting that the stock market would move to new heights.[6] By early September, the market had reached an 18-month low with August proving to be one of the worst trading months in 40 years.[7]

There are also recent examples of the reverse situation. At the end of 1990 and the beginning of 1991, because of a clear economic recession and the threat of war in the Persian Gulf, most professional investment strategists were predicting that stocks would go lower in the months ahead. Then, in February 1991 with the successful conclusion of the war, the stock market made a dramatic comeback and reached record heights. Rarely have so many stock market professionals been so wrong.[8] As stated by one stock market expert, "There are plenty of pitfalls out there and maybe a few cliffs."[9]

Placing an Order

Most investors have their brokers buy and sell stock on one of the major exchanges. The general pattern of this transaction is the same regardless of where the actual purchase or sale occurs. The investor begins by placing an order, that is, informing the stockbroker what stock and how much to purchase or sell. For example, an investor might call the broker and say, "Buy me 100 shares of General Electric." In this case, the investor is buying at the best current price for GE stock. This is called a **market order,** which is an order to purchase or sell a stock at the best possible price at the present time. The broker who receives the purchase order will have it conveyed to an exchange member on the trading floor. If the stock brokerage has a seat on the stock exchange, an exchange member affiliated with the brokerage will carry out the order. If the brokerage is a small company, it will have its order executed by a member affiliated with a larger brokerage.

In either event, if the most recent sale of GE's stock was at 60¼ (60.25), the broker on the floor attempts to get a better price for the buyer by offering a little less. For example, the broker might offer 60 and see if someone will sell at this price. Depending on the number of buyers and sellers at that particular time, the broker will settle on a final price. If the investor were selling, the broker would attempt to get a slightly higher price, by offering, say, 60½.

Whatever price is worked out, the final sale will then be electronically relayed by an employee on the trading floor back to the broker who placed the order. Within minutes, the investor knows the stock's purchase or selling price.

Limit Orders In some cases, investors are not willing to issue a market order because they have a specific price in mind. The investor will place a **limit order,** which is an order that specifies the highest price at which the broker may buy or the lowest price at which the broker may sell. The broker on the trading floor will attempt to accommodate the investor immediately. If this is not possible, the broker will place the investor's order in a sales book and execute it in order of priority.

For example, if a buyer is willing to pay no more than 58 for GE and the current price is 60¼, no one may be willing to sell for the lower price. Perhaps the stock will rise to 62 per share. However, if it comes down to 58, everyone who has a limit order at this price will be sold the stock, in the order in which the requests came in. If the buyer in our example is fifth in line, the

Brokers at work in a trading room keep in touch with clients and monitor stock prices. Computers have had a major impact on Wall Street because they make possible more and faster transactions.

Source: © K. Garrett/Westlight.

Market order An order to purchase or sell a stock at the best possible price at the present time.

Limit order An order that specifies the highest price at which the broker may buy stock or the lowest price at which the broker may sell stock.

broker will fill this order after the first four buyers are accommodated. Conversely, if the investor wants to sell at 62 and the current price is 60¼, the seller must wait and hope that the price goes up. If it does, the first person to place a sales order at this price gets to sell the stock, and this continues as long as there is remaining demand for GE stock at this price.

Limit orders are good only for one day. An investor who wants to keep the order on the books must issue an open order. An **open order** instructs the broker to leave the order on the books until it is executed or the investor cancels it.

Open order   An order that instructs the broker to leave it on the books until it is executed or the investor cancels.

Discretionary Orders   Sometimes the broker on the trading floor has a better idea of what is going on than does the investor at home. The investor may therefore want the broker to exercise judgment in making money. In that case, the investor will give the broker a discretionary order. A **discretionary order** is one that gives the stockbroker the right to execute it immediately or wait for a better price. For example, the broker on the trading floor might determine that the price of GE is going to rise dramatically over the next 3 hours of trading. If buying, the broker will therefore complete the transaction right away. Conversely, if selling the stock, the broker would wait, because in a few hours the stock will reach a much higher price.

Discretionary order   An order that gives the stockbroker the right to execute it immediately or wait for a better price.

Round Lots and Odd Lots   Many people buy and sell 5, 10, or 20 shares of stock at a time, while institutions may trade 10,000 shares at a time (sometimes called a block sale). An **odd lot** is any number of shares less than 100. A **round lot** is 100 shares of stock. To facilitate purchases, brokers usually trade stocks in lots of 100, although some will handle odd lots at a slightly higher price per share. Most often, however, when an investor orders a broker to buy 15 shares, this odd-lot order will be combined with a series of other small orders to form a round lot, at which time the broker executes the order.

Odd lot   Any number of stock shares less than 100.

Round lot   100 shares of stock.

Paying for Stock Transactions

In addition to the price of the stock, the investor pays the broker a commission for buying or selling the securities. Commissions vary among brokers. In recent years, a number of discount brokers have emerged. These firms charge lower commissions than the major brokerages but provide fewer services. Schwab & Company is the best-known discount broker.[10]

Sometimes investors pay less than the full amount when they buy stock. Buying stock without putting up the full value of the transaction is called **margin trading.** The Federal Reserve determines the minimum margin required. For example, if an investor bought 100 shares of General Electric at 60, the total price would be $6,000. In recent years, the stock margin has been around 50 percent, so the investor could buy the 100 shares by paying only $3,000. The investor would then pay interest on the amount borrowed (in this case, the other $3,000).

Margin trading   Buying stock without putting up the full value of the transaction.

To ensure that the investor does not sell the stock and abscond with the funds, the broker keeps stock certificates of margin accounts at the brokerage as collateral. Also, if the stock were to plummet, the brokerage would act to protect its interests. Before the stock reached $30 a share, the broker would call the investor and request more money or have the stock sold.

National Computer Systems' ShareMaster computer software is a comprehensive stock transfer accounting and shareholder record keeping system, used for speedily transferring ownership of a corporation's common stock from one shareholder to another. Citizens and Southern Trust Company of Atlanta processes over 350,000 shareholder accounts with ShareMaster.

Source: Courtesy of National Computer Systems.

Bulls and Bears

Investors who are active buyers of stock are called bulls. A **bull** is an investor who believes the prices of stock are going to rise. Bulls follow the old Wall Street adage of "buy low, sell high." In a "bull market," many investors think the stock market is on the upswing. The heavy demand for buying stocks keeps the prices high. The mid-1980s witnessed a very long bull market. Investors kept the prices of stocks going steadily upward for reasons such as favorable interest rates and a slowing of the previous inflationary spiral. Some individual stocks, however, move counter to the trend.

As the crash of 1987 and the 1991 crisis in the Middle East attest, even bulls become bears. A **bear** is an investor who believes that stock prices are going to fall. In a "bear market," the majority of investors believe the stock market is on the downswing. For example, bears dominated the market in October 1987, when stock values plunged, and they did again following the Iraq invasion of Kuwait. Bears follow the adage "sell high, buy low." One high-risk strategy the investor can use to do this is called selling short.

Selling Short

An investor who expects the price of a stock to decline may sell short. **Selling short** involves selling stock that one does not own (it is borrowed from the

Bull An investor who believes that stock prices are going to rise.

Bear An investor who believes that stock prices are going to fall.

Selling short Selling borrowed stock in the hope of later buying it on the open market at a lower price.

broker) in the hope of later buying it on the open market at a lower price. At some point, the borrowed stock has to be returned to the broker. Investors make money selling short if the price of the stock goes down; they make the difference between what they sell the borrowed stock for and what they paid for the stock on the open market. The broker makes money on the commissions charged for the transactions.

For example, suppose the investor closely followed AT&T and, because of declining revenues, predicted that the company was going to declare a cut in its dividend and that the price of the stock would therefore drop. The investor would be better off selling now, when the price is higher, and buying later, when the price will be lower. If AT&T's stock is selling at 37 now but will drop to 34 after the company announces a cut in the dividend, the investor could borrow 1,000 shares from the broker and sell them now for $37,000. When the price went down, he or she could purchase the shares for $34,000 on the open market, give back the 1,000 shares to the broker, and make $3,000. Of course, if the investor is wrong about the reduced dividend or if other circumstances cause the price of a share to rise, the investor could lose as much or more.

During the stock market crashes of 1929 and 1987 and the rapid downturn following Iraq's invasion of Kuwait in 1990, a few investors made a fortune selling stocks short. For example, in the 1929 crash, President John Kennedy's father, Joseph Kennedy, made millions in the market because he realized the wisdom of selling high, buying low. Had he misjudged the market, the Kennedy fortune might well have been totally wiped out. Such risks are the biggest danger of selling short. A $100 stock that is sold short can, at its best, give the investor a gain of $100. (The stock can only drop 100 dollars.) However, there is no limit to which the stock can climb. The more the stock goes above $100, the more the person selling short loses.

Options

Options   Contracts that permit an investor to either purchase or sell a particular security at a .predetermined price and within a certain time period.

Options are contracts that permit an investor to either purchase or sell a particular security at a predetermined price and within a certain time period. The investor pays for the option but does not have to exercise it by buying or selling the security. Depending on the investor's expectations, he or she may buy a put option or a call option. Figure 21.1 illustrates how these work.

Why would anyone want to buy or sell an option? The answer is that this can be an inexpensive way to play the market. If the price of a stock does not change enough to warrant exercising an option, its owner will let the option expire and lose only the cost of the option. On the other hand, if the price of the stock changes dramatically in the expected direction, the option owner can make a great deal of money with a small investment. Selling options can also be profitable, although the seller must have the stock on hand if the option sells a right to buy. If the option's owner does not exercise it, the seller gets to profit from the payment for the option. Despite the risk, options are popular among speculators.

Put option   An option to sell a specific security.

Put Options   An option that grants the owner the right to sell a security is a **put option.** An example of a put option is a $500 option to sell 100 shares of Motorola at $75 a share within 90 days. An investor might buy this option if he or she believes that the price of Motorola will drop over the next 90 days.

FIGURE 21.1
How Options Work

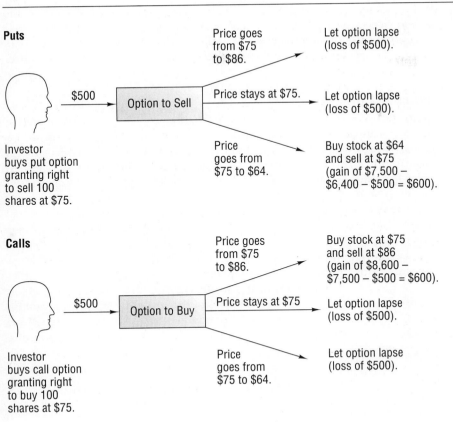

Puts

$500 → Option to Sell

Investor buys put option granting right to sell 100 shares at $75.

Price goes from $75 to $86. → Let option lapse (loss of $500).

Price stays at $75. → Let option lapse (loss of $500).

Price goes from $75 to $64. → Buy stock at $64 and sell at $75 (gain of $7,500 – $6,400 – $500 = $600).

Calls

$500 → Option to Buy

Investor buys call option granting right to buy 100 shares at $75.

Price goes from $75 to $86. → Buy stock at $75 and sell at $86 (gain of $8,600 – $7,500 – $500 = $600).

Price stays at $75 → Let option lapse (loss of $500).

Price goes from $75 to $64. → Let option lapse (loss of $500).

If it does, the investor will benefit from selling the shares at the option price to the person who sold the option. The put option therefore guarantees that the shares will be worth at least $75 a share. But because the investor has paid $500 for this right, the put will not generate a profit unless the stock drops below $70. If the price of Motorola drops to 64 during the 90-day option period, the investor can force the person who sold the option to buy 100 shares of Motorola at $75 a share.

Call Options If investors predict that the price of a stock will rise in the near future, they will buy a call option. A **call option** grants its owner the right to buy a specified amount of a stock at a predetermined price within a designated time period. For example, if investors believe that the price of Motorola will rise during the next 90 days, they could buy a 90-day option that allows them to call 100 shares of the stock away from the seller of the option. If this option costs $500, then the buyer will profit if the stock price rises enough to earn the investor more than $500. For every dollar the stock rises, the investor makes $100. If the exercise price is $75, then at $80 the price difference covers the cost of the option. Everything above $80 is profit. If the price of the stock rises to $90, the holder of the option can buy 100 shares of a $90 stock for only $75 a share. Even if the price of the stock rises

Call option An option to buy a specific security.

to less than $80, the investor can cut his or her losses by exercising the option. Of course, if the stock drops below $75, the investor will not exercise the option and will lose the cost of the option. Those investors who held call options at the beginning of January 1991 made considerable money after stock prices surged ahead during and after the war with Iraq.

Mutual Funds

Mutual fund An investment company that pools the contributions of investors: the fund is carefully managed by buying and selling securities to meet the investment objectives.

Many people today purchase stock indirectly; they buy shares in mutual funds. A **mutual fund** is an investment company that pools the contributions of investors; the fund is carefully managed by buying and selling securities to meet the investment objectives.[11] No-load funds do not have sales charges. Mutual funds are particularly well suited to small investors without a lot of money to invest, because the funds enable them to buy a variety of stocks; when one stock does poorly, another might be making up for the loss. Mutual funds also attract investors who do not want to manage their holdings closely.[12]

A mutual fund typically buys large blocks of stock in many different types of firms. Sometimes the fund invests in any type of company that appears to be a good investment. In other cases, the fund limits itself to specific types of firms such as growth companies or enterprises that promise a high yield. Other funds stick strictly to money market investments, which do particularly well when interest rates are high, as they were during the early 1980s.[13]

1. What are put and call options?
2. An investor wants to buy a specific stock but not at more than $25 per share. How can the investor place such an order?

CHECK ✓ POINT

Making Money in the Stock Market

While the approaches to investing in stocks are varied and often complex, investors buy stock for one simple reason: to make money. Most investment experts would agree that the surest way to earn money from stocks is to create as diverse a portfolio as possible and hang on to it for a long time, preferably decades. Investors who jump from stock to stock seeking quick profits have more opportunities to make mistakes.[14] Even when they manage to avoid mistakes, the brokerage fees can eat up most or all of the profits. Nevertheless, enough investors have reaped sizable gains from selective investing to attract others to the idea of beating the market. To succeed at this, investors need good sources of information.

Using a Broker

Much information about the market comes from stockbrokers. Brokers devote a considerable amount of time and resources to studying market reports and getting information on the forecasted financial performance of companies. Large brokerage houses, in particular, have in-house research departments that carry out these investigations and keep company brokers alert to potential market developments. Having this type of information does not guarantee that brokers will pick a winner every time. However, having as

CLOSE-UP / *International*

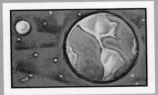

Investing Around the World

Most American stock investors own issues that are listed on local or national stock exchanges. However, in recent years more and more brokers have been recommending investment in issues on international exchanges. There are two reasons for this interest: (a) many of the stocks on these exchanges have lower price-earnings ratios than those on U.S. stock exchanges, so there is greater opportunity for growth; and (b) the coming years are likely to see dynamic economic growth in many regions of the world, thus driving up the prices of stocks listed on these exchanges. Particular interest is being paid to the stock markets in Europe, Asia, and Latin America.

On European exchanges, the price-earnings ratios of stocks tend to be significantly lower than those in the United States. Additionally, as the full economic effect of the European Community begins to be felt, many of the large firms are likely to prosper and enjoy higher stock prices. Many stock analysts believe that Siemen, the huge German electronics firm, will be a very good investment over the next five years. Another firm in this "recommended for buy" group is Volvo, the well known Swedish auto maker. Although Volvo has recently experienced some problems, a number of stockbrokers believe that the firm is soon due for a turnaround. A third often-cited choice is Ciba-Geigy, the internationally-known Swiss drug maker. If the European market begins to boom during the next few years, as many economists believe it will, these three stocks are likely to do extremely well.

Some stock market experts believe that Asian stocks also hold the potential for large profits, particularly those within the housing and communications industries. During this decade more and more homes will be built in crowded but prosperous Asia, proving to be a boon for not only construction firms, but for land developers and banks as well. Specific examples of potentially profitable stocks include the Development Bank of Singapore and Hutchinson-Whampoa, a Hong Kong telecommunications company.

The same investment advice holds for Latin America where analysts see growing economies and underpriced stocks. In Brazil, Souza Cruz, the country's leading cigarette maker, holds 85 percent of the local market and is likely to grow rapidly as the government continues to scrap price controls. In Mexico, Telefonos de Mexico, which has the phone monopoly, is viewed as an excellent investment.

Of course, the stocks mentioned above may not prove to be big winners, but the logic of internationally-focused stock brokers is not to be taken lightly. The world market will grow rapidly during the years ahead, which means that many companies that are quite small today will be extremely large tomorrow. In addition, some large firms that previously have had marginal profits may enjoy very large ones. Picking the best individual firms in various parts of the world will not be easy. However, by using the services of stockbrokers who are backed by research staffs keeping track of international stock prices and staying up-to-date on the performance of leading foreign companies, many investors will find that an effective portfolio strategy contains many international stocks.

Source: William Galsgall, Ted Holden, and Elizabeth Weinger, "The World According to Stock-Pickers," *Business Week,* June 22, 1992, pp. 96–97.

much information as possible to pass on to their customers undoubtedly increases the brokers' chances that they will be right.[15] What the individual investor reads in the business section of the morning paper is often information that brokers have acted on the day before.

The amount of assistance an investor can expect is reflected in the broker's fees. Some brokers are more than willing to discuss the market and recommend opportunities, but their fees may be heavy. Others provide special services such as newsletters. At the other extreme are discount brokers. These brokers charge small fees, but their services are generally limited to executing orders. Although many individual investors in recent years began using discount brokers, they are unlikely to dominate in the years ahead. One reason is that the amount of stock trading on a worldwide basis is expected to increase. As discussed in the accompanying International Close-Up (Investing Around the World), investors will need additional rather than less service as they begin global trading.

Going It Alone

Many investors prefer to avoid high brokerage fees. They pay a small fee to a bank to buy and sell securities but plan and implement their own investment strategy. Most successful approaches to investing on one's own depend on getting good information and avoiding common pitfalls. Serious investors often subscribe to investment newsletters from brokerage houses and financial experts that carefully study the stock market. Such newsletters provide insights about specific stocks or the market in general. To the degree that the newsletter is accurate, investors can do quite well. Some investors are very loyal to such a service.

One way investors can get ahead of the crowd is to become an expert in a particular industry. Investors might study an industry such as telecommunications or machine tools and identify the firms that appear to be the strongest and most likely to grow over the next couple of years. If the industry looks healthy and one of the companies is superior to the others, it may be a good investment. Another way to obtain expertise is to watch developments in one's own field of employment. Companies the person has first-hand knowledge of that have introduced new technology or competitively advantageous techniques may be good candidates for investment. However, this investor must be careful to avoid illegal insider trading (obtaining advantageous information that is not available to the public at large in order to make investment decisions).

A simpler investment strategy is to choose a handful of reliable blue-chip stocks that have performed well in the past and stick with them. Examples include American Express, Disney, General Electric, and PepsiCo, which have been popular among investors in recent years. This technique may not make a quick fortune for the investor, but it is relatively safe and over the long run can earn money. Another strategy is to invest in up-and-coming firms and hang on for the long run. For example, a $1,000 investment at the beginning of the 1980s — $100 in each of these 10 stocks — would have grown to more than $50,000 by the end of the decade:

• Circuit City	$ 9,287
• Hasbro	6,606
• The Limited	6,357
• Mark IV Industries	6,257
• Marion Laboratories	3,973
• Wal-Mart Stores	3,767
• The Gap	3,791
• Dillard Department Stores	3,706
• Shaw Industries	3,554
• Tyson Foods	3,317
	$50,615

The catch is, of course, that these 10 highly successful stocks were selected after the fact. Even in good economic times, investors would be very fortunate to have their stocks perform this well.

Investors using any of these strategies should also recognize common mistakes so that they can avoid making them. Here are the ones that seem to occur frequently and some suggestions on how to avoid them.[16]

- Failure to diversify, or spread the risk over several different investments. Depending on one's financial goals (growth or income), it is usually wisest to divide investments up into bonds and various types of stocks.
- Paying too much for a stock with the mistaken belief that it will continue to go up. This can be avoided through careful research of industry and company performance and trends in the overall economy.
- Not knowing when to sell, or hanging on to a stock and then riding it down. This can be avoided by setting a selling price and sticking to it.
- Buying fad stocks. Stay away from fads and stick with the long-standing quality stocks.
- Buying on the basis of a "hot tip" without realizing that it is old news to insiders. Rumors and tips usually are cold, not hot; it is best to ignore them.
- The mistaken belief that an investor can identify the market's peaks and troughs while they are occurring. Imagine the surprise of those who believed that after 3 days of record losses on October 14 to 16, 1987, the market had bottomed out and therefore bought stocks. The following Monday the market crash occurred. Most small investors are a step behind; relying on such intuition is difficult if not impossible.

Techniques and Strategies for Predicting Stock Market Activity

If investors could predict where a stock's prices were heading before anyone else could, they would make a killing in the market. Unfortunately, no sure-fire methods exist for predicting the stock market's future. However, many investors — especially the professionals — try to improve on chance alone by becoming experts in techniques and strategies used for making predictions about the market. Two common approaches used by knowledgeable investors are fundamental analysis and technical analysis, and two unique but maybe as effective approaches, the random walk theory and contrarianism.

Fundamental Analysis　To evaluate an individual company's stock, most serious investors begin with **fundamental analysis,** which is the process of comparing a company's current financial position and future prospects with those of other firms in the same or different industries. For example, an investor might compare the financial and managerial prospects of Ford, General Motors, and Chrysler in deciding which has the brightest outlook for the next 2 or 3 years. The ratios discussed in Chapter 18 are often part of a fundamental analysis. Conducted properly, this type of analysis can help an investor decide whether the price of a particular stock is likely to go up or down based on estimates of future sales and profits.

Fundamental analysis The process of comparing a company's current financial position and prospects for the future with those of other firms.

Technical Analysis　Some investors, called "chartists," select stocks based on patterns they identify in the movement of stock prices. This approach is called **technical analysis.** Chartists spend a great deal of time charting the prices of specific stocks over time and then deciding whether these securities are ready to move up or fall back. By looking at the pattern of a stock's price, these analysts try to identify the stock's "behavior" and use this as a basis for predicting future price movement.

Technical analysis The process of using the pattern of a stock's price over time to predict the stock's future price movement.

In recent years, some financial experts have challenged this approach, arguing that one can select better stocks by throwing darts at the financial pages than by using technical analysis. Nevertheless, some market analysts still firmly believe that a stock's price follows a set pattern of behavior and that watching a stock closely enough makes it possible to forecast what is going to happen next.

Random walk theory
An investment strategy holding that future stock prices are independent of past stock prices.

Random Walk   Some investors not only doubt that stock prices follow patterns, they believe that the prices are random. The **random walk theory** holds that future stock prices are independent of past stock prices. Therefore, investors who hold this view say that stock prices follow a random walk, as opposed to a predictable pattern. Based on this theory, technical analysis is a waste of time. To choose stocks that are about to move up, investors might simply identify what brings about increases in stock prices, such as sound management and favorable government policies, and hold on to stocks in companies that meet these criteria.

Contrarianism   An investment strategy based on the belief that the market will move in the direction opposite to that predicted by the general public.

Contrarianism   Some investors have adopted an unusual approach, **contrarianism,** which holds that the market will move in the direction opposite to that predicted by the general public. This view is based on an assumption that the average investor is usually wrong. Most investors get information too slowly, so they buy just as a stock's price is topping out and sell just before the stock starts to go up. A favorite motto of contrarians is "buy on bad news, sell on good news." In other words, these investors do the opposite of what the general public does.

Supporters of contrarianism defend their position by noting that most investors cannot make big profits in the stock market; in the end, only a small minority comes out ahead. Once the public hears an idea or fact, it acts on it, and then its usefulness is at an end. For example, if word gets out that a company has just developed a new product with great potential, the sudden surge of interest in that company's stock will drive up the price before most investors can get in on the ground floor. Contrarians therefore believe that the little guy always winds up losing. Fortunately, such a view is not totally accurate. Small and large investors can both make money in stocks, but investing takes hard work, skill, and, perhaps, a dose of luck.

Understanding the Financial News

A key to any investment strategy is to keep as informed as possible. Every day financial news is broadcast over radio and TV and is published in the newspapers. Investors can find out which stocks have moved up, which have fallen back, and what new developments are taking place that are likely to affect security prices. Detailed feedback is also available through electronic data services. In addition, serious investors should review stories and forecasts about particular companies and the market in general in such financial papers as *The Wall Street Journal* and *Barron's.*

At the heart of this information are price quotations. Prices for a variety of securities are published in the business section of most newspapers following every business day. This information is important to investors because it shows how well their investments are performing and provides a basis for detailed comparison with other securities. In addition, managers of compa-

FIGURE 21.2
Reading a Stock Market Quotation

Highest and lowest prices during the past 52 weeks

Name of the company, in this case, Texas Instruments

Current annual dividend paid per share, in this case, $2.68

Yield, which is the dividend divided by the selling price

P–E (price–earnings) ratio, which is the market price divided by earnings per share

Number of shares (in hundreds) traded this day

Highest and lowest prices at which the stock traded this day

Closing price of the stock

Net change in the price of this stock over that of the previous business day's close

| 52 Weeks | | | | Yid | P-E | Sales | | | | Net |
High	Low	Stock	Div.	%	Ratio	100s	High	Low	Close	Chg
57¹/₂	48⁷/₈	TxETpf	5.35e	10.9	...	6	49¹/₂	49	49	+ ¹/₈
35	25⁵/₈	TexInd	.80b	3.1	11	14	26¹/₄	26	26	- ¹/₄
148¹/₄	87¹/₂	Tex Inst	2.00	1.8	...	876	111¹/₂	109¹/₂	109⁵/₈	- ¹/₈
33	23³/₄	TxPac	.40	1.5	18	16	27¹/₄	27	27¹/₄	...
35¹/₄	25⁷/₈	TexUtil	2.68	8.1	8	4683	33⁵/₈	33¹/₈	33¹/₄	...
5⁶/₈	2⁵/₈	Texfi In			68	26	3¹/₂	3³/₈	3³/₈	- ¹/₄
65¹/₄	44¹/₈	Textron	1.80	3.5	9	912	52	51³/₄	52	...
71	48¹/₂	Textr pf	2.08	3.7	...	2	56¹/₂	56¹/₂	56¹/₂	...
12¹/₂	7³/₄	Thack		...	56	30	10	10	10	+ ¹/₈
34¹/₂	18⁷/₈	ThrmE s		...	30	188	32¹/₄	31⁷/₈	32	- ¹/₄
48¹/₂	33³/₄	ThmBet	1.52	3.7	18	206	41	40	40⁵/₈	+ ³/₈
26³/₄	17	Thomin	.68b	3.2	11	66	21⁵/₈	21¹/₈	21¹/₈	- ¹/₄
21	11³/₄	ThmMed	.40	2.8	13	105	14¹/₄	14	14¹/₈	+ ¹/₈
40³/₈	18¹/₈	Thrifty	1.17e	3.1	23	1117	37¹/₂	37¹/₄	37³/₈	- ¹/₈
16³/₄	4¹/₄	Tidwtr	.27i	...	...	281	5	4⁵/₈	5	+ ¹/₄
9³/₈		TigerIn		...	...	612	5³/₄	5¹/₂	5³/₄	+ ¹/₈
91³/₈	52	Time	1.00	1.2	25	537	81¹/₈	80³/₄	81¹/₈	- ¹/₈
23⁷/₈	13³/₄	Timplx		...	14	2116	15¹/₄	14³/₄	14⁷/₈	- ³/₈
73⁷/₈	43³/₄	TimeM	1.50	2.4	12	358	65	63¹/₂	63⁵/₈	- 1¹/₂
53³/₈	40	Timken	1.00	2.5	...	159	41¹/₄	40¹/₂	40⁵/₈	+ ¹/₈

nies that issue publicly traded securities follow price quotations to see how investors view their company's prospects.

Stock Prices   Regardless of which paper lists them, stock prices appear in the basic presentation shown in Figure 21.2. To understand the entries, consider Textron, the seventh stock down. The price is stated in dollars and eighths of a dollar. This stock had a high price of $65.25 and a low of $44.125 during the previous 52 weeks. It paid a dividend of $1.80, which is a yield of 3.5 percent (dividend divided by the stock price) on its current selling price of $52.00. The stock's price-earnings (P-E) ratio is 9, meaning that the stock is selling for 9 times the company's earnings per share; and on this particular trading day, 91,200 shares were traded. During this day, the stock sold at a high of $52.00 and a low of $51.75, and it closed the day at $52.00. This closing price was the same as it was on the previous business day.

Any additional information supplementing this list appears in a footnote or explanatory table. For example, in Figure 21.2 there is a letter "e" after the $5.35 dividend of the first stock listed. This letter is explained at the bottom of the stock market page, as are any other letters or symbols.

Over-the-Counter Stocks   Listings for over-the-counter stocks are easier to read than most others because they provide less information; specifically they do not show dividends, yields, or P-E ratios. Figure 21.3 provides an example. Taking the third stock, Apple Computer had 52-week high and low prices of $39.125 and $14.25, respectively. On this trading day 670,000

FIGURE 21.3
Reading an Over-the-Counter Quotation

High and low prices over the last 365 days

Name of the company

Number of shares (in hundreds) traded this business day

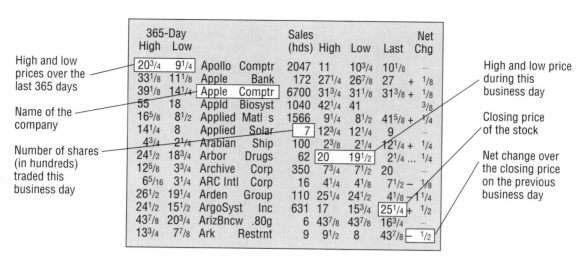

High and low price during this business day

Closing price of the stock

Net change over the closing price on the previous business day

shares were traded, with the high and low for the day being 31¾ and 31⅛, respectively. The stock closed at 31⅜, which was ⅛ of a dollar higher than the closing price on the previous business day.

Stock Averages   Some investors are as interested in the stock averages or indexes as they are in what has happened to a particular stock. Three stock averages are most widely recognized and quoted. The most popular is the Dow Jones, which is really three different indexes based on market prices of 30 industrial, 20 transportation, and 15 utility stocks. The Dow Jones industrials include a host of popular blue-chip stocks, including AT&T, General Electric, Eastman Kodak, IBM, and Wal-Mart.

While individual stocks may go up or down, the index provides a general gauge of market activity for a given time period. For example, the Dow was below 1000 in 1981 and closed above 3,000 for the first time on April 18, 1991. This indicates that the market made a major advance in recent years and that investors were in a bullish mood.

Two other popular averages are the Standard & Poor's Index and the New York Stock Exchange Composite. The Standard & Poor's Index is based on 400 industrial, 40 financial, 40 utility, and 20 transportation stocks. The New York Stock Exchange Composite includes every stock traded on the Big Board. Like the Dow Jones averages, these two indexes serve as a guide to overall stock market performance and can be found in the daily financial section of all major newspapers.

Will these averages go up or down this year? Some investors who are less than thrilled with the accuracy of sophisticated forecasting techniques propose, with tongue in cheek, that the easiest way to predict this is to find out who won the last Super Bowl. Some observers have found a correlation between whether a team from the original National Football League or a

FIGURE 21.4
Reading a Bond Market Quotation

Bonds	Cur Yld	Vol	High	Low	Close	Net Chg.
Coleco 14³/₈02	14.4	115	100¹/₈	100¹/₈	100¹/₈	...
Coleco 11s89	cv	30	106⁷/₈	106⁷/₈	106⁷/₈ +	¹/₈
ColuG 9¹/₈95	9.0	1	101¹/₂	101¹/₂	101¹/₂ +	¹/₂
ColuG 9⁵/₈89	9.5	25	102	101¹/₂	101¹/₂	...
CMdis 8s03	cv	10	99³/₄	99¹/₂	99¹/₂ -	¹/₄
CMdis 9.65s02	11.0	5	88¹/₂	87⁵/₈	87⁵/₈ -	1³/₈
CmwE 8s03	9.1	3	87⁵/₈	87⁵/₈	87⁵/₈ -	¹/₄
CmwE 8¹/₈07J	9.4	15	86	86	86 -	³/₄
CmwE 9¹/₈08	9.6	9	95⁷/₈	95⁷/₈	95 -	¹/₂
CmwE 14s91	12.9	10	108³/₄	108³/₄	108³/₄ -	⁷/₈
CmwE 16¹/₄89	15.2	10	107	107	107	...
CmwE 16s90	15.0	30	107¹/₈	107¹/₈	107 -	¹/₈
CmwE 14³/₈94	12.4	5	116	116	116	
CmwE 16³/₄11	14.5	20	115⁷/₈	115⁷/₈	115⁷/₈	...
CmwE 12¹/₄91	11.2	68	109¹/₈	109	109¹/₈ +.	1¹/₂
Compq 9¹/₂05	cv	50	133	133	133 +	3¹/₂
ConEd 4³/₄91	5.4	1	87³/₄	87³/₄	87³/₄ +	3¹/₂
ConEd 4³/₄92V	5.3	10	83	81¹/₄	83 -	2
ConEd 4⁵/₈93	5.8	5	80¹/₈	80¹/₈	80¹/₈ +	³/₄
ConEd 9³/₈00	9.3	25	101¹/₄	101	101	...
ConEd 7.9s01	8.6	17	91¹/₂	91¹/₂	91¹/₂ +	¹/₂
ConEd 7.9s02	8.5	45	92³/₄	92	92³/₄ +	1⁵/₈
ConEd 9¹/₈04	9.1	34	99³/₄	99³/₄	100 +	¹/₈

Name of the bond (Coleco), interest rate (14³/₈), and maturity date (the year 2002)

Current yield, which is the interest payment divided by the selling price

Number of bonds traded this day

Highest and lowest price at which the bond sold this day

Bond price at the close of the business day

Net change in the price from that of the previous day of trading

team from the original American Football League wins and the direction stock indexes head during the years. Specifically, when a team from the original NFL wins, the stock market indexes that year are usually higher than they were the previous year. When a team from the original AFL wins, these averages tend to drop.

Bond Prices Bond quotations are stated as percentages of par or face value. The prices are quoted in hundreds of dollars. Thus, on a bond with $1,000 face value, a quotation of 66⅛ means $661.25, not $66.125. Figure 21.4 describes what each of the entries means. The last bond is a Consolidated Edison bond that pays 9⅛ percent on a $1,000 bond that is due to expire in 2004. The current yield on the bond is 9.1 percent ($91.25 interest ÷ $1000 selling price), and 34 of these bonds were traded on this day. Because bonds are issued in denominations of $1,000, the prices in the last four columns are shown without the last decimal place. Thus, the highest price paid was $1,000, and the lowest was $997.50. The bond closed at $1,000, which was an increase of $1.25 over its closing price on the previous business day of trading.

Mutual Fund Prices Figure 21.5 provides a newspaper report of a mutual fund quotation. Information on these funds is provided in a manner similar to that of bonds and over-the-counter stocks. In the Dreyfus mutual fund, the growth fund is one of many in the group. The net asset value (NAV) of 11.37 is the value of one share of the growth fund and the price is what

FIGURE 21.5
Reading a Mutual Fund Quotation

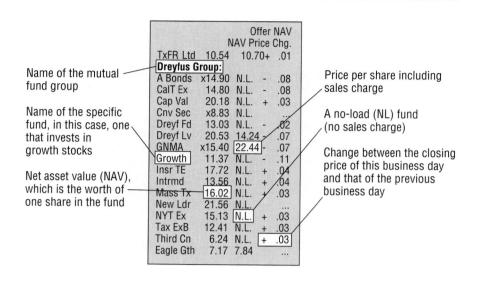

Name of the mutual fund group

Name of the specific fund, in this case, one that invests in growth stocks

Net asset value (NAV), which is the worth of one share in the fund

Price per share including sales charge

A no-load (NL) fund (no sales charge)

Change between the closing price of this business day and that of the previous business day

buyers are willing to pay per share, including sales charge. The N.L. stands for no load, which means there is no sales charge when shares of this fund are bought and sold. The +.02 under the NAV Chg column for the growth fund is the change between present buy price and the previous day's buy price. By following price changes, an investor can evaluate a fund's performance and decide whether to stay with that fund or switch to another.

CHECK ✓ POINT

1. What are three strategies for investing in the stock market?
2. Many small investors believe that it is wisest to invest in mutual funds rather than in specific stocks. What do you think is the logic behind this investment strategy?

Closing Comments

This chapter examined the process of investing, with emphasis on the stock market. Buyers and sellers of securities are both affected by price changes, so they need to know how to read and interpret financial news. These investors are also interested in the various investment strategies and how well they work. The humorist Will Rogers gave the following advice for those investing in the stock market: "Don't gamble; buy some good stock, hold it till it goes up, and then sell it. If it doesn't go up, don't buy it." Unfortunately, this type of advice may work about as well as the more sophisticated advice on investing in the stock market. Yet, by understanding the mechanics of the stock market, being as informed as possible, and following the guidelines provided in this chapter, investors may be able to improve their chances of achieving their investment objectives.

VIDEO CASE / *Buy Low, Sell High*

The war in the Middle East made some stockholders very rich, while for others it had a negative effect on their holdings. For example, those who bought oil futures in the days immediately following the Iraq takeover of Kuwait made a lot of money because the price of oil zoomed from $18 a barrel to over $40. By the same token, several months later when oil prices declined, those who bought oil futures at high prices found themselves facing large losses.

Investors who stay the course during times of turmoil with their blue-chip stocks have usually done well. For example, Wal-Mart, presented in the Chapter 18 vignette and video case as the very successful, fastest growing retailer in America, announced plans to acquire a major wholesale operation and continued to show increases of 10-plus percent growth annually, com-

pared with 5 percent or less for most competitors. In turn, the company's stock, which had fallen from $35 a share to $25, had rebounded back to the $31 range and there was talk that it would reach $50 within a year thanks to Wal-Mart's tremendous growth rate. In early 1991, Wal-Mart passed Sears as the largest retailer in America, and the founder and owner, Sam Walton, announced that sales would be even greater in the years ahead. Given that Wal-Mart stock had split 2:1 three times during the 1980s, many investors looked forward to Sam's predictions coming true. They felt that holding on to this stock would provide them a lot more return on their money than speculating in oil futures. To take a lesson from history, those wise investors who bought a couple thousand dollars of Wal-Mart stock when it went public in

the early 1970s and have held onto it over the years are millionaires today.

Source: Richard Behar, "Mr. Sam Stuns Goliath," *Time*, February 25, 1991, 62–63.

Case Questions

1. If investors felt that the price of oil was going to rise rapidly in the near future, would they be best served by buying a put or a call option?

2. What are the investment objectives of an individual who buys or sells oil options? Would these be the same objectives as someone who invests in Wal-Mart stock?

3. Would an investor looking into buying Wal-Mart stock be interested in fundamental analysis or random walk theory? Why?

Learning Objectives Revisited

1. **Identify the types of investors and their major objectives.** Institutional investors are organizations that buy securities with their own funds or funds from pension contributions or insurance premiums held in trust for others. Personal investors are individuals who trade securities for their own account. Investors pursue large profits through speculation, steady growth, a flow of income, and safety in the form of relatively low-risk investments.

2. **Describe securities exchanges.** A securities exchange is a central marketplace for the trading of securities. Its purpose is to provide a place where securities are bought and sold. Most exchanges are physical entities. To trade on the exchange floor, brokers become members by buying a seat. These exchanges include the New York Stock Exchange, the American Stock Exchange, and the Chicago Board of Trade. In addition, securities trade on regional and international exchanges. The over-the-counter market has a large network of brokers but no physical location.

3. **Relate the mechanics of buying and selling stock.** The purchase begins when a client places an order with

a stockbroker. This can be a market order, a limit order, or a discretionary order. Most orders are in round lots of 100 shares. The broker who receives the order communicates it to an exchange member affiliated with the brokerage, who executes the order on the floor of the exchange. The results are then reported back to the client, usually within minutes. The client pays the price of any stock bought plus the broker's commission. Variations on this basic approach include selling short, buying options, and investing in mutual funds.

4. **Discuss how investors try to make money in the stock market.** The most certain approach to making money from stocks is to buy a variety of stocks and hold them for a long time. But to do better, many investors attempt to gain an edge by having good sources of information. Some investors try to keep up-to-date by relying on a stockbroker for advice. Others prefer to reduce their expenses (commissions to brokers) by conducting their own analysis of particular stocks or the market in general, and they may use fundamental analysis, technical analysis, the random walk theory, and/or contrarianism.

5. **Explain how to read and understand financial news.** Stock market quotations typically list the highest and lowest prices during the past 52 weeks, followed by the name of the company, the dividend paid, the yield, the price-earnings (P-E) ratio, the number of shares (in hundreds) traded that day, the highest and lowest prices of the day, the closing price, and the amount by which the closing price differed from that of the previous business day. Over-the-counter quotations are similar, except that they do not show dividends, yields, or P-E ratios. A bond quotation lists the name of the bond, the interest rate, the maturity date, the current yield, the number of bonds traded that day, the highest and lowest price that day, the closing price, and the amounts by which the closing price differed from that of the previous business day. A mutual fund quotation gives the name, the net asset value per share, the price per share including the sales charge for load funds, and the change between the day's closing price and that of the previous business day.

Key Terms Reviewed

Review each of the following terms. For any that you do not know or are unsure of, look up the definitions and see how they were used in the chapter.

securities
institutional investors
personal investors
speculation
blue-chip stocks
yield
securities exchange
stockbroker
stock exchange
New York Stock Exchange (NYSE)
American Stock Exchange (AMEX)

regional stock exchanges
over-the-counter (OTC) market
market order
limit order
open order
discretionary order
odd lot
round lot
margin trading
bull

bear
selling short
options
put option
call option
mutual fund
fundamental analysis
technical analysis
random walk theory
contrarianism

Review Questions

1. Which type of investor has a greater impact on stock market activity — institutional investors or personal investors? Why?
2. Which investment objective — growth, income, speculation, or safety — would each of the following investors have? You may indicate a combination of objectives if that seems most appropriate. What securities might best meet these objectives?
   a. Cathy Brown is a 25-year-old salesperson. Every year, she has received a bonus, which she has saved with the goal of accumulating enough to travel extensively some day. But Cathy is tired of watching her funds grow slowly in the bank.
   b. Arnold Gray is a 55-year-old welder. Through conscientious budgeting and careful investing, he has been able to accumulate almost enough funds to provide him with a comfortable retirement.
3. Chuck Siller is interested in buying only blue chip stocks. Is this a wise investment strategy?
4. Andy Grove, president of Grove Enterprises, has decided not to apply for listing on the New York Stock Exchange. He prefers to have his company's stock listed in the over-the-counter market. Why might Andy feel this way?
5. How can an investor rely on a stockbroker's judgment about the best price at which to sell a stock? How can an investor use his or her own judgment about the best price?
6. How can an investor use leverage (described in Chapter 20) in stock purchases?

7. Why do investors buy options? When would an investor buy a put option? When would an investor buy a call option?

8. Mutual funds charge a fee or a percentage of earnings in return for their services. What services do they provide? Why do investors use a mutual fund rather than invest directly in the stock market?

9. Where do investors get information about the stock market?

10. Marilyn Danby wants to invest her $20,000 inheritance in the stock market. What are some common mistakes she should seek to avoid?

11. Stock in All Things Enterprises rose steadily for 10 years and then declined for 10 years. The price has just begun rising again, and investors are growing interested in the company. How would you expect each of the following to respond to this news?
    a. Fundamental analysts
    b. Chartists
    c. Adherents of the random walk theory
    d. Contrarians

12. To answer this question, refer to the following stock quotations:

c. What is the stock's price-earnings ratio? What does this tell you about the company?

13. To answer this question, refer to the following bond quotations:

Bonds	Cur Yld	Vol	High	Low	Close	Net Chg
Chvrn 5¾92	6.5	44	88⅝	88¼	88½	+1⅝
Chvrn 7s96	8.3	35	84⅛	84⅛	84⅛	+1⅛
Chvrn 8¾05	9.8	23	89¼	89¼	89¼	+1⅜
Chvrn 8¾96	9.3	45	93⅞	93⅞	93⅞	…
ChckFul 7s12	cv	25	94	94	94	+1
ChCft 13s99	12.7	5	102¼	102¼	102¼	…
Chrysl 8⅞95	9.2	29	96	96	96	− ⅛

a. What is the interest rate on Chrysler bonds?
b. In what year do these bonds mature?
c. What was the closing price of Chrysler bonds on this trading day? What was the closing price on the preceding business day?

52 Weeks High	Low	Stock	Div.	Yld %	P-E Ratio	Sales 100s	High	Low	Close	Net Chg
20¼	12½	RLI Cp	.32	2.2	6	40	14⅜	14¼	14⅜	+ ⅛
7	1¾	RPC	…	…		259	7	6⅝	6¾	− ¼
39	22¾	RTE	.68	2.3	18	72	29¾	29⅜	29⅜	− ⅜
10¼	4½	Radice	…		238	116	4⅞	4⅝	4¾	…
94	60	RalsPur	1.24	1.5	16	2179	85¼	83¾	83⅞	−1⅝
9¾	6	Ramad	…		27	2203	7⅞	7⅝	7¾	− ⅛
6¾	3¾	RangrO	…		84	323	5⅞	5¾	5⅞	…
156	69⅝	Raycm	.44	.3	22	140	148	144¾	146	−1
25¾	10⅝	RjamFn	.16	.9	10	26	17¾	17⅝	17¾	…
26	18⅝	Rayonr	2.60	12.8	8	58	20½	20¼	20⅜	…
13	4⅞	Raytch	…		11	231	12½	12	12	− ¾
84⅞	60	Raythn	1.80	2.2	15	1315	81⅞	80¾	80⅞	− ⅞

a. On this trading day, what was the closing price for stock in Ralston Purina?

b. How does this price compare to the closing price on the preceding day? To the highest and lowest prices in the preceding year?

Applied Exercise

An investor holds five put options and five call options. The following indicates the number of shares covered by each option, the cost of each option, and the current price of the stock. How much money will the investor gain or lose in exercising the options on the basis of current market price? Analyze each of the ten options and then calculate overall figures for the five puts and the five calls. Show your work.

	Cost of the Option	Current Market Price	Current Gain or Loss
Put Option			
100 shares of Stock A at $30	$ 300	$31	_____
500 shares of Stock B at $40	1,000	37	_____
200 shares of Stock C at $50	600	56	_____
100 shares of Stock D at $60	300	68	_____
200 shares of Stock E at $70	600	64	_____
Call Option			
100 shares of Stock F at $30	$ 300	$36	_____
500 shares of Stock G at $40	1,000	40	_____
200 shares of Stock H at $50	600	47	_____
100 shares of Stock I at $60	300	72	_____
200 shares of Stock J at $70	600	89	_____

YOU BE THE ADVISER / *The Personal Investor*

Over the past 6 months, Andy Farr, a retired machinist, has done extremely well in the stock market, earning approximately 18 percent on his money. His broker, Charles Bentley, certainly knew what he was talking about when he put together a list of securities Andy should buy. Andy followed this advice to the letter and has never regretted it.

This past week, Andy called Charles and asked if they could meet for lunch. During their meeting, Andy explained that he had been doing a great deal of reading about securities markets and how they work. "I think I know a lot about the stock market and how to make money. That's why I wanted to talk to you. I have about $19,000 in savings at my bank. I'd like to draw out half this amount and begin playing the market on my own. I'd have two stock portfolios: you'd manage the large one, and I'd manage the small one."

Charles told Andy that his idea sounded fine. Andy was a reasonable investor and should have no trouble picking some good stocks on his own. "What do you have in mind as a strategy?" Charles asked. Andy outlined two specific plans of action that he had been thinking about. The first involved oil stocks: "I've been doing a lot of research on the oil firms," said Andy, "and I think I know when they are going up and when they are coming down. I've been playing with them on paper

and have already made more $10,000 on a fictitious $25,000 investment. I have bought a couple and sold a few more short. In each case, I have made money. I'd like to put about $6,000 in about four selected oil stocks. The rest of the money I'd like to put into entertainment or movie stocks like Disney Productions and MCA. I read every issue of *Variety*, and I think I can pick out blockbuster movies the minute I've seen them. I've been playing these stocks on paper, too, and I've made almost 70 percent on my money in the last four months."

Charles listened carefully. When Andy was finished, he congratulated him: "I never realized how much time and attention you were giving to the securities markets. You certainly seem to know a lot. I'm particularly impressed by your knowledge of the entertainment business. Maybe I can call on you for advice sometime. But about the oil stocks, let me warn you about going short. That can be a lucrative strategy, but you can also end up losing a pile of money. Watch out, and if you do go short, promise yourself that if the stock goes up more than three or four points, you will go back in and take your losses." Andy agreed and promised to follow Charles's advice. Before they parted company, Charles wished him luck and told Andy to call if he needed any assistance.

Your Advice

1. What should Andy do?
   ___ a. Put most of his money into oil stocks.
   ___ b. Put most of his money into entertainment stocks.
   ___ c. Divide the investment evenly between the two types of stocks.
2. Should Andy put more of his money into oil or entertainment stocks, or should he divide it evenly? Why?
3. What do you think of Charles's advice regarding how to handle short sales? Is it good advice? Why or why not?
4. What investment pitfalls should Andy be concerned about?
5. Is Andy likely to make money with his investment strategy?

Career Opportunities in Business

The finance industry offers a variety of promising career opportunities. During the 1990s this sector has had some problems, but opportunities for employment still exist because the economy depends so heavily on this industry. For example, today virtually everyone needs the services of accountants and bankers, and more and more people own and trade stock. Thus, some of the most promising careers in the finance field include positions in accounting and banking and as brokers dealing in stocks and bonds.

Internal Auditor

An internal auditor is someone who monitors an organization's internal accounting controls. This individual works with both operating employees and managers and provides important financial information to both.

Job Description. An internal auditor evaluates accounting records in order to determine whether funds are being properly handled and are being accurately recorded by managers and employees. These findings are then reported to higher levels of management. As a result, the auditor must be both thorough and comprehensive when conducting accounting reviews.

Employment Outlook and Earnings. Internal auditors can be found in private firms, government agencies, and nonprofit organizations. When first starting out, internal auditors are usually assigned to duties such as verifying the accuracy of accounting records. After gaining experience, a staff auditor may be placed in charge of special audits and may have several other auditors reporting to him or her. Internal auditors have undergraduate degrees in accounting and initial salaries are in the $25,000 to $30,000 range. For those who work their way up to be the head of the department or director of auditing in a large company, annual salaries are $75,000 and above.

Bank Manager

A bank manager is an individual who supervises and coordinates the activities of one of the bank's departments. They also directly interact with customers, especially large depositors, who have special needs and want to talk directly to them.

Job Description. A bank manager coordinates the activities of one of the departments such as consumer lending, commercial lending, or credit cards. The individual oversees programs to control and minimize losses that may arise from financial transactions and interacts directly with other department heads and customers. The bank manager also participates in community projects and works closely with the bank's board of directors.

Employment Outlook and Earnings. Approximately one-half million bank managers are employed in the United States. During recent years, because of the problems in the financial industry, the number of managers has decreased somewhat. For example, thousands were laid off by some of the major banks such as Citibank. However, most banks are still financially sound and the services they are offering to customers should expand during the years ahead. Bank managers typically have college degrees, many of them in finance, economics, or other business-related areas. Beginning salaries are in the $17,000 to $27,000 range, depending on experience and the region of the country. Top level bank managers of large institutions make $100,000 and over.

Stockbroker

Stockbrokers explore and recommend overall investment strategies to customers and analyze and evaluate specific stocks and bonds as potential investments for clients.

Job Description. A stockbroker buys and sells stocks and bonds for clients. In this capacity, as a salesperson and advisor, the broker discusses investment strategies and financial planning and learns the type of stocks and bonds that each client would be interested in purchasing. In working within these guidelines, the stockbroker reads research reports and the financial news in order to make recommendations. The broker also offers advice on the purchase of mutual funds, tax shelters, and other specialized investments.

Employment Outlook and Earnings. Stockbrokers in the United States number around 80,000. A college degree is not required, but many brokers have an undergraduate degree in finance, economics, or business. Before working with clients, stockbrokers must pass a series of examinations given by the Securities and Exchange Commission and by the state where they are employed. They also take short courses and training from their employer. New hires can expect to make $20,000 to $50,000 in their first year, depending on their commissions. As the list of clients increases and they become more experienced and knowledgeable, annual income can rise very high.

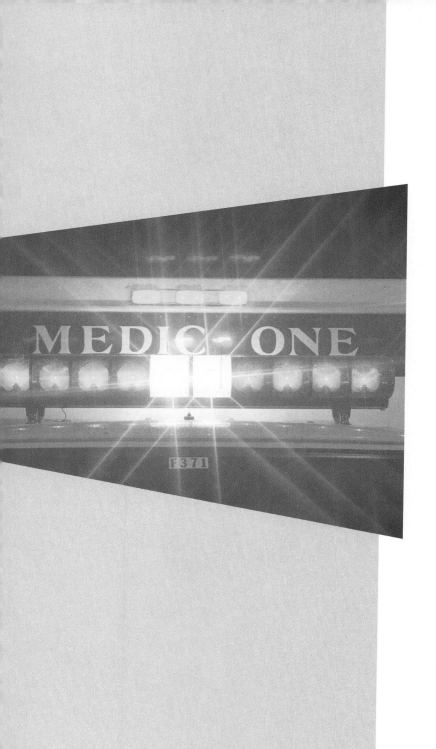

GET HIP TO REDUCING HEALTH COSTS

Over the past 20 years, health care costs have increased at a much faster rate than inflation. As a result, many businesses and individual consumers are finding that medical expenses and insurance premiums take a bigger bite out of their budget than they did a few years ago. The Health Insurance Plan (HIP) of Greater New York is an insurer that is helping to do something about this.

HIP is a health maintenance organization (HMO), which means that it offers managed health care.

Risk Management and Insurance

22

Chapter Learning Objectives

- Specify the types of risk and ways to manage each.

- Describe the criteria of insurability and sources of insurance.

- Identify the major types of property and liability insurance.

- Discuss the key types of health insurance.

- Present the major types of life insurance.

- Relate the special insurance needs of international businesses.

The traditional health insurance company serves merely as a go-between, paying hospitals and physicians for medical services provided to individuals covered by a particular insurance program but leaving these individuals free to choose their own doctors and hospitals. Insurers that offer managed health care, on the other hand, actively control the facilities that provide the services. They secure the participation of doctors and hospitals to provide health care to members of the plan.

At present HIP has the second largest health care plan in the country with over 1 million members. The plan covers employees in both the public sector (such as New York City employees) and the private sector (including Citicorp and American Airlines). Fifty hospitals in New York, New Jersey, and south Florida participate in HIP, and the future is likely to see many more as this form of insurance coverage increases.

Many companies are now balking at paying increased premiums for medical coverage for employees.

They are demanding that health care providers find ways of reducing their costs so that premiums can be stabilized. Insurance companies that sell the coverage are sending the same message to the providers. In both cases, pressure is growing on hospitals, in particular, to find ways to reduce overhead and contain expenses. The Health Insurance Plan of Greater New York and other HMOs offer one approach to dealing with the industry's number one headache: rising costs.

Photo source: © Walter Hodges/Westlight.

Introduction

There are very few certainties — things that a manager can count on 100 percent of the time — in modern business. The same is true of the other extreme, pure uncertainties — things that have never happened before and with which there is no direct or even indirect experience. In between is risk with some uncertainty of a loss and some experience from which to draw, even though it may be indirect. Risk is an unavoidable part of modern business, and there is considerable risk in most management decisions. For example, when businesses invest in their operations (Chapter 20) or in securities (Chapter 21), they take a risk of losing money or earning less than they could have with a different strategy. This chapter discusses other kinds of risks that businesses incur and describes how insurance helps the organization manage them. Because businesses are subject to many risks, managing them is a challenging and important task. The chapter begins with a broad look at risks. It then identifies the kinds of risks that insurance may cover, examines the structure of the insurance industry, and describes the many different types of insurance available to companies and individuals.

Risk and How to Manage It

The existence of risk is a fact of life for individuals and businesses. For example, if a company has a communications satellite put into orbit, any number of things could go wrong, destroying the satellite or causing it to malfunction. No matter how often a manufacturer stresses safety, someone is injured on the job eventually. At any type of company, a key employee could die, leaving the firm scrambling for new talent. A company that produces consumer goods may someday be sued for injury caused by the product. These are only some of the risks businesses face today.

Types of Risks

Speculative risk The threat of a loss coupled with the chance of a gain.

Notice that none of the risks just mentioned involves investing. An investment is a **speculative risk,** one in which there is a chance of either gain or loss. Betting on a racehorse is a speculative risk. So is gambling that the value of a stock is going to go down. So is taking a chance on backing a new rock group and sponsoring a national tour for them. Investors can increase or decrease speculative risk by adjusting their investment strategy.

Pure risk The threat of a loss without the possibility of a gain.

This chapter discusses pure risk. **Pure risk** is the threat of a loss without the possibility of a gain. For example, if a K mart warehouse burns down, the company may lose millions of dollars in inventory. If no fire occurs, however, the lack of a fire will not add millions of dollars to the company's earnings. The risk of a fire involves a possible loss but no expectation of a gain. Figure 22.1 shows the possible outcomes of these two kinds of risk.

Risk Management

Risk management The reduction of loss caused by uncontrollable events.

Because every company is subject to risk, businesspeople practice **risk management,** the reduction of loss caused by uncontrollable events. There are four ways to manage pure risks: avoiding, reducing, assuming, or shifting them.

FIGURE 22.1
Risk: Possible Outcomes

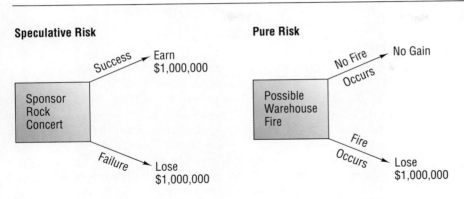

Speculative Risk

Sponsor Rock Concert — Success → Earn $1,000,000

Sponsor Rock Concert — Failure → Lose $1,000,000

Pure Risk

Possible Warehouse Fire — No Fire Occurs → No Gain

Possible Warehouse Fire — Fire Occurs → Lose $1,000,000

Avoiding the Risk   If the possibility of a loss is great enough, a company may avoid it altogether. For example, a retailer may choose not to open stores in Beirut because of the unstable political climate there. When an airline cancels flights during a blizzard, it too is avoiding a risk. The airline is eliminating the uncertainty over whether one of its planes will crash and cause a substantial loss. It is certain that no planes will crash when parked. Of course, the airline has eliminated the possibility of producing revenue. Customer service also suffers, since customers get upset when their plane is grounded.

Businesses cannot avoid every risk, however. To eliminate all risk of property damage, the company would have to eliminate all property. To eliminate all risk that employees will become ill, sustain an injury, or die, the company would have to eliminate all employees. Any line of work carries risks. Most companies do, however, avoid the risk of high-frequency, high-severity losses.

Reducing the Risk   When they can, businesspeople try to reduce or prevent risks. For example, managers may promote plant safety by training personnel and instituting safety rules and procedures. To reduce the risk of uncollected accounts, the financial manager might tighten up credit or offer incentives for prompt payment. The company might also deny further credit to customers who are constantly delinquent in paying. These actions do not eliminate the possibility that accidents will occur or customers will fail to pay, but they do reduce the likelihood of these losses.

In deciding whether to reduce a risk, businesspeople may weigh the cost of doing so and their social responsibility against the size of the risk. For example, a store might find that the additional sales that result from a generous credit policy outweigh the expected losses from bad debts. In that case, the company probably would not try to reduce the risk. But even though making a product or workplace safe can be costly, many companies bear the expense in order to fulfill their social responsibility.

Assuming the Risk   When a company decides that a particular risk is worth taking, it assumes the risk. If the risk seems likely to result in an occasional,

Workers remove asbestos from a building. The protective coverings and face masks that workers are required to wear and the safety procedures they follow are designed to reduce or prevent the risk of exposure to asbestos, which is linked to various types of cancer.

Source: © James Joern.

moderately serious financial loss, the firm may set up a self-insurance fund. In some instances companies are forced to self-insure because they cannot get insurance coverage from the outside. A self-insurance fund is a fund into which the company periodically sets aside cash, called reserves, to cover financial losses. The company pays for its own losses, but the fund enables it to spread out the expense.

Shifting the Risk   Another way to manage a worthwhile risk is to shift it. The most popular way to shift risk is to buy **insurance.** This is a financial arrangement under which the cost of unexpected losses is distributed among those who are insured. Insurance spreads the losses incurred by a few over an entire group, therefore substituting average loss for actual loss. Each party desiring insurance pays a **premium,** which is a fee to cover the costs of the insurance policy. In exchange for this fee, the insurance company will pay the agreed-upon amount if the insured suffers a specified loss. For example, if a store buys a policy insuring it against losses from theft up to $10,000 and suffers a $4,000 theft loss, the insurance company will pay the store $4,000 minus the deductible. A **deductible** is the amount that a policyholder must pay before the insurance company pays for any part of a claim. If the store suffers a $4,000 loss from fire, the insurance company will not pay.

Buying insurance can be the easiest way to manage risk; the business merely pays a premium, and the insurance company covers any insured loss.

Insurance A financial arrangement under which the cost of unexpected losses is distributed among those who are insured.

Premium A fee to cover the costs of an insurance policy.

Deductible The amount that a policyholder must pay before the insurance company pays any part of a claim.

Especially when used alone, however, insurance can be a costly approach to risk management. Most companies use some combination of risk management techniques. For example, a supermarket might refuse to carry dangerous products, carefully screen employees to minimize the likelihood of pilferage, and buy fire insurance.

1. How does a pure risk differ from a speculative risk?
2. What are four ways to manage risk?

CHECK ✓ POINT

Criteria for Insurability

No matter how much a business is willing to pay, an insurance company will assume a risk only under certain circumstances. More specifically, the coverage must be for an insurable interest and must cover an insurable risk.

Insurable Interest

A person or business wanting coverage must have an insurable interest. This means that the person or business would suffer a financial loss if the event being insured were to happen. For example, a company can buy life insurance on its key managers; if one or more of them were to die, the company would suffer a financial loss. Even if another manager could do the job well, the company would incur expenses in hiring a replacement. If there were no chance of financial loss, there would be no risk to insure. For example, if the fan of a movie actor thought the actor seemed to be in poor health, the fan could not purchase a life insurance policy on the actor's life. Although the fan might feel sad if the actor died, he or she would suffer no financial loss. Therefore, no insurable interest is present. The actor's dependents could, however, insure the actor's life.

Insurable Risk

Besides having an insurable interest, the other criterion for insurability is that there must be an insurable risk. Specifically, an insurable risk involves prerequisites such as a lack of control, calculable losses, economic feasibility, and widespread coverage. These criteria enable insurers to manage their own risks involved in issuing insurance.

Lack of Control   The peril that is being insured against cannot be under the policyholder's direct control. Any losses must happen by chance or be accidental. For example, if a retailer insures his store against fire, he cannot burn down the building and collect. If an investigation finds that the retailer is implicated in the fire, the insurance company can refuse to pay the claim.

Calculable Losses   For a risk to be insurable, the losses related to it must be calculable. This means that the insurer must be able to predict how many losses will occur and how big they will be. The insurance company determines this by hiring **actuaries,** people who collect statistics about losses and use this information to make predictions. For example, actuaries calculate statistics that give average life expectancies for various groups of people, as well as the number of deaths likely to occur in each group during the course

Actuaries Experts in collecting statistics about losses and using this information to make predictions.

CLOSE-UP / *Ethics*

Are New Car Consumers in Danger?

In order to conserve energy, the government has mandated that autos must be more fuel efficient. Some federal legislators want to see a 20 percent increase in gas mileage in 1995 cars compared to those at the beginning of the decade, and they want to see a 40 percent increase for the model year 2001. Opponents are arguing that this is a dangerous goal because it will decrease auto safety.

The Insurance Institute, which is funded by the insurance industry, has just completed a study showing that cars that have been downsized since 1977, mainly for fuel-efficiency reasons, have had significantly higher death rates of passengers involved in accidents than those riding in earlier, larger autos. Moreover, although smaller cars such as those by Toyota and Nissan at one time had much higher passenger death rates than those for the larger domestic autos produced by Ford and General Motors, the death rates have become much closer in recent years because on the whole the Japanese cars have become relatively bigger and the American cars have become smaller. A recent study by a Brookings Institution researcher and a Harvard

University professor predicts that over the next decade fuel-economy rules will be responsible for up to 3,900 additional fatalities involving smaller 1989 models alone.

These alarming statistics do not mean that downsized, lighter cars are destined to become death traps. Supporters of more fuel-efficient autos note that improved technology can do more than save gas; it can also save lives by providing increased safety. As the executive director of the Center for Auto Safety put it, "You can build safety into small cars if you want to do it." One of the most effective ways is through the installation of air bags. Another is by putting more safety equipment on board and improving the auto's ability to stop quickly and safely.

These arguments have not been successful in swaying the Insurance Institute, which continues to contend that downsized cars are more dangerous. For example, after examining 11 types of GM cars that were downsized between 1985 and 1989 the Institute found that the death rate of occupants had increased in 10 of these types of cars and remained the same for the 11th. Simply put, they claim that "large cars seem to offer a greater degree of protection." So, is the welfare of auto buyers being put in greater danger with each new annual model? Insurance statisticians think so, but opponents believe that improved auto design can offset these dangers and allow the public to attain both of the desired ends: safe and fuel-efficient autos.

Source: Laurie McGinley, "Gas Savings vs. Safety Sours Debate," *The Wall Street Journal,* September 6, 1990, B1.

of a year. These expectancy figures do not show the likelihood that you or any other individual will die this year. They only show the proportion of deaths in the population. The accompanying Ethics Close-Up (Are New Car Consumers in Danger?) provides an interesting discussion related to calculable losses and auto safety.

In recent years, some people have criticized insurance companies for determining premiums for certain types of insurance on the basis of sex. For example, women may pay higher premiums than men for the same health insurance coverage, but may pay lower premiums than men for an equal amount of life insurance. On the surface this may appear to be discriminatory, but the insurance companies are charging premiums according to the risks associated with each group. Whether they have a social responsibility to charge men and women the same, regardless of the statistical risk, is still being debated.

To be calculable, a loss must also be measurable. For this reason, insurers cover only risks that involve a financial loss. For example, fire insurance covers the cost of the assets — building, furniture, and other belongings — lost in a fire. Life insurance replaces the income policyholders might have earned or the expenses of a funeral. Most insurance policies specify a maximum amount they will cover, which also helps the company predict the extent of losses it must cover.

Economic Feasibility   The insurance company uses the information its actuaries gather to decide whether risks are economically feasible. Employees called underwriters decide what insurance the company can offer profitably. For example, if the company sells 1,000 insurance policies, each paying $50,000, and expects two deaths per thousand, the company can expect to pay out $100,000 in a year. It will sell the policies if it can charge more than $100 for each. If customers won't pay that much, the insurance company cannot make a profit and will look for other risks to insure.

Besides premium size, the insurance company considers the size of the potential loss. Most losses are small enough that the insurer can sell enough policies to cover the claims filed. But liability claims in some industries (such as those that made, sold, or installed asbestos) have been so large that insurers refuse to provide liability insurance to them. And the damages of war are so great that insurers won't cover the risk of a war.

Economic feasibility is linked to the insurer's profits. If an insurer predicts that product liability lawsuits will cost $5 million to defend and pay but that the company can raise only $4 million from selling the policies, it won't sell the insurance. However, if an insurer can make up the difference by investing the premiums until it has to pay out losses, the company may sell the insurance even if the premiums themselves fall short of expected payouts.

Widespread Risk   Linked to the other criteria is the requirement that an insurable risk be widespread. To calculate the expected frequency of losses, the insurer must have a large number of cases to compare. For example, in determining the frequency with which office buildings are struck by tornadoes, an insurer must be able to weigh the experience of more than a handful of office buildings. Because damage from tornadoes is widespread, the insurer can calculate this risk and sell enough policies to spread the risk widely and lower the cost borne by each customer.

Another dimension of widespread risk is that for many risks to be economically feasible, the insurer needs to spread them geographically. In the case of fire insurance, an insurer would not want to insure 25 large buildings in the lower Manhattan financial district and no others; a fire in this locale might wipe out all of the buildings. For example, when the Philadelphia police fire-bombed a house a few years ago, and the entire neighborhood burned down, if the same company had insured all these homes, it could have been wiped out, unless it could have recovered money from the city. However, if the insurer has covered buildings spread out across the state or country, a fire in one location will damage only a small percentage of all the insured buildings. Similarly, a life insurance company would not want to limit coverage to people in one city, because a calamity in this city, such as a tornado or hurricane, could wipe out the insurer's revenues.

CHECK ✓ POINT

1. What is an insurable interest?
2. What makes a risk insurable?

An insurance industry advertisement supports the practice of charging different rates for men and women. As it explains, the risks in each group are statistically different; women tend to live longer and, before age 55, tend to use health care services more than men. Thus, women typically pay less for life insurance and more for health insurance until they are 55. Critics of the practice of charging different rates contend that the distinction is artificially imposed.

Source: Courtesy of ACLI (American Council of Life Insurance) and HIAA (Health Insurance Association of America).

The Insurance Industry

The insurance industry consists of two basic types of companies: public and private. The best known are privately owned. However, public insurers provide a wealth of benefits and services to millions of people.

Public Insurance Companies

A public insurance company is a governmental agency established to provide insurance protection. These agencies exist at both federal and state levels and provide a wide range of coverage.

Federal Protection   At the federal level, perhaps the best-known insurance program is **Old-Age, Survivors, Disability, and Health Insurance (OASDHI),** commonly known as social security, which provides retirement, medical, disability, and death benefits. This insurance program was estab-

Old Age, Survivors, Disability, and Health Insurance (OASDHI)   A federal insurance program (commonly known as social security) that provides retirement, medical, disability, and death benefits.

lished by the Social Security Act of 1935. It was originally intended to be a retirement benefit program, but Congress has added other coverages over the years. For example, in 1965 Congress added **Medicare,** a form of hospital insurance for the elderly.

Medicare A federal program providing hospital and medical insurance to the elderly.

Many people think of social security as a kind of retirement savings plan, but it actually operates under a "pay as you go" approach. In 1990 employees paid 7.65 percent of the first $51,300 of their pay to social security and the employer contributed another 7.65 percent. Self-employed persons, on the other hand, paid 15.3 percent of $51,300 to social security in 1990. In other words, employees, employers, and entrepreneurs contribute funds to finance the benefits currently provided to the elderly, the infirm, and others covered by this form of insurance. In turn, when those workers retire, they will receive benefits financed by those who remain in the workforce.

Other forms of federal insurance protect individuals in diverse ways:

- The Federal Deposit Insurance Corporation (FDIC) insures deposits in financial institutions (see Chapter 19).[1]
- The Federal Housing Administration (FHA) provides mortgage insurance to protect lenders against default by homeowners.
- The National Flood Insurance Association protects property owners against floods and mudslides.
- The Federal Crop Insurance Corporation provides farmers with crop insurance, protecting them against losses from crop failure.
- Federal crime insurance is available to people who have property in high crime areas and are unable to purchase this coverage from private insurance firms.

State Protection At the state level, the two basic types of insurance are unemployment insurance and workers' compensation insurance. **Unemployment insurance** provides benefits to workers who have been laid off. These weekly payments typically extend for 26 to 39 weeks, although in some states this time period is much shorter and in others it runs for a year or more. For the duration of the time they receive these benefits, the unemployed must be able, available, and actively seeking work. Many states offer placement services. Unemployment insurance is funded from employer contributions, and the more workers a company lays off, the higher its contribution.

Unemployment insurance A state program that provides benefits to workers who have been laid off.

Workers' compensation insurance provides benefits to workers who suffer a job-related injury or illness. This compensation generally covers a percentage of wages or salaries, medical care costs, rehabilitative services, and, for certain types of injuries such as a loss of an arm or foot, a lump-sum payment. The employer pays the premiums, which are based on the company's record of past claims and type of industry. Today, every state has workers' compensation laws requiring companies to carry this type of insurance. Even though required by state law, companies normally contract with private insurers to provide this benefit.

Workers' compensation insurance A state program that provides benefits to workers who suffer job-related injury or illness.

Private Insurance Companies

Most of the insurance in the United States is provided by private firms. These firms may be stock insurance companies or mutual insurance companies. A **stock insurance company** is a corporation operated for profit. As

Stock insurance company A corporation that sells insurance for profit.

TABLE 22.1
The 10 Largest Life Insurance
Companies

ªMutual Company.
Source: "The Service 500," *Fortune*, June 4,
1990, 322.

Company	Assets (in billions)
Prudential of Americaª	$129.1
Metropolitan Lifeª	98.7
Equitable Life Assuranceª	52.5
Aetna Life	52.0
Teachers Insurance & Annuity	44.4
New York Lifeª	37.3
Connecticut General Life	34.0
Travelers	32.1
John Hancock Mutual Lifeª	30.9
Northwestern Mutual Lifeª	28.5

with any other corporation, those who invest by purchasing shares expect a return in the form of dividends or an increase in the value of the stock. Although the problems are not as severe as those facing the financial industry (see Chapter 19), in recent years the profits of these companies have been shrinking[2] because of some poor investments and loans to builders[3] and slowing premium income.

A **mutual insurance company** is a type of cooperative; the policyholders become shareholders of the company. Any profits the company makes go back to the policyholders in the form of dividends or reductions in premiums. Most mutual insurance companies sell life insurance. As Table 22.1 illustrates, more than half of the 10 largest life insurance companies in the United States are mutual companies.

Private insurance companies offer many different types of insurance relevant to modern business, and these are basically the same types that individuals would buy to insure against risk. Today, there are so many different types of insurance, and variations of the same type, that consumers may be getting confused. Ralph Nader, the well-known consumer activist, feels that consumers sometimes spend too much for too little insurance coverage.[4] To help ease some of the confusion, the basic types of insurance — property and liability, health, and life — should be understood.

Mutual insurance company
A type of cooperative in which the policyholders become shareholders of the insurance company.

CHECK ✓ POINT

1. What types of benefits are provided by social security?
2. Who receives the dividends paid by a stock insurance company? A mutual insurance company?

Property and Liability Insurance

Businesses risk losses from damage to their buildings and equipment, from theft or other crimes, and from lawsuits resulting from negligent actions or faulty products. They shift the risk of these losses by purchasing property

Engineering representatives at Aetna Life & Casualty's hydraulics lab demonstrate fire control to customers' safety managers. The reps also conduct 275,000 surveys annually of customers' operations to identify hazards and recommend solutions to potential problems. Intended to prevent or minimize losses, these activities can benefit the insurance company's customers through lower rates.

Source: Courtesy of Aetna Life & Casualty.

and liability insurance. These insurance policies include fire, fidelity and surety, business interruption, marine and aviation, public liability, and automobile insurance.

Insuring against Loss of Property Due to Fire

The property component of property and liability insurance most commonly provides protection against loss of property due to fire. In the United States, about five fires happen every minute, and many of these damage business property. This makes fire insurance coverage very important. The policies for fire insurance can and usually will be expanded to cover other perils such as losses stemming from wind, ice, water, and smoke. These policies pay the value of the loss or the amount of the policy, whichever is lower. For example, if a corporation carried a $10 million fire insurance policy on its headquarters building, but the building was valued at $8 million, the insurance company would pay only $8 million if the structure were completely destroyed by fire. If the structure were valued at $11 million, the insurance company would pay the maximum $10 million.

Few buildings are completely gutted by fire. A typical fire does only partial damage to a structure. For example, a building worth $10 million might suffer $1 million in fire damage. To prevent firms from underinsuring their buildings and taking a chance that the fire will not destroy the entire structure, insurance companies put a coinsurance clause in the policy. This clause requires the firm to cover at least 80 percent of the value of the building in order to receive full coverage for any loss.

Insuring against Income Loss

Another form of property and liability insurance is to protect against income loss. There are several types of this insurance.

Fidelity bond Coverage of losses caused by employee embezzlement or theft.

Surety bond Coverage against the risk that someone will fail to perform on a contract.

Fidelity and Surety Bonds When employees handle money, the company risks losing some of the money to a dishonest employee. The company can insure against such a loss by purchasing **fidelity bonds,** which provide coverage against loss caused by employee embezzlement or theft. If a bonded employee were to abscond with funds, the bond would cover the loss up to its face value. The insurance company will then try to recover the funds.

A **surety bond** provides coverage against the risk that someone will fail to perform on a contract. For example, a corporation that is having a new headquarters built might want to insure itself against the risk that the builder will not finish on time or will walk away from the job. If either of these does happen, the bond provides the funds necessary to hire someone else to complete the project.

Crime Insurance Employees are not, of course, the only people who might steal from a business. To protect against losses arising from theft by outsiders, a company can buy crime insurance, also called theft insurance. This policy may cover robbery, which is taking property from someone by force or threat of force, and burglary, which is taking property by forcible entry into the premises.

Business interruption insurance Coverage of losses from temporary business closings.

Business Interruption Insurance A number of problems, such as a strike or flood, may cause a business to shut down temporarily. To protect themselves, companies buy **business interruption insurance,** which is designed to cover losses from temporary business closings. Without this protection, many temporary closings would become permanent ones. For example, if a store has a fire, it may need a week or two to clean up the mess and replace its inventory. Fire insurance would pay for the damage but not the lost revenues. Business interruption insurance can cover that loss.

Many movie production firms buy this insurance to handle losses caused by the injury or death of a lead actor. The production has costs for the crew and other actors and for the set or location that are normally committed and cannot be put on hold. Should such a calamity occur, the entire crew would have to either wait for the actor's recovery or hire a replacement. In either case, business interruption insurance would help minimize the financial losses.

Marine insurance Coverage of losses to boats, ships, trucks, railcars and engines, planes, and their cargo.

Ocean marine insurance Coverage of losses that occur to ships or their cargo on the high seas or in port.

Inland marine insurance Coverage of damage to or loss of goods shipped by rail, truck, airplane, or inland barge.

Aviation insurance Coverage of losses involving airliners and their passengers.

Marine and Aviation Insurance Companies that transport cargo or passengers take on special kinds of risks. To protect against losses involving their boats, ships, trucks, railcars and engines, planes, and their cargo, companies buy **marine insurance.** As transportation modes expanded beyond ships, the word marine became too limiting. **Ocean marine insurance** covers losses that occur to ships or their cargo on the high seas or in port. **Inland marine insurance** covers damage to or loss of goods shipped by rail, truck, airplane, or inland barge.

Aviation insurance provides coverage of airliners and passengers. Airlines carry aviation insurance to cover the liabilities arising from damage to the aircraft or the passengers. A typical policy provides $500 million of liability insurance on small-body aircraft and $800 million on wide-body craft, and has a deductible of $250,000.

Norfolk Southern Corporation's innovative Triple Crown® service uses truck trailers with road wheels and rail wheels to transport cargo. Some transportation companies take on special risks and protect against losses with inland marine insurance.

Source: Courtesy of Norfolk Southern Corporation.

Credit and Title Insurance   Buying and selling goods also carry risks. When a company sells goods on credit, it risks not receiving full payment. The debtor may die before the total payment is due, leaving the seller to bear the loss. To protect against this risk, many sellers buy credit insurance or require that borrowers pay for such insurance when they take out a loan.

Buyers of real estate risk finding out that someone other than the seller has an interest in the real estate. For example, a buyer may find out one day that the seller was an imposter or that the seller had a spouse who now says that he or she never wanted to transfer ownership of the property. To cover the costs of any resulting lawsuit and possible loss of the property, buyers of real estate often purchase a title insurance policy.

Insuring against Loss from Liability

Large losses can arise if a court finds that a business is liable for causing personal injury or property damage. Even if the company is found innocent, the costs of legal defense are often substantial. To protect against these losses, businesses buy personal or public liability insurance, which is designed to protect individuals and businesses from lawsuits arising from injuries or property damage. This form of insurance covers many different types of liabilities.

Personal Liability Insurance   Many homeowners' policies include personal liability insurance to protect the owners from claims by individuals who injure themselves on their property. In addition to their regular coverage, many individuals with considerable risks, such as parents who are responsible for teenage drivers, or people in the public eye who are exposed to suits such as for slander, buy an umbrella liability policy, which extends coverage to $1 million or more.

Professional Liability Insurance   A special type of personal liability insurance is professional liability insurance, which covers professionals against

Directors' and officers' liability insurance Coverage of the costs of lawsuits against board members and senior corporate executives arising out of their actions.

lawsuits arising from accusations of malpractice. Doctors, lawyers, architects, and even college professors have been sued in recent years by irate clients or students. Professional liability insurance helps protect the insured from financial losses resulting from successful lawsuits.

A special kind of professional liability insurance is **directors' and officers' liability insurance,** which provides coverage to board members and senior corporate executives in the case of lawsuits arising out of their actions. For example, as Chapter 3 pointed out, stockholders have recently sued some directors and officers, claiming that negligence on the part of directors resulted in needless corporate losses.

Product Liability Insurance   To protect themselves from lawsuits related to their products, companies buy a form of personal or public liability insurance called product liability insurance. Product liability claims can pose a serious problem for companies. For example, the widow of a man who died of cyanide poisoning after taking a Sudafed decongestant capsule filed a negligence lawsuit against the manufacturer Burroughs Wellcome Company.[5] Merrell Dow Pharmaceuticals withdrew Benedectin from the market after a jury awarded $750,000 to a family who claimed that the drug, designed to fight morning sickness, caused their child to be born with a birth defect. Union Carbide continues to face millions of dollars in product liability claims from the toxic-gas leak in its plant in Bhopal, India, which resulted in the death of several thousand people.

Although the crisis in liability insurance that saw premiums skyrocket in the mid-1980s now appears to be over, except in a few high-risk areas such as ski resorts and medical malpractice, the insurance world may never be the same. Some insurance companies are facing charges that they illegally got together to offer liability policies with less coverage for more money. In addition, more businesses than ever are self-insuring (up to about one-third of the product liability market and growing). For example, Hardee's Food Systems now pays for losses up to $2 million itself and just buys insurance against catastrophes. Hardee's believes the key to this approach is to manage risk in ways other than insurance by taking steps such as installing nonskid floors to minimize falls. Other companies such as DuPont and Control Data have helped create new insurance companies to stabilize the market. As a result of these efforts and good old supply and demand at work, insurance companies are once again offering better policy terms.

Automobile Insurance
Combining elements of property and liability coverage is automobile insurance, which provides protection from such perils as theft, fire, collision, and personal injury in the operation of an auto. Private individuals as well as firms that own autos almost always carry insurance on them, and an increasing number of states require proof of insurance before they will register a vehicle and issue a license plate. A number of important types of coverage are available:

* *Comprehensive insurance.* Covers damage to the car from a variety of mishaps, including fire, theft, falling objects, earthquakes, broken glass, and

malicious vandalism. This coverage also often includes the cost of renting a car in case of theft or disabling damage.

- *Collision insurance.* Covers damage to the car if it collides with another car or object. Most policies have a deductible of about $250 for collision. Thus, in the case of a $500 claim, the insurance company would pay only $250. If the damage was less than $250, the insurance firm would not pay.

- *Liability insurance.* Provides coverage for bodily injury and property damage. Bodily injury liability insurance provides coverage against claims by anyone inside or outside the car who suffers bodily injury because of the driver; property damage liability insurance provides protection against claims or damage to other people's property in an accident. The policy sets liability limits, or maximum amounts of coverage. These are typically expressed as three numbers, such as 100/300/50, which means that up to $100,000 for bodily injury is payable to any one victim of an accident, up to a total of $300,000 is payable to all victims of the accident, and up to $50,000 may be paid in settlement of property damage caused to another person's car or personal property.

- *Medical payments insurance.* Provides a wide range of coverage for reasonable medical or funeral expenses that occur within a year's time of an auto accident. The bodily injury liability insurance may pay for damages beyond medical bills, for example, for loss of earning power because of resulting loss of time or a disability. The insurer usually pays for the medical expenses, regardless of who caused the accident.

- *Uninsured motorist insurance.* Covers expenses from injury to anyone in the car when an uninsured motorist or a hit-and-run driver causes an accident.

Insurance that provides for compensation regardless of who was at fault during an auto accident is called **no-fault insurance.** The insurance company pays for financial losses suffered by anyone involved in the accident. However, the insurance also limits the right of victims to sue. As Figure 22.2 shows, 25 states require no-fault insurance, and the number is growing. Although these no-fault laws were passed to put a rein on spiraling auto insurance premiums, some states (for example, Nevada) found that costs kept rising rapidly and have repealed their no-fault laws.

No-fault insurance Coverage providing compensation regardless of who was at fault in an auto accident.

1. What are three types of property and liability insurance?
2. What type(s) of insurance coverage would you purchase for your brand new automobile?

CHECK ✓ POINT

Health Insurance

The great majority of Americans carry some form of health insurance. Health care costs have risen so high that this type of insurance has become a necessity (see Figure 22.3). Most employees receive group coverage through their employer, who pays part or all of the premium. These premiums have been increasing 20 to 30 percent a year. The large firms typically spend over $100 million a year to provide employee medical coverage, and the cost of

FIGURE 22.2
States with No-Fault Auto Insurance

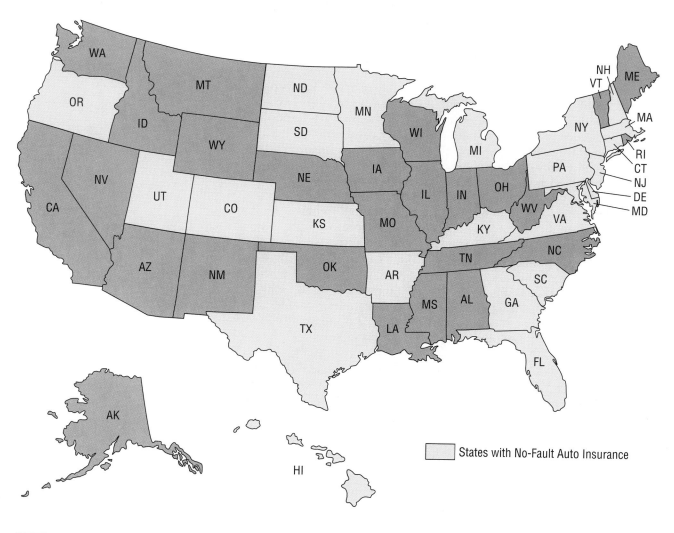

States with No-Fault Auto Insurance

medical benefits to the average employer is 13 percent of payroll, compared with less than 4 percent a decade ago.[6] Because of these dramatically escalating costs, some companies have developed their own approaches to negotiating lower rates. As seen in the Innovation Close-Up (Containing Escalating Health Care Costs), these programs can result in hefty savings.

Major Types of Health Insurance Coverage

The basic components of most health care coverage are hospitalization, surgical and medical, and major medical insurance. Hospitalization insurance covers the expenses of a hospital stay up to a coverage limit. Typically included are a semiprivate room, food, routine nursing care, and medication. Extras

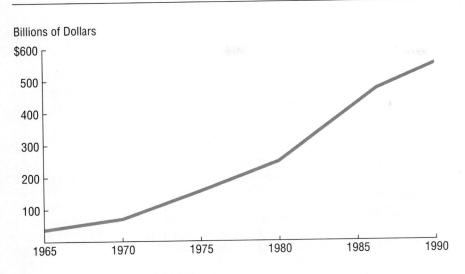

FIGURE 22.3
The Cost of Health Care in
the United States

Billions of Dollars

such as a TV or a private room are seldom covered. Surgical and medical insurance covers the costs of surgeons and medical specialists. In addition to any operating expenses, this coverage includes in-hospital visits by the doctor, as well as office visits or house calls after the patient's release. In an attempt to better manage escalating health care costs, many employers and health care insurers are attempting to control inappropriate or unnecessary care. For example, 3M requires doctors to obtain approval before performing inpatient surgery, and Hershey uses data on treatment patterns to determine which hospitals have the lowest rates of complications and deaths and the lowest costs.[7]

Hospitalization and surgical and medical coverage often carry limits. When a person exceeds those limits, major medical takes over. Major medical insurance covers health care expenses that exceed the coverage limits of other insurance.

Other Types of Health Insurance Coverage

Sometimes health insurance policies include dental and vision insurance, which covers a fixed percentage of expenses for dental and optical care. This insurance typically covers periodic checkups by a dentist, plus routine fillings and other dental work. The vision portion usually covers eye exams, eyeglasses, and medically prescribed contact lenses. The insurance seldom covers cosmetic work such as capping all of the teeth or providing orthodontic care for purely aesthetic reasons, nor does it cover corrective eye surgery undertaken to eliminate the use of glasses.

Many companies are now beginning to offer their employees some form of mental health insurance. Mental health insurance provides coverages for psychiatric care and sometimes counseling. This coverage varies widely. Some firms have programs with little if any deductible and cover the individual up to a predetermined limit such as $50,000; other programs require the

C L O S E - U P / *Innovation*

Containing Escalating Health Care Costs

In recent years, business firms have experienced skyrocketing health care costs. In many cases these costs are at least partially passed on to employees. However, some employers are using an innovative approach by which they regularly track these expenses and develop cost containment strategies for reducing them. There are a number of such approaches that are currently being implemented in an effort to control the escalating health care costs.

One option is the shifting of some of the health coverage to alternative suppliers. For example, some firms have found that they can negotiate extremely low pharmaceutical coverage with discount chains and cut a significant percentage of their overall costs.

Some companies have elected to have a physician conduct a no-frills physical for all employees and identify areas of health where each employee should be encouraged to make changes. At one firm the doctor was able to identify employees who had weight, cholesterol, and blood pressure problems. Over the next year the affected employees lost an average of eight pounds; the average cholesterol reading dropped 19 points; and no one's blood pressure increased. Result: The company's medical bill went down by $39,000.

Another strategy is to form a coalition with other companies and collectively negotiate bids for services from local hospitals. One group of 45 companies asked three local hospitals to bid on their combined business, with the result that the companies were able to cut 30 percent off their hospital bills.

Some organizations conduct a detailed analysis of the claims filed with the insurance carrier in order to identify those areas where costs are the highest, and set up a committee to study how these costs can be driven down. Armed with this information, the firm can then take the proper steps. One company's analysis revealed that many of its employees were going to the very expensive emergency room with their problems instead of visiting a doctor's office. Once the employees learned that the cost of obtaining the emergency room treatment was 2 1/2 times that of most doctor's offices, they stopped this practice and saved the company thousands of dollars in unnecessary expenses.

These strategies are helping firms reduce their medical expenses and keep them low. Because the costs of employee health care are a significant portion of overall expenses, these strategies are also helping firms become more competitive and profitable.

Source: Terri Lammers, "The Examined Health-Insurance Bill," *Inc.*, May 1992, pp. 45–47.

insured to bear more of the costs. Mental health coverage is becoming more common as the importance of such care gains recognition.

In addition to medical expenses, being sick for more than a few days can lead to lost income. Disability income insurance provides income to those who are unable to work because of a disabling illness or injury. These policies generally have a waiting period of a week or more before payments begin. The payments are usually a percentage of the worker's former earnings. Many employers provide this insurance, although individuals can also buy it themselves if they are not covered by their employer or want to supplement what the employer provides.

CHECK ✓ POINT

1. What are the major sources of health insurance coverage?
2. What losses does major medical insurance cover?

Life Insurance

Millions of Americans have life insurance. This coverage provides money to the insured's beneficiary (the person or persons, usually family members, whom the policy owner names to receive the insurance benefits) upon the insured's death. In addition, some types of life insurance function as a form of investment. The purchaser's risks and objectives determine the most appropriate type of life insurance to buy. While the most common forms of life insurance are term life and whole life, insurance companies are offering an increasing number of alternatives.

Term Life Insurance

The least expensive type of coverage is **term life insurance,** which provides coverage for a death benefit during a stated number of years; if the insured dies during this time, the insurance company will pay the stated or face value of the policy. Term insurance can be purchased for a term of 1, 5, 10, or 20 years and may have a fixed or declining death benefit. With a fixed benefit such as $100,000, the premium will increase every year or two. With a declining or decreasing benefit, the benefit declines every year while the premium is fixed. For example, the premium might buy $100,000 of coverage the first year, $99,000 the second, $97,000 the third, and so forth.

The cost of term insurance is based on the insured person's age. The older the insured, the greater the premium, with rates tending to rise rapidly beginning at around age 50. For this reason, it is most popular among young people who want to buy as much insurance as possible at as low a price as they can.

Term life insurance Coverage for a death benefit during a stated number of years.

Whole Life Insurance

Whole life insurance combines a death benefit with savings. Premiums remain the same from year to year and, usually, beginning in the second year, the policy begins to accumulate cash value. The **cash value** of life insurance is the amount of money in a policy that the insured can borrow or obtain by canceling the policy. If the insured borrows the cash value, he or she must pay interest (usually at a variable rate); if the insured dies, the company subtracts the borrowed amount from the face value of the policy before paying the death benefit.

Whole life used to be the most common form of life insurance, but it has recently accounted for less than half of all policies sold. The reason is that it is expensive compared to other forms of insurance. Fewer people find the accumulating cash value worth the additional cost. Many other attractive investment opportunities are vying for people's savings, and rarely charge the investors interest when they want to borrow some of their investment.

Whole life insurance
A combination of a death benefit and tax-deferred savings.

Cash value The amount of money in a life insurance policy that the insured can borrow or obtain by canceling the policy.

Limited-Pay Life Insurance

Some whole life insurance, called **limited-pay life insurance,** limits the number of years the insured must pay premiums. A typical limit is 20 years; such a policy is commonly referred to as "20 pay life." The major benefit of this type of policy is that the insured can limit premium payments to the years when he or she expects to be making the most money. However, this form of insurance provides less protection for the money than does whole life.

Limited-pay life insurance
Whole life insurance that limits the number of years the insured must pay premiums.

Endowment Life Insurance

A policy that combines a death benefit with a great deal of savings is **endowment life insurance.** The premium on this type of policy is greater than that of whole life or limited-pay life, but the cash value also increases a lot faster.

Endowment life insurance Life insurance that combines a death benefit with a great deal of savings.

Many consumers choose universal life when purchasing life insurance because this form provides not only a death benefit but also a living benefit by building up a considerable cash value. Universal life is Safeco Corporation's best-selling individual life insurance product.

Source: © John Terence Turner.

In fact, at the end of a stated time period, such as 20 years, the cash value is equal to the face value of the policy, and the insured can cash it in. If the insured dies before this time, the company pays face value of the policy to the beneficiary named in the policy. This form of policy has diminished in popularity in recent years because there are a number of alternative ways to save money.

Universal Life Insurance

Universal life insurance Life insurance that combines term insurance with a tax-deferred savings plan.

Recently very popular, **universal life insurance** combines term insurance with a tax-deferred savings plan. By the early 1990s, universal life was accounting for about half of all life insurance sales. This form of insurance is even growing in popularity as a benefit offered by companies to their employees. Premiums are used to cover losses, just as they are in a term insurance policy. However, any remaining funds are invested at competitive rates of interest. As a result, the cash value of the policy may, depending on interest rates, go up faster than that of a whole life policy. Some of these policies also allow the insured to change the premium or the coverage or to withdraw savings from time to time. This kind of flexibility makes it different from whole life and has made the universal policy attractive to buyers. However, the interest earned on the savings is subject to tax when it is withdrawn.

Universal life was developed by the insurance industry to meet changing customer needs. Other products such as variable life insurance, which allows the policyholder to designate a certain amount of premium dollars to investments in stocks, bonds, or a money-market mutual fund, are also available. As in other industries, the insurance industry is offering an increasing number of alternatives. Businesses and individuals need to be aware of their options when considering their life insurance needs.

Business Life Insurance

As with health insurance, many businesses buy life insurance as an employee benefit. Typically, they provide group life insurance, which is term life insurance on all members of a particular group, such as the employees of a company. Unlike most individual life insurance policies, a group plan does not require the employees to take a physical exam. The death benefit goes to the insured's estate, and its size is usually tied to the insured's salary.

To protect themselves, businesses buy **owner or executive insurance,** also called key employee insurance, which reimburses the organization upon the death of a key employee. Often, small partnerships buy key employee insurance on the life of the owners so that, if one dies, the others can buy out the deceased's interest in the firm. In larger enterprises, the funds from this insurance compensate for the contribution a senior executive or vital manager would have made and to cover the costs of finding and hiring a replacement.

Owner or executive insurance Life insurance that reimburses an organization upon the death of a key employee.

1. What are three types of life insurance?
2. What risks does a company shift when it buys owner or executive insurance?

CHECK ✓ POINT

Special Insurance for International Business

As more and more businesses enter the international arena, they develop special insurance needs. For example, businesses operating in other countries run a greater risk of losses from actions such as the kidnapping of an employee or nationalization of the company's overseas operations. To protect themselves, many international businesses buy kidnap, ransom, and extortion insurance, and expropriation and inconvertibility insurance.

Kidnap, ransom, and extortion insurance covers costs associated with these criminal acts. Firms sending their personnel into risky overseas areas, such as the Middle East, are particularly interested in this form of insurance. The coverage typically reimburses the business for extortion payments, ransom paid to kidnappers, and expenses associated with negotiating a victim's release. Also covered are medical, legal, travel, and other costs related to activities conducted before and after a victim's release.

Kidnap, ransom, and extortion insurance Political risk insurance that covers costs associated with these criminal acts.

Expropriation and inconvertibility insurance covers losses associated with the nationalization of property and conversion of currency. If a foreign government seizes a firm's plant and equipment (as when Iraq took over Kuwait), expropriation insurance compensates for the assets. If a company is unable to convert its foreign currency back into U.S. dollars, inconvertibility insurance helps the firm cover any losses or pay for the costs of negotiating a solution. In most cases, the insurer delays reimbursement for at least 30 days, during which time the company tries to work out the problem. If these efforts fail, the insurer reimburses the company based on the exchange rates prevailing on the day the period of inconvertibility began.

Expropriation and inconvertibility insurance Political risk insurance that covers nationalization of property and conversion of currency.

1. Why do international companies need special forms of insurance?
2. What risks are covered by expropriation and inconvertibility insurance?

CHECK ✓ POINT

Closing Comments

Modern businesses encounter a variety of risks, such as damage to their property, losses stemming from crime, lawsuits over faulty products, and the loss of a key employee. Businesses manage these risks in one or more of several ways: avoiding, reducing, assuming, and shifting the risks. When the risk is insurable, risk management almost always includes insurance. The major types of insurance are property and liability insurance, health insurance, and life insurance. International companies buy special insurance to protect them against political risks.

VIDEO CASE / *Keeping the Lid On*

One reason why the Health Insurance Plan (HIP) of Greater New York is so successful is that it focuses on the primary challenge facing health care today: cost control. More and more health care insurers and providers are looking for ways to reduce expenses. Three results of these efforts have been the emergence of managed health care provided by health maintenance organizations (HMOs), the acceptance of higher deductibles by the insured, and the introduction of cost-saving techniques in hospitals and other health care institutions.

Managed health care, such as that provided by HIP, gives individuals the right to choose a family doctor from among those who have agreed to participate in the plan. This doctor becomes the primary physician. If a problem is beyond his or her expertise, the physician will bring in a specialist, who is also part of the medical team recruited by the HMO. The objective of this approach is to offer a type of "supermarket" medical care in which all of an insured's medical needs can be handled by doctors who are part of the HMO plan. This extends from office visits to the primary physician or specialists to hospitalization and surgery. In fact, most HMO plans charge the insured very little, if anything, for in-hospital services. These expenses are all covered by the insurance premiums. Physicians in the plan are paid a fixed amount or

are salaried and, as a result, are motivated to keep the patient well. This emphasis on wellness, as opposed to curing illness, is an important recent development and is one of the most critical aspects of effective cost control. Because of this philosophy and its cost focus, HMOs and similar health care organizations have become very popular over the past decade.

The acceptance of higher deductibles by the insured allows insurance companies to lower premiums. As an example, if an insurer pays 90 percent of all expenses after a $100 deductible and a family has $2,000 of health care costs in a year, the insurer will pay out $1,780 ($.90 \times $1,900$). If the deductible is increased from $100 to $200, however, the insurance company will save $100 of expenses; and because there is a far greater likelihood that a person will have $200 of medical expenses in one year than $2,000 of expenses, the insured has assumed more of the risk. The problem with this approach is that there is a limit to the amount of risk that can be passed on to the insured. In addition to the premiums and the deductible, the insured typically ends up paying part of the bill as well. (In the example, the insured would pay 10 percent.) This results in a great deal of pressure on insurance companies to keep deductibles to a minimum. In turn, insurance companies are demanding that hospitals and other health care

providers reduce their in-house expenses.

A wide variety of cost controls have been implemented in health care institutions over the past decade, and these have helped slow the rising tide of costs. One approach that is proving particularly helpful is that of better inventory control. Hospitals, for example, purchase and store a wide assortment of medicines and supplies. A major hospital may require a 20,000-square-foot warehouse in order to avoid running out of critical supplies. Some major health care institutions are now finding that they can reduce or eliminate their warehouses by having outside suppliers provide them what they need when they need it. A good example is St. Luke's Episcopal Hospital in Houston:

. . . To achieve economies as the pressure to control costs intensified, St. Luke's shut its warehouse and sold the inventory to Baxter International, a major hospital supplier. Baxter is becoming a full-time partner with the 950-bed hospital in managing, ordering and delivering Baxter's wares as well as the products of 400 other companies. Baxter's daily "just-in-time" deliveries to the hospital loading dock were only the first step. In an innovative system that hospitals call stockless inventory, Baxter fills orders in exact, sometimes small, quantities and delivers directly to departments, including the operating rooms and nursing floors, inside St. Luke's.

The stockless method shifts all inventory responsibilities to the suppliers and calls for daily deliveries, often directly to the individuals or departments that need them. However, some hospitals are reluctant to accept a stockless approach because they are concerned that they will run out of critically needed inventory. Instead, they have opted for a just-in-time supply method, whereby they store small quantities in their storeroom and use them as needed. This approach is more costly than the stockless method, but it reduces the likelihood of stockouts. Hospital administrators must weigh the advantages and disadvantages of the systems before deciding whether to adopt either one.

As hospitals and other health care institutions continue to work on cost containment, more and more new approaches will be tried. Although expenses are unlikely to go down dramatically, these methods will certainly help keep the lid on recently escalating costs.

Source: Milt Freudenheim, "Removing the Warehouse from Cost-Conscious Hospitals," *New York Times*, March 3, 1991, Sec. F, 5.

Case Questions

1. How do health plans like the HIP help contain health care costs?
2. Why are increased deductibles proving to be of limited value in the effort to reduce health care costs?
3. In what way can stockless and just-in-time inventory help reduce health care premiums?

Learning Objectives Revisited

1. **Specify the types of risk and ways to manage each.** Pure risk is the threat of a loss without the possibility of a gain, while speculative risk involves the uncertainty of a loss or a gain. Risk management is the reduction of loss caused by pure risk. The four ways of managing such risk are avoiding the risk, reducing the risk, assuming the risk, or shifting the risk. The most common way to shift risk is to buy insurance.

2. **Describe the criteria of insurability and sources of insurance.** Insurability requires an insurable interest and an insurable risk. An insurable interest means that a person or business would suffer a financial loss if the risk being covered were to happen. An insurable risk is outside the control of the insured, involves calculable losses, is economically feasible to cover, and is widespread. Insurance is available through public insurance companies (government agencies) and private insurance companies, which may be stock companies or mutual companies.

3. **Identify the major types of property and liability insurance.** Property insurance includes fire insurance and protection against loss of income in the form of fidelity and surety bonds, crime insurance, business interruption insurance, marine and aviation insurance, and credit and title insurance. Personal or public liability insurance protects individuals and businesses from lawsuits and includes personal and professional liability insurance and product liability insurance. Automobile insurance combines property and liability coverage for risks associated with the ownership and operation of an auto.

4. **Discuss the key types of health insurance.** Health insurance includes hospitalization insurance, surgical and medical insurance, and major medical insurance. It also may cover dental and vision care and mental health care. Disability income insurance provides income to an insured person who is unable to work because of a disabling illness or injury.

5. **Present the major types of life insurance.** The major types of life insurance include term life insurance, whole life insurance (which includes limited-pay life insurance), endowment life insurance, and universal life insurance. Businesses often buy group life insurance, which provides term life insurance on all employees, and owner or executive insurance, which reimburses the organization for the loss of a key employee.

6. **Relate the special insurance needs of international businesses.** International businesses buy kidnap, ransom, and extortion coverage to protect against costs related to these risks. Expropriation and inconvertibility insurance covers nationalization of property and conversion of currency. These political risks are encountered by businesses operating overseas.

Key Terms Reviewed

Review each of the following terms. For any that you do not know or are unsure of, look up the definitions and see how they were used in the chapter.

speculative risk	workers' compensation insurance	no-fault insurance
pure risk	stock insurance company	term life insurance
risk management	mutual insurance company	whole life insurance
insurance	fidelity bond	cash value
premium	surety bond	limited-pay life insurance
deductible	business interruption insurance	endowment life insurance
actuaries	marine insurance	universal life insurance
Old Age, Survivors, Disability,	ocean marine insurance	owner or executive insurance
and Health Insurance	inland marine insurance	kidnap, ransom, and
(OASDHI)	aviation insurance	extortion insurance
Medicare	directors' and officers'	expropriation and
unemployment insurance	liability insurance	inconvertibility insurance

Review Questions

1. Identify each of the following as a pure risk or a speculative risk, and explain why you made each choice.
   a. An investor's risk that the price of stock might fall
   b. The risk to a company that someone might kidnap an employee and demand that the company pay ransom
   c. The risk of a retailer's security guard detaining a suspected shoplifter who turns out to be innocent of any wrongdoing
2. What approaches are available for managing each of the risks in Question 1? Be as specific as you can.
3. Why might a company avoid a risk rather than buy insurance to cover it?
4. Which of the following are insurable interests? Explain.
   a. A manufacturing firm's interest in its machinery
   b. The plant manager's interest in the machinery
   c. The plant manager's interest in his job
   d. The manufacturing firm's interest in the plant manager's life

5. If Safe First Mutual Automobile Insurance Company makes a profit this year, what can it do with the profits?
6. What are the differences among fidelity bonds, surety bonds, and crime insurance?
7. Pat Blount buys an auto insurance policy that includes comprehensive and collision insurance, each with a $100 deductible. The liability coverage is described as 100/300/25. What risks has Pat shifted? What risks has Pat retained?
8. If Patty Sheffield's retail store is fully covered by a fire insurance policy, why would she also want business interruption insurance?
9. How can Artis Manufacturing, an appliance maker, protect itself from lawsuits concerning its products? How can a law firm protect itself against lawsuits over poor advice?
10. If you were to buy insurance today, which of the types described in the chapter do you think you would select? Why?
11. Spedling Inc. is thinking about going international. How can the firm protect itself against the special risks of doing business overseas?

Applied Exercise

Read the following 10 requests for insurance and determine which are acceptable and which are not. In doing so, consider whether each involves an insurable interest and an insurable risk.

Person Requesting Insurance	Insurance Requested	Acceptable (A) or Unacceptable (U)?
1. Lee Iacocca	Fire insurance on the headquarters of General Motors	_____
2. Owner of the *Titanic*	Insurance covering loss of ship on the high seas	_____
3. Jessie James	Robbery insurance for a bank	_____
4. Leonard Bernstein	Broken baton insurance	_____
5. George Burns	Personal life insurance	_____
6. Noah	Flood insurance on his home	_____
7. Carl Sagan	Insurance to cover kidnapping by aliens from another planet	_____
8. Johnny Carson	Earthquake coverage on his Malibu home	_____
9. Houdini	Accident insurance in case he is injured during one of his escape tricks	_____
10. Steven Spielberg	Business interruption insurance covering his filming of *ET II*	_____

YOU BE THE ADVISER / *Reviewing the Plan*

In the past, managers of the Wolfson Company gave a very superficial, informal annual review of its insurance coverage and decided what changes were needed. Now, however, insurance costs and potential liabilities have reached the point where the company has appointed a full-time risk manager. Chuck Stevens, who had previously worked in employee benefits, was given the job. Chuck does not yet know a lot about insurance, but whatever recommendations he makes to the insurance company that handles the firm's business, as well as any recommendations they make to Chuck, must be submitted to the board of directors for final approval.

The insurance company representative has made a number of recommendations to Chuck, who intends to pass them on to the board for review. The recommendations fall into two major categories:

1. The company owns a large warehouse in which chemicals are stored. The warehouse has a value of $20 million and is insured for 80 percent of its value. The insurance firm has recommended that fire coverage be extended to the full $20 million, because a fire near these highly flammable chemicals would undoubtedly burn the entire structure to the ground.
2. The firm intends to start manufacturing a product that will be distributed by a large pharmaceutical marketing firm. The insurance company feels that Wolfson should

purchase product liability insurance to protect itself from any problems arising from the potential side effects of the product.

Before passing these recommendations on to the board, Chuck wants to evaluate them. He would like to develop basic knowledge in the subject and determine whether he agrees or disagrees with each recommendation. He is also concerned that these recommendations come from a source that would profit from selling the company more insurance.

Your Advice

1. What should Chuck do?
   a. ___ Leave the insurance coverage at 80 percent.
   b. ___ Increase the insurance coverage to 100 percent.
   c. ___ Decrease the insurance coverage to below 80 percent.
2. If Chuck leaves the coverage at 80 percent and there is a $10 million fire, how much will the insurance company pay?
3. If Chuck extends the coverage to 100 percent and there is a $17 million fire, how much will the insurance company pay?
4. Should the firm buy product liability insurance? Why or why not? Besides buying insurance, how can the Wolfson Company manage its product liability risk?

A TRUCK IS A CAR IS A TRUCK

Lobbying has always been a major
part of the Washington scene. Large
business firms and entire industries
use lobbyists to inform and persuade
lawmakers to enact legislation that is
favorable to their special interests or
to block legislation that might hurt
them. All industries as well as
education, health care, and other
such groups have significant lobbying
efforts in Washington, but the largest
of all are the Japanese. Many of the
lobbyists representing Japanese
special interests are Americans who
have worked for the U.S.
government as trade representatives

Government Regulations and Business Law

23

Chapter Learning Objectives

- Describe the major laws that regulate business and ensure competition.

- Identify the major types of federal, state, and local taxes.

- Present the major dimensions of contract and sales law.

- Discuss negotiable instruments and property law.

- Explain the responsibilities under agency and tort law.

- Relate the different ways of handling bankruptcy.

---

or in administrative positions that gave them insights regarding how to circumvent or change American trade policies.

Like all lobbyists, these insiders use their knowledge to help the Japanese in the American marketplace. For example, until 1987 Japanese auto importers paid a 25 percent tariff on light trucks shipped into the United States. The Japanese firms then reclassified these trucks as passenger cars in order to pay only the 2.5 percent auto tariff. When the U.S. Customs Service discovered this, it ordered that the vehicles be reclassified back to trucks. However, the Japanese lobby convinced the Department of the Treasury to override the Customs Service and it was soon announced that, for purposes of the tariff, light trucks would pay the same tariff as passenger cars. The lobbyists next convinced the U.S. administration to let the vehicles be reclassified back to trucks once they were through customs. The reason the Japanese firms wanted this is that passenger auto requirements for fuel efficiency, safety, and emissions are higher than those for light trucks. To achieve this unique arrangement cost the Japanese firms approximately $3 million for lobbyists, public relations advisors, and political consultants, but it has been estimated that they saved more than $500 million a year in import duties.

As these events came to light, Congress began looking into the Japanese lobby and its effect on U.S. trade. If nothing else, lobbyists are likely to be more closely regulated than they have been in the past. The revolving door used by some American public servants with inside information and contacts who leave their jobs and go to work as lobbyists for special interest groups may be closed much tighter.

Photo source: © Adam Smith/Westlight.

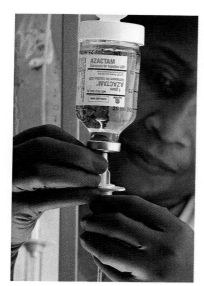

Pharmaceuticals is an example of an industry that is heavily regulated. Bristol-Myers Squibb developed Azactam and received approval from the U.S. Food and Drug Administration, the federal agency charged with regulating the industry, for the antibiotic's use against serious hospital-acquired infections. Subsequent studies show Azactam is effective against other types of infections and the company filed supplemental applications with the FDA seeking additional approval. Many pharmaceutical firms employ a special staff to ensure compliance with FDA regulations, monitor product safety, and obtain approval of new drugs.

Source: Courtesy of Bristol-Myers Squibb Company.

Sherman Antitrust Act
A federal law that prohibits all agreements created for the purpose of restraining trade in interstate commerce.

Introduction

Businesspeople need to be informed enough about the law to prevent problems and to know when to consult their lawyers. Two bodies of law are of particular interest. The first is regulatory law. For example, marketers developing an advertising campaign should be aware that the Federal Trade Commission has certain regulations to uphold and will monitor the ads. A second major area of the law pertains specifically to business. Categories of business law include contracts, sales, negotiable instruments, property, agency relationships, torts, and bankruptcy.

Government Regulation

Government assists business in many ways, as previous chapters have shown. At the federal level, for example, the Departments of Commerce and Agriculture provide technical assistance and the Department of Labor helps with training employees. At the state and local levels, government also helps business by providing tax incentives and help in securing favorable locations and services. Even the Internal Revenue Service provides assistance in tax preparation. In addition to this assistance, government plays a major role in the regulation of business. Some regulatory legislation is designed to promote competition; other laws regulate particular industries.

Regulation to Promote Competition

A market economy assumes that consumers benefit when businesses must compete for their money. To keep competition strong, Congress has passed a number of laws that prohibit businesses from engaging in unfair practices and restraining trade and competition. Some of the laws that are designed to prevent unfair business practices have been discussed in previous chapters. For example, Chapter 6 outlined the various equality in employment and environmental and consumer protection laws. The laws that have been passed through the years to promote competition and prevent the restraint of trade are summarized in Table 23.1. An example of a recent test case of the government's antitrust policy involves the agreement of MCI (the second-largest long distance telephone company) to buy Telecom USA (the fourth largest). MCI has countered the government's antitrust allegation by claiming that the acquisition of Telecom will actually increase competition, because the acquired assets will allow it to better compete with giant AT&T.[1]

Sherman Antitrust Act One of the earliest and most famous laws affecting business is the **Sherman Antitrust Act** of 1890. This act outlaws all agreements created for the purpose of restraining trade in interstate commerce. The act was initially used to break up giant monopolies of the late 1800s and early 1900s, which were preventing free competition. Probably the most famous case was that of the Standard Oil trust of John D. Rockefeller, Sr. At the time, Standard Oil held 90 percent of the nation's oil-refining capacity. The government used the Sherman Act to break up the trust. Today the Justice Department still uses this act to prevent what it believes is monopolis-

TABLE 23.1
Major Procompetition Legislation

Year	Federal Law	Consequences
1890	Sherman Antitrust Act	Outlaws all agreements created for the purpose of restraining trade in interstate commerce
1914	Clayton Act	Outlaws tying agreements, interlocking directorates, and certain anticompetitive stock acquisitions
1914	Federal Trade Commission Act	Outlaws unfair trade practices and established the Federal Trade Commission
1936	Robinson-Patman Act	Prohibits unfair pricing practices
1950	Celler-Kefauver Antimerger Act	Extended the prohibition of anticompetitive stock acquisitions of the Clayton Act to include mergers and major asset purchases that decrease competition in an industry
1974	Antitrust Procedures and Penalties Act	Increases fines and legal penalties for violation of the Sherman Act
1976	Antitrust Improvements Act	Requires companies planning to merge to notify the FTC in advance; allows injured parties to file lawsuits

tic power. AT&T was broken up into the seven Baby Bells for this reason. The early 1990s saw a rash of fines, settlements, and allegations against the Baby Bells for not living up to the antitrust ruling.[2] For instance, U.S. West recently agree to pay the largest fine ever in an antitrust case — $10 million.[3]

Clayton Act   To close loopholes in the Sherman Act, Congress amended it by passing the Clayton Act in 1914. The **Clayton Act** prohibits tying agreements, interlocking directorates, and certain anticompetitive stock acquisitions. In a tying agreement, sellers require customers to purchase unwanted merchandise in order to obtain what they want to buy. For example, a manufacturer of men's suits might require retailers to buy shirts and ties in order to get the suits, or a manufacturer of equipment might require that the buyer also purchase all of the materials and supplies needed to run the equipment. Recently, some computer manufacturers ran afoul of this law by requiring purchasers of their computer hardware to buy software and other related products. The government successfully argued in court that this constituted a violation of the Clayton Act.

An **interlocking directorate** is an arrangement in which a majority of the board of directors of two or more competing corporations with assets in excess of $1 million are the same people. Such an arrangement would enable the board members to establish company policies that would lessen competition between the companies. For example, they could raise prices at the same time. Today, many people serve on the boards of two or more corporations, but these directors must take care to avoid serving on the boards of competitors.

Clayton Act A federal law that prohibits tying agreements, interlocking directorates, and certain anticompetitive stock acquisitions.

Interlocking directorate An arrangement in which a majority of the board of directors of two or more competing corporations with assets in excess of $1 million are the same people.

TABLE 23.2
Cholesterol Confusion

Common Food Labels	Potential Contribution to High Cholesterol Levels
"Cholesterol-free"	Many consumers believe this phrase, used on products ranging from cooking oils to prepared foods, means they are also free of saturated fat. Not so; they may contain palm or coconut oil.
"Health foods"	Not all "health foods" are good for the heart. About 10 percent of a bran muffin's calories come from saturated fat. Nature Valley Granola has 30 times more saturated fat than Sugar Smacks.
Nondairy creamer	Think dairy products are dangerous? Consider that powdered "coffee whitener," rich in coconut or palm oil, may contain twice as much saturated fat per tablespoon as half-and-half.
Two percent milk	Almost the same as skim? Not really; whole milk is only 3.3 percent fat to begin with. Some critics question the FDA law that allows 2 percent milk to be labeled "low fat." Skim milk has no fat.

Source: *Newsweek,* October 19, 1987, 97.

Federal Trade Commission Act
A federal law that prohibits unfair trade practices and established the Federal Trade Commission (FTC).

Federal Trade Commission Act   In 1914, Congress passed the **Federal Trade Commission Act,** which prohibits unfair trade practices and established the Federal Trade Commission (FTC). The unfair trade practices mainly involve unfair competitive practices. For example, the agency recently investigated Nintendo, the Japanese video game giant, for allegedly using product designs and licensing policies to lock others out of its business and keep prices artificially high.[4] The FTC's job is to help enforce the Clayton Act and to issue cease-and-desist orders when it finds a violation of antitrust laws. Over the years, the FTC has become known for "policing the business world."

Today, the commission surveys business practices, watches for false or misleading advertising, and investigates claims made by manufacturers. Because of the recent public interest in the impact that a high blood cholesterol level may have on heart problems, food companies are trying to capitalize on this concern in their packaging and labeling. As Table 23.2 shows, products that are portrayed as being healthful and cholesterol-free may in fact contain saturated fat and palm and coconut oils, which are known to contribute to high levels of cholesterol. Another questionable practice is the loose use of "light" labels with regard to fat and calories. According to government guidelines, use of "light" on a food product is supposed to mean at least a one-third reduction in calories from the original product.[5] The agency may prosecute companies for making inaccurate or misleading claims. For example, it recently prohibited Kraft General Foods from misrepresenting nutrient claims of cheese-related products.[6]

In other examples, the FTC has asked some aspirin manufacturers to support their claims regarding the potency of their product, has asked tire manufacturers to demonstrate the performance of their tires, and has required that some food manufacturers stop claiming their products provide

CLOSE-UP / *Ethics*

Hitting Back at the Big Guy

A recent Supreme Court ruling is forcing the Eastman Kodak Company to go to court and defend itself against charges of unfair competition against some of its customers. This dispute dates back to 1985 when Kodak began limiting the availability of parts for its high-volume copiers and micrographics machines. The company is accused of telling its customers that they could get replacement parts only if they agreed not to use outside service companies.

Kodak's defense during the initial hearings was that there was vigorous competition in the sale of this equipment; they could not have exerted monopolistic power over the market for service and parts. In a 6-3 decision, the Supreme Court rejected this defense. Writing for the majority, Justice Harry Blackmun concluded that Kodak's tactics did not leave customers free to switch vendors because the overall cost of doing so would have been too high. The case is now scheduled to go to trial. The customers who are bringing the lawsuit are contending that

Kodak's strategy cost them large sums of money, and they are asking for damages.

Regardless of the outcome, the court's decision will set the precedent for future relationships between manufacturers and third-party service companies. A decision against Kodak will mean that big manufacturers will lose much of their power to tie customers into lucrative service and repair contracts; and this end of the business often accounts for a large percentage of profits. For example, in recent years Wang Laboratories made over 40 percent of its $2 billion from service contracts, and other large computer manufacturers have similar percentages. Given that service and repair work often carries a 40 to 50 percent profit margin, the future may be less bright for many firms, depending on the court's decision.

On the other hand, insurance companies will be delighted if Kodak loses because this will weaken the power of the Big Three automakers in the replacement car market; and thus make it cheaper to fix cars that have been damaged in accidents. Such a decision will also be good news for independent auto-parts makers. However, the group that will benefit most will be consumers for whom such a court ruling will mean lower prices for repairs and service in industries dominated by manufacturers.

Source: Tim Smart, Gary McWilliams, and Alice Z. Cuneo, "Kodak Takes a Shot in the Mug," *Business Week*, June 22, 1992, p. 40.

special dietary benefits.[7] The accompanying Ethics Close-Up (Hitting Back at the Big Guy) provides an example of a recent court ruling that may prevent Kodak from cornering the service market for its suppliers.

Robinson-Patman Act   Passed in 1936, the **Robinson-Patman Act** is designed to eliminate unfair price competition. The act prohibits a number of specific pricing practices. One is selling the same product at different prices unless the price differential is based on cost or the need to meet competition. For example, if a manufacturer receives an order from one wholesaler for 1,000 electrical components and a second order from a different wholesaler for 100 electrical components, the manufacturer may charge less per unit for the larger order, because manufacturing, packaging, and shipping big orders cost less per unit. The company may pass on the savings in the form of lower prices. However, if two wholesalers purchase the same number of units, the manufacturer may not charge one more than the other in an effort to drive one out of business or to provide the other with an unfair competitive advantage.

Other treatment must also be evenhanded. The Robinson-Patman Act also forbids sellers from discriminating against customers in interstate commerce by selling basically identical goods but at different prices. Advertising allowances must also be given to all buyers on a proportionately equal basis. If a company that buys $100,000 of merchandise receives $1,000 toward its

Robinson-Patman Act   A federal law designed to eliminate unfair price competition.

local advertising of the products, a firm that buys $50,000 of merchandise is entitled to $500 for local advertising.

The Robinson-Patman Act is regarded as fairly controversial because of the broad powers it gives to the FTC. For example, many economists believe that the act does more to discourage price competition than to eliminate monopolies. This is because the act does not focus enough attention on non-price competition such as the domination of market channels, as is the case with giant goods manufacturers. In any event, the act has made businesspeople acutely aware of the risks involved in unfair price competition.

Celler-Kefauver Antimerger Act   To prohibit mergers and major asset purchases that decrease competition in an industry, Congress passed the **Celler-Kefauver Antimerger Act** in 1950. This law broadened the scope of the Clayton Act, which had limited itself to forbidding companies to acquire the stock of competitive firms for the purpose of preventing competition. The Celler-Kefauver Act extended the prohibition to include mergers and major asset purchases that decrease competition in an industry. It also gave the FTC authority to approve mergers before they take place.

More Recent Regulatory Acts   The 1970s saw the passage of additional antitrust legislation. One was the **Antitrust Procedures and Penalties Act** of 1974, which increased the fines and penalties imposed for violation of the Sherman Act. Under the terms of this law, violation of the Sherman Act could result in a fine up to $100,000 for an individual and $10 million for a corporation. Such a violation was also made a felony and now carries a possible jail sentence of up to 3 years.

In 1976, Congress passed the **Antitrust Improvements Act,** which requires companies planning to merge to notify the FTC in advance and allows injured parties to file lawsuits. This act resulted in a host of suits designed to prevent mergers of firms in unrelated industries, for example, traditional manufacturing firms and high-tech companies, chemical firms and movie studios, and fast-food retailers and transportation companies.

In recent years, there also has been more vigorous enforcement of laws. A good example is the cracking down by the Securities and Exchange Commission (SEC) on insider stock trading by overseas investors.

Regulation of Limited-Entry Industries

At certain times in history, the government has been concerned that too many businesses are unable or unwilling to look after the interests of workers and consumers. Congress has responded by passing laws encouraging companies to make safe products in safe workplaces and to provide accurate product information to consumers. In addition, the government has paid special attention to industries into which there has been limited entry because of size and resource commitments (for example, utilities and communications industries). The accompanying Ethics Close-Up (Ripping Off Phone Customers) provides an example.

Electric and Gas Utilities   Most electric and gas utilities could be called pure or natural monopolies. As discussed in Chapter 2, a pure monopoly is a

Celler-Kefauver Antimerger Act A federal law that prohibits mergers and major asset purchases that decrease competition in an industry.

Antitrust Procedures and Penalties Act A federal law that increases fines and penalties imposed for violation of the Sherman Antitrust Act.

Antitrust Improvements Act A federal law that requires companies planning to merge to notify the FTC in advance and allows injured parties to file lawsuits.

C L O S E - U P / *Ethics*

Ripping Off Phone Customers

Government regulators closely monitor the utility industry to ensure that they do not violate the public trust. The result of one of these recent monitoring efforts has been the charge of the Florida state attorney general that Southern Bell rewarded its salespeople for fraudulent practices. According to the charge, company salespeople signed up hundreds of thousands of Floridians for phone services they never ordered. Southern Bell rewarded its salespeople with color televisions, video games, and Caribbean vacations.

The state attorney general's office alleges that Southern Bell set up boiler-room telemarketing techniques designed to sell customers a wide variety of services such as touch-tone service, call waiting, call forwarding, and speed calling. Southern Bell salespeople admit that in some cases, such services were added to accounts without customer consent. Since these costs are quite low (call waiting is $3.50 a month; call forwarding is $2.45 monthly), many customers did not notice the addi-

tional expenses and simply paid the bill every month. The most common addition to customers' bills was a wire maintenance service charge ($2.50 monthly) which covers repairs to wires and jacks. According to *Consumer Reports* magazine, this service is a waste of money for most people.

Southern Bell salespeople have also been accused of attempting to "bash" customers. This practice consisted of contacting customers who had been overcharged and persuading them to accept less than what was actually owed to them. Still another tactic identified by the state attorney in the charge was the failure to give customers credits when their phones were out of service for more than 24 hours. Such a refund is required by state law.

Southern Bell has denied the last two practices, and claims that it had been cooperating with the state attorney's office from the moment it learned something was amiss. The phone company also announced that it had stopped giving prizes to salespeople and had taken steps to prevent the recurrence of illegal selling practices. However, these statements have not had much influence on the state attorney general, who has filed a $14 million lawsuit against the utility to recover overcharges by the company.

Source: Peter Whoriskey, "State: Bell Rewarded Sales Fraud," *Miami Herald*, July 14, 1992, pp. 1A, 5A.

business that provides services that are impractical to duplicate. For example, Consolidated Edison of New York serves the greater New York metropolitan area; Interstate Power Company supplies power to parts of Iowa, Illinois, Wisconsin, and Minnesota; and Florida Power & Light serves the greater Miami area. It is thought to be cheaper for one large company to provide the energy than to have two power companies serving these areas, because they would unnecessarily duplicate costly power generation and distribution systems and the resulting higher costs would be passed on to the consumers.

However, the existence of pure monopolies eliminates the advantages of competition. For example, the utilities may lack an incentive to keep their rates low. Many people believe that a state or local government agency should monitor the firm and regulate how much it may charge — and this is exactly what happens throughout the country. Besides state and local public utility commissions, the federal government, through the Department of Energy, also oversees utility operations in areas such as preventing potentially catastrophic accidents like the one at the Three Mile Island nuclear power plant in Pennsylvania.

Cable television control room technicians prepare to direct a program. The 1984 Cable Communications Policy Act deregulated the industry, freeing most cable systems from local control over their rates and service. Since then, consumer complaints about the rising cable rates and poor service in some parts of the country have lead Congress to try to re-regulate the industry. Bills to establish legal rates for basic cable service and other regulations are regularly introduced.

Source: Index Stock International.

Communications   Broadcasting is an example of limited entry into the communications industry, because the number of radio and television stations is physically limited. Radio and TV stations are therefore regulated by the Federal Communications Commission (FCC), which Congress originally created to license radio stations and set rates. Today, the FCC also licenses and regulates cable TV networks and ham radio operators.

Deregulation of Industry

Regulation in the United States has tended to occur in waves. For example, the initial procompetition laws were passed around the turn of the century, and many of the major consumer protection laws were passed during the 1930s and 1970s. During the 1980s, the government turned from regulation to deregulation of such businesses as telephone services, the airlines, and banking, as was discussed in earlier chapters.

The debate over the merits of regulation versus deregulation will certainly continue. Some observers contend that many governmental rules and regulations continue to stifle business creativity and growth without providing substantive benefits to the general public. Others are concerned that deregulation has resulted in safety and financial risks and higher consumer

FIGURE 23.1
The Federal Budget Dollar

Where It Comes From...

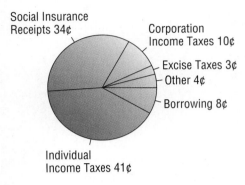

Social Insurance Receipts 34¢

Corporation Income Taxes 10¢

Excise Taxes 3¢
Other 4¢

Borrowing 8¢

Individual Income Taxes 41¢

Where It Goes...

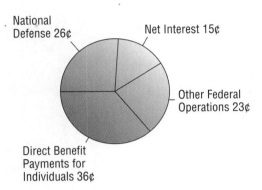

National Defense 26¢

Net Interest 15¢

Other Federal Operations 23¢

Direct Benefit Payments for Individuals 36¢

prices as seen in the airline and banking industries. As a result, the pendulum may swing back toward more regulation in these industries.[8]

1. What are two major laws that ensure competition?
2. Why are utilities subject to greater regulation than most businesses?

CHECK ✓ POINT

Taxation

Besides making and enforcing regulations, government affects business in a fundamental way by collecting money in the form of taxes. Corporations pay taxes themselves, and they withhold taxes from the paychecks of employees and remit these monies to the government. With the passage of the Tax Reform Act of 1986, some major tax law changes began to go into effect. Because of the increasing concern over our huge federal debt, there have been modifications and refinements over the years, and more major changes are sure to be coming.[9] Although the rates and impact will be changing, the types of taxes discussed in the balance of this section will remain the same.

Federal Taxes

The federal government spends billions each year to pay its employees, operate the military, support social security and other programs, pay interest on its debts, and cover a variety of other expenses. While the government currently borrows 8 cents out of every dollar it spends, over half of its income comes from taxes. Figure 23.1 shows the sources and uses of federal funds.

Income Taxes   The largest source of federal revenue is taxes on the income of individuals and corporations. As shown in Figure 23.2, top tax rates for each group have varied throughout this century. Top individual rates have varied from less than 10 percent in the early part of the century to more than

FIGURE 23.2
Top Federal Income Tax Rates

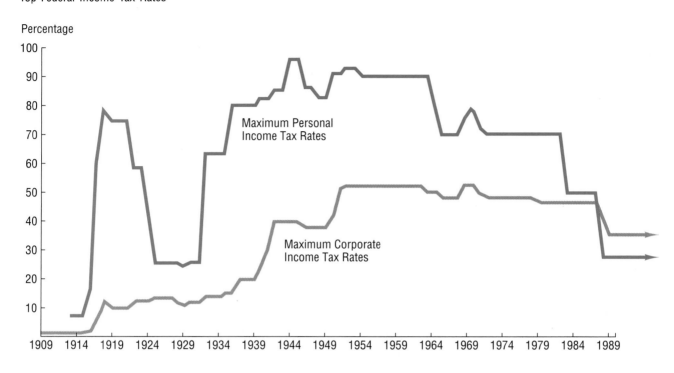

Percentage

90 percent in the mid-1940s to mid-1950s. Top corporate rates have been less than top individual rates, ranging from under 10 percent to slightly over 50 percent.

Congress periodically adjusts tax rates and regulations, not only to alter the amount of revenues, but to set policy as well. For example, the government has a policy of encouraging home ownership, which it carries out by currently allowing individuals to deduct from their taxable income the interest they pay on their mortgage. In the past, the government has encouraged businesses to invest in equipment by allowing them to deduct from their taxes a percentage of the cost of new equipment. The government has also encouraged investment by allowing investors to pay a lower rate on gains from long-term investments than they pay on other income. Congress ended these last two incentives with its 1986 tax law, in order to lower tax rates without reducing total tax receipts. Only time will tell what other changes are made.

As shown in Figure 23.1, the largest source of federal revenue is individual income taxes. These revenues come not only from employees, but also from sole proprietorships and partnerships, which pass their income to the owners for taxation at individual rates. In addition, certain small corporations may choose to be taxed as individuals, in which case they are called S corporations (see Chapter 3). Other corporations pay corporate rates, which are scheduled to run up to 39 percent as of 1991. Whether taxed at individual or corporate rates, all corporations file returns.

The federal income tax on individuals is sometimes referred to as a **progressive tax.** This means that people with low incomes pay tax at a lower rate than people with high incomes. The tax is progressive because it places a greater burden on those presumed to be in a better position to shoulder it. As of 1991, there were three tax brackets, one at 15 percent, one at 28 percent, and one at 31 percent for high-income taxpayers. In the years ahead these rates will be changing.

Progressive tax A tax that charges lower rates to taxpayers with lower incomes.

Excise Taxes The federal government also taxes certain purchases, using an excise tax. An **excise tax** is a levy designed to limit the purchase of goods or to make the users of certain services help pay for them. The excise tax on gasoline does both. It is designed to discourage excessive consumption and to pay for highway and road construction. In contrast, revenues from the excise tax on cigarettes are earmarked for general spending, not specifically for health research and medical care of smokers. Besides generating revenue, the tax provides an incentive to smoke less.

Excise tax A levy designed to limit the purchase of goods or make the users of certain services help pay for them.

Customs Duties In the 1800s, the major source of federal revenue was **customs duties,** taxes levied on imported goods. The importer pays the government a percentage of the value of the goods. Besides generating revenue, duties give a price advantage to American producers. Currently, as evidenced by the huge U.S. trade deficit (imports are greater than exports), duties seem to have little impact on the desire of foreign companies to export their goods and on the desire of Americans to buy them.

Customs duties Taxes levied on imported goods.

State and Local Taxes

State and local governments also use taxes as a source of revenue. Some states and local governments have an income tax. However, the major source of revenue for most state governments is sales taxes, and the major source of revenue for local governments is property taxes.

Income Taxes Most states today assess an income tax. So do many local governments, especially large cities. Often, the state or local income tax is a fixed percentage of income, rather than a progressive tax. In calculating their income for federal income tax, taxpayers may deduct the state and local income taxes they paid for the year.

Sales Taxes Most states and some cities assess sales taxes. A **sales tax** is a levy on specified purchases. The taxing body decides the products on which the sales tax will apply. For example, in the state of Florida, the sales tax on retail goods is 6 percent. This means that a shirt that sells for $20 will cost the consumer $21.20. The retailer collects these taxes and forwards them to the appropriate state agency.

Sales tax A levy on specified purchases.

Some people object to sales taxes because they are a regressive tax. A **regressive tax** is one that hits low-income people harder than high-income people. Anyone who buys a $20 shirt in Florida must pay a $1.20 sales tax, but a rich person can more easily afford this tax. However, a sales tax is one of the easiest ways to raise money. With the federal government reducing the

Regressive tax A tax that hits low-income persons harder than high-income persons.

funds it sends to the states and the costs of state governments continuing to increase, most states will undoubtedly continue to assess and even increase sales taxes.

Often people are less aware of the effect of the sales tax on their pocketbook than they are of the impact of income taxes, because they pay sales tax a little at a time but see their total income tax when they file each spring. Also, under current tax laws taxpayers are not able to deduct sales taxes from their taxable federal income, which will in effect increase the bite that sales taxes take out of their gross income.

Property Taxes   Local governments turn to property taxes for revenue. A **property tax** is a levy based on the assessed value of a piece of real estate. A tax assessor estimates the value of the property, and the tax is a proportion of that amount. If a house is assessed at $150,000 and the tax levy is $2.50 per $100, then the owner must pay $3,750 in property taxes ($150,000 ÷ $100 = 1,500; $1,500 × $2.50 = $3,750). The same approach is used in taxing office buildings, hotels, condominiums, and apartment buildings. Property taxes are deductible from income in the calculation of federal income tax.

A property tax is an example of a **proportional tax,** a tax in which the rate remains the same regardless of the base. If the house in the example above were to double in value over the next 5 years, the yearly tax bill would grow to $7,500.

Property tax   A levy based on the assessed value of a piece of real estate.

Proportional tax   A tax in which the rate remains the same regardless of the base.

CHECK ✓ POINT

1.   What are three federal taxes?
2.   What are the major sources of revenue for state and local governments?

Business Law

Every day businesses and their employees undertake activities governed by laws. Most businesspeople are not, and need not be, lawyers, but they do need a fundamental understanding of business law.

Sources of Law
In the United States, law arises from federal and state constitutions, federal and state statutes, administrative regulations, and court precedent. The U.S. Constitution is the highest law in the land; all other laws must be consistent with it. Each state has its own constitution, and the laws of the state are subject to its constitution.

The Congress of the United States and the state legislatures have the power to enact laws consistent with the Constitution. Together these laws form **statutory law.** These statutes may grant various administrative bodies the power to enact regulations, which retain the force of law, subject to legislative revision. Statutes and administrative regulations are sometimes called written law, because they are created as written documents.

Many businesses conduct their activities across state boundaries and therefore must keep up with the statutory law of various states. To simplify this, most states have adopted uniform codes governing a variety of activities. Of particular interest to business is the **Uniform Commercial Code (UCC),** which is a set of statutes that govern the legal dealings of business.

Statutory law   Law enacted by Congress and the state legislatures.

Uniform Commercial Code (UCC)   A set of statutes that govern the legal dealings of business.

Because legal considerations affect so many aspects of business, companies often hire experts in the law. This paralegal on the staff of Ohio Bell is gathering data in the law library of the Cuyahoga County courthouse. The legal department at Ohio Bell handles about 500 cases a year. Many of the cases are defenses against claims of personal injury or damage to property.

Source: Courtesy of Ohio Bell, an Ameritech Company.

The UCC has been adopted in its entirety by all states except Louisiana, which has adopted about half of it. The UCC covers a number of important areas of business law, including sales, commercial paper, bank deposits and collections, letters of credit, and investment securities.

Courts in the United States also rely on **common law,** the precedents established by prior court decisions, going back to English law. (However, reflecting that state's French heritage, Louisiana courts follow the Napoleonic Code instead.) Common law is sometimes called unwritten law, even though court decisions are recorded, to differentiate it from the documents of statutes and regulations. Today, statutes cover most areas of law, but judges rely on common law for guidance in interpreting statutes.

Common law The precedents established by prior court decisions, going back to English law.

Contract Law

The branch of business law that governs most transactions is contract law. A **contract** is a legally binding promise. The promise stipulates that something shall or shall not happen. For example, a sporting goods manufacturer may promise to deliver 100 football helmets in exchange for $50 each, and a university may promise to deliver a check for $5,000 in exchange for 100 helmets. The same manufacturer might promise to pay a refuse collector for its services and also promise to refrain from hiring any other refuse collector that year, no matter how much refuse needs to be removed.

Contract A legally binding promise.

Forming a Contract To form a contract, at least one of the parties must make a promise. In many cases, good business practice is to put contracts in writing to make sure that both sides exactly understand the terms and conditions of the agreement. A clear understanding at the outset can prevent lawsuits later. If a lawsuit does arise, a written contract can make the conflict easier to resolve. Moreover, the law requires that contracts for the following transactions must be in writing:

- The sale of real estate
- The sale of goods valued at $500 or more
- Acts that will be performed one year or more after the contract is made
- The assumption of another person's financial obligation
- A promise made in contemplation of marriage

Most contracts are for such routine or immediate transactions that they are unwritten. The time and effort required to draw up formal written contracts does not justify the benefits to be gained. Often the contract is oral. For example, when a company calls up a regular supplier and orders ten boxes of computer paper to be delivered later that day, the company and the supplier have entered into an oral contract. A contract may even be formed by a person's actions. If you drive into a gas station, fill up your car, and hand the attendant $15, you have entered into a sales contract without saying a word. Your action of filling up the gas tank implied a promise to pay.

Express contract One in which the parties make oral or written promises.

Implied contract One created by the actions of one or more parties.

Types of Contracts Depending on how the contract is formed, it may be express or implied. An **express contract** is one in which the parties make oral or written promises. Contracts involving important dealings should always be express contracts. An **implied contract** is one created by the actions of one or more parties. For example, when people eat in a restaurant, the restaurant implies a promise that the food is fit for consumption. If a diner were to become sick from food poisoning, the restaurant would be responsible. Similarly, the diners imply that they will pay for the meal.

Conditions of an Enforceable Contract Any promise may form the basis of a contract, but not all promises are enforceable in court. Several conditions must be present to make a contract legally enforceable. The contract must be based on a voluntary agreement between competent parties exchanging consideration for the performance of a lawful act.

A contract requires a voluntary agreement, or meeting of the minds. The parties must agree on the specific terms. For example, if a seller says, "I will sell you this shirt for $20 right now," the buyer must realize that there is a time limit. The customer cannot return a week later and legally hold the seller to the $20 price. Nor can the buyer accept by saying, "I'll give you $18." Proposing a different price is making a counteroffer. If the seller accepts the counteroffer, then an agreement exists. The parties to a contract must also enter into the agreement voluntarily. If someone is threatened into signing a contract, the courts will not uphold it.

All parties to a legal agreement must be competent to contract. Convicts, persons under the influence of alcohol, and people suffering from severe mental illness are not regarded as legally competent. Neither are minors, which is why many stores or car dealers refuse to sell expensive merchandise to minors unless their parents also participate in the agreement. The minor may be able to set aside the contract, return the merchandise, and ask for a full refund.

For a contract to be binding, consideration must be present. Consideration is something of value given in exchange for something else. For example, a business owner might give a real estate developer a $1,000 deposit on a parcel of land in return for the seller's promise to hold the land for 10 days while the business owner lines up the necessary financing. The $1,000 is consideration given in exchange for the promise not to sell the lot during the 10-day period.

To be enforceable, a contract must have a lawful purpose. An agreement in which a company promises to pay a competitor's employee to steal trade secrets is not legally binding. If the employee took the money without providing any secrets, the company could not sue to recover the money. Similarly, financial contracts that specify payment of interest at rates higher than those permitted by law are unenforceable. The courts typically require the borrower to repay the loan but not the interest. This condition of enforceability means that changes in the law may result in changes in contracts.

If the law requires that a contract be in writing, this is a necessary condition of enforceability. For example, a buyer could not enforce an oral contract to sell real estate.

Breach of Contract   If one of the parties fails to perform according to the terms of the agreement, this person has caused a breach of contract. When a party breaches an enforceable contract, the other party may sue to recover damages or to obtain specific performance.

Many problems can cause a breach of contract, including financial setbacks that make it too costly to continue with the agreement, and the decision to walk away from the agreement because it is not financially rewarding. For example, during the recession of the early 1980s, some owners of shopping centers found that the costs of operating the center exceeded revenues. The owners told their banks that they would discontinue running the center and would make no further payments on their outstanding loan. The banks stepped in, sold the shopping center, and, when the proceeds did not satisfy the mortgage on the property, sued the previous owners for the remainder of the debt. The owners, in essence, just walked away from their contracts with the banks.

In this case, the banks were the **plaintiffs** — the party that brought the legal action. The **defendant** is the party against whom a legal action is brought.

Plaintiff The party that brings a legal action.

Defendant The party against whom a legal action is brought.

Statute of Limitations   In cases of breach of contract, the plaintiff is restricted by the **statute of limitations.** This is the law that specifies the time period during which a wronged person may sue. After this statutory period, the defendant is protected from legal action.

Statute of limitations The law that specifies the time period during which a wronged person may sue.

Sales Law

All businesses enter into contracts to buy or sell. Therefore businesspeople must be familiar with **sales law,** which involves the sale of goods for cash or

Sales law The branch of law that involves the sale of goods for cash or credit.

FIGURE 23.3
An Express Warranty

Source: Courtesy of Whirlpool Corporation.

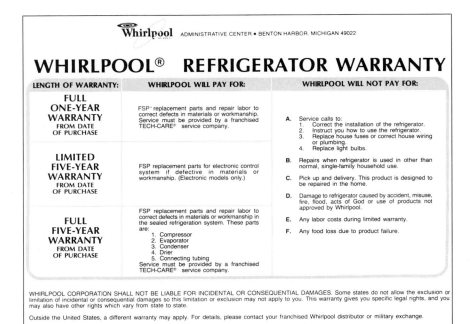

credit. This law is exclusively concerned with transactions involving tangible property such as machinery, materials, supplies, or equipment.

Article 2 of the Uniform Commercial Code (UCC) covers sales contracts. For example, it spells out when sales contracts need to be in writing and provides for remedies should one or more parties fail to carry out the agreement. Article 2 also gives buyers the right to accept, reject, and inspect merchandise for sale. Finally, Article 2 addresses the use of warranties. A **warranty** is a guarantee.

Warranties may be express or implied. An **express warranty** is a guarantee offered orally or in writing. Figure 23.3 shows an example. By reading the warranty, the buyer is able to determine what guarantees the seller is making. An **implied warranty** is a guarantee that automatically accompanies the sale of a product. For example, products for sale are presumed to be safe for their intended use. General Motors does not need to provide an express warranty that its new cars are safe. This guarantee is implied by the fact that the firm has offered the autos for sale. Some companies such as G. D. Searle, a large pharmaceutical firm, have gone a step further. They now offer guarantees on all of their drug products. If customers find the drug ineffective or that it has any unpleasant side effects, they need only fill out a card, attach the sales receipt, and Searle will refund the money.

Negotiable Instruments

In completing sales transactions, businesses use negotiable instruments. A **negotiable instrument** is a form of business paper that can be transferred

Warranty A guarantee.

Express warranty A guarantee offered orally or in writing.

Implied warranty A guarantee that automatically accompanies the sale of a product.

Negotiable instrument A form of business paper that can be transferred from one person to another as a substitute for money.

FIGURE 23.4
Basic Forms of Endorsement

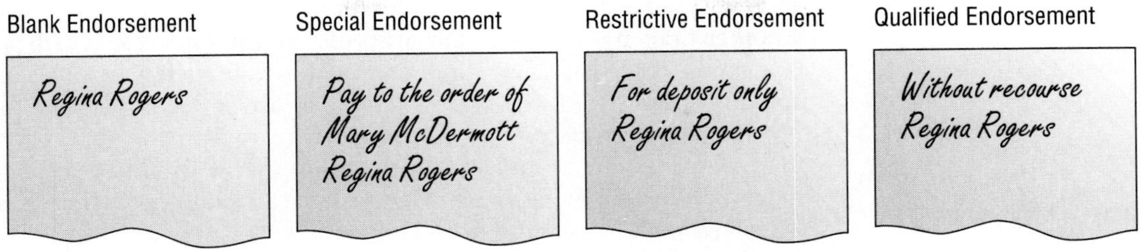

Blank Endorsement	Special Endorsement	Restrictive Endorsement	Qualified Endorsement
Regina Rogers	Pay to the order of Mary McDermott Regina Rogers	For deposit only Regina Rogers	Without recourse Regina Rogers

from one person to another as a substitute for money. The most common example of a negotiable instrument is a check. Negotiable instruments facilitate the transfer of funds and make it easier to consummate business deals.

The value of negotiable instruments is in their negotiability, or transferability. To be negotiable, the instrument must meet certain criteria:

- The instrument must be in writing and signed by the payer.
- It must contain an unconditional promise to pay a specific amount of money. An instrument that says "pay John upon delivery of my car" would not be negotiable, because the promise is conditional and the amount is not specified.
- The instrument must be payable on demand or at a specific future date. A check may be cashed on or after the date entered on it.
- The instrument must be payable to bearer on order. Most checks say "Pay to the order of _____," meaning that only the person named may use it. If a check says only "Pay to _____," then anyone who has it (the bearer) may receive payment.
- The payee, or recipient of the payment, must be indicated with reasonable certainty.

Properly filling out a standard check form creates a negotiable instrument.

To transfer the rights to a negotiable instrument, the payee endorses it. In the case of a check, the payee typically endorses it by signing it on the back. The endorsement is often designed to transfer to the bank the right to collect on it and deposit funds in the payee's account. The type of endorsement used determines the specific rights transferred. Figure 23.4 shows the basic types of endorsement.

As shown, a blank endorsement is simply the owner's signature at the top of the reverse side of a negotiable instrument. If you lose a check with a blank endorsement, anyone can cash it. That is why a restrictive endorsement, which specifies how the instrument may be used, is safer. A special endorsement specifies the person to whom the instrument is being transferred, and a qualified endorsement sets forth conditions on the transfer of the instrument. The most common wording on a qualified endorsement is "without recourse," which means that the endorser does not accept liability for payment of the instrument. For example, someone who accepts an instrument with the qualified endorsement of "without recourse" agrees not to pursue the endorser if the account has insufficient funds to cover the check.

Property Law

Property law The branch of law that involves the rights and duties associated with the ownership or use of real or personal property.

Another branch of law that concerns sales is property law, which addresses ownership as well as sales. More precisely, **property law** involves the rights and duties associated with the ownership or use of real or personal property.

Real property Land and property attached to land.

Land and property attached to land are **real property.** The property must be permanently attached in the sense that it would be difficult to remove or that removing it would destroy it. Examples include a house, a factory, a warehouse, and a parking lot.

Deed A document that establishes property ownership and is transferable to other parties.

The instrument that conveys ownership of real property is typically a deed. A **deed** is a document that establishes property ownership and is transferable to other parties. The owner of real property may also grant use of the property by renting it. Small and medium-sized enterprises and businesses in major metropolitan areas often find it more economical to rent than to own property. The tenant signs a **lease,** a document that allows the tenant to use the owner's property for a predetermined time period in exchange for consideration (a rental fee).

Lease A document that allows the tenant to use the owner's property for a predetermined time period in exchange for consideration.

Any property that is not real property is **personal property.** Furniture, videocassette recorders, personal computers, and pencils are all examples of personal property. So are stock and bond certificates. Personal property may be tangible or intangible. Tangible personal property consists of physical items such as equipment and inventory. Intangible personal property is property whose ownership is represented by a document or written instrument. For example, a person with a $500 check has a valuable property but the value is contained in what the check represents ($500 in cash) rather than what the check is (a mere piece of paper). Mortgages, stock certificates, and trademarks are also examples of intangible personal property.

Personal property Any property that is not real property.

Understanding the difference between real and personal property is important because the laws and practices for transferring the two often differ. In addition, a businessperson buying or selling real estate, such as an office building, needs to know what items are real property and are therefore automatically included in the sale.

Patent, Trademark, and Copyright Law

Certain intangible property — patents, trademarks, and copyrights — provides its owner with protection from competition. To promote fair competition, a body of law protects owners' rights in these intangible assets.[10]

Patent A federal government grant of exclusive control over and use of a discovery or a new product or process for 17 years.

Patents Developing a new product or manufacturing process often takes enormous amounts of time and money. Few businesses would bother with research if any competitor could immediately put the new idea to use. Thus an inventor with a new idea obtains a **patent,** a federal government grant of exclusive control over and use of a discovery or a new product or process. The U.S. Patent Office protects inventions for 17 years. The patent owner may manufacture the product exclusively or may sell other firms a license to use the patent.

An applicant for a patent must demonstrate that the discovery is indeed new. Howard Head, famous for his invention of metal skis, later developed the now popular oversized tennis racket, the Prince. Initially, the government claimed he had not developed anything new — tennis rackets have been around for centuries. However, Head showed the patent office that the "sweet spot" (the part of the racket head used for returning a volley) on this racket was much larger than that on any conventional-sized racquet. The patent office then awarded him the legal right he sought. Within 5 years, the Prince oversized racket had become the best-selling racket in the United States.

Trademark   **A trademark** is a word or symbol used to distinguish a company's products. To protect the trademark from use or exploitation by others, the company must register it with the federal government and renew it every 20 years.[11] In some cases, a trademark is a brand name such as Cadillac, Polaroid, or Excedrin. In other cases, it includes a logo such as McDonald's golden arches or Apple Computer's apple. Companies must protect their trademarks, because they will lose their exclusive right if the trademark becomes generic, describing a class of products rather than that of a particular company. For example, see the discussion of trademarks in Chapter 15.

Copyright   The contents of creative works such as books and compact discs varies because each new release is a unique endeavor requiring an investment of time and talent. A **copyright** is a legal protection of a particular work that allows its owner the exclusive right to reproduce, sell, and adapt the work. Copyrights protect literary and intellectual works such as books, magazines, plays, musicals, movies, videotapes, and computer software. The owner of the copyright registers this right by filing with the U.S. Copyright Office. Copyrights obtained before 1977 last 75 years, provided they are renewed before the end of the initial 28-year period. Subsequent copyrights last for the lifetime of the creator plus 50 years. It is up to the owner of the copyright to protect this right, going to court if necessary.

One of the most common copyright infringements is unauthorized photocopying of materials. Ready access to photocopiers makes it easy and inexpensive to copy parts of or entire books and magazine articles. As a result of recent lawsuits, however, many companies and universities now restrict the use of photocopying in order to protect themselves from possible legal entanglements.

Some foreign countries have no copyright agreement with the United States or are very lax about it. As a result, publishers in those countries often translate and sell American textbooks without paying the American authors or publishers for the right to do so. Both authors of this text have experienced this problem firsthand. On a trip to Korea, Professor Luthans met numerous Korean professors who told him how much they and their students enjoyed using one of his textbooks, from which he had never received royalties. Professor Hodgetts was equally surprised when he recently received a copy of a book he had written that had been translated into Chinese for use at the University of Beijing. He had never received royalt̶ ̶ ̶ ̶ ̶ ̶ ̶he book. Inside the front cover, the translator had autographed th̶ ̶ ̶ ̶ ̶ ̶ ̶ked whether he had written any other texts that could also ̶ ̶ ̶ ̶ ̶ Chinese!

Trademark   A word or symbol used to distinguish a company's products.

Copyright   A legal protection of a particular work that allows its owner the exclusive right to reproduce, sell, and adapt the work.

This basket of fruit combined with the name *Welch's* is the trademark of Welch Foods Inc., a cooperative. The trademark shows that the company's products are based on fruit and uses the company's widely recognized, longstanding brand name.

Source: Courtesy of Welch's.

Agency Law

Some dimensions of business law emphasize relationships between people rather than property rights. An important legal relationship is that of agency. An **agency** in business law is a legal relationship between an agent and a principal. An **agent** is a person authorized to act on behalf of another. A **principal** is a person represented by an agent. When an agent acts within the sphere of his or her agency responsibility, the principal is bound by those actions. Consequently, an agency relationship is one of trust. Any agent therefore owes the principal certain duties: care, obedience, accounting, and loyalty. This means that the agent must act carefully and follow instructions, must keep the principal informed about money and other matters, and must act in the best interests of the principal. The principal must compensate the agent and should be sure that the agent understands his or her duties.

Agents are important to business because they are a way to delegate authority. For example, a company may empower an attorney to enter into contracts for the firm. After hammering out an agreement, the attorney can commit the company to the contract. Businesses also authorize sales and purchasing agents to bind the company to sales contracts.

If agents exceed their authority, the enterprise can find itself embroiled in serious problems. If agents commit an illegal or harmful act while representing a company, they may be held liable for the act. For example, even though it may be unaware of the activity, a firm can find itself in trouble when an employee makes unauthorized sales to an unfriendly country. Principals must keep a careful eye on agents to make sure they are fulfilling their duties to the principal.

Tort Law

Not every right and duty arises from a formal contract, as the discussion of agency showed. In fact, the law recognizes that people inherently have certain rights, such as freedom from injury and the right to possess property. An infringement of another person's inherent right that injures or damages that person is a **tort** (once a synonym for a wrong). For example, someone who punches or threatens another person is committing a tort. So is someone who steals or interferes with contractual relations.

Sometimes one person injures or damages another unintentionally. For example, another student might walk off with your textbook, thinking it was his or her own. Carelessness that leads to an injury is called negligence. Tort law covers both intentional tort and negligence. Therefore, the following examples fall within the bounds of tort law:

- The driver of a company truck loses control of the vehicle and strikes a pedestrian.
- A security officer arrests a suspected shoplifter after wrestling the alleged offender to the ground, but the person turns out to be innocent of the charge.
- A key financial officer absconds with $500,000 of the company's money.

An area of tort la[w] [th]at is becoming increasingly important to business is that of product lia[bility] [m]entioned in Chapter 22 in the discussion of product liability insu[rance.] [Year]s ago, the courts established that a company was

---

Agency A legal relationship between an agent and a principal.

Agent A person authorized to act on behalf of another.

Principal A person represented by an agent.

Tort An infringement of a person's inherent right that injures or damages that person.

liable for the products it manufactured. In more recent years, this responsibility has been extended through the use of **strict product liability,** which holds that people or businesses are responsible for their acts, regardless of their intentions or degree of negligence. This means that even if a company tries very hard to make the best and safest product possible, if the product causes an injury, the company is still responsible. Consumers can now sue a manufacturer under this law if they can prove the following conditions: the product was defective; the defect caused the product to be unreasonably dangerous; and the defect was the probable cause of their injury. Companies can be found guilty of product liability even if they were not negligent or were unaware that the product was dangerous.[12]

Court cases illustrate the seriousness of product liability. In one of the most famous product liability cases to date, Ford Motor was charged with reckless homicide in the death of three young women who were burned to death in a Ford Pinto. The charge was that the company knew of the hazards of the car's design and did nothing about them. While the court found the company not guilty, the case helped show manufacturers how serious an area of concern product liability has become. Another example is the tragedy of the space shuttle *Challenger*. The families of some of the crew members have brought lawsuits against the designers and manufacturers of the shuttle's defective O-rings, which, along with mismanagement, have been implicated in the explosion.

In addition to manufacturers being liable for product defects, service firms such as banks are also beginning to be sued by unsatisfied customers. For example, a company that went broke sued their banker (who had given advice on how to avoid a hostile takeover) for negligence.[13]

Bankruptcy Law

Huge lawsuits, poor sales, and economic slumps are among the problems that have made some businesses unable to pay their debts and continue operating. **Bankruptcy law** specifies the legal steps for securing relief from debts. This law establishes procedures to protect an individual or business that cannot meet its financial obligations. The Bankruptcy Reform Act of 1978, as amended in 1984, spells out these procedures in three of the act's chapters: liquidation (Chapter 7 of the act), repayment (Chapter 13), and reorganization (Chapter 11).

Liquidation One approach (Chapter 7) to bankruptcy is **liquidation,** which is the sale of all assets to meet outstanding debts. Liquidation is often referred to as "straight" bankruptcy, because individuals or firms use it when they simply are unable to continue. A person who makes $30,000 a year and has debts of $600,000 will typically choose liquidation, because there is no way that person can hope to repay such a large debt. The best approach is to wipe the slate clean and start over again. When the court judges a person bankrupt, the person is relieved of all outstanding financial obligations.

The decision to declare bankruptcy is often, but not always, voluntary. A voluntary bankruptcy is a legal proceeding brought by an individual or business that is unable to meet its financial obligations. An involuntary bankruptcy is a legal proceeding brought by creditors against an insolvent debtor. The creditors try to force the debtor to liquidate his or her assets and pay

Strict product liability The principle that people or businesses are responsible for their acts, regardless of their intentions or degree of negligence.

Bankruptcy law The branch of law that specifies the legal steps for securing relief from debts.

Liquidation The sale of all assets to meet outstanding debts.

them their money. If the debtor has three or more creditors with total unsecured claims of $5,000 or more, the creditors may join together and file the petition. If the debtor has fewer than 12 creditors, one or more creditors with a claim of at least $5,000 may bring the involuntary bankruptcy action. If the debtor challenges these claims, the court will hear both sides and decide whether the bankruptcy proceeding may continue.

If the court rules that the individual or company is bankrupt, it appoints a trustee to preside over the debtor's property. The trustee administers the assets or operates the business during bankruptcy proceedings. If the assets are eventually sold, the Bankruptcy Act exempts certain property, including the following:

- Up to $7,500 in equity in a home and burial plot
- Equity of up to $1,200 in a motor vehicle
- Up to $200 each for household goods and furnishings, such as clothing, appliances, books, and so forth (recent amendments, however, limit the aggregate total of all items to $4,000)
- Up to $500 of jewelry
- Any other property up to a total of $400
- Up to $750 in tools of the person's trade

In dividing up the assets, the court begins by allowing creditors with secured claims to repossess the collateral that backed up their claim. Any remaining funds then go to pay creditors who have unsecured claims, in this order:

1. The cost of the bankruptcy case
2. Business claims that arose after the bankruptcy proceedings began
3. Employee wages, salaries, and commissions up to a limit of $2,000 per person
4. Claims for contributions to employee benefit plans
5. Claims by creditors who have purchased products that have not been delivered, up to $900 per claimant
6. Federal and state taxes

Repayment   Sometimes a person who is bankrupt can pay off the debts if given some time to do so. Repayment arrangements under Chapter 13 typically involve suspending interest on the debts and putting the bankrupt person on some type of repayment schedule. Individuals with a regular income, those with unsecured debts of less than $100,000, and those with secured debts of less than $350,000 can use this approach. Many creditors will go along with the plan because this is the only practical and realistic way of getting paid.

Reorganization   Corporations often file for Chapter 11 reorganization rather than liquidation. For example, in Texaco's court problems with Pennzoil over the attempted purchase of Getty Oil, the judgments against Texaco eventually forced it to file for Chapter 11 reorganization to set in motion the biggest case in bankruptcy-law history. Under this form of bankruptcy, the creditors and the debtor prepare a plan under which the debtor will pay a portion of the debts and is discharged from the remainder. The company continues to operate as usual. If the court finds that the management is grossly incompetent, it will appoint a trustee to run the company. Large firms whose liquidation would cause a hardship for many people are often allowed to reorganize rather than to liquidate.

CHECK ✓ POINT

1. What are two sources of law?
2. What are some legal obligations that are not spelled out in contracts?

Closing Comments

Business and the government influence one another in many ways — through laws, through taxes, through political influence, and through the exchange of goods and services. The government tries to protect business and consumers by ensuring fair trade and competition. Businesses must abide by laws governing contracts, negotiable instruments, property, patents, trademarks, copyrights, agency, torts, and bankruptcy. These laws are designed to ensure equity and honesty, not only for the general public, but for business itself.

VIDEO CASE / *The Third Major Political Party*

The Japanese lobby is the largest in Washington. This lobby spends over $100 million a year to hire 1,000 Washington, D.C., lobbyists who are superlawyers, former high-ranking public officials, public relations specialists, political advisors, and even past U.S. presidents. Another $300 million is spent on a nationwide grass roots political network for influencing public opinion; and another $400 million goes into political campaigns for advancing Japanese economic interests. The amount of money spent annually on political activity in the United States by the Japanese government and Japanese business firms is equal to that spent by all of the Democrats and Republicans in both houses of Congress in an election year. This has led some people to call the Japanese lobby the third major political party in America.

What does this lobbying effort get for the Japanese? For one thing it helps ensure them favorable trade legislation. For another, it lets them know what is happening on Capitol Hill. In fact, the Japanese have commissioned a study of the role and career patterns of the 30,000 people in Washington who serve as congressional and administrative aids. These staff people have great influence on the legislators and the Japanese want to keep track of them, know how to influence them, and learn how to get information from them. Is this intelligence network effective? There is evidence that it is. For example, a week before Carla Hills was named U.S. trade representative to Tokyo, Japanese officials knew about it, and 2 days before the American announcement Japanese papers had already broken the story to their readers.

Those who question the Japanese lobby point out that between 1973 and 1990 one-third of the principal trade officials in the Office of the U.S. Trade Representative left to become registered foreign agents, in many cases going to work for Japanese firms. This includes 15 assistants to the President of the United States, 9 representatives, 6 senators, 4 retired generals, and a chairman and a vice chairman of the U.S. International Trade Commission.

Should something be done to regulate lobbyists? Some experts believe the first step must be to slow up the revolving door that people are taking to move from top positions in the U.S. government to lobbyists for a foreign company or country. A "cooling off" period of one year was recently enacted by Congress, but some believe that a 5- to 10-year period would be a more substantial safeguard of public interest. Another suggestion is to have all foreign agents — lobbyists, journalists, public relations advisors, lawyers — provide full disclosure to the Justice Department. A third possibility is to prohibit foreign companies from participating in and contributing to U.S. elections. Some feel that the existing Corrupt Foreign Practices Act should be complemented with a Corrupt Domestic Practices Act. As one observer recently noted about the current lobbying situation in Washington, "It goes on because Americans tolerate it. Americans are the only ones who can stop it."

Source: Pat Choate, *Agents of Change* (New York: Alfred A. Knopf, 1990); and Pat Choate, "Political Advantage: Japan's Campaign for America," *Harvard Business Review*, September–October 1990, 87–103.

Case Questions

1. In what way do lobbyists such as those who work for the Japanese get around the Sherman Antitrust Act?
2. How do lobbying efforts undermine organizations such as the Federal Trade Commission?
3. What types of changes are needed in lobbying regulations in order to ensure a more equal balance of power between business and government?

Learning Objectives Revisited

1. **Describe the major laws that regulate business and ensure competition.** The Sherman Antitrust Act outlaws all agreements created for the purpose of restraining trade in interstate commerce. The Clayton Act outlaws tying agreements and interlocking directorates. The Federal Trade Commission Act established the Federal Trade Commission (FTC). The Robinson-Patman Act forbits types of unfair price competition. The Celler-Kefauver Act prohibits anticompetitive mergers. The Antitrust Procedures and Penalties Act increased penalties imposed for violating the Sherman Act. The Antitrust Improvements Act requires merging companies to notify the FTC in advance and allows injured parties to sue.

2. **Identify the major types of federal, state, and local taxes.** The major types of taxes levied at the federal level are individual and corporate income taxes, excise taxes, and customs duties. The major taxes assessed at the state and local levels are income taxes, sales taxes, and property taxes.

3. **Present the major dimensions of contract and sales law.** A contract is a legally binding promise. The promise may be expressed in words or implied by actions. For a contract to be enforceable, the parties must reach a voluntary agreement, they must all be competent to contract, consideration must be involved, and the contract's purpose must be lawful. In some cases, the agreement must be in writing. Sales law specifies when sales contracts must be in writing and what the buyer's rights are. It also addresses the use of warranties. An express warranty is a guarantee offered orally or in writing. An implied warranty is a guarantee such as the assurance of safety that automatically accompanies the sale of a product.

4. **Discuss negotiable instruments and property law.** A negotiable instrument is a form of business paper that people can transfer as a substitute for money. The payee transfers the instrument by endorsing it. Property law addresses the ownership and transfer of real and personal property. Real property consists of land and the things attached to it. Personal property is all other property. It includes intangible property such as patents, trademarks, and copyrights, which are governed by additional laws.

5. **Explain the responsibilities under agency and tort law.** Agency law governs the actions of agents—persons authorized to act on behalf of another (the principal)—and their principals. Agents owe the principal the duties of care, obedience, accounting, and loyalty. Principals should keep track of agents to make sure that they are fulfilling their responsibilities fully and behaving appropriately. A principal may be held liable for the unlawful acts of an agent. Tort law addresses breaches of duties held generally in the absence of a contract. This law addresses both intentional tort and negligence.

6. **Relate the different ways of handling bankruptcy.** One approach to bankruptcy is liquidation—selling all assets and paying debts with the proceeds. In voluntary bankruptcy, the debtor initiates this legal proceeding. An involuntary bankruptcy is a legal proceeding initiated by creditors. In some cases, the debtor will follow a repayment procedure, which involves repaying creditors on some type of schedule. Corporations also have the option of filing for reorganization rather than liquidation. Under Chapter 11 reorganization, the debtor pays a portion of the debt and is discharged from the remainder.

Key Terms Reviewed

Review the following terms. For any that you do not know or are unsure of, look up the definitions and see how they were used in the chapter.

Sherman Antitrust Act
Clayton Act
interlocking directorate
Federal Trade Commission Act
Robinson-Patman Act
Celler-Kefauver Antimerger Act
Antitrust Procedures and Penalties Act
Antitrust Improvements Act
progressive tax
excise tax
customs duties
sales tax
regressive tax
property tax

proportional tax
statutory law
Uniform Commercial Code (UCC)
common law
contract
express contract
implied contract
plaintiff
defendant
statute of limitations
sales law
warranty
express warranty
implied warranty
negotiable instrument

property law
real property
deed
lease
personal property
patent
trademark
copyright
agency
agent
principal
tort
strict product liability
bankruptcy law
liquidation

Review Questions

1. A large group of investors is planning to start a company that will make and sell snowblowers. So far, they have lined up $1.5 million in start-up financing. However, they are worried about how they will be able to compete with Toro. They are considering a scheme, proposed by one of the investors, in which they will ask some of Toro's board of directors to serve on the board of their company, in exchange for shares of stock. These directors would be interested in their company and would therefore give them tips on how to compete with Toro. What federal law addresses this arrangement? How does the law apply?

2. What is the role of the Federal Trade Commission?

3. Why are electric utilities regulated? Why are broadcasters regulated but not newspapers and magazines?

4. What is the major source of tax revenue for the federal government? For the state and local governments?

5. What general objectives does Congress try to meet by adjusting tax rates and regulations?

6. Identify one progressive tax and one regressive tax. What was your basis for selecting these taxes?

7. Who pays customs duties?

8. The Knapps have learned that their home has just been reassessed at $95,000. The tax rate for their suburb is $1.50 per $100 of assessed value. Last year they paid $8,000 in income taxes. How much do they own in property taxes this year?

9. What are the major sources of law in the United States?

10. Which of the following are enforceable contracts? Explain your reasoning.
    a. Two adults arrive at an oral agreement to sell a parcel of real estate for $87,500.
    b. Two workers on their lunch break enter a restaurant and order hamburgers with grilled onions.
    c. When he turns 16, Phil buys a CD player on a deferred-payment plan. Five years later, Lucille tricks Phil into signing an agreement to sell his CD player to her for $5.

11. A cleaning company in Des Moines signs a contract in which it agrees to provide window-cleaning services for an office building in the city. Why might the cleaning company's lawyer need to be familiar with Iowa's statute of limitations?

12. To reduce the company's risk of liability, the managers of Grand Furniture Company have decided

that in the future Grand's furniture will carry no warranties, express or implied. Can the company do this? If so, how? If not, why not?

13. What criteria make business paper negotiable?

14. Which of the following are real property? Which are personal property?
    a. Trees growing in a lot
    b. Lumber in a lumberyard
    c. Lumber constructed into a house

15. What is the difference between a patent and a copyright?

16. Why do agents have special duties to the principal? What are those duties? Considering the risk that an agent may violate those duties, why do businesses use agents?

17. If you were a judge, would you impose stricter penalties for intentional torts or for negligence? Why?

18. If you burn yourself on your toaster, what do you have to demonstrate in order to win a lawsuit based on strict product liability? (Of course, any damages you could win would likely fall far short of the court costs.) Do these requirements seem fair to you? Why or why not?

Applied Exercise

For each of the following situations, decide whether the action described is legal.

1. Barry's professor assigned an article from a business journal to be read by next week. Barry has gone to the library and photocopied the article without getting permission from the publisher. Is this a violation of the publisher's copyright?

2. Frances would like all of the people in her department to read a new book on effective sales techniques. She has no budget for purchasing enough books for each of them, but she does have an unlimited budget for copying. She has her secretary make 30 copies of the book and distributes them to her staff. Is this a violation of the publisher's copyright?

3. George recently attended an auction and bought a painting for $2,000. He was convinced that the painting had been mislabeled and was not the work of a minor artist but that of a famous 18th century artist. George estimated that the painting was worth at least $50,000. George then had the painting appraised by an art expert and learned that it was indeed the work of a minor artist and was worth around $1,700. George showed the painting to Mark, who also believed that the work was worth $50,000. George sold it to him for $45,000, but Mark has now learned that the painting is worth very little and he has been duped by George. Can Mark have the contract set aside and get his money back?

4. Roberta, a minor, purchased a VCR from a local dealer. The terms of the sale were "cash and no returns allowed." When she arrived at home with the machine, Roberta learned that her parents had just bought her a VCR for her birthday. If Roberta returns the machine to the dealer, can she get her money back?

5. Richard has been offered $5,000 if he will make a copy of his company's bid to sell computer equipment to the county. Richard does so and gives the information to John, whose company then underbids Richard's firm and wins a $1.5 million contract. John then gives Richard $1,000 for his help. Can Richard successfully sue John for the other $4,000?

YOU BE THE ADVISER / *The $100 Million Deal*

Clara Bartlett is a special assistant to Sam Davis, the chief executive officer (CEO) of a large, prosperous firm. Sam often sends Clara on assignments that require her to represent the firm and conclude business agreements in the company's name. Clara is an attorney, and much of this work falls within her area of expertise.

Last month, Clara and Sam spent 3 days negotiating with a competitor who wants to retire and sell his business for $110 million. Sam has had his accountants go over the company's books, and this asking price is in the ballpark. However, Sam believes that they can purchase the company for $100 million.

After discussing the matter with Clara, Sam arranged a meeting with the competitor, Winston Green. He then told Clara, "I want you to represent me in this meeting. Have contracts drawn up promising to pay Green $100 million. Then negotiate him down to this price. You might consider starting out at about $90 million and letting him work you up the last $10 million. I'm going to have the people in the accounting department issue you a check for $1 million that I want you to use to seal the deal. Give it to Green as consideration, with the other $99 million due in 90 days. I will have the check made out to you."

At the meeting, Clara and Winston Green discussed many details of the deal. Winston was initially concerned about Sam's absence, but he seemed satisfied when Clara ex-plained that she had the authority to strike a deal "if is right." The meeting lasted 6 hours, and when it w Winston had agreed to sell his company for $100 m Clara would pay the first $1 million as soon as they signed initial agreement. Another $24 million was due in cash in days. The last $75 million was due in 90 days.

After Winston had signed the papers, Clara signed on the line designated for her company's signature. She then re-moved a check for $1 million from her briefcase, turned it over, endorsed it, and then gave it to Winston. He looked at both sides of the check, stood up, and extended his hand across the table. "Congratulations," he said, "you've just bought yourself a company."

Your Advice

1. What type of endorsement should Clara have used on the check?
   a. ___ A blank endorsement
   b. ___ A restricted endorsement
   c. ___ A qualified endorsement
2. From what you have learned in this case, do the two parties have a contract, or has Clara failed to do something? Explain.
3. Is the $1 million that Clara gave Winston Green adequate as consideration or should she have given him more? Explain.

ities in Business

...able in the areas of risk
...ce and business law. Occupa-
... command good salaries. In most
... egree is required for employment, and,
... an attorney, a law degree. The following
... three promising careers: actuary, insurance
...sperson, and corporate attorney.

Actuary

An actuary is an individual who helps insurance companies determine the risk involved in providing insurance for different types of situations. Through higher mathematical calculations, the actuary is able to advise management on appropriate insurance rates.

Job Description. Actuaries typically work for the home offices of insurance companies. They assemble and analyze statistics for calculating the probabilities of death, sickness, injury, disability, property loss, and other hazards. In order to perform these duties effectively, the actuary must be informed and use data concerning general economic and social trends, as well as legislative, health, and other developments that can affect insurance practices. Most actuaries specialize in either health or life insurance or property and liability insurance. In addition, a growing number of actuaries are beginning to specialize in pension plans.

Employment Outlook and Earnings. Around 12,000 actuaries are employed in the United States, and the employment outlook is good. Growth in this occupation is expected to be much faster than the average of all occupations through the mid-1990s. An actuary will typically have a bachelor's degree with considerable work in mathematics and statistics or a degree in actuarial science. The individual must also pass a series of difficult examinations. New college graduates entering the field without having passed any actuarial exams can expect to earn in the range of $22,000 to $27,000. Those who pass the first exam can expect to make about $4,000 more, and those who pass subsequent exams can expect additional increments in salary. Top actuarial executives with the large insurance firms earn about $100,000 annually.

Insurance Salesperson

An insurance salesperson sells various types of insurance coverage to both individual customers and to companies that offer insurance coverage to their employees. In each case, the objective is to provide the insured with protection against loss in the case of some particular event such as a hospital stay as a result of being in a car accident.

Job Description. An insurance salesperson sells policies that provide individuals and businesses with financial protection. The salesperson helps people plan for the financial security and risk management of themselves, their families, and their businesses. The salesperson will also sell and advise clients regarding protection for auto, home, business, and property; will prepare reports and maintain records; and will help policyholders obtain settlement of their insurance claims. In most cases the salesperson will specialize in a particular type of insurance such as life, property-liability, health, auto, or comprehensive planning services. In some cases the salesperson will sell all types of coverage.

Employment Outlook and Earnings. Today the United States has approximately one-half million insurance salespeople. Employment in insurance sales is expected to grow more slowly than the average for all occupations through the mid-1990s. Although many insurance companies and their agencies prefer college graduates, most will also hire people with only some college work, people with potential or proven sales ability, or people who have been successful in other types of work. For example, schoolteachers often are hired for insurance sales. Starting salaries for new insurance salespeople depend greatly on commissions but generally are around $20,000 annually. However, those who have 5 to 10 years of experience and good sales skills can make considerably more — possibly even more than industry executives.

Corporate Attorney

Businesses have many legal needs. Large corporations, in particular, handle their legal requirements and problems through the services of their own attorneys or by hiring outside attorneys who are skilled in business law.

Job Description. A corporate attorney can be a generalist or a specialist. A generalist will handle most legal problems because they fall within the realm of his or her expertise. However, in the case of specialized problems such as tax issues, labor disputes, or patent suits, a specialist will be relied upon. In either case, the corporate attorney will remain abreast of his or her field and will typically discuss legal problems with clients, and will arrive at decisions regarding the best course of action to pursue. The attorney will then advise the client regarding the law and recommend the course(s) of action that he or she deems best in resolving or avoiding a given legal problem.

Employment Outlook and Earnings. There are about 300,000 corporate attorneys in the United States today and the number is likely to increase during the years ahead. One reason is the growing number of businesses that require legal assistance. A second is the attractive salaries. General counsels for large corporations can make substantially more than the average private sector attorney. Starting salaries are in the $30,000 to $40,000 range, and with experience a corporate attorney can make well over $100,000 annually.

The purpose of this appendix is to provide you with some insights and guidelines on how to pursue a career in business. You have learned a great deal about the world of work from this book, but this information alone will not get you a job. You need a well-formulated career plan. This plan should contain a number of important parts including a self-appraisal, development of a job search strategy, an effectively written resumé, and a well-handled job interview. Before examining these steps, however, you should look at how prepared you are to pursue a career and what else needs to be done. Table A.1 provides a career planning checklist that will give you some insights on how far along you are in your job search. Read the table closely and note everything that needs to be done. By the time you have finished reading this appendix, you will know how to carry out each of these major steps.

Plan Your Career Direction

The first step in forming a career plan is to determine the overall direction. There is more to getting the job of your choice than just having the necessary college courses or degree. Your formal education will open many doors for you, but you still need to know which specific doors you want to enter. This can be accomplished by carrying out a careful self-appraisal.

A self-appraisal involves two primary areas of consideration: identifying your personal career goals and making an honest evaluation of the things you do well. Such an appraisal helps you to focus on what you would really like to do and what you would be good at and then to use this information to help you get the appropriate job. After all, you want to do something in life that you find enjoyable and that you would be good at, and at the same time you need to find an organization that is willing to pay you to do these things.

The Key Questions to Ask Yourself

A self-appraisal does not have to be a time-consuming activity. It can be carried out by asking yourself some basic questions.

First, who are you? This may seem like a difficult question because you may have never asked it before, but it is critical to an effective self-analysis. What are your interests? Your strengths and weaknesses? Your special talents? Are you good with people? How would you describe yourself to an interviewer who asks, "Tell me about yourself." By being frank and honest, how would you convince the job interviewer that you have the necessary abilities and knowledge?

Second, what do you want to do? This is a question commonly asked by recruiters. After all, the company that employs you is going to pay you to do something; what can you do for it? If you can answer this question effectively, the recruiter will feel that you have given some attention to a career. If you cannot, the interviewer may feel that you are not very well prepared to seek a career with the company.

TABLE A.1
A Career Planning Checklist

Below is a checklist to see how far along you are in your job search. Check off the areas you have completed.

Setting Assessment

☐ I have chosen the setting in which I would like to work (i.e., large industrial, small business, government, non-profit).

☐ I have chosen one of the following locations: rural, urban, suburban.

Skills Assessment

☐ I have listed my three most useful job skills.

☐ I know what I am most successful doing.

☐ I have identified whether I want to work with people, data, or things.

☐ I know whether I want to be supervised or be the supervisor.

☐ I know if I want to work with others or work alone.

Interests Assessment

☐ I have listed some of the main career areas I might be interested in.

☐ I have decided whether I like "doing" or "thinking" activities at work.

☐ I have listed my favorite activities (hobbies, sports, etc.).

Values Assessment

☐ I have listed some of the most important values to me (i.e., prestige, security, variety).

☐ I know the kind of rewards that are important to me in a job (i.e., social, monetary, job flexibility).

Career Information Research

☐ I am familiar with the career information in the placement office library so I am able to further explore my options.

☐ I have developed a list of career possibilities to research.

☐ I keep up with current trends in my field (salary, job requirements, growth).

☐ I have identified employers interested in interviewing people with my academic background and experience.

☐ I have compiled a list of potential employers who may not have immediate openings, but would be good prospects in the future.

☐ I have a list of three or more employers in the field I am considering.

☐ I have made at least three contacts in my field.

☐ I have sought information and advice from people in my field.

Work Options

☐ I have narrowed down the career options I am considering.

☐ I have identified the needed additional educational or experiential background I need to better prepare for, or help test my choices (i.e., course work, part-time work, extra-curricular activities).

☐ I have discovered ways my academic course work supports my career objective.

☐ I have participated in some work experience or internship program in my field of interest.

☐ I am aware of the daily realities of the occupational area I am approaching.

☐ I have visited several of the work sites being considered as my career choice.

☐ I have become an active member in at least one professional association to enhance my job awareness.

Resumé Readiness

☐ I have a clear job objective.

☐ I have written a resumé which:

　☐ shows how my skills and experience fit my objective

　☐ speaks in terms of accomplishments and uses action verbs

　☐ is one, or at the most, two pages

　☐ has no spelling or grammatical errors

　☐ has been typed and professionally duplicated

☐ I am ready to compose a specific cover letter to accompany each resumé.

Interview Readiness

☐ I have thoroughly researched the employer with whom I am to interview.

☐ I have completed informational interviewing to gather information about employers.

☐ I have practiced my interviewing technique and am prepared to answer most interview questions.

☐ I have questions to ask employers during the interview.

☐ I will arrive at the interview on time and looking professional.

☐ I will write a thank-you letter after each interview.

Source: Florida International University, *Placement Manual, 1990/91*, 5.

Third, why do you want to do the work you have in mind to do? This follow-up question gets at your motivation. For example, if you tell the recruiter, "I want to be a salesperson," the individual will want to learn more about the characteristics you feel you possess that would make you effective in this job. Typical examples would include: high motivation, a self-starter, goal-oriented, competitive, a need to accomplish things, a desire for feedback regarding how well you are doing, and an opportunity to be directly rewarded for your own performance.

Fourth, where do you want to work? This is a broad question and can have a number of different answers. For example, the recruiter will likely want to know if you want to stay in the local area or are willing to relocate. Are you willing to travel as part of the job? Are you interested in a large company or a small one? Do you want to be in accounting or sales? These answers help the person decide how well you will fit in the organization. For example, if the recruiter is looking for a salesperson to cover a five-state area and you say you are willing to travel, this would be a point in favor of your landing the job. However, if you have elderly parents and must stay nearby to help them out, the recruiter will conclude that you are not the right person for this job. If there are a number of job openings, the recruiter may then explore other areas where you might fit. So this question helps the recruiter mesh your desires with the company's needs.

Finally, what are your goals? What do you hope to attain during your business career? This question is designed to help the recruiter understand the types of things you want out of a job. For example, you might be interested in a job that gives you a great deal of relevant experience so that you will be in a position to be promoted quickly. Money may be a secondary consideration for you. By understanding these objectives, you are in a position to show the recruiter the link between your goals and the company's needs. Sometimes recruiters will ask job candidates where they hope to be in the company in 10 years or 20 years. It also pays to give some early thought to your long-range goals and the positions you hope to attain along the way.

The Outcomes of the Self-Appraisal

The intended outcomes of the self-appraisal are to help you better understand the direction of your career. By knowing your likes and dislikes, abilities and shortcomings, you are most likely to get the best possible fit between yourself and the job. Some of the most important things you should get out of the self-appraisal are the following:

1. *Know yourself.* Make an honest appraisal of your interests, abilities, and shortcomings.
2. *Determine your interests.* Analyze the activities that interest you most (outdoors, helping people, mechanical, clerical).
3. *Recognize your aptitudes.* Identify the special abilities you have at present and for the future, and determine your best combination of abilities.
4. *Evaluate your work experience and education.* Determine the knowledge or skills you have acquired through your academic training and work experiences and how this knowledge will transfer to your desired career path.
5. *Recognize your personal qualities.* Evaluate the traits that will make you an outstanding candidate and be able to discuss them clearly and concisely.

6. *Understand your physical capacities.* Do you have any physical problems that would prevent you from functioning in certain jobs? If so, concentrate your efforts on obtaining employment where these physical problems will not be a limitation in accomplishing your short- and long-range goals.

7. *Identify your leisure time activities.* Evaluate your personal interests and hobbies. Determine how these can be an asset to you in accomplishing your goals.

8. *Determine your vocational goals.* Establishing goals is important. However, goals are short-lived. They are either attained, at which time new goals are set, or they are not attained, for whatever reason, and then alternative goals are established. In any case, at the very outset establish short-term as well as long-term goals. Doing so provides a target and helps keep you on the proper path.[1]

1. Of what value is a self-assessment?
2. How can the self-assessment help you plan your career direction?

CHECK ✓ POINT

Know Where the Jobs Are and How Much They Pay

The self-analysis should reveal a number of career paths. For example, if you want to be a salesperson, you might opt for on-the-road travel or choose to work in a retail store or maybe even take a job as a public relations trainee or some other sales-related position. In short, most people are flexible and can expand their career choices to include a number of options. This is important because the availability of jobs greatly varies and so does the pay.

Job Supply and Demand

Table A.2 reports the recent supply and demand for jobs by field of study. Although there will always be exceptions, generally speaking graduates in engineering, the sciences, health professions, and business have found that demand exceeds supply. However, even in these fields there may be industries and locations where supply exceeds demand. For example, going into the 1990s with the troubles experienced by the financial industry (see Chapter 19), savings and loan institutions and banks — which traditionally hired a lot of business graduates — cut way back on their hiring. Also, certain parts of the country that are experiencing economic difficulties (such as the recession in the early 1990s) are not in a hiring mode for any type of majors. Those graduating in such fields as the humanities or the social sciences usually find that the supply is equal to or greater than the demand. However, students with liberal arts majors can increase their marketability by taking three or four courses in business.

Salaries

Graduates who majored in engineering, business, scientific fields, and computer science are able to command higher starting salaries than those majoring in liberal arts, retailing, journalism, and home economics, as shown in Table A.3. However, in using this information, you need to keep a couple of

TABLE A.2
Supply and Demand of Jobs in
Academic Majors
(Projections to the Year 2000)

	Estimated Number	Percent of Total
More Jobs Than Candidates		
Business and management	242,047	24.33%
Engineering	74,070	7.44
Health professions	63,439	6.38
Computer and information sciences	39,935	4.01
Physical sciences	20,048	2.01
Engineering technologies	19,348	1.94
Total	458,886	46.12%
Jobs Equal to Candidates Available		
Education	87,437	8.79%
Mathematics	16,550	1.66
Protective services	12,978	1.30
Architecture and environmental design	8,955	0.90
Communications technologies	1,444	0.15
Other	1,706	0.17
Total	129,070	12.97%
More Candidates Than Jobs		
Social sciences	96,540	9.70%
Communications	44,131	4.44
Psychology	43,026	4.32
Life sciences	38,255	3.84
Letters	37,270	3.75
Visual and performing arts	36,357	3.65
Liberal/general studies	21,444	2.16
Multi/interdisciplinary studies	16,463	1.65
Agriculture and natural resources	15,046	1.51
Home economics	14,997	1.51
Public affairs	14,213	1.43
Foreign languages	10,222	1.03
Philosophy and religion	5,998	0.60
Theology	5,731	0.58
Parks and recreation	4,122	0.41
Area and ethnic studies	3,352	0.34
Total	407,168	40.92%
Grand Total — All Fields	995,000	100.00%

Source: Supply/demand ratios and numbers of graduates estimated by John D. Shingleton, Director Emeritus of Placement Services, and L. Patrick Scheetz, Director of the Collegiate Employment Research Institute, Michigan State University. Grand total of bachelor's-degree recipients from *Projections of Education Statistics to 2000* (Washington, D.C.: National Center for Education Statistics, U.S. Department of Education, 1989), 67.

TABLE A.3
Estimated Average Starting Salaries
by Academic Major

Academic Majors	Estimated Average Starting Salaries
Chemical engineering	$34,715
Mechanical engineering	33,546
Electrical engineering	33,391
Computer science	32,958
Industrial engineering	31,779
Physics	29,640
Civil engineering	28,538
Nursing	28,452
Accounting	28,133
Chemistry	26,976
Mathematics	25,967
Financial administration	25,090
Marketing/sales	24,823
Geology	24,802
Agriculture	23,258
General business administration	22,500
Social science	21,949
Personnel administration	21,664
Telecommunications	21,506
Education	21,476
Hotel, restaurant, and institutional management	21,375
Communications	21,357
Liberal arts/arts and letters	20,851
Advertising	20,448
Retailing	19,476
Natural resources	19,405
Journalism	18,803
Human ecology/home economics	18,702
M.B.A.	41,832
Master's	35,090
Ph.D.	38,224

Source: Estimates by John D. Shingleton, Director Emeritus of Placement Services, and L. Patrick Scheetz, Director of the Collegiate Employment Research Institute, Michigan State University, using data from *Recruiting Trends 1989–90.*

things in mind. First, salaries will vary based by geographic region. If you are going to be working in large cities in the Northeast such as Boston or New York, or on the West Coast in San Francisco or San Diego, you will probably get a higher salary than if you work in smaller cities in the Midwest or South. Second, other factors besides your major such as your grades, activities, and relevant experience will have an impact on your starting salary. Third, while the technical, specialized fields may have higher starting salaries, this edge does not necessarily last indefinitely. Many top salespeople make far more money than chemical or mechanical engineers. The same is true for those who rise into top level management positions. For example, Lee Iacocca of Chrysler started out as an engineer but he switched to sales and made much better money there. Next, he moved into management and, of course, today makes much more than anyone else in the firm. So remember that Table A.3 reports only starting salaries. You should look at more than just where you will be starting; you have to consider the route your career will take over the years. You may have to start low today in order to reach the heights tomorrow.

CHECK ✓ POINT

1. How can students majoring in the liberal arts improve their beginning salary?
2. What besides the academic major is important to getting a job and obtaining a good starting salary?

Develop a Job Search Strategy

Once you have decided on the type of job you want to pursue, the next step is to develop a strategy for finding that job. This calls for a well-formulated job search plan. There are many approaches that can be taken. The following examine the most popular and effective strategies that can be used alone or in conjunction with one another.

College Placement Services

Many students use their college placement office to help them find a job. As seen in Table A.4, recruiters hire more new college graduates through the placement office than any other source. However, this is not the only route for finding an employer, and research shows that the greater the number of contacts and interviews, the greater the number of job offers that will be received. It pays to tap a wide number of sources. In using the job placement office, sign up for on-campus interviews as soon as possible because a limited number of people will be interviewed by each recruiter. The placement office can provide you with the names of employers who will be interviewing on-campus and the type of jobs they are trying to fill. You can then use this information to identify the ones with whom you would like to interview.

Referral Campaign or Networking

A referral campaign, more commonly known as networking, may be the most popular strategy used for finding a job. This approach consists of drawing up a list of multiple contacts — people who have the power to hire you, individuals in companies or professions that are relevant to the job you are trying to get, or friends and relatives who have contacts that can help you. Once you have completed this list, you should then select individuals on the list who can provide you with information and suggestions that can help you in your job search. In particular, ask your contacts about job openings and the names of others who can be of assistance. To a large extent, the referral

Source	Percentage of New Hires
On-campus interviewing	42.2%
Write-ins	10.2
Responses from want ads	8.5
Job listings with placement offices	7.7
Referrals from current employees	5.5
Walk-ins	4.4
Cooperative education programs	3.7
Internship programs	3.6
High-demand major programs	3.5
Summer employment	2.9
Part-time employment	2.4
Minority career programs	1.8
Referrals from campus organizations	1.7
Unsolicited referrals from placement offices	1.4
Women's career programs	0.5
Total	100.0%

Source: John D. Shingleton and L. Patrick Scheetz. *Recruiting Trends 1986–87* (East Lansing, Mich.: Placement Services, Michigan State University, 1986). Reported in *CPC Annual, 1990/91*, 34th ed. (Bethlehem, PA: College Placement Council, 1990), 19.

campaign becomes a numbers game. The more people you contact, the better will be your chances of eventually getting the job you want. For example, if you want an accounting job, you might ask three faculty members and ten friends and relatives for relevant individuals they know in the accounting profession. You would then write or call each of these relevant people about job possibilities and try to arrange for an interview.

Internal Campaigns

An internal campaign is a type of self-marketing strategy. Typically, the person taking this approach would take voluntary positions, company internships, or even a low-paying job. The purpose is to get a foot in the door, gain some experience, and let management see how well you can perform. Normally, this would be done before graduation on a part-time basis. However, in some cases you may have to do this for a few months after graduation. In pursuing this strategy, check with your college placement office and learn about the types of opportunities that are available.

Job Opening Lists

Job opening lists consist of newspaper ads, bulletins, and newsletters that announce job openings. These lists detail the types of jobs that are available in a variety of fields. Your college placement office can tell you which newsletters and bulletins in your field carry advertised openings. Some of the current ones include:

- *National Business Employment Weekly*, 420 Lexington Avenue, New York, N.Y. 10017
- *Affirmative Action Register*, 3856 Olive Boulevard, St. Louis, Mo. 06312
- *YMCA National Vacancy List*, 101 N. Wacker Drive, Chicago, Ill. 60606-7356
- *National Arts Job Bank*, 207 Shelby Street, Suite 200, Sante Fe, N.M. 87501
- *Athletics Employment Weekly*, P.O. Box 86, Warsaw, Ill. 63379

Direct Mailings

Another approach is to use direct mailings in the form of customized cover letters and resumés. Some individuals will send these mailings to any company that they believe might be interested in recruiting someone with their education and abilities. However, this kind of blind mailing typically results in only a few interviews. Targeted mailings sent to a specific person such as the human resources manager, who has the authority to hire you, will improve your chances. Figure A.1 is an example of a cover letter that can be used in direct mailings.

Job Search Club

Increasingly, college placement offices organize groups of students who are conducting job searches and get them together in a club format to share resources, exchange job leads, and plan strategies. Sometimes faculty will also participate in these groups. Joining this type of club could be particularly valuable in helping you network and providing you with support and confidence in your job search. Check with your college placement office to see if it has organized such a club. If not, talk to the director of placement about starting one yourself; this would be great experience and would look good on your resumé.

Cold Calls/Walk-Ins

Not all job openings are publicized or require letters of inquiry or applications. In rare instances, you may call on a firm asking about job openings and be granted an immediate interview. This strategy obviously has a very low percentage of success and can be extremely time consuming. On the other hand, it does show that you are very interested in getting a job, and you may meet some people while you are there who will help you with leads or in the future. A walk-in approach is also a good idea if you have been unable to reach anyone on the phone to set up an interview and feel that your only chance is to go to the organization and make a formal application.

Job Centers/Employment Offices

If you do not have a college placement service available to you or if you have had extensive work experience in a particular area such as engineering, accounting, or nursing, you may want to consider using public or private employment agencies or working with executive search firms, commonly called "head hunters." A private employment agency will charge a fee, but this is sometimes paid, in part or in full, by the employer. Before signing anything be sure to ask what your financial liability would be. In any case, an employ-

FIGURE A.1
Sample Cover Letter Accompanying
a Resumé

Source: *CPC Annual, 1990/91*, 34th ed.
(Bethlehem, PA: College Placement Council,
1990), 41.

849 Baldwin Avenue
Virginia Beach, VA 23467
January 5, 19xx

Mr. Timothy T. Mellon
Director of College Recruiting
Midwest Mercantile Company
4500 Randolf Drive
Chicago, IL 60601

Dear Mr. Mellon:

I read your company's description in the CPC Annual and would like
to inquire about employment opportunities in your management
training program. I want to work in retail management and would
like to relocate to the Chicago area after graduation.

I shall receive my B.S. degree this May. My interest in business
started in Junior Achievement while in high school and developed
further through a variety of sales and retail positions during
college. My internship with a large department store convinced me
to pursue a career in retail. When I researched the top retailers
in Chicago, Midwest Mercantile emerged as having a strong market
position, an excellent training program, and a reputation for
excellent customer service. In short, you provide the kind of
professional retail environment I seek.

My resume is enclosed for your consideration. My education and
experience match the qualifications you seek in your management
trainees, but they don't tell the whole story. I know from
customer and supervisor feedback that I have the interpersonal
skills and motivation needed to build a successful career in
retail management. And my relatively extensive experience gives me
confidence in my career direction and in my abilities to perform
competently.

I know how busy you must be during this time of year, but I would
appreciate a few minutes of your time. I shall call you during the
week of January 22 to discuss employment possibilities. In the
meantime, if you need to contact me, my number is 804-683-8843.
Please leave a message if I'm not in, and I'll return your call
the next day.

Thank you very much for considering my request. I look forward to
talking with you.

Sincerely,

Craig S. Watson

Craig S. Watson

ment agency should not be at the top of your list of ways to get a job, because
college graduates typically are able to find employment without having to use
such services. An executive search firm may be interested in you if you have
previous experience or are currently employed. You will usually find out
very quickly, because such firms work on a fee basis, and it is paid by the
employer.

State and federal public employment agencies can be another good
source because they can provide realistic information about the job market in
your desired location. They are also aware of job opportunities in the public

sector. Every year these agencies help thousands of people get a job. One thing to keep in mind about these agencies is that you must fill out your applications very carefully. Incomplete forms are often used to eliminate applicants and these forms will be part of your permanent file should you be hired.

Telemarketing Yourself

In most cases companies will not talk to you until they have seen your resumé. They want to know something about you before entering into a formal face-to-face interview. In some cases, the prospective employer may also want to talk with you over the phone, especially if you have to travel a great distance to interview. The company may feel it is in both its and your best interest to talk with you before bringing you in for an interview. If possible, try to talk directly to a department head or someone who has authority over the hiring decision. Make notes before placing the call so that you are able to market yourself and your work interests as effectively as possible. You would then follow-up with a letter and your resumé.

A Bridging Position

A bridging position is a temporary or part-time job that you take while you are waiting for a more desirable position to open up. You should try to get the closest job possible to a preferred one so you can build relevant experience. You might even find that the company you want to work for is willing to hire you but, because of budget cuts or delayed plans, cannot do so right away. Again, you need employment for a brief time period. When interviewing for a bridging position, be honest about the fact that you are looking for only short-term work. It is unethical to allow the interviewer to think you are seeking a career position with the company and then suddenly quit. You will not receive a good recommendation. Be sure to give advance notice before leaving to take another position.

Long-Distance Search

Many of the strategies already discussed can be incorporated into a long-distance search. For example, if you currently live on the East Coast and would like to move to the San Francisco area, subscribe to one of that city's major newspapers and check the want ads and employment trends. Your university or city library may also carry the newspaper of the city in which you want to locate; if so, drop by every couple of days and review the want ads. Also, check with the college placement office to see if it has any books and directories on the city that can be helpful to you in your search. Finally, find out from your placement office if any colleges in the area where you wish to locate offer reciprocal placement services. If so, you can call to discuss your situation long distance. Eventually, however, you will have to be on-site to land a job. You may visit during vacation breaks to drop off resumés and do some interviews.

Other Approaches

Some college graduates have offered to work free for a company for a brief period of time as a trainee or intern. This allows them to get a foot in the door and show the firm what they can do. They hope, at the end of this time, to be hired full time. Another approach is to have business cards printed and distribute them at professional meetings or to develop a unique resumé. An example of the latter is a resumé printed on the label of a wine bottle that a student sent to the recruiter for a wine distributing firm.

Never Say Die

All of the strategies described can be useful, but there is no guarantee that they will produce immediate results. Depending on the type of job, the location, and the state of the economy, to land the job you are after may take months rather than weeks. You must be patient and continue to carry through on your strategy. You might also consider some of the following steps:

1. Join a different job-search group.
2. Try a strategy you have not used before.
3. Rework your contacts, calling on people you have not contacted for 3 to 4 weeks. Ask them for new suggestions and friends of friends.
4. Attend a workshop or seminar to improve your search and job interview skills.
5. Call interviewers you met 2 or 3 months ago to see if the person they hired worked out. State that you are still interested in the firm and wondering if anything new has opened up.
6. Attend a different professional association meeting and make new contacts.
7. Reassess your marketing package; redo your materials.
8. Analyze your competition — what methods are they using to land jobs?
9. Ask for the job. Let employers know you want to work for them.[2]

CHECK ✓ POINT

1. Which three job search strategy steps would be most effective for you? Identify and explain your choices.
2. What would you do if nothing seemed to be working?

Research the Companies that Interest You

An important but often overlooked step in planning a career is to research the companies in which you are most interested. The knowledge you gain will help you to write resumés and prepare for interviews. Moreover, many recruiters feel that an applicant who knows something about the company shows the type of interest and enthusiasm they seek. Begin your research on a particular company by determining whether it is publicly owned, a subsidiary or division of a parent company, privately owned, foreign-owned, or local or regional in scope. Once you know this, you can focus your research.

Publicly Owned Companies   One way to find out whether a company is publicly owned is to see if its stock is being traded on one of the stock exchanges. Do this by looking through the stock listings in *The Wall Street Journal* or your local paper. To get more information on the firm, you can then consult *Ward's Business Directory*, which provides data on both public and large private companies arranged alphabetically, geographically, and by sales volume. *Moody's Manuals*, another good source, provide operational and financial data on companies listed on the organized U.S. stock exchanges. An annual report, which may be available from your local brokerage house, will also be a valuable source of information on publicly owned companies.

Subsidiaries If the firm you are researching is not listed among publicly owned companies, it may be a subsidiary or division of a larger firm. Two useful sources in finding out the parent company are (a) *Directory of Corporate Affiliations*, which is a guide to corporate linkage for more than 4,000 major U.S. public and private companies, and (b) *Standard & Poor's Register of Corporations, Directors, and Executives*, which provides a corporate family index in Volume 3. From here you can seek additional information that will tell you something about the operations of the subsidiaries. If the parent firm is publicly held, the annual report may also provide some useful information about the subsidiary in which you are interested. Other good sources are periodical and newspaper articles that deal directly with the company. Your librarian can help you search for these articles.

Privately Owned Firms If any of the companies you are researching are privately owned but have sizable assets or sales, you may find them listed in directories such as *Ward's Business Directory*. Otherwise, you will have to conduct a computer search in the library to find out whether any articles have been written about them. If time allows, you may also call or write directly to the company for information that has been put together by its sales or public relations department.

Foreign-Owned Businesses As you know from your study of international business, an increasing number of foreign-owned businesses have a U.S. division or subsidiary. To find out if the company you are researching is foreign-based or foreign-owned, look at *Principal International Businesses*, a publication from Dun & Bradstreet that provides information on more than 50,000 leading companies in 133 countries. Two other good sources, especially for financial information, are *Moody's International Manual* and *World Directory of Multinational Enterprises*.

Local Or Regional Companies The easiest way to get information on these companies is to call or write directly and ask for printed material on their operations. Other useful sources of information include the local chamber of commerce, local newspapers, and the city or state industrial directory.

Many libraries offer access to company information through the use of computer data-base search services. Check with your librarian to find out whether this service is available. In some cases, a librarian will conduct the search; in others, you will find that the data bases are user-friendly and you can do the search yourself. Armed with all the information, obtained through research, you can write resumés directed at specific firms as well as prepare for job interviews.

CHECK ✓ POINT

1. What type of organization would you be interested in as your future employer?
2. How would you gather information on this company?

Write an Effective Resumé

Constructing your resumé is one of the most important steps in starting your career. Because your resumé will be scanned for only about 20 seconds, it must be well-written, have an appealing appearance, and provide the necessary information. The following are some specific guidelines for putting together an effective resumé.

Format of Resumés

The resumé is a sales tool. It must quickly identify for the employer: who you are; what you want; what you have accomplished; what you would like to do; and what you can offer to the company. It should emphasize the job qualifications and personal strengths that are of interest to the reader. There are three basic formats for resumés: chronological, functional, and targeted.

Chronological Resumés Chronological resumés are the most popular and they are easy to prepare. The basic format is to begin with your name and address and then move on to your objectives and education. This is followed by a brief description of your work history, special skills you possess, and any past and present activities that are relevant to the job application. This information is presented in chronological order beginning with the most recent. Figure A.2 provides an example.

Functional Resumés Functional resumés focus on the skills, aptitudes, and qualities that can be applied to a number of situations. Skills are organized into categories that tell prospective employers what you will be able to do for them. The functional resumé is especially valuable for candidates who lack direct job-related experience, who want to work in fields not related to their academic background, or whose education is so general that they must find a way of bridging the gap between their education and the job requirements. This type of resumé is also suitable for candidates who have considerable work experience, because it allows them to portray the skills they will be able to put to immediate use. Figure A.3 provides an example of a functional resumé.

Targeted Resumés A targeted resumé emphasizes a special career objective and is constructed to highlight your capabilities and accomplishments along the lines of the targeted job. The top of the resumé page should contain your job objectives and your education. After researching the job you are seeking and identifying the qualities, characteristics, or experiences that are necessary to success in that career, three or four capability statements should be written that clearly identify what you can do in that position. This should be followed by an accomplishment or experience section stressing accomplishments in past work and nonwork activities that demonstrate your skills and abilities. This resumé style can work well if you know specifically what you want to do and have the credentials to back it up. The resumé should demonstrate to the employer that you can make an immediate contribution. Figure A.4 provides an example of a targeted resumé.

FIGURE A.2

Example of a Chronological Resumé

Source: Florida International University,
Placement Manual, 1990–1991, 9.

Ivan T. Brown	1910 Sunrise Drive Miami Beach, Florida 33139 (305) 578-9823
Objective	To secure a programming/information systems position with a mid to large size organization.
Education	Florida International University Miami, Florida Degree: Bachelor of Science Major: Computer Science GPA: 3.8 Anticipated Date of Graduation: December 19xx
Work History	Computer Operator – American Republic Bank Miami, Florida. (July 19xx – present) Review computer program instruction sheets and determine necessary equipment setup for each job. Load computer with tapes and discs and monitor control console. Solve error problems when they occur. Retrieve data upon request from various departments. Maintain work logs and prepare reports on computer use. Data Entry Clerk – Trust Savings Miami, Florida (March 19xx – June 19xx) Copied coded data from documents. Verified entries and checked for errors.
Computer Skills	COBOL BASIC FORTRAN Assembler Pascal VAX & IBM Systems Macintosh & Apple Computers Lotus 123 Wordstar DBase III DisplayWrite 3
Activities	Data Processing Management Association August19xx – December 19xx National Wildlife Federation June 19xx – Present
References	Available upon request.

Construction and Layout

In developing an effective resumé, there are some useful rules to keep in mind regarding construction and layout. First, be sure there are no typographical or content errors and use an attractive word processing layout and a quality printer. A good resumé is functional rather than ornate in appearance; unusual type styles or too many kinds of type get in the way of the content. The safest color for paper is white or eggshell.

Second, the resumé should be one to two pages in length. If you have more than this amount of information that you would like to convey, write a

FIGURE A.3

Example of a Functional Resumé

Source: Florida International University, *Placement Manual, 1990–1991*, 9.

Luke Norman
2530 S.W. 2nd Street
Miami, FL 33135
(305) 666 - 9987

Career Target

A position in the field of public relations which will utilize my educational background.

Education

Florida International University
Miami, Florida
Graduation Date - April 1991
Master of Science - Public Relations 8/xx-12/xx

University of Miami
Miami, Florida
Bachelor of Science - Education l/xx-6xx

Skills

Fundraising – Identified immediate and long range financial needs of nonprofit community center. Established a series of goals. Completed research on sources of funds. Developed plans for soliciting funds from local business and government sources. Organized fundraising events for elementary schools in conjunction with parents' association.

Communication – Composed written press releases and promotional handouts. Supervised production of school newspaper. Utilized effective teaching skills in instructing classes. Interfaced with community officials, representatives from business and industry and parents of school children.

Planning Planned advertising events for community center. Prepared daily lesson plan for educational instruction. Organized and executed annual school events.

Employment History

Intern – Community Relations Department, Miami Civic Center, Miami, Florida (Summer 19xx)

Teacher – South Dade Elementary School, Miami, Florida (9/xx–Present)

Interests

Reading; graphic arts; photography; piano.

References available upon request

---

longer resumé and then cut it back to two pages. Notice that the three examples provided in Figures A.2, A.3, and A.4 are all one page in length.

Third, do not use personal pronouns and try to be as concise as possible. Use phrases instead of lengthy sentences and start these phrases with an active verb in the past tense. Here is a contrasting example:

Use of personal pronoun and lengthy sentence

I was one of four people who were charged with planning and implementing a workshop on mental health issues that was presented every March and September.

FIGURE A.4
Example of a Targeted Resumé

Source: Florida International University,
Placement Manual, 1990–1991, 8.

Wendy Wissel
987 E. 29th St., Hialeah, FL 33164
(305) 694-1342

Job Objective
A position in social services which would utilize my planning and counseling skills.

Education
Bachelor of Arts - Psychology
Florida International University
Miami, Florida - August 19xx

Capabilities
- Able to plan and implement workshops and activities.
- Able to utilize effective communication skills.
- Able to practice a variety of counseling techniques.

Experience
- Assisted in planning and implementing a workshop on mental health issues presented twice a year.
- Planned activities for groups of 30 adolescents at residential summer camp.
- Contributed to several departmental publications and monthly newsletters.
- Presented research findings on teenage suicide to group of community service volunteers.
- Utilized behavior modification techniques in facilitating recreational activities for children.

Work History
- Student/Assistant - Counseling Center, Florida International University. Miami, Florida. September 19xx – Present.
- Camp Counselor - Everglades National Park, Miami, Florida. Summer 19xx, 19xx.

Activities
Peer Advisor; University Host; Golden Panther Cheerleader; Church Youth Group.

References Available upon Request

Briefer and more direct sentence

Assisted in planning and implementing a workshop on mental health issues presented twice a year.

Fourth, run your resumé by knowledgeable people for their opinion and suggestions for improvement. They may be in the placement office or may be human resource management experts. Also, check to see whether your placement office has a resumé-writer program that can help you organize and present your information. For example, the office may have a computerized tutorial guide that takes you through each step of resumé development. The program also organizes your information and then has a word processing program that designs a customized resumé. If this is not available to you, check to see whether the bookstore sells the "Resume Expert Student Module." This program, which costs only around $15, allows you to input your data on the student data disk and then go to a master module site and edit and print your typeset resumé.

CHECK ✓ POINT

1. What type of resumé would be most beneficial for you: chronological, functional, or targeted? Defend your answer.
2. What type of assistance is available for constructing your resumé?

Know How to Interview

The employment interview is a two-way street. It provides the interviewer an opportunity to get to know you better and to learn how well your abilities and talents mesh with the company's needs. At the same time, it gives you the opportunity to size up the company and decide if this is the type of firm you would like to join. Typically there are at least two interviews: preliminary and follow-up. If you pass the first interview, you will be invited for a second one. Many recruiters acknowledge that their primary objective in the first interview is to screen out those whom they feel are not suited for their company. So your objective in the preliminary interview is to avoid being eliminated from further consideration. In doing so, there are a number of guidelines that can help you.

Preparation for the Interview
During the interview you should think the way a salesperson thinks. In other words, you should be prepared to convince the interviewer that you are the person he or she is seeking. If you have given careful attention to self-analysis, you should be in a good position to handle most of the interviewer's questions. In addition, if you have done background research on the company, you should find that many of the questions can be answered in such a way that the interviewer realizes you have done your homework and are indeed interested in the company. Typical questions you may be asked are listed in Figure A.5.

Attitude and Appearance
The interviewer is going to try to determine an answer to the important question, "How will this candidate be accepted by our current employees?" For this reason, you must have a positive attitude and good appearance. Be alert and enthusiastic; convey a feeling of "I'm happy to be here." During the interview, maintain eye contact and nod every now and then to indicate your understanding and approval. From time to time the interviewer will ask if you have any questions. Do not hesitate to ask some, but be careful about coming across as negative or picky. Discuss things in a positive and constructive way. For example, if you are asked, "What subject did you like least?" do not dwell on how difficult the course was or that the instructor was no good. Instead talk about how you wished the course were more practical or that

FIGURE A.5

Typical Questions Asked by Employers during Job Interviews

1. What are your long-range and short-range goals and objectives, when and why did you establish these goals, and how are you preparing yourself to achieve them?

2. What specific goals, other than those related to your occupation, have you established for yourself for the next 10 years?

3. What do you see yourself doing 5 years from now?

4. What do you *really* want to do in life?

5. What are your long-range career objectives?

6. How do you plan to achieve your career goals?

7. What are the most important rewards you expect in your business career?

8. What do you expect to be earning in 5 years?

9. Why did you choose the career for which you are preparing?

10. Which is more important to you, the money or the type of job?

11. What do you consider to be your greatest strengths and weaknesses?

12. How would you describe yourself?

13. How do you think a friend or professor who knows you would describe you?

14. What motivates you to put forth your greatest efforts?

15. How has your college experience prepared you for a business career?

16. Why should I hire you?

17. What qualifications do you have that make you think you will be successful in business?

18. How do you determine or evaluate success?

19. What do you think it takes to be successful in a company like ours?

20. In what ways do you think you can make a contribution to our company?

21. What qualities should a successful manager possess?

22. Describe the relationship that should exist between a supervisor and those reporting to him or her.

23. What two or three accomplishments have given you the most satisfaction? Why?

24. Describe your most rewarding college experience.

25. If you were hiring a graduate for this position, what qualities would you look for?

26. Why did you select your college or university?

27. What led you to choose your field of major study?

28. What college subjects did you like best? Why?

29. What college subjects did you like least? Why?

30. If you could do so, how would you plan your academic study differently? Why?

31. What changes would you make in your college or university? Why?

32. Do you have plans for continued study? An advanced degree?

33. Do you think your grades are a good indication of your academic achievement?

34. What have you learned from participation in extracurricular activities?

35. In what kind of a work environment are you most comfortable?

36. How well do you work under pressure?

37. In what part-time or summer jobs have you been most interested? Why?

38. How would you describe the ideal job for you following graduation?

39. Why did you decide to seek a position with this company?

40. What do you know about our company?

41. What two or three things are most important to you in your job?

42. Are you seeking employment in a company of a certain size? Why?

43. What criteria are you using to evaluate the company for which you hope to work?

44. Do you have a geographical preference? Why?

45. Will you relocate? Does relocation bother you?

46. Are you willing to travel?

47. Are you willing to spend at least six months as a trainee?

48. Why do you think you might like to live in the community in which our company is located?

49. What major problem have you encountered and how did you deal with it?

50. What have you learned from your mistakes?

Source: Florida International University, *Placement Manual*, 1990–91, 18.

you understand the need to know the subject, but that it was something that has never been able to hold your interest.

Dress well and be on time. Wear a business suit or similar outfit. Being well dressed will not get you the job, but a sloppy appearance will reduce your chances of getting even a follow-up interview. To avoid being late, plan ahead and allow yourself plenty of extra time in case you are caught up in heavy traffic, have trouble finding a parking space, or encounter some other problem.

Structure of the Interview A job interview typically has three parts: introduction, body, and close. The introduction is the ice-breaking portion of the interview. The interviewer will set the tone by trying to establish a positive atmosphere and put you at ease. This will usually take about 5 minutes.

The second part of the interview, the body, deals with requests for specific information. The interviewer will typically use a question-and-answer format to evaluate your qualifications and suitability for employment with the firm. The individual will be seeking information about your specific skills, knowledge, abilities, and attitudes. During this time you should be prepared to discuss your career objectives, academic qualifications, work experience, and personal goals. At the same time, you should avoid some subjects. For example, do not bring up the issue of salary. If the recruiter asks you what salary you are seeking, say "I'd like a salary that is commensurate with my abilities, but I'll let the company decide what that is." Remember, you did not say you would take whatever is offered. You are simply trying to indicate that money is not the only thing you are interested in. You can always counter a salary offer with a counteroffer later on.

The last part of the interview, the close, is used to answer any questions you have. The interviewer will also give you an idea of when the company will make a decision. Should the interviewer fail to tell you, feel free to ask. Also, be sure to convey to the interviewer your sincere interest in the company and the opportunity to explore the possibility of future employment.

These suggestions should be useful in helping you make a good impression. Here are some other specific hints for the interview:

1. Always check your appearance before being greeted by the interviewer.
2. Introduce yourself in a firm, confident manner.
3. Shake hands firmly.
4. Use the interviewer's last name in a friendly but businesslike manner. Do not address the interviewer by his or her first name unless specifically advised to do so.
5. Remain standing until you are offered a seat. However, if the interviewer has not offered you a seat after a reasonable time, ask: "May I be seated?"
6. Sit erectly but not rigidly. Place your arms and hands on the armrests of the chair or in your lap if there are no armrests. Avoid uncalled-for gestures.
7. Avoid writing notes during the interview. However, immediately after, take a few moments to jot down key points that you want to remember.
8. Avoid a boring presentation. Retain the interviewer's attention by varying the tempo of your speech and the tone of your voice.

9. Remember that this is your sales presentation. Take the opportunity to present yourself in a logical, confident manner.
10. Write a thank-you letter to the interviewer. An illustration is provided in Figure A.6.

The Follow-Up Interview

If you have favorably impressed the recruiter you will normally be given a second, or follow-up interview at the facility where you would be employed. The invitation will typically be conveyed in a letter that tells you when to arrive and with whom to coordinate the visit. The first thing to do is be sure that you are available on the date mentioned in the letter. Then call your contact person and get all of the information you need. If traveling expenses are involved, the company will reimburse you but may want to recommend a particular mode of transportation. For example, if you will be flying from Chicago to Los Angeles, the contact person will either have a ticket reserved for you at the airport or will ask you to purchase one and add that you will be reimbursed. Unless you are told otherwise, buy a coach ticket, not a first-class ticket, and keep copies of all your out-of-pocket expenses. The firm will reimburse you for everything that is reasonable.

Second, review your notes on the firm so that you are prepared to talk about company operations. Also review any notes you wrote after leaving the initial interview. These can be useful to you in remembering things you want to ask when you are on-site.

Third, when you are on-site be sure to dress professionally, unless you are instructed otherwise, and remain calm and poised. Do not smoke. During lunch refrain from ordering an alcoholic beverage, unless you are interviewing with a brewer or distiller, in which case you should have whatever everyone else is having. Be aware of your table manners, and when making "small talk" stay away from controversial topics such as politics and religion.

Fourth, in addition to the physical environment and the compensation package, be aware of the overall working climate. Do the people seem to like what they are doing? Does the work seem interesting and challenging? Do the managers appear to be effective? Do you think you will like working for the individual identified as your direct supervisor? What type of people will you be working with? In other words, will you be comfortable and challenged in this environment?

Fifth, after the visit is over file your expenses and send a thank-you letter to the key people you have met including your contact person and the individual who will be your supervisor.

Sixth, if you do not hear from the company within 10 days to 2 weeks, call your contact person and discuss where the firm is in the hiring process. Perhaps they have two more people to interview. Maybe they have completed the interview process and are now getting ready to make an offer. If you have other pending offers and must hear soon, let the contact person know this. Otherwise, sit tight for a while, but do not stop interviewing with other firms. It is better to have alternative offers to choose from rather than just one.

Finally, if you do get an offer, evaluate it carefully. Figure A.7 provides some important questions you should answer before making a decision. If you have two or more offers, you can use these questions to help you make a

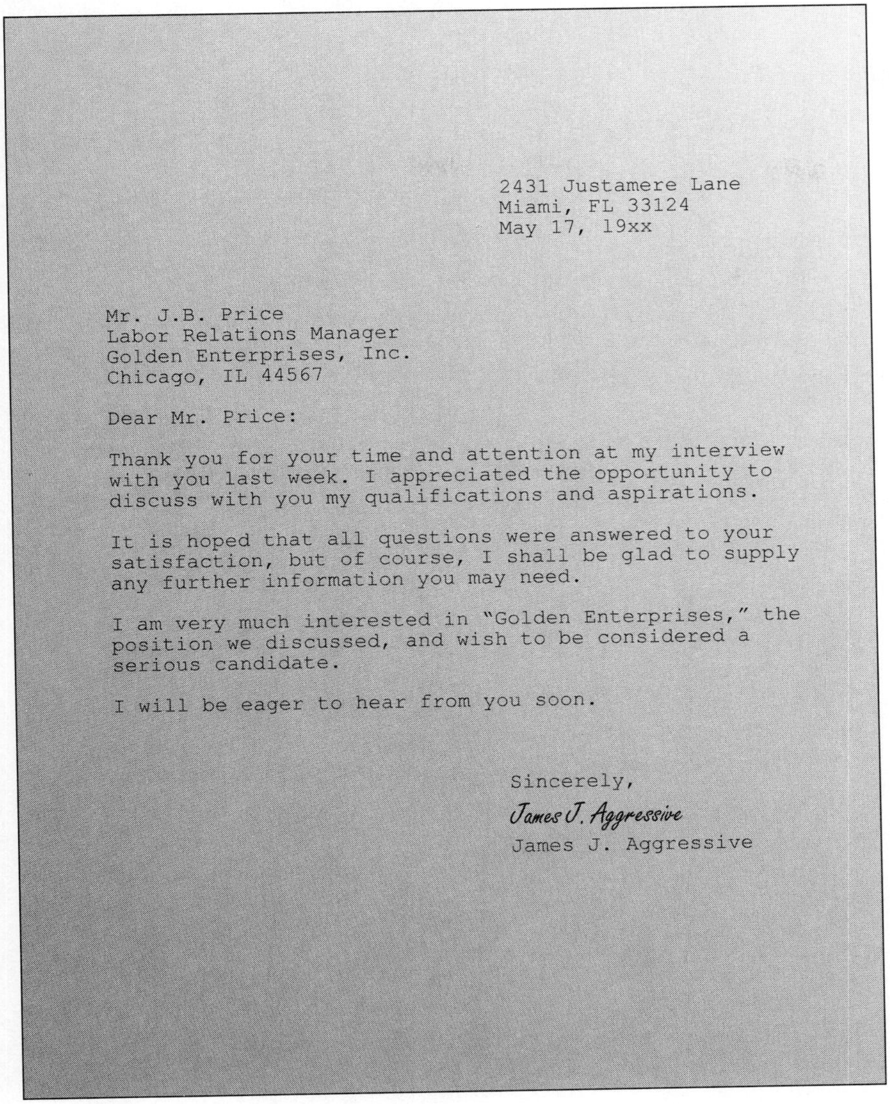

FIGURE A.6
Sample of a Thank-You Letter Written
after a Job Interview

Source: Florida International University,
Placement Manual: 1990–1991, 11.

```
                                    2431 Justamere Lane
                                    Miami, FL 33124
                                    May 17, 19xx



Mr. J.B. Price
Labor Relations Manager
Golden Enterprises, Inc.
Chicago, IL 44567

Dear Mr. Price:

Thank you for your time and attention at my interview
with you last week. I appreciated the opportunity to
discuss with you my qualifications and aspirations.

It is hoped that all questions were answered to your
satisfaction, but of course, I shall be glad to supply
any further information you may need.

I am very much interested in "Golden Enterprises," the
position we discussed, and wish to be considered a
serious candidate.

I will be eager to hear from you soon.



                              Sincerely,

                              James J. Aggressive
                              James J. Aggressive
```

comparison. If you have only one offer, after answering the questions you will have to decide whether the pluses outweigh the minuses. Whatever your decision, it will be based on a careful analysis rather than a gut feeling or emotional reaction.

In conclusion, keep in mind that a job search strategy is only the first step in your career. Now that you have taken the first step up the career ladder, you should begin thinking about your longer range plans and what you would like to accomplish over the next 3 to 5 years. After you have been on the job for a few months, talk to your new boss about these goals and

FIGURE A.7

Key Questions to Ask in Deciding Whether or Not to Take a Particular Job

- Will this position result in a significant promotion?
- Will it help broaden my experience and build a salable background?
- Would the company's management policies enhance my work performance?
- Will I get along well with the people with whom I will be working?
- Will I want to work for this company for 5 years or more?
- Is the offered salary satisfactory now?
- Will the anticipated salary 1 or 2 years from now be satisfactory?
- Am I sure that I can contribute substantially to the net worth of this company in the position involved?
- Is there a realistic opportunity for advancement beyond the starting scope and level of employment?
- Is the position itself interesting and challenging?

- Is the geographic location satisfactory to me and my family?
- Are desirable community, cultural, and religious facilities available?
- Has the company had a stable management team?
- If this is a new position, does the management decision to add this function seem well planned, and does it seem to have the support necessary?
- If this is not a new position, what happened to my predecessors?
- Is this a growth industry?
- Is the company growing faster than its competitors?
- Are the negative factors in my former position likely to exist in this new company?
- How good is my bargaining position?
- Is the company really sold on me, or do they appear to be merely willing to take a chance?

Source: Florida International University, *Placement Manual: 1990–1991,* 23.

C H E C K ✓ P O I N T

begin working to formulate an early career plan. It is never too soon to follow up your early success with a strategy for even greater accomplishments.

1. What three things are most important in interviewing effectively? Identify and describe each.
2. What will be most important to you in deciding whether or not to take a job?

Glossary

Absolute advantage A monopoly on certain products or the ability to produce them for considerably less than anyone else.

Accounting The process of measuring, interpreting, evaluating, and communicating financial information for the purpose of financial control and effective decision making.

Accounting equation The relationship stating that assets equal liabilities plus owners' equity.

Acid-test ratio The ratio of highly liquid assets to current liabilities.

Acquisition The purchase of one company by another, in which the purchasing company takes over the acquired company's operations and property.

Activity format Classifies cash inflows and outflows in terms of operating, investing, and financing activities.

Actuaries Experts in collecting statistics about losses and using this information to make predictions.

Advertising A nonpersonal form of promotion in which a firm attempts to persuade someone to a particular point of view.

Affirmative-action programs Programs designed to seek out minorities, women, those with a disability, and others with problems finding work and to hire, train, develop, and promote them.

Agency A legal relationship between an agent and a principal.

Agency shop A company at which the employees do not have to join the union but nevertheless have to pay union dues.

Agent A person authorized to act on behalf of another.

Agent intermediaries Wholesalers that do not take title to the goods they distribute.

Alien corporation A business incorporated in one country but operating in another.

American Federation of Labor (AFL) The most important craft union federation in the United States.

American Stock Exchange (AMEX) The second largest exchange in the United States.

Analytic manufacturing process A process that reduces a raw material to its component parts for the purpose of obtaining one or more products.

Antitrust Improvements Act A federal law that requires companies planning to merge to notify the FTC in advance and allows injured parties to file lawsuits.

Antitrust Procedures and Penalties Act A federal law that increased fines and penalties imposed for violation of the Sherman Antitrust Act.

Apprentice training Training a new employee by assigning a more experienced employee to teach procedures, rules, and techniques over a relatively long period.

Arbitration A resolution method in which a neutral third party listens to both sides and then directs each side in what to do.

Artificial intelligence (AI) Information technology for developing computers that can mimic human logic and allow the user to interact with the computer in English rather than a computer language.

Assets Everything of value owned by an enterprise.

Authority The right to command.

Authorization card A request that the union represent the workers.

Automatic teller machine (ATM) A machine that takes bank customers' debit cards and secret access codes to automatically deposit or withdraw funds from their accounts.

Aviation insurance Coverage of losses involving airliners and their passengers.

Bait and switch Advertising a product at a very low price and then telling customers the product is either out of stock or of low quality and recommending a higher priced alternative.

Balance of payments The total cash flow out of a country minus the total inflow of cash.

Balance of trade The difference between the value of a nation's exports and the value of its imports.

Balance sheet A financial statement showing the position of a firm as of a particular date.

Bank money market accounts Short-term special deposit accounts that offer competitive interest rates.

Bankruptcy law The branch of law that specifies the legal steps for securing relief from debts.

Bear An investor who believes that stock prices are going to fall.

Benefit segmentation Dividing up a market on the basis of the benefits that people seek.

Binding arbitration Arbitration in which both parties agree to follow the arbitrator's decision.

Blue-chip stocks Stocks of large, high-quality companies with a proven track record.

Blue-collar jobs Jobs in manufacturing or ones that call for employees to work with their hands.

Board of directors The top governing body of a corporation.

Bonds Long-term debts with a term of 20 to 30 years that are sold to raise funds.

Boycott An organized effort to convince people to refrain from buying goods or services from targeted businesses.

Brainstorming A creative technique for groups in which participants generate as many ideas as possible for solving a problem without considering at first the merits of each idea.

Branch organization An operation set up by a parent company in a foreign country for the purpose of accomplishing specific goals such as sales.

Brand A name, term, symbol, or combination of these used to identify a firm's products and differentiate them from competing products.

Breakeven point The level of production at which total revenues from selling the products equal total expenses incurred in making them.

Broker An agent intermediary that brings buyers and sellers together.

Budget A financial plan that specifies revenues and expenses for a given time period.

Bull An investor who believes that stock prices are going to rise.

Bumping An arrangement permitting employees laid off from one department to go to another department in the company and replace, or bump, someone there who has less seniority.

Burnout Mental and/or physical exhaustion caused by excess stress.

Business An organized, profit-seeking approach to providing people with the goods and services they want.

Business cycles Fluctuations in business activity.

Business ethics Standards that govern business behavior.

Business interruption insurance Coverage of losses from temporary business closings.

Buying Deciding the type and amount of goods to be purchased.

Byte A character of data.

Call option An option to buy a specific security.

Call provision A bond provision that allows the firm to repurchase the bonds before maturity.

Capital The money and technology used for operating the enterprise.

Capital goods Machinery, equipment, tools, and facilities.

Carrying costs The expenses associated with keeping inventory on hand.

Cash discount A discount given for paying a bill within a predetermined time period.

Cash value The amount of money in a life insurance policy that the insured can borrow or obtain by canceling the policy.

Celler-Kefauver Antimerger Act A federal law that prohibits mergers and major asset purchases that decrease competition in an industry.

Centralization An approach to delegation in which upper management levels retain most of the important decisions.

Central tendency error A rating error in which a manager tends to rate all employees as average regardless of how well or poorly they performed.

Certificates of deposit (CDs) Fixed-term accounts that pay a predetermined rate of interest.

Certified management accountant (CMA) A private accountant who has met certain education and professional requirements and has passed a series of exams.

Certified public accountant (CPA) A public accountant who has met state certification requirements of education and job experience and has passed a comprehensive examination.

Channel of distribution The path a product follows from production to final sale.

Checkoff Deducting union dues directly from each member's paycheck.

Class-action suit A lawsuit in which a group of buyers join together to sue the seller.

Clayton Act A federal law that prohibits tying agreements, interlocking directorates, and certain anticompetitive stock acquisitions.

Collateralized loan A loan that is backed with something of value that the lender can claim in case of default.

Collective bargaining The process in which management and employees, represented by the union of their choice, negotiate over wages, hours, and conditions of employment.

Commercial bank A financial institution that accepts deposits and provides a wide array of financial services.

Commercial finance company Lending institution that provides short-term, collateralized loans to businesses.

Commercial paper An unsecured promissory note.

Common carrier A transportation company that performs services within a particular line of business for the general public.

Common law The precedents established by prior court decisions, going back to English law.

Common stock Ownership shares in a corporation.

Communism An economic system in which the government owns all property and makes all decisions regarding production of goods and services.

Comparable worth The idea that jobs requiring equal amounts of skill and responsibility are of equal value to the employer and therefore should receive equal pay.

Comparative advantage The ability to sell certain products for relatively less than producers in most other nations can.

Composite of leading indicators A set of measurements that provides clues about which way the economy is moving.

Computer-integrated manufacturing (CIM) A manufacturing system that automates all of the factory functions and links them with company headquarters.

Computer network A system that allows for multiple users and multiple activities.

Computer program A series of coded instructions that tells the computer what to do.

Computer virus A small piece of computer code that can automatically hide duplicates of itself inside legitimate programs and when activated can destroy data and software.

Concentrated marketing Focusing marketing efforts on a single market segment.

Concurrent engineering A process in which people involved in designing new products work together as a group to create the final product.

Congress of Industrial Organizations (CIO) The most important industrial union federation in the United States.

Conscious motives The reasons for buying that people are willing to express.

Consumer behavior The way consumers go about making their purchase decisions.

Consumer finance company Financial institution that makes short-term loans to individuals.

Consumer good or service A good or service destined to be used by a consumer.

Consumerism A movement designed to provide buyers with the information and bargaining power necessary for obtaining high-quality, safe products and services.

Consumer-oriented marketing Based on the belief that a company must find out what the customer needs before providing a good or service.

Consumer pretest A test of advertising effectiveness that asks people to examine ads and rank them on their ability to capture and retain interest.

Contingency leadership The leadership technique of using the style that will be most effective in a specific situation.

Continuous production A production sequence in which the flow of materials is steady and constant.

Contract A legally binding promise.

Contract carrier A transportation company that performs services called for by an individual contract.

Contrarianism An investment strategy based on the belief that the market will move in the direction opposite to that predicted by the general public.

Controlling Comparing actual results against expected performance within a predetermined time.

Convenience store A limited-line store that specializes in fast service.

Conversion privilege A provision permitting conversion of bonds into a stated number of shares of common stock.

Cooperative advertising Advertising for a product in which the manufacturer and merchant share the costs.

Coordination A systematic, unified group effort in the pursuit of common objectives.

Copyright A legal protection of a particular work that allows its owner the exclusive right to reproduce, sell, and adapt the work.

Core hours Those times when everyone must be on the job under a flexible work schedule.

Corporate officers Individuals legally empowered to represent the corporation and to bind it to contracts.

Corporation A body established by law and existing distinct from the individuals who invest in and control it.

Cost of goods sold The costs involved in producing or acquiring a product to sell.

Couponing A sales promotion technique that offers buyers a specified discount if they redeem a coupon.

Creative process Generating new or unique ideas, involving four steps: preparation, incubation, illumination, and verification.

Creative selling Determining the buyer's needs and matching them with the products for sale.

Credit card An instrument used for obtaining a short-term loan for a cash purchase.

Credit union A savings cooperative that lends money to its members.

Critical path The sequence of activities that identifies the longest possible time a project will take.

Cross training An expanded version of job rotation, in which the employee learns different skills or perspectives.

Culture The beliefs, attitudes, values, and behaviors that people learn in their society.

Currency Coins and paper money.

Current assets Assets that the company will use or convert into cash within the year.

Current liabilities Financial obligations that will fall due within the year.

Current ratio The ratio of current assets to current liabilities.

Customer departmentalization The structure of a level of an organization on the basis of customer needs.

Customs duties Taxes levied on imported goods.

Data base An organization of data for rapid search and retrieval.

Debenture An unsecured bond.

Debit card An instrument that allows a merchant to deduct purchases directly from the buyer's bank account.

Debt-equity ratio The ratio of total debt to total equity.

Decentralization An approach to delegation in which many important decisions are made by lower management levels.

Decertification The process of dropping a union as the bargaining agent for the workers.

Deductible The amount that a policyholder must pay before the insurance company pays any part of a claim.

Deed A document that establishes property ownership and is transferable to other parties.

Defendant The party against whom a legal action is brought.

Delegation The distribution of work and authority to subordinates.

Delphi A group technique in which a panel of experts (and sometimes nonexperts) makes anonymous contributions, receives composite feedback, and then repeats the process until completion.

Demand The various amounts of a product that will be purchased at varying prices.

Demand deposits Checking accounts.

Demographic segmentation Dividing up a market on the basis of socioeconomic characteristics.

Departmentalization The structure of a given level of an organization on the basis of some common characteristics.

Department store A large store that offers a wide variety of merchandise grouped into departments.

Depreciation A deduction from the value of a fixed asset to account for its gradual wearing out.

Depression An economic period characterized by prolonged recession, massive unemployment, low wages, and large numbers of people living in poverty.

Deregulation The removal of government controls in certain industries.

Derivative plan The plan for a series of actions that convert the strategic plan into an operational plan.

Desktop publishing A computer system that allows companies to publish newsletters, charts, brochures, and other printed material in-house.

Desktop video (DTV) A new technology that combines both audio and visual effects to create sales or financial analysis in the form of an animated video.

Differentiated marketing Selling a range of related products to specific market segments.

Direct channel A distribution channel that bypasses all intermediaries.

Directing Getting human resources to work effectively and efficiently.

Directing function A management approach that brings employees and the organization together to achieve the objectives of both.

Directors' and officers' liability insurance Coverage of the costs of lawsuits against board members and senior corporate executives arising out of their actions.

Discount An amount subtracted from the list price; the amount by which a bond's price is less than its face value.

Discount rate The interest rate that the Fed charges member banks for loans.

Discount store A retail store that offers lower prices and fewer customer services than other retailers.

Discretionary order An order that gives the stockbroker the right to execute it immediately or wait for a better price.

Divestiture The selling off of a business holding.

Dividend A payment to stockholders from the corporation's earnings.

Domestic corporation A business operating in the state where it is incorporated.

Door-to-door retailer A salesperson who sells products house to house.

Dormant partner A partner who is not known as a partner to the general public and plays no active role in the company.

Double-entry bookkeeping The use of two entries for every transaction.

Downward processing A materials flow in which different parts of the same product are produced on different floors.

Durable goods Goods that do not wear out quickly.

Earnings per share The ratio of net income to common stock shares outstanding.

Ecology The interrelationship of living things and their environment.

Economic environment An environment in which buyers and sellers are brought together through an elaborate series of markets.

Economic order quantity (EOQ) model An inventory-ordering model that balances order and carrying costs and reduces the likelihood of running out of inventory.

Economics The study of how societies use limited resources to fulfill their needs and wants for goods and services.

Electronic funds transfer system A computerized system for depositing and withdrawing funds electronically.

Electronic mail A system for sending and receiving messages through computers.

Employer associations Employer-sponsored lobbying and public relations organizations primarily designed to promote promanagement legislation.

Employment at will The principle that the employer can retain or dismiss personnel as it wishes.

Endowment life insurance Life insurance that combines a death benefit with a great deal of savings.

Entrepreneur The creator and/or organizer of a venture.

Entrepreneurship The process of organizing, operating, and assuming the risks associated with a business venture.

Equal Employment Opportunity Commission (EEOC) The commission charged with overseeing enforcement of the Civil Rights Act of 1964 by investigating complaints and taking appropriate action.

Equilibrium price The price at which demand equals supply.

Equity financing The sale of ownership in a firm.

Ethics The use of proper conduct and behavior.

Exception principle The principle that management should concern itself only with significant deviations or exceptions.

Excise tax A levy designed to limit the purchase of goods or make the users of certain services help pay for them.

Exclusive distribution A channel strategy in which only one intermediary distributes a product in a given area.

Export-Import Bank (Exim Bank) A U.S. government lending agency that makes loans to importers and exporters unable to obtain private funding.

Exports Goods or services sold to other countries.

Express contract One in which the parties make oral or written promises.

Express warranty A guarantee offered orally or in writing.

Expropriation and inconvertibility insurance Political risk insurance that covers nationalization of property and conversion of currency.

Fabrication Combining materials or parts in order to form or assemble them into a finished product.

Facsimile machine (fax) A machine that transmits and receives documents via telephone lines.

Factor A financial institution that purchases accounts receivable.

Family brand A brand used with all of the products a firm sells.

Fast freight The rapid conveyance of perishable goods by train.

Federal Deposit Insurance Corporation (FDIC) A federal agency that insures the deposits of at first banks and now also S&Ls up to $100,000 in case of failure.

Federal Reserve System (Fed) A network of regional banks that regulate banking in America.

Federal Trade Commission Act A federal law that prohibits unfair trade practices and established the Federal Trade Commission (FTC).

Fidelity bond Coverage of losses caused by employee embezzlement or theft.

FIFO An inventory valuation system under which the first goods produced or acquired are considered the first ones sold (**F**irst **I**n **F**irst **O**ut).

Financial manager The person responsible for developing, implementing, and controlling the financial plan.

Fiscal policy The use of government spending and tax collection to attain full employment and a noninflationary high level of GNP.

Fiscal year The 12 months that constitute an organization's annual operation.

Fixed assets Assets that the company intends to keep for more than one year and use in the operation of the business.

Fixed-price technique A pricing technique in which the marketer sells at the announced price.

Flat structure Structure with few levels and wide spans of control.

Flex benefits approach An employee benefit arrangement that allows each worker to tailor his or her own benefit package.

Flexible manufacturing system (FMS) A manufacturing system in which computer-controlled machining centers produce complicated parts at high speed.

Flexible pricing Selling a product at a price that is negotiable.

Flexible work schedule An approach that allows workers to control their own schedule, within limitations established by the organization.

Flextime A flexible work schedule built around core hours.

Foreign corporation A business that has been incorporated in another state.

Formal organization structure The explicitly established lines of authority and responsibility designed by management.

Franchise A system of distribution in which a producer or supplier arranges for a dealer to handle a product or service under mutually agreed-upon conditions.

Franchisee The dealer in a franchise system.

Franchisor The supplier in a franchise system.

Freedom of choice The freedom of businesses to hire people, invest money, purchase machinery and equipment, and choose the markets where they wish to operate.

Free enterprise system An economic system under which businesses are free to decide what to supply and are rewarded based on how well they meet customer needs.

Free-trade zone (FTZ) A geographic area into which foreign goods can be imported without payment of duties.

Freight forwarder A common carrier that leases or contracts space from other carriers and resells it to small-volume shippers.

Functional departmentalization The structure of a level of an organization on the basis of major activities.

Fundamental analysis The process of comparing a company's current financial position and prospects for the future with those of other firms.

Gantt chart A tool for production scheduling and control that keeps track of projected and actual work progress over time.

General Agreement on Tariffs and Trade (GATT) An international agreement and organization designed to eliminate tariff barriers to worldwide trade.

General partner A partner who is active in the operation of a business and has unlimited liability.

Generic product A product with no brand and simple packaging.

Geographic departmentalization The structure of a level of an organization along territorial lines.

Geographic segmentation Dividing up a market on the basis of where people live.

Goal setting The process of establishing specific objectives for an individual to pursue.

Grading Sorting goods into classes based on quality.

Grievance A complaint brought by an employee who feels that he or she has been treated improperly.

Gross national product (GNP) The total market value of all goods and services produced in the economy in one year.

Group incentive plan Compensation to units, departments, and sometimes the entire organization for meeting or exceeding a goal.

Halo effect The tendency to allow an overall positive evaluation of a person to influence the specific characteristics being rated.

Hardware The machinery and physical components of a computer.

Hawthorne studies Pioneering research studies on worker behavior and motivation.

Horizontal flow A materials flow in which all production takes place on the same floor.

Human resource managers Managers responsible for staffing the organization and training, developing, appraising, and maintaining its employees.

Human resource planning The process of forecasting personnel needs and developing the necessary strategies for meeting those needs.

Hygiene factors Job characteristics that do not motivate people but that cause dissatisfaction when absent, including money, working conditions, and job security.

Hypermarket A giant store selling a combination of groceries and general merchandise at low prices.

Illumination State of the creative process during which the answer to the problem or issue becomes apparent.

Implied contract One created by the actions of one or more parties.

Implied warranty A guarantee that automatically accompanies the sale of a product.

Imports Goods or services brought into one's own country.

Impulse items Goods that consumers buy on the spur of the moment.

Income statement A financial statement that summarizes the firm's operations for a given period of time, usually one year.

Incubation Stage of the creative process that involves sitting back and letting the subconscious mind work on the problem.

Indenture agreement A document that sets forth the terms of a bond issue.

Individual brand A brand used exclusively for one of the products a firm sells.

Individual incentive payment plan Compensation that rewards a specific worker for high performance.

Industrial good or service A good or service used to produce still other goods or services.

Inflation A general increase in the level of prices.

Informal organization structure The structure created by the personnel on the basis of friendship and common interests.

Inland marine insurance Coverage of damage to or loss of goods shipped by rail, truck, airplane, or inland barge.

Innovation The introduction by business of a new product or service or the application of a new way to produce a product or service.

Input Any resource needed to produce a desired good or service.

Inside directors Directors who are employees of the firm.

Institutional advertising Advertising designed to create goodwill and build a desired company image.

Institutional investors Organizations that buy securities with their own funds or with funds held in trust for others.

Insurance A financial arrangement under which the cost of unexpected losses is distributed among those who are insured.

Insurance benefit programs Benefits designed to provide various forms of coverage against accident, illness, or death.

Intangible assets Assets such as patents or goodwill that do not have physical presence.

Integrated circuit A network of dozens of tiny transistors etched onto a silicon wafer.

Intensive distribution A channel strategy in which the producer sells its product through every available outlet.

Interlocking directorate An arrangement in which a majority of the board of directors of two or more competing corporations with assets in excess of $1 million are the same people.

Intermittent production A production sequence in which the flow of materials is noncontinuous.

Internal auditor In-house accountant who checks the accuracy of the organization's records and accounting methods.

Internal research Collecting and analyzing information contained in company records.

International Bank for Reconstruction and Development (World Bank) An agency that lends to underdeveloped countries to help them grow.

International Development Association (IDA) An organization that lends to underdeveloped countries.

International Finance Corporation (IFC) An organization that invests in private enterprises in underdeveloped nations.

International Monetary Fund (IMF) A UN organization that tries to stabilize exchange rates between world currencies.

In-transit privileges Permission to stop a train shipment along the way in order to perform a function and then continue the shipment.

Intrapreneur Manager or staff expert who creates and controls new, usually risky projects within an existing business.

Intrapreneuring Creating and controlling of new, usually risky projects by managers and staff experts within an existing business.

Inventory management Efficiently balancing inventory with sales orders.

Inventory turnover The number of times that inventory is replaced during the year, expressed as the ratio of costs of goods sold to average inventory.

Investment bank A financial intermediary that purchases and resells bonds and stocks.

Job enrichment A technique for motivating employees by adding motivator factors to their jobs.

Job rotation Development of broad experience by moving an employee from one job to another.

Job sharing Employing two or more part-time workers to fulfill the requirements of a single full-time position.

Joint venture An arrangement in which two companies pool their resources to create, produce, and market a product; when viewed as a partnership, is usually temporary and created for the purpose of carrying out a single business project.

Junk bonds High interest-bearing but very risky bonds that were mainly issued in the 1980s.

Just-in-time (JIT) inventory A system of receiving inventory just before it is needed in the production process.

Kidnap, ransom, and extortion insurance Political risk insurance that covers costs associated with these criminal acts.

Knights of Labor The most important federation of unions for skilled and unskilled workers in the years following the Civil War.

Label The part of a package that presents information about its contents.

Labor The people who produce the goods and services that the business provides.

Land The geographic territory, including water and natural resources, used in producing goods and services.

Leadership The process of influencing people to direct their efforts toward the achievement of particular objectives.

Lease A document that allows the tenant to use the owner's property for a predetermined time period in exchange for consideration.

Leniency error A rating error in which a manager rates most employees above average or excellent.

Leverage The use of borrowed funds to increase the return on equity.

Liabilities Creditors' claims on an enterprise's assets.

License A legal agreement in which one firm gives another the right to manufacture and sell its product in return for paying a royalty.

LIFO An inventory valuation system under which the last goods produced or acquired are considered the first ones sold (Last In, First Out).

Limited partner A partner whose liability is limited to his or her investment in the business.

Limited-pay life insurance Whole life insurance that limits the number of years the insured must pay premiums.

Limit order An order that specifies the highest price at which the broker may buy stock or the lowest price at which the broker may sell stock.

Line-and-staff organization structure A structure in which specialists help those directly responsible for attaining organization objectives.

Line of credit A stated cash reserve available whenever the business wants to draw on it.

Line organization structure A structure in which authority flows directly from the top of the organization to the bottom.

Line position Those who give orders and make decisions in their area of responsibility.

Liquidation The sale of all assets to meet outstanding debts.

Liquidity The ease with which an asset can be converted into cash.

List price The price announced for a product.

Local ad A television ad carried only in the immediate area.

Local union The basic unit of the union structure, representing members in a limited area.

Lockout A company's refusal to allow workers to enter a facility.

Long-term liabilities Debts that will be due one or more years in the future.

Long-term loan A loan that has a term of at least one year.

Loss leader A product that is priced below cost to attract people into a store.

M1 A measure of the money supply equal to currency and demand deposits.

Macroeconomics The branch of economics that is concerned with the overall economy.

Mail-order house A retailer that sells goods through a mail-order catalog.

Mainframe computer A large computer system with considerable storage capacity and fast processing capability.

Maintenance-of-membership provision A requirement that those who join the union must remain members.

Management The process of setting objectives and coordinating employees' efforts to attain them.

Management by objectives (MBO) The system in which managers and subordinates jointly set objectives to use as the basis for operating the business and evaluating performance.

Management by walking around (MBWA) The management practice of visiting the workplace to find out what is going on.

Management information system (MIS) A method for collecting, analyzing, and disseminating timely information to support decision making.

Margin trading Buying stock without putting up the full value of the transaction.

Marine insurance Coverage of losses to boats, ships, trucks, railcars and engines, planes, and their cargo.

Market A group of customers who have the money and desire to purchase goods and services.

Market economy An environment in which prices and wages are determined by the competitive environment, rather than by central planners, as in socialist countries.

Marketing Identifying the goods and services the customer needs and providing them at the right price, place, and time.

Marketing mix The combination of a firm's strategies for product, price, place, and promotion.

Marketing research Investigating marketing problems and identifying market opportunities.

Market order An order to purchase or sell a stock at the best possible price at the present time.

Market segmentation Dividing markets into groups that have similar characteristics.

Master production schedule A plan that coordinates all of the raw materials, parts, equipment, manufacturing processes, and assembly operations necessary to produce goods.

Materials handling Overseeing the movement of goods within the company's facilities.

Matrix organization structure A structure that combines elements of a line organization with elements of a project organization.

Mediation A resolution method in which a neutral third party with no formal authority helps both sides reach a settlement.

Medicare A federal program providing hospital and medical insurance to the elderly.

Mentor An experienced employee who coaches and counsels a less experienced employee in the latter's training and development, providing advice and assistance and helping the person achieve career goals.

Merchant wholesalers Intermediaries that take title to the goods they distribute.

Merger The joining together of two companies to form a new company.

Microcomputer A small desktop computer that relies on a microprocessor.

Microeconomics The branch of economics that is concerned with the individual firm or household.

Microprocessor An integrated circuit on one chip that is the equivalent of the central processing unit in a larger computer.

Minicomputer A medium-sized computer in terms of physical dimensions and storage capacity.

Minority enterprise small business investment company (MESBIC) An SBIC that provides capital and equity financing to small businesses whose owners are economically or socially disadvantaged.

Missionary selling A type of personal selling in which one salesperson supports the sales efforts of others.

Mixed economy An economy combining the characteristics of free enterprise, Communist, and/or Socialist economies.

Modification The process of changing raw materials into a product.

Monetary policy Government regulation of the money supply to attain full employment and a noninflationary high level of GNP.

Money Anything a society generally accepts in payment for goods and services.

Money market mutual funds Shares in mutual funds that make short-term investments in securities of the federal government and major corporations.

Monopolistic competition A market structure in which there are many firms, each producing only a small share of the total output demanded.

Motivation The process through which needs or wants lead to drives aimed at goals or incentives.

Motivator factors Job characteristics that make people feel exceptionally good about their jobs, including challenge, recognition, and responsibility.

Multinational corporation (MNC) A company having operations in more than one country, foreign sales, and/or a nationality mix of managers and owners.

Mutual fund An investment company that pools the contributions of investors: the fund is carefully managed by buying and selling securities to meet the investment objectives.

Mutual insurance company A type of cooperative in which the policyholders become shareholders of the insurance company.

Mutual savings bank State-chartered bank that offers many of the same services as S&Ls.

National banks Commercial banks chartered by the federal government.

National brand A brand owned by a manufacturer.

National union The parent organization for local unions, which focuses on long-range considerations that affect all of the locals.

Near money Certain highly liquid assets that do not function as a medium of exchange.

Negotiable instrument A form of business paper that can be transferred from one person to another as a substitute for money.

Negotiable order of withdrawal (NOW) account A checking account that pays interest.

Net exports The amount by which foreign spending on American goods and services exceeds American spending on foreign goods and services.

Net profit margin ratio The ratio of net income to net sales.

Network ad A television ad directed at a major audience around the country.

New York Stock Exchange (NYSE) The largest and best-known exchange in the United States.

No-fault insurance Coverage providing compensation regardless of who was at fault in an auto accident.

Nominal group A group in name only, consisting of individuals whose independent ideas are pooled or combined; they are not allowed to have face-to-face interaction with one another.

Nominal grouping technique (NGT) A group technique including benefits of both nominal grouping and normal interacting groups; it follows these steps: silent generation of ideas, round robin input, full interactive discussion, and decision making.

Nominal partner A partner who lends his or her name to the partnership but plays no role in the operation.

Nondurable goods Goods that are used up or wear out quickly.

Nonprice competition The effort to win over customers with advertising and personal selling rather than price.

Ocean marine insurance Coverage of losses that occur to ships or their cargo on the high seas or in port.

Odd lot Any number of stock shares less than 100.

Odd pricing Setting a price just below a round number for psychological reasons.

Old Age, Survivors, Disability, and Health Insurance (OASDHI) A federal insurance program (commonly known as social security) that provides retirement, medical, disability, and death benefits.

Oligopoly A market in which a small percentage of the firms dominate the industry.

On-the-job training Informal instruction conducted at the job site.

Open-market operations The buying and selling of government securities by the Fed.

Open order An order that instructs the broker to leave it on the books until it is executed or the investor cancels.

Open shop A company at which the workers do not have to join a union or pay union dues.

Operational objectives Short-range objectives that help management control its internal resources and implement the strategic plan.

Operational plan A short-range plan.

Operations The process of transforming inputs such as raw materials and labor into outputs, or finished products or services.

Operations planning The process whereby managers determine the most profitable way to produce the goods and services the company will sell.

Options Contracts that permit an investor to either purchase or sell a particular security at a predetermined price and within a certain time period.

Order costs The expenses associated with ordering inventory.

Order processing Taking sales orders, checking them, and then seeing that the product is shipped to the customer.

Order taking Processing orders from customers who have decided they want to buy.

Organizational culture An organization's norms, beliefs, attitudes, and values.

Organizing Efficiently bringing together human and material resources to attain objectives.

Output The finished good or service that results from the production process.

Outside directors Directors who come from outside the company.

Over-the-counter (OTC) market A marketplace for unlisted securities that trade outside the organized securities exchanges.

Owner or executive insurance Life insurance that reimburses an organization upon the death of a key employee.

Owners' equity The owners' claim on the assets of an enterprise.

Partnership An association of two or more persons to carry on as co-owners of a business for profit.

Passbook savings accounts Non-checkable interest-bearing accounts.

Patent A federal government grant of exclusive control over and use of a discovery or a new product or process for 17 years.

Paternalistic approach Taking care of employees similar to the way that parents take care of children.

Peak The phase of the business cycle when national output reaches its highest level.

Peer rating A performance appraisal in which the workers all rate each other.

Pension fund A pool of money set aside and invested to take care of retirement obligations.

People-meter An electronic instrument attached to a TV that records the channel to which the set is tuned.

Perpetual inventory A system for keeping track of inventory by subtracting what the company uses up or sells and adding what the company purchases.

Personal investors Individuals who trade securities for their own account.

Personal property Any property that is not real property.

Personnel managers Human resource managers.

Physical distribution The activities necessary to move goods from the producer to the final user.

Physical inventory The process of counting the amount of inventory on hand.

Picket An assembly of workers stationed outside the premises for the purpose of calling attention to their grievances.

Piggyback service The shipment of a fully loaded truck trailer on a specially designed railroad flatcar.

Place The location where a good or service is available for purchase.

Plaintiff The party that brings a legal action.

Planning Setting objectives and formulating the steps to attain them.

Point-of-purchase (POP) displays In-store displays of a product that draw attention to it.

Point-of-sale terminal A computer terminal that allows retail customers to use a debit card to transfer funds from their bank account to that of the merchant.

Pollution Contamination of the air, water, land, or environment in which life exists.

Portfolio analysis A method for developing a product strategy based on the attractiveness of a market and the product's share of that market.

Preferred stock Stock that provides preferential treatment in the payment of dividends and the distribution of assets.

Premium A fee to cover the costs of an insurance policy; the price paid for a bond above its face value.

Premiums Goods offered to potential customers as an incentive to purchase a product.

Preparation Stage of the creative process that involves gathering information on the problem or issue under analysis.

Price The cost of the product or service to the purchaser.

Price level The price being charged in the industry.

Primary-demand advertising Advertising designed to increase the total demand for a good or service, rather than for a particular brand.

Primary needs Physiological needs such as food, water, sex, sleep, clothing, and shelter.

Primary research Obtaining information for the first time through interviews or direct observation.

Principal A person represented by an agent.

Private brand A brand owned by a retailer.

Private carrier A transportation company owned by the company whose goods it transports.

Private investment Total expenditures for capital goods during a year.

Private warehouse A storage facility owned or leased by the company whose goods it stores.

Process layout A production layout that groups machines and equipment on the basis of function.

Product Any good or service that the firm offers to the customer.

Product departmentalization The structure of a level of an organization on the basis of product lines.

Product design The process of deciding the specific dimensions of the good or service to be produced.

Production-oriented marketing Based on the belief that a good product or service will sell itself.

Productivity The amount of output divided by the input.

Product layout A production layout in which all machines are set up along a product-flow line, and the units to be manufactured move down this line.

Profit The difference between revenues and expenses.

Program evaluation and review technique (PERT) A planning and control tool useful on complex projects requiring coordination.

Progressive tax A tax that charges lower rates to taxpayers with lower incomes.

Project organization structure A structure formed for the purpose of attaining a particular objective and then disbanded.

Promotion The process of stimulating demand for a company's goods and services.

Property law The branch of law that involves the rights and duties associated with the ownership or use of real or personal property.

Property tax A levy based on the assessed value of a piece of real estate.

Proportional tax A tax in which the rate remains the same regardless of the base.

Prospecting Researching potential buyers and choosing those who are the most likely customers.

Proxy A written authorization that allows a specified person to cast a stockholder's vote.

Psychographic segmentation Dividing up a market on the basis of the customer's lifestyle, values, or personality.

Publicity Product- or company-related information that the firm does not pay the media to carry and that the firm does not control.

Public relations All activities directed toward creating and maintaining a favorable public image.

Public warehouse A public storage facility whose owner is not the company storing goods there.

Purchasing The process of buying inventory and other assets.

Pure competition A market structure in which there are many independent sellers, each offering products at the current market price.

Pure monopoly A market in which there is only one seller or producer and there are no substitutes for the product or service.

Pure risk The threat of a loss without the possibility of a gain.

Put option An option to sell a specific security.

Quality control The process of ensuring that goods and services are produced or provided within predetermined specifications.

Quality-control circle A group of workers who meet regularly to discuss the way they do their jobs and to recommend changes.

Quality of work life (QWL) Efforts to improve the job environment and make work life more enjoyable and meaningful.

Quantity discount A discount given to buyers who place larger-than-average orders.

Quota A restriction on the quantity or value of an item that may be imported.

Random walk theory An investment strategy holding that future stock prices are independent of past stock prices.

Readership report A test of advertising effectiveness that asks people to look at ads that have appeared in publications and identify those that they recognize and those that they have read.

Realistic job previews Orientations that attempt to tell the full story about the job instead of creating false expectations.

Real property Land and property attached to land.

Recession An economic period during which the economy begins to slow and move downward.

Recovery An economic period during which demand for goods and services is on the rise.

Redemption premium A bonus the company pays bondholders for early redemption of bonds.

Regional stock exchanges Exchanges that trade the stocks of firms that serve regional markets.

Regressive tax A tax that hits low-income persons harder than high-income persons.

Regular checking An account that pays no interest but allows the depositor to write checks on the funds.

Reliable test Test that gives consistent and accurate results.

Reserve requirement The percentage of all deposits that a bank must keep on hand at the bank or on deposit with the Fed.

Resolution methods Approaches used to overcome union–management disagreements.

Resolution Trust Corporation (RTC) A group set up by Congress in 1989 as part of the S&L bailout to administer the sale of failed S&Ls.

Retailer An intermediary that sells goods and services to the final consumer.

Retained earnings Profits that have been reinvested in the company.

Return on owners' investment The ratio of net income to total owners' equity.

Right to private property The right to own, use, buy, sell, or give away property.

Right to rewards The owner's right to all of the profits, after taxes, that accrue from business activity.

Right-to-work laws State laws that prohibit union shops and other such union security arrangements.

Risk management The reduction of loss caused by uncontrollable events.

Robinson-Patman Act A federal law designed to eliminate unfair price competition.

Robot A machine capable of doing a variety of tasks based on computer-programmed manipulations of materials and tools.

Round lot 100 shares of stock.

Sales finance company A financial institution that purchases installment sales contracts.

Sales law The branch of law that involves the sale of goods for cash or credit.

Sales promotion Promotional activities other than advertising and personal selling that stimulate consumer purchasing and dealer effectiveness.

Sales tax A levy on specified purchases.

Sampling The process of inspecting some of the goods and using the results to judge the overall quality of all the goods.

Savings and loan association (S&L) Financial institution that emphasizes savings accounts and home mortgage loans.

Scientific management An approach started around 1900 that used engineering techniques such as time-and-motion analysis to increase plant efficiency by establishing the one best method for each task.

S corporation A corporation that has fewer than 35 stockholders and is taxed as a partnership but maintains the rights and liabilities of a corporation.

Scrambled merchandising Diversifying the store's selection of products in order to increase sales volume.

Seasonal discount A discount given during particular times of the year.

Secondary needs Psychological needs such as friendship, recognition, power, and achievement.

Secondary research Gathering information from sources such as newspapers, books, magazines, and government reports.

Secret partner A partner who is not known as a partner to the general public but who plays an active role in running the business.

Secured loan A loan backed up with collateral.

Securities Evidence of ownership (stocks) or debt (bonds).

Securities exchange A marketplace where securities such as stocks and bonds are bought and sold.

Selective advertising Advertising designed to increase the demand for a particular brand of product.

Selective distribution A channel strategy in which only a few intermediaries distribute a product.

Self-managed teams Employee teams that have no supervisor and manage themselves by determining their own approach to getting the job done and sometimes hire their own members and determine their own pay.

Self-rating A performance appraisal in which the employees evaluate themselves.

Selling Identifying buyers, developing a promotion campaign to attract their business, and concluding the sale.

Selling short Selling borrowed stock in the hope of later buying it on the open market at a lower price.

Semistructured interview An interview that consists of prepared questions to direct the interview but that allows the interviewee to develop ideas that seem important.

Severity error A rating error in which a manager rates all of the subordinates lower than they deserve.

Sexual harassment Any unwelcome sexual advance or hostile environment.

Sherman Antitrust Act A federal law that prohibits all agreements created for the purpose of restraining trade in interstate commerce.

Short-term financing Raising funds to meet obligations that will come due within the next 12 months.

Silent partner A partner known to be an owner in the business but who plays no active role in running the operation.

Small business Independently owned and operated business that is not dominant in its field of operation and meets certain standards of size in terms of employees or annual receipts.

Small Business Administration (SBA) The principal government agency concerned with the economic welfare of small U.S. firms.

Small business investment company (SBIC) A company licensed by the SBA for the purpose of providing venture capital to small businesses.

Socialism An economic system under which the government controls primary industries, but most other businesses remain in private hands.

Social responsibility The obligation of business to the society in which it operates.

Social security A legally required benefit that provides disability payments, old-age benefits, and survivors' benefits.

Software The series of instructions, or programming, that tells the computer what to do.

Sole proprietorship A business owned by one individual.

Span of control The number of subordinates directly reporting to a supervisor.

Speculation The assumption of large risks in the hope of large returns.

Speculative risk The treat of a loss coupled with the chance of a gain.

Spot ad A television ad broadcast over one or more stations at various times.

Spreadsheets Data arranged in tables of rows and columns.

Staff position Those who give advice and assist the line manager.

Stagflation Stagnant economic growth coupled with inflation.

Standardizing Establishing specifications or categories for products.

Standard of living The measure of how well off people of a country are economically.

State banks Commercial banks chartered by individual states.

Statement of cash flows Provides information regarding a firm's cash receipts and cash payments.

Static layout A production layout in which the product stays in one place and the workers come to the product.

Statute of limitations The law that specifies the time period during which a wronged person may sue.

Statutory law Law enacted by Congress and the state legislatures.

Steel-collar jobs Jobs performed by robots and computers.

Steward An on-site union representative whose job is to protect the rights of members.

Stockbroker An individual who has demonstrated knowledge by passing a series of exams on buying and selling securities and who, for a fee, performs this function for clients.

Stock exchange An organization whose members provide a trading place for buying and selling securities for clients.

Stockholders Individuals or institutions who have purchased shares of stock in a corporation.

Stock insurance company A corporation that sells insurance for profit.

Storing Warehousing goods.

Straight piecework A compensation plan in which employees are paid in direct relation to their output.

Strategic objectives Long-range objectives that help an organization compare itself with the competition.

Strategic plan A long-range plan.

Stress The body's response to an action or situation that places demands on a person.

Strict product liability The principle that people or businesses are responsible for their acts, regardless of their intentions or degree of negligence.

Strike A collective refusal to work until a dispute is resolved.

Strikebreaker A nonunion worker hired to do the job of a striking union employee.

Structural Unemployment The loss of work because of basic changes in the structure of the economy.

Structured interview An interview that follows a prepared format that consists of a series of direct questions.

Subordinate rating A performance appraisal in which the workers evaluate their superior.

Subsidiary A company organized under the laws of a foreign country for the purpose of carrying out tasks, such as production and sales, assigned by the parent firm.

Supermarket A large store that sells a wide variety of food products as well as some nonfood offerings.

Supervisory appraisal A performance appraisal in which the immediate supervisor evaluates the performance of a subordinate.

Suppressed motives The reasons for buying that people are unwilling to express.

Supply The various amounts of a product that will be provided at varying prices.

Surety bond Coverage against the risk that someone will fail to perform on a contract.

Syndicate An association of individuals or corporations formed to conduct financial transactions.

Synergistic effect An effect that leads to the whole being greater than the sum of the parts.

Synthetic manufacturing process A process that converts a number of raw materials or parts into a finished product.

Tall structure Structure with many levels and short spans of control.

Target market A group of customers who are likely to buy a company's goods and services.

Tariff A duty or fee levied on imported goods.

Technical analysis The process of using the pattern of a stock's price over time to predict the stock's future price movement.

Technology The application of knowledge to production, physical equipment, and machinery.

Telecommunicating Using a modem to send information between two computers or between a terminal and a processing unit.

Term life insurance Coverage for a death benefit during a stated number of years.

Theory X The assumption that people are basically lazy and have to be coerced or threatened before they will work.

Theory Y The assumption that people are creative and responsible and will work hard under the proper conditions.

Theory Z The assumption that the key to productivity is to create a climate or culture of openness and trust that leads to increased employee involvement.

Time deposits Savings accounts that require the depositor to give notice before withdrawing funds or to pay a penalty for withdrawing the funds before a specified date.

Tort An infringement of a person's inherent right that injures or damages that person.

Trade credit The purchase of merchandise on an open account.

Trade deficit A negative balance of trade.

Trade discount A discount given to merchants in the distribution channel.

Trademark A brand the owner has the legal and exclusive right to use.

Transformation process Those activities that change inputs into the desired outputs.

Transnational corporation (TNC) A firm that views the world as one giant market; it is "stateless" or "borderless."

Transporting Moving goods from where they were manufactured or purchased to where they are needed.

Traveler's check A check that is sold with a preset value and is redeemable if lost.

Type A personality A personality characterized by a drive to get more and more done in less and less time.

Unconscious motives The reasons for buying that people are unaware of.

Undifferentiated marketing Selling a single product to all customers.

Unemployment The involuntary idleness of people who are actively seeking work.

Unemployment insurance A legally required benefit that provides subsistence payments to employees who have been laid off.

Uniform Commercial Code (UCC) A set of statutes that govern the legal dealings of business.

Union An organization of workers who have joined forces to achieve common goals, such as higher wages and improved working conditions.

Union shop A company at which all employees, as a condition of employment, must join the union after a predetermined time period.

Unity of command The principle that every person should have only one boss.

Universal life insurance Life insurance that combines term insurance with a tax-deferred savings plan.

Unlimited liability Total responsibility for all debts of a company.

Unsecured loan A loan that requires no collateral.

User-friendly program A computer program that is easy to understand and master.

Valid test Test that measures what it is intended to measure.

Value-added network (VAN) A system providing electronic links between an organization and outside personnel.

Value analysis The evaluation of current products to determine how they can be improved.

Value engineering The evaluation of new products and the application of research and development to design the highest quality, lowest priced output.

Vending machine A mechanical retail outlet that stores products and dispenses them directly to customers.

Venture A new business or a new or different approach or product/service in an existing business.

Venture capital firms Financial intermediaries that specialize in funding ventures with special promise.

Venture capitalist An investor who specializes in small firms that offer potential for rapid growth and high returns.

Verification Stage of the creative process that involves testing the solution and, if necessary, modifying it.

Vertical marketing system (VMS) A planned distribution system in which all levels are brought under unified control.

Warehousing Storing goods until they are ready to be shipped.

Warranty A guarantee.

Whistle-blowers Employees who alert management or public bodies to illegal or unethical practices.

White-collar jobs Jobs that involve clerical, office, or managerial work.

Whole life insurance A combination of a death benefit and tax-deferred savings.

Wholesaler An intermediary that normally purchases goods and sells them to buyers for the purpose of resale.

Word processing A system to store, retrieve, edit, and print text.

Workers' compensation insurance A state program that provides benefits to workers who suffer job-related injury or illness.

Work ethic A belief that people should work hard and save their money.

Work slowdown A union action in which workers cut back their efforts and do only the minimum amount of work required.

Yield The percentage return from stock dividends, or the dividend divided by the selling price per share.

Notes

Chapter 1

1. "The Best New Products," *Business Week*, January 14, 1991, 127.

2. Calvin A. Kent, "Enterpreneurship Suffers Textbook Case of Neglect," *The Wall Street Journal*, September 4, 1987, 10.

3. Gifford Pinchot III, *Intrapreneuring* (New York: Harper & Row, 1985).

4. Paul Hofheinz, "The Soviet Winter of Discontent," *Fortune*, January 28, 1991, 78–85.

5. Lee Smith, "Can You Make Any Money in Russia?" *Fortune*, January 1, 1990, 104, 106.

6. "The Time Bomb in Beijing Keeps Ticking," *Business Week*, January 29, 1990, 50–51.

7. Craig R. Whitney, "East Europe Joins the Market and Gets a Preview of the Pain," *New York Times*, January 7, 1990, 3E.

8. Richard M. Hodgetts and Fred Luthans, *International Management* (New York: McGraw-Hill, 1991), Chapter 1.

9. Gene Koretz, "No Service Sector Pain, No Productivity Gain," *Business Week*, January 21, 1991, 20.

10. "Services Will Spur Job Growth in the '90s," *The Wall Street Journal*, January 9, 1990, B1.

11. James B. Treece, "Here Comes GM's Saturn," *Business Week*, April 9, 1990, 56–62; and S. C. Gwynne, "The Right Stuff," *Time*, October 29, 1990, 74–84.

12. Richard Brandt, "The Future of Silicon Valley," *Business Week*, February 5, 1990, 54–60.

13. John Naisbitt and Patricia Aburdene, *Megatrends 2000* (New York: Morrow, 1990), 38.

14. Louis S. Richman, "The Coming World Labor Shortage," *Fortune*, April 9, 1990, 76.

15. Alex Taylor III, "The New Drive to Revive GM," *Fortune*, April 9, 1990, 54.

16. Tom Peters and Robert Waterman, "Still No. 1," *USA Weekend*, June 30, 1989, 4.

17. John Naisbitt and Patricia Aburdene, *Megatrends 2000* (New York: William Morrow, 1990), 33.

18. Carla Rapoport, "You Can Make Money in Japan," *Fortune*, February 12, 1990, 85.

Chapter 2

1. See, for example, Craig C. Baig, "Products to Watch," *Fortune*, April 4, 1990, 106.

2. Clyde H. Farnsworth, "Japanese Pledge to Lower Barriers to Trade with U.S.," *New York Times*, April 6, 1990, A1, C5.

3. Also see Jay Finegan, "Do You See What I See?" *Inc.*, April 1990, 53.

4. Karen Pennar and Mike McNamee, "The New Face of Recession," *Business Week*, December 24, 1990, 58.

5. Michael J. Mandel, "1991 Won't Be a Pretty Year," *Business Week*, January 14, 1991, 62.

6. "The Toll that War Could Take on the Economy," *Business Week*, January 28, 1991, 32–33.

7. Reginald Rhein, Jr., "Patent Pirates May Soon Be Walking the Plank," *Business Week*, June 15, 1987, 62–63.

8. Eric Weiner, "For Airlines, A Heated Push to the Pacific Rim," *New York Times*, January 7, 1990, 6F.

9. Agis Salpukas, "Deregulation Left Only the Strong," *New York Times*, March 18, 1990, 10F.

10. Calvin Sims, "The Baby Bells Scramble for Europe," *New York Times*, December 12, 1989, Sec. 3, 1, 8.

11. For example, see John A. Byrne, "The Prophet of Quality," *Business Week*, January 28, 1991, 14.

12. See: David E. Bowen, Richard B. Chase and Thomas G. Cummings (Eds.), *Service Management Effectiveness* (San Francisco: Jossey-Bass, 1990).

13. Peter Newcomb, "Can Video Stores Survive?" *Forbes*, February 5, 1990, 39–41.

14. Fred Luthans, "Quality Is an HR Function," *Personnel*, May 1990, 72.

Chapter 3

1. *Statistical Abstract of the United States*, 1986, 1989.

2. Don Wallace, "Giant Killers: How to Fight the Big Guys and Win," *Success*, April 1990, 36–42.

3. Susan Benway, "Presto! The Convenience Industry: Making Life a Little Simpler," *Business Week*, April 17, 1987, 86–94.

4. See: Richard L. Daft, *Management*, 2nd ed. (Chicago: Dryden Press, 1991), 477–478, for an expanded discussion of the different types of conflict.

5. Rose Brady, Peter Galuszka, and Maria Shao, "Big Deals Run into Big Trouble in the Soviet Union," *Business Week*, March 19, 1990, 58–59; and Mark Maremont, "Investors Are Shaken — But Nobody's Packing," *Business Week*, January 28, 1991, 43–44.

6. *U.S. Statistical Abstract*, 1989, 517.

7. Dean Foust and Eric Schine, "Who's In Charge Here?" *Business Week*, March 19, 1990, 38–39.

8. Julie Amparano, "A Lawyer Flourishes by Suing Corporations for Their Shareholders," *The Wall Street Journal*, April 28, 1987, 1.

9. Alison L. Sprout, "America's Most Admired Corporations," *Fortune*, February 11, 1991, 54.

10. Albert B. Ellentuck, "S Corporations Losing Their Glitter," *Nation's Business*, February, 1991, 60.

11. Peter Coy, Mark Lewyn, and William C. Symonds, "Should the U.S. Free the Baby Bells?" *Business Week*, March 12, 1990, 118–126.

12. Christopher Farrell, "The Best Worst Deals of the '80s," *Business Week*, January 15, 1990, 53; and Jaclyn Fierman, "Deals of the Year," *Fortune*, January 28, 1991, 90–92.

13. "You Just Can't Mail Out 132 Prospectuses Anymore," *Business Week*, January 28, 1991, 62–63.

14. Walecia Konrad, Keith H. Hammonds, and Deidre A. Depke, "Survival of the Biggest," *Business Week*, April 2, 1990, 66–68.

15. "Strategy for the 1990s: Bankruptcy," *Fortune*, February 11, 1991, 13.

Chapter 4

1. John Case, "The Most Entrepreneurial Cities in America," *Inc.*, March 1990, 42.

2. *Information Please Almanac*, 1990, 54.

3. Steve McCracken, "Job Market Trends," *U.S. News & World Report*, September 25, 1989, 61.

4. "New Franchises," *Entrepreneur*, April 1990, 146.

5. "Are Money and Status Losing Their Allure?" *The Wall Street Journal*, January 12, 1988, 31.

6. Joan C. Szabo, "Finding the Right Workers," *Nation's Business*, February 1991, 16–22.

7. Bradford McKee, "Small Firms' Top Concerns," *Nation's Business*, February 1991, 45.

8. Steven P. Galante, "Small Manufacturers Shifting to 'Just-in-Time' Techniques," *The Wall Street Journal*, December 21, 1987, 21.

9. Nancy Croft Baker, "Franchising into the '90s," *Nation's Business*, March 1990, 61.

10. "Why Franchising Is Taking Off," *Fortune*, February 12, 1990, 124.

11. "New Franchises," *Entrepreneur*, April 1990, 132, 138.

12. Jeffrey A. Tannenbaum and Barbara Marsh, "Firms Try to Tighten Grip on Franchisees," *The Wall Street Journal*, January 16, 1990, B1, 2.

13. Meg Whittemore, "Franchising: An Inexact Science," *Nation's Business*, February 1991, 65.

14. "McDonald's: Food Called Too Fatty," *Miami Herald*, April 5, 1990, Sec. C, 1 and 3.

15. Barbara Marsh, "Franchisees See Home as Place to Set Up Shop," *The Wall Street Journal*, February 12, 1990, B1.

16. For more on this, see Nancy Croft Baker, "Franchising into the '90s," *Nation's Business*, March 1990, 61–68; and Suzanne Alexander, "More Working Mothers Opt for Flexibility of Operating a Franchise from Home," *The Wall Street Journal*, January 31, 1991, B1.

17. Meg Whittemore, "Franchising's Growth Patterns," *Nation's Business*, March 1990, 69.

18. Ibid.

19. "Handicapped Sought As Firm's Franchisees," *The Wall Street Journal*, April 3, 1989, B6.

Chapter 5

1. See: Richard M. Hodgetts and Fred Luthans, *International Management* (New York: McGraw-Hill, 1991).

2. William J. Holstein, "The Stateless Corporation," *Business Week*, May 14, 1990, 103.

3. Shawn Tully, "The Hunt for the Global Manager," *Fortune*, May 21, 1990, 140. Also see Bob Hagerty, "Firms in Europe Try to Find Executives Who Can Cross Borders in a Single Bound," *The Wall Street Journal*, January 25, 1991, B1.

4. See, for example, John Templeman, Gail E. Schares, and Igor Reichlin, "One Germany," *Business Week*, April 2, 1990, 46–54.

5. Peter Petre, "Lifting American Competitiveness," *Fortune*, April 23, 1990, 56.

6. Mack Ott, "Trade Deficit Myths," *The Wall Street Journal*, January 19, 1990, A8.

7. Carla Rapoport, "You Can Make Money in Japan," *Fortune*, February 12, 1990, 85.

8. Dinah Lee and Jonathan Levine, "AT&T Slowly Gets Its Global Wires Uncrossed," *Business Week*, February 11, 1991, 82–83.

9. Steven Prokesch, "G. M. Europe: How to Get Something Done Right," *New York Times*, February 4, 1990, Sec. 3, 1 and 6.

10. Edward O. Welles, "The Tokyo Connection," *Inc.*, February 1990, 52–63.

11. Richard Brandt, "The Future of Silicon Valley," *Business Week*, February 5, 1990, 58.

12. Alecia Swasy and Carol Hymowitz, "The Workplace Revolution," *The Wall Street Journal*, February 9, 1990, R6.

13. Karin DeVenuta, "Education Openers," *The Wall Street Journal*, February 9, 1990, R5.

14. Robert L. Bartley, "Pacific Rim: Wave of Future Hits Some Rocks," *The Wall Street Journal*, April 17, 1990, A14.

15. Heinz Weihrich, "Europe 1992: What the Future May Hold," *Academy of Management Executive*, May 1990, 7.

16. Lee Smith, "What Comes Next," *Fortune*, February 11, 1991, 36–43.

17. Christopher Hunt, "Exodus of Talent from Hong Kong Crimping Business," *The Wall Street Journal*, April 10, 1990, A18.

18. Gary Hector, "Why Mexico Is Looking Better," *Fortune*, January 15, 1990, 135–137.

19. Jeff Ryser, "Turning the Hemisphere into a Free Trade Bloc," *Business Week*, December 24, 1990, 37.

20. Steven R. Weisman, "The Negotiations with Japan Get Personal," *New York Times*, April 1, 1990, Sec. 4, 1–2.

21. Paul Magnusson and Blanca Riemer, "Carla Hills, Trade Warrior," *Business Week*, January 22, 1990, 50–55.

22. Richard Brandt, "The Future of Silicon Valley," *Business Week*, February 5, 1990, 58.

23. Bill Javetski, "One Germany," *Business Week*, April 2, 1990, 47–49.

24. Vivian Brownstein, "A Weaker Dollar Will Help Keep the Trade Deficit Shrinking," *Fortune*, April 23, 1990, 23.

25. Ted Holden and Stanley Reed, "Saying Sayonara Is Such Sweet Sorrow," *Business Week*, March 12, 1990, 52–53.

26. See: Rose Brady and Peter Galuszka, "Shattered Dreams," *Business Week*, February 11, 1991, 38–42; and Richard A. Melcher, "From Gung-Ho to Uh-Oh," *Business Week*, February 11, 1991, 43–46.

27. See: Rose Brady, "And Now, A Crackdown on Cash," *Business Week*, February 4, 1991, 64–65.

28. Lee Smith, "Can You Make Any Money in Russia?" *Fortune*, January 1, 1990, 106.

29. See: Fred Luthans, *Organizational Behavior*, 6th ed. (New York: McGraw Hill, 1992), Chapters 2, 19–20.

30. "GATT Split on Subsidies," *New York Times*, April 19, 1990, C7.

31. Shawn Tully, "Europe Hits the Brakes on 1992," *Fortune*, December 17, 1990, 133–140.

32. "Dogfight," *Business Week*, January 21, 1991, 56–62.

33. Monci Jo Williams, "Rewriting the Export Rules," *Fortune*, April 23, 1990, 96.

34. Stephen D. Solomon, "The Accidental Trader," *Inc.*, March 1990, 84–89.

35. Monci Jo Williams, "Rewriting the Export Rules," *Fortune*, April 23, 1990, 92.

36. Ibid., 89–92.

37. Robert J. Cole, "Western Firms Rush to Get Foothold in Eastern Europe," *Miami Herald*, January 7, 1990, 3F.

38. Lee Smith, "Can You Make Any Money in Russia?" *Fortune*, January 1, 1990, 107.

39. Shawn Tully, "What Eastern Europe Offers," *Fortune*, March 12, 1990, 52.

Chapter 6

1. Emily T. Smith, "The Greening of Corporate America," *Business Week*, April 23, 1990, 96.

2. See: Alexandra Peers, "Some Famous Corporate Insiders Get Big Gains from Buying Stock," *The Wall Street Journal*, January 30, 1991, C1.

3. "Labor Letter," *The Wall Street Journal*, January 19, 1988, 1.

4. Emily T. Smith, "The Greening of Corporate America," *Business Week*, April 23, 1990, 97.

5. "Swimming with the Dolphins," *Newsweek*, April 23, 1990, 76.

6. "The Working Disabled Face a Growing Pay Gap," *The Wall Street Journal*, September 20, 1989, B1.

7. Joel Dreyfuss, "Get Ready for the New Work Force," *Fortune*, April 23, 1990, 165.

8. "Affirmative Action Lost Some Steam in Mid-'70s," *The Wall Street Journal*, January 14, 1991, B1.

9. Amanda Bennett, "As Pool of Skilled Help Tightens, Firms Move to Broaden

Their Role," *The Wall Street Journal*, May 8, 1989, A1.

10. Barbara Mandell and Susan Kohler-Gray, "Management Development that Values Diversity," *Personnel*, March 1990, 43.

11. Linda Johnson Rice, "Black Capitalism Is on the Rise," *Fortune*, March 26, 1990, 52.

12. David Kirkpatrick, "Environmentalism: The New Crusade," *Fortune*, February 12, 1990, 44.

13. Mark Maremont, "Eastern Europe's Big Cleanup," *Business Week*, March 19, 1990, 114–115.

14. Talbot Page, "More Cooperation on the Environment," *Fortune*, March 26, 1990, 92.

15. John Naisbitt and Patricia Aburdene, *Megatrends 2000* (New York: William Morrow, 1990), 24–25.

16. Doran P. Levin, "Auto Makers' Plea on Pollution," *New York Times*, July 21, 1989, 25, 32.

17. John R. Luoma, "Coal-Cleaning Process Could Cut Pollution," *New York Times*, July 18, 1989, 17, 19.

18. John Schwartz and Harry Hurt III, "Catching Hell for Smoking," *Newsweek*, April 23, 1990, 25.

19. "As Cars Multiply, Dreams of Clean Air Get Stuck in Traffic," *New York Times*, March 11, 1990, 4E.

20. "Pollution Rules Affect Commuting in Southern California," *The Wall Street Journal*, January 15, 1991, A1.

21. "Judges Get a Primer in Environmental Law," *The Wall Street Journal*, January 29, 1991, B1.

22. Jerry Adler, "Troubled Waters," *Newsweek*, April 16, 1990, 66–80.

23. Michele Galen and Vicky Cahan, "The Legal Reef Ahead for Exxon," *Business Week*, March 12, 1990, 39.

24. Richard Lacayo, "A War Against the Earth," *Time*, February 4, 1991, 32–33.

25. Melina Beck, "Buried Alive," *Newsweek*, November 27, 1989, 67.

26. Ibid.

27. Sharon Begley, Hideko Takayama, and Mary Hager, "Teeing Off on Japan's Garbage," *Newsweek*, November 27, 1989, 70.

28. David Kirkpatrick, "Environmentalism," *Fortune*, February 12, 1990, 44.

29. "Leading the Crusade into Consumer Marketing," *Fortune*, February 12, 1990, 50.

30. Ibid.

31. Alex S. Jones, "Newsprint Poker Gets Expensive," *New York Times*, April 21, 1990, 17, 21.

32. James Cook, "Garbage into Gold," *Forbes*, January 22, 1990, 48–49.

33. Alain L. Sanders, "Battling Crimes Against Nature," *Time*, March 12, 1990, 54.

34. Barbara Posewicz and Rose Gutfeld, "Clean-Air Legislation Will Cost Americans $21.5 Billion a Year," *The Wall Street Journal*, March 28, 1990, A1.

35. David Kirkpatrick, "Environmentalism," *Fortune*, February 12, 1990, 44.

36. *USA Today*, April 13, 1990, 10A.

37. Matt Moffett, "Mexican Consumers Have a Stout Friend in Arturo Lomeli," *The Wall Street Journal*, January 18, 1988, 1.

38. See: Joanne Lipman, "FTC Is Cracking Down on Misleading Ads," *The Wall Street Journal*, February 4, 1991, B5.

39. For other examples, see John Holusha, "Some Smog in Pledges to Help Environment," *New York Times*, April 19, 1990, C1.

40. "Stick with Toy Truck Is Given as Example of Dangerous Toys," *Omaha World Herald*, November 11, 1989, 10.

41. Scott Toy and Lisa Driscoll, "Can Perrier Purify Its Reputation?" *Business Week*, February 26, 1990, 45.

42. "Having It All, Then Throwing It All Away," *Time*, May 25, 1987, 22.

43. Calvin Sims, "U.S. Suspends a Phone Company from Bids for Government Work," *New York Times*, April 8, 1990, 1, 17.

44. Kurt Eichenwald, "Milken Set to Pay a $600 Million Fine in Wall Street Fraud," *New York Times*, April 21, 1990, 1, 19.

45. Scott McMurray, "Tapes Depict Traders Routinely Scheming," *The Wall Street Journal*, January 9, 1990, C1.

46. Andy Pasztor and Rick Wartzman, "How a Spy for Boeing and His Pals Gleaned Data on Defense Plans," *The Wall Street Journal*, January 15, 1990, A1.

47. Paul Barrett, "FTC's Hard Line on Price Fixing May Foster Discounts," *The Wall Street Journal*, January 11, 1991, B1.

48. Jeffrey Rothfeder and Michele Galen, "Is Your Boss Spying on You?" *Business Week*, January 15, 1990, 74.

49. "Doing the 'Right' Thing Has Its Repercussions," *The Wall Street Journal*, January 25, 1990, B1.

50. Tim Smart, "Soon Corporate Crime May Really Not Pay," *Business Week*, February 18, 1990, 35.

51. "Ethical Behavior," *The Wall Street Journal*, January 18, 1988, 13.

52. Craig Torres and Kevin G. Salwen, "New Hot Line Hunts Program Trading Abuse," *The Wall Street Journal*, February 8, 1990, C1.

53. "Business Ethics Get Renewed Push," *The Wall Street Journal*, February 6, 1990, A1.

54. Ibid.

Chapter 7

1. Jennifer Katz, "The Creative Touch," *Nation's Business*, March 1990, 43.

2. Charles Fuller, "Boy Oh Buoy," *Entrepreneur*, March 1990, 64.

3. Charles Fuller, "Second Hand Prose," *Entrepreneur*, May 1990, 76.

4. "The Entrepreneurs' Best," *Business Week*, January 14, 1991, 132.

5. Alison L. Sprout, "America's Most Admired Corporations," *Fortune*, February 11, 1991, 56.

6. Thomas A. Stewart, "Lessons from U.S. Business Blunders," *Fortune*, April 23, 1990, 128.

7. Robert S. Feldman, *Understanding Psychology*, 2nd ed. (New York: McGraw-Hill, 1990), 242–243.

8. Jacquelyn Wonder and Priscilla Donovan, *Whole-Brain Thinking* (New York: William Morrow, 1984), 102–104.

9. Brian Dumaine, "Who Needs a Boss?" *Fortune*, May 7, 1990, 52–53.

10. Fred Luthans, *Organizational Behavior*, 6th ed. (New York: McGraw-Hill, 1992), Chapter 17.

11. See: Ibid. for a summary of this research.

12. Pascal Zachary, "Slow Start for Next Doesn't Worry Jobs," *The Wall Street Journal*, January 19, 1990, B1.

13. Deirdre Carmody, "Beating Time Warner at Its Own Game," *New York Times*, April 8, 1990, Sec. 3, 6.

14. Robert D. Hisrich, "Entrepreneurship/Intrapreneurship," *American Psychologist*, February 1990, 209.

15. Walter Guzzardi, "The National Business Hall of Fame," *Fortune*, March 12, 1990, 119.

16. Jill Andresky Fraser, "The New American Dream," *Inc.*, April 1990, 42–51.

17. Tom Peters and Nancy Austin, *A Passion for Excellence* (New York: Random House, 1985), xxii.

18. Sanford L. Jacobs, "Big-Firm Alumni Apt to Be Growth-Oriented Entrepreneurs," *The Wall Street Journal*, March 31, 1985, 27.

19. Linda Watkins, "Minority Entrepreneurs Venturing into Broader Range of Businesses," *The Wall Street Journal*, March 31, 1987, 31.

20. Robert D. Hisrich, "Entrepreneurship/ Intrapreneurship," *American Psychologist*, February 1990, 216.

21. Brian O'Reilly, "Is Your Company Asking Too Much?" *Fortune*, March 12, 1990, 38–46.

22. Charles N. Weaver and Michael D. Matthews, "What White Males Want from Their Jobs: Ten Years Later," *Personnel*, September 1987, 62.

23. Thomas J. Peters and Robert H. Waterman, Jr., *In Search of Excellence* (New York: Harper & Row, 1982).

24. Thomas J. Peters, *Thriving on Chaos: Handbook for a Management Revolution* (New York: Knopf, 1987).

25. Patricia Sellers, "What Customers Really Want," *Fortune*, June 4, 1990, 58.

26. Karl Albrecht and Ron Zemke, *Service America* (Homewood, Ill.: Dow Jones-Irwin, 1985), 49.

27. S. C. Gwynne, "The Right Stuff," *Time*, October 29, 1990, 74–84.

28. Alecia Swasy and Carol Hymowitz, "The Workplace Revolution," *The Wall Street Journal*, February 9, 1990, R8.

29. Albrecht and Zemke, *Service America*, 149, 152.

30. For a critical analysis of the Peters and Waterman work, see Michael A. Hitt and R. Duane Ireland, "Peters and Waterman Revisited: The Unended Quest for Excellence," *Academy of Management Executive*, May 1987, 91–98.

31. William Taylor, "The Business of Innovation," *Harvard Business Review*, March–April, 1990, 98.

32. "Say It with Napkins," *Entrepreneur*, January 1990, 327–329.

Chapter 8

1. Aimée L. Stern, "GF Tries the Old Restructure Ploy," *Business Month*, November, 1987, 37–39; also see Richard M. Hodgetts, *Modern Human Relations at Work*, 4th ed. (Hinsdale, Ill.: Dryden Press, 1990), 299.

2. Richard L. Daft, *Management*, 2d ed. (Hinsdale, Ill.: Dryden Press, 1991), 17.

3. Marc Beauchamp, "We Need To Be First," *Forbes*, February 5, 1990, 112–116.

4. See, for example, Rita Koselka, "When a Partner Becomes a Competitor," *Forbes*, April 30, 1990, 133–138.

5. For example, see Tom Peters, *Thriving on Chaos: Handbook for a Management Revolution* (New York: Knopf, 1987); and Fred Luthans, Richard M. Hodgetts, and Stuart

A. Rosenkrantz, *Real Managers* (Cambridge, Mass.: Ballinger, 1988).

6. Anne B. Fisher, "Is Long-Range Planning Worth It?" *Fortune*, April 23, 1990, 281–284.

7. Warren E. Leary, "Designing an SST: Noise and the Ozone," *New York Times*, April 10, 1990, B8.

8. "Steel Nerve," *Business Week*, January 14, 1991, 131.

9. Jonathan Kapstein, Thane Peterson, and Lois Therrien, "Look Out, World, Philips Is on a War Footing," *Business Week*, January 14, 1990, 44–45.

10. Thomas A. Stewart, "Lessons from U.S. Business Blunders," *Fortune*, April 23, 1990, 132.

11. John Harris, "The Window Frame Is a Fashion Item," *Forbes*, April 30, 1990, 125–130.

12. Keith H. Hammonds, "How a $4 Razor Ends Up Costing $300 Million," *Business Week*, January 29, 1990, 62–63.

13. Benjamin B. Tregoe and Peter M. Tobia, "An Action-Oriented Approach to Strategy," *Journal of Business Strategy*, January/February 1990, 16–21.

14. Thomas R. King, "For Perrier, New Woes Spring Up," *The Wall Street Journal*, April 26, 1990, B1, 6.

15. Keith Bradsher, "MCI to Acquire Telecom USA," *New York Times*, April 10, 1990, C1, 17; and Keith Bradsher, "MCI Deal Called Antitrust Test," *New York Times*, April 12, 1990, C2.

16. Peter Coy and Mark Lewyn, "Sounding More and More Like a Three-Man Band," *Business Week*, April 23, 1990, 30.

17. Mary Lu Carnevale, "Bell Companies Are Facing Delays in Moving into Information Services, Some Analysts Say," *The Wall Street Journal*, April 13, 1990, C2.

18. Tom Peters and Nancy Austin, *A Passion for Excellence* (New York: Random House, 1985), 313.

19. Ibid.

20. Anne T. Lawrence and Brian S. Mittman, "Downsizing on the Upswing." *Personnel*, February 1991, 14–15.

21. Fred Luthans, Stuart A. Rosenkrantz, and Harry W. Hennessey, "What Do Successful Managers Really Do?" *Journal of Applied Behavioral Science*, August 1985, 255–270.

22. Fleming Meeks, "'Fail' Is Not a Four-Letter Word," *Forbes*, April 30, 1990, 92–102.

23. Keith H. Hammonds, "The Baggage Weighing Marriott Down," *Business Week*, January 29, 1990, 64–65.

24. Bruce Hagen, "The Pet Food That's Fattening Colgate's Kitty," *Business Week*, May 7, 1990, 116.

25. John Harris, "The Battle of the Paper Clips," *Forbes*, May 14, 1990, 108–109.

26. James Brian Quinn, Thomas L. Doorley, and Penny C. Paquette, "Beyond Products: Services-Based Strategy," *Harvard Business Review*, March–April 1990, 65–66.

27. Andrew D. Szilagyi, Jr. and Marc J. Wallace, *Organizational Behavior and Performance*, 5th ed., (Glenview, Ill.: Scott, Foresman/Little Brown, 1990), 499.

28. Alison L. Sprout, "America's Most Admired Corporations," *Fortune*, February 11, 1991, 57.

29. Ralph H. Kilmann, "Corporate Culture," *Psychology Today*, April 1985, 63.

30. Much of the material in this section can be found in Terrence D. Deal and Allan A. Kennedy, *Corporate Cultures: The Rites and Rituals of Corporate Life* (Reading, Mass.: Addison-Wesley, 1982).

31. For other examples see John J. Keller and Mark Maremont, "Bob Allen Is Turning AT&T into a Live Wire," *Business Week*, November 6, 1989, 140–152.

32. See: Deal and Kennedy, *Corporate Cultures*, Ch. 6. Barbara Buell, "The Second Comeback of Apple," *Business Week*, January 28, 1991, 68.

Chapter 9

1. John W. Verity, "Computers Will See Lots of Downtime," *Business Week*, January 14, 1991, 101.

2. Brenton R. Schlender, "Hot New PCs that Read Your Writing," *Fortune*, February 11, 1991, 113–123.

3. Joseph B. White, "Stumbling Auto-Makers Face Tough '91," *The Wall Street Journal*, January 7, 1991, B1.

4. Anne T. Lawrence and Brian S. Mittman, "Downsizing on the Up-Swing," *Personnel*, February 1991, 14–15.

5. David Churbuck, "Starting Over," *Forbes*, May 14, 1990, 128.

6. Claire Poole, "Southwestern Belle," *Forbes*, April 16, 1990, 89.

7. See: Neil Gross, "How Sony Pulled Off Its Great Computer Coup," *Business Week*, January 15, 1990, 76–77.

8. Peter Nulty, "The Soul of an Old Machine," *Fortune*, May 21, 1990, 67–72.

9. See: Constance A. Gutske, "Making Big Gains from Small Steps," *Fortune*, April 23, 1990, 119–122.

10. "IBM Discovers a Simple Pleasure," *Fortune*, May 21, 1990, 64.

11. Andrew Kupfer, "Success Secrets of Tomorrow's Stars," *Fortune*, April 23, 1990, 78.

12. Otis Port, Zachary Schiller, and Resa W. King, "A Smarter Way to Manufacture," *Business Week*, April 30, 1990, 110–117.

13. Mark L. Blazey and Karen S. Davison, "Keeping Up with the Factory of the Future," *Training*, February 1990, 51–55.

14. Alecia Swasy and Carol Hymowitz, "The Workplace Revolution," *The Wall Street Journal*, February 9, 1990, R6.

15. Andrew Tanzer and Ruth Simon, "Why Japan Loves Robots and We Don't," *Forbes*, April 6, 1990, 153.

16. Ibid., 148.

17. Jeremy Main, "Manufacturing the Right Way," *Fortune*, May 21, 1990, 54–64.

18. Ibid., 64.

19. For example, see *Business Week*, June 15, 1990; the entire issue is devoted to technological innovation and the role it plays in the global competitive race.

20. Constance A. Gustke, "Making Big Gains from Small Steps," *Fortune*, April 23, 1990, 119–122.

21. Quoted in Joesph Oberle, "Quality Gurus," *Training*, January 1990, 47. Also see John A. Byrne, "The Prophet of Quality," *Business Week*, January 28, 1991, 14.

22. For example, see Patricia Sellers, "What Customers Really Want," *Fortune*, June 4, 1990, 58–61.

23. Joshua Hyatt, "Surviving Chaos," *Inc.*, May 1990, 60–71.

24. Peter F. Drucker, "The Emerging Theory of Manufacturing," *Harvard Business Review*, May–June 1990, 94–102.

25. Tom Peters and Nancy Austin, *A Passion for Excellence* (New York: Random House, 1985), 99. Also see: Frank Rose, "Now Quality Means Service, Too," *Fortune*, April 22, 1991, 99–108.

26. Ibid., 57.

27. Gary McWilliams, "If It Ain't Broke, Why Pay to Fix It?" *Business Week*, March 5, 1990, 82–84.

28. Terence P. Pare, "Why Some Do It the Wrong Way," *Fortune*, May 21, 1990, 76.

29. Jeremy Main, "How to Win the Baldrige Award," *Fortune*, April 23, 1990, 101–116.

30. D. Keith Denton, "The Service Imperative," *Personnel Journal*, March 1990, 66–74.

31. The quote comes from George F. Will and is found in Karl Albrecht and Ron Zemke, *Service America* (Homewood, Ill.: Dow Jones–Irwin, 1985), 1. This book champions the role of the service industry in American business.

32. This estimate comes from Frederick F. Reichheld, a management consultant for Bain & Co. See: Ronald Henkoff, "Make Your Office More Productive," *Fortune*, February 25, 1991, 72–84.

33. Patricia Sellers, "What Customers Really Want," *Fortune*, June 4, 1990, 60.

34. Ibid., 61.

35. Fred Luthans, "Quality Is an HR Function," *Personnel*, May 1990, 72.

36. "Sharpening Service Skills," *Personnel*, March 1990, 4.

Chapter 10

1. "Information Systems Services," *Fortune*, June 4, 1990, 212.

2. See, for example, Barnaby J. Feder, "Why Wall Street Likes Scientific Atlanta's," *New York Times*, April 1, 1990, F5.

3. Paul B. Carroll, "Computers Cut Through the Service Maze," *The Wall Street Journal*, May 1, 1990, B1.

4. Marc S. Miller, "Keep Flexible," *Personnel*, February 1991, 23.

5. Paul C. Judge, "Computers to Help Drivers Find Their Way," *New York Times*, April 25, 1990, C6.

6. Michael Schroeder, "More Computers — and Humans — Are Saying 'Checkmate,'" *Business Week*, November 6, 1989, 50.

7. Naomi Freundlich, "These Computers Would Make Supercomputers Look Slow," *Business Week*, December 18, 1989, 87.

8. Carmen Mead, "Machines Will Understand the World," *Fortune*, March 26, 1990, 69.

9. Michael Schroeder, "More Computers — and Humans — Are Saying 'Checkmate,'" *Business Week*, November 6, 1989, 50.

10. David Churbuck, "The Ultimate Computer Game," *Forbes*, February 5, 1990, 154–155.

11. Kathleen K. Wiegner, "A Computer for the Defense," *Forbes*, February 19, 1990, 158–159.

12. Fred V. Guterl, "Computers Think for Business," *Dun's Business Month*, October 1986, 32.

13. G. Pascal Zachary, "Opening of 'Windows' Shows How Bill Gates Succeeds in Software," *The Wall Street Journal*, May 21, 1990, A1.

14. "Tabling the Move to Computer Graphics," *The Wall Street Journal*, January 30, 1991, B1.

15. See: "Supercomputers: Brute Strength and a Sensitive Issue," *Business Week*, April 30, 1990, 83.

16. William M. Bulkeley, "PC Networks Begin to Oust Mainframes in Some Companies," *The Wall Street Journal*, May 23, 1990, A1.

17. Russell Mitchell, "The Genius," *Business Week*, April 30, 1990, 81.

18. "Chipmakers' Sneak Preview of Tomorrow's Memories," *Business Week*, February 4, 1991, 85.

19. Tim R. V. Davis, "Information Technology and White-Collar Productivity," *Academy of Management Executive*, February 1991, 55–67.

20. Robert Koester and Fred Luthans, "The Impact of the Computer on the Choice Activity of Decision Makers: A Replication with Actual Users of Computerized MIS," *Academy of Management Journal*, June 1979, 416–422.

21. "Virus Set to Attack Personal Computers," *Omaha World Herald*, October 7, 1989, 1–2; and Dori Jones Yang and Maria Shao, "Hackers: Is a Cure Worse than the Disease?" *Business Week*, December 4, 1989, 37.

22. Jeffrey Rothfeder, Michele Galen, and Lisa Driscoll, "Is Your Boss Spying on You?" *Business Week*, January 15, 1990, 74–75.

23. Dan Gutman, "Hollywood on Your Desktop," *Success*, May 1990, 18.

24. For other insights to technology and data presentation, see "Technology Will Serve Individuals More," *Fortune*, March 26, 1990, 120.

25. Jill MacNeice, "Calls by Computer," *Nation's Business*, July 1990, 29–31.

26. John Markoff, "Marrying the PC and the Fax Machine," *New York Times*, May 2, 1990, C8.

Chapter 11

1. Today, the term *Hawthorne effect* refers to a change in the behavior of research subjects caused by the fact that they are being studied and given special attention.

2. A quote by Edward E. Lawler III in "Let Workers Make White-Knuckle Decisions," *Fortune*, March 26, 1990, 49.

3. Michael Albert, "HR Profit Power," *Personnel*, February 1990, 47–49.

4. For example, see "Today's Leaders Look to Tomorrow," *Fortune*, March 26, 1990, 30–53. A common theme of the business leaders interviewed is the importance of enhancing human resources through motivating and leading them more effectively.

5. "Unappreciated Workers," *Journal of Accountancy*, June 1989, 154.

6. "Labor Letter," *The Wall Street Journal*, January 16, 1990, A1.

7. Richard M. Hodgetts and Fred Luthans, *International Management* (New York: McGraw-Hill, 1991), Chapter 11.

8. See: Christopher Knowlton, "11 Men's Million-Dollar Motivator," *Fortune*, April 9, 1990, 65–68.

9. Michael J. Mandel, "Those Fat Bonuses Don't Seem to Boost Performance," *Business Week*, January 8, 1990, 26.

10. Alecia Swasy and Carol Hymowitz, "The Workplace Revolution," *The Wall Street Journal*, February 9, 1990, R6.

11. Claudia H. Deutsch, "Asking Workers What They Think," *New York Times*, April 22, 1990, Sec. 3, F29.

12. In addition to those discussed here, see J. Barton Cunningham and Ted Eberle, "A Guide to Job Enrichment and Redesign," *Personnel*, February 1990, 56–61.

13. Brian Dumaine, "Who Needs a Boss?" *Fortune*, May 7, 1990, 52–53.

14. Cathy Trost and Carol Hymowitz, "Careers Start Giving In to Family Needs," *The Wall Street Journal*, June 18, 1990, B1.

15. See: Douglas T. Hall, "Promoting Work/Family Balance," *Organizational Dynamics*, Winter 1990, 5–18.

16. The most recent and comprehensive review of the considerable goal setting research is Edwin A. Locke and Gary P. Latham, *A Theory of Goal Setting and Task Performance* (Englewood Cliffs, NJ: Prentice-Hall, 1990).

17. For the news releases on these studies, see "Jobs with Little Freedom Boost Heart Risk," *Lincoln Journal*, April 11, 1990, 1; and "Heart Disease Anger Linked, Research Shows," *Lincoln Journal*, January 17, 1989, 4.

18. "Labor Letter," *The Wall Street Journal*, January 29, 1991, 1.

19. Bruce G. Posner, "Role Changes," *Inc.*, February 1990, 95–98.

20. For some recent thinking on leadership, see David A. Nadler and Michael L. Tushman, "Beyond the Charismatic Leader: Leadership and Organizational Change," *California Management Review*, Winter 1990, 77–97; John P. Kotter, "What Leaders Really Do," *Harvard Business Review*, May–June 1990, 103–111; and Jay A. Conger, "Inspiring Others: The Language of Leadership," *Academy of Management Executive*, February 1991, 31–45.

21. Marc Beauchamp, "We're All Rejuvenated," *Forbes*, March 19, 1990, 124–126.

22. Fred E. Fiedler, *A Theory of Leadership Effectiveness* (New York: McGraw-Hill, 1967).

23. Douglas Harbrecht, Amy Borrus and Bill Javetski, "Managing the War," *Business Week*, February 4, 1991, 34–37.

24. Joseph Weber, "With This Lifeguard It's Sink or Swim," *Business Week*, February 18, 1991, 56–58.

25. Fred E. Fiedler, *A Theory of Leadership Effectiveness* (New York: McGraw-Hill, 1967).

26. Steve Swartz, "How Eccentric Chief Built Up Hutton, Hastened Its Demise," *The Wall Street Journal*, February 17, 1988, 1.

27. See: Max DePree, "It's Not What You Preach but How You Behave," *Fortune*, March 26, 1990, 36, for an example.

28. John F. Welch, Jr., "We've Got to Simplify and Delegate More," *Fortune*, March 26, 1990, 30.

Chapter 12

1. See: Y. K. Shetty, "Regaining Competitiveness Requires HR Solutions," *Personnel*, July 1990, 8–12.

2. Dyan Machan, "Rent — An Exec," *Forbes*, January 22, 1990, 133.

3. Neil B. Krupp, "Overseas Staffing for the New Europe," *Personnel*, July 1990, 20–25.

4. See: Kathleen A. Hughes, "Pregnant Professionals Face Subtle Bias At Work as Attitudes Toward Them Shift," *The Wall Street Journal*, February 6, 1991, B1; and "Mothers-to-Be Sue, Charging Discrimination," *The Wall Street Journal*, February 6, 1991, B1; for how this issue is changing.

5. Kenneth A. Kovach and John A. Pearce II, "HR Strategic Mandate for the 1990s," *Personnel*, April 1990, 52. Also see: Joan C. Szabo, "Finding the Right Workers," *Nation's Business*, February 1991, 16–22.

6. Marcus Mabry, "Past Tomorrow," *Newsweek*, May 14, 1990, 37.

7. Joel Dreyfuss, "Get Ready for the New Work Force," *Fortune*, April 23, 1990, 168.

8. See, for example, Bill Richards, "Wanting Workers," *The Wall Street Journal*, February 9, 1990, R10–11.

9. Eric Rolfe Greenberg, "Workplace Testing: The 1990 AMA Survey," *Personnel*, June 1990, 45.

10. Eric C. Gottschalk, Jr., "New Test Quantifies the Way We Work," *The Wall Street Journal*, February 7, 1990, B1.

11. Brooks Mitchell, "Interviewing Face-to-Interface," *Personnel*, January 1990, 23–25.

12. Jolie Solomon, "The New Job Interview: Show Thyself," *The Wall Street Journal*, December 4, 1989, B1, 4.

13. See: Elliot H. Shaller, "Avoid Pitfalls in Hiring, Firing," *Nation's Business*, February 1991, 51–54.

14. Jolie Solomon, "Reference Preference: Employers Button Lips," *The Wall Street Journal*, January 4, 1990, B1.

15. Dillard B. Tinsley, "Computers Facilitate HR Function," *Personnel*, February 1990, 32–35.

16. Marc S. Miller, "Keep Flexible," *Personnel*, February 1991, 23.

17. Anne Ritter, "Training Wheels Are Turning," *Personnel*, February 1990, 7.

18. Paula Popvich and John P. Wanous, "The Realistic Job Preview as a Persuasive Communication," *Academy of Management Review*, July 1982, 570–578.

19. Marc J. Rosenberg, "Performance Technology: Working the System," *Training*, February 1990, 43.

20. Richard M. Hodgetts and Fred Luthans, "Japanese HR Management Practices," *Personnel*, April 1989, 42–43.

21. Thomas F. O'Boyle, "Mentor–Protege Ties Can Be Strained," *The Wall Street Journal*, June 12, 1990, B1.

22. *The Wall Street Journal*, October 3, 1989, A1.

23. See: Eric Sundstrom, Kenneth P. DeMeuse, and David Futrell, "Work Teams," *American Psychologist*, February 1990, 120–133.

24. See Cynthia D. Fisher, Lyle F. Schoenfelt, and James B. Shaw, *Human Resource Management* (Boston: Houghton Mifflin, 1990), 415–421, for a more in-depth discussion of rating errors.

25. See Gisela Bolte, "Will Americans Work for $5 a Day?" *Time*, July 23, 1990, 12–14.

26. Lynne Kilpatrick, "In Ontario, 'Equal Pay for Equal Work' Becomes a Reality," *The Wall Street Journal*, March 9, 1990, B1.

27. For example, see Amanda Bennett, "Pay for Performance," *The Wall Street Journal*, April 18, 1990, R7–8; and Claudia H. Deutsch, "Using Money to Change Executive Behavior," *New York Times*, May 20, 1990, Sec. 3, 29.

28. For example, see Bradley A. Stertz and Melinda Gernier Guiles, "Top Salaries Rise, But Bonuses Fell at GM, Ford, in '89," *Wall Street Journal*, April 10, 1990, B8.

29. Michael Siconolfi, "Wall Street Sees Bonuses Decline By 40% for 1990," *The Wall Street Journal*, February 6, 1991, C1.

30. "All Pulling Together, To Get the Carrot," *The Wall Street Journal*, April 30, 1990, B1.

31. Robert P. McNutt, "Achievement Pays Off at DuPont," *Personnel*, June 1990, 5–10.

32. Roger Thompson, "The High Cost of Employee Benefits," *Nation's Business*, February, 1991, 34.

33. Fred Luthans and Elaine Davis, "The Healthcare Cost Crisis: Causes and Containment," *Personnel*, February 1990, 24–30. Also see: Bradford McKee, "Small Firms' Top Concerns," *Nation's Business*, February 1991, 45.

34. "Labor Letter," *The Wall Street Journal*, March 27, 1990, A1; and Betty A. Iseri and Robert R. Cangemi, "Flexible Benefits: A Growing Option," *Personnel*, March 1990, 30–32.

35. See Alpert R. Karr, "Disabled-Rights Bill Inspires Hope, Fear," *The Wall Street Journal*, May 23, 1990, B1.

36. Timothy Noah, "Legislation Will Give Disabled People Greater Leverage to Gain Access to Jobs," *The Wall Street Journal*, May 23, 1990, B1.

37. Ibid. Also see: "Disabled Get Early Welcome At Some Firms," *Sunday World–Herald*, February 10, 1991, 1–G.

38. "Labor Letter," *The Wall Street Journal*, May 19, 1987, 1; also see "Enabling the Disabled," *Personnel*, July 1990, 2, in HR Focus section.

39. Sara M. Freedman and Robert T. Keller, "The Handicapped in the Workforce, *Academy of Management Review*, July 1981, 453.

40. Elliot H. Shaller, "Avoid Pitfalls In Hiring, Firing," *Nation's Business*, February, 1991, 51–54.

41. For a recent application of this to the education field, see Linda Greenhouse, "Universities Lose Shield of Secrecy in Tenure Dispute," *New York Times*, January 10, 1990, 1, 12.

42. "Workers Get Ways to Fight Age Bias," *Sunday World–Herald*, February 10, 1991, 15–L.

43. John Hoerr and Wendy Zellner, "A Japanese Import That's Not Selling," *Business Week*, February 26, 1990, 86–87.

Chapter 13

1. Conversation with U.S. Department of Labor, February 1991. The statistics on union membership include employee associations that act as unions.

2. "Labor Letter," *The Wall Street Journal*, July 10, 1990, A1.

3. "Labor Letter," *The Wall Street Journal*, April 17, 1990, 1.

4. "Labor Letter," *The Wall Street Journal*, January 29, 1991, 1.

5. Francine Schwadel, "Irate Nordstrom Straining in Labor Fight," *The Wall Street Journal*, April 6, 1990, B1.

6. Aaron Bernstein, "Been Down So Long," *Business Week*, January 14, 1991, 30–31.

7. Ronald Henkoff, "Cost-Cutting: How to Do It Right," *Fortune*, April 9, 1990, 40–49.

8. Robert Tomsho, "Employers and Unions Feeling Pressure to Eliminate Two-Tier Labor Contract," *The Wall Street Journal*, April 20, 1990, B1.

9. Gregory A. Patterson, "Hourly Auto Workers Now on Layoff Have a Sturdy Safety Net," *The Wall Street Journal*, January 29, 1991, 1.

10. "Chrysler Suggests Employee Ownership," *Omaha World Herald*, July 21, 1990, 58.

11. Todd Vogel, "Pittston Could Go From Settlement to Spinoff," *Business Week*, January 15, 1990, 23–24; and Joanne Zipperer, "Vote Today May End Long, Bitter Coal Strike," *USA Today*, February 19, 1990, 3A.

12. Shane R. Premeaux, R. Wayne Mondy, Art L. Bethke, and Ray Comish, "Managing Tomorrow's Unionized Workers," *Personnel*, July 1989, 61.

13. "Labor Letter," *The Wall Street Journal*, January 29, 1991, 1.

14. Aaron Bernstein and Jim Bartimo, "Wrong Time for Scare Tactics?" *Business Week*, April 16, 1990, 27–28.

15. "Labor Letter," *The Wall Street Journal*, February 5, 1991, 1.

16. "Labor Letter," *The Wall Street Journal*, April 17, 1990, 1.

17. Janice Castro, "Labor Draws an Empty Gun," *Time*, March 26, 1990, 56.

18. Aaron Bernstein, "For the Teamsters, It's Like in Eastern Europe," *Business Week*, March 5, 1990, 66; and Premeaux, "Managing Tomorrow's Unionized Workers," 61–64.

19. Louis S. Richman, "The Coming World Labor Shortage," *Fortune*, April 9, 1990, 74.

20. Aaron Bernstein, "Been Down So Long," *Business Week*, January 14, 1991, 30–31.

21. Anne Ritter, "Are Unions Worth the Bargain?" *Personnel*, February 1990, 13.

22. "Easier Organizing at Hospitals," *Personnel*, July 1989, 5.

23. See Douglas Ephlin, "The Unions' Role as Co-Manager," *Fortune*, March 26, 1990, 37.

Chapter 14

1. Stephen Philips, "King Customer," *Business Week*, March 12, 1990, 90.

2. Stephen J. Fansweet, "Dick Woolworth Builds a Better Mousetrap — and Falls Flat on His Face," *The Wall Street Journal*, September 24, 1970, 1.

3. See Andrew Pollack, "A Novel Idea: Customer Satisfaction," *New York Times*, May 27, 1990, Sec. 3, 1, 6.

4. Ronald Henkoff, "Big Mac Attacks with Pizza," *Fortune*, February 26, 1990, 87–89.

5. Stephen Phillips, "King Customers," *Business Week*, March 12, 1990, 91; and William McWhirter and Richard Woodbury, "Mr. Sam Stuns Goliath," *Time*, February 25, 1991, 62–63.

6. Judith Valente, "Northwest to Invest in Service," *The Wall Street Journal*, January 31, 1990, B1, 6.

7. Anthony Ramirez, "New Coke Conquest: Burger King," *New York Times*, May 2, 1990, Sec. C, 1, 10.

8. Bruce Hager and John Templeman, "Now They're Selling BMWs Door-to-Door — Almost," *Business Week*, May 14, 1990, 65.

9. George R. Walther, "Reach Out to Accounts," *Success*, May 1990, 24.

10. "Would You Buy a Car from This Woman?" *New York Times*, September 21, 1989, 131.

11. Bruce Hager, "The Pet Food That's Fattening Colgate's Kitty," *Business Week*, May 7, 1990, 111.

12. Charles Lazarus, "You Just Listen to Your Customers, Then Act," *Fortune*, March 26, 1990, 40.

13. "Journeying Deeper Into the Minds of Shoppers," *Business Week*, February 4, 1991, 85.

14. See: Kathleen Deveny and Peter K. Francese, "Shrinking Markets," *The Wall Street Journal*, March 9, 1990, R 29.

15. See: Joseph Pereira, "As Toy Makers Unwrap New Products, They Hope Video Games Are Peaking," *The Wall Street Journal*, February 11, 1991, B1.

16. See: Steven H. Star, "Marketing and Its Discontents," *Harvard Business Review*, November–December 1989, 148–154.

17. Stephen Kreider Yoder, "Motorola, Taking on Rivals, to Launch Line of Multi-

User Business Computers," *The Wall Street Journal*, March 5, 1990, B 4.

18. "The New Products Best," *Business Week*, January 14, 1991, 124.

19. Michael J. McCarthy, "New Coke Gets New Name, New Can, and New Chance," *The Wall Street Journal*, March 7, 1990, B1.

20. Peter M. Nichols, "Movie Rentals Fade, Forcing an Industry to Change Its Focus," *New York Times*, May 6, 1990, 1, 16.

21. Paul B. Brown, "How to Compete on Price," *Inc.*, May 1990, 105–107.

22. Jeffrey A. Trachtenberg, "A Buyer's Market Has Shoppers Demanding and Getting Discounts," *The Wall Street Journal*, February 8, 1991, 1.

23. Mark Lewyn, "PC Makers, Palms Sweating, Try Talking to Women," *Business Week*, January 15, 1990, 48.

24. Richard Gibson, "Kellogg Shifts Strategy to Pull Consumers In," *The Wall Street Journal*, January 22, 1990, B1.

Chapter 15

1. Jay Cocks, "Discs, DAT and D'Other Things," *Time*, January 14, 1991, 44.

2. Dennis Farney, "Inside Hallmark's Love Machine," *The Wall Street Journal*, February 14, 1990, B1, 4.

3. Isadore Barmash, "Make a Tie from a Dress?" *New York Times*, May 5, 1990, 12, 17.

4. Tim Smart and Seth Payne, "Smart Weapons: The Next Generation," *Business Week*, February 18, 1991, 33.

5. Amal Kumar Naj, "GE Claims Breakthrough in Plastics Development," *The Wall Street Journal*, September 14, 1989, B1.

6. Keith H. Hammonds, "How a $4 Razor Ends Up Costing $300 Million," *Business Week*, January 29, 1990, 62.

7. Michael J. McCarthy, "New Coke Gets New Name, New Can and New Chance," *The Wall Street Journal*, March 7, 1990, B1.

8. John Pierson, "Small Packages Bring New Economies of Scale," *The Wall Street Journal*, February 22, 1990, B1.

9. Ronald Henkoff, "Big Mac Attacks with Pizza," *Fortune*, February 26, 1990, 87–89.

10. Maria Mallory, "This Bright Idea Could Make GE a Billion," *Business Week*, December 4, 1989, 120.

11. Stephen Kreider Yoder, "Motorola, Taking on Rivals, to Launch Line of Multi-User Business Computers," *The Wall Street Journal*, March 5, 1990, B4.

12. Philip R. McDonald and Joseph O. Eastback, Jr., "Top Management Involvement with New Products," *Business Horizons*, December 1971, 24.

13. Michael E. Porter, *Competitive Advantage* (New York: Free Press, 1985), Chapter 8.

14. William H. Bulkalsy, "HP to Put Laser Printers within Reach of Everyone," *The Wall Street Journal*, September 13, 1989, B1.

15. *The Wall Street Journal*, March 7, 1990, A14.

16. See Geraldine Fabrikant, "Craig McCaw's High-Risk Phone Bet," *New York Times*, May 6, 1990, Sec. 3, 1, 6.

17. Anthony Ramirez, "Liggett to Change Its Focus with Shift from Cigarettes," *New York Times*, June 22, 1990, C1, 2; and Walecia Konrad, "If It's Legal, Cigarette Makers Are Trying It," *Business Week*, February 19, 1990, 52–54.

18. Laura Jereski, "Can Paul Fireman Put the Bounce Back in Reebok?" *Business Week*, June 18, 1990, 181–182.

19. Christopher Power, "And Now, Finger-Lickin' Good For Ya?" *Business Week*, February 18, 1991, 60.

20. For some examples, see Lois Therrien, "Kraft Is Looking for Fat Growth from Fat-Free Foods," *Business Week*, March 26, 1990, 100–101; Ronald Henkoff, "Big Mac Attacks with Pizza," *Fortune*, February 26, 1990, 89; and Richard Koenig and Alix M. Freedman, "FDA Clears Monsanto Fat Substitute, Giving It a Jump on the Competition," *The Wall Street Journal*, February 23, 1990, B1.

21. Peter Fuhrman, "Live All You Can. . .," *Forbes*, March 5, 1990, 120–122.

22. Also see N. R. Kleinfield, "Cashing In on a Hot New Brand Name," *New York Times*, April 29, 1990, Sec. 3, 1, 6.

23. "More Lawyers Caution: Watch That Trademark," *The Wall Street Journal*, February 8, 1991, B1.

24. See Ron Winslow, "Generic Drug Scandal Creates Opening," *The Wall Street Journal*, September 6, 1989, B1.

25. "What a Concept," *Business Week*, June 15, 1990, 182–191.

26. "Odds and Ends," *The Wall Street Journal*, January 29, 1991, B1.

27. "Leading the Crusade into Consumer Marketing," *Fortune*, February 12, 1990, 50.

28. Zach Schiller, "Procter & Gamble Tries Hauling Itself Out of America's Trash Heap," *Business Week*, April 23, 1990, 101.

29. Kenneth H. Bacon, "U.S. Proposes Nutrition Labels for Most Packaged Goods," *The Wall Street Journal*, March 8, 1990, B1.

30. See Teri Agins, "Low Prices or Low Practice? Regulators Cast Wary Eye on Retailers' Many Sales," *The Wall Street Journal*, February 13, 1990, B1, 6.

31. David Wessel, "The Price Is Wrong, and Economists Are in an Uproar," *The Wall Street Journal*, January 2, 1991, B1.

32. This discussion of quality is drawn from Fred Luthans, "Quality Is an HR Function," *Personnel*, May 1990, 72.

33. "Give Them Anything But Promise Satisfaction," *The Wall Street Journal*, February 13, 1991, B1.

34. Paul B. Brown, "How to Compete on Price," *Inc.*, May 1990, 105–107.

35. Jeffrey A. Trachtenberg, "A Buyer's Market Has Shoppers Demanding and Getting Discounts," *The Wall Street Journal*, February 8, 1991, 1.

Chapter 16

1. Laura Zinn, "Fewer Rings on the Cash Registers," *Business Week*, January 14, 1991, 85.

2. "Sears Ready to Cut Another 9,000 Jobs," *Omaha World Herald*, February 12, 1991, 11.

3. Joseph Weber, "The Practice of Making Perfect," *Business Week*, January 14, 1991, 86.

4. Alison L. Sprout, "America's Most Admired Corporations," *Fortune*, February 11, 1991, 52.

5. "Supermarkets Increase Share of Retail Sales," *The Wall Street Journal*, February 20, 1991, B1.

6. "K mart Uses Profits to Speed Makeover," *Omaha World Herald*, March 5, 1990, 13.

7. Patricia Sellers, "What Customers Really Want," *Fortune*, June 4, 1990, 56–68.

8. "Eye-Stopping Design in the Supermarket," *The Wall Street Journal*, January 21, 1988, 21.

9. Lori Kesler, "St. Louis' Dierbergs Serves More Than Usual Fare," *Advertising Age*, May 4, 1987, S4, S6.

10. Kevin Helliker, "Stop N Go's Van Horn Wants to Reinvent the Convenience Store," *The Wall Street Journal*, February 6, 1991, 1.

11. Antonio Fins, "Sunglass Huts: Thriving in Nooks and Crannies," *Business Week*, July 27, 1987, 77.

12. Chuck Hawkins, "Will Home Depot Be the Wal-Mart of the '90s?," *Business Week*, March 19, 1990, 124–126.

13. Steven P. Galante, "Bookshop 'Superstore' Reflects the Latest Word in Retailing," *The Wall Street Journal*, February 23, 1987, 21.

14. Brian Bremner and Keith N. Hammonds, "Lands' End Looks a Bit Frayed at the Edges," *Business Week*, March 19, 1990, 42.

Chapter 17

1. Robert Guenther, "Staid Private Bankers Turn Promotional," *The Wall Street Journal*, January 5, 1990, B1.

2. John Philip Jones, "Ad Spending: Maintaining Market Share," *Harvard Business Review*, January–February 1990, 38–42.

3. James C. Schroer, "Ad Spending: Growing Market Share," *Harvard Business Review*, January–February 1990, 44–48.

4. See Thomas R. King, "For Cola's the Fault Is in Too Many Stars," *The Wall Street Journal*, January 24, 1990, B1.

5. "As Ever, Advertising Mirrors How We Feel," *Time*, February 4, 1991, 59.

6. Joanne Lipman, "Ads That Sing Out, Pop Up, Getting Thumbs Down," *The Wall Street Journal*, October 18, 1989, B1.

7. Joshua Levine, "Drive Time," *Forbes*, March 19, 1990, 144–146.

8. See Lucy A. McCauley, "The Face of Advertising," *Harvard Business Review*, November–December 1989, 155–159; and Julia M. Collins, "On TV: Effective Ads of the 1980s," *Harvard Business Review*, March–April 1990, 150–155.

9. Joanne Lipman, "Super Bowl Is Advertisers' Biggest Turf," *The Wall Street Journal*, January 8, 1990, B1, 3.

10. Ronald Alsop, "More Companies Squeeze Ads into Bargain 15-Second Spots," *The Wall Street Journal*, January 19, 1987, 27.

11. "Video Magazines Find Rebirth in Specialization," *Omaha World Herald*, March 19, 1990, 13.

12. See Magid M. Abraham and Leonard M. Lodish, "Getting the Most Out of Advertising and Promotion," *Harvard Business Review*, May–June 1990, 50–60.

13. Thomas R. King, "Top Spots of '90 Reflect Marketers' Turn to Caution," *The Wall Street Journal*, January 22, 1991, B1.

14. Bill Carter, "ABC Plans to Impose New TV Rating System," *New York Times*, June 1, 1990, A1, C15; and Bill Carter, "NBC Alters Its Count on Viewers," *New York Times*, June 13, 1990, C1, 16.

15. "Networks Use Study Results to Ease Advertiser Concerns," *Omaha World Herald*, February 23, 1991, 52.

16. See Mark Laudler and Gail DeGeorge, "Tempers Are Sizzling over Burger King's New Ads," *Business Week*, February 12, 1990, 33.

17. "AT&T and MCI Trade Charges," *Business Week*, January 22, 1990, 38.

18. Michael Galen, "A Comeback May Be Ahead for Brand X," *Business Week*, December 4, 1989, 35.

19. "Suddenly, Green Marketers Are Seeing Red Flags," *Business Week*, February 25, 1991, 74.

20. See, for example, Mark Landler, Wendy Zellner, and James B. Treece, "Shirley Young: Pushing GM's Humble Pie Strategy," *Business Week*, June 11, 1990, 52–53.

21. See "Foes Claim Ad Bans Are Bad Business," *The Wall Street Journal*, February 27, 1990, B1.

22. See Mark J. Martinko, J. Dennis White, and Barbara Hassell, "An Operant Analysis of Prompting in a Sales Environment," *Journal of Organizational Behavior Management*, Vol. 10, No. 1, 1989, 93–107.

23. See, for example, Frank V. Cespedes, Stephen X. Doyle, and Robert J. Freedman, "Teamwork for Today's Selling," *Harvard Business Review*, March–April 1989, 44–52.

24. George R. Walther, "Reach Out to New Accounts," *Success*, May 1990, 24.

25. "Recession Feeds the Coupon Habit," *The Wall Street Journal*, February 20, 1991, B1.

26. Tom Ineck, "New Pictionary Draws Consumers," *Sunday Lincoln Journal Star*, February 7, 1988, 1C.

27. William McWhirter and Richard Woodbury, "Mr. Sam Stuns Goliath," *Time*, February 25, 1991, 63.

Chapter 18

1. See H. Thomas Johnson, "Managing Costs Versus Managing Activities — Which Strategy Works?" *Financial Executive*, January/February 1990, 32–36.

2. Alison Leigh Cowan, "S&L Backlash Against Accountants," *New York Times*, July 31, 1990, C1.

3. Anne B. Fisher, "How to Handle Your Accountant," *Fortune*, February 25, 1991, 117.

4. See Donald Westell, "Price Waterhouse Agrees to Review of Procedures," *Globe and Mail*, April 7, 1990, B1. For an example of a new accounting standard see: "Firms Do Have Options on Accounting Changes," *The Wall Street Journal*, January 18, 1991, B1.

5. These professional standards are changing in some cases, as in firms selling stock. See Alison Leigh Cowan, "C.P.A.s to Sell Stock in Practice," *New York Times*, June 14, 1990, C1, 6.

6. Earl C. Gottschalk, "CPAs Find Investment Role Too Taxing," *The Wall Street Journal*, January 16, 1991, C1.

7. Daniel Akst and Lee Berton, "Accountants Who Specialize in Detecting Fraud Find Themselves in Great Demand," *The Wall Street Journal*, February 26, 1988, 17.

8. For example, see Thomas A. Stewart, "Why Budgets Are Bad for Business," *Fortune*, June 4, 1990, 179–187.

9. "It's Fancy, It's Fun, It's an Annual Report," *The Wall Street Journal*, January 22, 1988, 21.

10. "Highest Salaries," *Lincoln Journal-Star*, February 9, 1991, 21.

11. "How the Oakland A's Make (Almost) A Million," *Fortune*, August 13, 1990, 98.

12. See Lourie Saunders, "Today California. . ." *Forbes*, May 14, 1990, 72–76.

13. John E. Gallagher, "Paying the Bill for the Party Next Door," *Time*, August 20, 1990, 42.

Chapter 19

1. For example, see: "Why Europe Is in Dollar Shock," *Business Week*, March 4, 1991, 36.

2. "Elegant Armed Robbery," *Newsweek*, April 2, 1990, 30.

3. For example, see: Mike McNamee, "The Fed May Be Seeing Things," *Business Week*, February 4, 1991, 48.

4. Michael Parkin, *Economics* (Reading, Mass.: Addison-Wesley, 1990), 707–711.

5. "Hitching a Ride on Tuition Bills," *Time*, October 5, 1987, 57.

6. John Meehan, "All That Plastic Is Still Fantastic for Citibank," *Business Week*, May 28, 1990, 90–92.

7. "They Don't Take Visa," *Time*, April 30, 1990, 72.

8. John Meehan, "Banks: Is Big Trouble Brewing?" *Business Week*, July 16, 1990, 146.

9. Bernard Banmohl and Deborah Fowler, "Breaking the Bank," *Time*, September 24, 1990, 66–67; and Geoffrey Smith, "From Bad to Abysmal in New England," *Business Week*, January 28, 1991, 64–65.

10. For more on this topic, see Paul B. Brown, "How to Deal with Your Bankers," *Inc.*, February 1990, 102–103.

11. Steven Waldman and Rich Thomas, "How Did It Happen?" *Newsweek*, May 21, 1990, 27–32.

12. "His Personal Piggy Bank," *Time*, March 12, 1990, 59.

13. Nathaniel C. Nash, "Savings Industry Lost $19.2 Billion, A Record, in 1989," *New York Times*, March 27, 1990, A1, C6.

14. Charles McCoy, "Hundreds of S&Ls Fall Hopelessly Short of New Capital Rules," *The Wall Street Journal*, December 7, 1989, A1, A8.

15. Howard Gleckman and Catherine Yang, "The Road to Bank Failure Is Paved with Federal Deposit Insurance," *Business Week*, August 16, 1990, 152.

16. John Davidson and Erik Colonius, "The Great S&L Fire Sale of 1990," *Fortune*, August 13, 1990, 60–66.

17. Catherine Yang, "Bail, Bail, Blub, Blub," *Business Week*, April 9, 1990, 20–21; Carolyn Friday and Rich Thomas, "How Not to Run an S&L," *Newsweek*, April 2, 1990, 44; and Terence P. Paré, "How to Hold Down S&L Losses," *Fortune*, February 11, 1991, 97–100.

18. John Meehan, "Is There Any Bottom to the Thrift Quagmire?" *Business Week*, March 4, 1991, 62–63.

19. Nathaniel C. Nash, "Savings Regulator Seeks $100 Billion for Bailout in '91," *New York Times*, July 31, 1990, A1, C2.

20. See Catherine Yang, Laura Jereski, and David Greising, "Credit Unions May Be Tempting Fate," *Business Week*, December 18, 1989, 112–113; and Ron Suskind, "Rhode Island Could Face Fiscal Crisis From a Bailout," *The Wall Street Journal*, January 4, 1991, A2.

21. Todd Vogel and Jon Friedman, "No Money Machine Can Run This Fast Forever," *Business Week*, April 30, 1990, 96–100; and Terence P. Paré, "Tough Birds that Quack Like Banks," *Fortune*, March 11, 1991, 79–84.

22. Lindley H. Clark, Jr., "Remaking the Fed: Maybe It's Time," *The Wall Street Journal*, September 18, 1989, A1.

23. See, for example, Lindley H. Clark, Jr., "The Fed Charts Slow, Steady Course," *The Wall Street Journal*, February 12, 1990, A1; and Paul E. Duke, "Fed Weighed Buying Commercial Loans from Banks to Help Ease Credit Crunch," *The Wall Street Journal*, February 22, 1991, A2.

24. Catherine Yang, David Zigas, and Vicky Cahan, "The $6 Trillion Monster That's Stalking Washington," *Business Week*, August 13, 1990, 98.

25. John Meehan, "A Shock to the System," *Business Week*, January 21, 1991, 24–26.

26. Karen Pennar, "Could Reforming Deposit Insurance Torpedo U.S. Banks?" *Business Week*, February 18, 1991, 22.

27. "S&Ls Can't Quit System, FDIC Says," *Omaha World Herald*, August 30, 1990, 18.

28. See Barry Hillenbrand, Thomas McCarroll, and Adam Zagorin, "Bareknuckle Banking," *Time*, July 30, 1990, 48–50.

29. Jeff Smith, "A Blend of Tragedy and Farce," *New York Times*, July 3, 1990, C1, 6.

30. John Meehan, "No Holiday for Banks," *Business Week*, January 14, 1991, 115.

31. Steve Jordan, "Author: Endless Service Is the Means to Success," *Omaha World Herald*, November 18, 1987, 58. Quotes author Nancy Austin, who coauthored the book *A Passion for Excellence* with Tom Peters.

32. Laura Jereski, "Small Towns Add Up to Big Banking for KeyCorp," *Business Week*, April 30, 1990, 104.

33. "Tom Peters Tells U.S. Businesses: Serve and Take Care of Customers," *Lincoln Journal*, March 16, 1987, 15.

Chapter 20

1. "Growth Capital Can Still Be Found," *The Wall Street Journal*, January 31, 1988, 31.

2. Vivian Brownstein, "Yes, You Will Be Able to Borrow," *Fortune*, March 11, 1991, 38–39.

3. Terence P. Paré, "Tough Birds That Quack Like Banks," *Fortune*, March 11, 1991, 79–84.

4. John R. Dorfman, "As Debt Becomes a Dirty Word, Low-Leveraged Firms Win Fans," *The Wall Street Journal*, January 31, 1991, C1.

5. N. R. Kleinfield, "Stemming the Losses: Trying for a Leaner Macy's," *New York Times*, March 18, 1990, Sec. F, 5; and Chris Welles, Gail De George, and Joseph Weber, "Welcome to the Nineties, Donald," *Business Week*, May 14, 1990, 118–124.

6. "Tyson Is Winging Its Way to the Top," *Business Week*, February 25, 1991, 57.

7. Brenton R. Schlender, "How Levi Strauss Did an LBO Right," *Fortune*, May 7, 1990, 105.

Chapter 21

1. Susan E. Kuhn, "How To Survive the Stock Market's Ups and Downs," *Fortune*, February 11, 1991, 27.

2. William Power, "Name-Dropping on Wall Street No Longer What It Used to Be," *The Wall Street Journal*, February 22, 1991, C1.

3. Steven Weisman, "Japan Sobered by Recent Stock Slide," *New York Times*, March 31, 1990, 17, 29.

4. Carla Rapoport, "What's Ahead Now," *Fortune*, May 7, 1990, 64–68; and John Schwartz, Bradley Martin, and Rich Thomas, "Has the Tokyo Bubble Burst?" *Newsweek*, April 2, 1990, 42.

5. Stanley W. Angrist, "Investors Get Hooked on Tools of Trades," *The Wall Street Journal*, January 8, 1991, C1.

6. Jeffrey B. Laderman, "Will the Rally Pull a Fast Fade? Not This Time," *Business Week*, June 25, 1990, 74–75.

7. Floyd Norris, "The Dow's Worst Postwar Months," *New York Times*, September 2, 1990, Sec. 3, 1.

8. Randall Smith, "Stock Market Swing Shows How Wrong Professionals Can Be," *The Wall Street Journal*, February 26, 1991, 1.

9. Louis S. Richman, "Is This Bull Real?" *Fortune*, March 11, 1991, 41.

10. Maria Shao, "Suddenly, The Envy of the Street Is. . .Schwab?" *Business Week*, March 19, 1990, 102.

11. See Gary Weiss, Jon Friedman, and Keith H. Hammonds, "Mutual Funds: The Battle for Your Dollars," *Business Week*, June 11, 1990, 56–62.

12. See William Baldwin, "How to Choose a Fund," *Forbes*, September 3, 1990, 122–124.

13. See Spyros Manolatos, "The Honor Roll," *Forbes*, September 3, 1990, 126–127.

14. See Richard Phalon, "Lincoln's Way," *Forbes*, April 2, 1990, 192–193.

15. See also Jeffrey Laderman, Chuck Hawkins, and Irene Recio, "How Much Should You Trust Your Analyst," *Business Week*, July 23, 1990, 54–56.

16. Anise Wallace, "Seven Mistakes Investors Make Over and Over," *New York Times*, November 18, 1984, Sec. 12, 18, 20.

Chapter 22

1. See Bruce Hager, "It's Time for Savers to Check Their Safety Nets," *Business Week*, February 4, 1991, 100–101.

2. Larry Light, "The Sky May Not Fall In, But. . ." *Business Week*, January 14, 1991, 116.

3. Susan Pulliam and Mitchell Pacelle, "Loans to Builders Haunt Life Insurers," *The Wall Street Journal*, February 26, 1991, B1.

4. Bart Ziegler, "Ralph Nader Tackles Insurance Industry," *Omaha World Herald*, October 11, 1990, 55.

5. "Widow Sues Sudafed Maker," *Omaha World Herald*, March 8, 1991, 7.

6. Fred Luthans and Elaine Davis, "The Healthcare Cost Crisis: Causes and Containment," *Personnel*, February 1990, 24–30.

7. Susan B. Garland, "Insurers vs. Doctors: Who Knows Best?" Business Week, February 18, 1991, 65.

Chapter 23

1. Keith Bradsher, "MCI Deal Called Antitrust Test," *New York Times*, April 12, 1990, C2.

2. Peter Coy and Mark Lewyn, "The Baby Bells Misbehave," *Business Week*, March 4, 1991, 22.

3. "US West to Pay $10 million Fine in Antitrust Case," *Omaha World Herald*, February 16, 1991, 38.

4. Paul M. Barrett, "FTC's Hard Line on Price Fixing May Foster Discounts," *The Wall Street Journal*, January 11, 1991, B1.

5. James S. Hirsch, "As 'Light' Foods Multiply on Shelves, Critics Contend Health Claims Are Thin," *The Wall Street Journal*, March 28, 1990, B1.

6. Joanne Lipman, "FTC Is Cracking Down On Misleading Ads," *The Wall Street Journal*, February 4, 1991, B5.

7. Joanne Lipman, "Some Food Marketers May Shelve Outlandish Health Claims," *The Wall Street Journal*, January 29, 1990, B1.

8. See "Brady Seeks Support for Plan to Overhaul Bank Laws," *Nation's Business*, March 1991, 12.

9. For a summary of the minor changes in the tax laws and some proposed major changes see: Joan C. Szabo, "What Will You Give to the IRS This Year?" *Nation's Business*, March 1991, 26–28.

10. See James Lyons, "Smash the Competition," *Forbes*, September 3, 1990, 46.

11. See: "More Lawyers Caution: Watch That Trademark," *The Wall Street Journal*, February 8, 1991, B1.

12. "Asbestos Makers Run Out of Breathing Room," *Business Week*, November 20, 1989, 36.

13. Judith H. Dobrzynski, "Should You Sue Your Investment Banker for Lousy Advice?" *Business Week*, February 18, 1991, 116.

Appendix

1. See Florida International University, *Placement Manual: 1990–1991*, 4.

2. *CPC Annual, 1990/91*, 34th ed. (Bethlehem, PA: College Placement Council, 1990), 12.

Name Index

Subject Index

Key terms and the page numbers on which they are defined appear in boldface type.